Travel and Tourism *for* Vocational A level

formerly Advanced GNVQ

Tony Outhart, Lindsey Taylor, Ray Barker and Alan Marvell

Series editor: Tony Outhart

Published by HarperCollins*Publishers* Limited
77–85 Fulham Palace Road
Hammersmith
London
W6 8JB

www.**Collins**Education.com
On-line support for schools and colleges

First published 2000
10 9 8 7 6

ISBN 0 00 329109 X

British Cataloguing in Publication Data.
A cataloguing record for this publication is available from the British Library.

Almost all the case studies in this book are factual. However, the persons, locations and subjects have been given different names to protect their identity. The accompanying images are for aesthetic purposes only and are not intended to represent or identify any existing person, location or subject. The publisher cannot accept any responsibility for consequences resulting from this use, except as expressly provided by law.

Series commissioned by Charis Evans
Designed, edited and typeset by DSM Partnership
Cover designed by Patricia Briggs
Cover picture by Tony Stone
Picture research by Thelma Gilbert
Illustrations by Barking Dog Art
Cartoons by Alan Fraser
Index by Julie Rimington
Project managed by Kay Wright
Production by Emma Lloyd-Jones
Printed and bound by Imago in Thailand

www.**fire**and**water**.co.uk
The book lover's website

Contents

Acknowledgements

The authors would like to thank everybody involved in supporting them during the writing and production of this book. In particular, thanks to Charis Evans, Kay Wright, Helen Evans, Peter Carr, Paul Stirner and Steve Moulds for their work throughout the project.

The authors and publishers would like to thank the following for permission to reproduce photographs and other material:

ACE Photo Agency: Christopher Lee (p. 18); Kevin Phillips (p.81); John Darling (p. 140 right); David Kerwin (p. 261); Vibert-Stokes (p. 335)

Ancient Art and Architecture (p. 239)

Bradford City Council (p. 148)

Brewers Fayre (p. 361)

Capital Radio (p. 286)

Center Parcs (p. 112)

Collections: Peter Wright (p. 111); Michael George (p. 119); John D Beldom (p. 125); Michael St Maur Sheil (p. 374)

CTV (p. 151)

English Tourism Council (pp. 55, 119 right, 102)

Guild of Registered Tourist Guides (p. 329)

Helen Evans (p. 289)

Hulton Getty: (pp. 10, 18); Fox photos (p. 150)

Northern Ireland Tourist Board (p. 30)

Oxford Scientific Films: Keith Gillett (p. 114)

PA Photos: Barry Batchelor (p. 198)

P&O Cruises (p. 313)

Popperfoto/Reuters (p. 35)

Portsmouth Harbour project (p. 111)

Rex Features (p. 245)

Robert Harding: Ian Griffiths (p. 15); A R Lampshire (p. 97); Michael Short (p. 136); R Richardson (p. 150); T Waltham (p. 172); (pp. 171, 179 bottom); Robert Francis (p. 260); Roy Rainford (p. 385); Paul Henning (p. 397)

Roger Scruton (pp. 119, 405, 133, 248)

Sally & Richard Greenhill: Richard Greenhill (pp. 260, 227)

Scotland Tourist Board (p. 30)

Solo Syndication (pp. 24 and 26)

Spectrum Colour Library (pp. 107, 140 left, 166, 172, 179, 187, 190, 224)

Thomson Holidays (p. 265)

Tony Stone: Bob Thomas (p. 32); H Rogers (p. 81); Jon Riley (p. 270)

Tourism Concern (p. 32)

Trailblazer (p. 315)

Trip: B Turner (p. 169, 179 top); M O'Brien (p. 189)

Wales Tourist Board (p. 30)

Welcome Host (p. 315)

V&A Museum (p. 289)

Every effort has been made to contact copyright holders, but if any have been inadvertently overlooked, the publishers will be pleased to make the necessary arrangements at the first opportunity.

Introduction

Vocational A levels

A **Vocational A level** is a qualification of the same standard as a traditional A level but with a different focus. It used to be called an Advanced GNVQ, which stands for **General National Vocational Qualification**.

The Vocational A level qualification relates to the world of work and employment. In contrast to **GCSEs** and traditional **A levels**, which are based on knowledge and understanding of academic subjects, Vocational A levels are based on developing an understanding of the ways in which people earn their living in travel and tourism, in leisure and recreation, in hospitality and catering, and in many other areas of work.

Vocational A levels introduce you to a general area of work rather than to a particular job. You may have heard of NVQs (**National Vocational Qualifications**). These relate to the skills you need to undertake particular jobs. A Vocational A level, on the other hand, covers a broad area of work and is designed for people who are usually studying full-time at school or college, and usually aged between 16 and 19.

How will I study?

If you have achieved an Intermediate GNVQ, you should already have a good idea of what it is like to study a Vocational A level. However, if you have taken GCSEs, you will find that studying for a Vocational A level is different in several ways from GCSE work and from studying for traditional A levels.

First, as a Vocational A level student, you will take more responsibility for your own learning, for planning your work, for making your own investigations and for keeping proper records of what you have done. Your tutor will play an important part in teaching you some of what you need to know and helping you to plan your work, to keep to your plan and to respond to problems and setbacks. However, in the end, you have to take responsibility for your programme of study, just as you will have to take responsibility for your work when you are employed in the future.

Second, much of your learning will be acquired through carrying out your own enquiries and investigations, often in connection with assignments agreed with your tutor. These investigations can involve a wide range of tasks and activities, drawing on several different sources of information. For example, you may:

- do research in libraries and resource centres
- visit work places and talk to people currently working in the travel and tourism industry
- learn from visits by local employers and business people
- carry out surveys of people's activities, preferences and opinions
- study company brochures and gather information from press and television reports
- study particular examples of people, places and firms that relate to your work
- learn from work experience with a local employer (if this can be arranged).

Overall, you will be actively investigating the real world of work and presenting your findings in various ways, including giving talks and presentations. All these activities develop skills which are essential in the world of work.

Third, two-thirds of your work will be assessed through assignments that you complete during the course, which you will assemble in a portfolio. Only one-third will be assessed through tests.

The structure of the course

The structure of the Vocational A level in travel and tourism is quite simple. There are 12 units in the full award. Six are **compulsory units**; every student takes them. Each of the compulsory units is covered in this textbook. Six are **optional units**. Each awarding body has produced its own set of optional units and you will probably choose which of these to study. These optional units are not covered in this book, although you will find the information contained in the compulsory units a useful foundation for your optional unit work.

All units are the same size. To gain the full award you have to take all 12 units and your overall result is worked out by adding up the results you get on each unit. Since the new A levels have six units, your 12-unit Vocational A level is worth two traditional A levels. You may be able to take a six unit Vocational A level award that is equivalent to one A level.

Course specifications

Your tutor will give you a copy of the specifications for the units you will need in your course and will go through them with you. All units have the same basic characteristics. They are addressed directly to you, the student. They have three sections:

- **about this unit** – this briefly describes what the unit covers

- **what you need to learn** – this clearly states the knowledge, understanding and skills you need to complete the unit

- **assessment evidence** – this sets out the evidence you need to produce for the unit, including what you need to produce to get higher grades, and the tasks you will be set in the units which are assessed through tests.

The unit specifications are designed to let you know exactly what skills and knowledge you have to demonstrate: if you demonstrate them, you achieve the qualification.

What are key skills?

There are six **key skills units**:

- communication

- application of number

- information technology

- working with others

- improving own learning and performance

- problem solving.

The first three key skills – communication, application of number, and information technology – make up the Key Skills Qualification, which is available to every student or trainee, whatever course they are following. To achieve the Key Skills Qualification, you have to pass these three units at any level. You can pass each one at a different level and still achieve the qualification. Most Vocational A level students will aim for Level 3 in these key skills.

How will I be assessed?

Four of your six compulsory units are assessed through a **portfolio of evidence** that you will compile. This is assessed by your tutors. The other two compulsory units – for tourism development and marketing – will be assessed by a test that is set and marked by the awarding body.

The portfolio is the heart of your course. Everything in it should be your own work and it must meet all the requirements set out in the **assessment evidence** sections of the unit specifications. It has to be carefully planned, organised and maintained, and it must have an index so that you can show how everything in it relates to the evidence requirements.

Evidence can take several forms. Much of it will be your own written work. However, some evidence will be provided by your tutor or some other person (maybe an employer) who has witnessed you taking part in a discussion, or dealing with a customer, or making a presentation. Your tutor, or other witness to your work, needs to provide a written statement that you have reached the required standard.

Your portfolio of evidence may contain video or audio recordings of role plays, work experience and research activities. It may also include letters, photographs, computer printouts and graphics, sketches and plans. All this evidence must be carefully recorded and indexed.

You need to build up a separate portfolio for your key skills evidence.

Grading

Vocational levels are **graded A to E**, exactly like traditional A levels. You will be given a grade for each unit. These grades will then be combined to give your overall grade for the whole qualification. When you have completed the course successfully, you will be awarded a Vocational A level certificate from your awarding body. This will list all the units you have completed, with grades, and will also specify your grade for the whole qualification.

How this book is organised

The content, structure and features of *Vocational A level for Travel and Tourism* are designed to help you to get the most out of your course. The content directly matches all the underpinning knowledge that you will need to complete the compulsory units. The units in this book are organised into sections that make them easier to follow. Each section is packed with information, case studies and activities to help you learn in an active and stimulating way. You can identify each section within a unit by looking at the top corner of every right-hand page.

The special features include **activities**, **case studies**, and **webstracts** that will help you to develop your understanding of what you have been reading and to apply it to your own experience and studies. A webstract is a case study that is based upon information gathered from the internet. All special features are indicated by distinct icons and banners.

You will be able to complete many of the activities in class, sometimes by working with other people. Some activities will require you to make enquiries or investigations outside the classroom. Some activities will ask you to analyse case studies, documents and figures that you will find in this book or that you can access easily in libraries. Whatever the type of activity, you will be given clear instructions on what to do.

Each section within a unit ends with a feature called **build your learning**. This lists the key words and phrases that you have covered. **Key words and phrases** are also highlighted in red when they first appear in the section, and are fully referenced in the index at the back of this book.

As you complete each section within the unit, there is an **end of section activity**. These are usually bigger than the activities and case studies that appear throughout the preceding section and can include some useful opportunities for you to generate evidence for your portfolio assignments.

Portfolio assessments

You will find portfolio assessments for each of the four compulsory units that are not externally assessed on pages 452–9 at the back of the book. These are based on the assessment criteria that you are required to meet in order to pass your Vocational A level. You are also given tips and suggestions on where to find information that will help you complete these assessments. Check with your teacher before starting any assessment work that will contribute to your portfolio of evidence.

There is no portfolio assessment for Unit 2, Tourism development, and Unit 4, Marketing in travel and tourism, as these will be externally assessed by the awarding body.

Resource directory

The resource directory provides you with useful information that will help you complete your assessment portfolio and also prepare for the externally set tests. You are provided with a list of key sources of information and data on the travel and tourism industry.

There is a massive amount of information about travel and tourism available on the internet. This section also provides you with a mini-directory of useful internet websites, listed in alphabetical order, to further help you with your research.

Good luck with your course!

Author biographies

Tony Outhart was formerly Curriculum Manager for Hospitality and Leisure at York College and has been involved in leading GNVQ Leisure and Tourism programmes since their introduction. Tony is a part-time FEFC inspector and has worked for QCA, Edexcel and FEDA in the development of the 2000 curriculum. Since 2000, he has been a freelance education and training consultant. He has been a professional footballer and a director of a children's activity company. Tony is Series Editor for Collins GNVQ Leisure and Tourism.

Alan Marvell is a Senior Lecturer in Tourism Management at Bath Spa University College. He was formerly Head of Department at New College Swindon, leading and developing Travel, Tourism and Leisure courses. Alan has also worked as an educational consultant for various national organisations.

Lindsey Taylor is a Senior Lecturer in Leisure, Tourism and Sport and GNVQ Coordinator at Yorkshire Coast College. She was involved in the original pilot GNVQ and has worked extensively with awarding bodies in the development of the revised qualification. She has worked in marketing consultancy within the leisure and tourism industry and as a personnel and training manager for Forte Hotels.

Ray Barker is a Senior Lecturer in Leisure and Tourism Management at University College Scarborough. He has worked as an outdoor activity and events manager and an independent consultant organising personal and staff development courses.

Preview

Travel and tourism is one of the fastest growing industries in the world. We are going to investigate the reasons for the rapid growth in travel and tourism since the end of the Second World War. You will learn about the key features of the present UK travel and tourism industry and find that it is made up of a wide variety of components such as tourist attractions, accommodation and catering, travel agents and tour operations. We will investigate a selection of commercial and non-commercial organisations within these industry components and look at the way they interact to supply a wide range of products and services. We will investigate the structure and scale of the UK travel and tourism industry and consider its economic significance. Finally, we explore the wide-ranging career opportunities available in the industry and help you to identify employment opportunities that match your own aspirations, skills and abilities. The portfolio assessment for this unit is on pp. 452–3.

1

Investigating travel and tourism

Defining travel and tourism

TRAVEL AND TOURISM IS ONE of the fastest growing industries in the world. In the UK it is one of the key drivers of the economy, supporting around 1.7 million jobs and generating £61 billion per year in revenue in 1998. The industry is extremely diverse and covers a wide variety of interests, including at least 200,000 businesses.

In order to begin to understand the enormous size and diversity of the travel and tourism industry, it is necessary to define some key terms. Tourism is a broad area to define, but it usually involves travelling away from home, whether for leisure or business purposes. The World Tourism Organisation defines **tourism** as:

> *...the short-term movement of people to destinations away from the communities in which they live and work, and their activities during their trip, including travel, day visits and excursions.*

So tourism includes short-term travel for all purposes, whether for leisure or business. An essential part of tourism is the intention of the traveller to return, whether this is from a day trip, a holiday or a short business trip.

Most tourist activities take place during people's leisure time. Going on holiday, visiting relatives and day trips can all be classified under the general heading of **leisure travel**. If the reason for travel is business, then we class this as **business travel**.

Leisure travellers are sometimes divided into tourists and day visitors. If people stay one or more nights away from home they are classed as **tourists**; if they travel and return home, or pass through an area, without staying overnight, they are classed as **day visitors**. The distinction is not always important, but you may come across it when you are reading or doing research.

ACTIVITY

Defining tourism

What do you think are the key words and phrases in the World Tourism Council's definition of tourism? With a classmate, identify and discuss each of them. For example, why does the definition include the phrase short-term movement?

Travel is to do with how people get to their chosen destination and how they travel around the area they are visiting. There are many methods of travel, including air, rail, ferry, bus, taxi, car hire and coach. In this book, we use the term **travel and tourism** to cover the whole phenomenon of people travelling away from home on a temporary basis (whether for business or leisure), and the industry that supports this activity.

In this unit you will investigate key industry components including:

- tourist attractions
- accommodation and catering
- tourism development and promotion
- transportation
- travel agents
- tour operators.

Types of tourism

We have already seen that tourists can visit destinations for leisure or business purposes (or a combination of both), and that they can be also grouped according to the duration of their stay (**day visitor** or **tourist**). Tourists can also be grouped into further three categories, which are based on where they come from:

- **domestic tourism** – UK residents taking day trips or holidays in the UK
- **inbound tourism** – overseas tourists visiting the UK
- **outbound tourism** – UK residents taking holidays outside the UK.

Overseas visitors to the United Kingdom are therefore often referred to as **incoming tourists** (inbound tourism) while British residents travelling abroad are referred to as **outbound tourists** (outbound tourism). Another commonly used term is **domestic tourist** (domestic tourism) which describes British residents visiting places inside the UK. Use these descriptions to complete the activity opposite.

ACTIVITY

What kind of tourist?

Complete the table below by filling in the boxes appropriately.

Description of visitor	Business or leisure	Day vistor or tourist	Domestic, incoming or outgoing
Joan Dumas from Lille attends a one-day business meeting in London	Business.	Day visitor.	Incoming.
Jack and Doris Brooks from Durham go on a day trip to London	leisure.	Day visitor.	Domestic.
The Jones from Bargoed in Wales take their annual two-week hoilday in Ibiza	leisure.	tourist.	outgoing.
Batholomew Tapp from Brussels visits relatives in Norwich for five days	leisure.	tourist.	Incoming.

Throughout this textbook you will come across a number of key industry terms. You will need to apply this terminology to your own investigation into the industry as part of the unit assessment. The most important of these terms are defined in Figure 1.1.

Figure 1.1: Key industry definitions

A **long holiday** is a holiday of four nights or more away from home.

A **short-break holiday** (or short break) involves one to three nights away from home (but specified as on holiday).

Holidays abroad divide into short haul and long haul. **Short haul** refers to holidays within Europe, dominated by flights to Spain, the Balearic Islands, Portugal, Greece, Cyprus, Turkey and the Canary Islands (which are treated as part of Spain) of no longer than five hours duration. **Long haul** refers to flights of more than five hours duration, outside Europe (apart from the Canary Islands). The main long-haul destinations visited by UK residents are the US and Canada, the Caribbean, India and the Far East, Australasia and North Africa.

Inclusive tours, or **package holidays**, are defined to cover the simultaneous sale of at least two elements of a holiday to the traveller: fares on public transport (for example, flights) and commercial accommodation (for example, hotels or self-catering apartments). Other elements such as meals or excursions are not essential to the definition of an inclusive tour, but are included in **all-inclusive holidays**, which are usually based in one hotel or holiday complex and include all meals, drinks and an entertainment programme within the price of the holiday.

Independent holidays are those which the traveller organises, booking transport and accommodation from separate sources (for example, a Channel ferry crossing and a caravan site in France). **Seat-only** is used to denote holidays in which travellers only purchase a return fare, usually to a known destination (for example, Florida or Majorca) and then book their own accommodation, car hire and other services. **Fly-drive holidays** include flight and car hire. Classified statistically as inclusive tours, fly-drives are a hybrid of seat-only independent holidays and inclusive tours. They sometimes include the first or last night's accommodation.

Purpose of travel

Tourists have a range of reasons for travelling. The purpose of travelling could be going on holiday, sightseeing, visiting an attraction, attending a business meeting, visiting relatives and friends or going to a sports event. The most popular purpose of visit by both UK residents and overseas visitors is holidays, as you can see from Figure 1.2. (See also Figure 4.27 on p. 278.)

Figure 1.2: Purpose of tourism, 1998

Millions	UK residents		Overseas visitors	
	Trips	Spending	Trips	Spending
Holiday	65.1	£9,800	10.5	£4,488
Business	13.7	£2,200	6.9	£3,820
To visit friends or relatives	38.4	£1,595	5.4	£1,970
Other	5.1	£435	2.9	£2,393
All purposes	122.3	£14,030	25.7	£12,671

Source: BTA/ETC

BUILD YOUR LEARNING

1 Use the definitions and information provided in this section to identify:

- the difference between domestic, inbound and outbound tourism
- the most popular reasons for travel by UK residents in 1998
- the percentage increase in the number of holidays taken by UK residents between 1951 and 1998 (see Figure 1.4, p.9).
- five short-haul tourist destinations for UK residents
- five long-haul tourist destinations for UK residents
- five popular UK tourist destinations.

2 Describe the difference between an inclusive tour, an all-inclusive tour and an independent holiday.

Keywords and phrases

You should know the meaning of the words and phrases listed below. Go back through the last three pages to refresh your understanding if necessary.

- All-inclusive holiday
- Business travel
- Day visitor
- Domestic tourism
- Domestic tourist
- Fly-drive holiday
- Inbound tourism
- Incoming tourist
- Inclusive tour/package holidays
- Independent holiday
- Leisure travel
- Long haul
- Long holiday
- Outbound tourism
- Outbound tourist
- Seat-only holiday
- short-break holiday
- Short haul
- Tourism
- Tourist
- Travel

Post-war development of travel and tourism

WE ARE GOING TO EXPLORE THE factors and major steps in the development of the UK travel and tourism industry from the end of the Second World War to the present day. Some of the key milestones in the rapid development of the industry are shown in Figure 1.3. It is important to realise, however, that travel and tourism existed long before this time. Indeed, many of our present day leisure activities can be traced back to ancient times. Roman citizens used to get away from the unbearable heat of Rome in mid-summer by going to their villas on the coast and in the Middle Ages, many monasteries made a good living from providing accommodation for people going on religious pilgrimages.

Since the Second World War, which ended in 1945, the global travel and tourism industry has grown so much that it is now regarded as the largest industry in the world. The total number of holidays taken by UK residents has risen steadily from 1951 to the present day, as shown in Figure 1.4. In 1998 it was estimated that UK residents took over 60 million holidays both at home and abroad.

Figure 1.3: Some key milestones in the development of the UK travel and tourism industry

Date	Milestone
1936 *Domestic*	Billy Butlin opens his first holiday camp at Skegness *Butlins*
1938	Holidays with Pay Act introduced
1946 *Domestic*	Fred Pontin opens his first holiday camp near Weston-Super-Mare *Pontins*
1950	First packaged air holiday organised by Horizon
1952	First jet airline passenger service
1959	First jet airline passenger service to Australia
1960 *Domestic*	Number of domestic holidays taken exceeds 30 million for the first time and number of foreign holidays rises to 3.5 million
Early 1960s	First global distribution systems developed by American airline companies
1968 *Domestic*	Countryside Act passed to create national parks
1968	World's first commercial Hovercraft operated from Dover to Boulogne
1969 *Domestic*	Development of Tourism Act introduced. Formation of the British, English, Scottish and Wales Tourist Boards
1976	Concorde goes into service
1981	60 per cent of households in the UK have regular use of at least one car *mobility*
1987 *Domestic*	Number of holidays abroad exceeds 20 million for the first time, whilst domestic holidays fall to 28.5 million, the lowest number since 1955
1992	EU Directive on package holidays introduced
1992	Department of National Heritage formed
1995 *easyJet founded.*	Le Shuttle and Eurostar carry first passengers through the Channel Tunnel
1997	70 per cent of all households in the UK have regular use of at least one car
1998	Number of holidays abroad exceeds 30 million for the first time
1998	An estimated 1.4 million people purchased travel tickets on the internet
1999	The English Tourism Council replaced the English Tourist Board

transport
I = transport

Figure 1.4: Estimated number of holidays, 1951–1998

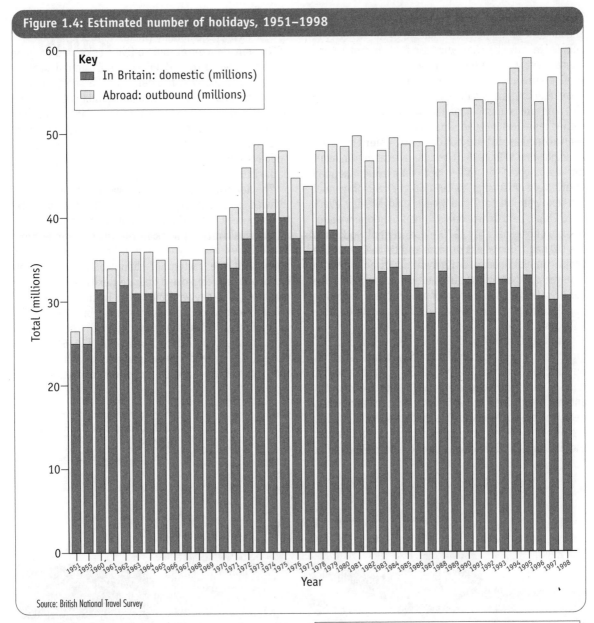

Source: British National Travel Survey

The development of the UK travel and tourism industry since the 1950s has been shaped by a complex set of interrelated factors. We are going to investigate four main factors which have combined to generate increased consumer demand for travel and tourism products and services, both in the UK and abroad. These are:

- changing socioeconomic conditions
- developing technology
- product development and innovation
- changing consumer needs, expectations and fashions.

Let's look at each factor in turn.

Socioeconomic conditions

Socioeconomic is the term given to the combination of social and economic factors. Many socioeconomic factors have contributed to the growth of the travel and tourism industry since the Second World War. They include:

- an increase in the time available for travel and leisure activities, including tourism
- an increase in disposable income for many people
- improved transport systems and greater personal mobility.

Time for travel and tourism

The amount of leisure time available to the majority of people in the UK has increased in recent years. Consequently, the number of facilities, products and services provided to satisfy consumer demands for travel and tourism has increased.

There are a number of reasons why people have gained more leisure time. One reason is that there has been an increase in **paid holiday entitlement** for those in employment. In 1938 it became a legal requirement for employers to give their employees holiday entitlement. Although by 1951 66 per cent of manual workers were allowed two weeks paid holiday every year, 28 per cent of workers still had only one week of holiday entitlement. By 1970, 52 per cent of workers in the UK had three weeks or more and by the 1990s the typical annual holiday entitlement had risen to four to five weeks. One obvious effect of increasing paid leave has been that a far higher proportion of the UK working population now has the time and money to take holidays.

The provision of paid holiday leave inspired the growth of the first seaside holiday camps such as Butlin's and Pontin's. Billy Butlin opened his first holiday camp at Skegness in 1936 and Fred Pontin entered the business in 1946 with his Brean Sands camp near Weston-Super-Mare. This made a seaside holiday accessible to the majority of working class families for the first time. Holiday camps proved extremely popular throughout the 1950s and 1960s and were the precursor to today's package holiday (inclusive tour).

The entitlement of four to five weeks paid holiday leave has helped the UK domestic tourism industry by encouraging many consumers to take short holiday breaks in addition to their main holiday. As a broad generalisation, domestic tourism is now used for additional holidays or weekend breaks, often involving brief trips to visit friends or relatives, or for short holidays such as city breaks, shopping trips and theme park visits.

The length of the working week has also been reduced substantially. In the 1950s, the average working week in the UK was 50 hours. The typical hours in a normal working week in the UK now range from 37–40 hours. Many workers also have greater choice now about the pattern of their working week. For example, some employers operate flexitime systems or operate a four-day working week. In these cases, the weekly hours worked remain the same, but the pattern of employees' leisure time has changed, as they move away from a typical Monday to Friday, 9–5 working pattern. These trends have stimulated growth in the UK short-break market and day trips to tourist attractions.

▼ Holidaymakers at Butlin's in the 1950s

A large number of people in the UK do not have jobs and therefore have significant amounts of free time. The unemployed and the retired are two such groups. The number of retired people in the UK has increased in recent years and demand for leisure activities to meet their needs has been a significant factor in the growth of companies such as SAGA, which specialises in holidays for people over 50. Most of the major tour operators now provide specialised holiday products for the over-50s market.

Disposable income

The amount of money that people have to spend on travel and tourism depends on the amount that is left after they have paid for necessities such as food, household bills, rent or mortgage. The remaining money is referred to as **disposable income**. Overall, individual disposable income has tended to rise in the UK in recent years and this has led to an increase in consumer spending on travel and tourism.

The general state of the economy is a major factor in the taking of holidays, particularly overseas travel. During the economic boom of the 1980s, when the economy grew rapidly, consumer spending on both domestic and outbound tourism rose in line with increasing levels of disposable income for many people. However, in periods of economic decline and recession, when average levels of disposable income fall, the taking of holidays is often the first item of household expenditure to be cut. For example, the early 1990s recession in the UK saw reduced demand for overseas holidays. Consumer confidence was low due to fears of unemployment and a slump in house prices. However, the domestic tourism industry benefited, as many

A World of Holidays

SAGA
Exclusively for people over 50

▲ Meeting the demand from older consumers for holidays

Britons took holidays in the UK rather than overseas.

Many other economic factors influence the development of the travel and tourism industry. Some of the key socioeconomic factors that have influenced the taking of holidays abroad by UK residents throughout the 1990s are highlighted in the case study.

CASE STUDY

How national economics affects travel and tourism

In 1999 the market research company Mintel investigated the key economic factors that have influenced the development of the UK outbound holiday market in the 1990s. Here are some of their key findings.

The general state of the economy has clearly operated as a major market factor in the taking of holidays abroad by UK residents throughout the 1990s.

Disposable income

Disposable income levels have been a determinant in holiday taking. For example, the UK travel and tourism industry was boosted by building society windfall payments in 1997.

Building society and friendly society flotations as public companies were valued at £36 billion in 1997, of which £6 billion went back to consumers who sold their shares. According to a MORI survey in August 1997, 25 per cent of the £6 billion, or £1.5 billion, was spent on holidays. However MORI estimates that the same consumers would have spent around half this amount on holidays anyway, so the travel industry only gained an extra £800 million in holiday spending. There will be further benefits from windfalls in future, since those who have retained their shares may be investing in order to afford a better holiday.

Life stage economics

Holidays are taken by all life stage groups of the population, from children to the elderly. For example, fear of unemployment was a major detractor for selling holidays during the recession, but it had less influence on the affluent early retireds, who constitute a significant market for independent and many specialist holidays.

Interest rates have a more significant impact on the retired population because of the importance of savings to these consumers. In the early 1990s, the higher interest rates which were introduced to help curb inflation had a negative impact on borrowers, who included the majority of younger families with mortgage repayments to consider before booking holidays. In contrast, higher interest rates benefited those relying on their savings to fund holidays. Meanwhile, the pre-family group which travels abroad extensively is less influenced by interest rates or the threat of unemployment. In this case, it is basic salary levels or the availability of student grants (or parental support) which are crucial

Exchange rates

Exchange rates have always been an important factor in determining patterns of holiday taking, for young or old people. In a mature, sophisticated travel market, any rise in the value of the pound will encourage outbound tourism, particularly if it involves the leading destination countries. This was never more apparent than in 1997, when the pound was riding high against most other currencies. This allowed the British to budget for their holidays abroad with unusual freedom of choice. Only two years earlier, travellers to France had found it difficult to maintain their usual holiday spending patterns, as the pound then bought less than eight French francs. In 1997 this rate had improved by 20 per cent.

Selected sterling exchange rates, September 1995 and September 1997

	1995	1997
US dollars	1.57	1.61
Austrian schillings	15.9	19.9
French francs	7.8	9.5
Dutch guilders	2.5	3.2
Italian lire	2,520	2,767
Spanish pesetas	194	238

Exchange rates obviously depend on the strength or weakness of sterling but they are also affected by the internal strength of currencies in main destination countries such as France or Spain. Inflation is also important in the holiday resorts, which may change more rapidly locally than in the rest of the country.

Source: Adapted from the Mintel Special Report into Holidays, *Marketing The Travel Business*, 1999

ACTIVITY

How national economics affects the travel and tourism

Read the case study and carry out these tasks.

- List the main economic factors that Mintel believes influenced the taking of holidays abroad in the 1990s.

- For each factor that you list, identify whether it has had a positive or negative effect on the taking of holidays abroad by UK residents.

- In small groups, identify possible socioeconomic factors and trends that you think will influence domestic, incoming and outbound tourism over the next five years.

- Look at the table showing exchange rates against the pound in 1995 and 1997 for selected popular tourist destination countries. For each currency, find out the present exchange rate and decide if you think the current rate is likely to have a positive or negative effect on outbound travel by UK residents to that country. Repeat the exercise, but this time consider the effect of the current exchange rates on inbound travel to the UK from each country.

Improved transport networks and personal mobility

Most people in the UK now have access to efficient transport networks which have made travel and tourism facilities, products and services much more readily accessible. Ports, airports and railway stations are able to handle millions of passengers each year, and the opening of the Channel Tunnel has stimulated increased cross-Channel travel. However, the greatest single transport factor that has promoted increased demand for tourism has been the rise of car ownership in the UK. There was a fivefold increase in the number of private cars on UK roads between 1951 and 1970, and around a tenfold increase between 1951 and the mid-1990s. It is now estimated that there are over 20 million privately owned cars in the UK and that 70 per cent of all households have access to at least one car (see Figure 1.5). Increasing car ownership has been a major factor in the rising popularity of visits to tourist destinations and attractions in the UK. The predominance of the car as the preferred mode of transport for domestic holidays in the UK is shown in Figure 1.6.

In 1951, trains, coaches and buses were the main modes of transport used by domestic tourists, yet by 1998, 80 per cent of all trips were taken by car. The improvement in road networks and increasing car ownership have also been major factors in opening access to the countryside for leisure activities. For those living in towns and cities, the countryside is now often just a short car journey away. Until the mid-1960s, recreational use of the countryside in Britain was still fairly limited. However, the numbers visiting the countryside for leisure purposes increased significantly after the 1960s and it is now estimated that over three-quarters of the UK population now visit the countryside on at least one occasion per year.

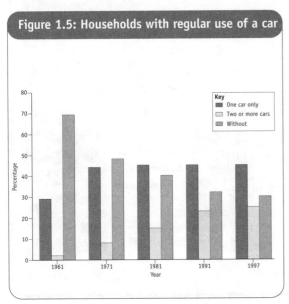

Figure 1.5: Households with regular use of a car

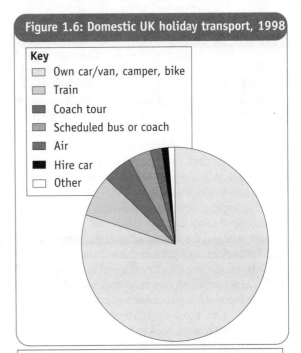

Figure 1.6: Domestic UK holiday transport, 1998

Key
- Own car/van, camper, bike
- Train
- Coach tour
- Scheduled bus or coach
- Air
- Hire car
- Other

Developing technology

A vast number of **technological developments** have influenced the development of the travel and tourism industry from the 1950s to the present day. Two of the most important are:

- transport technology
- communication and information technology.

Let's look at each in turn.

Transport technology

Improved transport technology has revolutionised passenger travel. Aircraft, ships and trains can today carry large numbers of passengers quickly, safely and cost effectively to their chosen destinations.

Technological advances in aircraft design after the Second World War meant that air travel became available as a means of mass transport from the 1970s. The development of the jet engine meant that air travel became fast, comfortable and relatively inexpensive, compared to sea travel. As the potential for air travel increased, entrepreneurs realised that there was scope to offer holidays to foreign destinations which combined transport, accommodation, meals and resort services in one package. This marked the emergence of the tour operator and inclusive tour (package holiday) as we know it. Thomson, one of the largest and best known tour operators today, was launched in 1965 and its development is described in the case study. Over 20 million holidays are now taken by British residents to overseas tourist destinations such as Spain, Italy and Greece every year.

Try & get up to date figures on car ownership.

The Boeing 707 jet airline service was introduced in 1958, and the development of State and privately owned airline companies provided the capacity to transport large numbers of passengers on package holidays. However, foreign holidays did not really emerge as a mass market phenomenon until the 1980s. According to estimates from Target Group Index (TGI), less than 10 per cent of UK adults took inclusive tours abroad as their main holiday in 1979. By 1998, however, this figure had risen to 22 per cent. So the growth of the overseas inclusive tour only became significant in the UK from the 1980s onwards.

The continuing development of transport technology throughout the 1990s has continued to increase demand for travel. As aircraft have become more technologically advanced they can carry larger numbers of passengers over longer distances more quickly and cost effectively than ever before. This has made air travel more affordable and convenient to the mass market in the UK and resulted in increased demand for both short-haul and long-haul flights and inclusive tours.

It is not just developing aircraft technology that has influenced the travel and tourism industry. Most forms of passenger travel have developed rapidly in recent years, including rail, ferry and cruise services.

The impact of developing transport technology on travel and tourism is highlighted by the cross-Channel market. Following the opening of the Channel Tunnel to passenger traffic in 1995, the continued development of new rail and ferry services, and the availability of low cost air services, tourists now have many cross-Channel travel options. Cross-Channel operators such as Le Shuttle, Eurostar, Hoverspeed, P&O and Brittany Ferries have all improved their services and lowered prices in order to remain competitive. Airline companies such as RyanAir, Go, EasyJet and British Midland have also been drawn into this competitive situation in order to retain their market shares. Given this situation it is not surprising that the volume of cross-Channel travel has increased throughout the 1990s, a trend that is likely to continue in the next decade.

CASE STUDY

The Thomson Travel Group

Thomson started in 1965, when Lord Thomson acquired three companies to meet the increasing demand for package holidays: Universal Skytours, Riviera Holidays and Britannia Airways. Market leaders at the time were Clarksons, Global and Cosmos. In 1968, Gay Tours and Luxitours were added to the family. At the same time, Lord Thomson was the first to introduce winter sun holidays, cruises and lake and mountain destinations.

In 1972, with the advent of wide-bodied jets and the lifting of restrictive price rulings, tour operators became able to expand the volume of the holidays available and to offer keen prices. Lord Thomson amalgamated his companies to form Thomson Holidays, which used Britannia Airways flights. He also acquired Sunair and Lunn Poly, a small retail chain. By 1974 Thomson Holidays had become the UK's leading tour operator.

Today, Thomson Travel consists of Thomson Tour Operations (a tour operator), Portland Holidays (a direct-sell tour operator), Britannia Airways (a charter airline) and Lunn Poly (the travel agency chain). Thomson, Portland, Skytours and Horizon are well-known brand names and Thomson Tour Operations is now Britain's number one tour operating company.

...to an even bigger choice of holidays

...to even more places to visit, with more things to do

Look forward...

...to the best value and best priced Thomson holidays

...to an even better service from your

THOMSON
preferred agent

CASE STUDY

Cross-Channel travel

In 1998 the *Mail on Sunday* sampled a selection of cross-Channel operators and marked each one out of ten.

no longer in operation.

Hoverspeed hovercraft

Operates: Dover-Calais, 12 crossings a day in each direction

Return fare for car and four passengers: from £115

Journey time: on schedule. Dock gate to dock gate 58 minutes. Time on hovercraft 36 minutes

Nausea factor: Low

Our rating: Fast, efficient and smooth. But let down by tacky cabins

8/10

32 yrs 1/10/00

Hoverspeed Seacat catamaran

Operates: Dover-Calais (five a day) and Folkestone to Boulogne (four a day)

Service tested: Dover to Calais

Return fare for car and four passengers: £115

Journey time: on schedule. Dock gate to dock gate 74 minutes. Time on catamaran 51 minutes

Nausea factor: Low

Our Rating: Very comfortable, but takes longer than the hovercraft

7/10

P&O Stena Line Elite catamaran

Operates: Newhaven-Dieppe (three services a day)

Return fare for car and four passengers: from £169

Journey time: Five minutes late. Dock gate to dock gate two hours 50 minutes. Time on catamaran two hours 20 minutes

Nausea factor: Low to medium

Our rating: Good for speed and scores well for general comfort

8/10

P&O Superstar Express catamaran

Operates: Portsmouth to Cherbourg three times a day

Return fare for car and four passengers: from £150

Journey time: Seven minutes late. Dock gate to dock gate three hours 35 minutes. Time on ferry two hours 52 minutes

Nausea factor: Low to medium

Our rating: Best of breed – spacious, well appointed and quiet

9/10

Eurotunnel car shuttle

Operates: Channel Tunnel car shuttle service between Folkestone and Boulogne – up to four services an hour at peak times

Return fare for car and four passengers: from £110

Journey time: Thirty minute delay. From motorway to motorway 90 minutes (long waiting time caused by 'disruption to services')

Actual journey time on train 37 minutes

Nausea factor: Nil

Our rating: Excellent marks for speed and efficiency

9/10

Source: Adapted from the
Mail on Sunday, 12 July 1998

ACTIVITY

Cross-Channel travel

The cross-Channel market is now extremely competitive. Obtain up-to-date information about the various transport options available to someone wishing to travel to Paris from your own locality. You should include at least one road, rail, ferry and air option. Present your findings in a comparison chart like the one below.

You will need to obtain travel brochures and timetables, or have access to the internet to complete this activity.

Method of travel	Departure point	Journey time	Return fare
Road			
Rail			
Sea			
Air			

Communications and information technology

Developments in communications and information technology systems have made a significant impact on the global travel and tourism industry. **Computer reservation systems (CRS)** or **global distribution systems (GDS)** have revolutionised the sales of airline tickets, package holidays, hotel accommodation and other travel and tourism products since they were first developed in the USA in the late 1960s.

GDS systems were developed from individual airline reservations which eventually amalgamated into four major global reservations systems: Sabre, Galileo, Amadeus and Worldspan. These huge distribution systems have enabled multinational corporations such as Thomson and Carlson to operate commercially throughout the world and develop global partnerships with airlines, hotel groups, travel agency chains and tour operators. The systems make it possible to obtain the latest information about an enormous range of travel and tourism products and services, make bookings and process payments. Their importance is shown in the Worldspan case study on p. 33.

Many consumers can now access information and purchase travel products from their own homes. In the 1980s, teletext services enabled many people to purchase travel products direct. However, the subsequent development of the internet and introduction of interactive digital television is likely to revolutionise the way consumers make their travel purchases in the future. The internet, in particular, is further stimulating the growth of independent holidays as growing numbers of consumers can now plan and book their holidays without needing to visit a travel agent.

Many airlines, tour operators and travel agents have recognised the potential of on-line bookings and are developing internet-based operations. One of the most comprehensive on-line travel information services is uTravel.co.uk (**www.uTravel.co.uk**). Some other examples of on-line travel service providers are shown in the newspaper article.

Surf the net for holiday bargains

Flights, insurance, package tours and car hire are cheap and easy to book on the internet, writes Matthew Wall, Web Wise.

There are thunderstorms and torrential downpours across Britain, so it must be summer again. And it is time to book that last minute jaunt to sunnier climes. If you want to save time, effort and money, start with the web.

Researching and booking holidays is one of the most popular internet activities. According to Fletcher Research, an internet consultancy, 1.4 million people bought travel tickets on-line in 1998. And it believes internet bookings will be worth £275 million by 2002.

Flights are ideally suited to web distribution because they are simple. And the later you are prepared to book, the greater the bargain, because the airline is desperate to fill the plane. But don't be too fussy about when you go.

You can either go direct to the airline or via an on-line travel agent. EasyJet (www.easyjet.co.uk) the discount airline, has had great success on-line and now sells about a third of all its tickets over the internet. It offers £1 off every one-way flight and £2 off every return flight bought on-line. There are no tickets involved – all you need to take with you is your confirmation number and passport. Go (www.go-fly.com) the low-cost arm of British Airways, has a similar service on its simple website. For a wider selection of flights and destinations you need to go to a broker, such as Cheap Flights (www.cheapflights.co.uk), which gives you a round-up of all the best travel agents' deals and links users to their websites. Flightbookers.com (www.flightbookers.com) is also useful. Last Minute (www.lastminute.com) will refund the difference if you find a cheaper flight.

Of course, the big travel websites, such as Expedia (www.expedia.co.uk), Travelocity (www.travelocity.com) and a2btravel.com (www.a2btravel.com) also offer flight booking, but include weekend breaks, package holidays, hotel reservations and car-hire booking. For last minute packages, Bargain Holidays.com (www.bargain-holidays.com) is a good bet. Even Bob Geldof has jumped on board with his own travel site (www.deckchair.com), while Virgin Net offers a well-designed all-round travel service. There are even websites, such as QXL (www.qxl.com) and Last Minute, that allow you to bid at auction for tickets and holidays. Be prepared to hunt for the best bargain and make sure that the travel sites you book through are accredited by a recognised body.

Sunday Times, 6 June 1999

Product development

The travel and tourism industry is dynamic and new products are continually developed in order to meet the **changing needs and expectations of consumers**. The development of the mass tourism market has been largely due to the ability of the industry to introduce **innovative travel products** and services for domestic, inbound and outbound tourists. The case study highlights the writer's top three travel innovations of the twentieth century.

ACTIVITY

Travel innovations

What do you think the top three travel innovations of the twenty-first century will be? Discuss your suggestions in small groups to identify the most likely innovations.

CASE STUDY

The top travel innovations of the twentieth century

The twentieth century has seen many travel innovations: factor 24 sun cream, suitcases with wheels, the bikini... Frank Barrett, the Mail on Sunday's travel editor chooses his (more serious) top three.

Disneyland

The modern shape of the tourist business effectively dates from the day in the early fifties when Walt Disney took his daughters to a California funfair and recoiled in disgust at the tawdry stalls and litter-strewn surroundings.

A man who ran a business which demanded the most painstaking standards of production was entitled to wonder why similar standards did not apply equally to amusement parks and Disney decided to create one where families would enjoy the highest levels of quality in a safe, controlled environment.

While friends and colleagues privately derided the idea of the creator of Mickey Mouse and Snow White becoming the proprietor of a glorified funfair, Disney bought a plot of land in Anaheim, California, and built his park called, with an impressive lack of modesty, Disneyland.

Its opening confirmed the slowly growing realisation that tourism had evolved into something quite different from the concept pioneered by Thomas Cook more than 100 years before. It was no longer simply the sum total of combining transport arrangements with accommodation bookings – holidays had become a branch of show business.

By creating his own world, Disney had taken the first steps towards a concept of controlled delivery, through which holiday suppliers endeavour to control every element of a package to ensure total satisfaction.

Disney realised that people deserve the best during their precious holiday time. The most complete realisation of his dream is to be found at the Disney theme parks which make up Walt Disney World in Orlando, Florida.

Laker

Like Disney, Freddie Laker with his Laker Airways was a man who had a vision and asked: 'Why not offer a low-cost transatlantic airline service with the bare minimum of on-board facilities – something like a flying train?' Until the mid-1970s, air travel was still largely the preserve of the wealthy. Laker, talked about the forgotten man, the ordinary person who was just as entitled to travel by plane. Laker was determined to bring air travel to the masses.

He proposed to call his service Skytrain. To achieve his dream he took on the airline establishment and national governments to break their monopoly on air fares. From the day Skytrain was launched, the travel business was never the same again. The cheap fare genie was out of the bottle. Laker's rapid success inspired the US government to usher in a new age of deregulated airlines that offered consumers better services and cheaper fares.

When the pound plunged against the dollar, Sir Freddie proved vunerable to a concerted attack from his competitors, who quickly seized the opportunity to shoot him out of the skies. His airline went bust in the 1980s recession.

Sir Freddie has never entirely left the airline business – Laker Airways flew the Atlantic again in the 1990s in a temporary but very admirable display of dogged defiance. Richard Branson picked up the Laker mantle, a fact which he happily acknowledged when he named one of his first Virgin Airways 747s the Spirit of Sir Freddie.

Horizon

Next year will mark the 50th anniversary of the charter flight-inclusive package holiday invented in its modern form by Horizon Holidays.

Its creator was Vladimir Raitz. Now 77, he's still energetic, helping to launch a programme of cigar holidays to Cuba a few months ago. A summer holiday on the island of Corsica in 1949 derailed him from a career in journalism into setting up his own holiday company.

He took the unprecedented step of specially chartering a plane to take his clients to a campsite on the island.

In doing so he effectively changed the face of the entire British holiday. Families who once saw Bognor Regis as the limit of their travel ambitions quickly became familiar with Spain, Greece and Portugal.

Source: *Mail on Sunday*, 26 December 1999

Domestic tourism

Domestic tourism in the UK peaked in the 1960s and early 1970s, with large numbers of holidays to seaside resorts such as Blackpool and Brighton. This era was also the height of the popularity of the many seaside holiday camps that had been developed by entrepreneurs such as Billy Butlin and Fred Pontin in the 1950s. However, by the late 1970s consumer expectations had shifted towards travelling abroad for holidays. The long seaside holiday was the main casualty of this trend, and many of the UK's traditional seaside resorts suffered as a result of falling tourist revenue.

Since the 1980s, the industry that supports domestic tourism in the UK has had to work hard to maintain its market share, despite increasing competition from overseas destinations. Although Figure 1.4 on p. 9 shows that the number of domestic holidays taken in the UK has fallen from its peak of 40.5 million in 1974 to 30 million in 1998, the industry has successfully retained a good share of the holiday market. It has

achieved this largely through the development of the **short break**. This is a weekend or mid-week break of three nights or less at discounted rates in hotels or other accommodation which would previously have insisted on offering discounts only for a full week's or fortnight's holiday.

Traditional seaside resorts such as Blackpool and Brighton have attempted to improve their image by developing new visitor attractions and some have also developed exhibition and conference facilities to encourage business visitors. The main holiday centre operators have also responded to changing consumer demands and the increasing competition from overseas destinations by developing new facilities and products, such as themed restaurants, sports facilities and swimming pools with slides and wave pools. The two case studies (on pp. 20–1) show how the traditional holiday camp market has responded to changing consumer expectations in the 1990s.

CASE STUDY

The changing face of UK holiday centres

Following the creation of the mass overseas inclusive tour market in the early 1970s, the UK sector saw its share of total holidays decline, despite the fact that, in absolute terms, the holiday business continued to grow. This development, plus the wider choice of home grown holiday arrangements and the popularity of the independent break, worked against the holiday centre vacation and market share was lost, particularly among middle income earners and younger holidaymakers.

The popular television sitcom of the early 1980s, *Hi-de-Hi*, also affected attendance levels, according to the industry. It mocked the holiday camp and its traditions and portrayed them as amateurish and downmarket. Some people still perceive holiday centres in terms of the images created by this series, although these images are no longer as widely held as they were.

The holiday centres invested considerable amounts of money during the 1970s and 1980s to improve their image and the investment was largely successful. Facilities were updated and standards improved, the range of amusements and activities was increased and entertainments were revitalised. Accommodation arrangements were also adjusted to be more flexible, increase product appeal and cater for the growing short-break market. Among the various arrangements were budget holidays, full-board, half-board, B&B, five and seven day breaks and self-catering. New holiday themes and styles included activity holidays, educational breaks, adult-only breaks and family holidays. Special arrangements were also introduced for single parents and pensioners.

Over the last 15 years, many mobile home and static caravan parks have also extended their facilities and entertainment provision to conform to the holiday centre format. In addition, some of the existing holiday centre operators, such as the Rank Organisation, have also established self-catering caravan parks with elaborate facilities and full entertainment and activity programmes.

A new dimension to these holiday businesses is the ownership option. Both Butlin's and Haven (Park World Holidays) have introduced schemes which allow holidaymakers to buy their own caravans at holiday camp sites. This is a useful means of increasing commitment to a holiday centre and of ensuring repeat business.

New holiday environments and themes have been important for the industry. The traditional format of swimming pool, mini-golf, bars, discos and night time entertainment still forms the basis for many holiday camps, although there is a growing emphasis on alternative activities.

Greater variety in catering facilities has also increased the appeal of holiday centres. Food courts are another improvement and restaurants provide a more sophisticated alternative to the traditional cafes. A move into different kinds of premises such as hotels and former stately homes has also been taking place and these have contributed to a more upbeat image for the holiday centre.

Investment in upgrading and extending the range of options and offerings by the holiday centres has been a positive move and has been instrumental in transforming the down-market image of these businesses. Mintel estimates suggest that spending on holiday centre breaks has grown from £405 million in 1990 to £750 million in 1996. These estimates relate to the booking price only and exclude extra goods and services purchased at the holiday centre.

The establishment of the Centre Parcs holiday village format in the UK in 1987 introduced a new concept which has appealed to groups that have traditionally stayed away from British holiday centres. The Centre Parcs holiday village is typically sited in unspoilt natural woodland and is designed to complement the ecology of the local environment. The range of leisure activities available emphasises a healthy lifestyle. Accommodation is self-catering, although there are also restaurants and brasseries to tempt holidaymakers.

Source: Adapted from the Mintel Report on Holiday Centres 1997

CASE STUDY

New image for Butlin's brand

In 1936, Billy Butlin opened his first holiday camp at Skegness. It could accommodate 2,000 people and offered chalet accommodation and a comprehensive recreational programme that included sport, dancing and other communal entertainments. Initially, Butlin's camps were aimed at clerical workers and their families, as the weekly charges of around £3.50 were beyond the reach of most manual workers. However, after the Second World War, Butlin's camps catered increasingly for the mass working class market and attracted huge numbers of visitors. Facilities typically included a ballroom, theatre, swimming pool, gardens, dining room and chalet accommodation.

By the 1970s, the number of people visiting Butlin's camps had fallen dramatically, due largely to the popularity of cheap foreign package holidays. The Rank Organisation took over Butlin's Holidays Camps in 1972 and decided that a major relaunch was needed for the 1990s. It closed many camps and opened five huge Holiday Worlds around the coast of Britain.

In 1997 Butlin's announced that it was channelling £150 million into its sites. In 1998 the holiday centres in Ayr and Pwllheli were transferred to sister company Haven and a £2.5 million investment transformed them into Haven All Action Holiday Parks. At Minehead, Bognor Regis and Skegness, more than £10 million was invested in new splash waterworld attractions. Other additions included new Noddy-themed accommodation units, Jaks bars and, in Minehead, a new Hotshots ten-pin bowling and family entertainment centre. The Coral Beach and Ocean Drive restaurants at Skegness were refitted and themed, and each centre had a new Pinewood Studios Café and Bar, as well as all-weather sports courts.

The redevelopment programme was completed in 1999. It included new-built and refurbished accommodation, and the addition of Skyline Pavilions which provide year-round, weather-protected entertainment venues, complete with live acts, bars and restaurants. Noddy and his friends from Toyland became permanent fixtures, as did high street names such as Burger King and Harry Ramsden's. The sites opened under the brand name Butlin's Family Entertainment Resorts in 1999.

www.butlins.co.uk — January – December 2000

Butlins Family Entertainment Resorts

SAVE UP TO 25%

Resorts at Minehead, Bognor Regis and Skegness

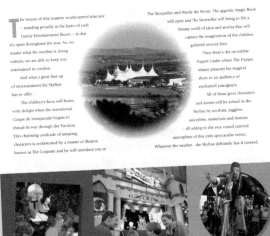

November 1999 to October 2000

the Skyline has it covered

Take a seat in the Skyline Pavilion...sip a drink or two, watch the world go by and enjoy the endless feast of fun served up in this fantastic venue.

'Once upon a time'

A magical show at the Puppet Castle

While holiday centres today offer the same basic products that their predecessors provided (namely, accommodation, recreation and entertainment for the whole family on one site) they now offer a much wider choice for consumers.

ACTIVITY

Holiday centres

Read the case studies on pp. 20–1 about the development of the traditional seaside holiday camps of the 1960s into modern holiday centres and answer the following questions.

- Why did the holiday camp concept became so popular in the 1950s and 1960s?

- What were the key factors that contributed to the decline of these camps in the 1980s?

- What types of product development and innovation have been introduced by the holiday centre operators throughout the 1990s to increase the level of business?

- How have changing consumer needs and expectations influenced the recent development of the holiday centre?

Outbound tourism

Tour operators, airlines, hotels and travel agents must constantly develop innovative products in order to meet consumer demand and retain their market share in an increasingly competitive market. For example, tour operators now provide a wide variety of holiday products that cater for all types of tourist. This diversity is highlighted by ABTA's A to Z list of special interest holiday categories (Figure 1.7). The list gives an indication of how much the industry has developed since the introduction of mass market package holidays in the 1960s and 1970s. In the early days of the package holiday, consumer choice was relatively limited, with tour operators concentrating on summer beach resort holidays to Spain, Greece and Portugal. However, today consumers can choose from an extensive range of holiday destinations and products and, because the travel and tourism industry is continually developing, the list of special interest holidays will change.

ACTIVITY

Special interest holiday categories

Select ten activities from the list of special interest holiday categories in Figure 1.7. For each, identify one tour operator that offers this type of holiday.

Suggest five new types of special interest holiday that you think might become popular in the future, and then identify five from the list that you think may cease to be provided due to falling consumer demand. When you have made your choices, discuss the reasons behind your selections in small groups.

The vast number of overseas holiday products can be divided and subdivided almost indefinitely, but the following indicators provide a basis for investigating product development:

- inclusive tours or independent holidays

- mode of transport out of the UK – air or sea or Channel Tunnel

- length of holiday – short break of less than four nights or longer holidays

- distance of destination from the UK – short haul or long haul

- season of departure – winter or summer.

These indicators can be combined in various ways to produce distinct holiday categories. Since the 1970s, the most popular type of holiday abroad has been the inclusive tour by air, lasting more than four nights, taken in the summer to short-haul destinations such as Spain and Greece. However, other holiday products have become popular and are now challenging the traditional short haul destinations. In particular, long-haul inclusive tours and all-inclusive holidays have grown in popularity following new product launches and sustained marketing efforts by tour operators.

Tour operators have successfully developed innovative new products to cater for specific markets such as families, single and retired people, honeymooners and special interest holidays. The industry is continually developing new products and services to cater for all markets.

Figure 1.7: Types of special interest holiday

Activity	Drama	Religious/ pilgrimages	Motor racing
Adventure	Dream machines	Romantic	Netball
Agricultural	Educational	Round the world	Olympics (summer)
Animal watching	Escorted tours	Safari/wildlife	Olympics (winter)
Archaeology	Expeditions	Sailing/boating/ yachting	Paragliding
Art and craft	Exhibitions		Paralympics
Ballooning	Festivals/carnivals	School tours	Parasailing
Battlefield tours	Floral/gardening	Scrabble	Polo
Bird watching	Fly-drive	Shooting	Rugby
Botany/naturalist	Ghost hunting/haunting	Singles	Skiing
Bridge		Single parent	Snow boarding
Camper/motor home	Groups	Sports – general	Squash
Camping/caravan	Health/spa/fitness	American sports	Tennis
Canal/river cruising	Historical/heritage	Archery	Volleyball
Canoeing	Incentive	Basketball	Water sports
Carpet weaving	Island hopping	Bowling (ten-pin)	Winter sports
Children's holiday clubs	Language tours	Bowls (greens)	Tailor-made
Christmas/New Year	Millennium	Boxing	The arts
Church and cathedral	Military history	Bungee jumping	Theme parks
City/short/weekend breaks	Motoring/self-drive	Cricket	Trade fairs
Coach	Mountaineering	Cycling	Trekking
Concorde experience	Murder/mystery	Diving	Upmarket
Cook/gastronomic	Music – jazz	Fishing	Walking/rambling
Corporate	Music – opera	Fishing (deep sea)	Weddings abroad
Cruise	Music – rock and pop	Football (playing)	Whale/dolphin watching
Crusader/castle tours	Naturist	Football (watching)	White water rafting
Cultural	Nostalgia	Golf (playing)	Wind surfing
Dancing	Older generation	Golf (watching)	Wine/beer tasting
Day trips	Outdoor pursuits	Hockey	Young people
Disabled	Photography	Horse racing	
	Rail/railways	Horse riding	
	Ranch holidays	Martial arts	

Source: ABTA Information Bureau, www.abtanet.com

Long-haul holidays

Long-haul holidays have in the past been identified with exotic destinations for the affluent and those with plenty of time on their hands, but this image has changed in recent years. Many consumers who would previously have holidayed within Europe are now taking long-haul holidays. At least five million holidays were taken to long-haul countries in 1998, of which around half were package tours and half independent. Earlier in the decade, independent travel was more important in the long-haul market, but the growth of package holidays to Florida and the Caribbean has shifted the ratio towards inclusive tours, as shown in Figure 1.8.

ROLL UP...

■ FIFTY years after inventing the package holiday, its founder Vladimir Raitz has embarked on a new venture. The man who blazed the trail to Majorca and the Costa del Sol is backing the hot new destination – Cuba. With independent operator Scantours, he has put together a programme of eight-day cigar tours for aficionados of genuine Havanas. Further information from Scantours 0171-839 2927.

▲ Vladimir Raitz invented the package holiday more than fifty years ago

The most important change in the pattern of British holidays in the 1990s was, arguably, the breakthrough of the USA as a mass market destination. In fact, the trans-Atlantic crossing is the focus of growth, since holidays to Canada and the Caribbean are also booming. The latter feature important long-haul **niche markets** like Caribbean cruises, all-inclusive tours (for example, to the Dominican Republic and St Lucia) and skiing in Canada. Florida has emerged as a mainstream destination for family, summer sun holidays.

Other long-haul destinations such as Kenya and South Africa, India and Thailand have also taken some summer sun share from the traditional Mediterranean destinations. Australia and New Zealand also continue to grow in popularity.

Despite the growth of long-haul holidays, they still account for less than 20 per cent of the whole holiday market, so it is worth stressing that France, Spain and the Canaries remain popular. Together they account for over 50 per cent of the holidays abroad taken by the British. However, in the future traditional European short-haul destinations will have to compete hard with long-haul destinations in order to retain their market share.

All-inclusive tours

The all-inclusive concept has been established for over 20 years, centred around exclusive upmarket destinations in the Caribbean. The concept was extended into the main market short-haul sector by the major tour operators during the summer season of 1996, with all-inclusive tours to countries such as Spain and Portugal that were targeted at families. However, the main all-inclusive holiday market caters to consumers who want a holiday in an exotic location and who are prepared to pay a premium for the indulgence of a plentiful supply of food, drink and entertainment.

All-inclusive holidays are profitable for the tour operators since they are relatively expensive. The more exclusive long-haul resorts attract a niche market and continue to be in demand for events such as weddings and honeymoons.

The all-inclusive concept is now well established and is likely to be attractive to many holiday makers who perceive it as good value for money and who appreciate the chance to budget by knowing how much they will spend in advance. All-inclusive holidays are widely believed to be attractive to families, offering sports facilities and activities for a range of different ages with plenty to keep children occupied.

Figure 1.8: Long-haul holidays abroad, 1991–98

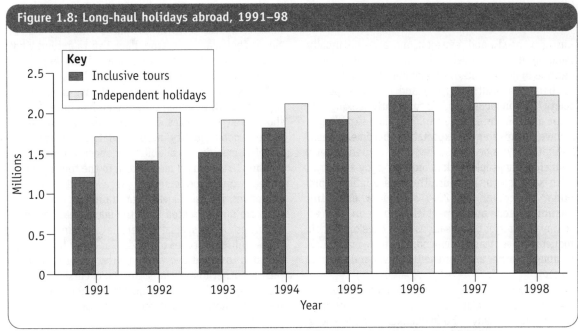

Key
- Inclusive tours
- Independent holidays

(y-axis: Millions, 0 to 2.5; x-axis: Year, 1991–1998)

First Choice
All inclusive

Save up to £180
Free child places
see page 17

Year-round

May 2000 - April 2001 1st Edition

THOMSON
All Inclusive

Smiles
in the Sun
made possible by
THOMSON

Look after Nº1. Let Nº1 look after you.

ACTIVITY

Products and services

Obtain copies of two tour operators' brochures that include holidays to long haul destinations such as the USA or the Caribbean. Look through the brochures and for each one make a list of any particular products or services that are provided for the following client groups:

- families with babies
- families with young children
- families with teenagers
- retired couples
- couples on honeymoon
- people celebrating birthdays and anniversaries.

Include products and services you find that are provided for client groups which are not listed above.

Compare the types of products and services provided by each tour operator and decide which one, in your opinion, has the most innovative products for the various client groups. You may find it useful to compare your answers with your classmates.

Needs and expectations

Consumer needs and expectations are continually changing and the travel and tourism industry must continue to develop innovative products. Today we are members of a healthier, fitter and more prosperous society than previously, that is constantly seeking new leisure and tourism experiences. The more experiences we have, the greater our expectations become. Indeed, Britain today has been described as a leisured society, in which many people work in order to enjoy a lifestyle which satisfies their needs. The case studies about holiday centres on pp. 20–1 show how **changing consumer needs and expectations** have influenced the way that major organisations have developed their products to meet market demand. There are many such examples in other areas of the UK travel and tourism industry.

As holidaymakers we are increasingly adventurous. Already familiar with Spain and other European destinations, many holidaymakers now seek destinations further afield. The introduction of charter routes to more exotic destinations has made them more affordable and accessible.

As holidaymakers become more experienced and adventurous they expect more from each holiday. What used to be perceived as added value or extra is now often expected as a standard part of any inclusive tour. The fierce competition within the package holiday market means that many operators have had to extend what they provide within the price of a holiday, especially those which are on a full or half-board basis.

The way we now choose our holidays is also more sophisticated. Research undertaken by Mintel (1998) shows that the basics expected today are value for money, good quality accommodation, trustworthy travel companies, availability of specific resorts and bonding to safeguard money paid to the tour operator. Added value products such as a broad choice of excursions, inclusive meals, entertainment and special deals are now expected from the mainstream holiday. Activities and special interests are increasingly important for all types of holiday, as fewer tourists are prepared to spend two weeks by the sea or hotel pool with no other distractions. Sports, excursions, group activities, evening entertainments and children's clubs are all now considered essential by many holidaymakers.

Consumer sophistication has been underlined by trends such as late booking, bargain hunting, independent booking (using teletext or the internet) and willingness to complain if holidays do not live up to their brochure promises, as highlighted in the article below.

Good moaning guide

We have had a week of interesting and curious developments in that strange, unpredictable circus known as the travel business.

Perhaps the most fascinating revelation is that the Association of British Travel Agents is preparing, in consultation with the Office of Fair Trading, a 'how to complain' guide for holiday-makers.

Can the sworn enemy of Watchdog's Anne Robinson really be encouraging its members' customers to 'whinge' (as the travel companies are wont to put it)?

Indeed, Keith Betton of ABTA admits that it does sound rather like turkeys reminding people that Christmas is just around the corner. He says: 'Last year we received calls from more than 50,000 consumers needing some on-the-spot advice and a further 17,100 letters detailing various holiday woes.

'It is a small percentage of the 16 million or so people who take an overseas package holiday, but it still requires a team of 12 consumer advisers to tell customers what options are open to them.'

Adapted from the *Mail on Sunday*, 5 September 1999

Friends, Britons, travel agents, lend me your ears.....

The trend towards late booking to gain discounts from travel agents and tour operators has affected profit margins. Major tour operators now try to increase profitability by encouraging early booking. Holiday prices are now often cheapest when first published, to encourage consumers to book well in advance.

The development of low-cost or no-frills airlines during the 1990s and their increasing popularity has boosted holidays within Europe, especially independent travel and visits to friends and relations. The press article highlights the impact of these no-frills airlines on the package holiday industry. However, as the article points out, it is a combination of factors, rather than simply the availability of cheap flights, that influences the package holiday market.

Will there be life for the traditional package holiday in the new millennium?

Fifty years after its birth, Britain's biggest tour operators are agonising over the future.

The package holiday market is rapidly losing ground to the fast-growing independent travel sector. Last year for example, of the 30.8 million people who took a holiday, 16.2 million people bought a package holiday, while 14.6 million travelled independently.

A key factor in this growth has been the no-frills airline revolution which has seen the rise and rise of EasyJet, Go and RyanAir. Last year more than 8.5 million people booked a flight independently in the UK, an increase of more than a fifth over the 1998 total. Not surprisingly, therefore, Airtours and Thomson have been making noises about ways to 'unpackage' the package. They plan to loosen the shackles of fixed period durations – and freshen up the product so their holidays are more closely matched to the increasingly sophisticated aspirations of their clients. Interestingly, Thomson is planning a short-break programme using the low-cost flights of the new no-frills airlines – if you can't beat them, join them.

The most detailed analysis of the future of the holiday business comes from Britain's third biggest operator, First Choice. In a fascinating report, the company analyses the social trends which are having a huge impact on our holiday plans. It found that in addition to becoming better educated, wealthier and better travelled, we're having fewer children.

The average family now has 1.7 children and women are having their children later, meaning that more and more of us will be holidaying with teenagers when we're in our fifties.

More women are choosing not to have children – one in five women of childbearing age – and fewer people are getting married. More are living together – seven in 10 couples nowadays, compared to one in 21 in the mid-1960s – and more are living alone. Put all these changing trends together – and toss in developments like the internet – and you can understand why the traditional package holiday no longer matches many people's needs.

There is a fast growing army of new Britons blazing a new holiday trail. Affluent, educated, energetic and keen for intelligent travel – the holiday business is racing to keep up with them.

Mail on Sunday, 29 August 1999

ACTIVITY

Consumer needs and expectations

In small groups, discuss how changing consumer needs and expectations have influenced the development of the following travel and tourism trends.

- Emergence of modern holiday centres such as Centre Parcs and Butlin's Holiday Worlds to replace traditional holiday camps.

- Increasing popularity of short breaks in the UK, at the expense of the traditional longer seaside holiday that was popular in the 1960s and 1970s.

- Growth of independently organised holidays to overseas destinations.

- Increasing popularity of long haul inclusive tours.

- Increasing popularity of all-inclusive tours.

To be able to take part in leisure and tourism activities in the 1990s we need to have time, money, access to transport and an awareness of the range of activities available. The factors which have stimulated the growth of the UK travel and tourism industry are all interrelated and it is their combined impact which has generated the huge consumer demand for the wide range of products and services that these industries now provide. It is highly likely that the factors which have generated increasing consumer demand for travel and tourism products and services will continue to stimulate growth. Indeed, tourism is now regarded as the world's largest industry and is set to continue to grow.

BUILD YOUR LEARNING

Keywords and phrases

You should know the meaning of the words and phrases listed below. Go back to refresh your understanding if necessary.

- Changing needs and expectations
- Computerised reservation system (CRS)
- Disposable income
- Global distribution system
- Innovative travel products
- Niche market
- Paid holiday entitlement
- Short break
- Socioeconomic
- Technological developments

End of section activitiy

1 Describe the key factors that have influenced the rapid development of the UK travel and tourism industry since the end of the Second World War. You should include:

- changing socioeconomic circumstances
- developing technology
- product development and innovation
- changing consumer needs, expectations and fashions.

Support your description with relevant examples and data.

2 Describe the key factors that you think will affect the development of the industry in the future. Support your views with appropriate examples and forecasts.

Features of the travel and tourism industry

THE TRAVEL AND TOURISM industry is continually developing in order to meet changing consumer needs and perceptions. Today's travel and tourism industry is extremely diverse in the products and services that it provides to customers, and is subject to continual changes in demand. The UK travel and tourism industry that has evolved over the relatively short period since the end of the Second World War has a number of features that reflect the highly dynamic and competitive nature of the business. Some of the key features are that it is:

- dominated by the private sector
- made up predominantly of small and medium-sized private sector enterprises
- often supported and promoted by public sector organisations
- dependent on the extensive use of new technologies
- vulnerable to external pressures
- can have a positive or negative impact on host communities.

Broadly speaking, we can divide travel and tourism organisations into two groups: **commercial** (the **private sector**) and **non-commercial** (the **public** and **voluntary sectors**). Commercial and non-commercial organisations often differ in terms of:

- defining and meeting objectives
- funding or revenue generation
- stakeholder or shareholder expectations.

The UK travel and tourism industry is dominated by the private sector. The BTA estimates that the UK industry is made up of at least 200,000 businesses, the majority of which are small to medium sized. Although there is a huge number of travel and tourism enterprises in the UK, most components of the industry are dominated by a small number of national and multinational corporations. For example, the holiday market is dominated by a small number of corporations such as Thomson and Airtours in terms of the total volume of business, although there are hundreds of small independent travel agents and tour operators. We shall consider the structure of the various components of the industry later.

The private sector

Private sector organisations are directly or indirectly in private ownership. Their main aim is usually to generate profits from the services and products which they provide for their customers, for the benefit of the owners or shareholders of the organisation. The main activities of the private sector in the travel and tourism industry are in the fields of retail sales, catering, accommodation, entertainment, travel services and tourism. Many private sector travel and tourism organisations such as Rank, P&O and Virgin are household names and make a major contribution to the wealth of the United Kingdom. Many of these major companies are **public limited companies** (plcs) that are owned by **shareholders**, who expect to gain a financial return from their share holdings. Travel and tourism facilities commonly provided by the private sector include hotels, theme parks, travel agencies and restaurants.

ACTIVITY

The private sector

1 Identify the types of facilities, products and services provided by each of these well-known private sector travel and tourism organisations:

- British Airways
- First Choice Holidays
- Forte
- Rank Organisation
- Thomas Cook
- Virgin.

2 Look at the financial section of any national broadsheet newspaper (such as *The Times* or *The Guardian*) and note all plcs listed in the shares column under the heading of leisure. What do you think they have in common in terms of defining and meeting objectives, funding or revenue generation and shareholder expectations? You may find it useful to obtain the annual report of a plc, as this often provides information on objectives, funding and shareholders.

The public sector

Public sector organisations are largely funded by central or local government, which also influences their strategies and policies. These organisations include tourist boards and local authorities, which run facilities such as museums, art galleries and tourist information centres. Often, the role of public sector organisations involved in the travel and tourism industry is one of support and promotion. The British Tourist Authority and the national and regional tourist boards are the key public sector organisations involved in supporting the UK tourism industry.

The British Tourist Authority

The **British Tourist Authority (BTA)** was established under the Development of Tourism Act 1969. This was the first piece of legislation specifically concerned with tourism. The BTA is responsible for promoting Britain as a destination for incoming (overseas) tourists. Its role and functions are described in the case study on p. 59.

BRITISH TOURIST AUTHORITY

The national tourist boards

The **national tourist boards (NTBs)** were established in 1969 when the Development of Tourism Act was passed. A tourist board for Northern Ireland had already been established in 1948. The **English Tourism Council (ETC)** replaced the English Tourist Board (ETB) in 1999.

BWRDD CROESO CYMRU
WALES TOURIST BOARD

SCOTLAND

Northern Ireland Tourist Board

While the British Tourist Authority promotes Britain overseas, the national tourist boards are responsible for promoting domestic tourism in their respective countries. There are four main national tourist boards, plus separate national tourist boards for the Isle of Man, Guernsey and Jersey. They all have broadly similar objectives, which include:

- advising the government and public bodies on all matters concerning tourism

- maximising tourism's contribution to the economy by creating wealth and jobs

- enhancing the image of their countries as tourist destinations

- encouraging sustainable tourism development

- researching trends in tourism and consumer requirements.

The regional tourist boards

The work of the national tourist boards in promoting domestic tourism in their respective countries is supported by regional tourist boards. There are now ten **regional tourist boards** in England and three in Wales, as shown on the map on p. 31. Although autonomous bodies, regional tourist boards operate some common programmes under contract from their NTBs such as information collection and the networked Tourist Information Centre (TIC) system.

Although the regional tourist boards receive grants from central and local government, they have to raise a large proportion of their income from commercial activities such as subscriptions from their members and revenue from advertising in their regional publications.

Local authorities

Many local authorities in the UK play an important role in developing, promoting and managing tourism in their areas. For example, Darlington borough council produces a visitor guide that describes attractions, accommodation in the surrounding countryside, events and festivals in the area in order to promote tourism. Many local authorities also work with a range of local agencies to provide web sites that promote tourism in their area, as in Poole in Dorset, (**www.poole.gov.uk**) and in Merseyside (**www.merseyworld.com**).

The voluntary sector

Voluntary sector organisations are usually non-profit making or charitable and are managed and operated largely by volunteers. Examples of voluntary sector organisations include travel clubs and a wide range of conservation, countryside recreation and heritage pressure groups, such as the Rambler's Association, Tourism Concern and the National Trust. The webstract on p. 32 provides details of the role and funding of Tourism Concern.

ACTIVITY

The regional tourist boards

The map shows the 13 regions which currently make up the English and Welsh regional tourist boards. Locate each of these tourist board regions on the map.

Key:

1	Cumbria		7	London
2	Northumbria		8	West country
3	North west		9	Southern
4	Yorkshire		10	South east England
5	Heart of England		11	North Wales
6	East of England		12	Mid Wales
			13	South Wales

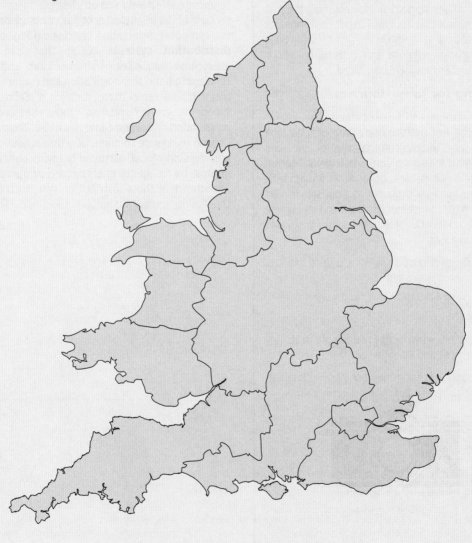

WEBSTRACT

Tourism Concern

Tourism Concern is:

- a membership network set up in 1989 to bring together people concerned about tourism's impact on communities and the environment, both in the UK and worldwide

- a catalyst for change. Tourism Concern influences and informs government, industry and education. It is an independent voice for justice and sustainability in tourism.

Why Tourism Concern?

Tourism is the world's largest industry, affecting the lives of millions of people. While it can bring benefits, these are seldom spread evenly. People in many tourist destinations are now counting the cost of development that has failed to put their interests and rights on a par with their visitors'. Livelihoods are being lost, religions and cultural traditions debased and environments degraded.

Working for fairer tourism

Tourism Concern is a UK-based charity working for constructive responses to these problems. We look at the way tourism affects the people and environments in tourism destination areas. Tourism Concern raises awareness of tourism's impact with the general public, with government decision makers and within the tourist industry itself and we provide a unique information base for campaigners and students of tourism.

Tourism Concern campaigns for a tourist industry that is:

- just – yielding benefits that are fairly distributed

- participatory – involving local people in its development and management

- sustainable – putting long-term environmental and social benefit before short-term gain.

Putting people in the picture

Source: www.tourismconcern.org.uk

ACTIVITY

Tourism Concern

Compare and contrast the objectives of Tourism Concern with two other travel and tourism organisations, one of which should be from the private sector and one from the public sector.

Use of new technology

We have already seen that developing technologies in areas such as transportation and communications have facilitated the rapid development of tourism throughout the world. Today's travel and tourism industry is truly global and one of its key features is that it requires extensive use of new technology in order to operate effectively and efficiently.

Most of the key industry components are now reliant on computer reservation systems (CRS) or **global distribution systems** (GDS) that can process everything from sales of airline tickets and package holidays to hotel accommodation and car hire. The four major global reservations systems of Sabre, Galileo, Amadeus and Worldspan have enabled major multinational corporations such as Thomson and Carlson to operate commercially throughout the world and develop global partnerships with airlines, hotel groups, travel agency chains and tour operators. The importance of these distribution systems is shown in the Worldspan case study.

CASE STUDY

Worldspan

Global Travel Information Services

See us on Stand No. TT409 at the World Travel Market.
For further information or a brochure call 0181 745 1922, or visit our web site at http://www.worldspan.com

Given the global nature of the travel and tourism industry and its dependence upon travel and communication technology, it is likely that the major corporations will need to make extensive use of technology in the future if they are to survive in this highly competitive market.

A global distribution system (GDS) is a worldwide network which provides central reservations systems in different countries to sell airline seats and related products such as car hire and accommodation. Many current GDSs are owned by airlines, such as the Sabre GDS operated by American Airlines. GDSs have been slow to develop because of the enormous investment needed in complex computer hardware which can link the reservations systems of major providers such as airlines. However, experts predict that, in the future, the majority of travel and related reservations systems will be provided by three or four main GDSs. The systems have a number of advantages. They are very cost effective for users and provide a wide range of information that is easily accessed. Many of the larger travel agents are already investing heavily in GDSs, particularly Trans World Airlines' (TWA) GDS, Worldspan.

Worldspan has introduced a system called power pricing which allows users to reserve a travel itinerary at the lowest possible price. Details of the itinerary are supplied by the user and the system provides details of the cheapest way of making the journey. This may mean that the customer takes advantage of a special offer, chooses a less direct route or travels on a different date or at a different time. Customers can reserve travel itineraries directly by using a credit card. Unlike the internet (which is also a global system) a GDS can only be used by its subscribers and is not open to everyone. This means that there is greater security when recording customer details and payments.

ACTIVITY

Worldspan

Consider the following technological developments and in small groups discuss how you think travel and tourism organisations will use them to develop their businesses in the future:

- the internet
- interactive digital television
- supersonic wide-bodied jet airliners
- commercial flights into space.

External pressures

A key feature of the travel and tourism industry is that it is vulnerable to a wide range of external pressures, ranging from the actions of governments to natural disasters, over which it has absolutely no control. Examples of such pressures include:

- currency fluctuation
- state of the economy
- government legislation
- climatic change
- natural disaster
- war, civil unrest, acts of terrorism or crime.

Currency fluctuation and the economy

Exchange rates have an unpredictable, uncontrollable influence on holiday demand. Any rise in the value of the pound encourages outbound tourism, as the strength of sterling against other currencies allows UK holidaymakers to get much more for their money. The rate of exchange with the Spanish peseta, the French franc and the US dollar influences over 60 per cent of the holidays taken abroad by the British.

Legislation

Government interventions are increasingly important to the travel and tourism industry, particularly economic ones. Growing tax revenue from travel and tourism operators has a significant impact on the industry. The introduction of air passenger duty (APD) has been the UK government's main levy on the growth of travel. Since 1997, APD has added £10 to every flight from the UK to another European country, and £20 to flights outside the EU. For a return flight to Florida, for example, this adds £40 to what is already a price sensitive market. A 1997 study by Deloitte and Touche estimated that the holiday industry lost £364 million worth of sales as a result of the deterrent effect of APD.

The government can also influence the structure and operation of the industry. The Monopolies and Mergers Commission's investigation of the UK travel industry in 1997 reported that the foreign package holiday market was broadly competitive and served the customer well, but three industry practices were stopped.

- Discounts on holidays which were conditional on buying travel insurance related to that holiday are now prohibited using an order under the Fair Trading Act 1973.

- Most favoured customer clauses in tour operators' contracts with travel agents were stopped.

- Lack of clarity about the ownership of travel agencies by major tour operators was stopped. Ownership must be made clear to consumers in company literature and in retail premises.

It is not only UK government legislation that affects the travel and tourism industry. European Union legislation has also had a significant impact in recent years. For example, following European Union legislation, duty free was abolished in 1999. This has indirectly increased the cost of holidays in two ways. Tour operators, airlines and ferry companies have had to put their prices up to cover the loss of profits from duty free sales, and holidays are now perceived as more expensive by consumers who no longer have the benefit of subsidised drink, tobacco and gifts.

One of the most significant pieces of European Union legislation has been the introduction of a Directive, in 1990, that has to some degree changed the nature of package travel.

The EU Directive on package travel

The intention of the European Union Directive on package travel was to harmonise consumer protection across the whole community. While ABTA had been operating its own system of financial protection successfully for many years, it had never been under any legal obligation to do so. ABTA made representation and contributed to the European Commission's financial protection arrangements and the result was a Directive that brought other European countries in line with the system that ABTA operated through its articles of association.

The significance of this new law to the industry is unparalleled. Financial protection for consumers is now imposed upon the industry, rather than the choice of individual companies, and there are new liabilities and criminal offences in respect of sales procedures. Anyone acting as an organiser of package holidays must now have a bond or other financial protection in place, otherwise he or she may be prosecuted by trading standards officers. The actual definition of organiser is very wide; an estimated 30,000 people are considered tour organisers under the terms of the Directive.

▼ABTA encouraged travellers to lobby against air taxes

A TAXING TIME ON HOLIDAY

Dear Traveller,

You may not be aware that a growing proportion of the cost of your holiday is made up of indirect taxes imposed by the Government. A few years ago, the Government introduced Air Passenger Duty (APD). As of 1 November 1997 APD doubled. This means that a typical family of four, every time they leave the country by air, will pay £40 APD travelling within the European Union and £80 APD travelling elsewhere. This is in addition to taxes imposed by foreign governments and represents a substantial proportion of the holiday cost.

We feel that APD is the equivalent of a poll tax on holidaymakers and hits families with children particularly hard. If you agree with us, we suggest you make your views known to your MP at the House of Commons. Suggested wording is on the reverse of this leaflet.

Climatic changes

Climatic changes affect the pattern of demand for tourist destinations. In the UK, a poor summer has a disastrous effect on tourism in the popular seaside resorts. A permanent long-term factor that influences the choice of holidays abroad made by the British is the search of warmer climates. Health warnings against long exposure to the sun have only had minimal impact on the mainstream package holiday market so far. If, in the long term, global warming leads to climatic changes in the popular destination countries, then there could be a shift in the pattern of overseas holidays taken by the British.

Natural disasters

In addition to their many more immediate effects, natural disasters can have a disastrous effect on the economy of tourist destinations. Earthquakes, tornadoes, hurricanes, floods, droughts and avalanches can all adversely affect tourism to a region for many years. The earthquake that devastated parts of Turkey in 1999 did not affect the country's popular tourist areas, but the media exposure and shocking scenes on television combined to reduce the number of visitors to Turkey.

▲ Natural disasters deter tourists

War, civil unrest, terrorism and crime

The travel and tourism industry is permanently vulnerable to war, terrorism, criminal violence and political unrest. Countries and regions affected in the 1990s include the Middle East, the former Yugoslavia, Cyprus, Morocco and Egypt.

The Luxor tourist massacre in 1997 severely set back tourism in Egypt and the Dominican Republic suffered similarly in the same year, when boom turned to downturn in the industry within two seasons, due to hygiene problems. Although the effect of the Luxor massacre was understandable, it only took a handful of incidents involving hygiene in the hotels of the Dominican Republic to change the market direction. This illustrates that international tourists are prepared to switch destination rapidly.

Impact on host communities

A key feature of the travel and tourism industry is the significant impact that it has on the people who live in a much visited area. These people are usually described as the **host community**. Depending on the circumstances of a particular area, tourism may have a combination of positive and negative effects on the host community. There are three main types of impact on the host community:

- economic
- social
- environmental.

Economic impact

The travel and tourism industry has a significant impact on the UK economy in terms of the income it generates, the numbers employed and its contribution to the balance of payments. On a local scale, income generated from tourism is often vital to the economic well-being of the host community, as it supports local trade and provides jobs. This is because a wide range of industries benefit from both direct and indirect income generated by visitors to the area.

Indirect income is generated through a process known as the **multiplier effect**. This occurs because a proportion of the money spent by visitors is recirculated in the local economy. For example, a hotel may buy its supplies from wholesalers in the area, and its employees spend a proportion of their wages on products and services provided by local businesses.

A survey by Touche Ross in 1994 highlighted the economic importance of leisure and tourism to the city of York. It was estimated that the four million people who visited the city in 1993 generated a total income of £250 million and that 10,000 people were directly employed in the industry. Because of the multiplier effect, it was also estimated that a further £100 million of indirect income was generated for the local economy.

The multiplier effect can also be applied to the numbers employed. In addition to those directly employed, it has been estimated that for every two jobs in the industry, a third job is created elsewhere. For example, an airport must employ a wide range of people to provide products and services for its customers. Staff on check-in and information desks, those working in shops and restaurants, baggage handlers and maintenance crews are all directly employed in the travel and tourism industry. But what about some of the people who supply the airport? The jobs of the manufacturers and wholesalers who supply the various retail and catering operations, of the engineers who build the aircraft and of the security services are all indirectly created by the travel and tourism industry.

Although the tourism industry usually has a positive **economic impact** on the host community, it can also have a negative economic impact. As many of the jobs created are seasonal and part-time, they do not always provide a stable or sufficient basis for supporting a family. Also, the wealth generated by the industry may not be reinvested locally, so that the multiplier income benefits are reduced. A further problem is the high turnover of staff in many travel and tourism organisations, due to long, unsociable working hours, poor career prospects and low pay.

Social impact

The UK travel and tourism industry has a significant impact on our lives. Local communities benefit from the provision of public, private and voluntary sector travel and tourism facilities and services, ranging from restaurants and shopping complexes to transport services and visitor attractions. Regeneration schemes have led to improvements and increased investment in many deprived or neglected areas. Cities such as London, Glasgow, Liverpool, Leeds, Bradford, Birmingham and Hull have undertaken urban regeneration schemes which have included investment in facilities to encourage tourism and to improve the quality of life for both residents and visitors.

In some respects, tourism has a positive social impact on host communities: it gives locals the opportunity to mix with people from other parts of Britain and from overseas and can help to preserve local cultures and traditions. Many arts and crafts have only survived because of the demands of tourism. Investment in public services and visitor attractions also leads to the creation of facilities and services which are of benefit to local residents.

Figure 1.9: Income generated by Euro 96

	Additional expenditure (£ million)	Expenditure per game (£ million)	Expenditure per visitor (£)
Total economic impact	120	3.88	77.00
London	34	3.10	67.09
Birmingham	11	2.73	56.72
Manchester	10	2.05	60.90
Liverpool	7	1.68	55.00
Leeds	4	1.34	59.37
Newcastle	5	1.65	55.54
Sheffield	5	1.65	55.25
Nottingham	7	2.38	60.87
Outside host cities	37	1.20	75.00

Source: Leisure Industries Research Centre

On the other hand, the **social impact** of tourism on host communities is more often negative than positive. Tourism may generate wealth, but it also tends to raise the price of services, food and houses, with the result that many locals cannot afford to continue living in the area. Property prices in many popular countryside tourist areas such as Devon are often high and only affordable to outsiders. This can lead to resentment between local residents and newcomers who purchase holiday properties and second homes. Host communities may also have to put up with disorderly behaviour, traffic congestion, violence and increased crime during the peak holiday periods.

Environmental impact

While tourism is almost universally welcomed for the economic benefits that it provides, there is growing concern about its detrimental **impact on the environment**. In extreme cases, badly managed tourism development has overwhelmed local cultures and permanently damaged sites and landscapes. The Castleton and Edale areas of the Peak District, for example, famous for their limestone caverns, are swamped by an estimated two million car-driving visitors a year. Likewise, the expansion of Manchester Airport has had a negative impact on the surronding countryside.

If our man-made, natural and cultural resources are to be maintained for future generations, then leisure and tourism activities need to be sustainable over a long period. This concept has led to growing demands for **sustainable tourism**, community tourism, **ecotourism** or green tourism. These terms describe tourism development that is in harmony with the visitor, host community and environment. Fuller definitions of these terms, together with case studies of what they involve, are provided in Unit 2.

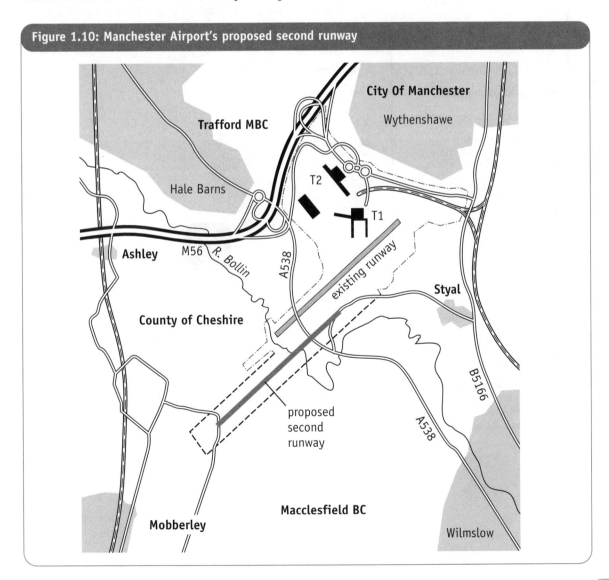

Figure 1.10: Manchester Airport's proposed second runway

BUILD YOUR LEARNING

You should know the meaning of the words and phrases listed below. Go back through the last seven pages to refresh your understanding if necessary.

- British Tourist Authority (BTA)
- Climatic change
- Commercial organisation
- Economic impact
- Ecotourism
- English Tourism Council (ETC)
- Environmental impact
- Global distribution system
- Host community
- Multiplier effect
- National tourist boards
- Non-commercial organisation
- Private sector
- Public limited company (plc)
- Public sector
- Regional tourist boards
- Shareholder
- Social impact
- Sustainable tourism
- Voluntary sector

End of section activitiy

1 Describe the key features of the UK travel and tourism industry, including the:

- role of commercial (private sector) and non-commercial (public and voluntary sector) organisations
- use of new technology
- vulnerability to external pressures
- positive and negative impact on host communities.

Support your description with relevant examples and statistics.

2 Evaluate the key features of at least two commercial and two non-commercial travel and tourism organisations to illustrate differences in their:

- objectives
- funding or revenue generation
- shareholder expectations.

Structure of the travel and tourism industry

THE INDUSTRY WHICH SUPPORTS domestic, inbound and outbound tourism contains two broad categories: travel and tourism. Travel and tourism providers are closely related and combine to provide facilities, products and services for people travelling away from their normal place of residence for leisure or business purposes. The main components which make up the UK travel and tourism industry are shown in Figure 1.11. We are going to explore each of the components set out in Figure 1.11, giving examples of the facilities, products and services available.

The private sector dominates provision in all the components except support and information services, which are often provided by the public and voluntary sectors. Before describing each of these components in detail, it is useful to consider the supply structure within the UK travel and tourism industry.

A massive range of products and services is required to meet the travel needs of leisure and business tourists. The relationship between producers, wholesalers and retailers forms the **supply structure**, or **chain of distribution** as it is sometimes described. The typical chain of distribution that operates within the UK travel and tourism industry is outlined in Figure 1.12.

Principals

Principals are organisations that provide products (for example, holiday insurance) and services (for example, accommodation and travel) which make up the holiday package. They can be divided into three groups:

- transportation carriers – for example, airlines, ferries, cruise companies, railways, road transport, coaches

- accommodation providers – for example, hotels, motels, guest houses, villas and apartments, camp sites, holiday centres

- ancillary services – for example, transfer agents, excursion operators, car hire and travel insurance.

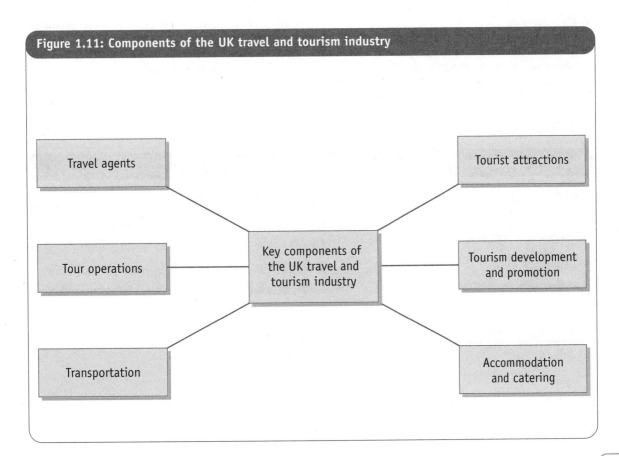

Figure 1.11: Components of the UK travel and tourism industry

Travel agents

Tour operations

Transportation

Key components of the UK travel and tourism industry

Tourist attractions

Tourism development and promotion

Accommodation and catering

Figure 1.12: Chain of distribution in the travel and tourism industry

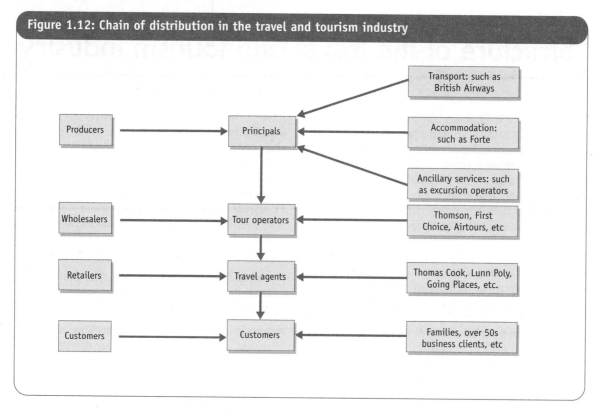

Figure 1.13 gives some examples of well-known UK principals providing transport, accommodation and ancillary services.

In the travel industry, principals often sell their services and products through others, such as tour operators, who then put together an inclusive holiday package. This is not always the case, however, and principals may sell direct to travel agents or customers.

The distinction between principals, tour operators and travel agents has become less obvious because of a process known as vertical integration. **Vertical integration** describes the way in which some major travel organisations have become both **producers** (**principals**) and sellers (**wholesalers** and **retailers**) of travel products and services. For example, Thomson Travel Group contains the Lunn Poly chain of travel agencies, Thomson tour operators and Britannia Airways.

Although the UK travel and tourism industry is dominated by the private sector, public sector organisations such as the British Tourist Authority and

Figure 1.13: Examples of UK principals

Service	Some major UK principles
Coach transport	Shearings, Wallace Arnold, National Express
Rail transport	Eurostar, Le Shuttle, Great North Eastern Railway
Air transport	British Airways, Virgin Airways, Britannia Airways
Sea transport	Stena Sealink, North Sea Ferries, P&O European Ferries
Hotels	Forte, Thistle, Novotel, Butlin's Holiday Worlds
Camp sites and caravan sites	Haven Warner, Ladbrokes
Holiday centres	Centre Parcs, Butlin's
Car hire	Hertz, Avis, EuroDollar
Guiding services	Guide Friday, Blue Badge Guides

the national and regional tourist boards liaise closely with the private sector to provide a number of important support services. These include national accommodation grading schemes and marketing the UK as a tourist destination.

Travel agencies

There are two basic types of travel agency; retail agencies and business travel agencies.

Retail travel agencies

Retail travel agencies sell a range of leisure travel products and services to outgoing, incoming and domestic visitors. They are usually located in the high street and the bulk of their business comes from consumers of outbound holidays. Retail travel agencies act as the link between customers and tour operators. They advise customers, suggest possible holidays and resorts, answer questions, and make bookings with tour operators by computer link or telephone.

Many retail travel agencies also make coach, flight, rail or ferry bookings for clients who want independent travel arrangements and provide specialist services for business travellers, including travel, car hire and accommodation. They also provide a range of ancillary products and services such as travel insurance, foreign currency and traveller's cheques, airport parking and information on health requirements.

The role of the retail travel agency is changing. The conventional high street agency is facing extremely tough competition from direct sell tour operators and customers who can access and purchase travel products from home via the internet or teletext. In the future, it is likely that high street travel agencies will concentrate on providing customers with tailor made holidays, individually designed to meet their needs, rather than providing package holidays for the mass market.

Figure 1.14: Largest ABTA travel agencies by number of branches, 1998

		Number of branches
1	Lunn Poly Ltd	797
2	Going Places	738
3	The Thomas Cook Group	390
4	Carlson Worldchoice	385
5	Co-operative Wholesale Society	255
6	American Express Europe Ltd	144
7	Hogg Robinson (Travel) Ltd	121
8	The Travel World Group	118
9	C W Travel UK Ltd	115
10	Midlands Co-operative Society Ltd	88
11	Bakers World Travel Ltd	68
12	R E Bath Travel Service Ltd	57
13	United Norwest Co-operative Ltd	57
14	Portman Travel Ltd	44
15	STA Travel Ltd	36
16	British Airways Travel Shops Ltd	29
17	Ilkeston Consumer Co-operative Society Ltd	28
18	Britannic Travel Ltd	21
19	Ayscough Travel Ltd	9
20	The Travel Company Ltd	3

Source: ABTA Information Bureau, Information sheet 5, August 1999

It is estimated that 90 per cent of the UK's package holidays are currently sold through retail travel agencies. There are around 7,000 travel agencies in the UK that are members of the **Association of British Travel Agents (ABTA)**. Figure 1.14 shows the top 20 ABTA registered travel agencies.

THE ONE STOP HOLIDAY SHOP
AT THOMAS COOK

HOLIDAY MONEY
All major currencies and Travellers Cheques available instantly*

TRAVEL INSURANCE
Excellent cover at competitive prices

AIRPORT HOTELS
FREE accommodation for children under 16

AIRPORT CAR PARKING
Secure parking at competitive rates and exclusive discounts

HOLIDAY CAR HIRE
Low cost hire option, in association with Hertz

SEE OVER FOR MORE DETAILS

*Subject to availability

▲ From a Thomas Cook leaflet

ABTA
You know the name, what does it mean?

6972 Travel Agent Office Members

795 Tour Operator Office Members

Combined Turnover £29 Billion

90% of the UK's package holidays sold through ABTA Members

Financial Protection for customers, ABTA Currently has bonds valued at:
£182 million for travel agents
£118 million for tour operators

To protect consumer's monies and holidays in 1997, ABTA paid out
£4 million in respect of Travel Agents failures
£500,000 in respect of Tour Operators failures

In 1997 ABTA dealt with 14,755 complaints. Of these, 879 went to ABTA's independent arbitration scheme, an alternative to a small claim's court

▲ ABTA facts and figures

Travel agencies range from **independent outlets** with one or two offices, to national chains, known as **multiples**, with branches in almost every town and city. Since the 1980s there have been numerous mergers and takeovers within this component of the industry and many of the smaller chains have been acquired by major corporations. The case study shows how takeovers and mergers have changed the structure of the retail travel industry.

The industry is now dominated by four leading **multiples**: Lunn Poly, Going Places, Thomas Cook and Carlson Worldchoice. Between them they are responsible for over 60 per cent of the inclusive tours sold in the UK, although they account for only one-third of the total number of high street travel agency branches in the UK.

There are also medium-sized travel agency chains that have multiple outlets in particular regions. The Midlands Co-operative Society, for example, has 88 branches. These chains are not classified as multiples because they do not have a national network of branches. However, they are much larger concerns than the many small, independent agencies, and these medium-sized chains of travel agencies are referred to as **miniples**.

CASE STUDY

The supply structure in retail travel

THE HOLIDAY MATCHMAKER

The largest tour operator, Thomson Travel Group (TTG) has developed its travel agent subsidiary, Lunn Poly, into the UK's largest multiple, with nearly 800 outlets. Thomson's main rival in the mainstream tour market, Airtours, has challenged the leader by creating Going Places, with over 725 outlets. (Many of these formerly traded as Pickfords or Hogg Robinson.) Another key development has been the emergence of multiples interested only in leisure travel rather than business travel.

Thomas Cook is still the most famous name in travel agency. However, its international structure was broken up in 1993 when its former owner, Midland Bank, sold the European branch of the company (separate from the US branch) to a German consortium, led by Westdeutsche Landesbank. The new owner, a regional German bank, also has major shares in German travel companies. The bank disposed of Thomas Cook's business travel accounts to concentrate on holidays. This led to the acquisition of a series of travel operators and, in

1998, to the proposed merger with Carlson Leisure. Carlson originally entered the UK travel market by buying AT Mays, a major regional agency with a wide presence across Scotland and Northern England. In 1997, the AT Mays chain was merged with the voluntary group, ARTAC, into a partly voluntary and partly Carlson-owned chain branded as Worldchoice, with 1,100 branches in total (of which 412 are owned by Carlson and the rest are independents). The proposed merger with Thomas Cook would create a chain of 1,447 branches, of which around 800 would be owned by the Carlson/Thomas Cook group (a similar number to the market leader, Lunn Poly).

The Carlson/Thomas Cook announcement was swiftly followed by news that Airtours was negotiating a tie-up with the Advantage Travel Centres, a consortium of independent travel agents. The group has 480 members with 950 branches, and Airtours anticipates that over 400 of the branches will be signed up with Airtours.

The Carlson/Thomas Cook and Airtours/Advantage negotiations contributed to a revolutionary year for multiple travel agents. Earlier in 1998, Thomson showed its hand by creating a preferred agents scheme, promising higher commissions on holiday sales to around 2,000 agents (other that its own Lunn Poly) which achieve the sales targets of Thomson holidays.

The next restructuring saw First Choice acquiring Bakers Dolphin, a medium-sized chain with 52 outlets in the south west, its first tied travel agency. In the same period (October-November 1998), First Choice also bought strategic shareholdings of at least 25 per cent in several other miniples. By the year 2000, First Choice had connections – ownership or preferential deals – with over 700 branches.

In 1999 Airtours announced plans to buy First Choice to further increase the size of its market share. This takeover would be dependent upon approval from the Monopolies and Mergers Commission (MMC).

Source: Mintel, Marketing the Holiday Business, 1999

ACTIVITY

The supply structure in retail travel

Read the case study on retail travel (p. 43) and answer these questions.

1 What benefits do tour operators gain from owning multiple chains of travel agencies?

2 What effect do you think that tour operator ownership of the multiple travel agencies has on the small independent travel agency?

3 List all the retail travel agencies in an area of your choice. Identify whether each agency is independent, miniple or multiple.

4 How do you think the increasing number of direct sell tour operators and on-line travel service providers will affect the structure of the retail travel industry?

ACTIVITY

Business travel agencies

Read the *Mail on Sunday* article (opposite) which gives examples of the types of products and services that specialist business travel agencies provide.

Make a list of the main advantages which companies derive from using these specialist business travel organisers or consultants.

Business travel agencies

Business travel agencies specialise in the sale of travel related products to business clients. This can involve everything from arranging flights and accommodation to rapid delivery of passports and visas. They do not usually have a high street presence unless they are part of a retail travel agency. They are sometimes located in-house, in other words in an office within the organisation for which they arrange travel.

The larger business travel agencies are members of the Guild of Business Travel Agents (GBTA), and together contract over 80 per cent of business travel arrangements made through travel agencies. The leading GBTA business travel agencies are American Express Travel, Britannic Travel, Carlson Wagonlits, Hogg Robinson, Portman Travel and Seaforth Travel. Many high street travel agencies also provide a business travel service for customers, particularly American Express and Thomas Cook.

With over 1,700 offices in 120 countries, American Express is the world's largest travel agent. It has 190 offices in the UK alone selling a whole range of products including insurance, foreign exchange as well as package tours and flights.

American Express is the biggest business travel agent in the UK. In conjunction with Microsoft, the company is developing an interactive booking facility on the internet, aimed at both business and leisure travellers. The company is also pioneering ticketless travel with the support of IBM and American Airlines, where a smart card holds all the information necessary to identify the traveller and confirm the reservation.

Tour operations

Around 700 tour operators in the UK provide a wide range of products and services for domestic, outgoing and incoming tourists. Tour operators arrange the transport, accommodation and leisure activities which make up the holiday package. Although they specialise in fully inclusive packages, many tour operators offer more flexible options for their customers, such as flight-only, fly-drive and multi-centre holidays.

Holiday packages are usually sold to clients through travel agencies which receive a commission for acting as the link between the customer and the supplier. The standard travel agency commission on a package holiday sale is around 10 per cent. Like the travel agency market described earlier, although there are hundreds of tour operators in the UK, the market is dominated by a handful of major companies. ABTA estimates that 70 per cent of inclusive tours are sold by travel agencies offering holiday products from the five largest UK tour operators. However, some tour operators such as Portland Holidays and Direct Holidays sell holidays direct to the public by telephone, teletext, the internet or through the mail. In 1998 it was estimated that 10 per cent of outbound inclusive tours sold in the UK were booked directly with the tour operator rather than via a travel agent. Given the increasing numbers of consumers who prefer independent travel, the option of getting lower prices by booking direct with the tour operator is likely to become more popular. Indeed, the major tour operators such as Thomson and Airtours have already introduced their own direct sell operations in order to protect their market shares.

Can the boss's secretary beat the travel agent by ringing round for the best deals?

Specialist business travel agencies are generally the first choice because they claim to do the job, and more besides, faster and more cost-effectively.

With 6,000 clients and £500 million annual turnover, Hogg Robinson BTI, Britain's second largest travel agency, has at least two advantages over the do-it-yourself business travel arranger — technology and buying clout. It can instantly pinpoint some of the cheapest and most appropriate air fares and hotel rates through its computer reservations system. Immediate confirmation can be given and tickets issued automatically.

Increasingly, however, companies such as Hogg Robinson and American Express are turning into travel management specialists. Mike Platt, commercial affairs director at Hogg Robinson BTI, says, 'A good business travel consultant can give instant advice on health requirements and arrange for the rapid delivery of currency, passports and visas. We also run a 24-hour worldwide emergency service, which can help with everything from lost tickets to getting you out of a country in a hurry if war breaks out.'

One of the agency's most important new roles is the preparation of reports outlining a client company's travel spending. The boss can tell who is going where and how, and whether the company's travel policy is being observed.

Consultants' preference for large operators should enable them to make savings. American Express, Britain's largest corporate travel consultancy, which has Marks and Spencer as a client, claims that 10 per cent reductions on a company's travel spending are not uncommon.

Eric Brannan, American Express senior vice-president for business travel operations in Europe, explains, 'We discuss with the company its travel plans for the year and then negotiate volume deals with the carriers, hotels and car rental companies. On a £10 million annual budget we can often save £1 million, plus the loss of productivity from the employee making the arrangements.'

This means that if a private traveller contacts the Hyatt Regency, Hong Kong, he will probably pay the going rate of £194 a night, particularly if the hotel is nearly full. If his company has an agreed corporate rate, the bill falls to £155. If a bulk-buying agent uses Hyatt as a preferred supplier the charge is £140, possibly with other privileges.

However, the greatest potential savings lie with air fares. Agents representing companies with a high number of trips on certain routes can consolidate their business with one carrier and earn additional commission. This may be passed back to the client.

Various airline perks must be assessed too. Peter Cornwall, UK and Ireland sales manager for KLM Royal Dutch Airline says, 'Professional consultants are of the utmost importance, particularly when one considers the value-added products airlines are now offering, such as free airport car parking, chauffeured limousine services and upgraded features of on-board service.

'The consultant's expertise is a further support for the business traveller in negotiating the maze of packages on offer.'

Adapted from the *Mail on Sunday*, 24 September 1995

CASE STUDY

Direct booking

Book direct from big tour operators

Just as direct banking and insurance have grown, so have direct holidays. The big four tour operators have each developed sales strategies to squeeze out the travel agent. On the one hand they have their own direct-sell brands: Thomson owns Portland Direct; Airtours owns Direct Holidays; and First Choice owns Eclipse. On the other hand, Thomson *et al* encourage direct bookings from their main brochures by including phone numbers for their in-house reservations staff. Thomas Cook doesn't have a dedicated direct-sell brochure, but it does have a huge call centre to take direct bookings.

Flights from Leeds/Bradford, Humberside, Newcastle, Teesside, Manchester, Liverpool.

FOLD HERE

24 HOUR BROCHURE HOTLINE

Is it cheaper to book direct?

We picked a package holiday in each of the four main tour operators' summer-sun brochures. We compared the price of each holiday when booked through various travel agencies, when booked direct using the reservations number in the brochure of each tour operator (when available). The cheapest prices were generally offered by the travel agents, thanks to the discounts they were offering at the time.

The direct-sell arms of the major tour operators featured only a few holidays that were exactly the same as those in the main brochure of their parent companies, but when they did, these were often cheaper. Only one direct-sell operator – Eclipse – was cheaper than the high street travel agent for a comparable holiday.

Pros and cons of booking direct

The pros

- You should be able to ask detailed questions about your package and get detailed and accurate answers.

- You don't need to leave your house (or even your armchair) to book a holiday.

- You can avoid the hard sell of a vertically integrated travel agent who wants to sell you a holiday with its in-house tour operator.

- Holiday Which? members are more likely to recommend direct-sell tour operators, of whatever size, than other tour operators.

- Direct-sell operators, both large and small, were considered to offer good value for money in our members' survey.

- Small specialist tour operators can be flexible and can often tailor-make a package to suit you.

The cons

- You won't get the sort of impartial advice and face-to-face service that should be the stock-in-trade of a good independent travel agent.

- If a package is available both by booking directly and through a travel agent, you may get a better price from a travel agent.

- It could be hard work trying to compare and contrast what different tour operators are offering you. This is something that a good travel agent should be able to do for you.

- If you can't find a package that suits your needs, you might be better off talking to a travel agent who can arrange flights and accommodation for you.

Source: adapted from *Which On-line?*, March 1999

The tour operations market provides products and services for three main categories of tourist:

- outbound
- inbound
- domestic.

Outbound tour operators

The majority of tour operators in the UK are **outbound operators** which organise package holidays abroad for UK residents. The largest operators in this market are Thomson Tour Operators, First Choice Holidays and Airtours. Their largest market is air-inclusive tours (AITs) to short-haul destinations in the Mediterranean.

There are also specialist long-haul operators such as Kuoni Travel and Page and Moy, operators which specialise in city breaks, such as Travelscene, and winter sports specialists, such as Crystal and Ski Bound. Figure. 1.15 shows the top 20 ABTA and ATOL registered UK tour operators in order of their market share of air inclusive tours.

The overseas holiday market in the UK is dominated by four large vertically and horizontally integrated groups which account for the dominant share of sales of inclusive tours. The remainder of the market is composed of a number of smaller specialists operating in niche sectors. Market shares are difficult to analyse due to merger and takeover activity.

Figure 1.15: Top 20 UK tour operators in terms of passengers carried, 1999

		Air inclusive tours ('000s)	percentage market share*
1	Thomson Holidays Ltd	4,333	22.5%
2	Airtours plc	2,972	15.5%
3	First Choice Holidays & Flights Ltd	1,972	10%
4	Sunworld Ltd	1,480	8%
5	Unijet Travel Ltd	942	5%
6	Flying Colours Holidays Ltd**	720	4%
7	Avro plc	604	3%
8	Inspirations East Ltd	573	3%
9	Trailfinders Ltd	518	2.5%
10	Cosmosair plc	362	2%
11	Gold Medal Travel Group	311	2%
12	British Airways Holidays Ltd	301	2%
13	The Thomas Cook Group	294	1.5%
14	Crystal Holidays Ltd	270	1%
15	Virgin Holidays Ltd	254	1%
16	Kuoni Travel Ltd	240	1%
17	Direct Holidays plc	226	1%
18	Going Places Leisure Travel Ltd	203	1%
19	MTG (UK) Ltd	186	1%
20	Lunn Poly Ltd	186	1%

* rounded to nearest 0.5%

** since acquired by Sunworld Ltd

Source: Civil Aviation Authority, ATOL Business, Issue 14 July 1999

Tour operators are generally taken to be air tour operators, selling air inclusive tours. They are licensed to sell these holidays by the Civil Aviation Authority (CAA) which issues an Air Tours Operators Licence (ATOL). ATOL holders make deposits (bonds) with the CAA with those flying with licensed operations. Other organisers of inclusive tours do not use flights and are not regulated by the CAA. These include organisers of holidays based on coach travel, railways or sea crossings.

These outbound tour operators offer a multitude of holiday products which reflect the differing needs of their customers. The obvious distinction between the different packages available is by holiday type. If you scan the holiday brochures in a high street travel agency you will no doubt find examples of the following types of package holiday:

- summer and winter sun beach holidays
- winter sports and skiing
- lakes and mountains
- activity and adventure holidays
- fly-drives or fly-cruises
- special interest holidays
- senior citizens' holidays
- young people's holidays
- short breaks or city breaks in Europe
- golfing holidays.

Figure 1.16 shows some examples of the types of package holiday products provided by one UK outgoing tour operator.

Vertical and horizontal integration
The largest outbound tour operators have integrated operations involving the three main elements:

- the creation and marketing of branded package holidays
- ownership of charter airlines
- ownership of multiple travel agencies, usually trading under names different to the tour operator's.

The fourth element, accommodation, is traditionally bought in from outside, although some large operators do own hotels.

Outbound tour operators

1 Study Figure 1.15, which shows the top 20 ATOL registered tour operators. Working individually or in groups, select a suitable sample of the tour operators listed. For each, obtain a list of its brand names. For example, Thomson tour operators' brand names are Thomson, Portland, Skytours and Horizon.

2 For each holiday type listed in the table below, find examples of short-haul and long-haul holidays currently available. You should give the name of the tour operators, the destination and the name of the brochure it can be found in.

Holiday type	Short-haul holiday	Long-haul holiday
Winter sports		
Fly-drive		
Fly-cruise		
Young people's holiday		
Golf		
City breaks		
Senior citizens's holiday		

Figure 1.16: First Choice's brochure

There are thousands of small and medium-sized tour operators, but the ten largest account for around 90 per cent of the market. The top three, Thomson, Airtours and First Choice have around 60 per cent between them.

Thomson and Airtours have expanded both vertically – owning travel agencies, airlines, direct sell and flight only divisions, and horizontally – selling long-haul, cruises, skiing and cottage holidays – while continuing to dominate the mainstream summer sun short-haul market.

Horizontal (or lateral) integration is just as important as vertical integration, as major tour operators have developed a wide range of products and brands to cater for the needs of a wide audience.

The structure of tour operating in the UK is therefore dominated by an elite group of a dozen companies which account for over 90 per cent of the air holiday market, most of which are integrated laterally (across various types of holiday) and vertically (owning either travel agents or charter airlines, or both). One characteristic which sets the larger operators apart from the thousands of small tour operators is their ownership of charter airlines. The most prominent examples are:

- Britannia (Thomson Travel Group), with 30 aircraft, the largest tour operator airline in Europe

- Airtours International (Airtours), with 20 aircraft

- Monarch, part of the Cosmos group, with 20 aircraft

- Air 2000 (First Choice), with 17 aircraft.

The case study gives an example of a major tour operator which has successfully achieved vertical and horizontal integration.

CASE STUDY

Airtours

Airtours is an independent UK company whose annual turnover exceeded £2 billion in 1999. Set up in the 1980s by David Crossland, the current chairman, Airtours has established a reputation for providing low-cost holidays and direct flights from northern UK airports, particularly to the Caribbean. In 1987 the company floated on the London Stock Exchange. In 1991, with the demise of Intasun, the short-haul market opened up for the company.

Airtours' market share of air inclusive tours (AITs) in the UK is second only to Thomson's, but the group has extensive international interests. Its international diversification has meant that less than 50 per cent of its turnover derives from UK outbound businesses. Purchases outside the UK have included

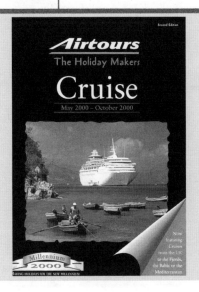

operators out of Canada, California and Scandinavia. Airtours is also looking to Eastern Europe for expansion.

In the UK, Airtours has its own charter airline, Airtours International and major travel agency, Going Places. To achieve vertical integration, Airtours bought several travel agencies and developed Going Places into a 715-branch group. Other acquisitions in the 1990s included Aspro, a budget brand of AITs, and Tradewinds, which offers exclusive and exotic long-haul holidays on scheduled flights. (A bid for First Choice, then called Owners Abroad, failed).

Like Thomson, Airtours manages its specialist holidays in a separate division which incorporates cruises, skiing, city breaks, lakes and mountains, and youth holidays.

Horizontal (lateral) integration of the group across holidays out of the UK has included the following developments:

- long-haul holidays, particularly to Florida, including flights using Airtours International, the in-house charter airline

- continental camping holidays: EuroSites is one of the five largest operators offering self-drive camping holidays from the UK to continental Europe

- outbound city breaks

- cruises.

Cruise developments are central to Airtours progress. The company started offering cruise holidays in 1994 and its success attracted the attention of Carnival Corporation, the world's largest cruise company, which now has a 29 per cent stake in Airtours. The Carnival deal was followed by the joint purchase of the major Italian cruise and ferry company, Costa Crociere, for £181 million. With ten ships, Crociere claims a 30 per cent share of passengers on Mediterranean cruises.

ACTIVITY

Integrated tour operators

Obtain information about a selection of major integrated tour operators other than Airtours. A good starting point is to gather a selection of holiday brochures for each of the operators you are looking at. You may also find it useful to look at the tour operators' websites on the internet. (Some websites are given in the resource and internet directory on pp. 460–4.) Use the information to complete a table like the one below.

Name of tour airline	Main holiday brands	Ownership of travel agent	Ownership of operator charter
Airtours	Eurosites, Airtours cruises	Going Places	Airtours International

Inbound tour operators

Inbound tour operators provide inclusive holiday arrangements for overseas visitors to the UK. We do not come across their names very often because their products are sold overseas, although if you are Japanese the name of Miki Travel would be as familiar as Thomson or Airtours! Other well-known incoming operators are Spectra, Anglo-World and See Britain.

The products and services of these companies range from fully-inclusive holiday tours of the UK, including transport, accommodation, meals and guiding service, to transfer handling services such as airport to hotel transfers. Often, the inclusive package holidays is based on a particular theme, such as heritage, the countryside or city breaks.

ACTIVITY

Inbound tour operators

Imagine you work for a UK incoming tour operator which specialises in holidays for North American tourists aged over 50. Your booking agent in the USA has identified a huge potential for 21-day escorted coach tours which include all accommodation, meals, guiding services and entry to attractions. Work in small groups to devise a suitable itinerary for this type of holiday that shows the destinations and schedules. You have been informed that the main reason why the clients wish to visit the UK is to see the many historic attractions, so your itinerary should be based on the theme of Historic Britain.

Domestic tour operators

Domestic tour operators organise inclusive holidays within the UK for UK residents. These are usually inclusive coach or rail holidays, although there is now a growing market for the independent traveller who requires accommodation only. Less than 10 per cent of domestic holidays involve any contact with a travel agent, largely because 80 per cent of holidays are self-drive, either by car or caravan.

There are many similarities between the types of domestic and outgoing package holiday available. For example, beach, city breaks, special interest, senior citizen and young people's holidays are all popular types of domestic holiday products sold in the UK.

The most important commercial suppliers of holidays, or elements of holidays, in the domestic market fall into two distinct categories:

- accommodation suppliers (hotel and other tourist accommodation)
- tour operators specialising in short breaks.

We are going to concentrate on the latter category here, as accommodation providers are covered later on.

Packaged holiday travel falls into three main areas in the domestic market:

- hotel break specialists
- coach operators
- activity and special interest companies.

Hotel break specialists came into being following the movement of hotel groups into the leisure breaks market in the 1980s. Tour operators were in a position to capitalise on the availability of rooms in good hotels at reduced weekend rates. Most of the operators which emerged during the 1980s remained independent until the 1990s. Recent years have seen the acquisition of some specialists by much larger companies. Among the most notable takeovers, Eurocamp bought Superbreak and Goldenrail; TTG is involved with its Holiday Cottages Group and Blake's Boating and Airtours owns London Travel Service.

Coach operators are the largest of these companies, in a locally fragmented market, and have made a major contribution to packaging the UK for holidays. Their main emphasis is on multi-centre sightseeing tours with a customer base biased towards the over 50s. The leading domestic operators are Shearings and Wallace Arnold, both of which were bought out by their managements in 1997.

Activity and special interest companies are usually very small. These independent companies (or sole traders) use a variety of accommodation, from camping and hostels or schools and universities to luxury hotels, depending on the activity they are providing. Some larger operators put together activity packages with accommodation at various UK locations. Property owners are also important, ranging from seaside hoteliers and private schools, to outdoor centres owned by local authorities.

CASE STUDY

With annual sales of over £100 million, derived from coach holidays in the UK and abroad, **Shearings Holidays** is the largest UK coach holiday brand. The company is based in Wigan, Lancashire. There are four major hub interchanges and over 1,000 pick-up points available from 250 joining locations.

The Shearings fleet stands at 320 coaches. In addition to its coach fleet, the company owns an expanding group of over thirty Coast and Country hotels around the UK. These are integral to its Britain by Coach programme.

Shearings' range of holiday brochures, available in travel agencies, covers Britain (including regional versions), Europe and North America. Festive breaks are featured in a separate brochure, along with shopping breaks to France before Christmas.

Wallace Arnold Holidays is second to Shearings in the domestic coach holiday market, with annual sales of around £60 million and a long heritage (70 years) in coach transport. It was bought out from the Barr & Wallace Arnold Trust in 1997.

Like Shearings, Wallace Arnold has its own chain of seaside hotels (but only five of them) to guarantee control of standards and facilities on some holidays. They offer four courses at dinner and sometimes have free wine offers. All the hotels have large ballrooms. The company also offers themed holidays including dancing, photography and card games.

Superbreak Mini-Holidays (Eurocamp) is the overall market leader in organising short hotel breaks, independently from ownership by a hotel group. The group includes Goldenrail, a budget brand of short-break holidays which originally focused exclusively on breaks by train.

The company was acquired in 1995 by Eurocamp, the leading operator for camping holidays in Europe. Eurocamp (renamed as Holidaymaker in 1998) needed to broaden its base after exchange rates – particularly the high value of the French franc – threatened to erode it core business.

Highlife Breaks was another pioneer in hotel breaks, run by the Scottish group of hotels, Thistle. The hotels were owned by Scottish & Newcastle and then Mount Charlotte Thistle before being floated separately in 1997. Unusually, Highlife Breaks is operated as a holiday programme at arm's length from Thistle, offering a choice of hotels including Queen's Moat Houses and Regal hotels.

London Travel Service is one of the city break programmes operated by the Bridge Travel Group, which was bought in 1997 by Airtours (the UK's second largest tour operator). London Travel Service is a relatively minor programme next to the Paris Travel Service and Amsterdam Travel Service, but gives Airtours a foothold in the domestic market. Breaks in London are promoted within and outside the UK, with theatre and event breaks a speciality for domestic travellers. Theatre and event tickets are bought separately from the travel and accommodation package, and the best seats in the house are usually guaranteed.

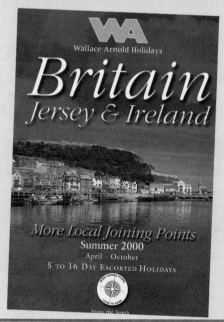

ACTIVITY

Domestic tour operators

Choose a well-known company that provides domestic holidays from those shown in the case study and produce a list of the types of holiday products that it provides. You may need to obtain a brochure to complete this activity.

Transport

Transport carriers form a significant part of the travel and tourism industry. In the UK they are now mainly private companies, using a well-developed network of roads, railways, inland waterways, shipping lanes and airways.

Transport can be divided into three categories: land-based, air-based and water-based. The most common modes of transport within each category are:

- land – car, coach, taxi, bus, bicycle, caravan, train, tube
- air – scheduled flights, charter holiday flights, air taxis (helicopter or plane)
- water – ferries, cruise ships, hovercraft, river boats, narrow boats.

The type of transport used usually depends on the distance to be travelled, how much the traveller can afford to spend, the time available, the purpose of the visit and the ease of access to departure points.

Two-thirds of international travel by both UK residents and overseas residents is made by air. The Channel Tunnel has been fully operational since 1995 and in 1997 accounted for approximately 10 per cent of all international travel by both residents and visitors. Although sea traffic has recorded little or no growth since the tunnel opened, it does not seem to have had an adverse impact on the growth of air traffic.

The transport network contains many **terminals** which people use at the beginning and end of their journeys. Bus and rail stations and ports and airports are therefore regarded as important facilities within the travel and tourism industry. The UK airports listed in Figure 1.17 handled over 133 million domestic and international passengers in 1998. Heathrow, the UK's largest and busiest airport, handled 60 million passengers in the same year.

Major airports such as Heathrow, Gatwick, Manchester and Glasgow have also developed into travel, retail and leisure complexes. Heathrow's Terminal Four, for example, contains 22 high quality

Figure 1.17: Traffic at the UK's main airports		
Airport	**Million passengers**	
	1988	**1998**
1 London Heathrow	37.5	60.4
2 London Gatwwick	20.7	29.0
3 Manchester	9.5	17.2
4 London Stanstead	1.0	6.8
5 Birmingham	2.8	6.6
6 Glasgow	3.6	6.5
7 Edinburgh	2.1	4.5
8 Luton	2.8	4.1
9 Newcastle	1.4	2.9
10 Aberdeen	1.6	2.7
11 Belfast International	2.2	2.6
12 East Midlands	1.3	2.1

stores, seven bars and restaurants and a wide choice of shops. In 1997, Heathrow generated £783 million of revenue.

The Heathrow Airport Visitor Centre is a great place to find out how an airport operates

ACTIVITY

Transport termini

1 Trace the outline map of the UK and locate the seaports listed below on the map. You may need to use an atlas, ferry brochures or shipping guides. State the destination which each port serves.

2 In addition, identify the locations of the airports listed in Figure 1.17. Add any other regional airports you can identify.

- Weymouth
- Plymouth
- Swansea
- Holyhead
- Liverpool
- Stranraer
- Larne
- Belfast
- Newcastle-upon-Tyne
- Hull
- Felixstowe
- Harwich
- Ramsgate
- Dover
- Folkestone
- Newhaven
- Portsmouth
- Southampton
- Poole
- Fishguard
- Aberdeen
- Scrabster
- Strommes
- Ullapool
- Oban
- Pembroke

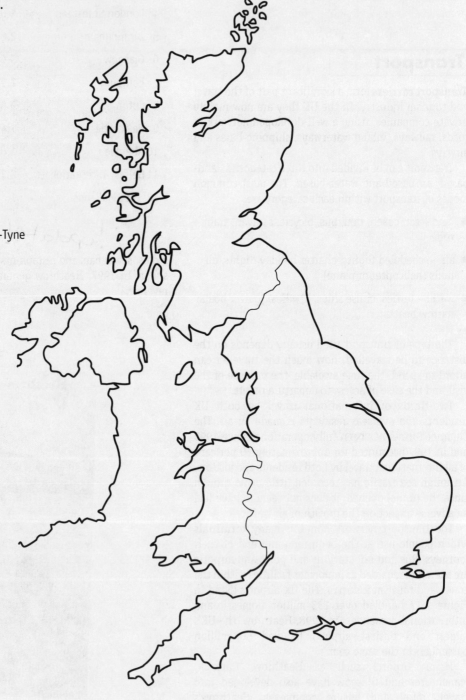

Accommodation

There is an enormous diversity of **accommodation providers** in the UK, ranging from small single outlet operations to major outlets such as Forte and Thistle hotels. Accommodation can either be serviced, which includes meals and housekeeping, or self-catering.

Serviced accommodation

Hotels and other serviced accommodation vary hugely in terms of their size, quality, turnover and the range of facilities and services they provide. Hotels, guest houses and other serviced accommodation can be categorised in a number of ways, including by number of bedrooms:

- small (ten rooms or fewer)
- medium (11 to 50 rooms)
- large (more than 50 rooms).

They can also be classified by turnover:

- less than £100,000
- £100,000-£499,999
- £500,000-£999,999
- £1 million and over.

There are several classification schemes that categorise providers according to the range of facilities, services and products they provide. For example, the national tourist boards for England, Scotland and Wales have developed classification systems for hotels, guest houses, bed and breakfasts, inns and farmhouses and for self-catering accommodation. Establishments are awarded ratings which indicate the range of facilities and services they provide. Figure 1.18 sets out the English Tourism Council's (ETC) classification scheme for hotels and guest houses, which was introduced in 1999. ETC inspectors check and grade over 20,000 hotels and similar establishments and 11,000 self-catering facilities a year.

Definitions of hotels are rather vague because UK accommodation is traditionally classified according to its status in alcoholic drinks licensing. The boundaries between the bed and breakfast (B&B) and the guest house, and between the guest house and the small, unlicensed hotel are particularly vague. The majority of unlicensed accommodation properties are referred to as guest houses or B&Bs. Many of these only operate in the main tourist season in summer, although larger guest houses may stay open longer, targeting out of season visitors. Seaside guest house traditionally insist on stays of a least a week, whereas B&Bs usually target the short-break visitor who stays for one or two nights.

Figure 1.18: ETC's classification scheme

Statistics on the UK hotel industry portray a fragmented industry with a concentration of large hotels in London. Mintel estimates that there are currently 10,500 companies trading primarily as hoteliers in the UK. These offer a combined total of 375,000 bedrooms and in 1998 generated a estimated turnover of around £10,000 million. Figure 1.19 provides a profile of the UK hotels sector.

Figure 1.20: Largest UK hotel groups, 1998

	Hotels	Bedrooms
Forte (Granada Group)		
Travelodge	160	7,000
Other	168	22,000
Total Forte/Granada	328	29,000
Whitbread		
Marriott	34	5,000
Travel Inn	190	9,500
Total Whitbread	224	14,500
Thistle/Mount Charlotte	70	10,000
Hilton (Ladbroke Group)	42	9,000
Stakis	55	8,000
Bass		
Holiday Inn	48	6,000
Toby Hotels/Inns	45	1,400
Total Bass	93	7,400
Queen's Moat Houses	51	7,000
Regal Hotels	100	5,500
Jarvis Hotels	68	5,500
Friendly Hotels	60	5,000
Millennium & Copthorne(CDL)	17	4,500
Swallow (Vaux Group)	30	4,000
De Vere/Village Leisure (Greenalls)	26	3,200

Source: Mintel

Figure 1.19: Key facts about UK hotels sector

- Around 25,000 outlets are known to the national tourist boards across the UK, of which 81 per cent are in England, 12 per cent in Scotland, 6 per cent in Wales, and 1 per cent in Northern Ireland.

- London hotels account for 3 per cent of the hotels in England, but for 15 per cent of the bedrooms available. The average hotel in London has 250 bedrooms; the average in a provincial hotel in England is 33 bedrooms.

- The other areas of hotel concentration are the West Country and north west England, each with over 3,000 registered hotels. The West Country is the leading destination for domestic long holidays and the north west's accommodation includes concentrations in Blackpool and the Lake District.

- In Scotland, concentrations of larger hotels are found in Edinburgh and Glasgow.

- In Wales, the heaviest concentration of hotels is in the Gwynedd region, which accounts for 34 per cent of the hotels in Wales.

- Eighty-four per cent of all hotels in the UK had turnovers of less than £500,000 in 1997 and, of these, 41 per cent had turnovers of less than £100,000 in the same year.

Concentration at the top of the industry is usually measured in terms of bedrooms rather than hotel units, since the major operators are those with the largest hotels, which tend to have fewer units. For example, the Hilton group has a much higher ranking by bedrooms (fourth largest group) than by hotel units.

For domestic tourism, hotels either market themselves independently, through their own holiday brochures, or through tour operators. Short-break tour operators developed in the 1980s, while the 1990s saw more brochured holidays produced directly by hotels groups including Marriott, Thistle and Stakis and offered for sale through travel agencies.

Forte hotels

Forte has 328 hotels with nearly 30,000 bedrooms in the UK. The units are currently divided equally between the Travelodge budget hotels and a range of other hotel brands, including Posthouse and Le Meridien. The acquisition of Forte, for many years the UK's (and Europe's) largest hotelier, by the leisure and retailing conglomerate, Granada Group, ranks among the most important events in UK hotel industry.

Granada first approached Forte in 1995. Following an acrimonious struggle, the acquisition was completed in 1996. By 1997, the hotels division of the Granada Group accounted for 26 per cent of group sales and 31 per cent of profits.

Granada's strategy for Forte has taken some time to evolve. Under Forte family control, a rebranding strategy had been incorporated just before the takeover, with the aim of using Forte as a stronger umbrella brand. There used to be hundreds of Forte hotels in which corporate branding was kept at a minimum; in the 1990s the company classified them strategically under groups such as Posthouse, Exclusive and Heritage, all under the Forte umbrella.

Granada decided to retain the Forte umbrella brand but to be more rigorous in disposing of hotels which did not fit into marketable categories. A group of 60 smaller hotels was given the temporary name of White Hart and put on the market as a parcel which was eventually sold to Regal Hotels. The Crest name, acquired by Forte from Bass, was dispensed with in favour of Posthouse to market modern, mid-market hotels aimed at business and stopover travellers. Forte had acquired Le Meridien, a major France-based chain of international, four-star hotels, and Granada has kept and developed this brand and its concept.

In London and other major cities of the world, Forte owns long established, luxury hotels which do not easily fit into the modern brand categories. These are retained as a separate group.

Self-service accommodation

A wide range of self-catering accommodation is available throughout the UK. Examples include holiday cottages and homes, chalets, camp sites, caravan parks and timeshare properties. Holiday centres that combine self-catering accommodation with activities and entertainment on a single site are popular. Butlin's, Centre Parcs, Pontin's and Haven Warner have all invested large sums to create purpose-built holiday and entertainment complexes. Butlin's, for example, has invested over £190 million in updating its five Holiday Worlds since the 1980s.

Accommodation providers

Make a list of the products and services offered by the following types of accommodation provider:

- a four or five-star hotel
- a caravan and camping site
- a holiday centre, such as Haven, Butlin's or Center Parcs.

You may be able to base your research on facilities in your area.

Catering services

The list of **catering establishments** serving food and drink is seemingly endless, from expensive à la carte restaurants and self-service cafeterias to burger bars, pizza houses and takeaways. Catering facilities which can be found in most UK towns and cities include:

- restaurants
- cafés
- bistros and wine bars
- fast food and takeaway outlets
- pizza houses
- pubs
- snack bars
- mobile snack bars.

Both the restaurant and takeaway markets have continued to grow in the UK. This growth is partly due to the increasing popularity of ethnic restaurants and takeaways, although pub meals still accounted for the largest proportion of consumer expenditure in 1997.

A taste for the exotic

Eastern cuisine accounts for almost a quarter of spending in restaurants and takeaways. With Britons spending £32 million every week on Indian food, it could be argued that curry is now as much a national dish as fish and chips.

Despite their substantial share of the market, Chinese and Indian restaurateurs should not be complacent. Other cooking styles such as Thai and Japanese are growing at a faster rate, with an increase in spending of 38 per cent over the past four years, compared with 12.5 per cent for Indian restaurants and 8 per cent for Chinese.

Travel to far-flung destinations has led to greater demand for more adventurous eating out among the more affluent. Interest in south east Asian cuisine is increasing, reflected by the good performance of such restaurants and the recent appearance in supermarkets of ingredients such as lemon grass and Thai fish sauce.

We may yet find coriander in our Cornish pasties and lime leaves on our Yorkshire pudding.

Adapted from the *Mail on Sunday*

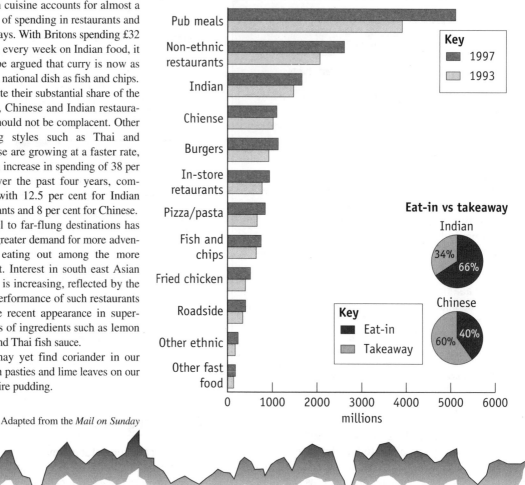

ACTIVITY

Catering

Give examples of catering facilities for each of the categories listed in the figure in the article in your area. You may find it useful to refer to a copy of Yellow Pages or to a local newspaper.

Tourism development

This component of the travel and tourism industry includes tourism support and promotion services, tourist information centres and guiding services. As we have seen, many local authorities have specific departments to support and develop tourism in their areas. This support may include marketing the area by producing and distributing holiday, accommodation and entertainment guides, or attending travel exhibitions to promote the area as a tourist destination.

National and regional tourist boards, together with local authorities, play a key role in promoting and developing tourism in their areas. This involves providing a wide range of services such as research, education, information, visitor guides and other publicity material. The role of the public sector in promoting and supporting the UK travel and tourism industry was discussed earlier (p. 30). The webstract shows how the British Tourist Authority (BTA) supports travel and tourism.

WEBSTRACT

The role of the British Tourist Authority

The British Tourist Authority (BTA) is an official government organisation, formed under the Development of Tourism Act in 1969, together with the national tourist boards for Scotland, Wales and England.

Our role

The BTA's role is to build the value of tourism to Britain, generating additional revenue throughout Britain and throughout the year. It sharpens the industry's competitiveness by promoting tourism in ways that a fragmented industry cannot do alone. Through its market intelligence, expertise and overseas marketing network, it helps the industry reach overseas customers cost effectively. The BTA also advises government and the industry on all matters of tourism, as well as conducting important research.

Our funding

The BTA's funding comes from two sources – grant in aid received directly from the government through our sponsoring department the Department of Culture, Media and Sport, and through commercial revenue and support in kind raised from public and private sector partners. The BTA's grant in aid for 1998–99 was £35 million. In addition it raises approximately a further £15 million annually in commercial revenue.

Return on investment

The BTA has a strong commercial focus, concentrating on customer markets and segments which will generate a financial return for Britain. For every £1 of State funds invested, the BTA generates a return of £27. The ratio is expected to rise to 30:1 within the next three years.

Cooperation

The BTA works in partnership with the Scottish, English, Welsh and regional tourist boards and with the inbound travel trade in the UK. It also works with the Department of Culture, Media and Sport and other organisations in its portfolio such as the Arts Council of Great Britain, the Sports Council and English Heritage. In overseas markets, BTA staff work closely with the British Council and diplomatic and cultural staff, the local travel trade and media to stimulate interest in Britain.

The BTA speaks for the whole of Britain on inbound tourism. Our mission statement is to build the value of tourism in Britain. So how do we approach that mission? We generate additional tourism revenue throughout Britain and at all times of the year by promoting Britain as a tourist destination all over the world. We:

- generate more value from customers in key overseas markets

- provide accurate, impartial tourist information

- gather and disseminate market intelligence

- encourage a sustainable level of tourism for visitors and residents alike

- develop new business for the longer term

- develop the quality and calibre of BTA staff as a key strategic resource.

Working in collaboration with UK national and regional tourist boards, a crucially important aspect in our advisory and liaison roles is as the industry's lead body in international tourism. The BTA is the definitive source of the information needed to plan for this enormously important sector.

The BTA represents Britain in overseas markets that cover some 90 per cent of inbound tourism. Each year, it handles 2.75 million enquiries from the public, the media and the travel industry.

There are over 700 tourist information centres in the UK and they play a key role in promoting and supporting the travel and tourism industry in their respective areas. Most of the 700 tourist information centres in the UK are funded and operated by local authorities or regional tourist boards. Tourist information centres offer a range of information services and travel products for visitors to the area. They provide information on local attractions and sell guidebooks, maps and souvenirs. They also operate booking services for accommodation, sightseeing tours, theatres and special events in their areas. Many tourist information centres also operate the Book A Bed Ahead service (BABA), which allows accommodation to be booked in advance through information centres in other localities.

Source: www.visitbritain.com

Guiding services

Guiding services provide specialist knowledge of an area, tourist attraction or historic building or site. The best known guiding services are the Blue Badge Guides and Guide Friday. The regional tourist boards validate Guild of Registered Tourist Guides training courses and award the Blue Badge to successful participants.

Some services are operated by commercial firms, of which Guide Friday is the largest. It caters for more than a million visitors a year and its distinctive green and cream open-top buses are a familiar sight in some of Britain's most popular heritage centres.

Many people work as voluntary guides, notably in historic buildings and churches. Volunteers often belong to voluntary guide associations, which provide free tours, training and support for their members.

Tourist attractions

The English Tourism Council (formerly English Tourist Board) defines a **visitor (tourist) attraction** as:

> *a permanently established excursion destination, a primary purpose of which is to allow public access for entertainment, interest or education, rather than being a primary retail outlet or venue for sporting, theatrical or film performances. It must be open to the public, without prior booking, for published periods each year, and should be capable of attracting day visitors or tourists as well as local residents.*

Tourist attractions are a vital component of the UK travel and tourism industry. The English Tourism Council (ETC) estimated that visits to attractions

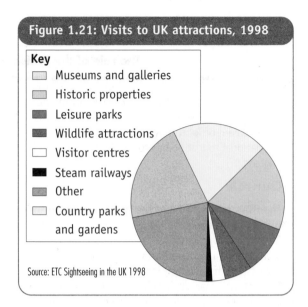

Figure 1.21: Visits to UK attractions, 1998

Key
- Museums and galleries
- Historic properties
- Leisure parks
- Wildlife attractions
- Visitor centres
- Steam railways
- Other
- Country parks and gardens

Source: ETC Sightseeing in the UK 1998

totalled 396 million in 1998. There are many different categories of tourist attraction in the UK. Figure 1.22 shows the ETC's eight main categories of attraction and identifies the leading attraction in each category.

Some attractions, such as Madame Tussaud's, are run by the private sector for profit, some are run by charities, such as the National Trust, and others are controlled by the public sector, either through local authorities or on behalf of central government.

The range of products and services provided at visitor attractions varies depending on the nature of the attraction, its size, location and customer profile. Most larger attractions have retail and catering operations in addition to the mains tours, rides and exhibitions.

A good idea of the range of attractions in an area can be gained by studying a road touring map. Most use key

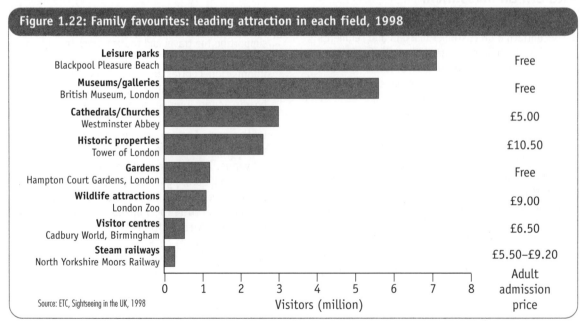

Figure 1.22: Family favourites: leading attraction in each field, 1998

Category	Visitors (million)	Adult admission price
Leisure parks Blackpool Pleasure Beach	7.1	Free
Museums/galleries British Museum, London	5.6	Free
Cathedrals/Churches Westminster Abbey	3.0	£5.00
Historic properties Tower of London	2.6	£10.50
Gardens Hampton Court Gardens, London	1.2	Free
Wildlife attractions London Zoo	1.1	£9.00
Visitor centres Cadbury World, Birmingham	0.5	£6.50
Steam railways North Yorkshire Moors Railway	0.3	£5.50–£9.20

Source: ETC, Sightseeing in the UK, 1998

symbols to denote various types of attraction. There are many such attractions in the UK, ranging from small local heritage sites and buildings to major leisure and theme parks. Many of the leisure and tourism facilities we discuss in this book can be regarded as visitor attractions, including theatres, museums, theme parks and country parks. Figure 1.23 shows the 20 most popular visitor attractions in the UK in 1999 and some of the most popular free visitor attractions.

Visitor attractions are often clustered in particular areas to form a tourist resort or destination area, such as Blackpool. Sometimes a single visitor attraction is the main purpose for a visit, for example Alton Towers, but more usually visitors travel to a locality with the intention of seeing several things, ranging from natural attractions such as beaches, lakes and hills to shops, museums, hotels, theatres and heritage sites.

In addition to established tourist destinations, many other locations are seeking to increase their tourist potential. Cities such as Glasgow, Liverpool and Leeds have invested huge sums of money in developing visitor attractions in an attempt to attract tourists.

Figure 1.23: Top 20 UK attractions charging admission, 1999

Rank	Attraction	Visitor numbers
1	Alton Towers, Staffordshire	2,650,000
2	Madame Tussaud's, London	2,640,000
3	Tower of London	2,422,181
4	Natural History Museum, London	1,739,591
5	Legoland, Windsor	1,620,000
6	Chessington World of Adventures, Surrey	1,550,000
7	Science Museum, London	1,480,000
8	Royal Academy, London	1,390,000
9	Canterbury Cathedral	1,350,000
10	Windsor Castle, Berkshire	1,280,000
11	Westminster Abbey, London	1,268,215
12	Edinburgh Castle	1,219,720
13	Flamingo Land Theme Park, Yorkshire	1,197,000
14	Drayton Manor Park, Staffordshire	1,174,448
15	Windermere Lake Cruises, Cumbria	1,140,207
16	St. Paul's Cathedral, London	1,076,222
17	London Zoo	1,067,917
18	Chester Zoo	965,721
19	Victoria and Albert Museum, London	945,677
20	Thorpe Park, Surrey	926,000

Free attractions with attendances of two million or more in 1998 include: Albert Dock, Liverpool; Blackpool Pleasure Beach; The British Museum; Eastbourne Pier; Magical World of Fantasy Island, Lincolnshire; The National Gallery; The Palace Pier, Brighton; Pleasureland Amusement Park, Southport; Strathclyde Country Park; Sutton Park, Sutton Coldfield; York Minster.

Source: www.staruk.org, ETC and BTA figures

▲ Blackpool is a popular seaside holiday resort with a range of visitor attractions

ACTIVITY

Visitor attractions

Trace an outline map of the UK and locate five examples for each of the following types of visitor attraction or destination:

- heritage or historic sites of national importance, (for example, Stonehenge)
- seaside resorts (for example, Brighton)
- towns or cities which are major tourist destination areas, (for example, Edinburgh)
- spa towns, (for example, Bath)
- major theme parks, (for example, Alton Towers)
- natural features or areas which are major visitor attractions, (for example, the Giant's Causeway).

Theme and leisure park attractions

The term **theme park** describes an action packed, family-centred leisure and entertainment complex. Parks often include high technology versions of traditional funfair rides and roller coasters (sometimes referred to as white knuckle rides), as well as amusement arcades, adventure playgrounds, computer simulations and laser games. They often have a variety of sports facilities, heritage activities, zoos and wildlife areas. Examples of well known UK theme parks include:

- Alton Towers, Staffordshire
- Chessington World of Adventures, Surrey
- Thorpe Park, Surrey
- Legoland, Windsor
- Drayton Manor Park, Staffordshire.

Theme parks usually charge a daily admission fee, covering the cost of all rides and entertainments. Alton Towers is the largest admission charging theme park in the UK, attracting over 2.7 million visitors in 1998.

Some theme and leisure parks do not charge admission fees, so it is only possible to estimate the total number of visitors each year. It is estimated that around eight million people visited Blackpool Pleasure Beach in 1998.

Theme and leisure parks are big business, attracting huge numbers of visitors and require major financial investment, running into millions of pounds. For example, the Pepsi Max Big One roller coaster at Blackpool Pleasure Beach cost £12 million, while the Nemesis ride at Alton Towers cost £10 million. Legoland Windsor cost £85 million to build.

Heritage or historic sites

This category of tourist attraction ranges from centuries-old historic sites, such as Stonehenge and Skara Brae, to castles, cathedrals and stately homes. There are around 450,000 listed historic buildings and sites in the United Kingdom. They include:

- stately homes, palaces and manors, for example Blenheim Palace and Castle Howard
- castles and forts, for example, Edinburgh, Caernarfon and Dover castles
- cathedrals, churches and abbeys, for example, Westminster Abbey and Coventry Cathedral
- monuments and ruins, for example Hadrian's Wall and Glastonbury Tor
- battlefields, for example, Naseby and Towton
- historic ships, for example, *Cutty Sark*, *HMS Victory* and *HMS Belfast*.

Many historic buildings and sites are owned and run by religious organisations, including Westminster Abbey and York Minster. Local authorities, the National Trust and English Heritage are also involved in preserving and maintaining historic buildings, while the five historic palaces — the Tower of London, Hampton Court, Kensington Palace, Kew Palace and the Banqueting House, Whitehall — are run by the government agency Historic Royal Palaces.

Figure 1.24: Top UK historic monuments, 1998

Historic house/monument	Visits
1 Tower of London	2,551,459
2 Windsor Castle	1,495,465
3 Edinburgh Castle	1,219,055
4 Roman Baths, Bath	905,426
5 Stonehenge, Wiltshire	817,493
6 Warwick Castle	777,500
7 Hampton Court Palace	605,230
8 Leeds Castle, Kent	551,377
9 Shakespeare's birthplace, Stratford	520,108
10 Chatsworth House, Derbyshire	475,000

Source: Visits to Tourist Attractions 1998, English Tourist Board

Figure 1.25: Top ten UK cathedrals, 1998

Cathedral/church	Visits
1 Westminster Abbey	3,000,000
2 York Minster	2,000,000
3 Canterbury Cathedral	1,500,000
4 St Paul's Cathedral, London	1,095,299
5 Chester Cathedral	1,000,000
6 Salisbury Cathedral	800,000
7 Norwich Cathedral	540,000
8 St Martin in the Fields, London	500,000
9 Truro Cathedral	500,000
10 Durham Cathedral	466,559

Source: Visits to Tourist Attractions 1998, English Tourist Board

Approximately a third of the historic properties in the UK that are open to the public are owned and managed by the private or voluntary sector. These include the properties owned by the National Trust.

Figures 1.24 and 1.25 show the most visited historic houses and monuments, and cathedrals and churches in the UK in 1998.

Heritage experience attractions such as the Jorvic Viking Centre in York are a relatively new group of attractions. They offer a simulated experience through technology-based techniques such as interactive displays, rides, animation, sounds and even smells. Such attractions are expensive to develop and build: most are run by the private sector and charge an admission fee. The Natural History Museum's (public sector) Earth Gallery Experience attraction cost £12 million and enables visitors to descend into a volcano to witness a lava flow, while a platform rocks in a mock earthquake.

Museums and galleries

Millions of people visit museums and art galleries in the UK every year for a variety of recreational, educational and cultural reasons. Museums are run by organisations in the public, private and voluntary sectors, although the principal ones are all publicly owned. Facilities range from large national museums, such as the British Museum and the National Gallery, to important regional and local collections and small local museums run by volunteers.

The Museums Association defines a **museum** as:

an institution which collects, preserves, exhibits and interprets material evidence and associated information for the public benefit.

This definition encompasses general municipal museums and those which specialise, for example, in social history, natural history, transport, science, military artefacts, past industrial processes and agriculture. The Campaign for Museums has developed the 24 Hour Museum, which provides extensive information about museums on the internet. The web site (**www.24hourmuseum.org.uk**) includes a museum finder, with museum collections placed in a number of categories.

The English Tourist Board lists about 950 museums in the UK, each attracting at least 5,000 visitors a year. London is the major centre for museums. It has 47 public museums and galleries which each attract 50,000 or more visits per year. London is also home to the six most popular national museums (see Figure 1.26).

Outside the capital, the largest museums are located in major cities, including the Glasgow Art Gallery and Museum which attracted over a million visitors in 1998.

ACTIVITY

The 24 Hour Museum

If you have access to the internet go to the 24 Hour Museum site (www.24hourmuseum.org.uk)

Undertake a detailed search for information on museums in a chosen locality and complete a table like the one below. If you do not have access to the internet you can complete this activity by gathering information from visitor guides, or by visiting the museums.

Museum	Owner and sector	Collection details	Facilities	Location

Figure 1.26: Most popular UK museums, 1998

Museums	Estimated attendance in 1998 (in millions)
British Museum	6.2
National Gallery	4.9
Natural History Museum	1.9
Tate Gallery	1.9
Science Museum	1.6
Victoria and Albert Museum	1.1

Countryside visitor attractions

The countryside provides significant opportunities for millions of people to enjoy a variety of leisure pastimes and activities, including drives, picnics, walks and visits to parks, monuments and historic properties.

Many areas have long had urban parks, gardens and allotments. More recently, new types of amenities have been developed, including children's play areas, walking trails and cycleways. Some of the best known urban parks include Hyde Park, Regent's Park and St James's Park in London, Kelvingrove Park in Glasgow, Sefton Park in Liverpool and Sophia Gardens in Cardiff. London also has two of the most visited gardens in the United Kingdom – Kew Gardens and Hampton Court.

Perhaps the best known areas of the countryside providing recreational opportunities are the national parks. There are now 11 national parks in England and Wales, with a twelfth, in the New Forest, planned.

Other designated areas of the countryside provide recreational opportunities in addition to the national parks. These include:

- areas of outstanding natural beauty, for example the Kent Downs and the North Pennines

- heritage coasts, for example, the south west coast and the Norfolk coast

- national trails and long distance paths, for example, the Cleveland Way and the Thames Path

- country parks, for example, Strathclyde Park, Motherwell and Crawfordsburn Park, Belfast.

There have also been a number of projects to create parks out of derelict industrial areas such as the Lee Valley and Colne Valley regional parks.

ACTIVITY

Countryside attractions

The map shows the location and names of the national parks in England and Wales. In small groups, select and investigate one national park. Try to find out:

- when the park was designated

- who owns the land

- how many people are employed by the park

- how many people visited the park

- the annual revenue generated by visitors.

You may find useful information in the annual reports published by each national park. When you have finished your research, present your findings and compare your research with the other groups.

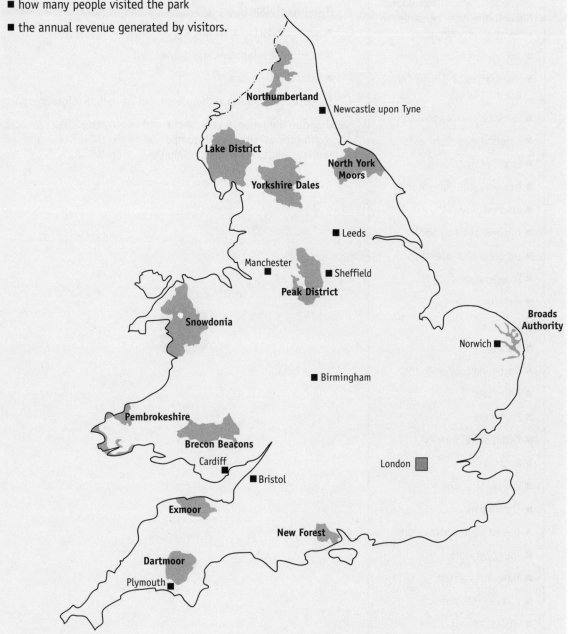

BUILD YOUR LEARNING

1 Explain the present structure of the UK travel and tourism industry, giving suitable examples. You should include all of the components below:

- travel agencies
- tour operations
- transportation
- accommodation and catering
- tourism development and promotion
- tourist attractions.

Support your findings with relevant and up-to date information.

2 Describe the range of commercial and non-commercial organisations within each component of the UK travel and tourism industry and give examples.

Keywords and phrases

You should know the meaning of these words and phrases. If you are unsure about any of them, go back through the last 27 pages to refresh your understanding.

- Accommodation providers
- Association of British Travel Agents (ABTA)
- Business travel agencies
- Catering establishments
- Chain of distribution
- Domestic tour operator
- Guiding services
- Horizontal integration
- Inbound tour operator
- Independent outlets
- Miniple
- Multiple
- Museum
- Outbound tour operator
- Principals
- Producers
- Retail travel agency
- Retailers
- Supply structure
- Theme park
- Tourist visitor attraction
- Tour operators
- Transport carriers
- Vertical integration
- Wholesalers

Scale of the UK travel and tourism industry

TRAVEL AND TOURISM IS A MULTI-BILLION pound industry in the UK. It has a major impact on the economy in terms of consumer spending and employment. However, because the industry is so diverse and fragmented, it is often difficult to assess its exact contribution to the national economy.

Several organisations produce statistics on the numbers employed in various sectors within the industry and the contribution they make to the national economy. Perhaps the best-known sources of data are government statistics published by Her Majesty's Stationery Office (HMSO), such as *Social Trends and the Annual Abstract of Statistics*. Other sources include the British Tourist Authority, national and regional tourist boards, industry bodies such as ABTA and market research companies such as Mintel and Keynote. Another useful source on information can be found on the internet at www.staruk.org

We now investigate some of these sources of information, in order to assess the scale of the UK travel and tourism industry. This is based on analysis of:

- UK travel and tourism revenue and its contribution to the national economy

- employment statistics

- inbound, outbound and domestic tourist numbers in the UK.

Travel and tourism revenue

The British Tourist Authority (BTA) and the English Tourism Council (ETC) estimate that the value of tourism to the UK in 1998 was £61,201 million, making the industry the fourth largest earner of foreign exchange. Figure 1.27 shows the main areas where this money was spent. Figures 1.28 shows how important tourism is to the UK economy.

Figure 1.27: UK spending by tourists, 1998

	Trips (millions)	Spending (£m)
UK residents	122.3	£14,030
Overseas visitors	25.7	£12,671
Total	148.0	£26,701

Source: BTA/ETC

Figure 1.28: Tourism in the UK economy

Economic indicator	£ billion 1998	Tourism's share
Gross domestic product	838	3.6%
Consumer pending	523	5.7%
All exports	351	4.5%
Services exports	60	26.5%

Source: BTA/ETC

In 1998, 25.7 million overseas visitors came to Britain, spending more than £12 billion. The British Tourist Authority estimates that by the year 2003, overseas visitors will spend around £18 billion a year in the UK, 44 per cent more than in 1998. The industry continues to grow as towns, cities and resorts increase their efforts to attract visitors from overseas and from other parts of the UK. The industry also caters for British residents who travel overseas for leisure or business purposes. Figure 1.28 shows that tourism was responsible for 5.7 per cent of all consumer spending in the UK in 1998, and accounted for 3.6 per cent of the country's gross domestic product.

The ETC and BTA both produce data that highlight the importance of tourism to the national economy. Their data considers the value of expenditure by foreign tourists visiting the UK (incoming tourists) in addition to expenditure by UK residents (domestic tourists). Some key statistics are highlighted in Figures 1.29, 1.30 and 1.31.

A wide range of industries benefit from both **direct and indirect income** generated by tourists. Indirect income is generated through a process known as the **multiplier effect** (see p. 35). This occurs because a proportion of the money spent by tourists is recirculated in the local economy. The travel and tourism industry also contributes to the national economy via central and local government taxation, including corporation tax and value added tax (VAT). On a local scale, travel and tourism enterprises also contribute to local government finances through the payment of business rates.

Figure 1.29: Value of tourism in the UK, 1995

Value of tourism to the UK 1995

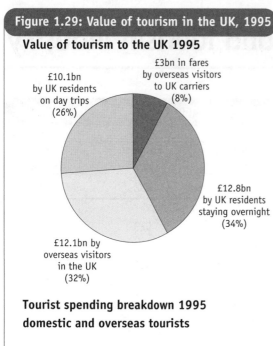

£10.1bn by UK residents on day trips (26%)

£3bn in fares by overseas visitors to UK carriers (8%)

£12.8bn by UK residents staying overnight (34%)

£12.1bn by overseas visitors in the UK (32%)

Tourist spending breakdown 1995 domestic and overseas tourists

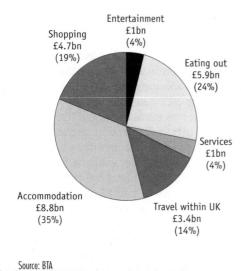

Shopping £4.7bn (19%)

Entertainment £1bn (4%)

Eating out £5.9bn (24%)

Services £1bn (4%)

Travel within UK £3.4bn (14%)

Accommodation £8.8bn (35%)

Source: BTA

Figure 1.30: Value of tourism in the UK, 1998

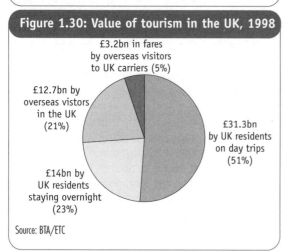

£3.2bn in fares by overseas visitors to UK carriers (5%)

£12.7bn by overseas vistors in the UK (21%)

£31.3bn by UK residents on day trips (51%)

£14bn by UK residents staying overnight (23%)

Source: BTA/ETC

Figure 1.31: Tourist spending, 1998

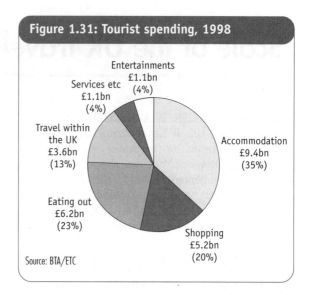

Entertainments £1.1bn (4%)

Services etc £1.1bn (4%)

Travel within the UK £3.6bn (13%)

Accommodation £9.4bn (35%)

Eating out £6.2bn (23%)

Shopping £5.2bn (20%)

Source: BTA/ETC

Contribution to the balance of payments

The **balance of payments** is the relationship between the value of what is imported to the UK and what is exported. It is easy to measure the balance of payments on manufactured goods such as cars because we know exactly how many British-made cars are exported overseas and how many foreign cars are imported into this country during any given period. If the value of British cars exported is greater than the value of foreign cars imported, there is a **surplus** on the balance of payments. However, if the value of imported cars is greater than the value of exported cars, the balance of payments is in **deficit**.

It is harder to assess the contribution which the travel and tourism industry makes to the balance of payments, because tourists are generally paying for services rather than for material goods. Some of the services may have been paid for in advance as part of a tour operator's inclusive holiday package, while others may be paid for in US dollars or in traveller's cheques. We also do not know exactly how much money a tourist will spend whilst on holiday and exchange rates vary from one day to the next.

The income which we receive from visitors to the UK is considered to be an **export** because it earns foreign currency, bringing money into the economy. Although nothing leaves the UK – in fact tourists come to the UK – visitors are buying a British product when they visit this country, in the same way that they might buy a British car. The money that we spend on holidays abroad is considered an **import**, because the goods and services are paid for in foreign currency, taking money out of the UK economy. Again, although nothing is brought into the UK, tourists are buying a foreign product when they travel overseas in much the same way that they might buy a foreign car.

Although the amount of tourism export earnings has increased in recent years, the balance of payments has moved from a surplus in the 1970s to a deficit in the 1990s. The main reason for the transition from surplus to deficit is the large increase in outbound tourism. In 1998, international (outgoing) tourism by the British reached almost 31 million trips, representing a spend of almost £15 billion, compared with an incoming tourist spend of just under £13 billion.

Changing tourism patterns and trends will continue to have an impact upon the UK's tourism balance of payments. For example, the UK is currently the fifth most popular tourist destination in Europe, behind France, Spain, Italy and Hungary. If the UK falls further, or rises in popularity, then it is likely that the balance of payments will change accordingly.

ACTIVITY
Tourism's balance of payments

In small groups, study the following scenarios and brainstorm the impact you think they could have on the UK's tourism balance of payments.

- The value of sterling rises against most of the world's major currencies.

- The value of sterling falls against most of the world's major currencies.

- The UK records its hottest summer on record and meteorologists predict another extremely hot summer for the following year.

- A group of extremists carry out a series of terrorist attacks on trans-atlantic airline carriers.

- The UK economy enjoys a boom period, with low interest rates, average incomes rising faster than inflation and increasing disposable income.

Discuss your findings with other groups to determine the most likely impact of each scenario.

Employment statistics

The travel and tourism industry is one of Britain's largest employers, with an estimated 1.7 million people currently employed in it and around 50,000 new jobs being created every year. This level of employment represents seven per cent of all UK employees, more than in construction or transport. The industry is

therefore regarded as a major provider of employment opportunities. Figure 1.32 shows the estimated numbers employed in selected industry components.

Figure 1.32: Numbers employed in tourism

	'000
Hotels and other tourist accommodation	318.7
Restaurants, cafes, etc.	356.0
Bars, pubs, clubs	364.1
Travel agents, tour operators	83.5
Libraries, museums, culture	77.0
Sport and other recreation	291.7
Self employment in tourism industry	94.0
Total employed in tourism industry	1,685.1

Source: Office for National Statistics, Annual Abstract of Statistics 1999

ACTIVITY
Employment in travel and tourism

1 Obtain up-to-date information on the numbers employed in various components of the travel and tourism industries. You will find the quarterly *Employment Gazette* and the annual abstracts of statistics useful starting points for your research. These are available at your school or college or local library.

2 Identify any seasonal variations in the numbers of people employed in the various industry components. Suggest reasons why the total numbers employed vary throughout the year.

3 Imagine you have been asked to give a talk to a group of 14–16 year olds about job opportunities within the travel and tourism industry. Produce a handout which presents your data in a format suitable for your intended audience from the national employment data you have gathered. This may include use of tables or charts.

Tourist statistics

The huge size of the travel and tourism industry can be appreciated if we consider the number of trips taken by UK residents and incoming tourists, as well as the volume of spending. We have already seen that the number of trips taken for leisure and business purposes continues to increase (Figures 1.33 and 1.34). Figures 1.35, 1.36 and 1.37 give an indication of the current scale of the UK industry, and will help you to complete the end of section activity on p. 71

Figure 1.34: Forecast incoming tourism growth

	1997	2003	% change 1997–2003	Yearly change %
Visits	25.7m	31.8m	+24	+4
Spend	£12.7bn	£18.2bn	+44	+8

Source: BTA forecasts

Figure 1.33: Incoming visitors to the UK

	Millions of visits	Nights	Spending
1988	15.8	173	£6,184
1989	17.3	187	£6,945
1990	18.0	196	£7,748
1991	17.1	186	£7,386
1992	18.5	186	£7,891
1993	19.9	190	£9,487
1994	20.8	192	£9,786
1995	23.5	220	£11,763
1996	25.2	220	£12,290
1997	25.5	223	£12,244
1998	25.7	231	£12,671

Source: www.staruk.org.uk

Figure 1.35: Distribution of tourism 1998 from staruk website

	UK residents		Overseas visitors	
	Trips (millions)	Spending (£m)	Trips (millions)	Spending (£m)
Cumbria	2.9	£380	0.29	£49
Northumbria	4.2	£340	0.49	£139
North west	8.4	£970	1.28	£423
Yorkshire	9.2	£940	1.02	£307
Heart of England	16.8	£1,160	2.24	£688
East of England	13.0	£1,290	1.78	£628
London	11.6	£1,055	13.48	£6,736
West Country	16.6	£2,670	1.69	£529
Southern	10.9	£1,245	2.23	£829
South east	10.5	£825	2.54	£885
England	101.9	£10,880	21.97	£11,204
Northern Ireland	0.8	£200	0.12	£50
Scotland	9.8	£1,540	2.14	£945
Wales	9.8	£1,100	0.79	£176
UK*	122.3	£14,030	25.7	£12,671

UK* includes Channel Islands and the Isle of Man

Source: www.staruk.org.uk

BUILD YOUR LEARNING

End of section activity

You have been asked to give a talk to a group of people about the scale of the UK travel and tourism industry. Write a speech or design a handout that starts, 'The industry that has developed in the UK to meet the needs of tourists is very extensive'. Describe the scale of the industry and highlight its economic significance, giving suitable examples and relevant, accurate data. You should include all of the following:

■ UK travel and tourism revenue

■ employment statistics

■ incoming tourist numbers to the UK

■ travel statistics for UK residents (domestic and outgoing tourists).

If you have access to the internet you may find it useful to check out the following website, which contains extensive information on tourism statistics and trends: **www.staruk.org.uk**

Keywords and phrases

You should know the meaning of the words and phrases below. If you are unsure about any of them, go back through the last four pages of the unit to refresh your understanding.

■ Balance of payments

■ Deficit

■ Direct income

■ Employment statistics

■ Export

■ Import

■ Indirect income

■ Multiplier effect

■ Tourism reverve

■ Tourist statistics

didnt no bout Sept 11th 2001, not wot sed it wuld b. ✗

2003.	Trips/visits millions	Wights millions	Spending millions
UK resi	167.3	531.9	26.699
Overseas resi	24.2	199.3	11.737

www.starbu.org.vu.

main purpose for overseas is holidays closely followed by buisness

Working in travel and tourism

YOU SHOULD NOW UNDERSTAND that the travel and tourism industry is very wide-ranging and consists of a wide variety of enterprises of different sizes. Travel and tourism is one of Britain's biggest growth industries. Few can match it for the range of employment opportunities it offers people of all ages. Taking account of both direct and indirect employment, the list of job opportunities for people with the right skills, knowledge and personal qualities is vast.

In this section we are going to look at the range of employment opportunities in the travel and tourism industry, at the personal and technical skills and qualities required by employers and at ways of finding a job in travel and tourism.

Part of the assessment for this unit requires you to select a job from the travel and tourism industry that best matches your own aspirations, skills and abilities. To do this you will need to be able to answer questions like:

■ what are my strengths, weaknesses and interests?

■ what sectors of the industry are available to me?

■ what job opportunities exist?

▼ There is a range of job opportunities in travel and tourism

■ what personal and technical skills are required to do my chosen job?

■ how can I prepare myself to pusue my career progression aims?

Employment opportunities

The vast range of jobs in the travel and tourism industry reflects the breadth and diversity of the key industry components. We cannot provide you with an exhaustive list of all types of employment opportunity within each of these components here. Instead, we investigate some of the most common employment opportunities across the industry. Before we do so it is important for you to understand that these jobs may be:

■ full time or part time

■ permanent or temporary (seasonal).

A distinctive feature of the UK's domestic tourism industry is the vast number of full and part-time seasonal jobs that it provides. For example, employment opportunities in most UK seaside resorts are drastically reduced outside the peak summer holiday months of July and August. See pp. 73–4 for an indication of the jobs available and skills required for selected industry components.

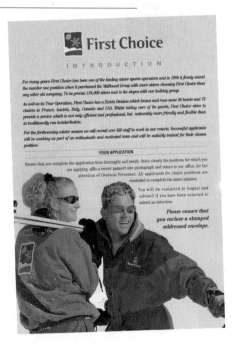

Jobs in travel services

Jobs available

- Leisure travel agents: Travel sales consultants, foreign exchange clerks, telephone salespeople.

- Business travel agents: Sales consultants, telephone salespeople, conference organisers.

- Tour operators: Staff in accounts, administration, brochure production, contracting, customer services, marketing, product development, resort representatives, children's activity leaders, reservations clerks, telephone sales, tour guides.

Working conditions

Similar to work in any retail outlet, except the sales product is travel rather than goods. Jobs initially offer low wages, but there is competition because travel is perceived as a glamorous.

What do employers look for?

- methodical working habits
- accuracy
- literacy and numeracy
- knowledge of travel geography
- ability to work with people
- keyboard skills

Skills

- literacy and numeracy
- attention to detail
- customer service skills
- IT skills
- financial ability
- organisational skills
- communication skills
- languages

Qualifications

- NVQs in travel services
- ABTAC (ABTA Travel Agent's Certificate)
- ABTOC (ABTA Tour Operator's Certificate)
- Vocational A level Travel and Tourism
- GBTA Introductory Certificate in Business Travel
- qualifications in languages, IT and customer care

Jobs in transportation

Jobs available

- General: administrative, sales, customer service, marketing, cleaning and maintenance staff

- Coach companies: drivers, traffic managers, tour guides, stewards/stewardesses

- Railways: conductors, drivers, catering staff

- Airlines: flight crew, cabin crew, passenger sales agents, check-in staff, telephone sales staff

- Airports: air traffic controllers, concession receptionists (car hire, hotel bookings), customs and excise, immigration, information staff, porters, retail staff, security staff

- Ferries: sales staff, deck hands, catering and retail staff*

- Cruise liners: chefs, catering staff, entertainers, fitness staff, hairdressers, purser's office staff, qualified nursery staff

Working conditions

Many jobs require stamina and staff cannot suffer from motion sickness. Hours worked are often unsocial and work shifts can be long. However, most employers offer staff perks such as free or discounted travel.

What do employers look for?

- literacy and numeracy
- IT skills
- customer service skills
- foreign languages are also useful

Jobs in tourist attractions

Jobs available

Jobs range from small specialist museums to internationally-known theme parks and visitor attractions. They include:

- general: administrative office staff, marketing and sales personnel, press, publicity and advertising staff, maintenance and security staff, tour guides
- staff for souvenir shops; car park attendants, guides and information staff
- catering and hospitality staff, cleaners and porters
- museums staff such as curators, guides, archivists.

Working conditions

Hours can be long and unsocial, but those who come in contact with visitors must be friendly and welcoming at all times. Jobs are frequently seasonal or on short-term contracts. There is work all over the UK, both at country venues and in cities. Some venues are open year-round, others close at the end of the season.

What do employers look for?

- customers care skills
- stamina and a can do attitude
- willingness to work long hours in the height of the season
- languages, if the venue has overseas visitors.
- Useful qualifications
- GNVQ in Travel and Tourism
- NVQs in Customer Service, Travel Services and Tour Guiding
- first aid qualifications
- food hygiene certificate
- languages

Jobs in tourism support and promotion

Jobs available

- Regional tourist boards need administration staff in planning, development, marketing, press and PR, publications, research, information, standards officers.
- Local authority tourism departments, tourism marketing groups and tourism agencies set up to promote attractions also need these administration staff.
- Tourist information centres need information staff.
- Stately homes and historic houses need room stewards/stewardesses, house guides, cashiers, sales and retail staff, car park attendants, gardeners and cleaners.

Working conditions

Work is often office based. Some is outdoors in all weathers and often requires staff to stay away in hotels (at the company's expense). Staff on the front line in tourist information centres need to have a calm temperament to deal with the public.

What do employers look for?

- languages
- marketing and sales experience
- customer care qualifications
- IT experience
- conservation and environmental awareness

Qualifications required

- Degree or diploma in Marketing
- language qualifications
- NVQs in Travel Services and Tour Guiding

Jobs in hospitality and catering

Jobs available

- Hotels: accountant, barman, chambermaid, cashier, chef, concierge, cook, conference and banqueting staff, doorman, duty manager/ess, general manager/ess, hall porter, health, fitness and beauty operator, florist, housekeeper, kitchen porter, linen room assistant, linkman, maintenance staff, marketing staff, night porter, porter, press and PR, reservation staff, sales staff, secretary, security, telephonist, valet, waiter/waitress, wine waiter/ess.

- Other hotels: in smaller hotels jobs are often combined, for example, receptionist, reservations and secretarial work can all be carried out by one person. Guest houses, bed and breakfasts, self-catering establishments and camp sites may employ chambermaids, cooks, maintenance staff and receptionists.

- Cruise ships and ferries: catering staff, chefs and kitchen staff. If passengers stay on board overnight then they employ some or all of the same staff as a hotel. Other jobs include entertainer, steward/ess, purser, secretary, deck cadet, engineer, nurse, fitness, beauty and hairdresser and retail staff.

- Pubs and inns: bar staff, cleaner, waiter/waitress, glass collector, cellarman/woman, chef, cook, licensee/manager, door supervisor, chambermaid.

- Agencies: hotel marketing groups, hotel consortia, hotel group reservations and hotel representatives all need sales and marketing staff with IT skills.

Working conditions

Many jobs involve teamwork. Chambermaids and everyone working in a busy kitchen have to work as part of a team. Hours are often long and unsocial. Shift work may be required, although split shifts (working at lunch time, and then again in the evening) are gradually disappearing. Early starts are often the norm.

What do employers look for?

- appropriate GNVQs and NVQs

- first aid and health and safety training

- a can-do attitude and customer service skills

ACTIVITY

Jobs in travel and tourism

1 Read through the information about the range of jobs available in the main components of the travel and tourism industry. In small groups, discuss the most common skills and abilities that employers look for.

2 Make a list of the travel and tourism jobs that are currently available in a selected locality. You will find it useful to look at your local paper and perhaps visit the local Jobcentre. From your investigation, identify the most common types of job available within the travel and tourism industry.

3 Select one of the jobs from your list and describe:

- working conditions

- qualifications required

- skills and useful qualification for the job.

The nature of employment

The travel and tourism industry is regarded as a people industry and there are a vast number of jobs that involve dealing with customers in person, such as waiters, resort representatives and air cabin crew to name but a few. There are many more jobs at a basic or operative level than there are in management. If you are a school or college leaver starting out on your career, your first job is likely to be at the operative level. Figure 1.36 gives some typical examples of jobs at this level.

Figure 1.36 Some jobs at operative level
Resort representative
Hotel receptionist
Waiter or waitress
Travel agency sales consultant
Tourist information centre assistant
Tourist guide
Coach driver
Airline cabin crew

The travel and tourism industry offers good promotion prospects and many people progress from basic jobs to supervisory and higher management positions. Some examples of career progression are shown in Figure 1.37.

For some people, promotion from operative to supervisory and management levels can be relatively quick, although competition for jobs at all levels is often intense. For example, thousands of people apply to airline companies every year for cabin crew positions, but only a small proportion are accepted.

Another feature of work in the travel and tourism industry is the potential for changing career paths. For example, if you work for an employer who owns a range of facilities, such as hotels, pubs, restaurants and leisure facilities, it may be possible to move from one to another. Even if this is not the case, there are numerous opportunities to diversify into different areas.

Finally, many jobs in the industry involve working unsocial hours, such as holiday periods, evenings and weekends. This may be a significant barrier for some people entering the industry as they may not be available to work unsocial hours on a regular basis.

ACTIVITY

Unsocial hours

1 List ten jobs in the travel and tourism industry that you think involve working unsocial hours. For each one, explain why you think the hours worked are unsociable.

2 In small groups, discuss how you think employers could compensate their employees for working unsocial hours.

Personal and technical skills

The personal and technical skills and qualities required by employers vary from job to job. However, many of the personal skills required by employers are common right across the industry. The list below gives an indication of the personal skills most commonly sought after by travel and tourism employers.

- good communication skills
- good customer service skills
- common sense
- good listener
- literacy and numeracy skills
- outgoing personality
- sense of humour
- enthusiasm
- flexibility
- stamina and good health
- organisational skills
- enjoy dealing with the general public
- ability to work well in a team
- smart appearance
- ability to think quickly
- willingness to work unsocial hours
- polite

Figure 1.37: Examples of career progression

Operative →	Supervisory →	Management
Travel agency sales consultant	Senior sales consultant	Travel agency manager
Waiter/waitress	Head waiter/waitress	Restaurant manager
Hotel receptionist	Front of house manager	Hotel manager
Holiday resort representative	Senior resort representative	Resort manager

ACTIVITY

Personal qualities and skills

Study the following list of comments from people working in the industry who were asked, 'What are the most important personal qualities, skills and knowledge requirements for your job?'

1 'I must understand how to motivate people and this means finding exactly the right approach for each individual. The most important skills are the ability to communicate, (sometimes in foreign languages) teach others and inspire confidence. I have to be physically fit as the job is very demanding.'

2 'I need business acumen and flair to develop new ideas and increase use of the facility. It is important to be able to handle people, both employees and customers. Good communication skills are important with staff and customers. Numeracy and information technology skills are needed in order to cope with the financial and management information aspects of the job. Finally, there is a high level of responsibility as I am accountable for the day-to-day running of the facility and for the health and safety of visitors and staff.'

3 'I have to be confident and outgoing whilst at work. It is important to get on well with people and deal tactfully and diplomatically with dissatisfied customers. I am very much in the public eye, so smart appearance and good social skills are vital. Also important are organisational ability, business skills, competence in financial matters and knowledge of a range of related practical skills such as cookery, food and beverage service and housekeeping. At peak times the work is hectic and the ability to work under pressure is vital.'

4 'Good customer service, communication and IT skills are essential for my job. I deal with customers face to face and I need to suggest the most appropriate products to meet their needs. It is very useful if I have specific knowledge about a destination or resort. Attention to detail is very important when making a booking.'

5 'Good customer service and communication skills are essential, combined with bags of enthusiasm. Many people regard the job as glamorous, but in reality its very demanding because of the unsocial hours and frequent stopovers away from home.'

6 'Many people think the work is glamorous, but it is frequently very demanding with long unsociable hours. The main requirement is the ability to communicate well with all types of people and deal effectively with customer complaints. It is very important to have a confident, outgoing personality and to get on with customers. Languages are also very useful.'

The comments on knowledge and skills came from:

- a hotel manager
- a holiday resort representative
- a travel sales consultant
- a tour guide
- a ski-ing instructor
- an air cabin crew member.

Match each description with the job role.

In small groups, discuss what knowledge and skills are common to all of these jobs. Record the main requirements in a table like the one below.

Description	Job role	Knowledge/skills required
1		
2		
3		
4		
5		
6		

Job descriptions and person specifications

Usually employers outline the personal and technical skills required to do the job in a job description and person specification. A job description describes the duties and responsibilities involved in a particular job. A person specification outlines the skills, knowledge and characteristics that are required to carry out the job. It is important that you understand the structure and content of a job description and person specification so that you can make appropriate choices for your own career progression.

The details included in a job description vary, as does the way in which it is laid out, but generally the following should always appear.

- The job title. For example, waitress, travel agency sales consultant, air cabin crew.

- The reporting structure. This should include details of who the job holder reports to and whether there is anyone who reports to the job holder. For example, the head waiter reports to the restaurant manager. The waiting staff, cashier and trainees report to the head waiter.

Figure 1.38: Job description for an hotel assistant

Sunnyhills Hotel
Job Description

JOB TITLE: **Hotel Assistant**

LOCATION: **Dartmouth**

RESPONSIBLE TO: **General Manager**

SCOPE AND GENERAL PURPOSE: To consistently deliver Sunnyhills Hotel standards ensuring a high degree of guest care at all times

PRINCIPAL ACCOUNTABILITIES

1 To report for duty in good time, clean and tidy and wearing the correct uniform.

2 To strive to anticipate guest needs wherever possible and to react to these to enhance guest satisfaction.

3 To treat all guests and colleagues in a polite and courteous manner at all times. To give full cooperation to any customer or colleague requiring assistance in a prompt, caring and helpful manner.

4 To consistently perform all tasks to standard as detailed and laid down within the Sunnyhills Hotel Service Standards.

5 To attend hotel meetings when required.

6 To attend training sessions and meetings when required and operate in line with training or information received.

7 To achieve action points arising out of six-monthly staff assessment.

8 To demonstrate a pride in the workplace and a high level of commitment.

9 To positively contribute to the sales activities within the hotel and maximise sales opportunities and to be knowledgeable of hotel products.

10 To minimise operating costs by using all equipment and products in accordance with company or manufacturer's guidelines.

11 To report all maintenance requirements and hazards in the workplace to your supervisor or manager.

12 To comply with statutory and legal requirements for fire, health and safety, licensing and employment. Your manager will supply you with current information.

13 To adhere to hotel rules at all times.

I confirm that I have read and agreed this job description explaining the main duties of my job.

SIGNED: JOB HOLDER

PRINT NAME:

DATE:

SIGNED: MANAGER

Job responsibilities are often categorised into main responsibilities and occasional responsibilities. The main job responsibilities are those carried out on a regular basis; occasional ones are those that may sometimes be part of the job.

The areas of responsibility in a job description often specify outcomes rather than responsibilities. In other words, it specifies what the job holder is expected to do. For example, the responsibility for delivering customer service may be expressed as 'to offer customers relevant information and assistance to meet their needs'.

The person specification identifies the specific skills and characteristics needed to fulfil the job description. A person specification may include sections on some or all of the following:

- personal attributes
- personal qualities
- personal achievements
- vocational qualifications
- academic qualifications
- competence.

Usually, job interviews cover each area identified on the person specification in order to distinguish the most suitable candidate from those of equal standing in other respects. Sometimes organisations indicate which skills and personal attributes are essential and which are merely desirable.

Personal attributes are personal characteristics. For example, people working in the travel and tourism industry deal with many people and need good communication skills. A resort representative needs to be confident, friendly and assertive and to have good communication skills.

Personal qualities are similar to attributes, but whereas attributes relate to personality, qualities refer to the way in which the person behaves. Many reference forms ask for specific details about the applicant, such as whether he or she is hardworking, reliable, honest, a good timekeeper, easy to work with and well-presented. These are all examples of personal qualities that are often required by employers.

Personal achievements can relate to both work experience and activities outside work. Work achievements might include the type of jobs held, the length of service or the nature of the duties and experience. Other personal achievements include interests, hobbies or activities that may reflect the ability to perform a job competently. For example, an assistant working for Camp America is required to work well as a member of a team. On the person specification under personal achievements it may say: 'provide clear

evidence of having worked successfully as a team member on a number of occasions.' One applicant may satisfy this requirement by explaining how he or she has had several holiday jobs in children's activity centres. Another applicant could satisfy this if he or she had been involved in organising a voluntary youth club. A third applicant may have been a leading member of the student's union at college, and perhaps been involved in coordinating rag week activities.

A **vocational qualification** is one that is based on a particular type of job and that is intended to lead to employment. Vocational A levels, General National Vocational Qualifications (GNVQs) and National Vocational Qualifications (NVQs) are all examples of vocational qualifications. There are many other vocational qualifications that may be important, such as the Basic Food Hygiene Certificate (for people involved in food preparation), first aid and health and safety qualifications.

Staff can get also get vocational qualifications by working for an organisation that has an efficient training programme. Many organisations provide excellent courses on specific topics such as complaint handling, selling skills, health and safety, and computer literacy. Many travel and tourism organisations provide on-the-job training, as it helps to build teamwork.

Academic qualifications include GCSEs, A levels, degrees and doctorates. Some jobs require an academic qualification at a high level. For example, an accountant working for a tour operator would probably require an academic qualification together with a vocational qualification taken after graduating. Other jobs may require more general academic qualifications. For example, a receptionist/cashier in a theatre may need GCSE mathematics and English to show that he or she has the required skills in literacy and numeracy.

Competence relates to the job skills required. For example, taxi drivers in London have to acquire the knowledge before they are able to operate a black cab service. This means that he or she must show familiarity with all routes and locations within the city. A travel agency sales consultant needs to be competent in computer literacy and telephone skills. A waiter must be able to provide silver service, lay tables correctly and serve wine.

Sources of information

There are many sources of information to help you choose a job in travel and tourism. Here are some of the main providers of careers guidance and information for jobs in travel and tourism.

Careers services

There should be someone responsible for providing careers education and guidance at your school or college who can help you. Alternatively, local careers services have extensive libraries and computer databases which provide information on most types of job. Careers service offices also display vacancies and, in some cases, will arrange interviews for you. Addresses of local careers service offices are listed in the telephone directory.

Libraries

There are many books and other publications on jobs and careers. Your local library is likely to contain a selection dealing with the leisure and tourism industries, together with information on how to apply for jobs. One title to request is the *Handbook of Jobs in Leisure and Tourism*, published annually by Hobsons.

Jobcentres

Jobcentres display vacancies that have been sent to them by employers. Their staff can also advise you about job opportunities in your area and on education and training schemes. Jobcentres are listed in the telephone directory under Employment Services.

Employment agencies

Many employers choose to place vacancies with private employment agencies rather than to advertise in local newspapers or jobcentres. Some employment agencies specialise in particular areas of the travel and tourism industry, such as catering and accommodation. Employment agencies in your locality will be listed in the Yellow Pages.

Professional associations

If you are a member of a professional body such as the Tourism Society or the Institute of Leisure and Amenity Management (ILAM) you will be able to obtain information about careers and job vacancies through their publications..

Talking to people already doing the job

Talking to people already employed in your chosen area can be an effective way of finding out about jobs and career opportunities. You may be able to do this as part of a work placement. Ask them how they got started and what skills and qualifications are required. Many schools and colleges arrange visits to local travel and tourism facilities to find out how they operate and what sort of jobs are available. Careers books provide accounts from people working in the industry that can also provide a useful insight into what a particular job is like. Three examples of such accounts are provided in the case study.

▲ A new way of looking for work

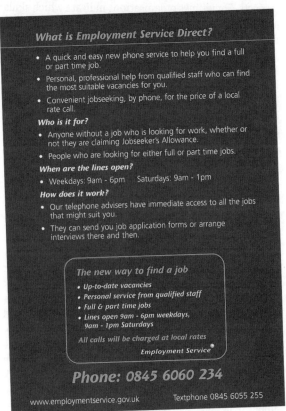

CASE STUDY

Career accounts

The cabin crew member

Susan, aged 24, is a cabin crew member with a large charter airline.

'People sometimes think that cabin crew are just waitresses in the sky, but nothing could be further from the truth. A huge amount of my job is about safety – making sure that all our passengers have a safe and enjoyable journey. We have intensive training on all aspects of safe air travel.

'Anyone interested in this job should understand how hard the work can be. You can be on continuous duty for 12 hours or more, with no chance to take a break. It is not a nine-to-five job, and you need to be very dedicated. I could be at home for several days at a time, but I may be on call to go anywhere in the world at a few hours notice. You have to like people to get on in this job, and I love meeting interesting passengers.'

The travel sales consultant

Marie, 21, is an experienced travel sales consultant in a well-known high street travel agency.

'I applied to the company because a friend worked for them and said they were a great company. I joined them four years ago – it's a tiny shop, but actually one of the most hectic branches in the country. I came in as a trainee travel advisor and the promotion opportunities have been very good so far.

'I love the variety of my job and everyone in the shop gets on brilliantly. No two days are ever the same, as we have to help each customer to find their ideal holiday. You have a computer to provide a lot of the information, but you need a knowledge of which destination will be right for each person. That's why I always ask customers to come back in and tell me about their holidays afterwards – so I'll know whether they had a good time.'

The holiday services executive (resort representative)

Simon, aged 23, has recently completed three years as a holiday services executive in Mallorca.

'I spent a lot of time in Spain when I was a teenager, and working there as a holiday services executive seemed like a natural idea, and also a chance to use my Spanish in a job. I'd met a lot of holiday services executives previously and they seemed like a really good crowd. When you actually do the job, you understand that it's certainly not just one big holiday! We operate in teams at each holiday resort and the work is fun, but hard – you need to be committed to it, flexible enough to deal with anything, and confident enough to stand up and give friendly welcome talks to dozens of complete strangers.

'My duties include administration, running welcome briefings and making sure that all customers I meet are having an enjoyable holiday. In the evenings, we might be leading excursions to local attractions. We also have to be ready to meet aircraft and see customers off on their trip home, which could happen at any time, day or night.

'It's seasonal work, of course – a lot of holiday services executives work until the end of October and then go back to the UK, or transfer to a winter resort. You very often see the same familiar faces come back year after year.'

ACTIVITY

Finding out about jobs

Interview someone who is currently working in the travel and tourism industry about his or her job. Try to obtain information about:

- how he or she got started and how long he or she has worked in the industry

- what qualifications are required to do the job

- what skills and qualities are required to do the job

- working conditions

- what he or she likes (or dislikes) about the job.

Writing to employers

Many of the larger employers in the leisure and tourism industries provide information about job opportunities, the skills and qualifications required, and how to apply. First Choice, McDonald's, Thorpe Park and Jarvis Hotels are four examples of companies that provide careers advice to people wishing to work in the industries.

▲ Example of career information provided by employers

Using the internet

There are now several excellent sites on the internet that provide information about career opportunities and job vacancies within the industry. Two of the most popular are: **www.careercompass.co.uk** and **www.leisureopportunities.co.uk**. Some employers also have recruitment sections on their web sites such as Thorpe Park (**www.thorpepark.co.uk**).

Travel Tourism Jobs

▲ Look for jobs on the internet

Identifying a suitable job

Your starting point is to decide what your personal aims and interests are and then identify jobs and career paths which suit these aims and interests. This will involve doing some research to find out about jobs, qualifications, prospects and employers. When identifying suitable job roles you should consider the following questions.

- Am I being realistic?

- What are my circumstances?

- What are my interests?

- What qualifications, skills and experience are required?

- What opportunities are available?

  Let's look at each in turn.

Am I being realistic?

Most employers expect prospective employees to be ambitious but you must also be realistic about the level at which you will enter the industry. As we have seen, most people enter at the operative level. It is best to discuss your plans with a careers adviser.

What are my circumstances?

You must take into account your personal circumstances when you are considering jobs. How far are you prepared to travel to find employment? Is your age an important factor? Some employers specify that you must be willing to work anywhere in the country, and some jobs have minimum age requirements (for example, bar staff must be 18 or over and most airlines and tour operators also require cabin crew or resort representatives to be at least 18).

If you are a 16 or 17-year-old school leaver, the range of full-time job opportunities in the industry will be limited, unless you are taking a training scheme which is sponsored by an employer. One such scheme is the ABTA Travel Training Company training programme, which recruits over a thousand young people every year and trains them for work in various occupations in the travel industry (see Figure 1.39).

▲ Travel Training Company leaflet

Figure 1.39: The Travel Training Programme

Aged between 16–18 years?

Take your first successful steps to a career in the travel industry.

Each year, the Travel Training Company arranges travel training courses throughout Britain, at over 60 regional training centres. All of the courses provide the opportunity to achieve National Vocational Qualifications at level 2 and 3.

The Travel Training Programme is regarded nationwide as a well run, quality scheme and should not be confused with other non-ABTA training programmes. A large number of travel companies have decided that the only method of entry for young people into their organisation will be through the programme. It is an equal opportunity scheme which does not discriminate on the grounds of race, religion, sex or disability.

We offer training in three different areas of the travel industry each leading to a National Vocational Qualification or Scottish Vocational Qualification.

- Business travel

    This part of the industry looks after the business person. Mainly working behind the scenes and using the telephone to arrange flights, car hire and hotel reservations.

- Tour operations

    Opportunities exist in the field of tour operations. However, there are only one-tenth the number of tour operators as travel agents, and therefore the number of openings is correspondingly lower. At present we are running courses in central London and Manchester.

- Retail travel

    This is by far the most popular programme which we operate and this area of the travel industry has the most openings for young people. All trainees work towards the NVQ/SVQ in Travel Services Levels 2 and 3. This includes Air Fares and Ticketing, Travel Geography, Package Holidays and Car Ferry Costings, and Ongoing Assessment of your Performance in the Workplace.

Source: The Travel Training Company

What are my interests?

Consider your current interests when looking for suitable jobs and evaluate your leisure pastimes and activities. For example, if you are interested in travel you may consider working as a holiday resort representative or a sales consultant in a travel agency.

What qualifications, skills and experience are required?

It is important to obtain advice on the qualifications, skills and experience required for your chosen job. A useful starting point is to list the relevant qualifications, skills and experience you have already, identify what others you are in the process of obtaining, and, finally, list any others you think you will need to obtain in the future. This may involve undertaking more training and work experience before you are ready to seek employment. You must also consider the type of person required by prospective employers and ask yourself the question, 'Do I have the personal qualities they are looking for?'

What opportunities are available?

You must also consider what opportunities are available for gaining employment. If you live in a popular tourist area you may be readily able to identify a number of opportunities in the travel and tourism industry within your locality. On the other hand, you may need to look outside your locality for suitable employment opportunities. Make sure you keep up to date with current developments by looking in newspapers, magazines and journals, as they can be a useful source of information on employers and potential job opportunities.

ACTIVITY

Thinking about jobs

Select at least one job from within the travel and tourism industry which you think is suitable for you, based on your personal aims, interests and abilities. In small groups, discuss why you have selected the particular job. You will find this exercise useful when undertaking the end of section activity on p. 85.

Training and qualifications

In the past, the travel and tourism industries have had a relaxed attitude towards qualifications. In many cases, the ability to do the job efficiently and possessing the right mix of personal qualities has been considered more important than an academic or vocational qualification. However, because of increased competition for jobs, and the need for higher standards in areas such as health and safety and customer service, many employers now value qualifications and training.

Skills and experience

Skills and experience are not the same thing but they are often grouped together. Your skills are the particular abilities you have to do things well. In most cases, you will acquire your skills through education and training, but you can also develop skills through experience and through learning from others at work.

Some of the skills you need to succeed in the travel and tourism industry are specific to the industry, (for example, the skill of successfully planning a package holiday), but many others are not and can be transferred from your other experience, not necessarily related to work. For example, the ability to supervise a group of people can be developed in many different contexts, including at school or college. Encouraging people to work together as a team in seeking to achieve a shared goal is something you may have done in a sporting context, or even in organising a party. You may have experience of organising a holiday for a group of friends or, more simply, of getting a group of people from one place to another. All this experience will have helped you develop skills which you will be able to use in your work.

Most employers will expect you to work hard, show commitment and work effectively in teams. They will also expect you to have a number of personal qualities which enhance your ability to deal with customers in a variety of situations. As many jobs in the travel and tourism industry involve working unsociable hours, including shift work, you will often have to work evenings and weekends.

Specific vocational knowledge and skill requirements obviously vary from job to job. However, as a general rule, staff working in the leisure and tourism industries need to be:

- cheerful and enthusiastic, focusing on solutions rather than problems

- polite and patient

- well organised and able to take responsibility

- able to work in teams

- good listeners and clear, fluent talkers

- smart in appearance

- numerate and literate.

Some of these personal qualities and skills can be developed through training and experience but others are closely related to the personality of the individual concerned. For example, someone who is extremely shy is unlikely to make a successful tour guide. What is important is to know one's strengths and weaknesses and to choose a job which is in harmony with them.

Part-time work

We have identified a range of qualifications and training opportunities which will help you gain employment in the leisure and tourism industry. You may be also be able to acquire useful skills and experience from part-time or voluntary work.

Due to the seasonal nature of the industry, there are many opportunities for temporary and part-time employment. If there is no way of finding part-time or temporary paid work you may be able to find voluntary work in order to learn about the job and make useful contacts. It is well worth doing voluntary work, even

though it is unpaid: you will gain experience and demonstrate commitment to the industry.

If you already have a job in the travel and tourism industry your employer may provide you with on-the-job training. For example, staff who have face-to-face contact with customers may receive training to develop their skills in a variety of situations. Some employers also encourage their employees to undertake qualifications and training programmes at local colleges and training providers through day or block release.

Whatever your chosen career path and personal circumstances, the acquisition of qualifications, skills and experience is of vital importance. Remember to seek advice before committing yourself to a particular training course or job; careful career planning at this stage could enable you to establish a successful career in your chosen field.

BUILD YOUR LEARNING

Keywords and phrases

You should know the meaning of the words and phrases listed below. If you are unsure about any of them, go back through the last 12 pages to refresh your understanding.

- Academic qualifications
- Competence
- Job description
- Person specification
- Personal achievements
- Personal attributes
- Personal qualities
- Vocational qualifications

End of section activity

1 Summarise the range of employment opportunities available within the travel and tourism industry. You should cover the most common employment opportunities for each industry component.

2 Find out about the types of job offered by one of the following travel and tourism organisations:

- travel agent
- tour operator
- airline
- hotel
- tourist attraction.

You may find it useful to visit or write to the organisation to obtain information about the range of jobs. For larger organisations, it may be possible to obtain information from the internet.

3 Select one job from the travel and tourism industry that best matches your own aspirations, skills and abilities. Gather information about the job, such as a job description and person specification, so that you can describe why the job is suitable for you. If possible, interview someone who has personal knowledge of the job and what it involves.

Presenting information to employers

COMPETITION FOR MANY JOBS in the leisure and tourism industries is intense. Many people may apply for a particular job, but few will get interviewed and, usually, only one person actually gets the job. It is important, therefore, for you to understand how to present personal information to prospective employers in order to increase your chances of being considered. We are going to give you some useful tips on applying for jobs, producing a curriculum vitae (CV) and preparing for interview.

Applying for jobs

When you hear of a job, or see one advertised in a newspaper, you usually have to write or telephone for further details. Remember, writing this letter or making the telephone call is the first chance you have of impressing the employer, so it is important to get it right. Always apply for a job as soon as you hear about it; it shows that you are genuinely interested and are actively looking for work.

When you have received more information, the next stage is to write a letter of application, complete the employer's printed application form, or send a copy of your curriculum vitae. It is important to do this well. The quality of your letter or form, both in terms of what it contains and how it is presented, often determines whether you get an interview. Always take steps to ensure that your application is with the employer before the closing date, as most will not consider late entries.

Letters of application

A **letter of application** should give all the relevant information in a logical sequence and without rambling. There are four stages in writing the letter.

1 State what job is being applied for, and where it was advertised.

2 Give brief details about your qualifications and experience.

3 Explain why the job is suitable for you.

4 Show enthusiasm.

The content of the letter is very important, but of equal importance is the way in which it is presented. The presentation creates the first impression that the organisation has of you as an applicant. A positive first impression can be achieved by following these guidelines:

- Make sure you set the letter out in the correct format (see p. 87), with your address, the date and the full address of the employer. Write to a named person if you have been given this information.

- Always write neatly and clearly and make a practice copy first. Better still, type your letter.

- Use plain, unlined white or cream paper and blue or black ink. Envelopes should match the paper. If you find it difficult to write straight on unlined paper, use bold lines under the paper to guide you.

- Always use a first class stamp on the envelope.

- Check spelling, or get someone else to check it if you are not certain.

- Letters to 'Dear Sir' or 'Dear Madam' end 'Yours faithfully'; letters to a named person ('Dear Mr Johnson') end 'Yours sincerely'.

- Make your signature clear and print your name underneath.

- Always say what job you are writing about, using a reference code if one is given in the job advert, and where you saw the advert. This is particularly important if a firm has several vacancies at the same time.

- Keep a copy of your letter, so that you can refer to it if you get an interview.

- If you include the names of people who will give you a reference, make sure you ask their permission first.

- Write the right letter. If you are responding to a job advert, follow the instructions. For example, do not include personal details if the advert asks you to write for further details or write for an application form. However, if you are asked to apply in writing you should give details about yourself and state clearly why you are applying for the job.

Even if no suitable vacancy is being advertised, it is still worth writing to a company to enquire if there will be any job opportunities in the near future. With this type of letter, too, you need to include details about yourself (or provide a CV) and identify areas of work you are interested in.

29 Westfield Road
Anytown
AL6 7DD

Mrs J Arkwright
Personnel Manager
Anytown District Council
Central Chambers
17 High Street
Anytown
AD1 3PQ

24 September 1999

Dear Mrs Arkwright

Trainee leisure assistant (Ref la1)

I would like to apply for the post of trainee leisure assistant as advertised in the Anytown Evening News on 17 September 1999.

I am 17 and left Anytown College this June after completing a General National Vocational Qualification (GNVQ) [6] in Leisure and Tourism at intermediate level, gaining an overall grade of Merit. During the one-year full-time course, I studied a range of leisure and tourism-related subjects, including customer service, marketing, organising events and tourist destinations, as well as developing skills in information technology, communication and numeracy.

I would really like to work at Faraway Travel because it is a well-established local agency. I am also keen to gain further vocational qualifications and would welcome the opportunity to work towards NVQs in Travel Services during the two-year training programme.

Since leaving college, I have worked at Shades restaurant as a part-time waitress at weekends and in the evenings. During my GNVQ course, I completed a three-week work placement at Elstree Travel Agency in Bambry. I thoroughly enjoyed this experience and found it very useful to observe experienced sales consultants and to assist in the processing of bookings, using the computer view data system.

I am a friendly, outgoing person who enjoys meeting people. My personal interests include travel, eating out and keep-fit. I am a member of Emperors Health and Fitness Centre and regularly attend Step classes. If you wish to obtain references, please contact:

Mr R Deacon
GNVQ Co-ordinator
Anytown College
Anytown
AD8 6DL

Mrs J Rose
Manager
Shades Restaurant
High Street
Anytown
AL5 7PQ

I am available to come for interview at any time.

Yours sincerely,

Jane Cook

Key	
1	Do not forget your address and the date.
2	Make sure you reply to the named person (if given) and correct address.
3	Say what job you are applying for.
4	Say where you saw the advert.
5	Give your age.
6	List your qualifications (you may also wish to include your GCSEs).
7	Say why you want the job.
8	Give details about any relevant skills and experience you have. Remember to include details of previous jobs or work placements.
9	Give brief details, including information about your main interests.
10	Give two references, remembering to ask their permission first.
11	Make sure you finish the letter in the correct manner ('yours sincerely' in this example), and print your name clearly below the signature.
12	The envelope should be the same colour as the paper (preferably white or cream) and a first class stamp should be affixed.

Figure 1.40: Job advertisement

Holiday services executive

You'll do everything you can to ensure our customers enjoy the most successful holiday ever! It's hard work, but very rewarding – so if you're the sort of person who enjoys helping people, are aged 21 or over (as at 1 April 1999) and have had some experience in a customer focused role, we want to hear from you. Apply in writing to Susan Bindley, Sunseekers, 7 High Street, Anytown AL1 3PH.

ACTIVITY

Writing a letter of application

Imagine that you want to apply for the job shown in Figure 1.40. Assume that you meet the minimum age criteria for your chosen job and that you have been asked to apply in writing. Write an appropriate letter of application.

Application forms

Many organisations send out **application forms**. This ensures that the organisation receives all the necessary information in a format that is easy to evaluate. This is important for jobs that require a lot of information, for example as a member of an airline cabin crew.

Not all application forms need be as detailed but most will include spaces to list:

- personal details
- qualifications
- employment history
- hobbies and interests
- referees (people who are willing to make a statement about the applicant's character, particularly in regard to the applicant's employment potential).

Here are some useful tips to help you fill in job application forms.

- Photocopy the form and complete the copy before filling in the original.
- Read through the whole form before you start to fill it in. Make sure you put all the information in the correct places and try to answer all the questions.
- Always use dark ink, preferably black on the final copy, as the firm may need to photocopy the form.
- Write clearly and neatly and check your spelling.
- Keep a copy of the form so that you can refer to it if you get an interview.
- Obtain permission from the people you are nominating as referees.
- Write a brief covering letter, like the one below, to send with the completed form. If the application form does not ask you to give reasons why you are applying for the job, or to outline why you feel you are suitable, then it is a good idea to make the covering letter longer to include these points.

29 Westbourne Road
Anytown
Someshire
AD1 3PO

24 September 1999

Mrs J Arkwright
Personnel Manager
Anytown District Council
Central Chambers
17 High Street
Anytown AD1 3PQ

Dear Mrs Arkwright,

Please find enclosed my completed application form for the post of trainee leisure assistant, reference LA1.

Yours sincerely,

Jonathon West

Jonathon West

Enc

ACTIVITY

Application forms

Copy and complete the application form opposite.

Strictly confidential

Application for Employment

Position for which you are applying _____

Where did you learn of the vacancy? _____

Personal details

Surname _____ Mr/Mrs/Miss/Ms
                              (delete as applicable)

First name(s) _____

Address _____

_____

_____

Telephone _____

Date of birth _____

Age _____

Nationality _____

Marital status _____

Full and part-time education (Please continue on a separate sheet if necessary)

School, College, University	From	To	Qualifications obtained
_____	____	____	_____
_____	____	____	_____
_____	____	____	_____
_____	____	____	_____
_____	____	____	_____
_____	____	____	_____
_____	____	____	_____

Present and previous employment (Please continue on a separate sheet if necessary)

Name and address of employer	From	To	Job title, duties and responsibilities
_____	____	____	_____
_____	____	____	_____
_____	____	____	_____
_____	____	____	_____
_____	____	____	_____
_____	____	____	_____
_____	____	____	_____

Curriculum vitae

Sometimes employers ask you to send a copy of your **curriculum vitae** (CV) in support of your application, although this is usually requested in the case of jobs for older people rather than school leavers. Nonetheless, it is important to understand what information to include in a CV and how best to present it.

Curriculum vitae is Latin and translates as an outline of your qualifications and career to date. As with a letter of application, a CV can be evaluated in terms of content and presentation. A CV generally includes:

- name
- date of birth
- address
- telephone number
- education to date
- vocational qualifications
- academic qualifications
- employment record
- skills
- other achievements (for example, hobbies or interests)
- referees.

A CV should be typed or wordprocessed on a single side of A4 paper. Experienced applicants may require more than one sheet of paper to present previous job experiences. There are no strict rules about the layout but it should be neat, logical and pleasing to the eye. Above all, it should be easy for the employer to find information quickly. This is usually achieved by using bold headings.

There are several acceptable layouts for producing a CV. Whichever you choose, here are some general points to guide you.

- A CV should usually be presented on one or two sheets of A4 paper and is preferably typed.

- Continually update your CV to take into account changes in your circumstances such as a change of address or a newly-gained qualification.

- Enhance the presentation by using clear, bold headings which are neatly arranged.

- Obtain several good quality copies of your CV so that you can use it in approaching other employers.

- Always write a covering letter with a CV explaining your reasons for applying for the particular job and outlining why you think you are suitable.

- If possible, produce your CV on a computer wordprocessing package so you can easily amend details. Using a computer should also enhance the quality of presentation, particularly if you can use a good quality laser printer.

- Always check spelling and grammar.

Figure 1.41: How to organise a curriculum vitae

Personal details	Age, address and telephone number.
Academic and vocational qualifications	Details of schools and colleges attended, dates, subjects studied and grades obtained plus details of qualifications you are currently pursuing.
Employment/work experience	Details of previous employment, including part-time, full-time and voluntary work. Give brief details of your duties and responsibilities and any specialist skills used.
Achievements and other qualifications	For example, driving licence, first aid certificate, lifesaving awards.
Personal interests	Leisure activities, pastimes, membership of clubs or societies. Highlight activities that show initiative and responsibilities.
References	The names of two referees with addresses, identifying in what capacity they know you, for example youth leader, manager during work experience placement.

Figure 1.42: A typical CV

Name:	Sarah Mills
Address:	17 West Park Avenue, Bisham, Woldshire WD1 7PQ
Date of Birth:	May 20 1981

Education

Bisham College of Further Education 1997–2000
GNVQ Advanced Level (2000) Leisure and Tourism Distinction
GNVQ Intermediate Level (1998) Leisure and Tourism Merit

Bisham Comprehensive School 1992–1997
GCSEs (1997)

English Language	B
Geography	C
History	D
French	D
Mathematics	D
Biology	E

Employment

1995–present Banton's newsagents, part-time sales assistant, Saturdays and Sundays. Duties include handling sales and using electronic cash register

1999 Member of the team that ran the college fashion show. The show was very successful and raised £250 for charity. My role was to coordinate the fundraising activities and ensure the project met its financial targets.

1998 College work placement (four weeks) at Rudston Mining Museum. I was involved in taking bookings and escorting groups on guided tours. During the placement I completed a project about the museum's marketing mix and made recommendations on how to increase visitor numbers.

1996 Trident project: completed three weeks of full-time work experience at Freedom Travel Agency. Duties included assisting with customer enquiries and bookings.

Interests

Wide variety of sports, including tennis, swimming and keep-fit. I have represented Woldshire County Tennis Association at under-15 and under-19 levels and am currently the Bisham under-19 district champion. I am also interested in tennis coaching and have gained the Lawn Tennis Association (LTA) Leader's Coaching Award. Outside of sport, my main interests include travel and pop music.

Other qualifications/awards

Clean driving licence; St John's Ambulance First Aid Certificate; LTA Leader's Coaching Award; Community Sports Leader's Award.

Referees

Mrs S Jameson	Mr J Tate
Head of Leisure and Tourism	Head Coach
Bisham College of Further Education	Woldshire Tennis Centre
Bisham	17 Parkland Centre
WI0 7LD	Rudston

Figure 1.42 provides an example of a layout, presentation style and range of content which would be suitable for sending to prospective employers. Before you send out your CV, make sure someone checks it for you. Teachers and careers advisers will usually give you advice and help.

Interview skills

When you are invited for an **interview**, there are some useful things that you should remember.

Before the interview

- Think positively, you have already done well to get this far!

- Think carefully about why you want the job, and why you believe you are the best person to do it.

- Be prepared for anything. Interviews can vary tremendously, from a very formal interview with several interviewers combined with a written test, to a more casual approach.

- Organise yourself. Make sure you know where the company is, where the interview is to be held, and how you are going to get there.

- Learn as much about the company as you can and, if possible, find out more about the type of work for which you are applying.

- Dress smartly. All employers will appreciate your effort to look good.

During the interview

- Put forward a positive image, smile and look interested.

- Avoid simple yes and no answers, they stop conversation. When you answer each question give as much relevant information as you can.

- Tell the truth. Untruths often come to light either during or after the interview.

- When you have a chance to ask questions, ask one that shows enthusiasm for the job. Your last question might be about clarifying pay and conditions.

ACTIVITY

Interviews

In groups, role play the following interview questions. The interviewees should consider exactly what is being asked and give an answer that satisfies the question.

'Why do you want to work in the leisure and tourism industry?'

'How do you feel that you have benefited from doing an Advanced GNVQ in Leisure and Tourism?'

'What job would you like to be doing in five years time?'

'Which aspect of your education and/or previous work experience has been of most benefit to you?'

'What would you say are your main strengths?'

'What do you consider to be your main weaknesses?'

'How do you feel that you could overcome your main weaknesses?'

'If you could choose anything, what would your ideal job be, and why would you choose it?'

'What do you think constitutes a good work team?'

'What role do you usually play when working in a team?'

BUILD YOUR LEARNING

End of section activity

Use the guidelines provided to put together your own CV in a format suitable for sending to a prospective employer. Your CV should highlight the skills and abilities that are important for the type of travel and tourism job that you selected in the previous end of section activity on p. 85. The assessment requirment for this unit is on pp. 452–3.

Keywords and phrases

You should know the meaning of the words and phrases listed below. If you are unsure about any of them, go back through the last seven pages to refresh your understanding.

- Application forms
- Curriculum vitae
- Interview skills
- Letter of application

Tourism development is the planned and on-going development of destinations, facilities and services to meet the needs of current and future tourists. It can involve many different aspects of tourism growth, from the improvement of existing facilities to the development of entirely new products and services.

When effectively planned and managed, tourism development can result in huge improvements and benefits both for visiting tourists and for the local population. However, the reverse is also true; lack of planning and effective management can mean that development has a negative impact. You need to understand how the process of tourism development operates and the factors that determine its level of success and effectiveness. We look at those involved in tourism development, the agents and the objectives that they set when undertaking tourism development initiatives. We also explore the ways in which responsible tourism developers can manage the process to maximise positive and minimise negative impact. This unit is assessed by an externally set case study or test.

Tourism development

Contents

The agents of tourism development

THE **AGENTS** INVOLVED IN **tourism development** are the range of organisations, bodies and individuals which influence or contribute towards the development of tourism products and services. These agents can include:

- development agencies
- landowners
- development companies
- consultancies
- leisure organisations
- entertainment organisations
- local authorities
- national governments
- national and regional tourist boards
- voluntary and community groups
- pressure groups.

It is important to understand that there is a wide range of different agents which contribute to the success of most tourism development projects. For example, the development of Sheffield's National Centre for Popular Music involved a range of agents including Sheffield City Council, English Partnerships, the European Regional Development Fund, the Arts Council of England and the National Lottery Fund, as well as support from a number of private companies.

The various agents involved in tourism development can be split into three distinct categories:

- private sector enterprises
- public sector organisations
- voluntary sector bodies.

Let's look at each in turn.

Private sector enterprises

Private sector enterprises are organisations that operate primarily to make a profit. Traditionally, the development of tourism has been dominated by the private sector, which has meant that many past decisions on development have been based on profit-making objectives. For example, the growth and development of the accommodation and hospitality sector has been almost exclusively carried out by private hotel, restaurant and retail licensing companies. Similarly, the development of the foreign

---

Figure 2.1: Agents supporting Sheffield's National Centre for Popular Music

The National Centre for Popular Music has been made possible by the generous support of the following:

APPLE	PHILIPS PROJECTS
CUAN AV	PIONEER
EMAGIC	SOUND CONTROL
EMAP METRO	THE ROYAL BANK OF SCOTLAND
EMAP RADIO	THE PERFORMING RIGHT SOCIETY
GUINNESS PUBLISHING	TRIMAC TECHNOLOGY
HMV	VAUX BREWERIES
MTV NETWORKS EUROPE	VIRGIN COLA
	WESTFIELD CONTRIBUTORY HEALTH SCHEME

The National Centre for Popular Music is a registered charity (no.104 8577).VAT registration number 599 9435 54. Company registration no.2512 807 We reserve the right to vary opening hours and admission prices without prior notice. Details correct at time of going to press.

package holiday market has grown predominantly from the activities of private tour operators.

Development agencies

Development agencies, companies and consultancies are private organisations that initiate, advise or coordinate the development of tourism projects. They usually rely on the cooperation and contribution of other tourism agents to ensure the success of the project. For example, the development of a multi-facility attraction such as an out-of-town shopping mall, where a wide range of tourist attractions, facilities and services are offered, may be coordinated by a development agency which brings together a number of tourism organisations such as catering, retailing, transport and visitor attractions, to provide the facilities and services within the development.

Landowners

Since most aspects of tourism development require development land, **landowners** are often key agents. In many situations landowners are keen to benefit from the large profits that can frequently be made by selling land to developers. However, there are a number of laws and planning regulations that restrict the use of land for tourism development.

CASE STUDY

Urban Space Management

Urban Space Management (USM) is a privately owned development company and consultancy that specialises in the renewal of run-down or under-utilised space for retail and community uses, in imaginative and cost-effective ways. Their many projects tend to focus on urban regeneration initiatives where derelict areas of cities and large towns are converted to tourist attractions and facilities. They work closely with a number of other agents such as central and local government, as well as private sector developers. Some of USM's initiatives in London have included:

- Camden Lock, an area of derelict Victorian warehouses which has been developed into a lively craft area with restaurants and entertainment

- Spitalfields Market, a former fruit and vegetable market that has been redeveloped into a new market whilst retaining many original features

- Gabriel's Wharf, on the south bank of the Thames, which has been developed into a craft workshop area with catering outlets

- Merton Abbey Mills, a derelict fabric printing factory in Wimbledon, converted into a multi-facility leisure attraction with a market, restaurants and entertainment venues

- Elephant and Castle, a dilapidated shopping centre that was developed into a modern shopping complex.

Source: abridged from BTA's *Insights* magazine, November 1998

Factors that are considered include the effect that development may have on the surrounding area and the number of similar developments in the area. For example, in the 1990s there was a rapid increase in the number of farmers wanting to convert large areas of farmland into golf courses. Many such applications were turned down because of similar developments within the particular region and the problems that would arise if too much farmland were lost to tourism development.

Leisure and entertainment organisations

Private leisure and entertainment organisations play a key role in the development of tourism products and services. They can include:

- hospitality and catering organisations
- theatres and cinemas
- tourist attraction providers
- tour operators
- shops
- transport providers.

ACTIVITY

Private sector enterprises

Find out about any tourism development initiatives in your area and identify the private sector organisations that are involved. For example, there may be plans for a new hotel, cinema or tourist attraction. You may find local newspapers a good source of information.

Public sector organisations

The large-scale involvement of public sector organisations in the development of tourism has been relatively recent. As we saw in Unit 1, the Development of Tourism Act established the British Tourist Authority and the English, Welsh and Scottish tourist boards in 1969. Since then, both central government and local authorities have played an increasingly important role in tourism development and many other public sector organisations have been established.

Central government

Central government supports many areas of tourism development through the provision of grants for specific projects. For example, in 1999, a major package of grants was announced for the regeneration of British coastal areas. More than £10 million was allocated from the single regeneration budget to support a number of projects and initiatives in seaside areas, with over 20 resorts, such as Torbay and Great Yarmouth, benefiting.

Overseas governments also play a crucial role in the development of tourism and of course, the agents involved in tourism development differ from country to country. Overseas governments as well as our own are continually looking for ways to ensure their policies maximise the benefits that tourism brings. In some situations this may involve sacrificing some areas of development in order to benefit other areas, as the webstract below shows.

WEBSTRACT

The Gambia

Gambia government bans all-inclusives

The Gambian government has banned all-inclusive holidays from November after a poll found that 99 per cent of Gambians dependent on the tourism industry were opposed to them.

Adama Bah, who runs Gambia Tourism Concern, is delighted with the decision. 'All-inclusives are not the best way for The Gambia to benefit from tourism,' says Adama. 'They keep the profits out of the local economy and keep the tourists cooped up in the hotel instead of getting out, which many tourists don't like. Everybody, tourists and tourism industry, seem to realise that tourism would be better if it had more connection to the local economy and to local people.'

Tourism Concern will be working with British tour operators currently operating in The Gambia to follow the phase-out of all-inclusives and work on an alternative package which has more trickle-down to the Gambian economy.

Source: www.tourismconcern.org.uk

WEBSTRACT

Tomorrow's Tourism

In February 1999, the government launched its Tomorrow's Tourism strategy, focusing on the development of tourism within the UK. The strategy has six main aims:

- the development of a coherent strategy for tourism in London
- regeneration of England's resorts
- improving the quality of tourism accommodation
- developing business tourism
- improving the quality and range of tourist attractions
- developing products which promote our culture, heritage and countryside.

Responsibility for ensuring that these objectives are met is shared between a number of agents.

London. Government will ensure that tourism funds provided to the Greater London Authority (GLA) are used to promote London as an overseas destination, having regard to London's role as a gateway to Britain and to contribute to the delivery of national tourism programmes.

Resorts. The Department of Culture, Media and Sport (DCMS) will encourage the regeneration of seaside resorts by providing resort action plans and encouraging the Department of the Environment, Transport and the Regions (DETR) and the Department of Trade and Industry (DTI) to provide assistance through the single regeneration budget and other schemes and to recognise the case for European funding for resorts

Accommodation. Government will review the effectiveness of the national accommodation schemes in raising the quality of accommodation and consider the implications of introducing a statutory scheme.

Business tourism. Government has set up the Business Tourism Partnership and has tasked the British Tourist Authority (BTA) with focusing its marketing activity on sectors that can most easily be influenced and with enhancing the quality and frequency of its contact with the business tourism industry.

Developing products which promote our culture, heritage and countryside. The Department of Culture, Media and Sport will address this as part of its broader remit in relation to the arts, lottery funding, sport and film. The Countryside Agency and the Ministry of Agriculture, Fisheries and Food (MAFF) will also contribute to this objective as part of their responsibilities.

Source: www.etb.org.uk

ACTIVITY

Tomorrow's Tourism

Select two of the agents mentioned in the webstract (other than the DCMS) such as the Ministry of Agriculture, Fisheries and Food (MAFF), the Department of Trade and Industry (DTI), the Department of the Environment, Transport and the Regions (DETR), the Greater London Authority (GLA), the British Tourist Authority (BTA), the Countryside Agency or the British Tourism Partnership.

Investigate the specific contribution that the chosen agents make to tourism development. You could choose a specific area to consider, such as their contribution to and involvement in the regeneration of rundown areas. You may find the internet a good source of information.

The Department of Culture, Media and Sport

The central UK government department that has responsibility for government policy on tourism development and related leisure provision is the **Department for Culture, Media and Sport** (DCMS). Its areas of interest include the arts, sport and recreation, the National Lottery, libraries, museums and galleries, the built heritage and tourism. Many of its activities are carried out through non-departmental public bodies, which are funded by the DCMS. These include:

- Arts Council of England (**www.artscouncil.org.uk**)
- The British Library (**portico. Bl.uk**)
- The British Museum (**www.british-museum.ac.uk**)
- British Tourist Authority (**www.visitbritain.com**)
- Crafts Council (**www.craftscouncil.org.uk**)
- English Heritage (**www.open.gov.uk/heritage/ehehome**)
- English Tourist Board (**www.visitbritain.com**)
- Millennium Commission (**www.millennium.gov.uk**)
- National Lottery Charities Board (**www.nlcb.org.uk**)
- Royal Commission on Historical Manuscripts (**www.hmc.gov.uk**)
- Royal Commission on the Historical Monuments of England (**www.rchme.gov.uk**)
- Sport England (**www.English.Sports.gov.uk**).

The Department for Culture, Media and Sport is responsible for tourism policy, sponsoring the tourism industry in England and ensuring that tourism is promoted in Great Britain as a whole. The Scottish and Welsh Offices, and the Department for Economic Development (Northern Ireland) are responsible for tourism policy for Scotland, Wales and Northern Ireland respectively. The DCMS has many other areas of responsibility including heritage, museums and the arts which also make a considerable contribution to the development of tourism products and destinations.

ACTIVITY

The DCMS

The DCMS allocates an annual grant to a wide range of non-departmental public bodies. Try to find out how much was allocated to the various bodies last year. You may find tourism journals, the internet or your local authority good sources of information. Why do you think that some bodies receive higher grants than others?

Local authorities

In 1972, the Local Government Act gave local authorities the power to develop tourist facilities and services and to promote their areas as tourist destinations. Many local authorities now have tourism departments which take responsibility for development and work closely with local groups and private sector organisations.

Regional development agencies

Central government is committed to increasing the involvement of the local community in tourism development. The **regional development agencies** (RDAs) were launched in 1999 to provide effective economic regeneration and development within the regions. They have four statutory responsibilities:

- economic development and regeneration
- business support, investment and competitiveness
- skills training and employment
- sustainable development.

Membership of the board of each RDA is made up of four members from local government and nine members from trade unions and business. The government hopes that the RDAs will help to bring decision-making on planning and development closer to local people.

ACTIVITY

Industrial cities

Read the case study about Bradford opposite. Then, as a group, research how other industrialised UK cities have developed into tourist destinations and identify the products and services that have been developed to meet the needs of the tourist market. Examples might include Glasgow, Sheffield, Leeds or Birmingham.

CASE STUDY

Like many industrialised towns and cities, Bradford experienced considerable decline during the economic recession of the 1970s. Many traditional industries closed down and unemployment ran high. The city soon achieved the a grimy and run-down image and outside investors were not keen to invest money in the city. In 1979 Bradford Metropolitan City Council established the first economic development unit (EDU), with the aim of creating employment and improving the city's image to encourage investment. In order to achieve this, the EDU set about developing Bradford as the UK's first industrialised inland tourist destination.

A number of unique selling points were identified which provided the basis for tourism development. Attractions included the area's Victorian industrial heritage and Haworth, the home of the Bronte sisters, close to the Yorkshire Dales. The first two package holidays to be launched, 'In the footsteps of the Brontes' and 'Industrial heritage', attracted extensive media coverage and 2,000 packages were sold.

In the years that followed, the tourism industry continued to develop and flourish.

- 1983. Bradford won an English Tourist Board award for the fastest growing tourist destination in England. The National Museum of Photography, Film and Television opened following a joint project between Bradford Council and the Science Museum. It is now the most popular provincial museum in the country.

- 1984. With over 30,000 people taking holidays in Bradford, the city launched a new themed package based on the area's mill shops, providing tourists with the opportunity to buy bargain priced fabrics from factory outlet shops – an idea that has since been copied around the country.

- 1987. Following the success of other themed packages, 'Flavours of Asia' was launched, building on the strong Asian roots in the area and the vast number of high quality, authentic Asian restaurants.

Bradford now attracts six million national and international visitors a year and in a recent survey was ranked sixth out of 38 cities in the UK in terms of quality of life.

MAKE YOUR OWN TELEVISION PROGRAMME

AT THE NEW NATIONAL MUSEUM OF PHOTOGRAPHY, FILM & TELEVISION

Bring your family - children go free!*

National and regional tourist boards

There are four national tourist boards, the Welsh Tourist Board, Scottish Tourist Board, Northern Ireland Tourist Board and the English Tourism Council (previously named English Tourist Board), each responsible for creating and implementing a strategy for tourism development.

The **English Tourism Council** (ETC) was launched in 1999 to replace the existing English Tourist Board. Following the government's Tomorrow's Tourism strategy, which provided a wide reaching framework for the development of tourism, the ETC introduced its framework for action, which outlined the ways in which this strategy was to be achieved. Through this framework the ETC upholds three main aims based on quality, competitiveness and wise growth.

The ETC works closely with the 11 regional tourist boards in England on all issues involving tourism development. Ten million pounds of their annual grant from government is allocated to the regional tourist boards for this purpose. Figure 2.2 shows the various bodies and organisations that the English Tourism Council works with in developing tourism.

The role of the regional tourist boards covers a wide range of responsibilities depending on their location and the nature of tourism within their region. For example, the London Tourist Board plays a key role in strategies for the development of accommodation in the capital. Resort regional tourist boards have responsibility for the allocation of resources to help regeneration. They are expected to work closely with local authorities and organisations by providing support for the development of tourism.

CASE STUDY

Yorkshire's farm tourism initiative

The Yorkshire Tourism farm initiative is a comprehensive programme of assistance and activity for new and existing farm tourism businesses. It is a key component of the European programme to help the area diversify and increase its economic base. Over the next three years, more than £4 million of public and private money will be spent in developing the farm tourism sector across the northern uplands. The initiative is intended to improve the quality and professionalism of existing businesses and to provide new developments with relevant expert advice and training.

Accommodation providers are required to join an approved inspection scheme and attractions must sign the visitors' charter. The initiative is managed by the Yorkshire Tourist Board working closely with the Farm Holiday Bureau.

Source: adapted from YTB Tourism Education Pack 2000

ACTIVITY

Local tourism development

In pairs, find out what impact the regional tourist board has on tourism development within your area. You may find information on the internet, in local newspapers or directly from your local authority. See p. 462 for a list of tourist board websites.

▲ The English Tourism Council is responsible for creating and implementing a strategy on tourism development

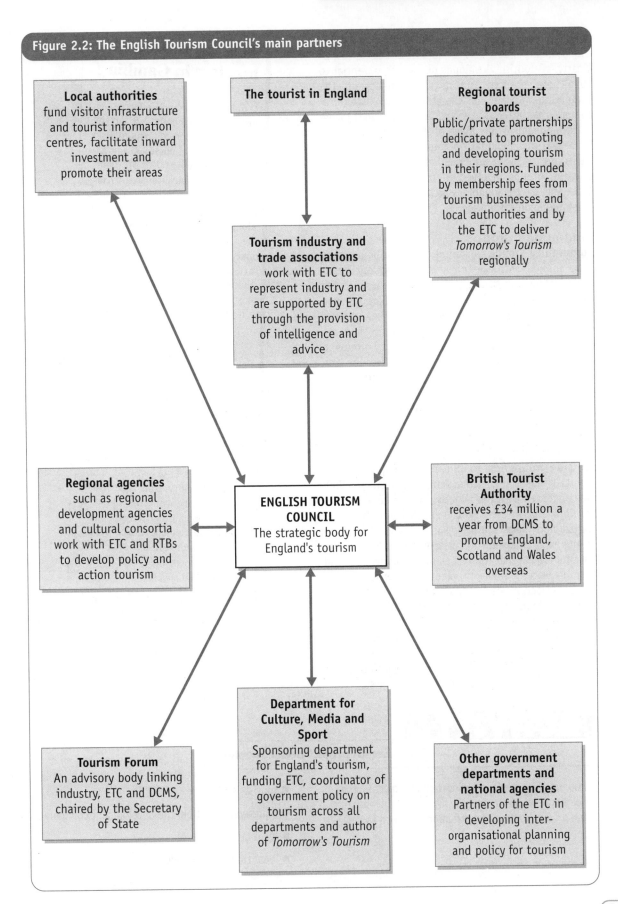

Figure 2.2: The English Tourism Council's main partners

Local authorities
fund visitor infrastructure and tourist information centres, facilitate inward investment and promote their areas

The tourist in England

Regional tourist boards
Public/private partnerships dedicated to promoting and developing tourism in their regions. Funded by membership fees from tourism businesses and local authorities and by the ETC to deliver *Tomorrow's Tourism* regionally

Tourism industry and trade associations
work with ETC to represent industry and are supported by ETC through the provision of intelligence and advice

Regional agencies
such as regional development agencies and cultural consortia work with ETC and RTBs to develop policy and action tourism

ENGLISH TOURISM COUNCIL
The strategic body for England's tourism

British Tourist Authority
receives £34 million a year from DCMS to promote England, Scotland and Wales overseas

Tourism Forum
An advisory body linking industry, ETC and DCMS, chaired by the Secretary of State

Department for Culture, Media and Sport
Sponsoring department for England's tourism, funding ETC, coordinator of government policy on tourism across all departments and author of *Tomorrow's Tourism*

Other government departments and national agencies
Partners of the ETC in developing inter-organisational planning and policy for tourism

Voluntary sector bodies

Clearly, all tourism development has the potential to have both positive and negative effects on the community and it is therefore vital that local communities are consulted and involved in the process of development. While much of this involvement may be based on individual opinions and contributions, there are an increasing number of community and pressure groups involved in tourism development. These include the Rambler's Association, the National Trust and English Heritage.

Community groups

Community groups are voluntary sector bodies that have formed with the objective of influencing or contributing towards specific tourism issues. For example, many areas have tourism forum groups such as the Stratford-upon-Avon's Residents' Week and the Cambridge Residents' Forum. In other areas, there are partnerships between different community groups to address tourism issues, such as the Windsor and Maidenhead Visitor Management Strategy Partnership. Community groups in overseas destinations also work together to raise awareness of tourism development issues, as the article on this page about Gambia shows.

Pressure groups

Pressure groups exist to influence development plans and strategies. Many, such as Tourism Concern and VSO, are concerned with the negative impact that tourism development can have on the environment and area. For example, many seaside resorts have local pressure groups that campaign for measures to minimise the harmful effects that tourism can have on beaches and bathing waters. Similarly, plans for new large-scale tourist attractions can often result in the formation of pressure groups of people concerned at the effects that such a development might have.

One of the problems that often arises in tourism development projects is that different community groups have differing opinions about the desirability of the project, as the case study on p. 105 shows.

Making an issue of hustlers in Gambia

Gambia Tourism Concern, an organisation recently set up by Gambians concerned about tourism development, has published a magazine in the style of *The Big Issue*, the British publication sold by the homeless. The 24-page monthly, *Concern*, was launched at the Bungalow Beach Hotel on Kotu Beach, a resort popular with British and Scandinavian tourists and aims to reduce antagonism between European tourists and the beach hustlers.

It will be sold by beach hustlers, or 'bumsters' at Banjul's airport and on the beaches for 15 dalais (£1), of which a third goes to cover production costs, a third goes to the vendor and a third to Gambia Tourism Concern.

Editor Adama Bah, explains: 'Over the years, the question of bumsters – or beach boys – who follow tourists, has been of prime concern to all those involved in the industry. The magazine is designed to address the concerns of such young people and give them some gainful employment. Concern will also deal with relevant issues on tourism and will endeavour to promote local initiatives.'

Source: *In Focus* magazine, Winter 1996–97

ACTIVITY

Zenith project public meeting

Role play a public meeting held to discuss the Scarborough Zenith development. Each member of the group should take a different role, such as:

- local residents
- representatives from the local authority

- tourists to the area
- representatives from the development company
- local business people
- local transport providers.

CASE STUDY

Scarborough's Zenith project

The Zenith project was heralded as the answer to Scarborough's declining tourism industry. Plans involve demolishing many of the existing tourist facilities and attractions in the north bay and covering a large part of the area with a futuristic domed construction which will house an indoor water park, dry-ski slope, restaurants, accommodation and a range of other attractions. The plans have met with mixed reactions from local community groups and business people. These letters are adapted from the *Scarborough Evening News*, 24 September 1999.

Sir

I am sure that Scarborough residents will take exception to being called blinkered. This expression could also be directed at the press and the Zenith developers. After all, the sole purpose of the Zenith development is to make a few bob for the share-holders. I believe they are taking a gamble and have not investigated all of the likely pitfalls.

The geographical and climatic conditions over a full year do not lend themselves to a development of this magnitude. Our Victorian road system will not be able to cope with the traffic. The North Side residents are bound to suffer loss of business by having a building site in their midst for the next three years. We, the public, would also question water supplies and sewage disposal. Would our treatment plants be able to cope? Holidaymakers like the sunshine and, unfortunately, we do not have this blessing all the time. Scarborough, sadly, is not the Costa Brava. The Zenith project will Costa Lot and could become the Costa White Elephant.

C. Cousins
Scarborough

Sir

Re the recent public meeting on the proposed Zenith development and the subsequent correspondence. While I fully appreciate the concerns expressed at the meeting, let us not forget that what is envisaged is a return to the number of visitors who used to come to Scarborough some years ago. Let us not forget that the development is not planned for a greenfield site, this site is already in leisure use and is desperately in need of improvement and up-grade. Let us not forget that the number of visitors to the town has been in steady decline for quite some period of time and as a result of this the number of facilities for the use of visitors and residents alike has also declined.

Business is suffering and I can, with certainty, state that companies such as my own will not invest here unless a project such as the Zenith, with that size and scale, actually does come to fruition. If we do not invest, the product (Scarborough as a seaside resort) will decline and we will, sooner rather than later, close. We have new competitors opening all the time and we cannot survive without investing substantial sums.

What future then for the young of Scarborough? Existing industry will find it more difficult to recruit from outside. Quality of life and the surrounding environment helps attract people to come here, to live and work. The sad spiral of decline will accelerate and any young person wanting a job and a secure future might have to look elsewhere. Do not throw away this lifeline.

Richard Smith
General manager
Sea Life Centre

BUILD YOUR LEARNING

1 Select a tourist area for investigation. This could be your local area, another area in the UK or an area outside the UK.

2 Produce a detailed map of the area showing all of the main tourist facilities and amenities.

3 Produce a brief summary about each of the main tourist facilities and amenities, explaining the specific products and services offered. You should also state when the facility or amenity was originally developed and explain any subsequent major development that has taken place. For example, the development of further facilities or change of use.

4 Describe the main agents involved in the development of the tourist destination, identifying their sector and role.

Keywords and phrases

You should know the meaning of the words and phrases listed below. Go back through the last 11 pages to refresh your understanding if necessary.

- Agent
- Central government
- Community groups
- Department of Culture, Media and Sport (DCMS)
- Development agency
- English Tourism Council (ETC)
- Landowner
- Leisure and entertainment organisation
- Overseas governments
- Pressure groups
- Regional development agency (RDA)
- Tourism development

The objectives of tourism development

WHERE A RANGE OF AGENTS ARE involved in a tourism development project it is likely that each will have specific and, possibly, different objectives. The various objectives for tourism development might be:

- economic objectives
- environmental objectives
- sociocultural objectives
- political objectives.

Economic objectives

One of the main objectives of tourism development is **economic gain**. This does not simply mean making a profit for the tourism providers, as there can frequently be economic objectives designed to benefit the community as a whole. Some of the more common economic objectives include:

- employment creation
- increased foreign currency earnings
- increased income for commercial operators
- economic development and regeneration.

Employment creation

A key objective of many tourism development initiatives is **job creation**. This is particularly true in areas where traditional industries have declined and unemployment has risen. As we saw in the case study about Bradford, tourism regeneration projects have been developed in many industrialised cities and towns to replace the jobs lost through failing industry.

Public sector organisations such as local authorities are especially likely to view employment creation as a main objective when developing tourism. For example, the East Midlands Development Agency specifies job creation as a key part of its overall strategy. The agency's objectives include:

recognising tourism and culture as a key generator of jobs and income, a channel for economic regeneration and a means of promoting the East Midlands image, building on the Heart of England Tourist Board's existing strategy and linking closely with the East Midlands Cultural Forum's forthcoming regional strategy.

In many of the less affluent overseas destinations, employment creation is a key issue in tourism development. Responsible developers look at ways in which local skills can be used and encouraged to provide employment opportunities through tourism trade. The webstract shows how local farming skills in St Lucia are used to provide food for tourists.

WEBSTRACT

St Lucia

How it's happening already: making the links

In St Lucia, Sunshine Harvest Fruit and Vegetable Farmers' Cooperative, consisting of 66 farmers, coordinates production and marketing to ensure regular supplies to hotels. The government and the private sector are agreeing to the need for a coordinated strategy. In 1994, the St Lucia Hotel Association and the Ministry of Agriculture, launched an 'adopt a farmer' pilot scheme, in which hoteliers buy produce from a specified farmer at a contract price agreed before planting. Smallholders are being encouraged to produce a wide range of fruit and vegetables instead of just bananas, which in the past have been imported from the USA. Loans from local banks are available to farmers at favourable rates to allow them to buy seeds and fertilisers. The potential for retaining more revenue from tourists in the island is greatly improved.

Source: www.vso.org.uk

Increased foreign currency earnings

Another objective of many tourism development initiatives is to increase the level of **foreign currency earnings** by attracting foreign tourists to an area to spend money on local products and services. Once again, this is particularly likely to be one of the main objectives of public sector organisations such as central government, which encourages foreign currency spending within the country.

However, one of the major concerns about income generation from tourism is **leakage**. This refers to the situation in which most of the income generated from tourism does not stay in the local economy but goes to boost the profits of airlines and tour operators. Leakage has been identified as a particular problem in many third world countries that have developed as tourist destinations. The problem has not been helped by the rapid growth in all-inclusive holidays, in which customers pay a single price for a holiday that includes all accommodation, facilities, food, drinks and often sporting activities. These holidays were originally offered in long-haul destinations such as the Caribbean, but are now also widely available throughout many of the prime short-haul European destinations as the following webstract shows.

WEBSTRACT

All-inclusives in Cyprus

Noel Josephides, managing director of Sunvil Holidays, is unequivocal about the economic damage caused by all-inclusives to Cyprus. In this article he explains how local traders want to know why their customers are being swallowed up by this alien concept.

Q: Why have all-inclusives come about?

A: The usual answer is because the rich and famous wanted to holiday in exotic locations without having to look at the abject poverty around them and without running the risk of being robbed by those less fortunate than themselves.

Q: In which case, why have they come to Cyprus, a recent addition to the all-inclusive club, when Aphrodite's island is one of the 20 richest nations in the world and probably one of the safest destinations on earth in which to spend a holiday?

A: You can walk around quite freely on the island and never feel threatened. We at Sunvil have probably had no more than five cases of theft reported by our 120,000 clients in 28 years of operating tours to Cyprus.

Q: So why on earth would travellers choose to be restricted to the confines of a single hotel?

A: Well, it started because Cyprus simply built too many hotels. In 1992, the boom year after the Gulf War, there was an almost magical increase in the flow of tourists as the island became flavour of the month. But no one stays flavour of the month for ever. And since building continued unabated in spite of the steady fall in tourist arrivals – especially from the UK, the island's largest supplier – the years

▲ Sunworld's all-inclusive holiday offers in Cyprus

1995 to 1997 were not good for Cypriot hoteliers. They have been ready to embrace anything that would help fill empty beds.

The all-inclusive concept, originally born out of necessity and the quest for top-of-the-range exclusivity had, in the meantime, gained popular recognition and had begun to attract the down-market mass operator. But this new market also demanded a low price tag and, as hotel rates in Cyprus were falling due to excess supply and some hoteliers in the more popular and more degraded resorts were beginning to panic, it was a concept they embraced as a quick fix for their troubles.

I do not know what studies have been undertaken as to the effects of the all-inclusive concept on local communities. It has certainly created problems in the Caribbean, but the authorities there seem reluctant to condemn a system embraced by large international hotel companies and tour operators. They are frightened in case they offend these organisations. Money talks it seems. But the fact is, the concept is now aggravating social problems, as local communities see themselves excluded not only from the obvious benefits derived from the tourist 'spend', but from the use of their own natural resources.

Of course, all-inclusives are still a novelty to Cypriots. Several hotels have attempted to cater for all-inclusive clients alongside others staying on a standard bed and breakfast basis. This has created confusion and ill-will between the two sets of clients. Individual customers no longer feel at home in the club-like, packaged atmosphere of such hotels.

The Cypriots have not been very impressed with the behaviour of their down-market, all-inclusive clients either. Many hoteliers mention the waste in food and drink which the concept encourages. Waiters are horrified at the glasses abandoned half-empty while fresh drinks are being ordered.

Costing an all-inclusive rate is also difficult. Like anything else, it takes time to get used to something new and many hoteliers have got it very wrong. And once in the all-inclusive game, reliance on mass market tour operators becomes total. Which is, of course, why the large tour operators are so keen on it. It works on the same principle as the cruise market and, in fact, provides the greatest competition to cruising.

It is the least successful hotels that have embraced all-inclusives. The better hotels which have built up a repeat clientele over many years are just not interested. They still feel that there is money to be made out of selling their clients optional extras, and they are understandably nervous about allowing the marketing of their properties to fall into the hands of large tour operators who may decide to withdraw from a hotel or a destination for no apparent reason other than that there is more money to be made elsewhere.

In Cyprus, the resentment from the restaurateurs, cafe owners and souvenir shop proprietors is now beginning to mount. In Cyprus there is no security risk – clients are being kept within the hotel for the sole benefit of the hotelier and tour operator, to the detriment of all others involved in tourism related industries. All-inclusives were never necessary in Cyprus and their presence can only do harm to the tourist industry as a whole.

Their proliferation in Cyprus at a time when the supply of beds and restaurants exceeds demand can only drive a wedge between the various tourist industry groupings. Yet no one is lifting a finger to research what is happening or trying to understand where it will lead. The tourist authorities are calmly presiding over a potential disaster.

Of course, there is still the chance that this is just a stop-gap, a passing fad until business picks up again. Let's hope so, before too much damage is done.

Source: www.tourismconcern.org.uk

ACTIVITY

All-inclusives in Cyprus

Read the webstract then complete the following tasks.

- identify the key areas where leakage occurs with all-inclusive holidays

- identify the main beneficiaries of all-inclusive holidays

- suggest ways international tour operators could continue to offer all-inclusive holidays whilst minimising the leakage factor.

You need to understand that **domestic spending** (money spent by residents within the country) is as important as foreign currency earnings and is another prime objective of tourism development. Ideally, tourism development aims to attract foreign tourists while also encouraging residents to take their holiday within their own country. The development of Benidorm in Spain is a good example of the way both domestic and foreign markets can be targeted.

Having experienced a decline in numbers of British holidaymakers in the early 1990s, the Spanish authorities undertook a process of development with the objective of increasing both foreign and domestic spending. This included the regeneration of rundown areas, up-grading of accommodation and a beach cleaning initiative. The numbers British visitors to Benidorm have now risen again and the number of Spanish tourists now visiting the area constitutes more than 40 per cent of the total visitor population. See also pages 149 and 203–6.

Increased income for commercial operators

The last two objectives that we looked at tend to be more common in the public sector. However, private sector commercial operators are key agents in the development of tourism and most operate with the main objective of **increasing income and profitability**. For such operators, the development of tourism facilities and services is based on their objective of financial gain. This is usually beneficial in terms of tourism development because it means that commercial operators will make sure that their proposals for development are cost effective and likely to be successful.

Economic development and regeneration

We have already discussed some examples of urban regeneration, where tourism development has helped revive areas and provide employment. Many agents involved in tourism development identify specific objectives that will encourage **economic development** and **regeneration**.

In areas that have become rundown there is the obvious objective of improving the physical environment for residents. This may involve eliminating unattractive buildings and wasteland or restoring them to their past glory. Even in well-maintained areas, tourism development may still provide considerable improvements in the conditions for local people. For example, the development of a multiplex cinema, theatres, restaurants and tourist attractions may occur because an area attracts a large number of tourists who will use the facilities. However, all of these facilities are also available to local residents all year round.

In most tourist areas, locals are able to use a wide range of facilities that are only available because the visiting tourist population helps to make them profitable. If such facilities were to rely only on local customers, many would soon prove unprofitable. However, locals do not always perceive the development of additional tourist facilities as of benefit to them. For example, local authorities which provide substantial grants to tourism development projects are often criticised by local people who feel that the money would be better spent on improving services that are provided purely for the local community.

It is important to understand that all four of the economic objectives that we have looked at may apply to a single tourism development initiative and are closely linked. For example, the objectives for the regeneration of an area may include increased employment in the area, greater foreign currency earnings, increased profits for commercial operators and regeneration of the environment and facilities for both locals and visitors.

ACTIVITY

Renaissance of Portsmouth harbour

The webstract opposite outlines the Renaissance of Portsmouth harbour millennium project and its proposed rapid transit system. As a group, discuss the benefits to the local community of the project. You should consider the economic, social and environmental benefits.

WEBSTRACT

Renaissance of Portsmouth harbour millennium project

Together, Gosport Borough Council, Portsmouth City Council, Portsmouth Historic Dockyard and the Portsmouth South East Hampshire Partnership, have been awarded a £38 million grant from the Millennium Commission to create an international maritime heritage arena. The £84 million Renaissance of Portsmouth Harbour project is one of 12 landmark schemes across the UK selected by the Commission to mark the new millennium. The scheme is made up of five inter-connected elements:

- two waterfront promenades on each side of the harbour, linking existing and new attractions

- a harbour tower, 165 metres high with three viewing platforms

- expansion and improvement of the historic dockyard

- development of Priddy's Hard heritage area in Gosport.

- A waterbus network across the harbour.

The Renaissance of Portsmouth harbour millennium project will create a world-class leisure and maritime heritage destination. It will bring new life to historic buildings and create new public access to the harbour's historic waterfront.

The scheme will attract an extra 1.64 million visitors each year and create 3,500 new jobs. It will act as a catalyst for over £300 million of investment in the local economy.

The South Hampshire rapid transit proposal is for a tram system running on and off-street to provide a fast, efficient, reliable and environmentally friendly public transport service between Fareham, Gosport and Portsmouth. With 16 stops along the 14 km, 28-minute route, the aim of the system is to relieve traffic congestion and improve quality of life in the area. Over two-thirds of the route uses a former rail corridor and there are links with two millennium national cycle routes. The vehicles are low floor and light weight, powered by an overhead electricity supply.

Most of the construction will take only a few weeks or months to complete, although construction in the harbour area will take about two and a half years.

With an estimated 17,000 trips made on the system each day, the project will relieve congestion and improve the quality of life in the area, bringing benefit in economic terms particularly to the Gosport peninsula. It offers:

- scope for regeneration and redevelopment

- a unique opportunity as part of the Renaissance of Portsmouth harbour millennium project

- a chance to raise the national and international profile of the area

- an enjoyable modern, comfortable and reliable means of travel.

Source: www.gosport.gov.uk/development/
millennium/elements

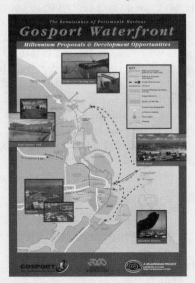

Environmental objectives

One of the key issues that arises with all tourism development is the potential effect upon the environment. Tourism is inextricably linked with the environment in which it is located. Some of the concerns are global issues, such as the impact on the ozone layer of the rapid increase in air travel, or the problems of pollution associated with increased road and water transport. Other issues may be more localised, such as erosion and overcrowding in popular countryside areas, or the loss of natural landscapes due to building development. Growing awareness of the importance of preserving and improving the environment has led many agents to embrace the principles of sustainable tourism. (We look at the implementation of sustainable tourism principles on p. 37 and p. 148.)

Many agents of tourism set out their **environmental** objectives in policy statements or strategies, as the example in Figure 2.3 shows.

Many of the environmental problems associated with tourism development are due to the seasonality of the product rather than to the actual product. For example, in the Lake District, mass overcrowding and congested roads present an environmental problem during the peak summer months.

During the last ten years, tourism providers have realised the importance of setting clear environmental objectives when initiating tourism development projects. Providers such as Center Parcs have led the way in developing tourist facilities in harmony with the local environment. All of the Center Parcs sites are situated in rural areas of natural beauty. The design, construction and layout of the sites is sympathetic, so that the natural beauty has been preserved and, in fact, incorporated within the tourism product.

WEBSTRACT

Center Parcs

Sherwood Forest, home of the legendary Robin Hood, is a nature-lover's paradise, renowned for its beautiful woodland, heathland and lakeside setting. The village has a magnificent, open village square, a spectacular subtropical swimming paradise, a country club with a golf driving range, a leisure bowl with a greenwood theme, and Center Parcs' own health and beauty centre.

Escape to Elveden Forest, set in the dramatic Breckland landscape, and enjoy one of the driest and mildest corners of England. You can relax and enjoy yourself, whatever the weather, in the flourishing Parc Plaza, subtropical swimming paradise, jardin des sports and new Mediterranean leisure bowl. Not far from the nine-hole golf course, you'll find the colonial-style country club, equipped with its own health and beauty centre.

Find yourself surrounded by hills and valleys in Longleat Forest's rich and varied landscape. The village has three distinct centres to suit your taste whether it be the classically French village square; the Mediterranean plaza or the magnificent jardin des sports with views of the sports lake. If you're not content with a European flavour, you'll be able to experience new North American-style apartments from Autumn 1999. Cycling is the best way to get around on the village, and there are cycle boardwalks to help you make light work of the hilly terrain, but if that still sounds too energetic, why not just hop onto the landtrain?

Source: www.centerparcs.com

Figure 2.3: Environmental objectives of the East Midlands Development Agency

east midlands
development agency

the catalyst for change

Our environmental objective is recognition that the quality of the East Midlands environment is an important factor in creating the right conditions for inward investment, tourism and overall quality of life. Maintenance and enhancement of biodiversity is a key test for sustainable development – the region has not had a good track record in recent years. We need to repair the damage of the past and create new assets to pass on to future generations.

The economic strategy can contribute by, for example:

■ encouraging economic development agents to understand the implications of their actions on biodiversity in the region

■ ensuring that important environmental assets are not damaged through growth and development

■ promoting environmental technology and service industries and encouraging best practice in environmental management among businesses, as a means of improving their competitiveness and developing new products in a fast expanding market

■ stimulating job generation through environmental improvements, regeneration of derelict sites, habitat management and housing rehabilitation.

Environmental objectives can cover a range of issues including:

■ the preservation of wildlife

■ environmental education

■ environmental improvement.

The preservation of wildlife

Tourism development can have serious effects on wildlife and many pressure groups have been established to safeguard the natural habitat of a wide range of species (habitat preservation). One of the most obvious examples of the potential effect upon wildlife is the building of new attractions or facilities that disrupt or destroy the natural habitat of local wildlife. However, there are many more, less obvious, potential effects, such as the impact of an increase in visitor numbers, increased litter, pollution and noise, as the case study about Zakinthos shows.

CASE STUDY

Zakinthos

In the early 1970s, the European package holiday market was booming, with tour operators searching for more destinations to tempt tourists and increase their market share. The first package holiday flights to the Ionian island of Zakinthos arrived at the single runway airport to find an authentic Greek island with few tourists and little tourism development.

Known as Fiore di Levante (the flower of the east wind), Zakinthos boasts some of the clearest waters and most stunning beaches of the Greek islands. However, these beaches can boast a further attraction. The island's Laganas Bay beach is the prime mediterranean nesting ground for the endangered loggerhead turtle. The sea turtles are an extremely long-lived species that spend their life in the sea but return to the sands at night to lay and hatch their eggs. The hatchlings (baby turtles) return to the sea once they are strong enough.

Early foreign visitors to Zakinthos were encouraged to visit Laganas Bay to view the turtles and some tour operators actually offered organised excursions. However, it soon became clear that what was being regarded as a tourist attraction was, in fact, endangering the existence of the turtles. Tourists arriving at night to see the turtles, were disturbing the nesting grounds and trampling on eggs. Increasing noise, both on the beach and on the newly built adjacent roads was disorientating the hatchlings so that they were unable to find their way back to the sea.

Under increasing pressure, the Greek government passed a law in 1987 to protect the turtles. This included making tourists aware of the danger to

turtles and asking them to observe the new law. Visitors are asked not to go to Laganas Bay beach between sunset and sunrise and to refrain from making a noise, leaving rubbish on the beach or using umbrellas which can break the turtle eggs. However, the temptation to promote the turtles as a Zakinthos attraction remains.

ACTIVITY

Zakinthos

As a group, discuss how you think the agents involved in tourism development in Zakinthos could ensure that their objectives effectively included the preservation of wildlife. For example, could the authorities develop a further visitor attraction that would satisfy the tourists' curiosity with the loggerhead turtles whilst ensuring that they did not visit the nesting grounds?

Environmental education

The case study on the loggerhead turtles of Zakinthos raises a further environmental issue that many tourism developers consider when setting their objectives. In many situations it is not sufficient for just the developers to be aware of and consider environmental concerns; it may also be necessary to provide environmental education to both local inhabitants and visiting tourists on environmental issues.

In Zakinthos, the local authority needed to ensure that the locals were aware of the dangers to the loggerhead turtles, so that they would discourage tourists from visiting the nesting grounds. It also need to educate visiting tourists about the steps that they could take to preserve the species.

Many resort destinations have development strategies that aim to educate locals and tourists about ways in which they can help to preserve the environment. For example, a large number of seaside resorts display signs on beaches about issues such as litter and dogs on the sands.

The concern about protecting the environment has become so strong in recent years that some tourism development has been based on the prime objective of educating people about environmental issues through tourist attractions as shown in the case study about The Earth Centre.

ACTIVITY

The Earth Centre, Doncaster

1 You will have noticed that the term sustainable occurs several times in the case study about the Earth Centre opposite. As a group, discuss what you think is meant by sustainability. Base your discussion on the information provided on the Earth Centre.

2 Try to find out how similar tourist attractions and facilities in the UK aim to educate visitors on environmental issues. You might find regional tourist boards and the national parks particularly good sources of information.

CASE STUDY

The Earth Centre, Doncaster

The Earth Centre in Doncaster opened in 1999 with the help of funding from the National Lottery Fund, the European Union, English Partnerships and partnerships with other organisations and private companies such as Railtrack.

The main objective of the centre is:

To promote understanding of sustainable development (development that sustains the environment and protects it for future generations) and to help people become involved in the process of achieving it in their own lives and the world.

Built on the site of the former Cadeby colliery, the Earth Centre is one of the largest Millennium Commission projects outside of the capital. The mining scars on the landscape are fast disappearing, and the trees and flowers are beginning to flourish once more.

Phase 1 of the Earth Centre is a 26-acre visitor attraction, packed with exhibitions and activities on the theme of sustainable development. Our aim is to challenge both adults and children to think about the way they live and how this impacts on the environment and on the lives of future generations. We demonstrate how today and in the future, we can sustain an enjoyable lifestyle without destroying the environment.

The future is in your hands right now. At the Earth Centre, we understand the problems and challenges, and without giving too much away, our line-up of entertainment and education for a sustainable future includes:

- Planet Earth gallery
- Action stations
- Action for the Future gallery
- Nature works
- Future Child gallery
- Wilderness Theatre
- Japanese sensory trail
- Earth arena.

A visit will be an educational and fun day out, an unforgettable journey of learning.

Source: adapted from the Earth Centre brochure

We're building the world's second biggest classroom.

Despite the excellent lead that providers such as the Earth Centre are taking in educating locals and tourists, research shows that many people may still have an unrealistic idea of the actual effect that tourism can have on the environment. A survey conducted by MORI in 1995 found that 37 per cent of the people surveyed believed that travel and tourism causes virtually no damage to the environment and that 21 per cent believed that it causes no damage at all. Only 9 per cent believed that it causes a fair amount of damage and 6 per cent that it causes major damage.

ACTIVITY

Tourism and environmental damage

A MORI survey has suggested that 64 per cent of the population believe that travel and tourism causes little or no damage at all to the environment or do not know of any damage.

As a group, discuss why you think so few people are aware of the possible harmful effects of tourism development. For example, does the fact that many tourists visit a destination after the damage has already been done lead them to believe that the destination has been unaffected by tourism development?

Environmental improvements

Many tourism development initiatives identify **environmental improvements** as one of their main objectives. This might include the renovation or regeneration of rundown areas or buildings to improve facilities and services. Such improvements may benefit local people and wildlife as well as tourists. The webstract outlines some of the environmental improvements that have been achieved by Norwich Council's parks and gardens department.

Apart from meeting their obvious environmental responsibilities, tourism providers also frequently find that planning applications meet with a more favourable response if they are able to show how the environment will be improved by a specific tourism development. For example, the conversion of a derelict building into a tourist attraction may be more enthusiastically received if the developer intends to retain the original features of the building and restore the frontage and interior to its former appearance. Locals may view this as a positive development in maintaining the area's character and visual appeal.

WEBSTRACT

Parks and gardens in Norwich

Green, open spaces are in abundance throughout the city, many with seasonally planted flowerbeds. There are more than 25 parks, gardens and recreation grounds which are also open-air venues for musical events, sports and play-schemes.

Norwich parks have an important role to play in providing leisure facilities. Many woodlands and marshes close to the city are now nature reserves, and there are riverside walks by the Wensum and Yare. After the First World War the council's policy was that new housing and parks should be planned together. In 1919 Captain Sandys-Wynch was appointed parks and allotments superintendent and his important influence on the parks of Norwich is evident to the present day. Sandys-Wynch planned each park in meticulous detail. Nothing was left to nature. The plans featured geometric patterns, with symmetrically placed tennis courts, football pitches and bowling greens, overlooked by a central pavilion. The work was carried out by unemployed people through the city council's Spend for Employment scheme.

Source: www.norwich.gov.uk

ACTIVITY

Environmental improvements

Investigate a small tourism development project in your area. For example, a disused building or area that has been converted (or is to be converted) into a tourism product, facility or service. Identify the ways in which the development could improve the local environment.

Much tourism development overseas has been criticised for failing to identify and achieve clear environmental objectives. However, there are numerous examples in which tourism development agents focus on environmental objectives, as the next webstract about the development of a resort in the Sinai shows.

WEBSTRACT

An eco-resort in the Sinai

Tourism is not just big tour operators – there are many small businesses that are trying to avoid the problems of mainstream tourism development. Basata, an alternative hotel built in an idyllic bay on the Gulf of Aqaba in Egypt is one such place. Sue Wheat talks to its owner, Sheriff El-Ghawrawy.

Q: How and why did you set up Basata?

A: I am from Cairo and was a civil engineer. In the big city you completely lose the feeling that you belong to nature, and people lose their identity as human beings. Also, as tourists, no one is active anymore. If you are on a tour, you are taken everywhere and given a programme to follow. The tourism industry calls it activities but I call it passivities. I came camping here and decided to change my life and set up business here. I had no idea about tourism, but I felt I'd come here and do something through which I could get a lot of messages across to people. I set up Basata (which means simplicity in Arabic) ten years ago, although it took 12 years to get through all the paperwork with officials who were very much against my ideas.

I bought this bay which is absolutely unspoiled and wanted to preserve it from damaging development. The development we have built here is as environmentally friendly as we can make it. At first the authorities wanted to kill me, then they realised I attracted a lot of people who weren't hippies, but ordinary people.

Q: Why do you think it is necessary to have environmentally run tourism?

A: Sinai is destroyed – or very soon will be – particularly from Nuweiba to Taba on the border of Israel. There is not a metre of the coastline that isn't sold to developers.

The authorities say, look we're environmentally friendly – we have all these green areas. They're even planning golf courses. But this is crazy. It's like going to Switzerland and putting in desert. I went to the Eco-Peace conference in Israel, between Egypt, Israel and Jordan, and there was a lot of back-slapping, but I just kept asking, but what did you DO? Apparently there had been an Aqaba clean-up campaign – but we hadn't heard of it, and we live here. We really need to prevent garbage being dumped into the sea, it will take 280 years to flush the Gulf of Aqaba. In a few years you won't be able to see the sea. It's terrifying. But this is a very fragile environment – and it's only a few metres from the coral to the beach and then the mountains. I know no one can ever produce zero pollution, but at least I'm trying to be less bad.

I think Egypt should be strong enough to choose the type of tourists we want. If I had built a disco I would have attracted party-goers, but if I build an ecological place I attract environmentally conscious people. Even if the number of tourists who wanted to visit environmentally run tourism projects equals one per cent of the world's tourists, Egypt couldn't cater to the demand. Sinai needs a focus – so why don't we try and corner that market?

Q: Can you describe the system you have here?

A: We have used natural materials for all the buildings. There are 18 bamboo huts which are very well made and comfortable. We are also now experimenting with mud houses built by Hassan Fathy's assistant. Hassan Fathy was an Egyptian architect famous for his ideas about architecture for the poor, and using just natural and locally-sourced materials. Many places now use Hassan Fathy's style because it is so attractive but we are the only place in Egypt to use the Hassan Fathy materials in the way that he intended.

Because of the very fragile desert and coastal environment, water is very scarce and we have to be very careful what we do with waste. Fresh water is made at our own desalination plant but this is conserved by having taps in the bathrooms that only run for six seconds per press. Waste water is our biggest problem and we keep it to a minimum by using the high-saline salt water from the desalination process for as many purposes as we can, particularly construction, the toilets and washing dishes (which are then rinsed in fresh water). There are recycling bins for plastic, organic waste, paper, glass, even cigarette butts. We also have a plastic shredding machine and the plastic is then sold to a company in Cairo.

Food waste is fed to the animals. We have ducks, pigeons, goats, donkeys, a camel and cats. Each animal is responsible for eating a certain kind of organic leftover food! The goats eat the macaroni, the camel eats the rice, ducks eat the fish – and they all produce wonderful fertiliser which we use in the greenhouse to grow tomatoes, peppers and aubergines, melons, cucumbers and other vegetables. Last year we even had enough to sell to hotels nearby. We bake our own bread and pizza, and evening meals are provided which are alternatively vegetarian and fish. We also have a small pharmacy and generate our own electricity with a generator.

Q: What information do you give to visitors?

A: We have a number of basic rules. No paper should be put down the toilets, no nude sunbathing, no alcohol, no sleeping in the public area, and no walking on the coral – you may kill yourself, or more importantly, kill the coral! In high season there are up to 300 visitors here, so it is important to have rules. Guests take their own food and drinks from the kitchen and write down what they've taken – the system works on trust and seems to work well.

Q: What are your plans for the future?

A: The country's plan is to have three million people working in this region within 20 years. Within three years all the planned hotels should be completed, so we need very good environmental regulations. From what I see, as a capitalist, an investor and an environmentalist, we need to teach the tourism industry what profits they'll make from being less environmentally damaging. I am setting up an environmental society with some other Egyptian friends and colleagues and we hope that we can help enforce Egypt's environmental regulations, educate the locals, tourists and investors. We need to get to all the specialists – the architects, engineers, labourers – everyone who is involved.

We also have plans to set up a kindergarten and school for local children. The Bedouins are very interested because they are not happy with the schools in Nuweiba. Its central philosophy will be on combining the environment, language and culture into every aspect of the normal curriculum – something between Montessori, Steiner and the normal educational styles. We will also have a cultural centre, so that the children can learn traditional handicrafts and we hope to start making paper there which will be very useful for the school. If the kids grow up studying in this way it will be easy for them to incorporate the ideas into adult life.

Source: www.tourismconcern.org.uk

ACTIVITY

An eco-resort in the Sinai

Identify the main environmental improvements that Sheriff El-Ghawrawy has achieved in his resort.

Sociocultural objectives

As we have already seen, most tourism development is closely linked to the location in which it takes place. Each location has its own specific resident population with its own characteristics and culture or **socio-culture.** The local population also has a range of opinions on the desirability of tourism development and the extent to which it will improve or hinder the local culture and social make-up of the area. The case study on the Zenith project in Scarborough (p. 105) showed that different sectors of the population may have very different ideas about tourism development within the area and its relative benefits. Where sectors of the local population are hostile towards tourism development, one of the main issues that often arises is the impact that the development may have on local socio-cultural values and characteristics.

Television and film productions have been responsible for developing many otherwise minor destinations into tourist destinations. For example, Glasgow attracted fans of the film *Trainspotting*, Sheffield benefited from its exposure in *The Full Monty* and Notting Hill in London has benefited from increased visitor numbers due to the success of the film of the same name. The British Tourist Authority actively encourages visits to some film and TV locations in the UK through its Movie Map.

Your guide to exploring Britain through film and tv
● LOCATIONS ● STARS ● ATTRACTIONS

▶ The Movie Map has helped to put places like Notting Hill Gate on the tourist circuit

CASE STUDY

Heartbeat

The development of TV's *Heartbeat* village of Goathland in north Yorkshire as a tourist destination caused a rapid transformation that had an enormous impact on the sociocultural characteristics of the local population.

Before the success of the programme, the destination was an isolated village with a limited number of small shops and pub-hotels. Within a few months the village was experiencing a mass invasion of organised coach excursions. Tourists trampled over residents' gardens, peered through their windows, and overcrowded pubs and restaurants.

Some of the locals were quick to capitalise on the unexpected boom. Local pubs advertised 'sandwiches as eaten by the *Heartbeat* cast' and shops turned away from many of their traditional products to introduce a wide range of *Heartbeat* souvenirs.

Research carried out jointly by the Yorkshire Tourist Board and the North York Moors National Park found that residents in Goathland voiced the following concerns.

■ It is not the TV production that is the problem, rather the number of visitors attracted by the programme.

■ Almost all residents feel there is visitor pressure in the village.

■ The main problems are congestion, erosion of land and a change in the atmosphere of the village.

■ Residents are proud of their village and would like to see it recognised for its traditional tourism and not just for its involvement in *Heartbeat*.

The graph shows the results of the research in terms of the residents' perceived positive (top graph) and negative (bottom graph) aspects of the filming of Heartbeat.

For those who embrace the tourism development the financial rewards are high. However, the impact on Goathland's sociocultural characteristics has meant that the days when residents could walk down their quiet high street and recognise almost everyone they met are long gone. Until, of course, Heartbeat ceases to be made and tourists no longer find it interesting to visit an isolated North Yorkshire village. When that happens, how easily will the village be able to return to its past?

Source: YTB's *Tourism Education Pack* 2000

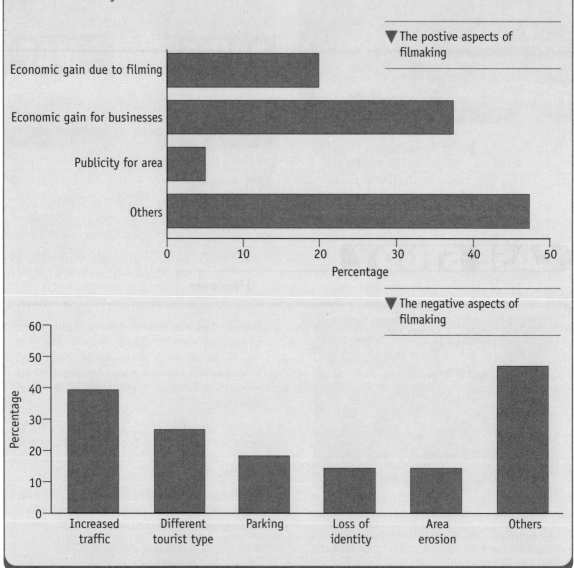

▼ The postive aspects of filmaking

▼ The negative aspects of filmaking

ACTIVITY

The impact of television

Find out about any TV programmes or films that have been made in your region. Have they been used to develop the area as a tourist destination and, if so, what have been the economic, environmental and sociocultural impacts on the area?

Responsible providers that are planning tourism developments always consider the sociocultural impact of their initiative and incorporate such concerns into their objectives. Issues they might consider include:

- the promotion of understanding between the cultures of tourists and those of the local population
- improvements to the quality of life of the local population
- provision of community facilities as well as facilities for tourists.

Promoting understanding

Responsible tourism development agents are aware that there are often significant differences between the cultures of tourists and of the host population and seek to promote an understanding between them. Many tourists travelling to foreign destinations rank the experience of a foreign culture as part of the attraction. Haggling in a Tunisian camel market, learning Turkish dancing from a hotel waiter or sampling tapas in a Spanish bar all help to create an experience that we feel is culturally different. However, tourists can have a profound effect on the cultures that they visit.

Perhaps the most obvious effect is created by tourists' lack of understanding of the local culture and the risk that they run of causing offence by, for example, failing to observe cultural standards for greetings, behaviour, body language or dress. Many Greek Orthodox churches now find it necessary to display signs advising visitors of the expected dress code in their churches. This is not because the local Greek population needs advice but rather because locals found the casual dress of visiting sightseers offensive.

While this example shows that local cultural values have been retained and take precedence over the values of tourists, there are many examples in which tourists' values have changed the local culture. Topless sunbathing is a prime example of the way that the cultural values of some destination countries have had to adapt to accept the behaviour of tourists. As recently as 15 years ago, tourists ran the risk of being arrested for indecency in some countries if they sunbathed topless. Today there are few resorts that are not willing to turn a blind eye to such behaviour in an attempt to maintain their share of the tourist market.

A second effect on local culture can be seen through a concept known as **staged authenticity**, in which cultural events or entertainments are put on for tourists. Often such events bear little resemblance to the actual culture of the area but are adapted to meet the expectations of tourists. For example, the Spanish flamenco night performed by the hotel staff and ending with versions of international pop songs bears little

resemblance to the traditional Spanish dance. Further examples include local craft markets that actually only sell tourist souvenirs and fake designer clothes. The effect of staged authenticity is that the authentic local culture becomes diluted in the attempt to create a culture that is attractive to tourists.

There have been some instances where the quest to provide authentic culture has been even more sinister as the webstract about the Padaung (see p. 122) shows.

A further impact that tourism can have on local cultures is to change the expectations or behaviour of the local population. For example, tourists in India sightseeing with camcorders and expensive cameras are displaying wealth that represents many weeks, if not months wages for the local population and the expectations of the local people can change. The opportunity to improve the local standard of living or to copy the culture of visitors can create a negative cultural impact in the form of crime, begging, prostitution and drug trafficking.

ACTIVITY

Club 18–30's mission statement

This is Club 18–30 mission statement, which has featured in one of their holiday brochures.

Leave the football shirt at home, find a new position, have fun, get the mother of all hangovers, stay out all night, sleep all day, get a tan with no white bits, try a paella sandwich, be silly because you can eat burger and chips at 5 a.m. Let someone else tidy up the room, fall down, dance until daylight, flirt blatantly with everyone, party on the beach, find an available six-pack, buy a crappy souvenir, forget your hotel, try sex in the surf, leave the British morals at home, try to pull, wake up on the beach, go non-stop clubbing, go on a bar crawl, laugh, 'til it hurts, have a vodka and Red Bull, get very physical, wear loads of outrageous new gear, show off and make a tit of yourself, fall madly in love (for an hour), lick ice cream out of his/her bellybutton, wake up in the wrong hotel, go skinny dipping, snog the waiter, drink all your duty frees on day one, try a bit of Spanish/Greek/Turkish at 5 a.m. Basically, have a bloody brilliant holiday!

Bear in mind that countries such as Spain and Greece used to have a cultural identity based on strict religious beliefs and conservative standards of behaviour for young people. As a group, discuss the effect that you think the typical Club 18–30 holidaymaker might have had on the local culture.

WEBSTRACT

The Padaung human zoo

A Thai businessman who kidnapped a Burmese community to make them into a tourist attraction is to stand trial. But their own fate is unclear. Andrew Drummond tells their story.

'Today God has come for sure,' said 67-year-old Mu Kyeh, hurriedly packing woven cloth and pots and pans into large plastic bags. Along with Mu Kyeh, 11 other adults and 21 children were handing up their belongings to helpers loading a truck. As they scurried about, the traditional brass rings on their necks caught the rays of the sun with bright flashes.

A group of Swedish tourists stood nearby, open-mouthed. They had paid Thai tourist operators to see 'giraffe women', the famous long-necked Padaung women whose tribe comes from Burma's Kayah state. What they were witnessing instead, in the tiny Thai border hamlet of Baan San Thon Du, was the hurried closure of a human zoo. A young Thai tourist guide ushered his charges back to their tour bus. 'We should go now,' he said. 'You don't want to stay. This is not a happy place.'

The camp's closure had been ordered by Prime Minister Chuan Leekpai, after reports in *The Times* of London. Indeed, when the senior official at the Thai Foreign Ministry first read the reports he said: 'What is this? Some sort of concentration camp?' A whole community had allegedly been kidnapped 18 months earlier from Burma by Thana Nakluang, a Chiang Mai businessman, who had turned one of the world's rarest tribes into a show for tourists.

Mu Kyeh and her relatives were lured from their homes in Panpet, in the south of Burma, in May 1996 by a Karenni tourist guide based in Thailand, who was working for Thana. The Padaung are a sect of the Karenni or Red Karen, and considered friends of insurgents by the Burmese military government. They had previously been moved out of their homes in the Kayah Hills and forced to live in a township under Burmese army control. Hence they readily fell for the guide's promise to take them to their relatives in Thailand's refugee camps.

The Padaung were allegedly trucked to a jungle area on the Thai-Burma border. Thana had approached the local district office saying he wished to help the penniless 'giraffe women' who had wandered into the area. He presented his scheme for a model tourist village at Baan San Thon Du.

Being a day trip from Chiang Mai, he said, it would attract a lot of tourists who would otherwise visit the three villages of long-necked Padaung refugees 200 miles south-west in Mae Hong Son. Everyone stood to benefit. Soon, tourist agencies throughout northern Thailand and in Bangkok were advertising the village of 'giraffe women'.

The Padaung said that Thana paid them in rations of rice and cooking oil, plus the equivalent of about 3,000 baht (some £42) per family per month, depending on his whim and their behaviour. There were no schools or medical facilities. Guards apparently ringed the village perimeter. Those refugees who dared wander beyond it claimed they were slapped and beaten.

In the camps at Mae Hong Son, members of the Karen Refugee Committee knew about the missing 34 Padaung from radio messages sent from Burma by the Karenni. But it was audio tapes delivered by sympathetic tourists that notified them where they were and the conditions of their captivity. 'I would rather die than continue to live here,' one woman grieved on the tapes. Another, Ma Bee, did die, of a broken heart, her fellow captives said.

When Thana, newspaper publisher and owner of a karaoke hostess club in the Chiang Mai Holiday Inn, was arrested, he said it was all a plot by the rival businessmen in Mae Hong Son. 'They want the money all for themselves,' he retorted angrily. Thana had promoted the camp in his newspaper, glorifying the rich cultural heritage of the 'giraffe women'. But police claimed his only consideration was how much money he could make from them.

The Padaung have now been returned to refugee camp 3 in Mae Hong Son, where they will stay to testify at the forthcoming trial of Thana and the camp manager.

The longer-term fate of the Padaung is in the balance. They remain illegal immigrants, subject to deportation to Burma, a country which, when it is not treating them as rebels, advertises them as a tourist attraction on its own internet website.

Source: www.tourismconcern.org.uk

Improvements to quality of life

Tourism development often creates considerable improvements in the **quality of life** of local people. This is particularly true in rundown areas where development represents an improvement in the physical environment. For example, many derelict dockland areas in inner cities such as London, Liverpool and Leeds have been successfully regenerated into thriving tourism, residential and business areas. The resident population has benefited from the substantial investment and improved environment. In less affluent overseas destinations, many host communities have also benefited from an improved quality of life.

Tourism development frequently provides a wider range of community facilities for locals. For example, populations in seaside resorts benefit all year round from the facilities and attractions that are primarily provided for visitors during the tourist season. If such attractions and facilities had to rely solely on the income generated from the local community, it is unlikely that they would be able to operate profitably and many would close.

WEBSTRACT

The hosts with the most

One of the principal goals of tourism development is enhanced quality of life for host communities. While this has not happened in all cases, there are success stories where the host community does win.

In a remote Lahu village in Mae Hong Son province, near the border with Burma, such a scenario exists. Here, the village members love having the foreigners come to stay. Empathic and responsible trekking companies have involved the headman and council of elders in decision making for the development of their community. As the headman explains: 'We feel like we are in control.'

Currently, only two companies visit the village weekly, with a maximum of ten people at a time, in compliance with a carrying capacity that has been set by the community. Together, the companies and villagers have targeted the problems and illnesses associated with poverty. There is now a tank providing clean and sanitised water and a small school built with tourist funds. All donations such as clothing and basic medical supplies go via the headman and benefit the entire community.

Village life has not been interrupted and there are no rubbish or elephants, while tourists wash only with biodegradeable soap. Educated guides explain traditional customs and monitor the behaviour of tourists.

Source: www.vso.org.uk

ACTIVITY

Quality of life

Select two towns with similar sized populations. One should be a tourist destination and the other should have little tourism trade. Compare the range of facilities in each. You might consider entertainment, tourist attractions, hospitality and catering. Set out your findings in a table like the one below, listing all of the facilities and the positive and negative impact that each has had on the quality of life of local people. We've put in one example.

Tourist destination			Non-tourist destination		
Facilities	**Positive impacts**	**Negative impacts**	**Facilities**	**Positive impacts**	**Negative impacts**
Multiplex cinema	Wide range of films	Local parking for residents	Single-screen cinema	Cinema in historic building	Lack of choice of films

Political objectives

We have already seen that public sector organisations such as local and central government are key agents in the development of tourism. Their involvement and support is often based on **political objectives** which might include the enhancement of an area's image or the creation of a regional or national identity.

Image enhancement

Agents such as local authorities often put the enhancement of their area's image at the forefront of their objectives for tourism development. Investment in new facilities and the regeneration of rundown areas, coupled with a marketing strategy that informs the public of the improvements, can all help to enhance the area's image. **Image enhancement** not only attracts more tourists to the area, but also improves the environment and quality of life for the local population.

A better image often results in more investment, the subsequent improvement of facilities and services, better employment prospects and increased prosperity.

The creation of regional or national identity

Some agents in tourism development aim to create specific identities. This may be conducted on a national scale, as in the creation of a positive national image of the UK as a tourist destination that the British Tourist Authority sets as one of its key objectives. Similarly, regional tourist boards and local authorities aim to establish unique identities for their areas.

The case study on pages 125–7 describes the Millennium Dome project, which aimed to revitalise an area of disused land at Greenwich and enhance the UK's image as a tourist destination through publicity linked to the new year millennium celebrations.

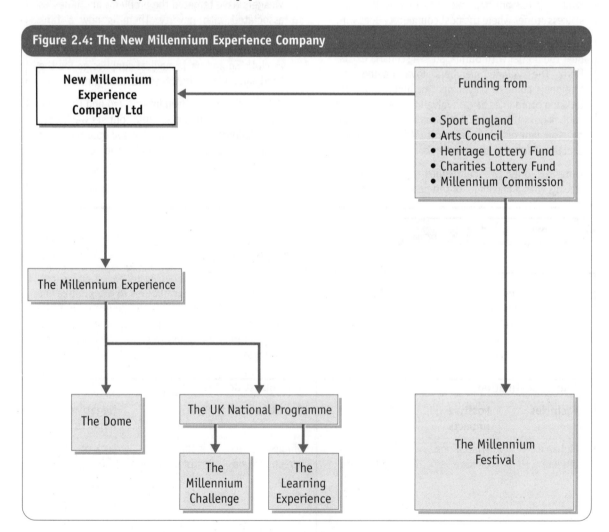

Figure 2.4: The New Millennium Experience Company

CASE STUDY

The Millennium Dome

The Millennium Dome, home to a spectacular exhibition, opened on 31 December 1999. The Millennium Commission promised that the Millennium Experience would be the biggest, most thrilling, most entertaining, most thought-provoking experience anywhere on the planet in the year 2000. It was designed to:

- be the world's biggest millennial celebration throughout the year 2000

- entertain, educate and inspire the nation

- offer over 12 million visitors a journey into the future

- focus on the theme of time and provide multimedia and interactive exhibits on our environment, society, culture and how we will live in the future

- take place on a 180-acre site on the meridian line at Greenwich.

Development of the site

The site of the Millennium Dome was a gasworks from 1871 until 1970 and the massive clean-up of the area was not completed until December 1997. The dome contains 12 masts, each of which was transported to Greenwich on 24 lorries. It is 365 metres in diameter, with a floor area of 80,000 square metres – enough room to house 1,100 Olympic size swimming pools, 18,000 double-decker buses or 3.8 million barrels of beer.

The huge structure is expected to last well into the next century with the aid of a comprehensive maintenance programme.

Agents

The dome formed part of the official UK millennium celebrations and is run by the New Millennium Experience Company (NMEC), an organisation established by central government to oversee millennium-based projects (see Figure 2.4).

The NMEC receives funding and grants from a number of sources including:

- Sport England

- Arts Council

- Heritage Lottery Fund

- Charities Lottery Fund

- Millennium Commission.

Economic and sociocultural impact

The economic decline of Greenwich during the early 1990s was dramatic. Five hundred businesses closed from 1991 to 1993, resulting in the loss of 10,000 jobs, the largest loss of any area of London. The creation of the dome has had a positive economic impact on the area. The cuttings from local newspapers highlight some local views on the economic benefits of the dome.

It is estimated that 7,000 jobs have been created that are directly related to the construction and operation of the dome. The British Tourist Authority has calculated that the Millennium Experience could earn more than £500 million from overseas visitors with a total financial gain of £1 billion. It is estimated that, once invested, this money could create up to 35,000 job years between 2000 and 2010.

Kibibe Onifade has worked in the Greenwich area for 12 years and is the coordinator of the West Greenwich Community Centre. She said, 'As a community worker I can see that there could be a lot of benefits with jobs and transport. But it has to be done in the right way and there has to be a way to involve local people'.

Ayesha Hussain, is the chair of the local Tenants' Forum. She said of the millennium experience, 'I believe in it. Greenwich is one of the worst blackspots for unemployment in London. With more jobs and more money in people's pockets it will also help the local shopping centres and the whole of the borough.'

Tessa Murphy has had a leather goods shop in Greenwich town for ten years. She said, 'The benefits will be an increased profile for Greenwich in the long term and that will benefit business for years afterwards.'

Environmental impact

Concern about the dome's environmental impact was a key issue amongst those who argued against its construction. However, the NMEC were keen to reassure local residents that the construction would be carefully managed to minimise any negative environmental impact. Concerns about the effects of the actual construction process were answered by the signing of the building industry's construction charter, as the article below explains.

Construction charter

The New Millennium Experience Co. Ltd has said that it will be a good neighbour to local people and the public after signing the building industry's construction charter.

The charter aims to minimise disruption to those people living and working near to the site. It includes:

- cleaning all vehicles leaving the site
- washing the footways outside the site
- limiting the activities which generate noise to certain times
- monitoring noise levels
- controlling dust levels
- ensuring that the perimeter of the site is secure and clean
- not tolerating abusive language or behaviour.

Further environmental initiatives have included the creation of 15 acres of parkland and landscape and the transformation by local schoolchildren of a section of the Thames by planting reeds to encourage native plants and wildlife to return to the area. In addition, the dome has a grey water system that recycles used water.

There were further local concerns about the huge rise in visitor numbers to the area and the obvious requirement for more transport. Apart from disabled visitors, access to the dome cannot be by car (unless dropped at the entrance), as there are no parking facilities within two miles of the site.

Transport is provided in a number of ways, all of which are aimed at reducing possible environment pollution:

- 12 minutes from central London using the Jubilee line
- regular Thames river boats
- park-and-sail boats
- park-and-ride buses.

The predicted method of transport for visitors:

- Jubilee line, 42 per cent
- park and ride, 17 per cent
- coach, 12 per cent
- boat, 10 per cent
- taxi/car drop off, 8 per cent
- rail/transfer, 4 per cent
- bus, 3 per cent
- cable car, 2 per cent
- walk/cycle, 1 per cent
- car (disabled), 1 per cent.

Access routes are clearly explained to visitors as the map below shows.

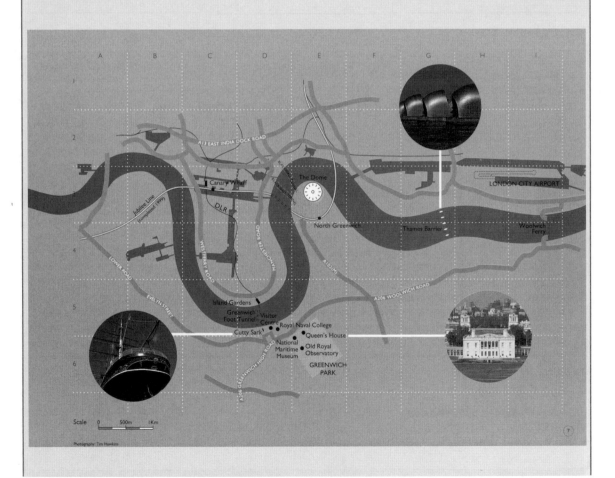

In anticipation of huge numbers of visitors, the dome uses time-linked tickets to avoid queuing. This means that each ticket states the times at which the visitor can view each exhibit.

Tickets are sold through National Lottery retailers, travel agents, rail and coach companies or directly from the Dome via the telephone or the website, as shown below.

The resource pack provided by the Millennium Experience gives a number of arguments for and against the Dome.

The dome debate

FOR:

- Good for Britain's prestige and morale.
- Will help to create 22,000 jobs in construction and other areas.
- Will help to regenerate a deprived part of south-east London.
- River boats will bring visitors to and from the site, bringing new life to the river.
- It is estimated that the dome will bring in an extra £300 to £500 million from overseas visitors.

AGAINST:

- An architectural eyesore.
- Money could be better spent on education, housing and tackling social problems.
- It will damage the environment and bring little benefit to local people.
- Rewards and prestige go to personalities and businesses involved, but the general public gains little.

BUILD YOUR LEARNING

1 Analyse the key advantages and disadvantages of the Millennium Dome in terms of tourism development.

2 Describe and evaluate the location.

3 Summarise the main visitor facilities and amenities.

4 Identify the agents involved and explain their main roles.

5 Clearly explain any potential conflicts in the objectives of the various agents involved. For example, possible conflicts between the economic objectives of commercial and public sector agents involved in the same initiaitive.

6 Explain the economic, environmental, socio-cultural and political objectives of the dome development.

Keywords and phrases

You should know the meaning of the words and phrases listed below. If you are unsure about any of them, go back through the last 22 pages to refresh your understanding.

- Domestic spending
- Economic gain
- Environmental education
- Environmental improvement
- Environmental objectives
- Foreign currency earnings
- Image enhancement
- Increasing income and profitability
- Job creation
- Leakage
- Political objectives
- Preservation of wildlife
- Quality of life
- Regeneration
- Sociocultural objectives

The impact of tourism development

WE HAVE ALREADY BEGUN TO EXPLORE the impact of tourism development. We are now going to look at some of these issues in greater detail and explore the ways in which tourism development can be effectively managed to maximise positive and minimise negative impact.

As we have seen, all tourism development has an impact both on the area in which it takes place and on the host population. However, it is important to understand that this impact will not always be positive. Some of the **positive and negative effects of tourism** development are outlined in Figure 2.5 and in the case studies and webstracts on pp. 131, 134, 136, 138 and 140.

Economic impact

Tourism development can generate increased income, create employment and attract outside investment. The city of Bath, for example, attracts two million visitors each year and generates 3,250 jobs of which 2,350 are directly linked to tourism and a further 900 indirectly linked. Tourism is worth between £150 million and £200 million to the Bath economy.

Tourism development also often provides **improvements in infrastructure**, for example, the creation of better public transport systems to cope with the influx of visitors. We look next at the economic impact of an major airport, Manchester shown in the case study opposite.

Figure 2.5: Pros and cons of tourism development

Jobs

Pros: Tourism creates jobs. It is relatively cheap to do this as tourism is labour intensive and there are limited opportunities for replacing people with new technology. It also enhances other sectors such as transport, agriculture and construction.

Cons: Jobs in tourism are often unskilled, seasonal, part-time and poorly paid. There is little chance of advancement.

Skills

Pros: Tourism diversifies the economy and provides alternative employment to traditional occupations, encouraging skills acquisition.

Cons: This can entail the loss of traditional skills because working in tourism is more lucrative.

Investment

Pros: Tourism brings in foreign exchange.

Cons: This means the sector is often dominated by large, multinational companies, and up to 90 per cent of the revenue generated by tourism can leak out of the local economy.

Stability

Pros: Tourism experiences fewer price fluctuations than many other export industries.

Cons: Tourism destinations experience life cycles and are vulnerable to recessions in rich countries.

Exports/imports

Pros: Tourism reduces reliance on primary exports.

Cons: It often involves importing food, materials and expertise.

Facilities

Pros: Tourism brings improvements to infrastructure, such as roads and airports.

Cons: Unfortunately the infrastructure developed for tourism can often bypass the local community and use up resources, particularly land and water.

Culture

Pros: Tourism promotes international understanding, offering a chance for visitor and visited to learn about other cultures.

Cons: The commercialisation of culture is also common, people are forced to sell and sometimes alter their culture for tourist consumption.

Source: www.vso.org.uk

CASE STUDY

Manchester Airport

Manchester Airport

Commitment to quality

Manchester Airport is much more than a place to catch a plane. It has many roles; major employer, business generator, regional resource, visitor attraction, service provider, community supporter and more.

Here are some key facts.

- Manchester Airport opened as an airstrip in 1938 and handled 4,000 passengers in its first year.

- Manchester is now the UK's third largest airport, with a passenger throughput of over 15 million people in 1998. In 1998 it was ranked 18th in the world for international passenger traffic.

- By 2005 the annual passenger throughput is expected to reach almost 30 million.

- Almost 90,000 tonnes of freight and mail are moved across the world to and from Manchester Airport per year using freight aircraft and in the cargo holds of passenger planes.

- The airport serves a catchment area of over 20 million people.

- Manchester has scheduled services to all five continents, serving 94 airlines, 274 tour operators and 175 long-haul and short-haul destinations.

Manchester Airport plc is the company which manages the airport. It is owned by Manchester City Council and the other nine Greater Manchester District Councils.

In 1992, the airport began planning to create a second runway. Despite extensive pressure from environmental groups, approval for the development was given by the government in 1997. The building of the runway will cost £170 million.

Economic benefits

Manchester Airport is the largest single generator of economic activity in the north west, with an influence that spreads far beyond the creation of direct on-site jobs. Many thousands of jobs depend on the airport, with over 15,000 people employed on-site, and many more away from the airport in related businesses.

Although the airport company is the largest on-site employer, with over 2,000 employees in 1998, there are approximately 250 other organisations which employ staff based at the airport. These range in size from the very large to those which employ only one or two people. The businesses include airlines and tour operators, passenger and freight agents, shops and hotels, and a host of maintenance and support activities. Figure 2.6 gives a breakdown of the proportion of jobs in each of the main operational areas that combine to provide the 15,000 jobs at the airport.

Figure 2.6: Jobs at Manchester Airport

Operational area	Proportion of jobs
Airlines	28.4 %
Handling agents	13.4 %
Catering	12.7 %
Manchester Airport plc	12.5 %
Control authorities	6.1 %
Freight	6.1 %
Retail	4.0 %
Cleaning	3.0 %
Engineering and maintenance	2.4 %
Hotels	2.2 %
Car hire	1.3 %
General aviation	0.8 %
Fuel agents	0.5 %
Others	6.6 %

The airport requires a wide range of jobs and skills, from highly technical to unskilled, and from full time to part time and seasonal. Typically, 1,000 new jobs are created on-site for every additional one million passengers. There are also a large number of jobs away from the airport, in a wide variety of locations and a broad range of industries. Taking into account employment in companies that have either relocated to the north west or expanded their activities due to services provided at the airport, it has been estimated that between 38,000 and 48,000 jobs in the region are indirectly dependent on the airport.

The economic benefits are not confined to the immediate area, but spread to all parts of the north west, Yorkshire and Humberside and other neighbouring regions. With the proposed second runway, up to 50,000 new jobs could be generated by 2005, excluding the effects on new and continued investment in regional businesses.

Manchester Airport's single runway is already operating at full capacity at peak periods. Without a second runway, air traffic would be lost to other UK or European airports.

Community relations

In 1998 approximately 7,000 complaints were received from members of the community surrounding Manchester Airport and each one was individually investigated. The most common areas of concern were:

- negative environmental impact of the second runway development

- increasing volume of road traffic to and from the airport causing congestion, noise and pollution

- aircraft noise

- pollution.

ACTIVITY

Economic and environmental impact

1 Imagine you are working for a public relations company that has been given the job of promoting the Manchester Airport second runway development. You have been asked to write a press release identifying the economic benefits of the proposed development to the host community. Produce a suitable press release using the facts given in the case study.

2 Imagine you are representing a conservation group opposed to a second runway at Manchester. Produce a press release which puts forward the case against this development. If you have access to a CD-ROM which contains newspaper articles, or to the internet, you may find it useful to look at what has already been published about this development.

We have already identified increasing employment opportunities as a positive benefit of tourism development, but one potential negative effect is the **loss of traditional employment opportunities**. For example, developments in rural areas can often encourage local people to leave traditional jobs such as farming to follow careers in tourism. When this happens on a large scale, the end result can be the loss of traditional skills and a skills shortage in local areas of employment.

A further negative effect of some tourism development is an **increase in the local cost of living**. This is a particular problem in poorer countries where the local population has a relatively low income. Development as a tourist destination often results in higher prices, simply because visiting foreign tourists are wealthier and can afford to pay more for products and services.

Local property and land prices can also increase dramatically after tourism development. Prime areas of land in developing tourist resorts often become valuable development land, making it too expensive for local buyers. Similarly, house and property prices can increase as tourism developers look for premises to convert or use.

ACTIVITY

The second home phenomenon

In the 1980s and 1990s, many wealthier UK residents bought second properties to use as holiday homes. This trend had a profound negative impact on many of the poorer areas of the UK. Property prices rose steeply and, while some local property owners made large profits from selling, others suddenly found that they were unable to afford a property in their area. Those unable to pay the high prices tend to be young adults buying their first house and many have been forced to move to other areas, where house prices are more moderate.

As a group, identify any further negative impact on the local community that the trend in second home ownership might have. For example, what effect might there be on local employment if a large number of young adults move away from the area?

Environmental impact

As we have seen, responsible and effective management of tourism development can have a positive impact on the environment. There are many instances of regeneration projects, for example, that have resulted in considerable improvements in the environment.

In some initiatives, areas and properties are actually improved upon and further assets are developed. The Garden Festival projects of the 1980s and 1990s, which landscaped areas of wasteland into countryside attractions and outdoor centres, often created an environment better than the original. With the support of various conservation groups, many of these areas have been able to create entirely new habitats for wildlife and plants that did not previously exist.

When badly managed, tourism development can have a serious negative impact on the environment. One of the key problems is that tourists frequently have to travel some distance to get to tourist attractions or destinations. Advances in transport coupled with increasing car ownership have meant that we can now travel further and faster then ever before, to visit an ever wider range of tourism options. However, all forms of transport, apart from bicycles and walking, have a negative impact on the environment.

The obvious negative impact is **pollution** caused by fuel consumption, but there are other effects to considered. Travel results in noise, congestion, the building of transport terminals and car parks, for example and problems arise when visitor pressure exceeds the capacity of the area to handle it.

- **Overcrowding** increases the risk of damage to resources, pressure on the host community and adverse effects on visitors' experience.

- **Traffic congestion** from cars and coaches is a problem in areas that cannot handle a large volume of traffic, such as small narrow streets in historic towns or minor roads in rural areas. At peak periods this can lead to disruption for local road users, damage to roads and verges, visual intrusion of traffic jams and noise and air pollution.

- **Increased wear and tear** on the physical fabric of buildings or the countryside is caused by the sheer volume of visitors.

- **Inappropriate development** detracts from the setting and antagonises the host community. Large increases in visitor numbers lead to pressure for new developments and problems can arise if these facilities are out of keeping with the setting.

- **Conflicts with the host community** can arise with noise, unruly behaviour or a change in the character of a place. A quaint, picturesque village can change in character if new tourism developments such as car parks, tea rooms, gift shops and hotels are not effectively controlled.

▼ Traffic jams are a frequent sight on approach roads to tourist destinations

CASE STUDY

North York Moors

The North York Moors National Park was designated in 1952. This was principally to conserve the extensive tracts of heather moorland, and to protect numerous areas of traditional farming, ancient deciduous woodland and 25 miles of rugged coastline. It is the largest heather moorland remaining in England today. The park covers an area of 1,432 square kilometres (553 square miles). It receives over 11 million day visits per year, making it the third most popular national park after the Peak and Lake Districts.

Tourism

Tourism is now the largest employer in the North York Moors, but it is subject to seasonal working patterns and part-time work. During August 1998 it was estimated that there were around 8,000 full-time equivalent jobs created by tourism, in January 1998 the figure was 2,000. In 1998, tourism generated £20 million in the North York Moors. It is estimated that 7 million visitor days were spent in the national park in 1998.

The largest employment sectors within the national park are farming (and jobs that are based on or dependent on farming) and tourism. Many of these jobs are both seasonal and part time. For an increasing number of families, the household income now comes from a number of part-time and seasonal jobs.

Farming

Traditional farming in the national park has created a landscape rich in variety and interest which is no longer present in much of the wider countryside outside the park. Many of the farms are small and family run. They are vital to the character of the national park but are increasingly under threat as incomes from agriculture remain low.

Traffic and transport

Traffic in the national park has grown by 28 per cent since 1992. Forecasts suggest that there could be a fourfold increase in rural traffic over the next 25 years. Moorsbus services have been very successful, but the proportion of people using public transport for recreational use is small and the majority of people still come by car. Problems from car use are increasing, with the highest levels of health-damaging ozone occurring in rural areas such as this.

Efforts are being made to increase the use and suitability of the Esk Valley railway, but if it is to continue to provide a service, initiatives to make it viable must be supported by both locals and tourists.

Housing

In 1998 the average house price in the national park was £118,000. Only about 10 per cent of the houses were on the market at £55,000 or less. Many local people are unable to compete in the local housing market.

Public rights of way

Erosion of footpaths and bridleways is a problem and in some places there are concerns about the sustainability of the rights of way network. In 1995, surveys identified 2,000 problems; the Park Authority dealt with 1,300 but with new problems developing all the time, there were still 1,500 outstanding at the end of the year. Increased use of about 160 km (100 miles) of green lanes by four-wheel drive vehicles has resulted in considerable damage to the surface of the tracks in some places. Increased use of bridleways by cyclists has led to some conflict with walkers.

Figure 2.7: North York Moors management plan

National park purposes
To conserve and enhance natural beauty, wildlife and cultural heritage. To promote opportunities for the enjoyment of the special qualities of the area by the public.

Economic and social well–being
To meet the needs of the present generation without compromising the ability of future generations to meet their own needs.

Sustainability
To meet the needs of the present generation without compromising the ability of future generations to meet their own needs.

Special characteristics and qualities of the North York Moors
Diversity of landscape, habitats and recreational opportunities, including...
- heather moorland
- traditional farming in central dales
- heritage coast
- industrial and historic heritage
- villages and buildings of architectural and historic value
- multipurpose forests.

ACTIVITY

North York Moors

1 List the advantages and disadvantages associated with tourism in the North York Moors National Park in terms of the economy, the host community and the environment.

2 In small groups, hold a discussion about the positive and negative impact of tourism in the park. Each group member should represent one of the following:

- visitor or tourist
- conservationist
- farmer
- local resident.

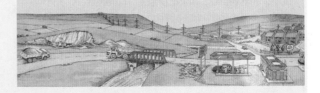

Sociocultural impact

Where an entire area or country is being developed, supporting and promoting the local culture may be a key feature of the tourism product offered. Grants and other means of support may be provided to allow local craftspeople to produce traditional products both for the local community and for visitors.

▲ Local crafts provide attractions for visiting tourists

Without such grants and support, the traditional products or methods of production may disappear. For example, visitors in Holland can visit clog-making factories where skilled craftspeople produce the traditional footwear by hand using methods passed down through generations. In reality, clogs can now be produced much more cheaply and efficiently in a factory by employees with limited craft skills. Similarly, Greek islands such as Rhodes have been able to revive and maintain ancient crafts such as fine lace-making because they provide an attraction for visiting tourists.

Further sociocultural benefits include the development of additional facilities and services that can be enjoyed by the local community as well as tourists. For example, tourist information centres may be provided primarily for visitors to the area but local residents also benefit by using the centre to book theatre tickets and tickets to other events.

We have already looked at much of the negative impact that tourism development can have on communities' socio-cultural identity and behavior. However, it is worth emphasising the importance of the problems that can arise from a loss of cultural identity and possible conflicts between the local culture and those of its visitors.

Some tourists visit expecting the local culture to adapt. Other tourists visit a destination because they want to experience the local culture and do not expect the population to treat them any differently. Clearly, the second type of tourist has a far less negative impact on the socio-cultural values and behaviour of the host destination.

The growth in sex tourism is yet another example of one of the negative impacts that tourism can have on sociocultural values, as the following webstract shows.

WEBSTRACT

Sex tourism: doing the hustle

Although tourism generates jobs in hotels, bars, restaurants and other leisure areas, this does not necessarily benefit local people. Foreign-owned companies operating in underdeveloped countries frequently bring in managers and staff from Europe and North America. As a result, the economic opportunities that tourism provides for local people are mainly in the informal sector, where women, men and children work as unregistered taxi drivers, guides, souvenir sellers, fruit sellers, shoe-shine boys, masseuses, manicurists, hairdressers and cleaners in private apartments. The informal economy also often includes prostitution.

A number of factors impact upon the level of control independent adult prostitutes enjoy in transactions with sex tourists. For a start, they are often under intense economic duress. On the whole, sex tourism flourishes in countries where a large percentage of the population lives in poverty, where there is high unemployment and no welfare system to support those who are excluded from the formal economy.

Those involved in tourist-related prostitution are very often migrants from rural areas or urban conurbations and may be attempting to support several dependants as well as themselves through their prostitution. It would be wrong to claim that all those involved in prostitution in sex tourist destinations are working from a base of absolute poverty, and it is important to recognise that the economic rewards are very often far higher than those associated with unskilled work in factories or the hotel or catering industries – or indeed with prostitution serving local demand.

For female prostitutes, exchanges are inherently dangerous and their physical vulnerability is exacerbated by both the absence of legal protection and the presence of laws which penalise prostitutes. In Cuba, the Dominican Republic, Venezuela and South Africa, for example, women who had been raped or cheated by clients told us that the last thing in the world they would do would be to go to the police. They would run the risk of being raped by police officers and would most likely find themselves charged with some prostitution-related offence.

The unpalatable fact is that prostitution is very often the best means of subsistence available to children as well as to adults. As child labour researcher Maggie Black points out, in Dakar, Senegal, street girls report that they earn between US$7 and US$90 per day trading in sex, whereas those who beg earn between US$7 and US$17.

Children in tourist-related prostitution are often attempting to support not just themselves but also their dependants (a UNICEF survey in the Dominican Republic found that, in one tourist resort, almost half of the female prostitutes aged between 16 and 18 had one or more children). But children are also vulnerable for other reasons, as illustrated by the case of one 15 year-old girl we interviewed in the Dominican Republic.

Catalina started to prostitute herself at the age of 14 to support herself and her unemployed, alcoholic father. She is slightly built and stands only 4 ft 7 ins tall. In relation to her adult male clients, then, she is physically powerless. Like many child prostitutes around the world, Catalina drinks heavily while she solicits, and by 1 a.m. (when sex tourists in the resort where she works tend to pick up girls and women) she is usually visibly drunk. 'I like to drink,' she says, 'it helps me to forget everything.' As well as helping her to forget, however, working in this condition leaves her even less in control of transactions with clients and even more vulnerable to violence than she would otherwise be. Catalina does not have lodgings of her own but accompanies the tourists and expatriates who pick her up anywhere they choose to take her. But perhaps most telling of her powerlessness is her inability to enforce condom use, despite her knowledge of AIDS and how it is contracted.

The UNICEF survey mentioned above suggests that condom use by child prostitutes in the Dominican Republic is also erratic. Not only had up to 48 per cent of their sample in some areas fallen pregnant but, further, 20 per cent of girls interviewed in beach areas had contracted at least one form of venereal disease.

Many layers of parasites skim a living from sex tourism. Quite apart from the opportunities for local men to enrich themselves by actively or passively colluding with local women and children's sexual exploitation, the economic benefits for national and international capital are striking. Indeed, the prime beneficiaries of sex tourism are probably the airlines, which transport prostitute users half-way around the globe, the hotels (many of which are owned by international conglomerates) in which they stay, and the travel agents which arrange their flights and accommodation.

Source: www.vso.org.uk

ACTIVITY

Sociocultural impact

1 Select a relatively new tourist destination such as the Dominican Republic or Slovenia. Obtain some brochures that feature the destination you have selected and identify the key sociocultural values and expectations that are described in the brochure (for example, the country's religion, customs and traditional crafts).

2 Investigate the country from other sources that are not brochures, such as geography and history books. Can you identify any differences in the descriptions of sociocultural values and behaviour between the two sources of information?

3 Discuss the extent to which tourism might conflict with the host community or lead to a loss of cultural identity.

CASE STUDY

Castlefield regeneration

Castlefield in Central Manchester was originally a market town characterised by heavy industry. From the 1970s, as industry declined and many local manufacturing companies failed, a large number of buildings in the town became derelict and the amount of disused land increased. Manchester City Council identified Castlefield as a conservation area in 1979 and the area became Britain's first urban heritage park in 1982. In 1988, Castlefield was earmarked as an area for regeneration based upon leisure and tourism development within an industrial heritage context.

Castlefield has been successful in establishing itself as a tourist destination and attracts over two million visitors a year. The area has won a number of national awards for many of its attractions and developments, that include canal side cafes, quality accommodation, regenerated warehouses and buildings and a wide range of outdoor events.

Castlefield has benefited from excellent transport links (motorway, metrolink and train) and its proximity to two of the region's most popular attractions, Granada Studios and the Museum of Science and Industry.

The development of Castlefield into a thriving tourist destination has had both positive and negative impacts as Figure 2.8 shows.

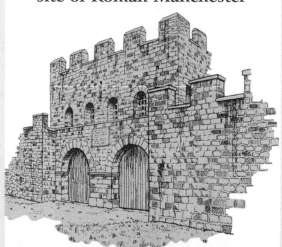

Castlefield

THE ROMAN TRAIL

welcome to mamucium

A 45 minute trail around the site of Roman Manchester

Castlefield Management Company
Castlefield Centre, 101 Liverpool Road,
Castlefield, Manchester. M3 4JN.
Tel : 0161 834 4026 Fax : 0161 839 8747

Registered Charity Number : 1054182

Castlefield Visitor Services are part funded by European Regional Development Fund.

Source: Castlefield Management Company,
Education Service factpack

Figure 2.8: Impact of tourism development in Castlefield

Positive impacts

Economic

- job creation
- attraction of inward investment
- encouragement of public, voluntary and private sector partnerships
- increase in facilities to support leisure and tourism trade
- secondary spend (spending on goods and services other than tourism, for example, in shops and hairdressers).

Environmental

- preserves areas of industrial heritage and encourages new uses
- has created green areas within the inner city
- improves the visual quality of the area
- has opened up the canals for new uses and encouraged wildlife
- encourages a mix of modern and ancient architecture.

Sociocultural

- encourages inward migration (new residents for employment and leisure)
- job creation
- increases pride in the city
- encourages cultural interaction.

Negative impacts

Economic

- seasonality
- visitor management and maintenance costs
- removes investment from other needy areas of city such as those that are seen as unsuitable for tourism development and remain rundown.

Environmental

- increased pollution (noise, litter, traffic)
- new areas often encourage crime and vandalism
- overcrowding.

Sociocultural

- residents antagonistic towards tourism
- potential for an increase in crime
- possible conflict with the host community.

WEBSTRACT

Tourism in the Gambia, the case for sustainability

The Gambia offers sun, sand and sea unlimited. But there's more to it than that. Adama Bah, founder member of Tourism Concern in the Gambia, explains what a more sustainable tourist industry could bring the Gambian people – and tourists too.

Q: What are some of the effects of tourism in the Gambia?

A: Tourism came to the Gambia through an investor, who came and found the Gambia ideal for tourism and decided to start a business there. There was no drive from the government to create economic development out of tourism; it was more an adventure for that investor. In 1971, a study was carried out by the United Nations to find out how the industry could best be developed to suit visitors coming to the Gambia. But the study did not look at how the industry could satisfy the basic needs and aspirations of the Gambian people; it was more directed at satisfying investors, so it came up with a one-sided vision geared only towards the sun, the beach and how friendly the local people are.

Following that model has had a lot of side-effects. Of course you cannot say that prostitution, drug addiction and all that was brought in by tourism, but it has certainly escalated, and right now we have a lot of young people who have no employment, no other means of survival but to look to the tourist. That is the cultural impact of tourism, where young people are reduced to begging and hassling tourists.

Q: At the same time, can tourism offer a country economic benefits?

A: The economic effects of tourism are indisputable; a lot of resources are generated through the development of tourism. The point is, what proportion of those resources stays in the country for the benefit of the people, and how much does the government use for the development of the people of that country? In the case of the Gambia, much more is siphoned off outside the country than stays behind: if you take into account the links between tourism and other areas of the economy it could be as much as 80 per cent that leaks overseas.

Some tourists who come to the Gambia are not just interested in the wine bar and the beach: they are also interested in going inland, in learning something, in having an exchange. This helps local people because they can build guest houses and small tourist resorts, provide the food from their own gardens and manage the whole thing themselves. The other advantage is that it is environmentally friendly.

Q: What sort of misconceptions do you face from Western tourists?

A: There are a lot of misconceptions about how Gambians live. People just think, 'Oh, they're African', but Africa is many different countries, many different cultures. So if you've been to Kenya it does not necessarily mean you understand what is happening in the Gambia. People need to know that.

Source: www.vso.org.uk

WEBSTRACT

Tourism development in the Gambia, Dawda's story

Before he started to speak about life in his village, a stone's throw from the multimillion dollar tourism development area, Dawda Gai took a deep breath. 'Forty years ago Kololi was a village with nothing more than 25 people. It was a small hamlet in the middle of the forest.

'We lived in huts that occupied a small piece of the land in an extended family setting. The rest of the land was used for farming cassava, sweet potatoes, maize, rice and tomatoes. Fruits like mangoes, guavas, avocados and plums grew in the wild. We looked after the forest and had farms on the outlying beaches. The young people were sent to guard the crops so that monkeys and birds would not destroy them. We lived in the heart of a forest. Today the distance to the capital, Banjul, is slight, but during our childhood it was titanic. There was no transport and bridges were made of wooden planks. Money was scarce, but we bartered our produce, grew our own food, caught our own fish in the tributary, drank milk from local herds and ate fruit from the forest.'

Dawda looked around him, and raised his eyes to the ceiling. 'Look at my house. The corrugated iron sheets are all worn out. This rainy season will be havoc as the roof leaks. I have trimmed my compound over and over again, selling bits off to make ends meet. My wife convinced me to transfer ownership to our children before we are left with no home of our own. Now it's only just big enough to hold my dilapidated house and another half-built shack. Everything is money. I do not have a job or business. Most of us are just sitting here from day to day without employment or cash to carry out petty trade. We are literally beggars. The sad thing is that our children are also joining the same boat. The Kololi of yesterday is no more. It is now a suburban area with some of the highest value land in the country. All the poor people are selling their land to rich prospectors. Apart from the swamps and vegetation which envelop the hotels, bars and restaurants, there is no forest now. Multistorey buildings have taken over the farm land, towering above the shacks of original settlers.

'There is improvement of infrastructure, I admit. But there are no primary schools or clinics in my village. Some people, taxi drivers, craftsmen and those able to establish restaurants, are gaining. But we, the traditional land holders in the area, are not. Here and there, a tourist gives gifts or pays for a child's schooling. That is all.

'Some years ago, they built a main road at the outskirts of the village heading towards the ocean. They first told us not to farm beyond the main road. We were not compensated for our rice and coos farms. Then fences were erected on our farm land. Eventually hotels emerged and the land was no longer ours. We later learnt that the government had transformed the whole area into a tourism development area, but we were left in the cold. Suddenly, we had no land to cultivate, no beaches to fish from and no employment. We have been like this for almost 20 years.

'When the hotels were established, our young people went to ask for work. But the hotel staff were provided by a hotel school – our children could not benefit. Our young people have been urbanised without employment. Many trawl the beaches in search of tourist friends day in and day out. Some girls even dress up to attract male tourists. At night, we see them marching across the village towards the bars and restaurants in search of western partners. It is not uncommon to find our young people taking drugs. Everything has changed.

'It is crazy – we hardly benefit from tourism at all. Most of the money goes out of the country. Even our farmers hardly benefit because so much of the food for tourists is imported. Tourism to the Gambia must change for the better. There is nothing idealistic about this. We have to make sure tourism is sustainable and viable for the future. For us, it's more or less a life or death struggle.'

Source: www.tourismconcern.org.uk

BUILD YOUR LEARNING

Read the webstracts about tourism development in the Gambia on pages 98 and 140–1. Identify the positive and negative effect that it has had economically, environmentally and socioculturally.

You may like to supplement your investigation by carrying out further research on tourism development in the Gambia, using articles in travel trade journals, newspaper reports and the internet.

Keywords and phrases

You should know the meaning of the words and phrases listed below. If you are unsure about any of them, go back through the last 12 pages to refresh your understanding.

- Conflicts with lost community

- Inappropriate development

- Increased cost of living

- Infrastructure improvements

- Living costs

- Loss of traditional employment opportunities

- Overcrowding

- Pollution

- Positive and negative impacts of tourism

- Traffic congestion

Managing the impact of tourism development

WHILE MANY OF THE EFFECTS OF tourism development may just happen, responsible tourism developers have the ability to manage and control its impact. A negative impact almost always occurs because irresponsible developers have not fully considered the implications of their initiatives. Similarly, where a positive impact is not maximised, this is largely due to the inefficiency of developers and their inability to identify appropriate objectives.

These are key issues in the successful development of tourism, both in the UK and globally. Effectively managed tourism development can bring great benefits to destinations, local communities, providers and the travel and tourism industry as a whole. We look next at some of the ways tourism development agents can maximise the positive and minimise the negative impact of tourism development initiatives.

Maximising positive impact

Responsible tourism developers are not only concerned with the potential positive impact of their initiatives, but also with ensuring that the positive impact is maximised. For example, the development of a new theatre may have a positive socio-cultural impact in that it provides an additional facility for the community. However, to maximise this impact the developer may look at ways of widening access to the new facility for local residents, for example by offering children's drama workshops or running loyalty schemes.

Maximising the positive impact of tourism development can involve a number of issues:

- retention of visitor spending
- investing tourism income in public projects
- widening access to facilities
- staff training, development and education.

Retention of visitor spending
Many tourism agents such as local authorities and local tourism groups are keen to ensure the **retention of visitor spending** so that visiting tourists spend their money at their destination rather than elsewhere. This clearly benefits the whole area by increasing tourism revenue and employment within the community. Therefore, one of the ways in which the positive impact of tourism development can be maximised is by

ensuring that visitors spend money at the destination by meeting all of their needs.

The development of purpose-built holiday resort centres is a good example of developers' attempts to maximise retention of visitor spending. Centres such as Disneyland, Paris, CenterParcs and Oasis have developed a wide range of facilities and services to ensure that visitors stay at the centre and spend their money there. Such facilities frequently include shops, catering, entertainment, special events and leisure facilities.

A recent study of the leakage of tourism revenue in Thailand estimated that up to 70 per cent of all of the money spent by foreign visitors went outside the country to foreign-owned tour operators, airline companies, and hospitality providers. Responsible tourism providers encourage foreign visitors to buy local goods and to use local services.

Investing tourism income
One way of maximising the positive impact of tourism development is by investing some of the income generated in projects that benefit the community. For example, planning permission for the development of a private sector tourist attraction may be granted on the condition that the developers improve the condition of access roads and parking facilities. You can see from Figure 2.9 that the Merry Hill Centre in Dudley invests a considerable amount of money in local community projects and improvements.

Sponsoring community projects

Look through some local and national newspapers and try to find examples of tourism organisations and providers that sponsor community projects.

Figure 2.9: Merry Hill sponsorship

Within the last year Merry Hill owners Chelsfield have sponsored community initiatives worth over £20,000 including:

- **Youth football academies** – Dudley MBC

- **Crime prevention poster design competition** – West Midlands Police

- **Young enterprise** – Dudley Training and Enterprise Council

- **School attendance campaign** – Dudley MBC

- **Provision of equipment** – Top Church Training Project

- **Provision of equipment** – Dudley Victim Support

- **Schools study resource pack** – Dudley Advisory Service/Sandwell LEA

- **Provision of fire training room** – West Midlands Fire

- **Dudley show** – Dudley MBC

- **110 not out** – Support for the Local History Group at Mount Pleasant School

These schemes highlight a few of the areas where contributions have helped benefit the local area and people.

Widening access

Another way of maximising the positive impact of tourism development is by **widening the access** that the local population has to the facilities and assets. For example, the development of Merlin Entertainments' Sea Life Centres in the UK has provided considerable educational access for local schools and colleges. Learning packs linked to the National Curriculum have been produced by Merlin Entertainments and discounted rates have been offered to educational groups.

Public sector tourism development agents are also often keen to maximise access for local communities. For example, the Brecon Beacons National Park Authority has developed a number of initiatives aimed at widening access.

CASE STUDY

Widening access

BRECON BEACONS NATIONAL PARK

The Brecon Beacons National Park Authority carried out extensive research in 1990 to evaluate the park's public right of way network. The results showed that:

- 43 per cent of the path links were obstructed

- 10 per cent of path links were completely impassable

- 56 per cent were difficult to follow on the ground

- only 14 per cent were signposted at the roadside.

After the research was carried out, considerable work was undertaken to widen access. By the end of 1996, 90 per cent of the path links were fully usable.

Staff training and development

Although tourism development almost always creates employment opportunities, there may also be a need for training and development of the local population so that they can take advantage of these employment opportunities. For example, a new tourist attraction may need guides, receptionists, cashiers, catering assistants, cleaning and maintenance staff. While members of the local community may have the general skills and personal qualities required, it is likely that they will need additional training to meet the responsibilities of their new job.

Training and education can take many forms. It may be provided by educational establishments such as universities and colleges, by individual tourism providers, by local authorities or by training organisations. The overall effect of maximising the level and quantity of training is to raise the general skills base of the local community. This can result in very positive social and economic benefits to the whole community and create a more employable workforce. Where training is combined with the opportunity to gain recognisable qualifications, the benefits to the individual are even greater, as the case study shows.

CASE STUDY

The HAVE project

While the hospitality industry is developing rapidly, there are not enough people with relevant qualifications to fill vacancies. Many key decision makers within the hospitality industry recognised the potential of providing students with the opportunity to achieve formal qualifications based on their work experience in the industry. With funding from the Department of Education and Employment, the Hotel, Catering and Institutional Management Association (HCIMA) launched the HAVE project in1998.

The Hospitality Adding Value for Education (HAVE) project aims to bridge the gap between employers, students and universities by providing valuable qualifications such as NVQs for students who have acquired skills through casual employment.

The HAVE pack explains to students how they can use their experiences of working in the hospitality industry to gain either NVQs or academic qualifications. The hope is that students will be able to use the skills that they have gained through training and experience and convert them into formal qualifications that will encourage them to follow a career in the hospitality industry.

ACTIVITY

Staff training and development

Investigate how a local tourism provider maximises the training and education of its workforce. For example, what training does the organisation provide? Does it arrange for external organisations to deliver training? Are staff encouraged to study for further qualifications such as NVQs or part-time courses with local colleges, training providers, or universities?

Training and employment of local people

Responsible tourism development can often lead to increased employment opportunities for the host community. This may be achieved by using their existing skills or by retraining them to provide new services to visiting tourists, as shown in the webstract on page 146.

WEBSTRACT

Training and employment of local people

Keeping tourists entertained, fed, watered, sheltered and moving involves a lot of people. Tourism provides millions of much-needed jobs and can transform standards of living. The World Travel and Tourism Council (1997) estimates that the industry, either directly or indirectly, creates one in nine jobs in the world economy today. Its employment impact is forecast to grow by 46 per cent by 2007, adding more than 100 million new jobs.

Tourism can be the making of small-scale entrepreneurs and their families. In Vietnam, for instance, where tourism was mainly government-owned ten years ago, 58 per cent of the industry is now in the private sector. Even the most basic jobs in tourism often have high social status, especially where there are few alternative opportunities. For women, especially in Muslim communities, tourism can also provide a lifeline to the wider world and to an independent income.

After I left school, I was a garden boy for two years, earning just Z$100 a month. As a sculptor, I am making between Z$4,000 and Z$5,000 in the same time. Now I am happy because I am working for myself. If you work for someone, you work hard and your boss gets richer. Things do get tough off-peak, but it is definitely better than being unemployed. My school friends are at home without jobs. Their lives are tough, they only earn once a year after harvest time when they sell their crops. They can't support their families, but I can. When I go home, 62 kms away, I take money, as well as essentials like sugar, flour, oil and soap. When I was a garden boy, I couldn't take them one cent. I couldn't even afford the bus journey home.

Admire Makuvise, a sculptor at Nyanga crafts village, Zimbabwe

Source: www.vso.org.uk

Tourism education

Much of the potential positive impact of tourism can be maximised by effective **tourism education**. There are numerous groups involved in the tourism industry whose activities include educating visitors so that they bring positive benefits to host communities rather than harmful effects. For example, Tourism Concern provides the following guide to better practice abroad, which it developed in consultation with local tourism groups.

- Save natural resources – try not to waste water; switch off lights and air conditioning if you go out.

- Support local trade and craftspeople – buy locally made souvenirs wherever possible, but avoid those made from ivory, fur, skins or other wildlife.

- Ask before taking photos or videos of people – don't worry if you don't speak the language; a smile and a gesture will be understood and appreciated.

- Don't give money or sweets to children – it encourages begging and demeans the child; a donation to a recognised project, health centre or school is a more constructive way to help.

- Respect local etiquette – in many countries loose clothes are preferable to skimpy tops or revealing shorts; and kissing in public is often inappropriate.

- Learn about the country – knowing about history and current affairs can help you appreciate many national idiosyncrasies and prevent misunderstandings.

ACTIVITY

Tourism education

Imagine that you are intending to go on holiday to the Gambia. You know it is a very poor country and you also know that tourism can help a country to develop economically. Look at the list of actions below that you could take to help Gambian people benefit from tourism. Rank them in order, starting with the one you would most prefer to take. Discuss your reasons for ranking the actions in the order you have chosen.

a. Bring pens and sweets to give to children you meet.

b. Agree to pay more for your accommodation.

c. Give money to a UK charity which supports development projects in the Gambia.

d. Make a point of using local shops, markets and restaurants.

e. Agree to pay a higher departure tax at the airport.

f. Give money or pens and notebooks to your tour operator to help a Gambian school.

g. Employ a bomsa (a local youth) to take you around the sights.

h. Decide to do something to challenge global inequality on your return.

Source: www.tourismconcern.org.uk

Minimising negative impact

Responsible, well-planned development can do much to minimise the negative impact of tourism development. This may include:

- planning control
- the use of the principles of sustainable tourism
- visitor and traffic management
- environmental impact assessment
- environmental audit.

Planning control

Most tourism development initiatives, whether to develop an entirely new tourism facility or convert existing land or buildings, require **planning permission**. One of the ways the negative impact of tourism can be minimised is by the careful control of planning permission.

Factors that may be considered can include the overall effect on the character of the area, the number of similar facilities already available, the destruction of existing buildings and land, and the effect of an increased number of visitors to the area.

Poor planning control may overlook some of these factors and allow tourism development to take place without recognition of the full impact that it will have.

For example, the conversion of some traditional pubs in quiet residential areas into themed pubs aimed at the youth market created many problems for some local communities.

One such community is in Farnham, Surrey where brewery owners have converted a local pub, the Wheatsheaf, into a themed pub and renamed it the Flyer. The pub has rapidly increased its level of trade by attracting young people from a wide area, particularly at weekends. Local residents in the elegant Georgian street report incidents of late night noise, drunkenness and vandalism. In this example, problems have been created not so much by the actual change of the pub's character, but by the type of customer it has attracted to the area and the conflict that has arisen with the local community.

ACTIVITY

Planning control

Look at a local newspaper and find articles about organisations that are seeking planning permission for a new development. Identify the factors that may affect the success of their application. For example, have local residents objected to the application and if so, on what grounds? As a group, discuss whether you think the proposed application will have a negative impact.

CASE STUDY

Queensland ecotourism plan

The Queensland ecotourism plan outlines the vision and policy for the future of ecotourism in Queensland. Its purpose is to provide a framework for planning, developing, managing, operating and marketing Queensland ecotourism.

The plan integrates environmental and economic considerations in natural areas in ways which ally environmental protection and the commercial viability of ecotourism operations. It complements the state government's economic development policy by providing opportunities for employment and development of small scale and larger scale businesses; ensuring skills development in ecotourism and natural area management; encouraging ecotourism in all Queensland regions; and favouring market enhancement while recognising ecotourism cannot occur without protection of the natural environment which attracts visitors.

Key policy issues which have been addressed in the development of the plan are:

- expanding the knowledge base and understanding of the natural resources and specific ecotourism opportunities within each biogeographic region

- managing natural areas for the various types of ecotourism

- developing diverse ecotourism opportunities which include a broader range of regions maintaining and, where necessary, providing additional infrastructure in popular ecotourism areas consistent with strategic and management plans and the protection of identified natural and cultural values

- improving and expanding basic tourism infrastructure in some of the more remote parts of the state

- improving environmental education and interpretation of the natural environment so visitors gain a greater understanding and appreciation of the environment

- developing ecotourism marketing plans through the auspices of regional tourist associations and regional economic development organisations as a means of targeting specific ecotourism opportunities within regions.

Implementation

The Queensland Tourist and Travel Corporation (QTTC) will be the agency responsible for coordinating the implementation of this plan. Each year, this agency will develop an operational plan in conjunction with the agencies and groups with major implementation responsibilities. These groups and agencies have been identified in relation to their policy, management and operational roles. Their implementation role will include consulting with the other relevant groups and agencies in Queensland.

Government departments and agencies identified as having responsibilities for implementation actions will, to some extent, be able to incorporate these within their current programs. New activities not currently included in departmental plans will need to be included in the development or review of corporate plans and budgets or applications for new funding. The QTTC will work with other agencies to ensure this occurs.

Implementation will need to be flexible to account for changes in priorities and available resources and will include a process of monitoring and annual reviews. Progress on the implementation of the plan will be reported annually to cabinet by the QTTC

Principles of sustainable tourism

It is now generally accepted that tourism needs to be effectively managed to ensure that the area's identity and natural resources are not damaged for future generations. The World Tourist Organisation defines sustainable tourism as:

tourism that meets the needs of present tourists and host regions while protecting and enhancing opportunity for the future.

Without an effective sustainable approach to tourism development, the impact can be devastating and permanent. Therefore, all agents involved in tourism development have the shared responsibility to maximise sustainability and make it a key objective.

The key sustainable development objective is to maintain the quality of the environment in which leisure takes place (and which is an essential part of the UK's attractiveness to tourists) for future generations to enjoy. This will contribute to the quality of life of those taking part in leisure activities, and maximise the economic contribution of tourism while protecting natural resources.

The British government recognised the need for sustainability and launched an initiative called A Better Quality Of Life in 1999. This stated that sustainable development means meeting four objectives at the same time, in the UK and the world as a whole:

- social progress which recognizes the needs of all

- effective protection of the environment

- prudent use of natural resources

- maintenance of high and stable levels of economic growth and employment.

It also set out some of the guiding principles for sustainability:

- putting people at the centre

- taking a long-term perspective

- taking account of costs

- creating an open and supportive economic system

- combating poverty

- respecting environmental limits

- using scientific knowledge

- making the polluter pay.

Sustainability has also been considered on a more global scale. In 1992, more than 150 governments from around the world agreed to work together on an action plan for sustainability in the twenty-first century. The resulting action plan is known as Agenda 21 and within the UK local authorities are expected to develop their own local Agenda 21. Bradford Council, for example has formulated its own policy to address local issues on sustainability (see Figure 2.10).

Figure 2.10: Extract from Bradford Council's sustainability policy

This council is committed to promoting a sustainable Bradford district. This requires the preservation and creation of jobs, the alleviation of want and fear, the promotion of equality, the valuing of diversity, and maintenance and development of the physical environment.

Partnerships for local regeneration

All regeneration programmes will be based on the principle of community participation to ensure that regeneration is sustainable.

All regeneration programmes will be based on the principle of partnership with other agencies to tackle all aspects of deprivation and disadvantage. As well as action on economic, social, environmental and housing issues, regeneration programmes will include measures to tackle health inequalities, such as heart health and accident prevention, and will include action to fight crime and deal with the problem of drug addiction.

We will ensure that all building programmes in regeneration areas are done in partnership with companies that provide training and jobs for the people who live there.

Wherever possible we will encourage the use of brownfield sites in preference to greenfield sites for new developments, in order both to regenerate the inner areas and protect the greenbelt.

We will carry out an audit of all council-owned land and property to ensure that its full potential to assist regeneration is realised.

CASE STUDY

Tourism development in Benidorm: past and present

Package holidays to the Spanish Costas boomed in the 1970s with the result that large areas of the coastline were quickly developed into tourist destinations. The small fishing village of Benidorm was transformed into one of the largest resorts aimed at attracting foreign package holidaymakers.

The sudden huge demand meant that large hotels and apartments had to be built hastily. In many buildings, quality was sacrificed in the rush to provide more bed spaces and maximise revenue from tourism. The landscape became unrecognisable as high-rise buildings dominated.

The tourist boom continued in Benidorm until the late 1980s. However, between 1988 and 1990, tourism dropped by 30 per cent. The area had been developed too quickly with little consideration for sustainability. Little of the original charm remained, and the infrastructure proved unable to cope with the huge influx of visitors.

As the original tourists began to go elsewhere, Benidorm started to attract the budget market, bringing hooliganism and rowdy behaviour. Many hotels and apartments remained empty.

In recent years, the Spanish authorities have taken a more responsible approach to tourism development based on sound sustainable principles. A programme for upgrading hotels has been introduced, traffic was rerouted away from the main tourist areas such as the beach, new quality leisure faciliites have been built, attractive outdoor relaxation areas created and an effective beach cleaning scheme resulted in Benidorm gaining Blue Flag status.

The major tourism development projects include creating an environmentally themed wildlife attraction, building an open-air arts centre, creating quality shops and restaurants and restoring Benidorm's old town to regenerate its local charm.

The action taken by the authorities has been largely successful, with the number of tourists visiting Benidorm each year steadily increasing. This increase has come resulted from targetting two new markets: local Spanish holidaymakers and retired foreign visitors who stay for long breaks out of season. However, the days when locals could be proud of their attractive fishing village are long gone.

▲ Benidorm before the tourist boom of the 1970s (top) and Benidorm today

ACTIVITY

Sustainable tourism

Try to find out the extent to which sustainable principles are considered in tourist development in a tourist destination area of your choice. You might find useful articles in your local newspaper or on the internet. Alternatively, you could contact local environmental pressure or community groups and ask for their opinions.

Can you identify any tourist development that does not comply with the World Tourist Organisation's definition of sustainable tourism as, 'tourism that meets the needs of present tourists and host regions while protecting and enhancing opportunity for the future'?

Visitor and traffic management

Road travel has risen by more than a third since 1996, with individuals making journeys that average a total of over 2,600 miles per year. Air travel has also risen considerably and UK airports have seen a threefold increase in passengers over the last 20 years.

The impact that this growth has is usually concentrated in particular destinations at specific times of the year. A growing concern of many agents involved in tourism development is how this seasonal increase in visitors and traffic can be effectively managed to minimise the negative impact on destinations. This is known as **visitor and traffic management**.

Many local authorities have made specific areas of towns and cities pedestrian zones. However, this raises the problem of how visitors in cars actually get to the main tourist areas. While it would be counterproductive to discourage visitors in cars, many current initiatives are designed to minimise the effect of excessive traffic in busy destinations. Measures taken include:

- park-and-ride services, where visitors park on the outskirts of a destination and make the remainder of their journey by bus

- improved public transport

- designated drop-off points and parking for coaches (since 50 visitors on one coach is preferable to 25 couples arriving in cars)

- improved road systems such as city ring roads that help to keep traffic away from the main tourist areas.

Managing the number of visitors in a destination is also a key issue. In an ideal world a destination would attract just the right number of visitors to fill all of the hotels and tourist facilities so that tourism revenue is maximised. In reality, many destinations experience too many visitors at peak times, resulting in overcrowding and unsatisfied customers.

In some destinations, such as Bermuda, authorities have taken dramatic action to manage visitor numbers. The Bermudan authorities have only authorised the building of an extra 464 hotel beds in the last 25 years and have set a maximum of 10,000 bed spaces for visitors to the island. The number of cruise ship passengers allowed on the island is limited to 150,000 a year.

The management of visitor numbers has undergone rapid change and improvement in the last few years, with the introduction of **destination management systems**. These are computer-based systems that provide instant access to direct reservations with tourism providers as well as information on availability and visitor profiles. One of the main destination management systems used in the UK is CTV.

CASE STUDY

CTV destination management system

Destinations can manage availability to beat the bookability problem. A computerised booking system offers accommodation providers the opportunity to manage their own availability and prices as they wish; as often as they like; simply using a touch-tone phone. Those providers not connected can be manually updated by staff with the use of a hot key. Flexible set-up options allow the destination to dictate how the availability information is used. When used correctly this can almost eliminate the possibility of calling a provider that does not have the necessary bed. In terms of visitor management, this system allows destinations to regulate the number of visitors to the area and reduce overcrowding at peak times.

Visitor and traffic management also includes procedures used to inform incoming visitors of the accessibility of specific areas. For example, radio stations frequently broadcast regional traffic reports and car parking availability and roadside display boards such as those used on motorways provide a similar service.

ACTIVITY

Visitor and traffic management

Select a large town or city in your area and investigate how incoming road traffic is managed. For example, how are visitors informed about long and short-stay parking facilities and park-and-ride services? Is information displayed only within the town or on approach roads as well? Are visitors given sufficient warning when car parks are full and provided with suitable alternatives?

Environmental impact assessment

Many developers concerned about the potential negative effects of tourism development on the environment carry out **environmental impact assessments** (EIA). The developers evaluate the overall effect of development and identify any ways in which negative impact could be minimised. Some of the issues that EIA considers include:

- the costs of the development

- all of the possible benefits and who will specifically benefit

- those who may be adversely affected by the development

- whether there is a different way of developing the initiative that would have fewer negative impacts

- how the negative impacts may be minimised.

ACTIVITY

Environmental impact assessment

Go back to the case study about the Millennium Dome (see pp. 125–8). Using the information provided, imagine that you are carrying out an environmental impact assessment before the plans for the dome were finalised. What key issues would you identify?

Environmental audit

Environmental audit is a process whereby an organisation identifies all of its key activities, the effects that these activities have on the environment and how the effects can be managed to minimise their negative impact. Many tourism development agents are beginning to recognise the importance of environmental auditing, as the article shows.

Silifke is 250 km west of Antalya at the edge of the Taurus mountains. As well as a folkloric past and sandy beaches, the region includes the Goksu Peninsula, a protected area of significant importance. Like many Mediterranean cities, Silifke faces environmental, economic and social problems. Inadequate infrastructure impedes investment. Poor funding restricts maintenance of historic sites. There is insufficient accommodation. Waste disposal is uncontrolled. Government aid is negligible.

Tourism is seen as a major factor in improving living standards. As a major step towards Local Agenda 21 in July 1995, the Silifke municipality drafted an environmental audit; a forward-looking plan for the sustainable development of the town, obtained in consultation with its citizens. Currently the municipality is meeting with potential investors in tourism ventures.

The plan promotes the green strategy of Silifke, with the involvement of the whole community. It emphasises such environmental priorities as the improvement of infrastructure and the protection of the delta, wildlife and archaeological sites.

Source: Tourism Concern, Summer 1998

The total system, of which environmental audit is a key feature, is often referred to as an environmental management system.

The standard ISO 14001 (previously known as BS 7750) was introduced in 1992 with the aim of encouraging organisations to look critically at the impact that they have on the environment and at ways they can improve their performance while minimising negative environmental impact. Organisations that have achieved this standard have demonstrated that they are able to regulate the effect that they have on the environment.

The Department of Transport, Environment and the Regions (DETR) suggests six steps to effective environmental management and auditing.

Step one involves defining the activity, product and services. This requires organisations to list all activities, products and services irrespective of their impact on the environment. So, for example, some activities, products and services for a restaurant might include:

- purchasing, delivery and storage of raw ingredients
- preparation of food items (these would be further broken down according to each food item)
- laundering of tablecloths, napkins, uniforms, etc
- disposal of food waste
- disposal of packaging waste
- washing-up of equipment, crockery and cutlery
- cleaning of furniture, fittings and fixtures.

Step two involves identifying the environmental aspects associated with each activity, product or service. These can be any aspects of an organisation's activity, product or service which can have a positive or negative impact on the environment and are split into inputs and outputs.

Inputs are what is needed for an activity to take place, for example:

- energy use (electricity, fuel, renewable)
- water consumption (mains, wells)
- use of fuels (petroleum, diesel)
- land use (natural habitats, open space, landscapes, sensitive areas, agriculture)
- use of raw or secondary materials (chemicals, oils, aggregates, metals, plastic, paper)
- services from suppliers
- use of natural resources.

Outputs are the end effects that are produced by the activity, for example:

- wastes and by-products (handling, storage and transportation)
- discharges to water courses, sewers or drains (controlled or uncontrolled)
- impact on land (contamination, natural habitats, open space, agriculture, sensitive areas)
- emissions to air of carbon dioxide, ozone depleting substances and other pollutants
- generation of noise, dust, odour or vibration
- transport
- products (packaging, transport, use and disposal)
- impact on natural resources and wildlife
- impact on built environment
- visual impact
- public (influence, education, regulation, enforcement).

Step three involves identifying the associated environmental impact of each aspect. The environmental impact is the change that takes place in the environment as a result of the aspect. For example:

- contamination of soil or water
- release of carbon dioxide to the atmosphere
- injury to wildlife
- destruction of natural habitat
- conservation of energy
- waste minimisation
- reduction in vehicle emissions and other pollutants.

Step four involves determining the significance of the environmental impacts. This means evaluating the importance of and likely impact of each activity, product or service. For example, how probable is a negative impact and how severe would it be?

Step five requires the organisation to draw up a register listing the aspects of its operation (activities, products and services) that are likely to have a significant impact on the environment.

Once the register is complete (**step six**) the organisation can begin to set specific objectives and targets for each significant aspect identified.

Using the chart in Figure 2.11, organisations can assess the significance of their environmental impact factors by adding up the ranking scores from each. The higher the score, the more significant the impact.

The six-step procedure set out above gives an idea of some of the very complex activities undertaken by large organisations when implementing environmental management systems and carrying out environmental audits. However, even the smaller tourism providers can use the concept of environmental audit to ensure that they minimise the negative impact that their activities have on the environment. This can be achieved by organisations asking themselves:

- what do we do?
- what possible effects could these activities have on the environment?
- how can we manage these effects to minimise their negative impacts?

ACTIVITY

Environmental audit

The takeaway fast food industry has expanded considerably during the last decade. In most large towns, visitors and locals can choose from a wide range of different themed and ethnic versions of the takeaway product; Indian, Chinese, Greek, burgers, fish and chips and pizza, to name but a few. One characteristic that they all have in common is that the operators need to provide packaging to allow customers to carry the food away.

An environmental audit of the operators' activities would highlight the potential for negative environmental impact. As a group, discuss the possible impact and identify how it could be managed to minimise negative effects. You should consider the materials used for the packaging, as well as the disposal of packaging after use. You might like to contact a local takeaway fast food outlet and find out how it is trying to minimise its negative impact on the environment.

Figure 2.11: Assessment tool for determining significance of environmental impact

Description of Effect Likelihood	Rank	Likelihood of occurrence	Rank	Likelihood of detection	Rank	Severity of consequence /nuisance
■ Negligible or no impact ■ No breach of legislation ■ Emergency situations would cause a breach of policy or procedure	0	None	0	Certain	0	None
■ Very small impact ■ Immediate action possible ■ Emergency situations would cause a breach of legislation ■ Results in breach of own policy or procedures under abnormal conditions	1	Very low	1	Very high	1	Minor
■ Small impact ■ Results in breach of legislation under abnormal conditions ■ Results in breach of own policy or procedures under normal conditions	2	Low	2	High	2	Low
■ Moderate impact ■ Activity has impact under normal operating conditions ■ Results in breach of legislation under abnormal conditions ■ No previous breach of legislation	3	Moderate	3	Moderate	3	Moderate
■ Severe impact ■ Results in breach of legislation under abnormal conditions ■ History of past breaches of legislation	4	High	4	Low	4	High
■ Extensive impact ■ Results in beach of legislation under normal operating conditions ■ History of past breaches of legislation	5	Very high	5	Very low	5	Very high

BUILD YOUR LEARNING

1 Select a tourist destination either in the UK or abroad for investigation. Explain how the development of tourism in your chosen area has had a positive impact in terms of:

- economic impact (such as increased income and employment)
- environmental impact (such as improved assets, landscaping)
- sociocultural impact (such as preservation of local customs).

2 Explain how the development of tourism in your chosen area has had a negative impact in terms of:

- economic impact (such as less traditional jobs, higher living costs)
- environmental impact (such as traffic congestion, pollution)
- sociocultural impact (such as crime, loss of cultural identity).

Obtain relevant statistics such as employment figures, property prices, visitor spending to support your findings. You might use pictures and press cuttings to illustrate key issues, for example, before and after photographs of tourism development and letters in newspapers that praise or criticise specific tourism development.

3 Select two tourism agents within your chosen area. One should be from the private sector and one from the public sector (for example, a privately owned tourist attraction and a local authority's tourism department). Explain how each has:

a) attempted to maximise the positive impact of tourism development by:

- maximising the retention of visitor spending at the destination
- investing the income from tourists in public and social projects for local communities
- widening access to facilities and assets
- staff training, development and education.

b) attempted to minimise the negative impact of tourism development by:

- use of planning control
- use of the principles of sustainable tourism
- visitor and traffic management
- environmental impact assessment
- environmental audit.

4 Suggest ways in which you think the positive impact could be further maximised and the negative impact further minimised in your chosen area.

Keywords and phrases

You should know the meaning of the words and phrases listed below. Go back through the last 13 pages to refresh your understanding if necessary.

- Agenda 21
- Destination management systems
- Environmental audit
- Environmental impact assessment (EIA)
- Investing tourism income
- Planning permission
- Retention of visitor spending
- Sustainable tourism
- Tourism education
- Visitor and traffic management
- Widening access

Preview

We are going to explore the range of holiday destinations that are visited by UK tourists and to identify the key reasons why people want to visit them. When you have completed this chapter you will be able to locate the most popular holiday resorts and to understand their attraction for different tourist groups.

Although the UK is part of Europe, most examples in this chapter reflect the title, they are worldwide travel and tourism destinations. Hence, this chapter focuses on major short-haul continental European and long-haul destinations, rather than tourist destinations in the UK.

The travel file (pp. 203–25) explains the importance of travel and tourism in five popular tourist destinations visited by UK tourists (two short-haul and three long-haul). The information will help you structure your portfolio assessment requirements for this unit, although you may want to research different tourist destinations.

To complete the assessment for this unit you will need to gather a wide range of information in order to investigate four different worldwide travel and tourism destinations. Advice on sources of information can be found in the resource and internet directory on pp. 460–4. The portfolio assessment for this unit is shown on pp. 454–5.

Worldwide travel destinations

Introduction

A **TRAVEL DESTINATION** IS THE end point of a journey. The purpose of that journey may be for a holiday, business or to visit friends or relatives (VFR). The distance travelled may be relatively short, or include a long journey to far-away continents. A **tourism destination** combines elements of travel with the mix of features, attractions and facilities that make the destination appealing to tourists.

Tourism destinations are diverse in their character and appearance. They can be grouped into five main types:

- towns and cities, for example, London, Edinburgh Paris, Vienna, Madrid, Prague, Athens, Berlin, Rome, New York

- seaside resorts, for example, Blackpool, Benidorm, Nice, San Tropez, Bondi Beach, Miami

- purpose-built resorts, for example, Alton Towers, Disneyland Paris, Disneyland World Resort

- countryside areas, for example, Lake District, Alps, Grand Canyon, Ayres Rock

- historical and cultural destinations, for example, Bath, Pompeii, Pisa, Athens, Jerusalem.

A further distinction between the types of destination can be made based on the duration and distance travelled by air transport. **Short-haul** and **long-haul destinations** were defined in unit 1 (p. 5). Popular short-haul destinations from the UK include resorts in Spain, France, Greece and Italy. The five-hour flying time extends this list beyond European countries to include Iceland and North Africa. Popular long-haul destinations visited by UK residents include North America, the Caribbean and Australia.

The International Air Traffic Association (IATA) is a voluntary body which represents 80 per cent of the world's airlines operating on international routes and aims to promote safe, regular and economic air travel.

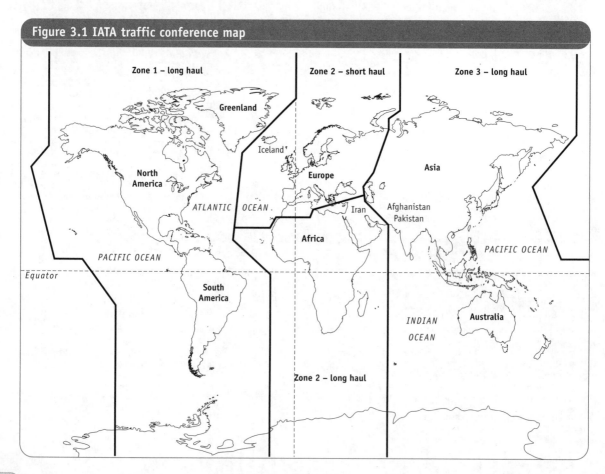

Figure 3.1 IATA traffic conference map

IATA divides the world up into three zones, known as **traffic conference areas** (see Figure 3.1). The UK is placed in the northern half of zone 2. Long-haul travel is to those countries which are in zones 1 and 3 or in the southern half of zone 2. Traffic conference areas represent the major airline routes and are used as the basis for drawing up air fares and timetables.

The pattern of where people go on holiday is mainly due to the geographical position of the UK. We are more likely to visit the countries closest to us than those which are further away. As the UK is an island, the British cannot simply drive across a border, like travellers in mainland Europe.

The most popular tourist destinations from the UK are France and Spain. Although more day trips are made to France, Spain is the top holiday destination for UK tourists, with a 26 per cent share of the holiday market in 1998. This includes its two main sets of islands, the Balearics (Mallorca, Ibiza and Formentera) and the Canary Islands (Lanzarote, Fuerteventura, Gran Canaria, Tenerife, La Palma, La Gomera and El Hierro). France, the second most popular destination, hosts 23 per cent of the UK holiday market. Spain has a greater share of the holiday market compared to France because more holidays to Spain are promoted as package holidays. The market shares of the leading tourist destinations are shown in the activity on p. 160.

ACTIVITY

Traffic conference areas

1 Use an atlas to identify ten countries that appear in each IATA zone.

2 Identify which countries you consider to be long-haul and which you consider to be short-haul.

3 Complete the following table, identifying whether the journey involved is short-haul or long-haul.

	Short-haul	Long-haul
Mr and Mrs Mitchell fly from Manchester to Florida on a two-week fly-drive		
Ramesh flies from Gatwick to visit his mother in India		
Jasmine flies from Heathrow to Australia to begin her round-the-world trip		
Mr White flies from Newcastle to Berlin to attend a business conference		
John flies from Bristol to visit his sister in Dublin		
Ruth and Harry fly from Heathrow to Miami to begin a Caribbean cruise		
Mrs Madhani flies from Heathrow to Paris to visit her daughter		
Enasha flies from Stansted to holiday in Greece		

ACTIVITY

Leading destinations for UK tourists

Country	1992 '000	%	1998 '000	%	% change 1992–98
Spain	5,119	22	8,500	27	+66
France	5,740	25	7,500	23	
United States	1,674	7	2,200	7	
Greece	1,821	8	1,700	5	
Italy	780	3	1,200	4	
Portugal	1,109	5	1,150	4	
Turkey	282	1	1,100	3	
Cyprus, Malta, Gibraltar	1,200	5	1,000	3	
Republic of Ireland	625	3	1,000	3	
The Netherlands	722	3	750	2	
Belgium	415	2	550	2	
Germany	565	2	500	2	
Eastern Europe	327	1	300	1	
Other short-haul	1,117	5	1,250	4	
Long-haul*	1,740	8	3,300	10	+90
Total	23,236,000	100%	32,000,000	100%	+38

* other than the United States

Source: Marketing The Travel Business, Mintel 1998

1 Look at the table and, in small groups, discuss why Spain and France are by far the most popular destinations for UK tourists travelling abroad. Make a list of your reasons and compare them with the rest of the group.

2 Calculate the percentage change of visitor numbers between 1992 and 1998 for each of the destinations listed. Percentage change is calculated using the formula:

$$\text{percentage increase} = \frac{\text{1998 figure} - \text{1992 figure}}{\text{1992 figure}} \times 100$$

3 Which countries have seen a rapid increase in the number of tourists from the UK between 1992 and 1998? Make a list of the factors that you think have contributed to the increasing popularity of these countries.

Short-haul destinations

Most of the most popular holiday destinations are short-haul. This is because accessibility plays an important part in their popularity. Countries which are closer to the UK, such as France, Belgium and the Netherlands have an advantage over destinations further afield. The growth of short-haul city break holidays to these countries, which are often taken as second holidays, is due largely to their accessibility. However, countries like Spain and Greece have other advantages over our closest short-haul destinations. They have warmer climates and are the most popular package holiday destinations for UK tourists. The travel files on pp. 203–11 describe two popular short-haul destinations, Paris and Benidorm.

Long-haul destinations

There has been a significant growth in the popularity of long-haul holiday destinations outside of Europe in recent years. It is important to be able to identify the most popular long-haul destinations at any given point in time and the reasons why they have become important. We will consider three key long-haul destination areas: North America (USA and Canada), the Caribbean and Australasia (Australia and New Zealand).

During the 1990s the trend was for tourists to travel further in search of a variety of different resorts for their holidays. Tourists are now more prepared to endure longer flights and transfer times to reach their holiday destination. For example, long-haul destinations such as Florida and the Caribbean have become popular, and this has affected tourist numbers to some of the more traditional Mediterranean resorts.

Figure 3.2 shows that the most popular long-haul destination is the United States, and Canada the second most popular. The Caribbean is the third, if all the countries of the Caribbean are grouped together. The table shows how popular the Dominican Republic is with UK tourists. Other important Caribbean islands include Jamaica, St Lucia and Barbados. Mexico has overtaken some of the Caribbean islands as an alternative holiday destination.

Africa also remains popular with UK tourists. Kenya

Figure 3.2: Leading long-haul destinations, 1996–98

Destination	1996 '000s	%	1998 '000s	%	% change in 1996–98
US	1,995	42.0	2,200	40.0	+10
Canada	275	6.0	350	6.5	+27
India	222	4.5	250	4.5	+13
Tunisia	222	4.5	250	4.5	+13
Egypt	187	4.0	200	3.5	+7
Dominican Republic	95	2.0	190	3.5	+100
Australia	123	2.5	150	3.0	+22
South Africa	96	2.0	140	2.5	+46
Thailand	112	2.0	130	2.5	+16
Kenya	85	2.0	100	2.0	+18
Other Caribbean*	332	7.0	400	7.0	+20
Latin America	125	2.5	200	3.5	+60
Middle East	142	3.0	160	3.0	+13
Other**	749	16.0	780	14.0	+4
Total	4,760,000	100%	5,500,000	100%	+16

*   excluding the Dominican Republic

**   other countries in Asia and Africa and all long-haul cruises

Source: Marketing The Travel Business, Mintel 1998

is the leading destination offering safaris, beach holidays or a combination of both. Egypt is included in the statistics for Africa and is a major attraction, although tourism figures have continued to suffer since the terrorist attack on a group of tourists at Luxor in 1997. A market for tourism is beginning to emerge in South Africa. Since the country abandoned its apartheid policies, the number of holiday bookings from the UK has increased by 46 per cent.

Despite the increasing popularity of long-haul destinations, the actual numbers of UK tourists visiting these countries are significantly smaller compared to the short-haul market.

The travel files on pp. 211–25 provide examples of three of the most popular long-haul destinations visited by UK tourists, North America, the Caribbean and Australasia. What these leading long-haul destinations have in common is the fact that they are English speaking. This suggests that the British prefer a degree of familiarity when they are on holiday.

Countries with colonial or Commonwealth connections are still important for the UK as well as other countries. The **Commonwealth** is an association of British-ruled territories (now sovereign states) and countries which depend on Britain and which recognise a British King or Queen as their own head of state. Such countries include Canada, Australia, many Caribbean islands and India. Visiting friends and relatives (VFR) is still an important factor in the tourism of these countries.

BUILD YOUR LEARNING

End of section activity

Look at Figure 3.2 and comment on the general trend of the leading long-haul destinations between 1996 and 1998.

Using statistics to support your answer, identify which countries have seen the highest increase in the numbers of visitors from the UK. Suggest reasons why these countries have seen an increase.

Keywords and phrases

You should know the meaning of the words and phrases listed below. If you are unsure about any of them, go back through the last five pages of the unit to refresh your understanding.

■ Long-haul destination

■ Short-haul destination

■ The Commonwealth

■ Tourism destination

■ Traffic conference area

■ Travel destination

Types of tourist destination

WE IDENTIFIED EARLIER that there are five main types of tourist destination:

- towns and cities
- seaside resorts
- purpose-built resorts
- countryside areas
- historical and cultural destinations.

Let's look at each of these in detail.

Towns and cities

Towns and cities have grown in importance as tourism destinations in recent years, especially for short breaks. The most popular European cities for British tourists are Paris, Amsterdam and Bruges. Amsterdam has been such a popular city break destination that at peak times most hotels have been fully booked. The shortage of beds in Amsterdam has enabled Bruges to draw tourists away from the Dutch city.

Although most visits to towns and cities by UK tourists are short-haul, some long-haul destinations are becoming increasingly popular. Visits to New York for shopping and entertainment have increased in popularity and New York moved up from the fifteenth most visited city in 1998 to the eleventh most visited city in 1999.

Figure 3.3 represents popular cities in terms of numbers of visitors, however, there are several cities which are not shown in the table but which have experienced dramatic increases in the numbers of visitors from the UK.

Figure 3.3: Top city breaks, January–June 1999	
1	Paris (1)
2	Amsterdam (2)
3	Bruges (3)
4	Brussels (4)
5	Rome (6)
6	Dublin (5)
7	Venice (8)
8	Barcelona (7)
9	Madrid (10)
10	Lille (14)
11	New York (15)
12	Prague (10)
13	Florence (13)
14	Seville (18)
15	Vienna (12)
1998 position in brackets	

Source: Travel Trade Gazette 12 July 1999

ACTIVITY

Popular destinations

Look at Figure 3.3 showing the top city breaks and identify which destinations are short-haul and which are long-haul.

Which cities increased in popularity between 1998 to 1999?

Suggest reasons why the top four destinations remain so popular with tourists from the UK.

People visit towns and cities for a variety of reasons including:

- sight-seeing
- night-life
- shopping
- special events
- theatre and concerts
- restaurants
- business
- pilgrimage.

Sight-seeing
Sight-seeing is one of tourism's main activities. Sights and attractions are often listed in guide books which suggest what to look for and how to get there.

Local companies organise tours around local sights, offering commentary and additional information. This is often an educational experience which helps tourists to understand something of the geography and culture of the area. Open-top tour buses are popular in many European capital cities. In Paris, tourists can buy a ticket for L'Open Tour, with the choice of three routes which take in sights such as the Arc de Triomphe, the Eiffel Tower, the Pompidou Centre and Notre Dame. Commentary is offered in both French and English.

Several tour operators offer a range of escorted tours for UK tourists who have not experienced a long-haul holiday before and for those visiting exotic countries. The main purpose of such a holiday is for sightseeing but with the benefits of having a guide who can advise on what to see and do. Such holidays are usually based around a comprehensive itinerary.

Night-life
Night-life is popular with tourists. Attractions include nightclubs, bars, theatres and casinos. Many European nightclubs have become popular with tourists by attracting internationally famous DJs and promoting themselves to an international audience. Promotions on radio, television and the internet have made islands like Ibiza popular with those seeking a range of top nightclubs. San Antonio in Ibiza boasts some of the most well-known nightclubs in Europe, including Cafe del Mar, Mambo and Savannah, which attract large numbers of tourists from the UK.

Shopping
Shopping has become one of our most popular leisure pursuits. Cheaper prices attract large numbers of people to France from the UK to visit hypermarkets offering a large range of discounted goods. This trend attracted UK-based chains such as Tesco and Sainsbury's to France. They have opened stores at Calais and other ferry ports or train stations and promote them to tourists travelling from the UK.

Paris and Milan are famous for their fashion industries and attract a significant number of visitors who seek to buy something that they could not purchase at home. People will travel large distances if they think that they will be able to buy something that is different or unique.

As we have seen, long-haul destinations are also becoming popular shopping destinations. Visits to New York are often advertised in national newspapers around Christmas time. Such packages include two or three nights accommodation in a centrally located hotel and the cost of transfers. The USA is also popular with visitors who want to save money by buying discounted goods from large factory outlet shopping centres. These centres are also becoming popular in the UK.

Some of the major items to purchase on holiday are souvenirs and gifts for friends and relatives. Tourists searching for a memento of their visit or a present for a friend often look for souvenirs that are unique to the area. Monuments and famous buildings are usually a focus for reproductions; for example, the Eiffel Tower in Paris and the Leaning Tower in Pisa. Most resorts and destinations sell a range of merchandise, with logos and pictures designed to evoke a memory of a visit.

Special events
Special events such as sporting competitions and festivals attract large numbers of domestic and incoming tourists. Large scale international events such as the Olympic Games attract millions of visitors. The World Cup held in France in 1998 attracted a total of 2.5 million spectators over a five-week period at the ten football stadiums used for the competition. Many English football fans travelled to Europe to support their national team and combined watching football matches with a short city-break holiday. The World Cup helped to promote French tourist resorts to a worldwide audience, as people who could not travel to the games saw images of France on their television screens and are now more aware of its attractions. The 2000 Olympic Games in Sydney will bring vast numbers of tourists to the area and help promote the city as a major tourist destination.

Theatres and concerts
Theatre shows and concerts in Europe are often advertised in UK newspapers offering concert tickets, transport and accommodation. Package deals to European concert venues are very popular, especially if the UK tour dates are inconvenient to those who wish to see their favourite band or singer perform.

Restaurants
Restaurants are popular with tourists. Even on self-catering holidays, tourists enjoy the choice of whether to eat in or out. Visiting another country and eating local dishes is part of the holiday experience. Many popular dishes in the UK are based on food from abroad that has become popular as more British people have travelled overseas. Tourists travelling to Italy often order a pizza in a restaurant because they are familiar with what they are ordering and want to experience what it is like to eat an authentic Italian pizza.

Business tourism
Business tourism is a major reason why people travel to towns and cities. Business tourism is based on the needs of the business traveller and includes travel for the purposes of meetings, conferences, trade fairs and exhibitions. Business people need to stay overnight due

to the distance travelled or because business is conducted over more than one day.

The amount earned by hotels and conference centres can be huge due to the large numbers of people and services involved. Business meetings may require accommodation, caterers and business services from the hotel, including secretarial support and the hire of audio-visual equipment.

In 1987, 13.3 per cent of all visits abroad by UK residents were on business. This compares to 15.6 per cent in 1997.

ACTIVITY

Business tourism

1 Look at Figure 3.4 and suggest reasons why the number of UK residents travelling abroad on business has increased in the last ten years.

2 Identify five short-haul and five long-haul destinations that you think attract large numbers of business tourists.

3 Suggest the benefits to towns and cities of promoting themselves as international conference and exhibition centres.

◀ There is a growing market for package deals to overseas music events

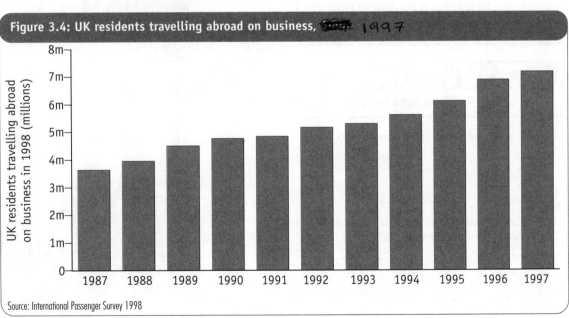

Figure 3.4: UK residents travelling abroad on business, ~~1987~~ 1997

Source: International Passenger Survey 1998

Pilgrimage tourism

People may have religious reasons for visiting towns and cities, for example, Christians who make pilgrimages to the shrines of Lourdes in France, or Muslims who travel to Mecca.

CASE STUDY

Lourdes

The tourist industry in Lourdes dates back to 1858 when Bernadette Soubirous, a local peasant, had a series of visions and discovered the healing powers of a local spa. The development of rail travel made the town accessible to pilgrims from all over France. They later came from Europe and North America. Lourdes has developed as one of the world's most famous Catholic shrines and attracts over four million tourists during the pilgrimage season, between April and October. A total room allocation of over 30,000 beds and a further 10,000 in private apartments and lodgings is provided to meet the needs of this influx of people.

ACTIVITY

Short-haul beach resorts

1 Select two short-haul beach resort areas from Figure 3.5 and explain the range of features that you think make each of them appealing to UK tourists. Compare the main strengths and weaknesses of each resort area.

2 What are the main types of customers that you think your chosen resorts attract?

3 Identify the peak holiday season for UK tourists for each resort. You may find it useful to look at brochure prices to identify the peak season.

Seaside resorts

In the past 20 years, the number of people taking their holidays at UK seaside resorts has declined. The number of trips to the seaside is, however, at a similar level to those taken in the 1980s. This figure is maintained by day visitors. The number of nights spent in British seaside resorts has fallen by approximately 20 per cent.

Whilst there has been a decline in the number of British seaside holidays, visits to short-haul and long-haul seaside resorts remain popular. The most popular short-haul beach resort destinations are found in Spain, Greece and Turkey. Popular long-haul beach resort destinations include Florida, the Caribbean islands, Bermuda and the Seychelles. The popularity of these areas is due to a combination of cheaper airfares, good levels of accommodation and almost guaranteed sunny weather for large parts of the year. Some of the most popular short-haul beach destinations areas are shown in Figure 3.5.

Figure 3.5: Popular short-haul beach resort destination areas

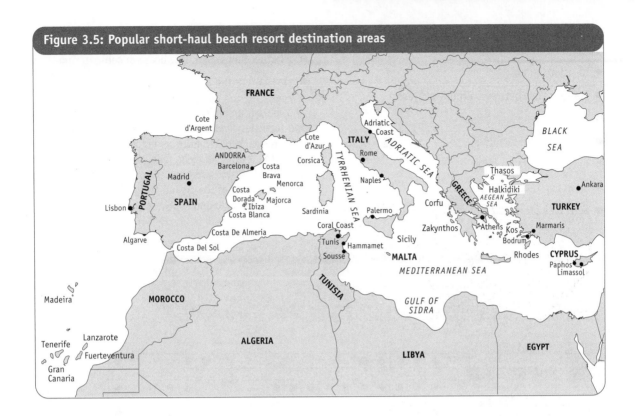

Long-haul beach resort destinations provide a warm, exotic location for UK tourists during the winter months. The extract from the First Choice Winter Sun brochure shows how tour operators describe these resorts in order to attract UK tourists.

The traditional beach holiday favoured by the sun worshipper has been modified over the last few years by increasing concerns over skin cancer and the rise of beach boredom syndrome. The link between skin damage and sunlight has been proven and many beaches now provide shady areas with parasols to offer shelter from the intensity of the midday sun. Many brands of sun cream are available and are an essential accessory to any summer sun holiday.

Beach boredom describes the lack of entertainment facilities or excitement provided in or around a beach. Many tourists are seeking local entertainment and attractions as well as the sun, sea and sand experience.

Holiday brochures promote a range of activities alongside views of sandy beaches and pictures of impressive looking hotels. The most detailed of these are the all-inclusive brochures for holidays in which all meals, drink and activities are paid for in advance. The level of detail varies between holiday brochures

If you're longing to laze on sun-drenched beaches, take a dip in warm waters, explore exotic landscapes and experience vibrant cultures, our Distant Shores collection is definitely for you.

Leave the cold British winter behind you and seek out the gorgeous Caribbean beaches of the Dominican Republic or Margarita, or explore the ancient cities and beautiful shores of Mexico. On the other side of the globe, Sri Lanka offers truly breathtaking scenery, while Goa is a tropical paradise. Wherever you decide to go you're due to receive a warm and friendly welcome.

Source: First Choice Winter Sun 1999–2000

although they all tend to give the same basic information. This includes:

- location
- transfer time between airport and resort
- distance to nearest beach
- description of facilities
- entertainment on offer
- sports on offer
- activities for children
- description of accommodation
- whether half-board, full-board or self-catering
- standard rating of accommodation.

The Airtours guide identifies the range of activities and facilities available to tourists staying on an all-inclusive package. To encourage tourists to stay near to the hotel, a range of extra incentives has to be offered to prevent beach boredom. These range from simple pleasures, such as ice-cream, to specialist water sports such as water polo and snorkelling.

Resort / Hotel		Grade	Local alcoholic/soft drinks	Breakfast, lunch and dinner	Snacks	Ice cream	Daytime and evening entertainment	Dolphins (3 to 5 year olds)	Sharks (6 to 10 year olds)	The Club (11 to 15 year olds)	Free child places	4 bedded rooms	Sailing	Snorkelling	Windsurfing	Water Polo	Tennis	Aerobics/keep fit	Gymnasium	Badminton	Volleyball	Bicycles	Table tennis	Jacuzzi and/or Sauna	Squash	Mini golf	Five-A-Side Football	Bowling
ALGARVE																												
Sol Club Quinta Nova	page 417	BRONZE	●	●	●	●	●											●	●			●				●		●
CORFU																												
Regency	pages 562/3	GOLD	●	●	●	●	●	●	●	●	●	●	●						●	●	●		●			●		●
COSTA DE ALMERIA																												
Aguamarina	page 313	SILVER	●	●	●	●	●												●	●	●		●			●		●
COSTA BLANCA																												
Monika Holidays	pages 342/3	GOLD	●	●	●	●	●												●	●		●						●	●
Fenicia	page 345	SILVER	●	●	●	●	●							●	●													●	●
Tropicana Gardens	page 349	SILVER	●	●	●	●	●								●						●					●		
Villa Venecia	page 353	SILVER	●	●	●	●	●														●					●		
COSTA BRAVA																												
Royal Beach	pages 394/5	SILVER	●	●	●	●	●	●	●	●	●	●								●				●				
COSTA DEL SOL																												
Gardenia Park	pages 322/3	GOLD	●	●	●	●	●	●	●	●	●	●	●	●	●				●				●			●	●	●
CYPRUS																												
Tsokkos Beach	page 498	SILVER	●	●	●	●	●						●						●			●						
Artemis	page 500	SILVER	●	●	●	●	●	●	●	●	●	●	●						●	●		●	●			●	●	●
Atlantica Bay	page 516	GOLD	●	●	●	●	●												●	●	●	●				●		
FUERTEVENTURA																												
Bristol Playa Hesperia	page 290	SILVER	●	●	●	●	●												●		●			●		●		
Green Oasis	page 300	SILVER	●	●		●	●													●	●		●			●		
GRAN CANARIA																												
Green Oasis	page 233	SILVER	●	●	●	●	●												●	●						●		
Monsenor	page 250	SILVER	●	●	●		●								●				●							●		●
IBIZA																												
Club Playa	pages 170/1	SILVER	●	●	●	●	●	●	●	●	●	●	●						●		●			●	●			
Sol Loros	page 173	SILVER	●	●	●		●												●	●			●			●		
KOS																												
Kanari Beach	pages 586/7	SILVER	●	●	●	●	●	●	●	●	●	●							●	●			●					
LANZAROTE																												
Green Oasis	page 269	SILVER	●	●	●	●	●	●												●	●			●				●
MAJORCA																												
Club Hotel Marte	pages 62/3	GOLD	●	●	●	●	●	●	●	●	●	●	●						●	●			●		●	●		
Don Pedro	pages 76/7	GOLD	●	●	●	●	●	●	●	●			●	●		●			●		●			●				
America I	page 87	SILVER	●	●	●		●								●				●	●	●			●	●		●		
Canarios Park	page 88	SILVER	●	●	●		●								●				●						●		●		●
Honolulu	page 101	SILVER	●	●	●		●								●				●		●						●		

▲ Extract from an Airtours brochure

Purpose-built resorts

Purpose-built resorts are specifically designed to meet the needs of tourists. The weather in northern Europe is often unpredictable and resorts like Center Parcs cater for this unpredictability with a range of outdoor and indoor activities.

CASE STUDY

Center Parcs

Center Parcs was established in Holland in 1967 by Piet Derksen as a purpose-built complex with 30 villas and an outdoor swimming pool. The villa in the forest idea was born out of Derksen's idea of getting away from the hustle and bustle of everyday life and escaping back to nature.

Center Parc resorts are designed using natural materials that are intended to blend in with the natural woodland environment. Buildings are typically designed with large windows in order to bring nature closer to those inside.

The company operates 13 villages across Europe, including five in Holland, two in Belgium, two in France, one in Germany and three in the UK. The villages offer a mix of bars, restaurants and retail outlets and a range of indoor and outdoor sports and leisure facilities.

Although there are many activities within each village, most people visit on short breaks. This generates a high rate of repeat business; 60 per cent of customers return within the same year.

ACTIVITY

Purpose-built resorts

Use a brochure from Center Parcs or from another purpose-built resort to identify the appeal of the destination to tourists.

Outline how different features of the resort appeal to different types of customer.

Theme park resorts

The most obvious type of purpose-built resort is the theme park. The most famous theme park in Europe is Disneyland, Paris. Located 32 kilometres east of Paris, it covers over 500 acres. Disneyland, Paris opened in 1992 with the declared aim of providing a place where everyone can be happy.

The resort includes:

- five themed lands containing 40 attractions
- six hotels containing 5,800 rooms in total
- a 27-hole golf course
- more than 50 shops
- more than 50 restaurants.

▲ Disneyland, Paris

The average length of stay in the six hotels is two to three nights. The hotels offer a range of packages to suit different target groups. Those on vacation in winter can book three nights for the price of two and special honeymoon deals are available. During the off-peak season the resort hosts many visits by schools and colleges, including an annual convention for students each December.

ACTIVITY

Theme park resorts

Gather information about a theme park resort of your choice. You could choose one in the UK, such as Alton Towers, or select an overseas resort, such as Disneyland, Paris or Disney World, Orlando. Make a list of the:

- facilities and attractions available at the resort
- main types of tourist catered for
- types of accommodation available.

Briefly describe why you think the resort is so popular with UK tourists.

Countryside areas

Countryside areas have always been popular with people who want to escape from the pressures of living in a town or city. Some countryside areas are more geared up for tourism than others. Accommodation can include:

- hotels
- farm houses
- rented cottages
- camping
- caravans
- youth hostels.

People visit the countryside for different reasons. Some will be attracted to the peace and quiet whilst others seek adventure. National parks throughout Europe combine active pursuits with the gentler activities of walking and sight-seeing.

Walking is a popular pastime as people from all ages can take part and engage with their natural surroundings. The Inghams lakes and mountains holiday brochure explains why walking holidays are so popular.

Some tour operators offer specialist guides to escort a group of walkers. Inghams has extended its range of support by producing guide books designed to be used by people on its walking holidays. Figure 3.6 outlines some of the most popular walking areas according to Inghams.

Enjoy the pleasure of walking

One of the greatest pleasures enjoyed by many Inghams guests on a lakes and mountains holiday is walking. There is no finer experience than wandering along twisting alpine paths, discovering the local flora and fauna, marvelling at the fascinating scenery and breathing in the fresh mountain air. It won't be long before you are filled with a sense of well-being bursting with good health – a feeling that will linger many weeks after your return to life at home.

Source: Inghams Lakes and Mountains brochure 1999.

Figure 3.6: Popular walking areas in Europe

Austria

Arlberg Region and Paznaun Valley

Lech, St Anton, Ischgl, Galtür

Ötz Valley

Obergurgl, Sölden

Innsbruck Region and Stubai Valley

Seefeld, Leutasch, Igls, Neustift, Fulpmes

Ziller Valley and Alpbach Valley

Mayrhofen, Alpbach

Kitzbühler Alps and Wild Emperor Mountains

Kitzbühel, Westendorf, Ellmau, Söll

Glemm Valley, Europa Sport Region and Gastein Valley

Zell am See, Saalbach, Hinterglemm, Kaprun, Badgastein

France

Chamonix Valley

Chamonix, Argentiére

Switzerland

Jungfrau region

Grindelwald, Wengen, Mürren

The Valais

Zermatt, Saas Fee

Italy

Val Gardena/Dolomites

Selva

Andorra

The Pyrenees

Soldeu, Western Andorra

Source: Inghams, 1999

Countryside areas throughout Europe have traditionally been favoured by the more mature traveller. Most tourists who visit Switzerland, Italy and Austria to view the scenery are over the age of 50. In Austria, 57 per cent of UK visitors to the lakes and mountains region are over 50 years old and 32 per cent are between 30 and 49 years old.

National tourist boards are keen to extend the attraction of these areas to a younger age group. Cheaper flight and accommodation packages are promoted in magazines along with articles which highlight sporting activities such as snow boarding, mountain biking, white water rafting, canoeing and cycling.

Ski resorts attract a younger crowd of holidaymakers who seek the excitement of winter sports. The slopes of Austria, Switzerland, Italy and France offer a range of facilities and ski runs for skiers of every level. A lively social scene exists around the sport and people enjoying apres-ski use local hotels, bars and restaurants.

ACTIVITY

Ski holidays

1 Use a range of ski holiday brochures to identify the major short-haul and long-haul ski resorts.

2 Which resorts appear to be the most popular? Give reasons for your answer.

3 By looking at the pictures in the brochures suggest the age group that skiing holidays attract.

4 What range of activities are on offer, on and off the slopes?

Historic destinations

Historic and cultural destinations attract tourists who want to learn about the past. Tourism that is based around historic features is often called **heritage tourism** and describes the part of the tourist industry that is based around some of the following features:

- ancient monuments
- historic buildings
- castles and abbeys
- ruined towns and cities
- historic sites
- museums.

Visitors to countries like Italy, France, Greece, Egypt, Jordan, Israel, Peru, India and China, can enjoy many historic and cultural sights. The city of Athens, for example, is dominated by the Acropolis, one of the most important historic monuments in the world. It is 2,400 years old and stood at the heart of the classical Greek empire. On the site stands the Parthenon, the temple of Athena. Surrounding the ruined site is the Theatre of Dionysius, the Temple of Heiphaistos, the Roman Forum, Hadrian's Arch and the famous water clock.

The term **culture** describes the intellectual development of a group of people or civilisation which includes new ideas and thinking. It also communicates how people lived, what motivated and inspired them and what gave them pleasure.

Tourists can find cultural experiences in:

- art, paintings and sculpture
- architecture
- inventions and discoveries
- language
- science and mathematics
- literature
- new ideas and education
- dress
- theatre and dance
- music
- food
- shopping
- sport
- lifestyle.

▲ The Acropolis

During the renaissance (awakening) between the fourteenth and the sixteenth century, Italy led the way in the new age of European discoveries and inventions. The town of Pisa, north of Siena, is famous for its leaning tower which stands 55 metres high. The tower is associated with the nearby medieval cathedral. The town is also famous as the birthplace of the astronomer and physicist Galileo, whose theories helped to lay the foundations of modern science.

Another Italian historical and cultural attraction is the Roman town of Pompeii. When the volcano Vesuvius erupted in AD 79 it buried the entire town, its buildings and many of its people. Rediscovered in 1748, Pompeii has some of the finest examples of Roman buildings and villas, with preserved murals and mosaics. Moulds of people and animals who were buried in volcanic ash are also on display and are a hugely popular attraction.

▲ Pompeii, one of Italy's many historical attractions

ACTIVITY

Historic and cultural destinations

Use a range of guide books and brochures to research your own example of one short-haul and one long-haul historic and cultural tourist destination. Describe its location, and explain the historic and cultural significance that makes it a popular destination for UK tourists.

ENGLISH HERITAGE

Stonehenge

The greatest mystery of the prehistoric world

BUILD YOUR LEARNING

1 Give two examples of each type of tourist destination (see list on p. 163) for each of the following countries:

- UK
- Spain
- France
- Greece
- USA
- Australia.

2 Select one tourist destination from your examples:

- describe its location
- explain its appeal for UK tourists
- identify the main travel routes and gateways by which UK tourists enter and leave the destination.

Keywords and phrases

You should know the meaning of the words and phrases listed below. If you are unsure about any of them, go back through the last ten pages of the unit to refresh your understanding.

- Beach boredom
- Countryside areas
- Culture
- Historic and cultural destinations
- Purpose-built resort
- Seaside resorts
- Towns and cities
- Types of tourist destination

Characteristics of tourist destinations

EACH OF THE FIVE DESTINATION types we have looked at has its own particular set of features. These appeal to visitors in different ways and in different combinations. People travel to particular destinations in order to experience the unique combination of features that the destination has to offer.

Characteristics of tourist destinations include:

- climate

- natural attractions and topography

- built attractions

- events

- food, drink and entertainment

- types of accommodation

- types of transport

- accessibility to travel and tourism gateways.

We are going to look at each of these features, the reasons why they appeal to tourists and at example destinations.

Climate

Climate is an important consideration when choosing a holiday destination. Most people prefer sunny warm weather to dull, cold or wet weather during their holiday. The difference between weather and climate is that weather is experienced on a daily basis. Climate describes the overall conditions that are likely to be experienced, such as temperatures based on yearly or monthly averages.

Figure 3.7 shows the main climatic areas that are found on the Earth's surface. Equal lines of temperature are shown on the map to distinguish between the various **climate zones**. These lines of equal temperature are known as isotherms.

Arctic and polar climates

Arctic and polar regions are characterised by extreme cold and little precipitation, for example rainfall and snow. As there is little evaporation they remain snow covered for most of the year. The temperature is below 6°C for more than nine months of the year and the summers are very short. Some tour operators organise

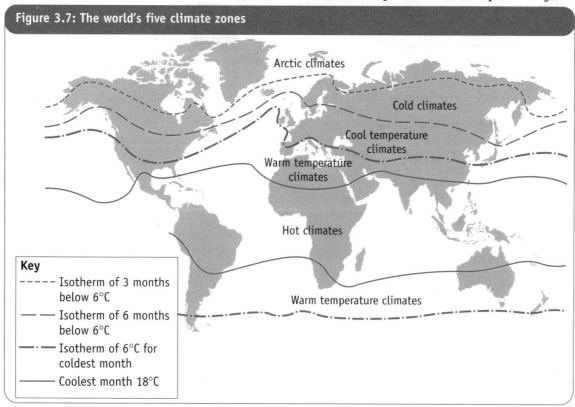

Figure 3.7: The world's five climate zones

Arctic climates

Cold climates

Cool temperature climates

Warm temperature climates

Hot climates

Warm temperature climates

Key
- - - - Isotherm of 3 months below 6°C
— — Isotherm of 6 months below 6°C
— · — Isotherm of 6°C for coldest month
——— Coolest month 18°C

visits to these regions, for example, to Antarctica to watch the wildlife. However, the tours are very expensive and few people can afford to visit. This is perhaps a good thing, as the Arctic and polar regions are very delicate ecologically and cannot sustain large numbers of visitors.

Cold climates

The temperature for this zone falls below 6°C for six months of the year. The range of temperature is extensive, with extremes of cold to minus 30°C and summer averages of 19°C. Summers are short and cool and the change between seasons is rapid. The tourist season is very short, with small numbers of tourists visiting for scenic tours and specialist activities such as mountaineering. Visits to Iceland, Norway and Sweden are popular with specialist tour operators such as Icelandair Holidays.

Cool temperate climates

These are typically experienced by countries in northern Europe including the UK, the Netherlands and Germany. Temperatures range from an average of 0°C in mid-winter to 16°C in mid-summer. Large numbers of tourists from these areas seek climates that are warmer than their own, for example, the great number of tourists from the UK and Germany who visit the Mediterranean each year.

Warm temperate climates

These areas, which include Greece and Spain provide near perfect conditions to support tourism all year round. Average monthly temperatures range between 10°C in winter to 25°C in summer. Winters are never very cold and rarely fall below 6°C.

Hot climates

These areas are found in a narrow band near to the equator. Temperatures are extremely hot; typically above 26°C all year round. It is very humid around the equator due to the large amount of water vapour in the atmosphere. Afternoon storms are almost daily events and give us the term rain forest. Tourists can find these conditions difficult as the excessive heat and humidity make outdoor activities and getting around in cities exhausting. Visits to the rain forests of the Amazon and the African Congo are usually only suitable for special interest groups seeking study tours or safaris and are organised by specialist tour operators. Earthwatch, for example, organises study tours and expeditions to help with scientific research and conservation projects.

Hot deserts are found near to equatorial rain forests, typically in the middle of hot continents away from the sea. They receive very little rainfall. The maximum

temperature in hot deserts can be over 40°C, whilst humidity is relatively low. Safaris to the Sahara desert are made possible by organised groups using jeeps and plenty of supplies. Visitors to countries such as Egypt and Morocco are often invited to explore desert environments.

Dehydration is a major problem facing many tourists who visit these inhospitable places. Visitors thinking of going to Egypt between June and August are often advised that, unless they are used to extreme heat, it is best to avoid holidays at this time of the year. Visitors to central Africa face similar problems. Climate has a direct effect on the numbers of tourists visiting these countries during the peak UK holiday season.

Climate graphs

Local differences in geography can mean that one tourist destination may experience different temperature and rainfall patterns to another in the same climate zone. **Climate graphs** show both temperature and rainfall as monthly averages. Rainfall is shown as a series of bars along the bottom (x axis) whilst temperature is shown as a line against the vertical (y axis) (see Figure 3.8). Climate graphs are found in most atlases, travel guides and holiday brochures.

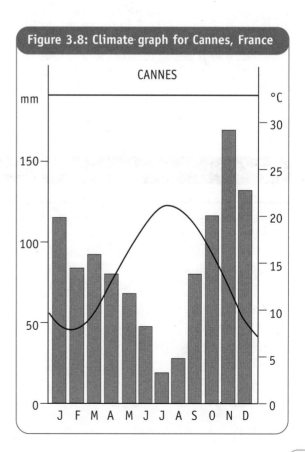

Figure 3.8: Climate graph for Cannes, France

ACTIVITY

Climate zones

1 Look at the climate graph for Cannes (Figure 3.8). Which is the hottest month of the year? What is the average temperature in °C?

2 Describe the temperature range (hottest to coldest monthly average) in °C.

3 Which is the wettest month of the year and what is the average amount of rainfall in millimetres?

4 Select one short-haul and one long-haul destination that you think appeal to tourists for their favourable climate. For each of your chosen destinations, answer questions 1 to 3 above. You will need to research the climate of each destination to answer these questions.

5 Compare and contrast the climate of each of your chosen destinations. What is it about their climates that makes them appealing to tourists?

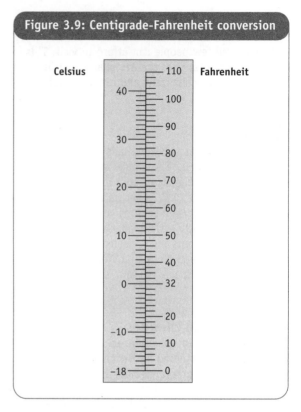

Figure 3.9: Centigrade-Fahrenheit conversion

In most atlases temperature is recorded in degrees Centigrade or °C whilst many holiday brochures prefer to use degrees Fahrenheit or °F. In Europe and the UK, the centigrade scale is preferred, although the Fahrenheit scale is used in countries such as America. For many tourists seeking hot summer temperatures, an average temperature of 70°F sounds more desirable than 21°C, although there is no actual difference between them. Figure 3.9 shows a centigrade and Fahrenheit conversion chart.

Average sunshine hours per day is another feature of holiday brochures and atlases. It presents the reader with an idea of what is to be expected from the weather, based upon an average figure. Tourists may experience more or fewer sunshine hours, depending on local weather conditions.

On average, the UK receives only 53 days of sunshine each year, so many Britons holiday overseas in search of better weather. The amount of sunshine is important to the UK holidaymaker as well as the strength of the

Figure 3.10: Comparison of UK and Ibiza climate data, 1999

	April	May	June	July	August	September	October
Average daily maximum temperature (°F) in the UK	55	60	67	70	69	65	55
Average daily sunshine hours in the UK	5	6	7	6	6	5	3
Average daily maximum temperature (°F) in Ibiza	67	72	78	84	84	79	72
Average daily sunshine hours in Ibiza	7	10	10	11	11	8	6

Source: based on Airtours 1999 Summer Sun Brochure p. 260

sun's rays. Although the sun can create a feeling of well-being and a tan, overexposure can lead to certain forms of skin cancer and to premature ageing of the skin. Most European and American weather reports during the summer months carry warnings about the time it takes for exposed skin to burn. Public awareness about the potential dangers of sunbathing and what to do in order to minimise the risk has been growing in recent years.

ACTIVITY

Climate graphs

1 Look at Figure 3.10, which compares climate data for the UK and Ibiza between April and October. Convert the maximum temperature figures in the UK and Ibiza from Farenheit to Centigrade.

2 How many more hours of sunshine, on average, does Ibiza have from April to October compared to the UK?

3 Suggest why tour operators use maximum average temperatures in their brochures rather than the actual average.

4 Use data from the table to explain which would be the most popular months for UK tourists to visit Ibiza.

Natural attractions

The term **topography** describes the natural shape of the planet's surface and includes features such as lakes, mountains and coastlines. Tourists are attracted to these natural features as they are visually appealing and provide scenic views. However, some of them have been modified by man-made developments over time in order to make them more appealing to tourists. For example, large areas of southern France once suffered from mosquitoes which threatened the development of the tourist trade along the wealthy tourist resort of Cote d'Azur. The local authorities decided to drain vast areas of wetland to prevent the mosquitoes from laying their eggs. Although most of the mosquitoes were eliminated, the ecological damage to other wetland species is now considered to be irreversible.

A varied topography provides sharp contrasts between natural features in the same view and creates a dramatic landscape. The lakes and mountains of Austria are popular tourist destinations, as tall and imposing mountains are contrasted with deep alpine valleys. In the summer months the lakes and mountains are a popular destination for walking holidays, whilst in the winter the scenery is transformed to provide some of Europe's leading ski resorts.

GROSSGLOCKNER
HOCHALPENSTRASSE

SEEING NATURE
EXPERIENCING NATURE
DREAM ROUTE
THROUGH THE NATIONAL PARK

▲ The Hohe Tauern National Park contains Austria's highest mountain, the Gross Glockner, which is 3,700 metres high

Coastlines are perhaps the most popular natural attractions as the majority of tourists seek sun, sand and sea. Throughout Europe, seaside resorts are inspected for cleanliness. The Blue Flag awards introduced in 1996 by the Foundation for Environmental Education in Europe allow beaches the right to display the Blue Flag when the conditions of the EU Bathing Water Directive are met. The European awards are decided on an annual basis and are only valid for a year. The Blue Flag award is removed when a beach no longer meets the standards required.

Figure 3.11: Blue Flags awarded in Europe, 2000

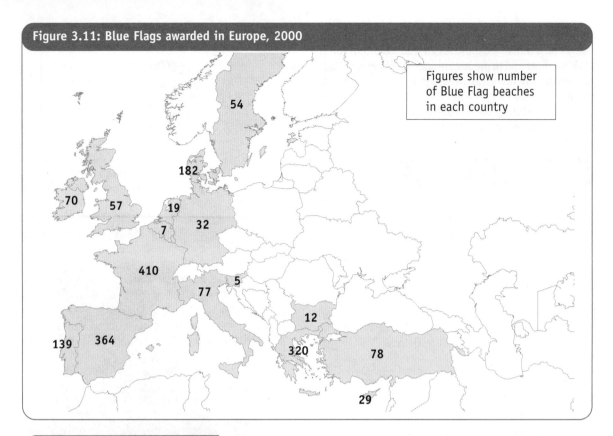

Figures show number of Blue Flag beaches in each country

ACTIVITY

Blue Flag awards

- Which countries have the most Blue Flag Awards? How does this compare to the awards given to UK beaches?

- In your opinion, do awards for cleanliness improve the attraction of the resort for tourists?

While some beach resorts offer relaxation and the chance to walk along remote coastal paths, others offer fun and excitement. Resorts such as Kavos in Corfu, Playa De Las Americas in Tenerife and San Antonio in Ibiza are popular with the 18-30 year old market because they offer a combination of hot weather, beaches, watersports and numerous bars, restaurants and nightclubs.

Other coastal areas attract tourists for their scenic beauty and unique wildlife. Australia's Great Barrier Reef is the world's largest coral ecosystem and has been granted special status both as a marine park and as a world heritage site. The reef attracts tourists from all over the world to view the coral and the brightly coloured fish that live in it. The reef has over 200 varieties of coral and over 1, 000 species of tropical fish.

Tourism in this area is growing at a rate of 30 per cent each year and has to be carefully controlled so the delicate coral ecosystem is not damaged. Tourists are able to see the coral from glass-bottomed boats, on diving trips as well as by helicopter, as the extent of the reef can be clearly seen by air. Tourists who visit the resort do so to experience a unique environment.

Built attractions

Built attractions are those which are purpose-built for tourists. They are diverse in their design and use, and include monuments, museums, art galleries and theme parks. Many built attractions are historic and include churches and cathedrals and stately homes. The Eiffel Tower, for example, was built for the 1889 World Fair to attract tourists and to demonstrate new building techniques using structural steel. When it was completed in 1889 it was the tallest building in the world. It was designed by Alexandre Gustave Eiffel who was also the engineer for the frame of the Statue of Liberty. At the time it was built, the Eiffel Tower was considered too modern and many called for it to be torn down. Its future was secured when it became a mast for a radio antenna to serve the people of Paris, and later to broadcast television. Today it is one of the world's most famous landmarks and attracts many visitors each year who make their way to the top of tower to gaze at the view which extends for 50 miles in every direction.

▲ The Eiffel Tower

The pyramids of Egypt attract visitors from all over the world. The largest pyramid is 137 metres high and contains over three million blocks of stone. Entrance to the pyramids is made possible by a series of tunnels and staircases. Next to the pyramids is the equally famous Sphinx, which has been admired over many centuries.

Visitors to these sites want to experience the wonders of this ancient civilisation and to admire the size and scale of the buildings. As tourism has grown, the area has also been used for open air concerts and a golf course has even been constructed nearby.

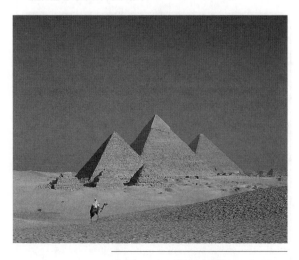

▲ The pyramids at Giza

Royal palaces, stately homes and country houses have become popular with visitors. The stately homes of the Loire Valley in France are popular with tourists. Many French kings and queens spent much of their time in the Loire Valley and attracted a number of wealthy noble families who also built magnificent country retreats known as **chateaux**. These buildings are highly decorated and have an almost fairy-tale appearance.

One of the most striking is Chambord, which is set in its own private forest. It was once a fortified hunting lodge which has over the years been transformed into a royal country house. It is the largest chateau in the region and is one of the most visited. It has been described as a massive film set and as a fairy-tale castle. The building has 440 rooms and 365 chimneys. The rooms exhibit furniture and ornaments that were fashionable at the time when the chateau was in use as a royal building. A unique feature is the double-helix staircase; it appears to be one staircase but has another built inside it, so that two people can walk down the staircase and never meet. This impressive building is set amongst 13,417 acres of forest of which only 3,000 acres are open to the public. The rest is used as a national hunting reserve and is home to a large collection of wild boar and deer.

▲ Stately homes like Chambord in France have become popular with visitors

The ultimate in built attractions are theme parks, which have been designed specifically for the purpose of managing vast numbers of tourists. Large car parks that can cater for thousands of vehicles per day are normally at their capacity during peak holiday periods. Queuing systems for the most popular rides are used, with games and activities provided along the length of the queues to keep the waiting visitors entertained. Some theme parks, like Disneyland, Paris, have rail terminals near the entrance to the park, so that visitors can walk off the train and straight into the park. The needs of tourists are paramount throughout theme park developments.

ACTIVITY

Copy and complete the table below. Give an example of each of the built attractions in a country other than the UK. Describe the main features that make each example appealing to visitors, and suggest the types of tourists that you think will visit.

	Stately home	Ancient/historic monument	Theme park
Main features			
Likely tourists			

Events

Some tourist guides promote a wide range of different **events** that appeal to a wide range of audiences. These include carnivals, music festivals, art festivals and sporting events.

Music festivals usually take place during the summer months and are held in a variety of settings such as parks, stadiums or on farmland. They can draw huge crowds of up to 100,000 people and attract international artists and performers. Open-air festivals often have temporary camp sites and facilities with showers and toilets, especially if the event occurs over a number of days. Every major city hosts a series of events each year, although some are more popular than others.

Major towns and cities play host to many festivals and events and each has been designed to attract a wide range of visitors. Some of the largest events revolve around sport. The football World Cup and the Olympic Games, both held every four years, are the biggest sporting events in the world. Between them they attract millions of visitors to the host countries.

WEBSTRACT

The Olympic Games

The 2000 Olympic Games take place in Sydney, Australia. Centred around the Homebush site, Sydney Olympic Park hosts many of the games, including athletics and football. Other areas used for the games include Darling Harbour for the water sports and Manly Beach for beach volleyball.

The Olympic Games is not just another sporting occasion but an important commercial operation. It enables the host country to increase its revenue through sponsorship and tourism, and at the same time develop world-class sporting facilities.

Source: www.olympics.com

Entertainment

When UK tourists travel abroad they are often keen to experience foreign **cuisine**, and **bars and restaurants** are common features of most tourist destinations. Cities, in particular, are cosmopolitan, attracting people from many different countries and cultures. Their bars and restaurants offer food and drink from many different nations.

Some resorts customise their restaurant menus to meet the needs and tastes of less adventurous tourists, offering international as well as traditional dishes. In some extreme cases, for example, in the popular resorts of Spain, restaurants only offer English menus to cater for the vast numbers of British tourists.

Some restaurant chains are international in their approach and structure. McDonald's, for example, is familiar the world over. Its standard menu ensures that no matter where the McDonald's restaurant is located, the food and customer service will be the same. Bars and restaurants also use this idea to attract tourists from the UK to visit familiar surroundings and to offer local people something different. Irish pubs are a common sight in many British towns and cities, for example and they are also found in major cities around the world.

▲ Irish theme pubs are found in major cities around the world

Entertainment is often a major feature of a tourist destination. Hotels often provide a programme of entertainments which are are displayed in holiday brochures to promote the holiday. Nightclubs are also popular and some hotels run nightclubs as part of their operation.

Many tour operators organise special events for children and offer a programme of activities. For example, Sunwing resorts offer many activities aimed at families, including a summer camp for children.

ACTIVITY

Entertainment

Suggest the type of tourist that you think prefers the following types of holiday entertainment:

- nightclub
- resident hotel band
- traditional dancing
- children's entertainer
- keep fit class
- juggling act
- portrait painting
- comedian
- guided tours and walks.

Accommodation types

Accommodation is available at a variety of different levels of quality and service, and at a variety of prices. Some tourists choose self-catering accommodation, while others prefer a hotel with breakfast and an evening meal provided, known as half-board. Others like to have a midday meal provided as well (full-board). All-inclusive accommodation extends full-board to include unlimited bar snacks, meals and drinks.

Many resorts vary the types of accommodation on offer to attract a wide range of holidaymakers and some hotels offer room only, bed and breakfast, half-board, full-board and all-inclusive accommodation.

European countries like the Republic of Ireland, Spain, Greece, France and the Netherlands have national systems of classifying the quality of accommodation, whilst the main tour operators have developed their own.

In France, the classification of hotels depends on the levels of comfort and service offered (see Figure 3.12).

Figure 3.12: French hotel classification system

L****	Very high class, de luxe hotel
****	High class, comfortable hotel
***	Very comfortable hotel
**	Comfortable hotel
* and HT*	Simple hotel with basic levels of comfort

Official ratings vary from one country to another. To enable holiday makers to compare one hotel with another, tour operators use their own ratings system. Thomson Holidays use a T rating system that is based on the standard of hotels displayed in their brochures.

Figure 3.13: Thomson's rating system

Ibiza Portinatx

Hotel El Greco
ⓣⓣⓣ

Your Opinion Customers rating good or excellent in Summer 98
0   25   50   75   100%
HOLIDAY OVERALL
ACCOMMODATION
LOCATION
FOOD QUALITY

ACTIVITY

Accommodation

Use a selection of holiday brochures to identify the different ways in which the quality of the resort and its accommodation are represented.

Look at the back or front of the brochures. Do they describe how the resorts and hotels have been graded?

Types of transport

The **type and cost of transport** available to travel to a tourist destination influences its appeal to UK tourists. There are an increasing number of ways in which tourists can travel to their holiday destinations. The main forms of transport that are provided are by coach, rail, ferry and air.

Travelling by road is a convenient form of transport when visiting countries in Europe or when exploring a holiday destination. Despite its popularity however, the car is not always a desirable option for long distance travel. Although flexible in terms of route and timing, drivers get tired on long journeys and often feel less confident driving in other countries. Coach travel provides an alternative to the car and offers a range of extra services such as toilets and on-board video. Coaches can offer local pick-up points and are a popular form of mass transport.

The benefits of rail travel are that seats may be reserved, meals are available and sleeping accommodation can be provided on long journeys. Rail travel into Europe has become a more popular option since the opening of the Channel Tunnel. Travelling between mainland Europe and the UK has been made easier as the travel time between London and Paris has been reduced to three hours. When the new high-speed rail link from London through Kent is opened it will reduce the journey time to two and a half hours.

Faster rail travel competes with short-haul air travel. The flight time between London and Paris is shorter than the rail journey, at an hour and five minutes, but check-in and baggage collection adds to the length of the trip by air.

The most frequently used sea routes to short-haul destinations are across the English Channel to France, the Irish Sea to Ireland and the North Sea to Holland and Norway. Travelling by sea includes cruising as well as using ferry or hovercraft services. On-board facilities can include:

- restaurants
- sun decks
- children's entertainment
- bars
- arcade machines
- shopping
- cinema.

The most popular method of travelling to a holiday destination, whether it be short-haul or long-haul, is by air. In a recent survey, 85 per cent of holidaymakers preferred to use this method of transport.

Improvements in the levels of comfort and service, and an increase in disposable income has encouraged people to travel further. This has also been helped by the advent of budget airlines offering cut-price seats on major routes.

Access

Access to a destination depends on a number of important factors such as location, convenience, cost and distance to be travelled. Travelling to and from remote locations involves greater effort and the journeys can be long. Even when several opportunities for travel are available, the decision on the route taken, time of departure, cost and level of services have already been determined by the tour operator, unless you are an independent traveller. (Access is described in more detail on pp. 199–200.)

We have now looked at the main types of tourist destination and the characteristics that make them appeal to visitors.

BUILD YOUR LEARNING

End of section activity

Select two short-haul and two long-haul tourist destinations and explain the appeal of each destination to UK tourists. You should cover:

- climate
- topography
- natural attractions and topography
- built attractions
- events
- food, drink and entertainment
- types of accommodation
- types of transport
- accessibility.

Make use of examples and statistics to support your explanation.

Keywords and phrases

You should know the meaning of the words and phrases listed below. If you are unsure about any of them, go back through the last ten pages to refresh your understanding.

- Access
- Accommodation
- Built attractions
- Climate
- Climate graph
- Climate zone
- Cuisine, bars and restaurants
- Events
- Topography
- Type and cost of transport

Travel and tourism gateways and routes

YOU NEED TO BE ABLE TO IDENTIFY the main gateways and **travel routes** that tourists use when travelling in continental Europe and to long-haul destinations.

Gateways

A **gateway** is a point of access to, or departure from, a country or holiday destination. Gateways include:

- airports
- seaports
- border crossings
- railway stations.

Gateways offer quick and easy access to holiday destinations and may also provide a range of facilities and services for tourists such as shops, restaurants, car hire, accommodation and currency exchange. Gateways are often involved in the movement of international traffic. For example people travelling to Paris by air from the UK mainly use Charles de Gaulle and Orly airports, rather than Beauvais or Rouen, as they have more international connections and are closer to the city.

A good transport system carries passengers quickly and safely to their chosen destination. Transport routes, which include roads, car parks, railway stations and terminals, are known as the **transport infrastructure**. A good infrastructure allows people to

Figure 3.14: World's 20 busiest airports, 1997

Airport	Location	Passenger arrivals
1 Hartsfield International Airport	Atlanta, Georgia	73,474,298
2 Chicago-O'Hare International Airport	Chicago, Illinois	72,369,951
3 Los Angeles International Airport	Los Angeles	61,216,072
4 Heathrow Airport	London	60,659,500
5 Dallas Fort Worth International Airport	Texas	60,482,700
6 Haneda Airport	Tokyo	51,240,704
7 Frankfurt Airport	Frankfurt	42,734,178
8 San Francisco International Airport	San Francisco	40,059,975
9 Charles de Gaulle International Airport	Paris	38,628,916
10 Denver International Airport	Denver, Colorado	36,817,520
11 Amsterdam Schiphol Airport	Amsterdam	34,420,143
12 Miami International Airport	Florida	33,935,491
13 Newark International Airport	Newark, New Jersey	32,445,000
14 Phoenix Sky Harbor International Airport	Phoenix, Arizona	31,771,762
15 Detroit Metropolitan Airport	Detroit, Michigan	31,544,426
16 John F Kennedy International Airport	New York	31,295,000
17 George Bush Intercontinental Airport	Houston, Texas	31,025,726
18 McCarran International Airport	Las Vegas, Nevada	30,217,665
19 Kimpo International Airport	Seoul, Korea	29,429,044
20 Gatwick Airport	London	29,173,257

Source: Airport Council International 1998

travel with ease and with minimum inconvenience.

A **terminal** is a building that is used to process passengers who are arriving and departing at an air or sea port. Facilities may include ticketing, check-in, immigration, lounges and catering. The term terminal should not to be confused with terminus, which is the final stop on a railway line or bus route.

Airports

The busiest airport in the UK is Heathrow. It handles over 60 million passengers a year, which accounts for approximately 40 per cent of all air passengers. The second largest is Gatwick Airport, which handles nearly 30 million passengers a year. Over the last 12 years both Heathrow and Gatwick have lost market shares of around 3.5 per cent as Stansted, Manchester, Birmingham and Luton have improved their share of the market. During this time UK airports have seen passenger traffic increase by 6.4 per cent per year. (See also page 53, Figure 1.17.)

ACTIVITY

The world's busiest airports

Figure 3.14 shows the top 20 busiest airports in the world. Suggest reasons why each of the top ten airports receive so many passengers. Identify reasons under the following headings for each of the top ten airports:

- holidays

- business travel

- visiting friends and relatives (VFR).

Why do you think that the USA has most of the world's busiest airports?

ACTIVITY

European airports

Working in groups, name each of the airports labelled on the map.

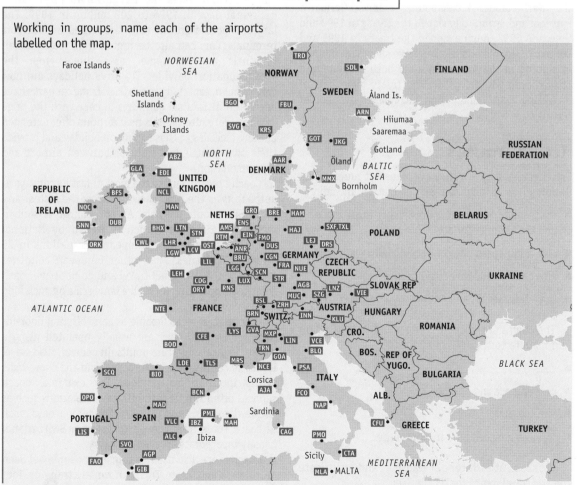

Seaports

As the UK is an island it has many seaports. The main seaports in the UK are Dover, Folkestone and Portsmouth, with ferry routes to France and Northern Spain. (See also the activity on p. 54.)

Land border crossings

Land border crossings are also gateways to other countries, offering points of entry between nation states. They can exist along major roads or railways. They are often carefully monitored and free passage is only possible with the right documentation. Such documentation varies from country to country but usually includes passport and visas. Some borders have been removed with permission between various countries. This allows easier movement, as no documentation is required.

Since 1995 border controls between member states of the European Union who have signed the **Schengen Treaty** have been relaxed and largely unrestricted movement of tourists is allowed between these countries. The countries which originally signed the treaty in the village of Schengen in 1985 were: Belgium, the Netherlands, Luxembourg, France, Germany, Portugal and Spain. Italy signed the treaty in 1990 and Greece in 1992. Austria signed the treaty in 1995 and Denmark, Finland and Sweden have shown an interest in signing in the future. In 2000 both Belgium and Luxembourg withdrew from the treaty over fears of increasing illegal immigration and concern over border security.

Travel routes

Travellers often have a choice of transport routes when deciding how to travel to their destination, including:

- road – motorways, autobahns, major trunk roads and the Channel Tunnel

- rail - high-speed lines and scenic railways

- air - charter and scheduled flights

- sea – ferry routes and cruises.

The choice of transport type and route is based on four main factors:

- cost

- convenience and availability

- journey time

- services provided by transport carrier.

Let's look at each type of transport and investigate the key travel routes for UK tourists.

Roads

Road travel includes both car and coach travel. The car gives greatest flexibility in terms of the choice of route, time of departure and of arrival.

The motorway networks are fast and efficient, although drivers often experience delays approaching major towns and cities at peak times. Some major urban areas are trying to encourage car users to park their cars and travel by public transport when entering a town or city. It is felt that congestion and pollution is unpleasant for residents and discourages repeat visits, so money has been invested in park and ride schemes in cities such as Paris, Amsterdam and Salzburg.

Motorway networks are made up of fast and efficient roads that have multiple lanes. Some foreign motorways impose a charge or toll to travel on them. Toll roads in the USA include the Florida Turnpike and the Central Florida Greeneway which links International Drive to Sanford International Airport. Bridges that levy tolls include the Sydney Harbour Bridge in Australia and the two Severn Bridge crossings between England and Wales.

Car hire has increased over the last ten years. The European car rental market has grown from 160 million car rental days in 1996 to 202 million in 1999. The largest reported growth is in cars rented from airport terminals. Cars can also be rented from seaports, rail terminals and in some cases direct from the accommodation provider. Fly-drive holidays are now very popular, especially in the USA. Large car parks have been built at tourism gateways to cope with the huge demand. Very often hotels near airports offer extended parking facilities to those going on holiday and provide their own shuttle-bus transfer between airport and accommodation.

Coach operators make the most of fast motorways or autobahns as the road network offers the fastest and most direct route possible. An autobahn is a German motorway. Eurolines, which is owned by National Express, travels to 450 European destinations in 25 different countries. Most other European countries encourage the use of rail travel and do not have coach companies operating on such a large scale on such long distance routes.

Coaches can be as flexible as cars, offering door-to-door service, but they are usually operated using a variety of local departure points. In general, road travel is mostly confined to domestic tourism and short visits across international borders. For example, coach services often run from the UK to destinations such as Amsterdam, Paris and Brussels. Longer journeys, such as coach tours from the UK to Spain or Switzerland, usually incorporate an overnight stay.

Coaches are also used to transport people between destination and resort. This is known as a **transfer**. Tour operators hire local coach companies at airports to drop

Great value coaches all around Europe

Regular departures to over
450 destinations throughout Europe

EUROPE'S EXPRESS COACH NETWORK

1st April 1999 - 31st March 2000

off and pick up people en route. Taxis are also used to transfer smaller groups of people, especially if their accommodation is remote. In the UK, AirLinks, which owns Flightlink, Jetlink and Speedlink offers an airport service travelling between the UK's main airports and local towns.

For further information, use the internet to look up National Express, Eurolines and AirLinks, which are all part of the National Express Group

- www.nationalexpress.co.uk

- www.eurolines.co.uk

- www.airlinks.co.uk

If you have ever travelled by road in mainland Europe, you may have noticed that some continental roads appear to have two numbers, a local motorway or autobahn number and an E number, identified by green and white signs. This is due to the European Agreement on Main International Traffic Arteries which came into force in 1983. It set out to coordinate a European road network known as the **European International Network**. The idea is to simplify the use of road numbers which often change when crossing country borders. Even numbers run east to west and odd numbers run north to south.

Although this appears to be a good idea, not all countries in Europe have adopted the system. In the UK a number of routes have been designated E roads, but none are signposted or nationally recognised.

ACTIVITY

Motorways

Obtain a European road atlas or find a route planner on the internet. Which motorway routes would you use to make the following journeys:

- Calais to Paris

- Calais to Brussels

- Calais to Salzburg?

Rail

▲ Few British holidaymakers travel by train to their European holiday destination

Rail travel currently represents only 7 per cent of holiday transportation in the UK. Centrally located stations and a wide supporting infrastructure makes rail travel a popular choice, especially with business travellers, but few people travel by train to their

European holiday destination. Criticism of cost, punctuality and safety has caused UK tourists to look towards alternative forms of transport.

In Europe, rail travel has been supported by successive governments and is generally more advanced than in Britain. Trains are faster and operate more frequently. The Eurostar rail service operates in direct competition to cross-Channel ferry services and short-haul flights. Destinations from London include a three-hour journey to Paris, a three-hour, fifteen-minute journey to Brussels, and a two-hour journey to Lille. Eurostar departs from Waterloo International terminal and travels via Ashford International terminal in Kent.

The difference between Eurostar and Le Shuttle is that Eurostar is a train with carriages whereas Le Shuttle accommodates cars, coaches and motorcycles, complete with their passengers. Journey time through the tunnel takes approximately 35 minutes, with loading and unloading at Folkestone and Calais.

Although rail travel has the advantage of comfort, there is a cut-off point in distance and time travelled at which rail travel is perceived as tiring and decidedly uncomfortable. Alternatives like domestic flights, which are on average three times faster than rail, become serious contenders, especially from regional airports. As Figure 3.15 shows, there are only a few high-speed rail routes in Europe.

ACTIVITY

Travel options

Identify the range of road, rail, air and sea travel options available to a UK tourist wishing to travel to the following tourist destinations:

- a seven-day skiing holiday in Soll, Austria
- a three-night city break in Paris
- A ten-day cycling holiday in the Netherlands.

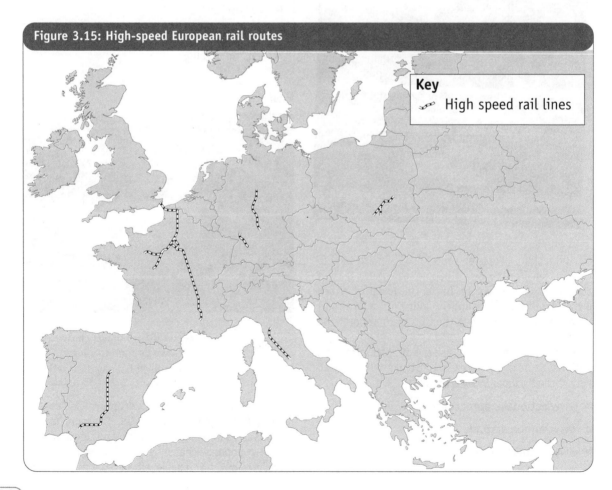

Figure 3.15: High-speed European rail routes

Key

〜 High speed rail lines

Several tour operators offer short and long-haul sightseeing excursions by rail. Perhaps the best known is the Orient Express, which transports tourists in luxurious surroundings, through scenic countryside from its starting point in London to Vienna. Alternatively, tourists can travel the 2,770 miles from California to Florida in just three days on Amtrak's Superliner Sunset Limited.

Air

Air travel falls into two main categories, scheduled and charter flights. **Scheduled flights** operate to a given timetable and depart whether or not the seats are filled. To offset these costs the flights tend to be more expensive and airlines offer discounts for group bookings known as **special group inclusive tours (SGITS)**. Package holidays which use seats on scheduled flights are referred to as **inclusive tours by excursion (ITX)**.

Charter flights are associated with package holidays. Aircraft are booked for a specific destination and length of time. They do not fly to a regular timetable. Package holidays which use chartered aircraft are referred to as **inclusive tours by charter (ITC)**. If the chartered flight maintains a regular pattern over a series of weeks, then it is known as a flight series.

If booking figures are low for specific flights then tour operators may require clients to travel from a different airport. Putting two sets of passengers together on one flight is known as consolidation. If this is inconvenient to some of the passengers, alternative transport arrangements are made by the tour operator.

Air travel has grown significantly over the last ten years and a price war between the major airlines has made travel seem cheaper and more accessible. Airports are increasing the capacity, range and frequency of destinations offered. Regional airports are also increasing in importance, as they compete for popular routes and attract people away from congested major airports such as Orlando International Airport.

Air routes are becoming increasingly congested as the numbers of aircraft using them grows. Air routes are monitored by air traffic control and link airports across the globe. Some long-haul routes include a series of stopovers, where the aircraft has to refuel. Tourists can take advantage of these stopovers to enjoy a short break in the country before travelling on.

CASE STUDY

Orlando International Airport

Although Miami Airport is the main international airport for Florida, Orlando International Airport is becoming the favourite airport for UK tourists visiting the American state. A travel industry survey voted Orlando Airport the USA's number one airport for customer convenience. Its emphasis on customer service includes:

- an automated monorail system allowing easy access between terminals

- moving walkways

- multi-lingual tourist information centres

- extended opening times of tourist information centres and assistance points.

Sea

Sea travel falls into two categories: ferries and cruises. Cross-Channel ferries transport foot passengers, cars and lorries, and provide modern on-board facilities including shops, restaurants, cabins, lounges, children's play areas, arcade machines and foreign exchange services. On the Kent coast, cross-Channel ferries are in direct competition with the Channel Tunnel (see the article on p. 190). With the abolition of duty free prices, the two compete on price, journey time, convenience and levels of comfort. The average time taken to travel between Dover and Calais is 50 minutes by ferry.

Hovercraft travel on a cushion of air which produces a very smooth crossing in calm waters, as the vessel travels above the waves rather than through them. Crossings are faster than those of conventional ships. When the weather is rough, however, the hovercraft service is one of the first to be suspended as it is not suitable for use in stormy seas. A new breed of hovercraft, known as a **sea catamaran** (Seacat) has now been introduced on cross-Channel routes. The Seacat has a distinctive shape due to its catamaran design, which has two hulls. It is described as the most advanced fast ferry in the world. The Stena HSS is operated by Stena Line between the UK, Ireland and Holland. It offers a range of services on board similar to those found on a cross-Channel ferry.

Agents feel the squeeze as cross-Channel growth slows

By Ian Taylor

Cross-Channel traffic may be peaking after passenger numbers soared with the opening of the Channel Tunnel, according to a new report by market analyst Mintel.

And there is evidence that agents are already suffering.

Mintel's report, Crossing the Channel, shows that in the first three months of this year there was a 33 per cent fall in cross-Channel ticket bookings through agents compared with the same period in 1998.

And Eurostar reported a mere one per cent increase in passengers in the first half of the year.

Last month's abolition of duty-free sales within the European Union removed a lucrative source of revenue for ferry operators which will have to be compensated for with higher fares.

UK cross-Channel traffic had risen every year for the past decade.

But last year saw a 3.2 million fall in ferry passengers to 28.9 million and the overall increase in cross-Channel traffic of one million was just two per cent up on 1997.

Mintel predicts "only a very modest growth rate – or even contradiction – during 1999".

Last year was the first year of uninterrupted operations for Eurostar and the Eurotunnel Shuttle Services. Passengers increased by 4.2 million to 9.4 million people.

By the end of 1998, the tunnel had more than 40 per cent of the market and Mintel expects Eurostar and the Shuttle to outstrip ferries by 2002.

The end of duty-free sales was another blow for ferry operators.

Typical prices for day-trips – a price-sensitive sector – have already increased from £10 to £40 since the start of the year.

But Mintel points out that higher fares mean higher commission for agents.

Ferry companies also want to expand their retail operations.

In the long term, Mintel predicts shopping – particularly to France – will be an important element of cross-Channel travel for ferry operators to exploit.

But it warns cost-cutting is likely to hit staffing levels.

TTG Newspaper, 9 August 1999

Cruise ships are large ocean-going vessels that can be described as floating five-star hotels with a wide range of services on board. Cruises are growing in importance as a holiday option and overall prices have been reduced by up to 20 per cent as they have become more popular with the public. Once the preserve of the rich and famous, more and more people are opting for high levels of service and a wide range of facilities.

One of the newest cruise liners is the *Disney Wonder*. Operating from Disney's private terminal, Port Canaveral in Florida, it sails to Nassau in the Bahamas and to Disney's private island, Castaway Cay. Disney offers a seven-day package with three or four days at Walt Disney World Resort and with three or four days on board the *Disney Wonder* or its sister ship the *Disney Magic*.

▲ The QE2 is one of the most famous ocean-going liners in the world

BUILD YOUR LEARNING

1 Describe the main transport types and routes that a tourist travelling from where you live could take to these tourist destinations:

- Benidorm, Spain
- St.Tropez, France
- Athens, Greece
- New York, USA
- Sydney, Australia.

2 For each route chosen, identify the most suitable UK departure gateway and destination arrival gateway.

3 Once you have decided on the main transport type, route and gateway, for each destination identify the:

- quickest route type
- cheapest route type
- most expensive route type
- most comfortable route type.

Keywords and phrases

You should know the meaning of the words and phrases listed below. If you are unclear about any of them, go back through the last eight pages to refresh your understanding.

- Charter flights
- European International Network
- Gateway
- Inclusive tours by Charter (ITC)
- Inclusive tours by excursion (ITX)
- Scheduled flights
- Schengen Treaty
- Sea catamaran
- Special Group Inclusive Tours (SGITS)
- Terminal
- Transport infrastructure
- Travel routes

The popularity of tourist destinations

THE POPULARITY OF TOURIST destinations fluctuates over time because of economic, social and political and environmental and geographical factors.

Let's look at each in turn.

Economic factors

The state of the UK economy plays an important part in the choice of holiday destinations. In times of hardship, income is more likely to be spent on necessities than on luxuries and in times of uncertainty holidays tend to be one of the first areas of spending that are reduced or forfeited altogether.

In times of economic growth, the reverse is true; personal disposable incomes rise and people spend more money on their holidays, stay longer, travel further and travel more frequently. Many supplement their main holiday with a short weekend break in the UK. People who feel more confident about their financial position are likely to spend more money on luxury items and holidays.

Cost

The **cost of holidays** is important. Destinations whose accommodation and transport costs are low provide excellent value for money. Mediterranean destinations remain competitively priced and attract the majority of UK tourists.

Increasing competition between tour operators and airline companies has also driven prices down, increasing demand for some short and long-haul destinations. The combined effect of increasing competition within the travel industry and overcapacity in some destinations is widespread discounting of holidays. For example, air ticket prices to America began to fall with the introduction of Laker Airways in the late 1970s. Virgin Atlantic continued the trend in the1990s. Both airlines undercut the prices of British Airways and the American Airline carriers.

Lower prices have helped places such as Florida to thrive as popular destinations for UK tourists. Short-haul airlines have also reduced levels of service to offer low-cost travel to many European destinations. These operators are sometimes known as low cost, no frills airlines. Budget airlines such as Go, EasyJet, Virgin Express and RyanAir are now competing on price against the major airlines. The reason that they are able to do so is that they heavily discount a percentage of their seats and only provide a basic level of service.

ACTIVITY

Budget air fares

Select a tourist destination gateway such as Dublin, Nice, Paris, Geneva or Orlando that is serviced by at least one UK based budget airline. Find out the cheapest return fare available for a selected departure date from the UK. What impact do you think the availability of this budget service has had on tourist destinations in the area served by your selected gateway?

Exchange rates

The value of sterling against foreign currencies plays an important part in the appeal of destinations to UK tourists. The value of foreign currency is often displayed in the windows of travel agents that have a bureau de change, in banks and in newspapers. The value of foreign currency is often referred to as the **exchange rate** and shows how much foreign money a British pound can buy.

Figure 3.16: Foreign exchange rates

Australia	2.4237	Ireland	1.1769
Austria	20.56	Italy	2911
Belgium	60.44	Japan	174.24
Canada	2.3638	Malta	0.6333
Cyprus	0.8631	New Zealand	3.0672
Denmark	11.19	Norway	12.47
Euro	1.54255	Portugal	298.57
Finland	8.9232	Spain	248.57
France	9.8176	Sweden	13.13
Germany	2.9372	Switzerland	2.3953
Greece	492.82	Turkey	737175
Holland	3.2953	USA	1.6106
Hong Kong	12.42		

Notes: Sterling-exchange rates, March 2000

ACTIVITY

Impact of exchange rates on travel

1 Which of the currencies in Figure 3.16 is not a national currency in its own right?

2 Suggest why the answer to question 1 will help people travelling throughout Europe.

3 Use the most up-to-date exchange rates that you can find to make a list of those currencies which have decreased in value and those which have increased from the rates shown in the table above. Make a prediction based on this information about which countries you think will increase in popularity with UK tourists.

Fluctuating exchange rates

The popularity of tourist destinations with UK tourists often fluctuates in line with the exchange rate. When sterling is strong against the destination currency, UK residents benefit from the greater buying power of the pound, whilst the opposite is true if the exchange rate is lower. For example, in 1999 UK tourists visiting France benefited from an exchange rate of just over ten francs to the pound, compared to a rate of around eight francs in previous years. The high exchange rate in 1999, and the availability of low fares due to the fierce competition between cross-Channel transport operators, led to an increase in UK tourist numbers to France in 1999.

The rate of inflation is also a significant economic factor in the popularity of tourist destinations. The **rate of inflation** shows how much goods and services are increasing in price. If a holiday destination is seen to be expensive or poor value for money then holiday makers will look for alternative resorts.

ACTIVITY

Price of holidays

1 Look at the holiday price guide (see Figure 3.17). Which are the most expensive destinations?

2 What type of target group do you think each of the resorts attracts?

3 Why do you think that the prices vary so much?

4 Suggest how economic considerations altered the popularity of these tourist resorts.

Figure 3.17: Long-haul destination price guide, 1998–99

	Florida	Barbados	Mexico	Thailand	Goa	Egypt	Sydney	South Africa
Three-course meal	£8.15	£14.90	£4.95	£7.15	£2.75	£8.00	£11.00	£7.60
Bottle of house wine	£4.40	£19.90	£11.20	£4.90	£1.89	£8.00	£4.40	£1.60
Bottle of beer in bar	£1.60	£1.65	£0.80	£0.50	£0.50	£2.40	£0.75	£0.30
Coffee in bar	£0.80	£0.85	£0.80	£0.15	£0.10	£1.00	£0.55	£0.30
Soft drink in bar	£0.95	£0.85	£0.50	£0.15	£0.20	£0.75	£0.55	£0.20
One-week car hire	£168	£165	£160	£176	£200	£320	£201	£126
Petrol per litre	£1.15 (gallon)	£0.50	£0.25	£0.15	£0.30	£0.20	£0.25	£0.20

Source: *Travel Trade Gazette*

Social and political factors

Social and political considerations such as personal safety, security and comfort are important to tourists. These considerations are influenced by the wider social and political factors at work in the host country. Some social and political factors that can affect the numbers of tourists include:

- promotion of the destination
- exclusivity
- overcommercialisation
- crime
- political instability or unrest
- media coverage
- tourism management
- growth of independent travel
- growth of short-break holidays.

Let's look at examples of the ways these factors can influence tourists.

Promotion

A lot of money goes into **promoting holiday destinations**. Many countries promote tourism through national tourist organisations, which are often located in capital cities. They provide tourist information, brochures, maps and advice for travellers. They organise and coordinate promotional events and advertising directed both at the general public and at the travel trade.

Exclusivity

Some destinations are geared towards meeting the needs of small but significant groups of tourists rather than catering for the mass market. Destinations such as those on the Cote d' Azur in southern France, which includes resorts such as Monte Carlo, Cannes and Nice, offer the rich and famous high-class accommodation and entertainment.

The popularity of these resorts will change if the mass market gains access to them. This has happened in the Greek and Spanish coastal resorts, including Falariki and Benidorm. Certain long-haul resorts still have an air of exclusivity about them, such as the Caribbean islands (Jamaica and Barbados) and far-eastern countries such as Japan and Thailand. However, as these destinations become more accessible to large numbers of UK tourists, they may lose an element of their **exclusivity**.

The price of holidays is not the only indicator of exclusivity. Many newspapers and magazines report the holiday destinations of famous people which creates valuable associations of fashion and glamour.

Overcommercialisation

Overcommercialisation is a negative term. It refers to the extent to which destinations lose their tradition and heritage to modern facilities such as bars and nightclubs, which are more to do with making money than the needs of local people.

Mass market tourist areas such as Torremolinos on the Spanish coastline have been criticised by locals and tourists alike for being overcommercialised. Holidaymakers wanting to explore local history, culture and tradition are disappointed in overcommercialised resorts. Massive hotel complexes, bars, nightclubs and restaurants dominate and offer nothing that is distinctive to the destination. Old buildings are cleared away to make space for new development, or are hidden amongst the sprawl of hotels and apartment blocks.

ACTIVITY

Overcommercialisation

1 Select a tourist destination that you think has become overcommercialised. Explain the reasons for your choice.

2 To what extent has overcommercialisation affected the resorts? Give examples or provide evidence to support your answer.

3 What impact do you think overcommercialisation has had on the type and number of UK tourists visiting the destination?

Crime

The **level of crime** in popular tourist destinations around the world is relatively low in most cases, but a few well publicised incidents can make tourists stay away. When major crime or acts of terrorism affect UK tourists abroad, widespread media coverage is generated that influences the appeal of the destination to UK tourists.

In Orlando, Florida, for example, a spate of car crime around Miami and Orlando airports caused a lot of worry in the 1990s as thieves were preying on holidaymakers leaving the airport in identifiable hire cars. The level of crime has since been reduced because car hire companies have made sure their logos are no longer visible, educated drivers to stay on the main tourist routes and recommended that tourists should not stop at the roadside unless requested to do so by a police officer.

WEBSTRACT

Advice on travelling in Florida

The UK government Foreign and Commonwealth Office gives the following advice on travelling in Florida.

- Most people visit Florida without experiencing difficulty. However, visitors should continue to be vigilant about their personal security.

- If staying in a hotel, do not leave your door open at any time.

- Do not wear ostentatious jewellery and avoid walking in obviously run-down areas.

- If arriving at night, take a taxi to your hotel and collect your hire car the next day.

- If departing on an evening flight, avoid leaving luggage and souvenirs on view in your hire car during the day. Gangs of thieves are targeting these vehicles and stealing the contents.

- Drive on main highways and use well-lit car parks.

- Do not stop if your car is bumped from behind. Instead, indicate to the other driver to follow you to the nearest public area and call for police assistance.

- Do not sleep in your car on the roadside or in rest areas.

Source: www.fco.gov.uk/travel/countryadvice.asp

Political instability and unrest

Political instability can lead to civil unrest and ultimately to crime, terrorism and even war. For example, Egypt has suffered political unrest since 1992, when an outlawed group which opposes the government began targeting tourists. Several bombings took place place in tourist areas, including a terrorist attack at the popular tourist site at Luxor in 1997.

British tourists angry at leaving Luxor

British holidaymakers were angry yesterday that they were being flown out of Luxor after the terrorist massacre. They said that the Foreign Office had over-reacted.

Convoys of coaches took visitors to Luxor airport as tour operators sent charter flights to evacuate the area. Buses came in their scores from such companies as Thomson, Kuomi and Golden Joy Holidays. Most big firms decided to pull out; only some of the small independent travel groups giving their clients the chance to stay on.

One group of tourists had arrived only last night for a two-week tour of the region and were going back to London within 12 hours. Jenny Reynolds, from Birmingham, was with her 85-year-old mother, Eileen Reynolds. "It's just pure panic," Dr Reynolds said. "We were asked at Heathrow last night if we wanted to go and we all said yes."

Geoff Gregg, of Luton, said: "I'm absolutely furious with the Foreign Office. What message will be we sending to the terrorists if the British pull out?"

Tourists had been advised to remain inside their hotels and boats after the attack at the Temple of Queen Hatshepsut. But a handful were mingling with local Egyptians outside the Luxor City Council office. Many tourists spoke of their respect for the Egyptian people, saying that they had done much to ease the situation.

The Times, 19 November 1997

ACTIVITY

Luxor

1 What effect do you think the Luxor massacre had on UK tourists visiting Egypt?

2 How did this affect the reputation of Egypt as a tourist destination?

3 What has been done to help restore confidence?

The threat of further incidents caused a drop in visitors, which did not begin to recover until Egypt increased security levels to help protect foreign tourists. A ceasefire was declared in 1999, but visitors are still advised to keep abreast of developments. Egypt receives over 200,000 UK tourists each year and most enjoy a trouble-free stay.

Some areas are definitely not for tourists. Sri Lanka welcomes visitors to the south of the country, but fighting between the Sri Lankan security forces and Tamil separatists in the north and east of the country makes these areas too dangerous for tourists. The Sri Lankan government restricts travel in these areas, including Wilpattu and Gal-Oya national parks. Hotels in Colombo, Sri Lanka's capital, have been directly affected by the threat of terrorism as they are close to strategic buildings. The Sri Lanka Tourist Office is trying to restore confidence, but the tourism is unlikely to recover until the political unrest has been resolved.

The war in the Balkans disrupted the tourist industry in the former Yugoslavia and throughout Eastern Europe. For example, the Czech Republic lost half of its tourist bookings in 1999 because of the Kosovo crisis, even though the war was being fought 600 miles away. The loss in bookings was greater than that experienced in Hungary, which shares its borders with the Federal Republic of Yugoslavia. Most of the cancellations were from North America and western Europe, costing the Czech Republic £600 million in lost tourism income.

ACTIVITY

The Kosovo crisis

1 Explain why areas other than Kosovo might see a reduction in the number of tourists.

2 How would reactions by people in those countries affect the tourist industry?

3 How did the tourist industry in the UK react to the war in the Balkans?

Frightened on the beaches

The Kosovo war may soon start having a harmful impact in countries far beyond the southern Balkans. Tourism throughout the eastern Mediterranean will swiftly collapse if fighting stretches into the summer, especially if Nato sends in ground troops. From Turkey to Italy, Hungary to North Africa, resorts face economic catastrophe.

Italy's Adriatic coastline is already predicting mass cancellations and along the southern shores shuttered hotels and deserted beaches are a foretaste of what tourist operators say will be one of Italy's most disastrous years in decades.

Cruise companies have begun to alter the routes of their pleasure ships and are notably avoiding Venice. Corfu, one of the closest resorts to the mayhem in Albania, will also suffer: Costa Paquet, one of the leading European operators, said it had cancelled stops in Corfu as well as Dubrovnik, and would sail instead to Tunis and Genoa.

The military build-up in the region has not yet provoked mass cancellations, but tourist authorities in Greece, Turkey, Italy and Croatia are clearly rattled.

The areas likely to see the biggest drop in tourism are those nearest to the theatre of war. Croatia has not been drawn into the fighting but tourism the length of the Dalmatian coast, including the holiday island resorts in the north, is at risk.

Other areas that may be affected include Slovenia, which has been quietly consolidating its summer Alpine tourism, Hungary, Bulgaria's Black Sea Coast and Turkey. But tourists are notoriously nervous: any hint of trouble could put off people going even to places safely out of the combat zone: Cyprus, Egypt and Turkey's southern coast could all see fewer tourists this summer.

The Times, 24 April 1999

Before travelling to an area that is potentially at risk, tourists are advised to seek information and guidance from the Foreign and Commonwealth Office. The Foreign and Commonwealth Office internet site provides travellers with information on travel and personal safety in other countries. It can be accessed at **www.fco.gov.uk/travel/**

Guidance for tourists

Other countries produce information and guidance for tourists and travellers. If you have access to the internet, have a look at the following sites:

■ United States Department of State

   travel.state.gov/

■ Canadian Department of Foreign Affairs and International Trade

   www.dfait-maeci.gc.ca

■ Australian Department of Foreign Affairs and Trade

   www.dfat.gov.au

Media coverage

Very often a decision to choose one resort over another is based on what we have seen or what we have heard. **Media coverage** can have a significant influence on the popularity of tourist destinations. Media coverage can be in the form of a dramatic news story or a report on a travel show or consumer programme. Forms of travel media include:

■ magazine articles

■ travel guides

■ internet sites

■ advertisements

■ radio, television and newspaper reports.

Most television channels have travel shows, for example, the Holiday Programme on BBC1, which review different holidays and offer information and advice. Travel programmes are entertaining and also serve as interactive brochures. Satellite and cable television channels like Travel Shop provide entertainment and a chance to book a holiday as you are watching the programme. A glowing report, complete with picturesque views, can tempt viewers to the point at which they reach for the telephone and make a booking.

Television programmes with negative content about a tourist destination can influence people to the extent that they take extra precautions, find out more information or cancel their holidays altogether. Stories of pickpockets, organised crime, natural disasters or terrorist attacks throughout the world cause people to reconsider holiday plans.

Tourism management

Tourism management is the process by which tourists are catered for by local, regional and national authorities within a holiday resort. Very often tourism officers are appointed to oversee the management and coordination of accommodation, catering, transport and entertainment providers. Evidence of good tourism management includes:

■ appropriate marketing of a resort which attracts tourists

■ clearly signposted routes and adequate car parking on arrival

■ clear information about what there is to see and do

■ minimising the risk of hazards to the public (health and safety issues)

■ encouraging the use of tickets and discount vouchers that can be used to gain entry for several attractions in the destination

■ encouraging the use of attractions that are not weather dependent

■ making use of local facilities out of the main tourist season

■ encouraging tourists to stay in the resort and to return at a later date.

CASE STUDY

Tourism management: The solar eclipse of 11 August 1999

Effective tourism management in the south west of England during August 1999 was vital, as four million people were expected to flock to Devon and Cornwall to view the total eclipse of the sun. Sensational stories were reported in the media that roads would be gridlocked, that Cornwall would run out of water, and that shops and restaurants would run out of food. All visitors were advised to bring everything they needed for their visit. Seats on Great Western trains were fully booked months in advance and hotel owners predicted that there would be few vacancies. Emergency camp sites were set up and extra supplies were brought in, including a whole field stockpiled with bottled water.

Unfortunately, the anticipated influx of visitors did not happen. Overcast weather and adverse publicity meant that many people stayed at home and watched the eclipse on television or directly from their back garden. Up to 500, 000 visitors made the journey to Devon and Cornwall for the eclipse, an increase of just 10 per cent on the number of tourists expected at that time of year.

Throughout Europe the weather prevented a good view of the eclipse. The best views were in Turkey, Iraq and Iran.

ACTIVITY

The solar eclipse

1 Why were so many people attracted by the eclipse?

2 What impact would this have on the tourist industry?

3 What would the situation have been like in Cornwall had the weather been hot and sunny?

4 Why do you think effective tourism management was seen as the answer to coping with the large number of expected tourists to the area?

The growth of independent travel

Independent travel is defined travel or holiday arrangements that are made independently of a tour operator. Travel itineraries are put together by the travellers themselves, who either book direct with travel companies and hotels or make their arrangements through a travel agent which organise the holiday to their individual requirements.

Just over half (54 per cent) of all holidays taken abroad by UK residents are defined as inclusive or package holidays. The statistic also includes numbers of tourists who took holidays on cruise ships.

Independent travel has risen modestly during the last ten years and currently represents 46 per cent of all holidays taken abroad (see Figure 3.18). Many British tourists, some of whom have gained in confidence through the package holiday market, seek experiences other than those on display in holiday brochures and want to take control of their own travel itineraries.

Independent holidays have increased in popularity as communication links to mainland Europe continually improve. Regular ferry crossings across the English Channel and the Channel Tunnel rail services have allowed British motorists the chance to explore European destinations using their own vehicles. The greatest amount of independent travel is experienced by people taking short-break holidays. In the UK, 90 per cent of short-break holidays are organised independently.

Independent travel is very popular with students. Discounted coach, rail and air fares allow students on a tight budget the freedom to travel. Many use these discount schemes to travel to and from their university or college, while others are more adventurous, travelling around Europe and in some cases around the world.

Figure 3.18: Type of holiday taken abroad

	Holiday abroad of more than three nights													
Year	'85	'86	'87	'88	'89	'90	'91	'92	'93	'94	'95	'96	'97	'98
Inclusive* or package	61%	62%	63%	63%	57%	56%	54%	61%	55%	58%	61%	57%	57%	54%
Independent	39%	38%	37%	37%	43%	44%	46%	39%	45%	42%	39%	43%	43%	46%

* From the 1989 survey onwards the definition of inclusive holiday was changed to a holiday in which a single price covered both travel and accommodation. In the above table the proportions of inclusive holiday in the years before 1989 have been recalculated according to the new definition. Inclusive includes cruises.

Source: British National Travel Survey 1998

CASE STUDY
Student travel: USIT

USIT is one of the largest student travel companies, with three call centres in the UK and 233 offices in 65 countries around the world. Last year USIT dealt with 500,000 clients in the UK, providing a range of travel services to students who spent an average of £130 per transaction. These travel services range from rail and coach discount cards to round the world trips. The most popular short-haul destinations are Spain, in particular Ibiza, Amsterdam and Dublin, whilst the cities that are showing the largest amount of growth in the student travel market are Prague and Budapest. Favourite long-haul destinations include Australia and America. Many students travelling to Australia head for Sydney or Melbourne where there are established communities of British expatriates. An expatriate is a person who lives in a country other than their country of birth. Students find work in local bars and restaurants owned by British expatriates in order to travel around Australia before coming back to the UK.

The growth of short breaks

Short breaks abroad are becoming increasingly popular because of improvements in the transport infrastructure and falling prices caused by increased competition between operators. People who live close to a tourism gateway can access a range of possibilities: short breaks in Paris and Brussels are advertised by the Eurostar service, while ferry companies offer shopping visits to France. Some airlines offer flight and accommodation breaks to Amsterdam, Paris and other

ACTIVITY
Student travel

1 Find out about the special deals that companies such as USIT and the Student Travel Association offer students for two long-haul and two short-haul destinations.

2 What are the main routes and gateways to these destinations for students?

3 Suggest why these destinations appeal to students.

European cities and other opportunities include weekend breaks to the New York, or short-break skiing holidays to European resorts. Some Mediterranean countries, such as Tunisia, have recently begun promoting themselves as short-break destinations.

Geographical factors

The four main areas of environmental and geographical consideration are:

- accessibility
- climate
- pollution
- natural disasters.

Access

Access to a holiday destination means being able to get there and being able to return home. Access may be restricted by natural causes, such as weather and climate, or by human factors, such as pollution or industrial action.

Industrial disputes can restrict movement through tourist gateways or close them temporarily. Some industrial action can happen with very little notice and with huge consequences for the airline and its passengers. In the past, industrial action by air traffic controllers in Spain and France closed airports and meant flights had to be diverted. Strikes are usually organised disputes over pay and working conditions.

Flying Colours Airlines spent £250,000 reuniting passengers with their luggage following the one-day illegal strike by Spanish baggage handlers at Lanzarote Airport. The Thomas Cook-owned airline chartered two cargo aircraft to collect 2,240 bags and return them to customers in the UK.

Source: *Travel Trade Gazette News*, 16 August 1999

Climate

Climatic conditions are important in choosing a holiday destination and many UK tourists escape the cold British winter to holiday in the Mediterranean. However, the recent rise in temperatures brought about by global warming has had an impact on the Mediterranean resorts. Temperatures have increased, making the heat during the summer months unbearable for many tourists. Reports of tourists who do not venture from their air-conditioned hotel rooms until late afternoon are becoming common. Despite the heat, these resorts remain popular. If the high temperatures of recent years continue, however, they may seriously affect the numbers of tourists during the height of the season in the future.

Winter ski resorts have also experienced new extremes, with greater amounts of snowfall than in previous years. This is also attributed to global warming, as more heat allows the atmosphere to retain more moisture and therefore produce more precipitation, which includes rain and snow.

During February 1999, ski resorts in Austria received more snow than expected. During one such storm, three metres of snowfall was forecast. The excessive amount of snow triggered an avalanche which engulfed an entire village at Galtur in the Austrian Tyrol and killed more than 30 people. Many of the nearby ski resorts were evacuated as a precaution against further avalanches.

Pollution

Pollution is not only undesirable but can also be hazardous to health. Some pollution is immediately evident; you may be able to see it or smell it. Other forms of pollution are not readily detectable until someone suffers from ill health. For example, the Dominican Republic, a developing tourist destination in the Caribbean, had widely reported health and hygiene problems in some of its main hotels. Some holiday tour operators have had to refund large numbers of UK tourists because they suffered from sickness throughout their holiday.

Two areas of pollution concern are highlighted in beach environments; the beach itself and the water quality.

Large numbers of people on a crowded beach can cause all sorts of problems. One of the most frequent reported causes of first aid treatment is cuts to feet from broken glass bottles and discarded drinks cans. Barbecues are often restricted to certain parts of the beach because the surrounding area is usually very dry and they represent a fire hazard. Fires can be caused by discarded cigarettes or by sparks from barbecues and can devastate huge areas.

Water quality is a difficult issue and one that is debated between government agencies and environmental pressure groups. The Blue Flag awards give an indication of water quality (see p. 178) but nearby beaches may be polluted by sewage outlets and industrial effluent. If a beach resort does not carry a Blue Flag then tour operators may favour beaches that do. This has begun to happen in the UK, as beaches which appear dirty are highlighted by lobby groups such as Surfers Against Sewage.

Air pollution can be a major problem in congested towns and cities. During hot weather the air above the city becomes polluted with exhaust gases and industrial emissions. These tiny particles of pollution, called hydrocarbons, react with sunlight to form photochemical smog. Cities such as Los Angeles, California, Bangkok and London have air pollution which can increase the likelihood of breathing problems, especially in asthmatics. Ozone is also created at ground level during these conditions. Although a useful gas in the atmosphere, it is harmful when inhaled. Weather bulletins give air quality indexes which provide an indication of the conditions.

Acid rain is perhaps one of the most frequently discussed forms of pollution. Caused by air pollutants reacting with water in the atmosphere, it produces carbonic and sulphuric acids which slowly dissolve the limestone which is used to construct buildings. Some of the world's most important tourism related buildings are slowly being eroded. Acid rain has caused damage to the Taj Mahal in India, the Acropolis in Greece and St Paul's Cathedral in London.

Deadly beaches

Beaches around the entire coast of Britain are harbouring the deadly bug which claimed the life of an eight-year-old holidaymaker, it was alleged yesterday.

The privatised water companies were accused of failing to spend enough to clean up sewage, with the result that 180 million litres of raw and partially treated waste are pumped into the sea every day.

Bathing water surrounding 75 beaches is registering dangerous levels of bugs, including e. coli, salmonella and hepatitis A – despite a ten-year clean-up.

Heather Preen contracted e. coli after playing on the beach during a family holiday at Dawlish Warren in Devon. The death of the schoolgirl stands at the tip of an iceberg of misery which includes stomach bugs and lung infections.

Many of the country's most famous beaches – including Blackpool, Bournemouth and Newquay – have been found to be contaminated with dangerous levels of human sewage.

A report from the Environment Agency has identified 44 beaches in England and Wales which are failing to meet minimum cleanliness standards – largely because of the presence of human waste. Research in Scotland has identified another 34 beaches where dangerous levels of such waste have been found.

But just three of the big ten water companies have agreed to spend the money needed to install state-of-the-art sewage disinfection systems across their networks.

Daily Mail, 18 August 1999

ACTIVITY

Unsafe beaches

Read the article about deadly beaches. What impression do you get about the standard of cleanliness on this beach? Who is largely responsible for this? What likely impact will this have on UK tourists taking holidays at this resort?

Natural disasters

Natural disasters occur throughout the world, having a dramatic effect not only on the lives of those directly affected but also on people planning to visit the area. Natural disasters include catastrophes such as floods, hurricanes, fire, earthquakes, avalanches and volcanic eruptions. Many occur without warning and are shocking when reported on television or in the press.

One of the most recent natural disasters in Europe was the earthquake in Turkey in August 1999. An earthquake measuring 7.4 on the Richter scale caused considerable damage in the north west of the country. Over 17,000 people died, although many of the bodies were never found. Hot weather caused dehydration and further suffering. This was followed by heavy rain storms which brought different fears of flooding and disease. Many people expected that further, smaller, earthquakes called aftershocks would send more buildings crashing to the ground and took to the streets in make-shift shelters.

Images like that of the Turkish earthquake are likely to deter tourists. Although travel advice given by ABTA and the Foreign and Commonwealth Office explained that the main tourist areas to the south of the country were unaffected by the earthquake, the constant stream of pictures shown on television news broadcasts presented a different story to those waiting to go on holiday to Turkey at the time and many tourists cancelled their holidays. It may take many years to fully restore customer confidence as the towns hit by the earthquake begin a long process of rebuilding their homes and businesses.

ACTIVITY

The Turkish earthquake

List the ways in which the disaster affected tourism in Turkey. How would you find out if there is a risk of earthquakes in an area that you intend to visit on holiday?

Transport principals

The popularity of tourist destinations can also be measured in terms of the number of **transport principals** serving the destination. Transport principals include the charter airlines used by tour operators, scheduled airline carriers, ferry, rail and coach services to and from the tourist destination. Some of the main travel principals serving the popular tourist destinations featured in the travel files that end this unit are highlighted in Figures 3.19, 3.22, 3.26 and 3.30. Popular destinations such as Benidorm, Majorca, Paris, Orlando and Sydney are served by a large number of transport principals to cater for the large number of tourists and visitors. Destinations that are more remote, and which receive fewer visitors, tend to be serviced by a small number of transport principals that tend to specialise in niche markets rather than the mass market tourist destinations. Examples of this kind of niche market include walking holidays in the Himalayas and world cruise holidays.

BUILD YOUR LEARNING

End of section activity

Use a range of examples to explain how four tourism destinations, (two long-haul and two short-haul) have experienced changes in popularity over the last ten years. Use a range of statistics to support your findings. For each resort you should consider the impact of:

- economic factors
- social and political factors
- environmental and geographical factors.

For each of your chosen destinations explain their current popularity in terms of visitor numbers from the UK and the number of transport principals serving the destination.

You may find it useful to use the same tourist destinations that you investigated in the earlier end of section activities on pp. 173, 183 and 191.

Keywords and phrases

You should know the meaning of the words and phrases listed below. If you are unsure about any of them, go back through the last 11 pages to refresh your understanding.

- Access
- Climatic conditions
- Cost of holidays
- Exchange rate
- Exclusivity
- Independent travel
- Level of crime
- Media coverage
- Natural disasters
- Overcommercialisation
- Political instability
- Promoting holiday destinations
- Rate of inflation
- Tourism management
- Transport principal
- Water quality

Spain

Spain is the leading holiday destination with tourists from the UK. The Spanish tourist market can be divided into four distinct areas: the Balearic Islands (Majorca, Minorca, Ibiza), the Spanish Costas (Costa Brava, Costa Blanca, Costa Del Sol, Costa Dorada), the Canary Islands (Tenerife, Gran Canaria, Lanzarote, Fuerteventura) and mainland Spain (Madrid, Barcelona and Seville).

Most of the holidays taken in Spain are through summer sun brochure promotions aimed at the mass tourist market. Summer sun brochures mainly promote beach holidays with hotel-based entertainment packages. However, alternative holidays are beginning to increase in popularity, with short-break city holidays to Barcelona and Madrid. These holidays not only emphasise the warm sunny weather but also Spanish culture and tradition.

None of the top three Spanish destinations are on the mainland. They are the island resorts:

- Majorca

- the other Balearic Islands, of which Ibiza and Minorca are the most popular

- the Canary Islands, led by Tenerife, followed by Gran Canaria and Lanzarote.

More tourists from the UK visit Majorca than any other tourist destination; 1.75 million holidays are taken there each year. The island is also popular with tourists from other countries, making it the most important destination in Europe.

The other Balearic Islands are also popular with tourists, and receive 1.55 million tourists each year. Young people are attracted by the nightclub scene in Ibiza whilst Minorca retains a relaxed family atmosphere.

TRAVEL FILE

The most popular mainland resort area is the Costa Blanca. Benidorm receives 600,000 UK visitors each year, of whom 200,000 visit in the winter months. This is followed by the Costa Brava, the Costa Dorada and the Costa del Sol.

Over 30 per cent of international arrivals to Spain travel by air. Nearly 50 million pass through Spanish airports each year, with 70 per cent travelling on chartered flights. Spain receives more charter flights than any other country, with 75 per cent of passenger traffic originating from other European countries.

Benidorm

Benidorm is the most popular tourist resort on the Costa Blanca, Spain's eastern coastline. It is situated between the bays of the Costa Valencia to the north and the Costa Calida to the south.

The main resorts on the Costa Blanca are:

- Cala de Finestrat, 3 km from Benidorm

- Calpe, a beach and sports resort north of Benidorm

- Albir, a family resort 7 km from Benidorm.

Benidorm attracts over 3.5 million staying visitors each year, who produce an estimated 40 million annual staying nights (including both hotels and self-catering apartments). Compare these figures to the leading British resort of Blackpool, which has four million staying visitors and produces 15 million staying nights.

Travel principals

Some of the main travel principals serving the Costa Blanca are set out in Figure 3.19

Figure 3.19: Principals serving Benidorm

Air Europa

Airtours

British Airways

Cosmos Coach Tours

First Choice Holidays

Iberia Airlines

JMC Holidays

Lufthansa

Monarch Airlines

Shearings Coach Holidays

Spanair

Thomson Holidays/Britannia Airways

Transavia Airlines

Unijet Travel

Other travel principals also offer services to Benidorm.
Source: ABTA 1999

Main routes and gateways

Access to the resort of Benidorm is by flying to Alicante airport and then travelling for 34 km along the E15 (or A7) coastal road, the main route between Alicante and Valencia. Most tour operators prefer to use Alicante rather than Valencia airport, as Valencia airport is 152 km north of Benidorm.

Appeal to UK tourists

Benidorm appeals to a wide range of UK tourists, from young adults and families during the summer to retired couples in the winter. The capital of the Costa Blanca is Alicante, known locally as the white city because of its characteristic white buildings and white sand.

Benidorm is built around two beaches, Playa Levante, which is 1.6 km long and Playa Poniente, which is 3.2 km long. The two beaches are separated by a rocky outcrop. There are fewer hotels close to Playa

Poniente compared to Playa Levante and the beach is generally less crowded. The water is very warm and clear and both beaches are gently sloping. This makes the sea relatively safe for both adults and children. The sea water is analysed daily to monitor its quality and the sand is cleaned on a weekly basis.

Climate

The climate is much warmer than that of the UK, and this attracts many British tourists. The hottest months of the year are July and August, when temperatures reach an average 30°C. This compares to a UK average temperature of 20°C in July and August.

Figure 3.20: Benidorm climate data

	Temperature (average daily maximum)	Sunshine (average hours)
April	20°C	9
May	25°C	9
June	26°C	11
July	30°C	12
August	30°C	11
September	26°C	8
October	25°C	7

Topography and natural features

Benidorm is a flat coastal area surrounded by several mountain ranges of the Sierra Helada, Bernia, Aitana, Puig Campana and El Tossal de la Cala. This creates a sheltered south facing valley with a warm climate. The high mountains create a rain shadow over the area, producing a noticeable lack of rainfall. This means that Benidorm is has 345 sunny days each year.

Natural attractions

The most famous natural attractions of Benidorm are its sandy beaches and warm climate. The rocky outcrop that separates the two beaches has been transformed into a star-shaped observation platform known as El Castillo.

Local attractions include the Algar waterfall, and excursions into the mountains to explore small villages, visit orange and lemon groves and view the spectacular scenery. Most of the mountain excursions are made by coach, although some are made by jeep. Other local visits are organised to the palm groves at Elche, the famous Rock of Ifach and the water fountains at Algar. Mud and water baths are popular in this area and are said to act as a beauty treatment and to cure aches and pains.

Built attractions

Most of the built attractions in Benidorm are the impressive hotels which dominate the coastal skyline. Very few of the original buildings are left, as the resort has developed rapidly over the years. Most of the built attractions are nightclubs, shops, restaurants and other places of entertainment. Shops are plentiful and there is an open-air market on Wednesdays selling locally produced souvenirs of leather, porcelain, wine and Turron, an almond and honey nougat.

Traditional buildings are best seen by taking a trip into the mountains. The village that receives the most visitors is Guadalest. The village was built by invading Moors over 1,000 years ago and still retains its medieval charm. Typical souvenirs from the villages include handmade lace, local honey, ceramics and almonds.

Events

Spain is known as the land of the fiesta and local towns and villages hold annual celebrations which often occur during religious holidays. One of the most popular fiestas in Benidorm is the San Juan Fiesta, which is held over two days around 23 and 24 June. Other important dates include Labour Day, usually on 1 May, and Assumption Day in August.

Food, drink and entertainment

Benidorm caters for the UK tourist by offering many home comforts. Restaurants include McDonald's and Burger King, as well as international cuisine including Indian, Mexican and Chinese food. Local Spanish restaurants are also popular and specialise in fish and paella.

The resort is extremely busy with hundreds of bars, restaurants, nightclubs, shops and a casino. Most of the entertainment is lively and noisy. The more sophisticated hostelries are situated in the old town. During the day, tourists occupy themselves with a range of sporting activities, including sailing, wind surfing, diving and fishing, tennis, horse riding and bowling.

Types of accommodation

There are some 32,000 rooms available in Benidorm. They range from luxury hotels to family run guest houses and camp sites. Most of the accommodation is based around large high-rise hotels and apartments which specialise in bulk bookings from the holiday tour operators. Very few cater for the independent traveller.

Types of transport

Eleven different public bus routes operate throughout the town. Visitors are particularly attracted to the local railway which runs from Alicante and Denia through the heart of Benidorm.

Recent trends in popularity

Fifty years ago Benidorm was a sleepy fishing village, but today the modern high-rise hotels have almost completely removed the character of the old town. Rapid development began in the 1950s and Benidorm is now the largest single resort town in Europe. Its image as a highly commercialised resort aimed at the mass holiday market is beginning to change. Publicity by the Spanish authorities is targeted at a different type of tourist, who is not just interested in clubs and bars but is also prepared to try the many sporting facilities and local sightseeing excursions.

The beaches are perhaps Benidorm's most precious asset, and they were awarded a European Blue Flag in 1997. Showers, children's play areas, exercise areas and refurbished bars have been established to encourage people to stay longer at the beach.

Very few tourists visit Benidorm for its historic attractions. In order to create a sense of tradition amongst the modern hotel apartment blocks, local authorities have built mock castles and historic-looking features. The local island of Plumbaria has been promoted to tourists staying in Benidorm as a local historical attraction. Visitors seeking a cultural experience have to leave the resort and find local places of interest, including picturesque hamlets, churches and castles.

The resort has rapidly expanded and new apartment blocks and hotels have been developed in the surrounding countryside. Villas and apartments, many owned by British and German tourists, are a common feature of the area. Previously used as holiday homes, sometimes on a time-share basis, more and more are being purchased as retirement homes. There are over half a million of these apartments in Benidorm and more are being built each year.

Further information

Spanish Tourist Office, 22–23 Manchester Square, London, W1M 5AP.
Tel: 020 7486 8077
Tel: 0891 669 920 (brochure request line)
Fax: 020 7486 8034
Website: **www.tourspain.es**

ACTIVITY

Benidorm

Find a tour operator's brochure that includes holidays to Benidorm and answer the following questions.

- Which airlines does the tour operator use?

- What is the nearest airport to where you live and how often are flights available to Alicante/Benidorm?

- What attractions are described in the holiday brochure?

- What types of accommodation are offered?

- Who is likely to be attracted to the destination, for example, families, single people?

- Is there any evidence of organised entertainment for children?

- Plan a holiday route to Benidorm from your own locality and provide details of costs for a family of four (two adults and two children) travelling in August.

France

France is the most popular day-trip destination for UK tourists. It is also the most important holiday market for independent holidays, including camping, skiing and city-breaks. An estimated 7.5 million holidays were taken in France in 1998. Of those, 2,400,000 were short-break holidays, which accounts for 57 per cent of all short-break holidays taken by tourists from the UK.

The main areas for tourism in France include:

- Paris, the leading city break destination

- Disneyland, Paris, the popular theme park often combined with visits to the capital city

- The Alps and Pyrenees, for skiing holidays

- Brittany and the Cote d'Azur, for camping and caravan holidays

- the Cote d'Azur, Nice and Provence, rural holidays and sophisticated seaside resorts

- Dordogne and Provence, traditional self-catering cottages known as gîtes.

The holiday industry is well developed in France, as the French often spend their holidays within their own country. This has enabled tourists to benefit from excellent road and rail services and well developed resorts. France receives more tourists than any other country in Europe, making it one of the most popular tourist destination countries in the world.

Paris

Paris is one of the world's great cities, located in northern central France. The capital city, it is built on the banks of the River Seine. The northern area is known as the Rive Droite (the Right Bank) and includes landmarks such as the Champs-Elysées and the Arc de Triomphe. To the south of the river, on the left bank, is the city's most prominent landmark, the Eiffel Tower.

▲ The Louvre, Paris

Travel principals

The city of Paris is served by two major airports; Charles de Gaulle, which has six main terminals and Orly airport, which has two. Other methods of travelling to Paris from the UK include ferry services across the English Channel, by road on Le Shuttle or by rail via Eurostar services.

Main routes and gateways

Charles de Gaulle airport is 23 km northeast of Paris. Transport to the city centre takes 45 minutes by scheduled bus services, or 27 minutes by rail. Orly airport is 14 km south of Paris. Transport to the city centre takes 25 minutes by scheduled bus services and 35 minutes by rail.

People who cross the English Channel by ferry or by Channel Tunnel, may continue the journey to Paris by road, following the main E 05 (A13) to Paris. Eurostar

runs rail services from London and Ashford direct to Lille and Paris.

Eurolines runs its coach service from Paris to most cities in Europe. Hoverspeed operates a bus-boat-bus service from London and there are also special routes between Ireland and France.

Climate

Paris has a cool temperate climate but its location in continental Europe means that winters tend to be slightly cooler and summers warmer than in the UK.

Figure 3.21: Paris climate data	
	Average monthly temperatures for Paris
January	7.5°C
February	7.0°C
March	10.0°C
April	16.0°C
May	16.5°C
June	23.0°C
July	25.0°C
August	25.5°C
September	21.0°C
October	16.5°C
November	12.0°C
December	8.0°C

Topography and natural features

The location of Paris on the banks of the River Seine offers scenic views and boat trips and river bank walks are popular with tourists who want to take in the sights and sounds of the city. There are also many parks and open spaces in the heart of the city. Paris is relatively flat and there are no large hills.

Built attractions

What Paris lacks in topographical attractions it makes up for in built attractions. The city boasts more than 80 museums and 200 art galleries, along with many fine examples of architecture and historic buildings. Some of the major tourist attractions include:

- the Pompidou Centre
- Notre Dame cathedral
- the Champs-Élysées
- the Louvre
- the Eiffel Tower
- L'Opera.

The Pompidou Centre looks like a building that has been turned inside out. It houses a collection of modern art and a large international library. It is the most visited site in Paris and the area surrounding the centre is popular with street entertainers and buskers.

Notre Dame is a Gothic cathedral which dates from 1163. It can hold up to 6,000 worshippers and is beautifully decorated throughout. Once inside, visitors gaze at its enormous rose windows and listen to a 7,800-pipe organ. Made famous by Victor Hugo's character Quasimodo in *The Hunchback of Notre Dame*, the cathedral attracts many visitors each year. The north tower is open to the public and its narrow staircase allows access to the west facade, providing spectacular views over Paris and close-ups of the cathedral's most terrifying gargoyles.

The Avenue des Champs-Élysées is a tree-lined avenue which has become synonymous with the style and high-class living that is associated with this romantic capital city. Two kilometres long and 70 metres wide, the Champs-Elysees is popular for evening walks from the Arc de Triomphe to Place de la Concorde. It provides frontage for numerous fashionable restaurants, car showrooms and cinemas.

The Louvre was built in the thirteenth century and has been used as a palace, the headquarters of the French Revolution and as a museum. A modern glass pyramid was added in front of the traditional palace-like building in 1988 to symbolise the meeting of the old and the new. Today, many visitors come to see the famous works of art on display, including Leonardo da Vinci's painting the Mona Lisa, and the French crown jewels which are also on display here. As there are so many exhibits it takes several days to see everything.

Events

The most important national day in France is 14 July, when the 1789 storming of the Bastille prison, the key event which triggered the French Revolution, is commemorated. The day is celebrated as a national holiday and many special events are organised, including street parties and firework displays.

ACTIVITY

Events

Look up *Pariscope* and *L'Officiel des Spectacles*, which publish a what's on guide in French with weekly information on entertainment. For an English version of events in Paris, look up the *Time Out* website www.timeout.com and click on information for Paris.

Food and drink

France is famous across the world for its food and drink. Cafes offer freshly baked bread in the form of baguettes and a range of pastries. Eating out in France is an experience with a unique character, flavour and service. Wine is the national drink and those who wish to learn more about the 450 French varieties are catered for with tours to local vineyards.

Accommodation

A huge range of accommodation is available in Paris. Hotel chains which offer a basic standard of accommodation with en-suite facilities include:

- Akena
- Balladins
- Bonsaï
- Etap
- Fasthotel
- Marmotte
- Formule 1
- Mister Bed
- Nuit d' Hötel
- Onestar Plus
- Premiére Classe
- Village Hotels

Some hotels offer special deals through the French tourist authority; Bon Weekend en Villes offers tourists two nights for the price of one. Other attractions include a weekend package which includes breakfast, free accommodation for children under 12, two metro or bus passes and a discount card. Other forms of accommodation range from bed and breakfast arrangements to gîtes, privately owned self-catering accommodation, although these are found mainly in rural areas.

Transport

Getting around the city is easiest on the Paris metro, an underground railway system which is integrated with the RER express train routes. These trains operate 20 hours a day and are more frequent than those on the London Underground. Buses are also frequent and both types of transport offer free route maps to help tourists to plan their journeys. Taxis are a common sight and fares are reasonably priced. To travel in style, the Batobus river taxi operates from May to September. There are five stops close to the capital's major tourist attractions and boats run every 30 minutes.

Recent trends in popularity

Paris was popular as a destination for UK tourists throughout the 1990s. Some of the factors which account for its popularity include:

- the opening of the Channel Tunnel in 1995 and the introduction of Le Shuttle and Eurostar services

- the availability of low-cost road, rail, air and sea transport options

- the opening of Disneyland, Paris

- the increasing popularity of short-break holidays

- the increasing popularity of independent travel and touring

- the development of camp sites with a full range of facilities and services

- the growing popularity of traditional gîtes in the villages surrounding Paris

- increasing interest in French cuisine (food and drink)

- the popularity of shopping in France following abolition of duty free allowances, especially for wine and tobacco

- favourable exchange rates with the French franc.

Major international events like the football World Cup in 1998 provided France with a world stage on which to promote itself as both a host nation and as a tourist destination. The event is said to have had an estimated 37 billion cumulative television viewers worldwide. The 10 football stadiums attracted a further 2.5 million spectators over the five-week tournament.

The Paris region is set to develop further as a tourist destination, as the number of Channel Tunnel passengers increases and ferry services become faster with an even greater range of on-board facilities. Improved transport helps to make France an attractive holiday destination which offers easy access to visitors from the UK.

Disneyland, Paris is also helping to increase the number of sightseeing visitors to the city as many Disneyland customers include a sightseeing tour of Paris as part of their holiday package. A recent advertising campaign by Disneyland, Paris highlighted the close proximity of France to the UK and the relative ease of travel. It also promoted France as a tourist destination with the slogan 'the magic is closer than you think'. (See also pp. 233–4.)

Further information

French Government Tourist Office
178 Piccadilly, London, W1V 0AL
Tel: 0891 244 123 (France information line)
Fax: 020 7493 6594
Website: **www.franceguide.com**
www.paris-touristoffice.com

ACTIVITY

Paris

You have been asked to plan a six-day tour of Paris for a group of 20 students aged between 16 and 19 from your school or college.

- Assess the suitability of travelling by road, rail, sea and air and include a comparison of cost and journey time. Also include a route plan from the point of departure in the UK to Paris.

- Devise an itinerary for the six-day tour, based on your chosen transport method and the range of attractions in and around Paris.

- Make a list of the travel principals which use Paris Charles de Gaulle and Orly airports.

- Use a range of holiday brochures to identify five chartered airlines that fly to Paris.

North America

TRAVEL FILE

The North American continent includes the countries of the United States of America and Canada.

Canada borders Alaska to the north west and the USA to the south. The Arctic Circle lies to the north. Much of Canada is sparsely populated and is characterised by stunning scenery. The climate varies according to location within this vast continent. It ranges from a polar climate in the north to a cool temperate climate in the south. However in southern Alberta, a warm dry wind known as a chinook, which is active in the spring, can raise temperatures by more than 25°C in an hour.

Canada offers the tourist a contrast of scenic beauty and vibrant city life. It attracts visitors who are predominantly from the USA and Europe. In 1997, 13,342,000 visitors to Canada came from the USA. The number of visitors from the UK was the second highest, at 744,000 trips, whilst the number of French visitors was the third highest at 440,000 trips. The large numbers of American tourists is due both to the geographical location of the country next door and the low value of the Canadian dollar in relation to the US dollar.

Canadian tourism is centred around the urban areas of Ottawa, the capital city, Vancouver, Montréal and Toronto, which are all cosmopolitan in character. From a distance, the Montréal skyline looks like any other north American city, yet on closer inspection the old city is distinguished by cobbled streets with restored eighteenth century warehouses. Montréal is a blend of the historic with the contemporary and the city has many exciting architectural designs, including the world's tallest inclined tower. Montréal is also the largest French-speaking city after Paris.

Canada promotes itself as the ideal location for rural tourism. It offers 38 national parks and marine conservation areas. Canada has the longest coastline in the world and when the shoreland of its 52,455 islands is included, it measures 243,792 km.

Canada's oldest national park is Banff, which was established in the 1930s. In the national parks visitors can witness rugged mountains, glaciers, alpine meadows and native wildlife which includes caribou and grizzly bears. Outdoor pursuits such as hiking, canoeing, skiing and the use of snow-mobiles, attract a wide range of tourists.

The United States of America shares its borders with Canada in the north and Mexico in the south. Forty-nine states are located on the mainland, with the state of Alaska on the north west corner separated by Canada. Hawaii, the fiftieth state, lies in the Pacific Ocean. The USA is made up of 50 states and the Federal District of Columbia, which contains the capital city, Washington.

Although the climate varies depending on location within this vast continent, it includes the two types of climate most popular with tourists; the warm temperate climate (also known as a Mediterranean climate) which is found on the west coast, and the subtropical climate of the coasts to the south.

Many of the American states have significant levels of tourism. The main areas of this activity are Florida, California, New York and Washington DC. DC stands for District of Columbia, an administrative district created to contain the capital city. Most European visitors are attracted by the east coast which includes New York, Orlando, Miami, Washington, Boston and Chicago. On the west coast, Los Angeles, San Francisco, San Diego and Las Vegas are also popular with UK tourists.

Urban tourism in the form of short city breaks to the east coast has grown over the last ten years. New York is the top destination for short-break holidays and attracts 25 per cent of all west European arrivals, whilst Orlando (Florida) receives 15 per cent visitors from western Europe. New York attracts 720,000 annual visitors from the UK, 40,000 from Germany and 300,000 from France.

Orlando, Florida

Orlando is the largest city in central Florida. It is located in an area known as the tourist quarter six km from Universal Studios, 16 km from Sea World and 32 km from Walt Disney World.

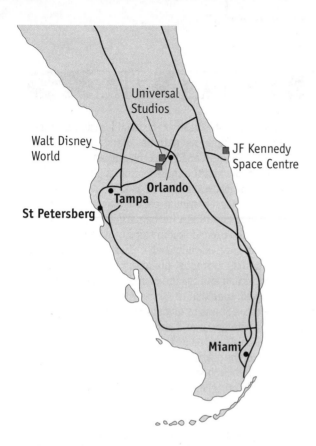

Florida has become the number one long-haul destination for UK tourists and receives the largest number of overseas visitors of any American state, approximately 7,225,000 people each year. The state of Florida receives 1.5 million tourists from the UK each year out of a total of 32 million tourists who visit Florida annually. Most of the tourists who visit Florida are American and Canadian. US and UK tourists are drawn to the many built attractions of Orlando. Those seeking a two-centre holiday may combine a week's stay in Orlando with a week on the coast in Miami or Clearwater. The city of Miami offers tourists both a beach holiday and a city break, as it is located on the coast. Miami is known locally as the city of the future because of its impressive skyline, a range of high-quality hotels and vibrant commercial districts.

The state is regarded as an all-year-round holiday destination. Southern Florida receives most of its visitors in the early spring, whilst the northern resorts receive the majority of their tourists during early summer.

Travel principals

Most of the major international airports offer daily flights to Florida. As the destination is so popular with UK holidaymakers, many tour operators offer packages. Figure 3.22 sets out some of the many names associated with holidays to Florida.

Main routes and gateways

Orlando Airport lies 14 km from the centre of Orlando and 35 kilometres from Walt Disney World resort. Transfer takes 20–30 minutes by taxi and 40 minutes by bus. Most visitors arrive by air and the range of airline carriers, rates and routes is diverse. The continuing development of tourism in Orlando has led to the creation of a second major gateway to the destination, Sandford Airport, which is situated approximately 35 km to the north of Orlando. Other airport gateways into Florida include Miami and Tampa.

Fly-drive package holidays are popular, as they give tourists the freedom to explore the state. Much of the USA is inaccessible without a car. Some fly-drive packages are inclusive of hotel vouchers which can be used to pre-book a number of hotel nights in a designated hotel chain at a discounted price.

Road access to Florida is from the north. Interstate 95 is the main routeway to the Atlantic seaboard states. Interstate 75 links the American midwest to the Gulf coast of Florida. Interstate 10 travels east from Los Angeles and California to Florida and joins Interstate 75 and 95.

Figure 3.22: Principals serving Florida
Airtours
American Airlines
British Airways
Continental Airlines
Cosmos Air
Delta Air Lines
JMC Holidays
Princess Cruises
Sabena Airlines
Thomson Holidays/Britannia Airways
TWA (Trans World Air)
Unijet Travel
United Airlines
Virgin Atlantic

Other travel principals also offer services to Florida.

Source: ABTA 1999

Climate

> Florida does not have an official rainy season. The general rule is that the hotter summer months also have the most rain showers. The usual pattern is that the afternoon heat usually brings mid-afternoon showers. By evening these have cleared. It is the summer months that also have the possibility of tropical storms and on rare occasions they reach hurricane force. The last hurricane in Florida was Andrew, in August 1995. Hurricanes lose their force over land, so Orlando is usually unaffected. Thanks to El Niño, strange weather patterns happened in 1998 all over the world and Florida had some tornados. This was very unusual. They are not expected again! By the way, Florida rain is usually warm!
>
> Source: Virgin Territory Florida and Caribbean brochure, January 1999 – March 2000

Florida is known as the sunshine state and it has over 300 sunny days each year. In January, temperatures can reach 80°F (26.5°C). Temperature in the US is recorded in degrees Fahrenheit rather than degrees Celsius. Southern Florida is subtropical, with hot and humid summer days. Winters tend to be cooler in the north.

Figure 3.23: Florida climate data

	Temperature (average daily maximum)	Sunshine hours (average daily hours)
May	88°F (31°C)	9
June	90°F (32°C)	9
July	91°F (32°C)	9
August	91°F (33°C)	8
September	90°F (32°C)	7
October	84°F (29°C)	7

Topography

Florida is located on a peninsula that has the Atlantic Ocean to the east and the Gulf of Mexico to the west. The eastern coast is called the Gold Coast because of its golden sandy beaches, while the eastern coast is known as the Gulf Coast. There is approximately 2,090 km of shoreline which includes 1,290 km of beach. The state is about the size of Great Britain and extends from Jacksonville and Tallahassee in the north to Miami and the Florida Keys in the south.

Over 10,000 square kilometres of Florida is water, originating from the Appalachian mountains. A number of rivers and streams offer tourists opportunities to take a boat ride, fish or canoe. The Everglades in the south are mangrove swamps which extend into grassland areas. Swimming is not recommended, as the waterways often contain alligators.

Florida contains large areas of national and state forests and is known for its exports of timber and paper. Most of the forests are accessible to the public.

Natural attractions

In addition to the many popular beaches, the Florida Keys and the Everglades are popular natural attractions. The Florida Keys are a string of small islands at the southern tip of the peninsula which extends from Key Largo. There are about 100 Keys, which are made of coral and surrounded by mangrove swamps with palm and pine trees. Forty-two bridges link the small islands along the Over Seas Highway, including the Seven Mile Bridge, named after the distance of water it crosses between islands. Watersports attract many visitors. With brightly coloured fish, coral reefs and accessible shipwrecks to explore, the Florida Keys offer some of the best diving and snorkelling in North America.

The Everglades National park covers 550,000 hectares. Most visitors enter the park through the main entrance near Homestead, south west of Miami. The main feature of the Everglades is an 80 km river of grass. The water is fed through a river system from Lake Okeechobee down towards the Florida Keys. Those who visit for the first time and do not leave their cars are sometimes disappointed by the miles of swampy grassland.

Built attractions

Orlando has three distinctive parts: International Drive, Kissimmee and Lake Buena Vista. Its largest attraction is Walt Disney World, which is located to the south west of International Drive.

Wet 'n' Wild is America's leading water park. Acres of water slides, flumes, chutes and pools provide entertainment and many rides are designed with groups in mind. Water rides are kept safe by qualified life guards and attendants. New attractions include the

Hydra Fighter, which launches 12 people at a time high into the air before sending them on a 'water adventure'. For the children who do not want to be left out, miniature versions of the park's most popular rides are available. Wet 'n' Wild is open all year round and uses heated pools in cooler weather.

Universal Studios is described as the number one movie studio and theme park in the world. With over 40 rides, movie sets and shows, it provides a wide range of family entertainment. Its rides have become famous across the world including Back To The Future, Terminator 2: 3D Battle Across Time, Jaws and ET Adventure. Recent additions include Twister! The Ride, and City Walk, which allows visitors to experience a variety of nightclubs, shops, cinemas and restaurants.

Islands of Adventure, opened in 1999, has been designed as a theme park for the twenty-first century. It is based on film and fictional characters and presented on five distinct islands: Seuss Landing, The Lost Continent, Jurassic Park, Toon Lagoon and Marvel Super Hero Island.

Belz Factory Outlet World is located 12 km from Walt Disney World resort and has 65,000 square metres of retail space. Shoppers can buy discounted goods direct from manufacturers in 160 stores. Designer labels in denim, sunglasses and trainers tend to be much cheaper than those for sale in the UK.

Sea World has a range of live sea creatures, including beluga whales, dolphins and stingrays as well as polar bears. Water-coaster rides take visitors on a Journey to Atlantis to explore the lost city and a jet-copter ride takes its passengers to the Wild Arctic.

The most famous of all the Orlando theme parks is the Walt Disney World resort. Much larger than Disneyland in California, Disney World is not just a theme park but a purpose-built resort in its own right. Visitors are encouraged to spend their entire vacation within the resort, although the resort does also receive many day visitors. The attractions here are known throughout the world; The Magic Kingdom, EPCOT and Disney MGM Studios to name but three. Disney's latest addition is a 200-hectare Animal Kingdom theme park, with rides, views and encounters with wild animals.

Disney World also offers three water parks: Disney's River Country Water Park provides family entertainment built around slides, chutes and rope swings. Disney's Typhoon Lagoon Water Park is primarily for the surf fanatic, with river rafting, rapids, twisting tides and water slides. The latest addition is Disney's Blizzard Beach Water Park, with the Summit Plummet, the world's tallest and fastest free-fall slide.

As the emphasis is on family fun, the Walt Disney World resort also includes a sports complex, five championship golf course, shopping and live music, as well as a range of entertainments.

Visitors to Orlando can purchase an Orlando FlexTicket, a prepaid ticket which permits access to either three, four or five parks. Purchasing a ticket can reduce the overall price if several parks are to be visited during a vacation.

Food, drink and entertainment

America has a reputation for offering large portions of high-quality food at reasonable prices and Florida is no exception. Traditional American steaks, burgers and fried foods are common, along with an abundance of seafood dishes. Tourists from the UK have a sense of familiarity, as many American restaurants and diners are common sights on British high streets.

Entertainment is provided with shows, live music, sport, exhibitions and a wide range of nightclubs. Almost every hotel offers some form of holiday entertainment and local bars show sporting events, often to a regular crowd of people. The main forms of entertainment can be found in the tourist attractions themselves, as they have become resorts in their own right and offer entertainment 20 hours a day.

Events

Florida covers a wide area and there are many annual events throughout the state. Most of the events take place out of the main tourist season. They include:

- January – Orange Bowl Football Classic, Orange Bowl, Miami

- January to April – Key West's Old Islands Days, Key West

- February – Miami Film Festival, Miami

- February – Florida State Fair, Tampa

- February – Speed Weeks, Daytona Speedway

- February – Kissimmee Livestock Show and Rodeo

- March – Miami Carnival

- March – Springtime Tallahassee

- April – Seafood Festival, Fort Lauderdale

- December– Grand Illumination, St Augustine

- December – Winterfest and Boat Parade, Fort Lauderdale.

Types of accommodation

Florida hotels and motels often charge room per night rates. Facilities are adequate, with private bathrooms, showers, television and air-conditioning. Many hotel and motel chains have voucher schemes which allow visitors to book accommodation ahead. Most of the popular accommodation is booked very quickly.

Accommodation with restaurant facilities may offer

full-board and half-board but these are given different names. American plan is full-board and modified American plan is half-board. If no plan is stated, an American continental breakfast is sometimes offered, which consists of coffee and doughnuts.

Major hotel chains in the state include Best Western Hotels, Clarion and Comfort Inns, Days Inn, Hilton Hotels, Holiday Inns, Hyatt Hotels, Marriott Hotels and Resorts, Ramada Inns, Sheraton Hotels, Motor Inns and Super 8 Motels.

There are many other types of accommodation, from condominiums (high-rise apartments) to guest houses, youth hostels and camping. Most camp sites are frequented by people using motor homes. Florida's state parks offer organised camp sites. Setting up camp away from designated areas requires special permission.

Recent trends in popularity

The most important change in the last ten years is the development of the US market as a mass holiday destination for UK tourists. Over 70 per cent of British package holidays to the US are based in Florida.

The recent trends have been to establish resort-based holidays and also create a new kind of package which combines resort holidays with independent travel, known as the fly-drive. UK tourists feel confident that they can travel independently in an English-speaking country whose culture appears to be familiar. Other developments that have led to growth in the market include improved tourism infrastructure, cheaper airfares due to intense competition on transatlantic routes and the ever increasing range of high-quality tourist attractions in the resorts.

Economic considerations have also had a positive impact on visitor numbers. Average living costs are lower in the US than in the UK. The lower costs of food,

accommodation, petrol and holiday gifts make Orlando an attractive proposition. The sterling exchange rate was relatively stable against the US dollar throughout the 1990s and ensured the state's reputation as a value for money destination.

Further information

In the USA each state is responsibly for its own tourist information and no national tourist office exists.
Central Florida Convention and Visitors Bureau, PO Box 61, Cypress Gardens, FL 33884, Florida, USA.
Fax: 001 941 534 0886
Website: www.goflorida.com/orlando

ACTIVITY

Florida

- Use a range of brochures to identify the resort characteristics that make Florida a popular destination for UK tourists.

- Produce a costing and itinerary of a two-week fly-drive holiday with a brief itinerary for a family of four (two adults, two children). Don't forget to include the types and timing of the transport used.

- What factors over the last ten years have contributed to the rising popularity of Florida as a holiday resort for UK tourists?

The Caribbean

TRAVEL FILE

Cuba
Haiti
Jamaica
Dominican Republic
St Lucia
Barbados
Trinidad and Tobago

The Caribbean is a not country in its own right, but a collection of 35 islands that stretch along a 4,000 km arc from Florida to Venezuela which encloses the Caribbean Sea. The most popular islands with tourists from the UK are the Dominican Republic, Barbados and Jamaica.

The tropical climate produces annual daily temperatures of over 25°C, which are cooled by the easterly trade wind from the Atlantic Ocean. Winters are milder and drier than the summers. The hurricane season is between July and October.

The attractions for tourists are the islands' climate and coastlines, which produce some of the world's most breathtaking beaches. Most islands capitalise on this by offering watersports and beach entertainment.

Each Caribbean island has its own particular characteristics. Some islands were created by volcanoes, others have been built over time by coral, sand and limestone and some are the tips of underwater mountains. A wide colonial background has brought a mix of cultures to each of the islands from the British, Irish, French, Dutch, Danish, Spanish, Indian, Chinese and African nations.

Cruises are very popular in the Caribbean and most of the cruise traffic can be described under three main headings:

- short one to four-day cruises from Miami or Port Canaveral to the Bahamas, and from Puerto Rico to the US Virgin Islands

- one-week cruises from Miami to the northern Caribbean and Yucatan, and from San Juan (Puerto Rico) to the US Virgin Islands

- two-week cruises from Florida to the whole of the Caribbean. These are declining in popularity and the southernmost islands have lost substantial numbers of cruise arrivals.

The island that has received most UK visitors during the last ten years is Barbados. This was a British colony from 1628 and became a sovereign state in 1966.

Country of origin	1993	1994	1995	1996	1997	% 1997
United Kingdom	551.1	644.5	683.6	742.2	957.3	23.0
France *	547.0	633.5	710.8	778.4	863.0	20.8
Germany	558.9	569.4	604.1	643.7	645.6	15.5
Holland	199.1	215.9	234.6	246.0	245.9	5.9
Italy	193.8	214.2	328.6	412.7	449.5	10.8
Spain	187.9	201.8	228.8	272.6	293.0	7.1
Sweden	29.7	21.3	25.9	27.2	41.5	1.0
Other Europe **	600.8	696.6	572.3	602.7	658.7	15.9
Totals ***	2,868.3	3,197.2	3,388.7	3,725.5	4,154.4	100.00

Figure 3.24: Tourist arrivals from Europe to the Caribbean (thousands)

* In some destinations, figures include arrivals from the French West Indies   ** Excludes Eastern Europe, includes arrivals from unspecified European countries

*** Includes estimates for missing data

Barbados

Barbados is a pear-shaped island of 430 square kilometres. It is 2,585 km south east of Miami and 860 km north east of Caracas, Venezuela.

Barbados has recently experienced six consecutive years of increased tourist arrivals. In 1998, 512,397 staying visitors came to the island, 8.5 per cent more than in 1997. This included 186,690 arrivals from the UK, up by 19.7 per cent on the previous year. UK tourists are the most important market and account for 36.4 per cent of long-stay arrivals. In 1998, Barbados received a total of 506,610 cruise ship passengers, a slight decrease of 2 per cent on the previous year.

In total, Barbados welcomed 1,019,007 visitors in 1998, its highest number ever and the first time in the island's history that tourist arrivals have exceeded one million.

The Barbadian people are known as Bajans and tourism has become the leading industry on the island. Holiday brochures describe Barbados as a place to relax in sophisticated style. The island has several typically British characteristics, such as stately homes, green countryside, cricket matches, championship golf, tennis and a tradition of serving afternoon tea.

Travel principals

Some of the major travel principals to Barbados are shown in Figure 3.26. The main cruise line companies that operate to Bridgetown include:

- Carnival Cruise Lines
- Chandris Cruises
- Costa Cruises
- Cunard Cruise Lines
- Epirotiki Lines (World Renaissance)
- Holland American Lines
- Norwegian Cruise Lines
- Ocean Cruise Lines
- Regency Cruises
- Royal Caribbean Lines
- Royal Cruise Lines
- Sun Line
- Wind Star Cruises.

Figure 3.26: Major principals serving Barbados

Air Canada

Airtours

American Airlines

British Airways

BWIA International

Cosmos Air

First Choice Holidays

Fred Olsen Cruises

JMC Holidays

KLM Airlines

Princess Cruises

P&O Cruises

Thomson Holidays/Britannia Airways

Virgin Atlantic

Other travel principals also offer services to Barbados

Source: ABTA 1999

Figure 3.25: Barbados facts and figures

Population Approximately: 254,000

Offical language: English

Currency: Barbados Dollar

Accommodation: caters for all tastes and budgets from luxury hotels and all-inclusive resorts to rooms in small hotels and self-catering apartments

Sports: Snorkelling, diving, fishing, sailing, waterskiing, tennis, squash. Two 18-hole and two nine-hole golf courses

Main routes and gateways

The main gateway by air to Barbados is through Barbados Grantley Adams International Airport, 11 km east of Bridgetown. Buses take on average 40-60 minutes, whilst taxis take on average 30 minutes to reach the centre.

The second most important gateway is by sea. Bridgetown's Deep Water Harbour is a kilometre from the centre and has a large cruise ship passenger terminal. Most people travelling by sea only visit the island for one or two days. The modern terminal is equipped with shops, banks and other associated facilities.

Climate

Barbados receives about 3,000 hours of sunshine each year, an average of over eight hours each day. The tradewinds help to keep the island cool. Rain is experienced in short showers, except during the hurricane season. These tropical storms usually pass to the north of the island. February to May are the driest months. In July, the wettest month, there is an average 18 days of rainfall. In April, the driest month, rainfall averages seven days.

Topography

Barbados has been created over many millions of years by coral building on top of sedimentary rocks. Water is evident in the island in underground streams, springs and limestone caves. Although most of the island is relatively flat, the northern part rises to a height of 340 metres at Mount Hillaby. Locally this is known as Scotland District, because of its rugged appearance.

The western coastline has white sandy beaches and clear blue waters. This contrasts with the eastern side of the island which faces the Atlantic Ocean whose waters are not suitable for bathing. Most of the island is surrounded by coral reefs.

Natural attractions

The beaches of Barbados are not just reserved for sun worshippers but are entertainment centres, hosting barbecues, steel bands and limbo displays. The island has over 112 km of coastline and gives plenty of opportunities to explore. Some beaches specialise in watersports, others have fine restaurants, whilst some are remote and undeveloped.

Harrison's Cave in St Thomas is a natural attraction that receives many tourists. It is a long cavern complemented by atmospheric lighting and is seen from a special train that runs for nearly two kilometres underground. Near to the lowest point of the cave system is the highlight of the tour, a spectacular 12 metre high waterfall that plunges into a large blue-green lake.

Near to Harrison's Cave is Flower Forest, 20 hectares of tropical plants on a former sugar plantation. It contains nearly every type of plant to be found on the island and has spectacular views of the Chalky Mountains and of the Atlantic Ocean.

Built attractions

The capital of Barbados, Bridgetown, is a relatively small city with a distinctly British character. The centre has a miniature replica of London's Trafalgar Square complete with a statue of Lord Nelson. This bustling city has a lot of impressive government buildings that reflect the naval and colonial history of the island. Other evidence of the country's colonial past includes a large Anglican cathedral, which was the home of the seventeenth century British garrison, and the Barbados Museum, which tells the history of the island.

Figure 3.27: Barbados climate data

	Temperature (average daily maximum)	Sunshine (average hours)
January	81°F (26.5°C)	8
February	81°F (26.5°C)	6
March	82°F (27°C)	8
April	84°F (29°C)	8
May	86°F (30°C)	8
June	87°F (30.5°C)	8
July	87°F (30.5°C)	9
August	88°F (31°C)	8
September	88°F (31°C)	8
October	86°F (30°C)	7
November	84°F (29°C)	8
December	82°F (27°C)	7

Local attractions include the open-air Rastafarian markets located in Temple Yard and Cheapside Market.

Old British colonial houses can be seen on the sugar plantations to the south of the island. Some of these houses have been turned into museums or restaurants, while others are still used as homes. Some of the many sugar factories have visitor centres which explain how the island's largest natural export is processed.

A popular tourist attraction for UK tourists is the Malibu Visitor Centre, which includes a tour around the West Indies rum distillery. A special day pass allows visitors to tour the facilities, take an all-inclusive lunch, sample the rum and take part in a range of sports and activities on Malibu beach.

Events

Annual attractions include the month-long Crop Over celebrations when street parties and parades are held to celebrate the end of the sugar cane crop. The grand finale is Kadooment Day, the first Monday in August. Visitors are often invited to take part in the revelry. Other festivals include the Oistins Fish Festival during Easter weekend and the National Independence Festival of Creative Arts held during November.

There are also a number of sporting events, including the Barbados Windsurfing World Cup, held in January and the Caribbean Surfing Championship, held in early November. A number of championship golf courses are also available on the island. Barbados has a range of international sports facilities and many specialist sporting activity tour operators include Barbados in their lists of destinations.

Food, drink and entertainment

Local cuisine includes many fish dishes. The most popular are flying fish, dolphin fish, red snapper and hot salt fish cakes. Bajan food is well seasoned and is accompanied by rice or macaroni pie. Fast food has an American flavour: pizza, chicken hamburgers and the local speciality, roti – a spicy parcel of chicken, beef or prawn that originated in Trinidad.

Rum is the main tropical drink on the island, although most locals drink fresh fruit juices and beer. Bottles of rum are popular as souvenirs with UK tourists.

Most restaurants in the major tourist areas offer entertainment from singers to fire-eaters in order to attract diners. Almost all hotels offer an entertainment schedule which is often combined with dinner-dances.

Rum and calypso tours, which offer boat trips around the island with food, drink and traditional calypso dancing are popular.

Although there are nightclubs in Bridgetown and other centres, the types of tourist that Barbados welcomes from the UK are more attracted by beach oriented entertainment.

Types of accommodation

There are more than 140 hotels, guest houses, apartments and holiday cottages on the island. Hotels offer a range of meal options which are bookable in advance:

- European plan – room only
- Continental plan – room plus continental breakfast
- modified American plan – room plus cooked breakfast and lunch
- American plan – room plus breakfast, lunch and dinner.

Each Caribbean island has a hotel rating system based on a number of stars, however this is not standardised across the islands.

It is becoming more common for resorts to offer all-inclusive packages to UK tourists. Packages vary between tour operators; some include the use of water sports, health and beauty treatments and laundry. Some of these packages are expensive, but contain a long list of extra services that are found in some of the Caribbean's top hotels. Some hotels, aware of their up-market image, are very strict about their policy towards children, to the extent that some hotels positively discourage them.

Staying with a family or booking a room in a guest house is a cheaper option than staying in a hotel. Guest houses have between six and eight rooms and are usually attached to a family home. They may offer room only and some offer evening meals.

Types of transport

The best way to travel throughout the island is by bus. There are three types of bus: government-operated buses which have the most extensive routes, a local minibus system and a taxi-bus system.

Taxis operate on a fare system set by the government but are unmetered, so tourists are advised to agree a price before travelling.

Although tourists can rent cars, all the car hire companies are locally owned which means that cars have to be hired upon arrival. Temporary driving permits are required which are available at the hire car companies.

Bicycles are also available for hire, and offer a relaxed tour of the island, especially in the south which is relatively flat.

Recent trends in popularity

The tourist attractions of Barbados are small scale compared to some other tourist destinations but that is part of the charm that makes Barbados popular. The Barbados Tourism Authority aims to increase the island's reputation as a high quality resort by improving its range of golf, sailing, villa and conference facilities. The number of golf courses, for example, is set to increase from four to seven by the year 2002. There are 1,000 fewer hotel rooms on the island than there were ten years ago, but they are generating three times as much income. Tour operators are increasing the number of flights to Barbados from the UK in a bid to make the island more accessible.

Further information

For more information on the Caribbean islands, visit the Caribbean Tourism Organisation website: www.caribtourism.com

For details on Barbados contact the Barbados Tourism Authority, 263 Tottenham Court Road, London, W1P 0LA.
Tel: 020 7636 9448
Fax: 020 7637 1496
Website: **www.barbados.org**

ACTIVITY

Barbados

1 You have been asked to arrange a visit for a mature couple who want to holiday in Barbados for two weeks. Produce a holiday costing and an itinerary of suggested activities, describing what there is to do and see on the island. As the couple have not been there before you will need to include a map.

2 The Barbados Ministry for Tourism has asked you to produce a written report on the tourism development of the island during the last ten years. You are expected to have researched tourism information (see Figures 3.24 and 3.25) and to have carried out your own independent research. The document is expected to include a list of recommendations that will help the government decide what it should do to encourage tourism during the next ten years.

Australasia

TRAVEL FILE

Australasia includes the countries of Australia and New Zealand.

New Zealand is 1,930 km south east of Australia and consists of two major islands separated by the Cook Straight. Smaller islands make up the rest of the country's land surface. To the north of North Island, the Auckland Peninsula is the most densely populated part of New Zealand and is home to nearly 75 per cent of the country's inhabitants. The area has fertile green fields as well as beaches. The island has four active volcanoes. South Island is dominated by the Southern Alps and has associated features of glaciers and fjords.

The climate is cooler on South Island than North Island and the mountains receive a lot of winter snowfall. On average, the country has a mild climate, with winter temperatures staying above 2°C. Rainfall is plentiful; the west of the country receives 2,540 mm of rain each year.

New Zealand relies on its neighbour, Australia, for its flow of tourists. Many Australians go to New Zealand when they are on holiday and some tourists visit New Zealand and Australia on a two-country holiday. Natural attractions and landscape form the basis of New Zealand's appeal. The country receives over a million international arrivals a year. On average North Island receives 5 per cent more arrivals than South Island. The main gateways are Auckland and Wellington on North Island, and Christchurch on South Island.

Australia is a huge country, nearly the same size as the USA. It has an extensive 36,738 km of coastline. It is surrounded by the Arafura Sea, Timor Seas, Coral and Tasman Seas, the Southern Ocean and the Indian Ocean.

Figure 3.28: Tourist arrivals from UK and Ireland to Australia		
	Arrivals	Change on previous year
1988	273,000	3.1%
1989	285,000	4.3%
1990	288,000	1.1%
1991	273,000	−5.2%
1992	299,000	9.3%
1993	321,000	7.6%
1994	350,000	9.1%
1995	365,000	4.2%
1996	388,000	6.3%
1997	436,000	12.3%
1998	499,000	14.4%

Source: Australian Tourist Commission

The climate varies widely. In the north, about 40 per cent of the country experiences a tropical rain forest climate. The central area which is mainly desert, is known as the outback. The large fertile plateau in the south east experiences milder temperatures. Most of the population is situated on the south east coastline, including Brisbane, Sydney, Melbourne and Adelaide. Perth is situated on the western coastline.

Australia receives an average 339,000 UK tourists each year, the majority of whom enter the country through the international gateways of Sydney and Melbourne. Many British tourists travel to Australia to visit friends and relatives (VFR) or have an adventure holiday in the Australian outback.

The tourist industry has increased steadily during the last ten years by 2 to 3 per cent each year. Approximately 77 per cent of tourism is generated by the domestic market and the remaining 23 per cent is generated by international arrivals.

The tourist season in Australia is the reverse of that experienced in Europe, as the country is located on the other side of the world in the southern hemisphere. Most UK tourists visit Australia between November and December, an ideal time to spend Christmas with friends and family, and to escape the UK winter for the Australian summer.

Sydney, New South Wales

New South Wales, an area six times the size of the UK, is in south east Australia. It is home to 5.5 million people and presents a wide range of natural attractions from golden beaches and the Snowy Mountains in the south to the subtropical forests in the north. The main focus of tourism in this area is found in the state capital, Sydney. The centre of Sydney has been described as a mini Manhattan with skyscrapers and harbour views.

A survey in 1997 revealed that 387,800 tourists from the UK aged 15 years and over visited Australia and that of those, 259,400 visited New South Wales (67 per cent of total UK visitors).

The top attractions that UK tourists visit in New South Wales are:

- Blue Mountains (36 per cent)
- Hunter Valley (11 per cent)
- Central Coast, Gosford, Terrigal (10 per cent)
- Kiama, Wollongong (10 per cent)
- Southern Highlands, Bowral, Mittagong (5 per cent).

Figure 3.29: Top ten regions visited, 1997

Region	Rank	Visitors
Sydney, NSW	1	2,315,600
Gold Coast, QLD	2	994,500
Melbourne, VIC	3	951,400
Far North, QLD	4	731,200
Brisbane, QLD	5	687,600
Perth, WA	6	467,800
Adelaide, SA	7	254,300
Petermann, NT	8	234,200
Canberra, ACT	9	197,000
Alice Springs, NT	10	194,700

Source: Australian Tourist Commission

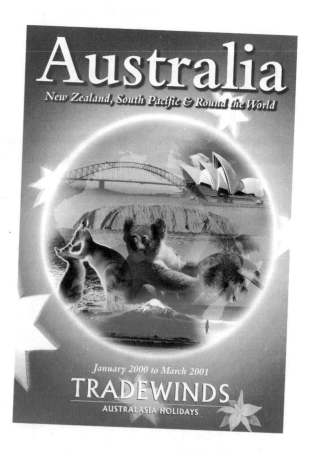

Australia
New Zealand, South Pacific & Round the World
January 2000 to March 2001
TRADEWINDS
AUSTRALASIA HOLIDAYS

Most of these are natural attractions. However, in the year 2000 the city will become the most important tourist attraction in the region when it hosts the Olympic Games.

Sydney has been described as Australia's premier city and is the oldest settlement in the country. According to the Australian Tourist Commission, the city is the economic powerhouse of the nation and the country's capital in everything but name.

Travel principals

Some of the main travel principals that organise tours of Australia are set out in Figure 3.30.

Figure 3.30: Main principals serving Australia

Air France

Austrian Airlines

British Airways

Cathay Pacific

Gulf Air

KLM Airlines

Korean Air

Lauda Air

Lufthansa

Malaysia Airlines

Philippine Airlines

Princess Cruises

P&O Cruises

Quantas Airways

Singapore Airlines

United Airlines

Virgin

Other travel principals also offer sewrvices to Australia

Source: ABTA 1999

Main routes and gateways

The two ways of getting to Australia are by air and by sea. Australia is considered to be the ultimate long-haul destination. The average journey time by air from London to Sydney is 24 hours. Most flights from the UK enter Australia via Sydney or Melbourne. Travellers seeking to avoid jetlag stop over in countries like Hong Kong or Singapore. Flights to Sydney land at Kingsford Smith Airport, 8 km south of Sydney. Transfer between airport and centre takes 20-30 minutes with direct bus routes and an efficient taxi service.

Internal flights are possible from major cities like Perth to Sydney, as most towns have a small airport.

By sea, the main routes are from the UK by air to Bali or Fiji and then by boat to Australia. Although the numbers on cruise liners are relatively small they are considered to be an important segment of the market.

Climate

The seasons in Australia are literally the reverse of those in the UK. Winter in Australia is from June to August, so Christmas takes place during the heat of the summer. As Australia covers such a wide area it extends from the tropics to the temperate zone. From April to September

Figure 3.31: Sydney climate data

	Temperature (average daily minimum)	Temperature (average daily maximum)
January	18°C (64°F)	26°C (79°F)
February	19°C (64°F)	26°C (79°F)
March	17°C (63°F)	25°C (77°F)
April	15°C (59°F)	22°C (72°F)
May	11°C (52°F)	19°C (66°F)
June	9°C (48°F)	17°C (63°F)
July	8°C (46°F)	16°C (61°F)
August	9°C (48°F)	18°C (64°F)
September	11°C (52°F)	20°C (68°F)
October	13°C (55°F)	22°C (72°F)
November	15°C (59°F)	24°C (75°F)
December	17°C (63°F)	25°C (77°F)

the tropics in north and central Australia are clear and warm. In the south, occasional rain can lower the temperatures to bring snow on the southern mountains.

Topography

Australia is a large country. It is 2,623 km from Adelaide to Darwin and 3,278 km from Sydney to Perth. The population is relatively small, with around 17 million living in a country the size of the USA (the American population is 265 million). The country can be divided in four distinct areas of the tropical north, the subtropical east coast, the Mediterranean south west and the desert and scrubland of the central region

Natural attractions

Sydney is surrounded with tourist attractions, including over 30 beaches, with a reputation for surfing, beach entertainment and scenery. Bondi beach is the closest ocean beach to Sydney and is famous for its surfing.

The spectacular Blue Mountains surround Sydney. When first seen they appear to have a blue colour as the light refracts through the haze of eucalyptus oil evaporating from the forest in the valleys below. The main town within the mountain range is Katoomba. Built in the nineteenth century, it attracts many tourists. From the town, the Three Sisters can be seen, an outcrop of rock that is shrouded in Aboriginal myth and legend as the sisters were said to have been turned to stone by their witch-doctor father. Another popular attraction is the Jenolan Caves and a view of the Jamieson Valley. This is made possible by boarding the scenic railway, the world's steepest railway line or the Scenic Skyway, a cable-car suspended high above the valley.

Hunter Valley is a famous wine producing area which attracts many tourists who visit the vineyards and sample the local produce. Australian wine, now a familiar sight on UK supermarket shelves, is an international industry. There are approximately 30 vineyards to explore in this region. The largest town in the Hunter Valley is the seaport of Newcastle. Newcastle's traditional industries are coal mining and shipbuilding. However, it is rapidly developing its tourist industry using its naval history and a beach that is renowned for its surfing.

Built attractions

When people think of Australia, and of Sydney in particular, they think of the famous opera house and its unique design. The roof is made of over a million tiles and 6,223 square metres of glass. The building houses five theatres, the largest of which seats 2,690 people. The opera house took more than 19 years to build and cost over Aus$100 million.

Sydney is a lively, cosmopolitan city. Amongst the array of theatres, museums and art galleries, there is a wide range of attractions for the tourist. The best views of the city can be seen from Sydney Tower at Centrepoint, high above the main shopping complex. At 305 metres high it is the tallest building in the southern hemisphere. At the top of the tower there are

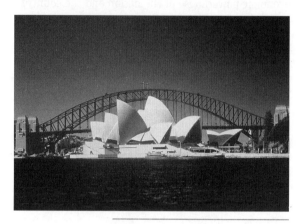

▲ Sydney Opera House

revolving restaurants and observation points.

The best shops and entertainment can be seen in George Street, Australia's oldest street. It contains the Queen Victoria Building which is now a shopping mall and houses 200 specialist shops, cafes and restaurants. Some of the leading attractions in Sydney include Taronga Zoo, the Harbour Bridge, the Australian Museum and Sydney Entertainment Centre.

Taronga Zoo is where most foreign tourists have their first meeting with native Australian animals: kangaroos, koala bears, platypus and over 1,500 species of native birds.

The Harbour Bridge, opened in 1932, is nicknamed the Coat Hanger. The bridge's single arch is 503 metres across and carries eight lanes of cars and two railway tracks, plus lanes for cyclists and pedestrians. Every year, over 40 million cars use the bridge, even though a new tunnel has been constructed to relieve congestion on its approach roads.

The Australian Museum is rated as one of the top five museums in the world. It tells the story of the history of Australia from fossil remains to the art, culture and history of the native Aborigines. Aboriginal arts and crafts are sold in the museum shop.

Sydney Entertainment Centre is set between Darling Harbour and Chinatown. It is designed for sporting events, concerts and other public gatherings and can admit 12,500 spectators.

Events

In January, the Festival of Sydney provides the scene for many outdoor events, from street entertainments to fireworks parties. The Royal Easter Show brings country life into the heart of the city during 12 days of celebration. The Sydney Film Festival takes place in June and the Rugby League Grand Final is held in September. A jazz festival is held in October and Christmas and New Year are celebrated on Bondi Beach.

Food, drink and entertainment

Many of Sydney's restaurants are to be found in Darlinghurst, King's Cross, Paddington and Glebe. Sydney's theatres are situated around the central business district and the famous opera house sits on the edge of Circular Quay.

Types of accommodation

Sydney has a variety of hotels and accommodation, from five-star penthouses to economy rooms. There are over 400,000 beds in the graded hotels alone. In Australia there is very little difference between a hotel and a motel. The main difference between the two is that a hotel has a bar that is open to the public, while a motel bar is strictly for guests only. Private hotels are often small guest houses and some private homes also take paying guests. Camping and youth hostelling are also popular.

Types of transport

The city has a reliable rail network including an underground service. The service can be slow but offers many discount deals and special rates. A more scenic way to travel is by ferry, which gives an excellent view of the harbour.

A monorail operates high above the city. Some locals see it as an ugly eyesore, others regard it as practical and futuristic.

Recent trends in popularity

A competitive tourist industry is considered important to Australia's future. Tourism is one of the fastest growing industries in Australia and contributes to over 10 per cent of the country's gross domestic product. More than four million visitors arrive each year and that figure is set to double within the next ten years.

Increases in the tourism market helped create 1.8 million new jobs in the service industries between 1984 and 1997. International tourism brought an estimated Aus$17 billion into Australia in 1997, which makes tourism one of the country's largest revenue earners.

The benefit of hosting the 2000 Olympic Games will be experienced in Australia for many years to come. It is estimated that during the three weeks of the previous games, televisions across the globe were switched on approximately 20 billion times.

Further information

Australian Tourist Commission, Gemini House, 10-18 Putney Hill, London, SW15 6AA.
Tel: 020 8780 2229
Tel: 0990 022 000 (Aussie helpline)
Fax: 020 8780 1496
Website: **atc.net.au**

ACTIVITY

Sydney

1 Describe the trend in visits to Australia from 1988 to 1998. Describe the rate of change that is taking place.

2 Explain why a fall in numbers in 1991 coincided with a long-running domestic strike by pilots.

3 Plan a working holiday to Australia for a student, using the most appropriate tour operators and the most cost-effective routes. The student wants to stay for two months. Suggest where the student would find out about visa requirements and find the latest information.

In this chapter we look at the ways in which travel and tourism organisations use marketing techniques and processes to achieve their objectives. Regardless of the type of travel and tourism organisation or the products and services that it offers, marketing plays a key function in its success. In this chapter you will learn that marketing is a continuous process that includes everything that an organisation does to attract and keep customers, identify and satisfy their needs, and continue to grow and develop successfully.

Marketing is particularly important in travel and tourism because the industry is fiercely competitive. Frequently, it is the effectiveness of a provider's marketing activities which determines if it is successful in attracting customers. This unit is assessed by an externally set case study or test.

4

Marketing in travel and tourism

The marketing process

THE INSTITUTE OF MARKETING describes **marketing** as:

the management process of identifying, anticipating and satisfying customer requirements profitably.

This means that those responsible for marketing within an organisation must be able to identify the needs of both existing and potential customers, in order to provide products and services that satisfy those needs. The main aim is usually to maximise income and generate profits. However, it is important to note that some organisations within the travel and tourism industry operate on a non-profit basis. In these circumstances, profitability may be measured in terms of benefit to the community rather than in financial terms. For example, many council-owned museums do not charge for entry and, so, do not make a profit.

Whatever the type of organisation and its motive for providing products and services, the basic principle that underpins the marketing concept is the same:

- getting the right product
- to the right people
- in the right place
- at the right time
- at the right price
- using the right promotion.

All travel and tourism providers need to recognise the important role that marketing plays in helping them to reach their organisational objectives.

Getting it right is vital, because if anything is wrong the customer will not be satisfied with the product or service, or the way in which it is delivered. If the customer is not satisfied, it is unlikely that the organisation will achieve its objectives. Even when an organisation gets everything right, that is not the end of the marketing process. It must continually monitor and evaluate progress to ensure that its products and services continue to meet customer needs.

This is particularly relevant to the travel and tourism industry, which is characterised by fierce competition and constantly changing customer expectations and needs. There are often a large number of providers of a given travel and tourism product and each aims to secure a larger share of the market than its competitors. For example, the package holiday market is highly competitive and providers are constantly trying to develop new products which are more attractive than those offered by competitors. Another example of the competitive and dynamic nature of the industry can be seen in the continuous development of new tourist attractions such as interactive museums and exhibits based on specific themes.

▼ Pitching copy at the right market

▲ The interactive Tower Bridge Experience in London

ACTIVITY

New tourist attractions

Find out the names of new or emerging tourist attractions that focus on:

- science and technology
- marine life
- pop music
- films and television
- areas of industry, such as mining or transport
- food.

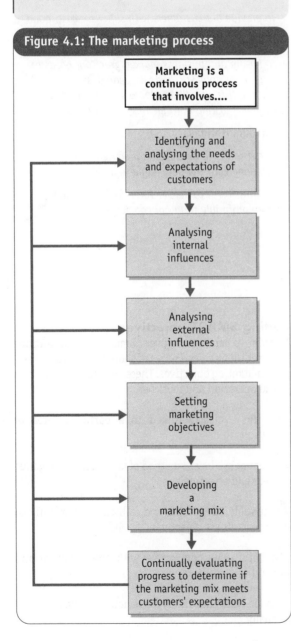

Figure 4.1: The marketing process

Marketing is a continuous process that involves....

- Identifying and analysing the needs and expectations of customers
- Analysing internal influences
- Analysing external influences
- Setting marketing objectives
- Developing a marketing mix
- Continually evaluating progress to determine if the marketing mix meets customers' expectations

Marketing is a **continuous process** that starts and finishes with the customer. It embraces everything an organisation does to identify, anticipate and satisfy customer needs and expectations (see Figure 4.1)

We are going to look at this process in more detail and will start by identifying marketing objectives in travel and tourism.

Marketing objectives

Before undertaking any marketing activity it is important that travel and tourism organisations focus clearly on what they hope to achieve. This involves setting **marketing objectives** from the outset and then continually reviewing and monitoring them to measure progress.

Organisations may have several key marketing objectives. They may include:

- analysing market needs
- satisfying customer requirements
- managing the effects of competition
- managing the effects of change
- coordinating a range of activities
- maximising income
- generating profit
- generating community benefit
- optimising customers' perception of the product.

Specific objectives are largely determined by the overall business objectives of the organisation. Private sector operators in travel and tourism usually gear their marketing towards achieving profit for their owners or shareholders. Consequently, their marketing objectives usually include a combination of the following:

- achieving a target level of sales
- expanding sales revenue to a specified level
- increasing market share
- entering new markets
- achieving an overall specified level of profit.

Figure 4.2 shows the marketing objectives of the New Millennium Experience Company.

Figure 4.2: Typical marketing objectives

The New Millennium Experience Company's objectives are:

- to deliver a once in a lifetime, high quality experience at Greenwich and a countrywide challenge programme to time and to budget

- to achieve at least 12 million visits to the Dome at Greenwich

- to deliver value for money to the Millennium Commission, sponsors and paying visitors

- to develop and implement the Experience (the Dome and the Challenge) in a way which:

  - optimises access, in the widest sense, by people of all ages, backgrounds and interests, achieving a nationally and socially inclusive event

  - involves, engages, entertains, educates and transforms the visitor and participant

  - makes best use of British and international creative talent and state of the art technology

- to create a world profile for the celebration of the millennium in the UK

- to assist and where possible, contribute to, the government's policy that there will be a lasting legacy for the nation from the Experience (the Dome and the Challenge).

Figure 4.3: Typical mission statements

The Natural History Museum

The museum's mission is to maintain and develop its collections and use them to promote the discovery, understanding, responsible use and enjoyment of the natural world.

The English Tourism Council

We drive forward to quality, competitiveness and wise growth of England's tourism, by providing intelligence, setting standards, creating partnerships and ensuring coherence.

easyJet

To provide our customers with safe, low-cost, good value, point-to-point air services. To offer a consistent and reliable product at fares appealing to leisure and business markets from our bases to a range of domestic and European destinations. To achieve this we will develop our people and establish lasting partnerships with our suppliers.

Airtours Holidays

Our vision is to be the UK's preferred holiday company with the best name in holidays.

Our mission is to deliver value for money holidays more profitably than our competitors.

Public and voluntary sector organisations that operate on a non-profit basis may also have some of the objectives listed above. However, they usually have other objectives, such as:

- generating community benefit

- targeting underrepresented and disadvantaged groups in the community

- promoting a cause, such as more active, healthy lifestyle

- increasing participation.

The general purpose or direction of an organisation is usually identified in a broad **mission or vision statement** or **philosophy of use**. This expresses the organisation's intent and can be used as a basis for developing specific objectives. Examples of mission statements in the travel and tourism industry are shown in Figure 4.3.

Setting SMART objectives

In order to achieve the overall mission, organisations must set themselves a series of short, medium and long-term marketing objectives. These are vital to the success of the operation and must be:

Specific – clearly linked to a particular area of operation

Measurable – have a method of measurement to gauge success and effectiveness

Achievable – be feasible and realistic, so that staff can work towards set objectives

Realistic – be compatible with the organisation's mission statement

Timed – have deadlines for review, weekly, monthly, annually.

Marketing objectives may cover financial, social and environmental issues. Some examples of **SMART objectives** are:

- increase income for the next month by 10 per cent

- reduce staffing budget by 15 per cent during January and February

- generate 50 per cent of all bookings from existing customers and repeat bookings

- achieve 10,000 paying visitors per month during next 12-month period

- give local youth organisations and disabled groups priority use of the facility between June and August

- generate 25 per cent of all bookings from people who are registered unemployed or those receiving income support

- give pensioners free use of the facility during off-peak periods

- reduce the number of customer complaints by 25 per cent in July and August

- increase the use of the park and ride scheme to 30 per cent of visitors to the city centre

ACTIVITY

Objectives and a mission statement for Creative Travel

Imagine that you are one of five candidates attending an interview at Creative Travel for the position of marketing manager. As part of the selection process you have been given the short written test that appears below. What would your answer be?

Creative Travel candidate selection test

Time: 30 minutes

Introduction: Creative Travel is a privately owned tour operator catering for the European package holiday market. It operates four distinct brands.

- **Hotspots** targets the family market by offering year-round package holidays to beach locations in European resorts.

- **Summer Sizzlers** caters for the 18–30 year market, offering budget holidays to popular resorts in Spain, Greece and Turkey.

- **Snowscene** focuses on the winter sports market by providing skiing and snowboarding package holidays in France, Switzerland, Austria and Bulgaria.

- **City Sights** offers short breaks throughout the year to five European cities.

Current trading figures show that demand for Hotspots packages has gradually declined over the last three years but still generates most of the company's profits. The main reason for the decline is thought to be the cheaper prices offered by the larger tour operators. Creative Travel is unable to reduce prices any further but feels that it offers better value for money because it is able to provide a personal touch.

Demand for Summer Sizzlers has shown the largest increase out of the four types of holidays offered. During peak season (June-September) demand exceeds the number of holidays available. Off-season (April- June and October/November), only 35 per cent of holidays available are sold.

Demand for Snowscene has remained the same for the last three years and 66 per cent of customers have been on a Snowscene holiday before.

Demand for City Sights has shown an increase each year for the last three years. Creative Travel is considering offering a further three European cities in the future.

Questions

1 If you were appointed as Creative Travel's marketing manager what would your first five SMART marketing objectives be?

2 Write a mission statement for the company.

Analysing internal factors

One of the first activities that organisations need to carry out in the marketing process is an analysis of the effectiveness of the company's operation and of the **internal factors** which influence success. This analysis is commonly carried out by conducting a **SWOT analysis**. This stands for:

Strengths

Weaknesses

Opportunities

Threats.

Strengths and weaknesses are internal factors that are within the control of the organisation. Opportunities and threats are outside the control of the organisation, for example, products offered by competitors or market forces such as seasonal fluctuations in demand.

A SWOT marketing analysis allows an organisation to plan future activities by considering a number of questions.

■ What are our strengths? How can we build on them to ensure that we offer a better product than our competitors?

■ What are our weaknesses? How can we eliminate them?

■ What are our opportunities? How are we going to use them to attract new customers or increase the number of products that existing customers buy?

■ What are our threats? How are we going to minimise them so that they do not affect sales of our products?

Figure 4.4 shows the SWOT analysis carried out by the Royal Armouries in Leeds.

Figure 4.4: Pre-launch SWOT analysis of the Royal Armouries in Leeds

Strengths

Attraction of royal status and connections
First national museum to be built outside London
Foremost collection of arms and armour
Wide educational opportunities
Management abilities – commercial and academic
Waterside environment
City centre accessibility
Mould breaker unique museum/attraction
Inspired use of technology
Interactive opportunities
Armouries at three locations

Weaknesses

Arms and armour
Perception of hunting and war
The name Royal Armouries
Lack of appreciation of what Royal Armouries is about
Perception of Leeds
Relevance of the museum in a changing world
The weather
Unattractive vicinity
Not in London
The use of technology off putting for the over 50s
Budgetary pressures, especially marketing
Lack of facilities for young children

Opportunities

Large potential target market
To become one of the UK's foremost visitor attractions
Widening the visitor experience through waterside use
Catalyst for development of tourism within Leeds
To create a sporting and cultural centre
To become leading corporate entertainment venue
Innovative merchandising
Joint ventures – tourism and leisure
To become the heart of Yorkshire tourist attraction
To generate important funding and sponsorship
International exhibitions
To develop a substantial business

Threats

Political disruption
Competition, especially enhanced regional attractions
Substitutes (sports, shopping etc.)
The Channel Tunnel (net exporter)
Change in economic climate
UK continuing to lose tourist revenue
Gun laws

CASE STUDY

Disneyland Paris, facts and figures

Welcome to Disneyland, Paris, Europe's most spectacular theme park and resort. Into a magic melting pot, Disney has tossed make-believe and charm, entertainment and innovation, creativity and technology. Travel with us and experience the adventure and excitement of Disney, its magic and fantasy.

There is something for everyone and for all ages, be it the thrill of Space Mountain, Disney's most exhilarating ride ever, the pageantry and colour of the daily parades complete with Disney characters, or perhaps, the dazzling entertainment and nightlife.

Quality service, the highest of standards and a dedication to fun and enjoyment, complete Disney's unique recipe for an unforgettable holiday.

Source: from the Paris Travel Service brochure

Paris is the most popular European city break destination in Europe.

The weather at Marne-le-Vallee is similar to southern England but there is quite a lot of rain throughout the year.

There were initial problems adapting French culture to the Disney magic. For example, Disney had to introduce wine into its restaurants because the French expected this as part of a restaurant meal.

One of the big successes of Disneyland, Paris is the business travel market. Facilities are available for conferences for between 20 and 2,000 delegates. Conference delegates tend to visit at low season and are unaffected by poor weather.

The Disney Corporation has a strong corporate image through its global operations, including films, merchandising, theme parks and other activities.

Channels of distribution include travel agents, direct sell, tour operators and ticket brokers.

Disney can afford extensive advertising campaigns that focus on the core promise of the Disney magic. European TV advertising tends to be broadcast at the end of the season to encourage visitors for the next season.

All staff are involved in the trials of new rides before they are offered to the public.

Disneyland, Paris provides one of the largest gardens in Europe, staffed by 120 full-time gardeners. State of the art technology is used to regulate planting, tending, irrigating and even predicting the weather.

Competition in Paris comes from the well-established Parc Asterix and the Futuroscope centre.

Eighty-four per cent of visitors state that they are very or totally satisfied with their visit. Ninety-seven per cent state that they will recommend the park to their friends. More than 30 per cent of visitors have visited the park at least once before.

Access to the park includes two Paris airports linked by shuttle and rail services to the park, direct motorway access and the Channel Tunnel link to the UK. Disneyland, Paris has its own railway station.

The Disney Village provides round-the-clock restaurants, bars and entertainment and is easily accessible from all of the resort hotels.

Visitors to Disneyland, Paris yield 20 per cent of all of the tourism revenue in the area.

Changes in European lifestyles have meant an increase in leisure time and higher disposable income.

Customer service is the main priority of the Disney Corporation and all staff are fully trained before beginning work.

Disneyland, Paris resort hotels provide almost 6,000 rooms. A further 800 rooms have been added to other hotels in the area to cater to the Disney market.

France currently has a low cost of living in comparison to many other European countries, including the UK, Germany and Belgium.

Sixty per cent of visitors to Disneyland, Paris are from outside France.

French is the first language used in the park. All cast members speak French, 70 per cent speak English and 25 per cent speak either German or Spanish.

Shopping is a major part of the Disney experience and visitors have a vast range of themed retail outlets to choose from.

There has been a rapid increase in the short break and second holiday market in Europe during the last ten years.

Unlike Americans, the majority of Europeans only take family holidays during the school holidays. Few take their children out of school during term time.

More than 50 million people live within a four-hour drive of Disneyland, Paris. Over 300 million are within a short-haul flight designated area.

Many of the attractions at Disneyland, Paris are covered or heated. Despite the cold weather, Christmas is one of the busiest periods for the park.

ACTIVITY

Disneyland, Paris

Using the descriptions, facts and figures in the case study, produce a SWOT analysis on Disneyland, Paris. You might also like to support your SWOT with further research. For example, you could find information on the internet, in brochures, newspapers and the trade press, as well as from people you know who have visited the park.

Analysing external factors

Travel and tourism organisations do not operate in isolation. A number of external factors influence the products and services that they offer and the extent to which customers decide to buy them. One of the activities in the marketing process is to look at these **external factors** and assess the effect that they have on the organisation, its products and services and its customers. These factors are often referred to as **market forces** or factors and include political, economic, social, technological, cultural and legislative influences.

Many organisations carry out a PEST (also sometimes known as STEP) analysis, so called because it uses the initial letter of the four main factors involved. The analysis considers:

Political factors

Economic factors

Social factors

Technological factors.

The purpose of carrying out a **PEST analysis** is to analyse the **external** environment in which the organisation operates and to identify how it should influence marketing decisions.

Political factors

The political actions of government can have major effects on business and markets, including creating or reducing demand for products and services.

At the national level, the government sets public spending levels, allocates funds for special programmes (such as the Millennium Fund), controls taxation and interest rates and is responsible for the introduction of new (or the abolition of existing) laws, regulations and licence arrangements. For example, the abolition of all duty free goods sales in 1999 had a profound effect on the products offered by transport operators and airports, and legislation which extended Sunday opening hours in pubs and licensed premises in 1995 has influenced the marketing decisions of many providers. (See also p. 34.)

At a local level, local authorities set spending levels for the provision of travel and tourism services in the communities they serve. In some cases this level of funding may allow for heavy subsidies for certain groups within the community, such as the elderly or the unemployed.

Economic factors

Customer demand in the travel and tourism industry is often determined by economic factors such as the distribution of wealth and the level of national income. In other words, the amount of money that people have to spend on travel and tourism influences what they actually decide to buy. Consumer spending may be controlled by a range of economic factors such as income levels, inflation, taxes, unemployment, exchange rates and mortgage rates. Look at Figure 4.5 and see some of the economic changes that have taken place in the last 20 years. (See also pages 11–12.)

Economic factors are often combined with political factors. For example, government changes in the amount of VAT on certain products can affect demand.

It is important to understand that when people have less money it does not necessarily mean that all travel and tourism products and services will suffer. Less money usually means that customers are more likely to buy alternatives to their usual tourism products. So, for example, customers on reduced incomes may not book their usual foreign package holiday but may instead go for days out to local tourist attractions. The foreign

Figure 4.5: Economic changes in the UK from 1979–1999

	May 1979	May 1989	May 1999
Prime Minister	Margaret Thatcher	Margaret Thatcher	Tony Blair
Inflation	13.4%	7.8%	4.6%
Interest rates	12.0%	13.75%	5.5%
Unemployment	4.1%	6.1%	4.6%
Women working	44%	49%	51%
Average income	£5,000	£11,700	£19,000
Manager's income	£19,000	£25,700	£36,400
Eating out	42%	47%	69%
Top holiday destination	Spain (1.9 million)	Spain (5.7 million)	Spain (7.7 million)
Percentage with video players		60%	82%
Percentage with CD players		15%	58%

package holiday tour operator may experience a decrease in demand, but local tourist attraction operators will benefit.

A further issue that needs to be considered is the impact of recession and rising unemployment on travel and tourism activities. In these situations people will not have as much money to spend on such activities but they usually have more time. Therefore, affordable activities are actually likely to benefit from an economic recession. (See also pages 11–12.)

Social factors

Social trends are important because they have a direct influence on the demand for particular types of product. For example, the UK has an aging population because people are having fewer babies and are living longer. By the year 2021 it is estimated that one in five of the population will be aged over 65, compared to only one in ten in 1951. In recent years, many travel and tourism providers have recognised this market opportunity and developed products and services targeted specifically at older customers. A good example is the success of SAGA Holidays, which caters specifically to retired people.

Demographic changes also have significance for marketing. Regions where the population is increasing may offer new market opportunities for travel and tourism providers. Conversely, a fall in population may provide a threat to travel and tourism organisations, as the size of their potential market diminishes. Further social changes can be seen in the increased amount of leisure time that many people now enjoy.

Technological factors

Developments in technology give rise to new products and market opportunities. The rapidly growing use of information technology, for example, allows customers to select and purchase products such as package holidays more quickly and more new travel and tourism products such as computer games, video systems and virtual reality are coming onto the market. An example of this can be seen at the Sellafield Interactive Experience, where technology is used to bring the exhibits to life for visitors.

▲ Sellafield is one the UK's technological visitor attractions

Transport has also been revolutionised by advances in technology. Thirty years ago it would have been unthinkable to go to Australia for a two-week holiday, but improvements in air travel have made this a realistic option. Further examples of the impact of technological change can be seen in the development of the internet and the effect that this has had on the way in which we are able to view and purchase travel and tourism products. (See also pp. 16–17 and 32–33.)

All four of these factors were used in the PEST analysis carried out by the National Centre for Popular Music in Sheffield, as the case study shows.

ACTIVITY

Technology

Make a list of tourist attractions that largely rely on technology to provide their facilities and services.

CASE STUDY

The National Centre For Popular Music

Situated in the centre of Sheffield, the National Centre for Popular Music opened in 1999. Its aim is to create a unique interactive arts and education centre that celebrates the diversity and influence of popular music. The centre boasts a range of interactive exhibits specially designed to appeal to people of all ages, musical tastes and experience. 'This is not a place where you walk around looking at memorabilia,' says creative director Tim Strickland. 'The National Centre is a place where you have a go; play an instrument, remix a video or design an album cover. Our aim from the beginning was to get people involved.'

PEST analysis of the National Centre for Popular Music.

Political

The political framework for the development and subsequent marketing of the Centre began in the early 1980s when the city council developed the Red Tape Studios, a council run studio where the community and education groups could record music in studios for a reduced fee. There was therefore a history of linking music with education and the community in Sheffield.

In 1988, Sheffield City Council's Department of Employment and Economic Development initiated research into the concept of a popular music visitor and educational resource. At the same time some media related businesses moved to the cultural quarter. The council policy was a help to the idea of the centre because the council's central idea was to create a media quarter in the area. This is a different direction to that taken by other big cities at the time. Places like Glasgow, Manchester, Birmingham and Leeds went for big cultural festivals and they are now trying to get local businesses to relocate in the areas they cleared for the big schemes. In Sheffield the council supported local, small businesses and helped them to relocate to the Cultural Industries Quarter, and now the city is developing the tourist potential.

Possible funding from local government dried up in the late 1980s, when the Conservative government wanted central control of funding for projects. Money became available through the private sector (via trusts) and through government sources like the Urban Programme and the Yorkshire and Humberside Tourist Board. The Urban Programme gave a one-off grant of £45,000 and this was spent on consultancy fees paid to Coopers and Lybrand in 1991. In 1993, after a positive report from the consultants, more than 30 applications were made to charities and trusts for development funding.

In 1994, Sheffield's new partnership body (private and public representatives) provided a plan for the future of Sheffield. The centre was a major stimulus to regeneration in the area. In 1995, an application to the European Regional Development Fund and a submission to the Millennium Fund were made. Later that year both applications were approved.

Economic

The overall depressed state of the economy in South Yorkshire has not been a factor in the development of the centre. The reduction in interest rates experienced at the beginning of 1999 has been an advantage because the centre borrowed £1 million from English Partnerships which is being paid back over ten years. Repayments have dropped along with interest rates. This is the only money that has to be repaid from the initial funding. All the rest was in the form of grants.

Social

Demographic patterns were taken into account in the initial research. This assessed how interesting people found the centre and the proportion who thought they were likely to visit. A second aim was to look at the attitudes of those likely visitors to the exhibition areas and proposed changes. A third aim was to establish the sociodemographic and leisure interests of likely visitors. The gender, age and socioeconomic profile of the total population living within a two-hour drive area was analysed.

The gender mix has almost equal numbers of males and females. The age profile of those likely to visit is markedly younger than the age profile in the catchment area. The two most important age groups were 25–34 year olds and 35–44 year olds. Retired people are a smaller proportion of likely visitors than they are in the catchment area. The two largest socioeconomic groups among likely visitors are A, B and C2. Compared with the catchment area population, the people who think they are likely to visit the centre includes a slightly lower proportion of A/B households and a slightly higher proportion of C2 household heads. For those that said that they were likely visitors to the centre, the most common

leisure interests were visits to pop and rock concerts, indoor sports events, nightclubs, jazz and outdoor sports events.

Technological

There is a core commitment to the use of technology in the development of the centre. This is reflected in the building design, the interactive nature of the activities and the constant commissioning of musical artists to use the technology. The use of technology is what makes the centre unique and it has been at the forefront of its marketing. The ability to update technology has been built into the design and forward planning of the centre.

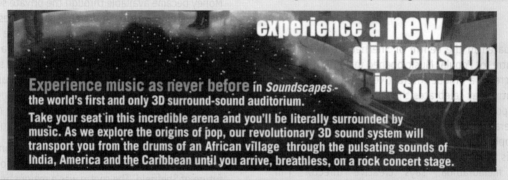

experience a **new dimension in sound**

Experience music as never before in *Soundscapes* - the world's first and only 3D surround-sound auditorium.

Take your seat in this incredible arena and you'll be literally surrounded by music. As we explore the origins of pop, our revolutionary 3D sound system will transport you from the drums of an African village through the pulsating sounds of India, America and the Caribbean until you arrive, breathless, on a rock concert stage.

The way the National Centre for Popular Music used a PEST analysis to help in the planning and development of the project can be used by any travel and tourism provider at any stage of product development. For example, a PEST analysis will give a useful insight into the reasons why the short-break holiday market has grown so rapidly in recent years.

The short-break holiday market has only really existed for about 30 years but in the last decade has boomed. More short-break holidays are now taken in the UK than long holidays. Over 37 million Britons took a short break in 1997.

The original idea for short-break holidays came about in the 1960s when hotel companies such as Trust Houses offered bargain break packages in city centre hotels in an attempt to fill empty bedrooms left vacant by the weekday business trade. In 1974, the then English Tourist Board launched the Let's Go campaign aimed at encouraging more people to take short breaks. The clear demand for short breaks led to the creation of specialist tour operators such as Rainbow Holidays. More recently, companies such as Oasis and Center Parcs have entered the market with phenomenal success by offering a self-catering product.

Figure 4.6: Growth in holidays in UK 1979–97

	1979–1988		1989–1997	
	Trips	Real spend	Trips	Real spend
All holidays	0%	–4%	+9%	+2%
Short holidays	+20%	+58%	+23%	+32%
Short breaks	+45%	+76%	+36%	+50%
Short breaks in serviced accommodation	+53%	+92%	+47%	+54%

Source: UKTS, BTSM

Note: Figures for 1979–88 have been adjusted to smooth out year on year fluctuactions

Figure 4.7: Social and economic change 1961–1997

	1961	1971	1981	1991	1997
UK population	52.8 m	55.9 m	56.4 m	57.8 m	59.0 m
Access to a car (percentage of households)	31%	52%	60%	68%	70%
Paid holiday entitlement (days)	n/a	16.5	21	n/a	24
Real disposable household income index	100	129	169	227	270

Source: *Social Trends 28, 1998*

Many of the reasons why short-break holidays have become so successful are due to PEST factors. Figure 4.7 shows some of the social and economic changes that have taken place between 1961 and 1997.

ACTIVITY

PEST factors and the short-break market

As a group, discuss why the social and economic changes set out in Figure 4.7 may have been responsible for the trend towards a growth in short-break holidays. Can you think of any political and technological changes that may also have had an effect? For example, how might developments in transport and car ownership have contributed to the increase in short breaks?

Needs of customers

The next stage of the marketing process is to identify the specific needs and expectations of the organisation's customers. Identifying and satisfying the needs and expectations of customers can be a long, complicated process, especially when those needs are implied rather than clearly expressed by the customer. For example, the single customer who books a tour of Italian cities may state that his or her expectations are to view the art collections and historical buildings of Italy.

However, there may be other unstated factors to take into account, such as the status and recognition attached to participating in such a tour or the opportunity to make new acquaintances.

▲ Art lovers flock to Florence

Organisations need to strive to identify both expressed and implied customer needs and expectations and use this information to develop products that meet or exceed those needs and expectations. This is known as the **customer oriented approach**.

Identification of the needs of customers only indicates the types of product that they are likely to buy. It is also necessary to understand what makes them want one product rather than another, or why they will use one service in preference to another. In other words, organisations need to know what specific product or service features and qualities will satisfy customers. These features are known as the **unique selling points (USPs)** and help to distinguish one product from another.

Customer satisfaction means that a product or service meets or exceeds the needs and wants of the customer. This is clearly an important principle, because an organisation does not usually aim to sell a product or service just once to one customer. Instead it strives to ensure that customers will continue to use the product, again and again. This can only be achieved if the organisation understands exactly what customers need and expect and how to satisfy them.

Often, the travel and tourism experience is a product that cannot be guaranteed in advance and may not be the same for two different people whose needs and expectations differ. For example, when a skiing holiday is booked, the customer has an expectation of the experience that will follow. If adverse weather conditions result in poor snow this will greatly affect the customer's assessment of the product.

Many summer holiday resorts rely heavily on good weather. If the weather is poor there is often little to keep visitors occupied. This can lead to dissatisfaction and may completely ruin the holiday experience.

▲ Adverse weather can tarnish the customer's experience of a skiing holiday

ACTIVITY

Budget accommodation

As a group, discuss why you think budget accommodation has proved such a success. Which types of customer do you think are particularly attracted by this type of product and how does it satisfy their needs and expectations?

CASE STUDY

Budget and limited service hotels

One of the major success stories of the last decade has been the rapid growth of budget or limited service hotels. The number of these hotels in the UK rose from 333 in 1995 to 570 in 1998, with an increase in bedrooms from 14,988 to 28,441 during the same period.

The multinational ACCOR hotel chain led the way in developing the concept of hotels aimed at guests who wanted reasonably priced accommodation. Prices were kept low by limiting the level of service offered and by providing comfortable but simply furnished accommodation. Since their introduction, many other hotel chains have recognised the potential of offering budget accommodation and have redeveloped existing hotels to satisfy demand from budget customers. Current budget brands include Travel Inns, Holiday Inn Express, Campanile, Travelodge and Premier Lodge. The ACCOR chain offers four distinct brands of budget hotel: IBIS, ETAP, MOTEL 6 and Formule 1. Each charges different rates depending on the facilities and services offered.

Budget hotels are usually situated in urban areas, or near transport termini or on major roads and cater for the short-stay visitor. Most offer bedroom accommodation that can sleep up to four people per room, and rates are based on the room rather than the number of occupants. A family of four can therefore have a room for the same price as a single guest.

The level of service varies across the brands, but some at the lower end of the market, such as Formula 1, have minimal staffing levels and services. Checking-in may be through a 24-hour automatic reception system using a guest's credit card and breakfast is often self-service. Some budget hotels do not offer restaurant or bar facilities but provide vending machines and are often situated next to restaurants or motorway service stations with catering outlets. Where private bathrooms are not available, facilities may be provided by self-cleaning toilets and showers.

Targeting and positioning

One of the main reasons for identifying customers' needs and expectations is that it allows products to be targeted at a specific market. **Targeting** means tailoring products and services to the needs of specific market segments. (We discuss market segmentation in more detail on p. 262.)

If an organisation can identify the specific needs and expectations of its customers, it can ensure that its product is tailored to meet them. For example, airport hotels know that their main target market is air travellers who may be checking in at all times of the day and night. They may therefore decide to offer catering facilities and transport to and from the airport throughout the day and night.

By targeting a particular type of customer, organisations are able to position themselves in a specific market. For example, Club 18-30 Holidays declares its market position in its title, whereas SAGA Holidays is positioned in the retired market. This is an important aspect of marketing. By establishing a strong **market position**, an organisation can ensure that its product is meeting the needs of customers in that particular market.

BUILD YOUR LEARNING

Keywords and phrases

You should know the meaning of the words and phrases listed below. If you are unsure about any of them, go back through the last 14 pages to refresh your understanding.

- Continuous process
- Customer oriented approach
- Customer satisfaction
- External factors
- Internal factors
- Market forces
- Marketing
- Marketing objectives
- Market position
- Market segmentation
- Mission statement
- PEST analysis
- Philosophy of use
- Smart objectives
- SWOT analysis
- Targeting
- Unique selling point (USP)

End of section activity

Select a travel and tourism organisation such as a tour operator, travel agency, transport provider or tourist attraction. Either write or arrange to visit in person to find out the following information:

- the organisation's mission or vision statement
- its marketing objectives
- its main strengths, weaknesses, opportunities and threats (SWOT)
- how external forces (PEST) influence its marketing activities
- which market segments it targets
- the needs and expectations of the target customers
- how it evaluates it marketing activities to ensure that they meet customers' needs and expectations.

Developing a marketing mix

THE **MARKETING MIX** REFERS to the factors that need to be combined, or mixed, to allow an organisation to achieve its marketing objectives. These factors are known as the four Ps:

Product

Price

Place

Promotion.

The four Ps involve matching the product or service to consumer needs, determining the price, deciding where and how the product or service should be placed (distributed) in the market and promoting it through advertising, sales promotions and public relations.

Product

In marketing, **product** refers to both goods and services. **Goods** are physical objects, such as food and drink or tourist souvenirs. **Services** involve the combination of skills, information or entertainment such as a package holiday, theatre production or guided tour. Some examples of travel and tourism products and services are shown in Figure 4.8.

There are three important factors to consider when developing a product. These are the:

- product characteristics

- brand image of the product

- position of the product within the product life cycle.

Product characteristics

When developing a marketing strategy for a product it is important to identify precisely what is being purchased in terms of the product characteristics and how these help to satisfy a particular customer need. **Product characteristics** are the specific features of a product or service that the customer sees as important and which attract them to buy it or use it. For example, a package holiday is a product that evokes a range of emotions, whose end result is the total customer experience. The determinants of this experience might include the mix and quality of attractions at the holiday resort, the range of services and the attitude of resort representatives towards children. Travel and tourism organisations must constantly review their product characteristics to ensure that they continue to meet customers' needs. Tour operators in particular are constantly developing new products to meet consumer demand. The webstract opposite provides an example.

Competition amongst visitor attractions is becoming increasingly fierce as more and more providers enter the market. One of the inevitable results is that individual providers look for new and innovative ways of developing unique product characteristics to attract customers. Such developments include interactive exhibits, computerised attractions and actors playing roles. This has meant that many travel and tourism customers now expect more than simply a static display or exhibit and want to be involved in the tourism experience.

Figure 4.8: Travel and tourism goods	
Goods	**Services**
Restaurant meal	Tour guide showing visitors around attraction
Range of souvenirs	London stage show such as Les Miserables
Theatre programme	Resort rep at welcome party
Duty free drinks	Tourist information clerk

WEBSTRACT

Thomson Holidays

Thomson Holidays, the UK's largest holiday company, has unveiled the first ever 'essentials only' holiday for a new, confident and independently minded type of holidaymaker. The new type of holidays, called Just, will offer customers the real essentials of both long-haul and short-haul holiday packages at an outstanding price; the flight, a hotel room or apartment in a property checked for safety and quality, and a dedicated 24-hour helpline in their holiday resort.

Prices are kept low by leaving out things like transfers from the airport to the resort, rep services and meals on short-haul flights; there are no accommodation or single occupancy supplements. Holidays are available from just £100.

Developed over a period of 18 months, Just is the result of research which identified holidaymakers who want a no frills, reduced but not inferior holiday package.

The launch of Just follows Thomson Holidays' unveiling of millions of new style package holidays this summer. Thomson Holidays managing director, Shaun Powell, commented: 'This new type of low cost holiday allows people to spend less on what we provide so holidaymakers can spend more on themselves.'

The Just guide will be much simpler than a holiday brochure, with holidays grouped by price. It's called a guide because it lists accommodation and flights; to get up-to-the minute prices customers must call Just Direct, visit the Just website or speak to a travel agent.

Source: www.thomsonholidays.com

In 1999, *Holiday Which?* carried out research to evaluate how a range of visitor attractions compared. High scores were awarded to Castle Howard, Chatsworth House, Alton Towers, the BBC Experience, the Roman Baths and the Natural History Museum for the range of facilities offered and the overall visitor experience.

Buckingham Palace did not fare so well. Comments ranged from complaints that it is sterile, stuffy and staid to the criticism that there is little that tells visitors about the history of the house. A spokesperson for Buckingham Palace was understandably annoyed and argued that as the headquarters of the British monarchy it could not be compared with a theme park.

▶ Castle Howard won a high score from *Holiday Which?* as a visitor attraction

CASTLE HOWARD
YORK
APPROX 20 MINUTES FROM YORK

HISTORY
still
IN THE MAKING

HOME TO
"Brideshead Revisited"

ACTIVITY

Product characteristics

Do you think there could be a possible conflict in trying to develop new product characteristics for a historical attraction such as Buckingham Palace to enable it to attract a wider market? For example, are the characteristics of being staid, sterile and stuffy actually in keeping with the historical nature of the attraction? If Buckingham Palace were to develop some of the more modern characteristics of other attractions, such as interactive displays, would it spoil its original appeal?

▶ *Holiday Which?* did not rate Buckingham Palace highly

Branding

Branding is the marketing process of giving a product or service a distinctive identity, with the aim of creating a unique image that will make it easily identifiable and distinct from its competitors.

A product's brand image can be created and reinforced in many ways, including by its name, logo, advertising, packaging, price and the use of specific colours. For example, look at the brochure cover for Club 18-30 and see how a distinct type of package holiday has been given a brand image. Compare it to the more traditional brochure front covers used by mass market tour operators such as Airtours and First Choice.

Four useful branding terms are as follows.

- **Brand awareness.** This means that a customer is able to identify a particular brand and its characteristics as opposed to others.

- **Brand leader.** This term refers to the brand with the highest share of the market in its category. For example McDonald's is the brand leader in fast food restaurants.

- **Brand extension** refers to situations in which a strong existing brand is used to create other products that carry the same brand title and image. For example, McDonald's is currently developing hotels in the UK which will be marketed under the general McDonald's brand image.

- **Brand loyalty** means that a customer is loyal to a particular brand and will buy it on a regular basis. Following the lead set by supermarkets, many travel and tourism providers are seeking to increase customer brand loyalty by introducing loyalty schemes such as Eurostar's Frequent Traveller.

Branding is a very powerful marketing tool and has a strong influence over the products and services that we buy. For example, in blind tests (where customers do not know the brand that they are trying) 51 per cent of people prefer Pepsi. However, when customers can see the brand that they are drinking, 65 per cent say that they prefer Coca-Cola. What these 65 per cent of people are in fact saying is that they prefer the brand rather than the product that is represented by the Coca-Cola image.

Branding is used both to establish customer awareness and loyalty, and to target specific segments of the market in order to achieve a higher market share. For example, tour operators have well established brands for particular market segments, such as Thomson's Young at Heart, which is aimed at people over 50.

In 1997, Prime Minister Tony Blair launched the Cool Britannia initiative. With the support of several high profile celebrities and a newly designed Union Jack for the British Tourist Authority, his aim was to create a trendy brand image of the UK by highlighting our music, arts and fashion industries.

▲ Club 18–30, a well-known holiday brand

▲ Noel Gallagher supports Tony Blair's launch of Cool Britannia

Since then many have argued that the initiative was ill founded and that it failed to consider Britain's brand characteristics. Research carried out in 1994, and then again in 1997, asked people in 30 different countries to choose five adjectives from a list of 40 that best described the British. In both 1994 and 1997, the words proud, civilised, cultured and cold were selected. The only difference was that arrogant was chosen in 1994 and replaced with witty in 1997.

The somewhat old-fashioned image that foreign visitors seem to have of the UK was further confirmed by some research conducted by the then English Tourist

▲ One of Eurostar's brand loyalty schemes

Board (now ETC). The study also found that the types of people most likely to visit the UK tended to be:

- aged over 35
- married
- in social classes A and B.

The most negative attitudes were found amongst under 25-year-old foreigners.

ACTIVITY

Branding Britain

As a group, discuss how you think Britain could benefit from the brand image that foreigners seem to have of us. What particular travel and tourism products and services could be highlighted to attract more overseas visitors?

The product life cycle

The concept of a **product life cycle** (PLC) is based on the idea that all products pass through four distinct stages.

- **Introduction**, when a product is first introduced. Demand may be low initially, as customers gradually become aware of the product characteristics and its brand image.

- **Growth**, as more customers become aware of the product, its image and characteristics and sales start to rise rapidly. This may be due to word-of-mouth recommendations and the beginning of customer loyalty.

- **Maturity**. At this stage of the PLC, sales are at their highest but tend to remain stable. Most of the demand comes from repeat customers who are loyal to the particular brand.

- **Decline**. At this stage demand starts to decline. This can be for a number of reasons such as increased competition, changing customer needs or any of the factors that we discussed in the section on PEST analysis (pp. 235–9).

In some circumstances there may be a fifth stage of revamping, when the organisation tries to stimulate increased sales by changing the product's characteristics or brand image. For example, many traditional seaside resorts such as Brighton, Torquay and Scarborough have attempted to reverse the decline in visitor numbers by revamping products and targeting the conference market.

The travel and tourism market is dynamic and subject to change. Even popular products can suffer declining sales or take-up numbers. For example, the popularity of the cinema reached its peak in 1947, when 1,460 million tickets were sold in the UK. By 1987 this number had fallen drastically to 80 million, due largely to the development of television.

Attendances increased again in the 1990s to around 150 million, due largely to the development of multiplex cinemas.

Figure 4.9: Cinema attendances 1937–97

	Millions
1937	954
1947	1,460
1957	915
1967	265
1977	105
1987	80
1997	140

Source: British Film institute, Screen Digest, Key Note

▲ The changing face of British cinema

Some other examples of travel and tourism products which have been revamped and relaunched following periods of decline include:

- holiday centres, including Butlin's Holiday Worlds (see also pp. 20–1)

- car ferries with limited leisure facilities on board – car ferries now provide a wide range of leisure facilities and attractions

- museums – many museums have been redeveloped to include interactive displays and simulators.

The change in product image or characteristics may be accompanied by a decision to target a different type of customer. For example, declining demand for package holidays in popular resorts on the Spanish coast during the late 1980s led to the development of long-stay, off-season holidays for the retired at heavily discounted rates.

Figure 4.10 shows the stages of the product life cycle as equal in length. In reality, each stage lasts a different length of time. A basic product such as milk or bread has been in the maturity stage for a very long time, whereas the skateboard had a relatively short maturity stage and then quickly declined in popularity.

Most organisations aim to keep the introduction stage as short as possible, as it tends to be the least profitable because of the amount of advertising that is needed to attract new customers. In fact, a lot of smaller travel and tourism organisations underestimate the costs involved at this stage and go out of business before even reaching the growth stage, as they cannot afford to maintain the amount of promotion needed.

The growth and maturity stages are the most desirable, as they represent increasing demand, customer loyalty and profitability. Successful travel and tourism organisations which understand the concept of the product life cycle, continually develop and offer a range of different products to ensure that they have products placed at each stage of the PLC. This means that as a particular product begins to pass from maturity to decline, there will be other products rising through the introduction and growth stages to take their place.

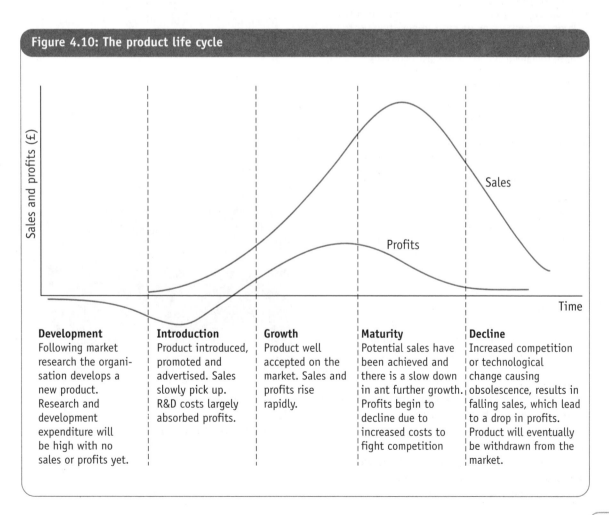

Figure 4.10: The product life cycle

Development	Introduction	Growth	Maturity	Decline
Following market research the organisation develops a new product. Research and development expenditure will be high with no sales or profits yet.	Product introduced, promoted and advertised. Sales slowly pick up. R&D costs largely absorbed profits.	Product well accepted on the market. Sales and profits rise rapidly.	Potential sales have been achieved and there is a slow down in ant further growth. Profits begin to decline due to increased costs to fight competition	Increased competition or technological change causing obsolescence, results in falling sales, which lead to a drop in profits. Product will eventually be withdrawn from the market.

ACTIVITY

The product life cycle

Where would you place the selection of attractions below on the product life cycle?

Southland's museum. Established in 1949 to commemorate the end of the Second World War. Free admission. Admissions peaked during the late 1980s following a series of exhibits on newly acquired local war memorabilia. Since then admissions have declined each year.

Gothic Tales. A privately owned interactive attraction that opened six months ago. Themed on Southlands' association with the filming of a major horror movie, the attraction takes visitors through a series of macabre film sets with actors playing the parts of famous horror movie stars. Initial admissions were low but in the last three months they have doubled.

Aqua-experience. A marine life attraction that has been operating for nine years. It is part of a national chain of aquariums which has pledged to invest large amounts of money in the next two years to develop further exhibits at their centres. Admissions have remained stable for the last two years.

Southland's Fayre. Based in a converted factory, Southland's Fayre is home to over 35 local craftspeople who exhibit and sell their products on stalls. It opened two years ago and there is already a long waiting list of other craftspeople eager to reserve space to sell their products.

Clippers. A newly opened attraction featuring the very latest in hairstyles and make-up based on popular TV and magazine make-over features. Trained stylists are on hand to offer hair care and make-up advice and products. Computer-based technology allows visitors to view themselves with different hairstyles and make-up and then allow stylists to create their chosen style. Initial interest was high but it is too early to predict whether this will be sustained.

Southland's Art Gallery. First opened in 1966 but due to declining attendance closed in 1998. In the last two months it has renovated its interior and now offers exhibits of work by local painters and a range of art workshops for all age groups.

Before we move on to look at the other three Ps of the marketing mix, it is important to stress that the product is vital. It does not matter how well the product is placed, priced or promoted – if it is not right it will not meet customers' needs and they will not buy it.

Place

Place describes the location and availability of the product or service and the method by which it is distributed to customers.

Location

When Charles Ritz, founder of the famous Ritz hotel, was asked what was important when opening a new hotel he replied that there were only three things that needed to be remembered: location, location and location!

While it is arguably an exaggeration to state that **location** is the only factor that is important, it is clearly something that travel and tourism providers need to give a lot of thought to. If a product or service is not accessible to potential customers, then no matter how well it has been developed, or how attractively it has been priced and promoted, it will not be successful.

▼ Tourist information centre in a main shopping area

Tourist information centres are usually located in the high street near to major tourist attractions or in travel terminals such as railway stations because they need to be accessible to their customers.

The case study on Alton Towers opposite details some of the factors about location that were considered when creating the theme park.

▲ All big cities have a variety of tourist attractions

CASE STUDY

Creating a theme park

Before undertaking a capital project such as Alton Towers, an in-depth study is essential. Certain criteria must be met before very considerable investment is made. Several factors must be taken into account.

The attraction must have a suitable catchment area. Alton Towers is a national brand and attracts visitors from all over the country and overseas. It is the UK's leading theme park and has a central position between the M1 and M6 motorways, making it easily accessible.

Smaller regional theme parks can operate with a more restricted catchment area. These parks have lower capital investment and overhead costs, so fewer visitors are required to meet company objectives. The average catchment area for regional parks tends to be within one and a half hour's drive.

In choosing the location of the park, you need to consider its planned size and design, and the mix of attractions, services and car parks. You also need to consider access to the park – road and rail links – and the impact on the local community. It is a question of assessing whether or not a chosen area is sufficient to accommodate these components.

As a rule, major theme parks require a minimum ride and attraction area of 50 acres, but they need considerably more to cater for the additional facilities, such as restaurants, snack bars, toilets and shops. For example, Disneyland in California has an attraction centre of 50 acres out of a 250 acre total area. Alton Towers is a 500-acre complex, part of which is gardens and parkland.

Source: Adapted from the Alton Towers' student information pack

ACTIVITY

Location

Josie Peters is planning to open a travel agency and has narrowed down her search for a suitable site to three properties. Look at the extracts from the estate agent's description of each property below. Which of the three do you think she should choose and why?

Property 1. This highly desirable property is situated on the outskirts of the town centre near to local offices and factories. There is ample local free parking and a regular bus service stops outside. Accommodation consists of a large shop frontage with salesroom, rear office space and extensive first floor accommodation. The property enjoys the benefit of being in a quiet area at weekends and during the evenings due to the mainly industrial nature of the area.

Asking price: £65,000

Property 2. Situated on the main high street, this extensive first-floor property has all of the commercial benefits that you would expect from a town centre location. Accommodation includes three separate offices and toilet facilities. Adjacent to a multi-story car park that provides parking for the nearby covered shopping mall, it enjoys an all-year passing trade. The ground floor property is currently occupied by a card and gift shop.

Asking price: £72,000

Property 3. Situated in the centre of the town's shopping mall on the second floor, this prime location is adjacent to many of the well-known household stores, including nine national clothing retailers, four travel agencies, two catalogue shops and a range of financial services. The centre is open six days a week with late-night opening on a Thursday. Accommodation comprises of a single sales area with small storeroom facilities at the rear. The centre also has comprehensive catering and security provision as well as a pay and display car park.

Asking price: £102,000

Chain of distribution

Another important aspect of place is the **chain of distribution** an organisation uses to bring its products and services to the market. Traditionally, manufacturers have sold products to wholesalers that are then sold to retailers in smaller quantities who then supply customers. This system can be seen in the way many package holidays are brought to the market (as illustrated in Figure 4.11). (See also p. 40.)

In recent years, a number of organisations in the travel industry have vertically integrated their operations. This means that they now cover all stages from manufacture to retail. As we saw in Unit 1, for example, the Thomson Travel Group today includes Britannia Airways, Thomson Tour Operators and the Lunn Poly chain of travel agencies. This allows savings to be made and provides a more efficient distribution system that can respond quickly to market trends such as fluctuations in demand. (See also pp. 48–50.)

However, many travel and tourism products are sold direct to the consumer rather than through third parties. Some tour operators such as Portland Holidays sell holidays direct to customers rather than through travel agencies. Many travel and tourism services are generally inseparable from the manufacturer and are sold direct to the consumer. For example, restaurants, hotels, cinemas and museums all provide products direct to their customers.

Figure 4.11: Channels of distribution

Manufacturers and providers	Hotels, tourist attractions, transport carriers
↓	↓
Wholesalers	Tour operators
↓	↓
Retailers	Travel agents
↓	↓
Customers	Tourists

CASE STUDY

Growing use of the internet has had a profound impact on the chain of distribution of travel and holiday products. Before the developments in information technology, customers wishing to book holidays or transport were faced with two basic options. They could either book directly with the provider or they could use the services of a travel agent. Today, internet reservation systems allow customers to search for the best holiday and travel deals, and to make reservations and payments on-line.

Travelocity is one of the largest internet travel agents and currently report sales of over £2 million each week.

This kind of use of the internet, as a means of reserving and buying travel products, is known as disintermediation. In other words, it cuts out the intermediary, or middleman, such as the travel agent. The wide-scale introduction of digital television further increases the likelihood that customers will turn to computerised systems to make their holiday and travel arrangements. Customers will be able to view holidays on digital television channels and then book their choice by accessing the internet through their television set.

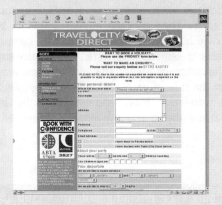

ACTIVITY

The use of the internet to make travel arrangements will clearly have profound effects on traditional channels of distribution in the travel and tourism industry. From a marketing point of view, what do you think are the advantages and disadvantages of these systems? You could consider this from a number of points of view. For example, of:

■ customers

■ travel agents

■ tour operators

■ transport providers

■ hotels.

Price

Once an organisation has identified a product or service, it must decide on the **price** at which it is going to be offered to customers. Decisions on price need to consider two main factors:

■ price determination

■ pricing policies.

Price determination

Whatever the price selected, it has to appear to customers as the right price; in other words, customers should feel the price offers **value for money**.

Costs involved in providing the product or service usually set the minimum level of the price. This is known as the **breakeven price**. The upper level is determined by:

- what customers are prepared to pay
- the market conditions, such as supply, demand, competition and seasonality
- the brand image of the product.

It is important to remember that lower prices are not always more attractive to customers. This is because the price charged often helps to reinforce the product's brand image. For example, customers may be suspicious if a price seems to be too low and assume that the product is of poor quality.

The process of communicating prices to customers in a way that the customer can easily understand is an important part of the marketing mix. Customers need to be able to identify what is and what is not included in the price charged. Tour operators face a number of difficulties when determining and communicating prices for their package holidays. This is because package holidays are complex products comprising a number of elements which often vary in price according to the customers' needs. Differences in prices may result from the time of year, the number of people sharing accommodation, meal requirements, flight time and departure airport and any number of selected extras

such as up-graded rooms, seaviews and cots. Tour operators try to make this as easy as possible for customers by using clear pricing panels in their brochures.

ACTIVITY

Working out the price of a holiday

Despite the fact that tour operators try to make the prices in their brochures as easy to understand as possible, many customers are surprised to discover that the actual cost of their holiday is often more that they thought it would be from their initial look through the brochure. Look at the pricing panels below for package holidays in Majorca. From the information provided, work out how much it would cost for two adults and a child to stay for 14 nights at the Fiesta Sahara, departing on 3 April.

As a group, discuss how well you think the various prices are communicated to customers.

Name and board: **Fiesta Sahara (self-catering)**

Flights: Mon, Fri, Sat

Prices based on: 1 apartment, 4 Adults

Nights	7	14	All
Per person price	Adult	Adult	Child

Departures on or between:			
01 Jan – 04 Feb	155	169	109
05 Feb – 11 Feb	149	175	119
12 Feb – 14 Feb	185	195	119
15 Feb – 19 Mar	175	195	119
20 Mar – 26 Mar	185	245	119
27 Mar – 31 Mar	239	309	129
01 Apr – 04 Apr	255	289	129
05 Apr – 23 Apr	239	259	109

Supplements per adult per night:

For 3 adults sharing	1.40
For 2 adults sharing	3.50

Figure 4.12: Pricing details from Club 18–30

	Marenapa		Marenapa	
Holiday Code	K02A0B		K02A0B	
Board base	SC		SC	
Number sharing	2–3		4	
Duration (nights)	7	14	7	14
01 May–17 May	269	289	265	285
25 May–01 June	319	335	315	329
02 June–08 June	299	335	296	329
23 June–29 June	335	399	329	395
14 July–20 July	365	455	358	449
21 July–05 Aug	395	465	369	457
17 Aug–23 Aug	375	425	369	429
02 Sept–15 Sept	315	369	308	365
29 Sept–13 Oct	285	326	279	319

Because of the high level of competition within the travel and tourism industry, the determination of price is often based on what competitors are charging. For tourist attractions, the comparison of admissions charges is looked at in relation to how long a visitor stays at the attraction; a concept known as **dwell time**. So, for example, a theme park may charge £12 admission with an average length of visitor stay of seven hours, whereas a museum may charge £4.50 with an average visitor stay of 1.5 hours. In terms of dwell time, the theme park works out at £1.71 an hour and the museum at £3 per hour. Dwell time is an important issue customers' perception of value for money.

Pricing policies

Getting the **pricing policy** right determines both the financial success of a product and, in part, the long-term success of the organisation. The exception to this pricing process is where an organisation provides free or subsidised products and services for its customers. For example, council-owned tourist attractions often provide free or subsidised services for certain groups within the communities they serve, such as pensioners, the unemployed, students and people on low incomes.

The type of organisation and the sector it operates in have a direct impact on the formulation of pricing policies, such as the need to make a profit, break even or operate at a loss. Several different pricing policies can be implemented by travel and tourism organisations when bringing products to the market, as shown on pp. 254–5.

ACTIVITY

Dwell time

Look through this information on average dwell time and admission prices of six major visitor attractions in the UK. Which represents the best value for money in terms of dwell time for adults, children and families?

Venue: Rock Circus, London

Average dwell time: 4 hours

Adults: £8.25

Children: £6.25

Family: n/a

Students/senior citizens: £7.25

Venue: Royal Armouries, Leeds

Average dwell time: 4 hours

Adults: £4.90

Children: £3.90

Family: £14.90

Students/senior citizens: £3.90

Venue: NCPM, Sheffield

Average dwell time: 2.5 hours

Adults: £5.95

Children: £4.00

Family: £18.00

Students/senior citizens: £4.75

Venue: Cadbury's World, Birmingham

Average dwell time: 2.5 hours

Adults: £6.75

Children: £4.90

Family: £20.20

Students/senior citizens: £5.75

Venue: Jorvik, York

Average dwell time: 1 hour

Adults: £5.65

Children: £4.25

Family: £18.00

Students/senior citizens: £5.00

Venue: National Railway Museum, York

Average dwell time: 3 hours

Adults: £6.50

Children: under 17 free

Family: n/a

Students: £4.00

Senior citizens: free

- **Market penetration pricing.** This is usually used by organisations which want to get into a new market in order to establish a product. It might involve setting a lower price to attract new business or to undercut competitors. Eurostar, for example, has adopted a market penetration pricing strategy by offering low prices to customers on selected services.

- **Cost-plus pricing.** This involves establishing the total costs of producing a particular product, adding a standard margin or mark-up and pricing the product accordingly. A hotel, for example, will typically have margins of 60–100 per cent on most of its menu items.

- **Competitive pricing.** Often the competition within the market dictates what price an organisation can set for a particular product. Where competitors' prices are low, this strategy may lead to very low profit margins and even to financial ruin. For example, many tour operators' profit margins are shrinking due to the fiercely competitive nature of the business and overcapacity at many of the resort destinations. The combined effect of these factors is discounted prices on many holidays.

- **Discount pricing.** This involves offering a reduced price for certain types and groups of customers. Discount pricing is widely used in the travel and tourism industries and includes numerous sales promotions and special offers such as two for the price of one, ten per cent off, free holiday insurance and child places.

If there is insufficient demand at their anticipated peak periods, then providers have to discount heavily in order to fill their capacity. This happened over the millennium holiday period when many holidays were offered by operators at vastly reduced prices due to lower than expected demand.

- **Variable pricing.** Organisations can vary price by customer types, levels and quality of service, times and days, season and so on. For example, an art gallery may set lower prices for certain groups, such as the unemployed, students and pensioners. Similarly, prices may vary according to peak and off-peak times during the day, week or year. The example of variable pricing at the Earth Centre in Doncaster is particularly unusual. In accordance with its eco-friendly aims, it offers discounted rates of admission to visitors who get to the centre using environmentally friendly transport or who share transport, such as a coach.

Figure 4.13: Discount pricing at Granada Studios

Figure 4.14: Variable pricing at the Earth Centre

Cost of admission	
Adults	£8.95
Children (under 14)	£6.95
OAPs and unemployed	£4.95
Family ticket	£30.00
Adults by coach (no minimum numbers)	£5.95
Children by coach	£4.95
Visitors by rail or bike	£4.95
Schools (per pupil, one in ten free)	£3.99

Within the travel and tourism industry, variable pricing is often used to maximise profits at peak times due to special events. For example, many providers increased their prices during the eclipse of August 1999 and for the millennium New Year's Eve celebrations. If you look in any holiday brochure you will see that the prices vary depending on the date of departure, with school holiday periods usually the most expensive.

- **Market skimming strategy.** As we have already seen, some products are not price sensitive. There may be limited competition or customers may be prepared to pay high prices for the quality and associated status. Up-market, long-haul holiday companies often adopt a high price strategy to retain their exclusivity, status and quality image.

Whatever pricing policy an organisation uses, it should be based on:

- the customers' perception of what constitutes value for money
- how much they can afford to pay
- what competitors are charging.

Most transport providers offer a range of fare types and conditions. One of the reasons for this is to spread demand for transport services and encourage more people to travel at off-peak times when demand is low. Look at the extract from the National Express fares structure below. Can you identify the peak and off-peak periods from the information provided?

Figure 4.15: National Express fares and conditions

Economy Single: Valid for a single journey on any day except Friday all through the year. Also not valid on any Saturday in July or August or at other times such as Christmas and Easter or as advertised.

Economy Return: Valid for a return journey where both outward and return journeys are on any day except Friday all through the year. Also not valid on any Saturday in July or August or at other times such as Christmas and Easter or as advertised.

Standard Single: Valid for a one-way journey on any day when an Economy Single is not available.

Standard Return: Valid for a return journey on any day where an Economy Return is not valid.

Day Return: On some journeys we offer Day Return fares which are lower than Standard and Economy returns. Where a Day Return fare is available it will automatically be offered by the enquiry system.

Advanced Purchase Fares:

If you book an Economy Return or a Standard Return more than seven days in advance it may qualify for an Advanced Purchase Discount.

Advanced Purchase Discount fares are not available on all routes and may not be offered at certain times of the year, such as Christmas.

Advance Purchase fares are not available to holders of National Express Discount Coachcards or children.

Restrictions Advanced Purchase tickets can be amended provided the amendment is made more than seven days in advance of the outward date of travel. Amendments made less than seven days in advance of the outward date or after the outward date can be made but an excess fare will be charged to bring the fare up to the normal Economy or Standard return fare.

Open Returns are not available on Advanced Purchase tickets.

Open Dated Returns:

Economy and Standard returns can be purchased with the return date left open. They are valid for three months from the date of outward travel. When the return journey is booked, a fee of £1.50 may be charged by the agent who makes the rebooking.

Earlybird Returns:

On some services we offer an Earlybird Day Return. These offer a very low day return fare but outward and return journeys must take place on specified outward and return journeys on the same day.

Promotion

Promotion is a vital component of the marketing mix. It includes all those activities used to communicate with existing and potential customers. For promotion to be effective, an organisation must be talking to the right people about the right product and convincing them that the price is right.

The ultimate aim of promotion is to encourage consumers to buy or use a product or service. In order to achieve this aim, promotional activities need to:

- create brand awareness of the product or service
- make consumers understand the characteristics of the product or service
- persuade them to buy the product or use the service
- encourage them to develop brand loyalty and therefore prefer it to alternatives provided by competitors
- encourage them to continue to buy the product and to recommend it to others.

In order to persuade consumers to go through these stages, organisations must identify who it is they are attempting to reach and target the promotion accordingly. Promotion therefore has an important role to play in positioning products in a market to specific target groups. The more precise the positioning and targeting, the greater the chance of the target audience buying the product.

Once an organisation has identified who is going to be approached, it must then decide how to approach them. This involves selecting a suitable medium to reach the target audience. For example, a local tourist attraction could reach its target audience by placing a leaflet in a local free newspaper which is delivered to every household in the area. This approach would not be suitable for a larger organisation with a national target audience, such as an airline or a tour operator, which would probably need to place advertisements in national newspapers or on television.

The choice of promotional activity is ultimately determined by:

- the budget (what the organisation can afford to spend)
- the type of product
- the target audience.

Most travel and tourism organisations use a combination of promotional activities. These include:

- advertising
- brochures and leaflets
- direct marketing
- public relations
- sales promotions
- sponsorship.

The combination of these activities is known as the **promotion mix.** We will look at them in greater detail in the section on marketing communications on pp. 283–304.

▲ Examples of promotional materials used in the travel and tourism industry

Evaluating the marketing mix

We have looked at the four factors within the marketing mix and their importance to ensuring the success of a travel and tourism organisation. However, it is not enough for an organisation to simply formulate an effective marketing mix; it needs continually to evaluate its effectiveness and to make changes when necessary. For example, customer needs and expectations may change, so that products or services must be redeveloped; competitors may change their pricing policies so that the organisation must revise its own prices in order to remain competitive.

We look at some of the ways in which organisations can evaluate the effectiveness of the marketing mix in the section on marketing research (see pp. 262–72). However, you need to understand now that the evaluation should focus on how effectively the marketing mix is able to meet the organisation's marketing objectives. For example, if one of an organisation's aims is to increase the number of new customers it attracts, an evaluation of its marketing mix might ask some of the following questions.

- Do our products and services meet the needs and expectations of the identified new market? Are the brand image and product characteristics appropriate for this market?

- Is the location and channel of distribution suitable for the new customers?

- Are our prices acceptable to the new customers?

- Is our promotion effective in attracting new customers?

CASE STUDY

McDonald's marketing mix

McDonald's is part of the British way of life, but in fact the famous red-fronted restaurants have only been with us for the last 25 years. The first restaurant opened in Woolwich, south-east London, in 1974. By 1977 there were 10 restaurants rising to 200 in 1985 and 738 in 1996. The thousandth McDonald's opened its doors in the UK in 1999. Globally, McDonald's operates 23,000 outlets in 109 countries. Over 38 million people in the world eat a McDonald's product each day.

The McDonald's vision statement

McDonald's sums up its mission in the following five global strategies.

- Develop our people at every level of the organisation, beginning in our restaurants.

- Foster innovation in our menu, facilities, marketing operations and technology.

- Expand our global mindset by sharing best practices and leveraging our best people resources around the world.

- Long term, reinvent the category in which we compete and develop other business and growth opportunities.

- Continue the successful implementation of changes underway in McDonald's USA.

Product

McDonald's product characteristics have been firmly embedded in its customers' minds through the extensive use of standardisation throughout its operations. Staff training, food and drink products, packaging and the design and decor of restaurants are consistent in all of their outlets.

Research carried out by Interbrand found that the McDonald's brand was recognised by more people throughout the world than any other, including Coca-Cola. The brand image has consistently been one of fast service, cleanliness, value for money and a fun experience for all of the family.

The initial introduction of the McDonald's product to the UK aimed to target the family market by offering catering as a leisure experience. Whilst still generating considerable revenue from this market, McDonald's has continuously developed new products to meet changing customer needs. Trends in healthy eating and the growing popularity of vegetarianism have seen the introduction of fish and bean burgers. More recently, ethnic influences have resulted in the development of Indian-style products. Targeting children, with the view that they are tomorrow's adult customers, has also been a prime objective, with the development of the hugely successful Happy Meals, offering food, soft drinks and a free toy.

Place

McDonald's restaurants seem to be located on every high street throughout the UK. The company has also developed outlets at airports, on ferries, at football grounds and even in hospitals.

Price

Price determination at McDonald's has always been governed by the company's desire to reinforce a brand image of good value for money. Special offers are frequently promoted, such as the very successful two for the price of one Big Mac offer in 1999; so successful, in fact, that when customer demand for Big Macs increased by 800 per cent the company ran out of burgers and had to put apology ads in the national press!

Promotion

A strong promotional strategy has always been one of the keys to McDonald's success. McDonald's original 1974 advertising slogan promised 'There's a difference at McDonald's you'll enjoy'. It aimed to persuade potential customers that the company was offering a new and fun product. In 1998, the company spent £44 million on advertising campaigns, compared to the £15.6 million spent by its competitor, Burger King.

Much of McDonald's promotion is carried out through television advertising and national newspapers and is designed to reflect the humorous side of the British way of life, with McDonald's at the centre.

McDonald's also uses promotional tie-ins extensively, particularly when targeting the children's market. In 1996, the company reached a ten-year agreement with Disney for the exclusive rights to merchandise new Disney films such as *A Bug's Life* and *Pocahontas*.

Point-of-sales displays and posters are also used at outlets to entice in hungry passers-by for a meal.

McDonald's undertakes a great deal of sponsorship, particularly of sporting events such as NASCAR racing and France '98 World Cup soccer.

McDonald's has 75 per cent of the UK hamburger market. Its nearest competitor is Burger King with just 15 per cent of the market.

BUILD YOUR LEARNING

Keywords and phrases

You should know the meaning of the words and phrases lised below. If you are unsure about any of them, go back through the last 17 pages to refresh your understanding.

- Brand awareness
- Brand extension
- Brand leader
- Brand loyalty
- Branding
- Breakeven price
- Chain of distribution
- Competitive pricing
- Cost plus pricing
- Discount pricing
- Dwell time
- Goods
- Location
- Marketing mix
- Market penetration pricing
- Market skimming stategy
- Place
- Price
- Pricing policy
- Product
- Product characteristics
- Product life cycle
- Promotion
- Promotions mix
- Service
- Value for money
- Variable pricing

End of section activity

Read through the McDonald's case study and carry out the following tasks.

1 Produce a SWOT and PEST analysis for McDonald's. You may find it useful to base your analysis of the business environment on a McDonald's outlet in your area.

2 Evaluate how McDonald's uses the marketing mix to satisfy its customers' needs and expectations.

3 Make recommendations about how the marketing mix for McDonald's could be improved.

4 Suggest any future trends that could affect McDonald's marketing mix, giving your reasons.

Market research

TRAVEL AND TOURISM ORGANISATIONS need to know who their customers are and the type of products and services that they want. To achieve this, effective market research must be a key marketing activity. **Market research** is the planned process of collecting, analysing and evaluating information and data about customers and markets.

▲ Market researchers are often seen in busy high streets

Effective marketing research helps organisations to make decisions about the types of products their customers want, the price they are prepared to pay, where they prefer to buy the product and how it should be promoted. The marketing research process is therefore closely linked the development of an effective marketing mix. By carrying out marketing research, organisations can identify key factors which contribute to achieving customer satisfaction, thereby increasing their competitiveness and improving performance.

Objectives

Marketing research can be used to obtain a wide range of information. The objectives of undertaking marketing research commonly involve identifying:

- customer needs
- markets
- trends and fashions
- changes in markets
- opportunities for market and product development
- competitors
- effectiveness of promotional activities.

Identifying customer needs

In order to be customer oriented, organisations must gather a range of information about what their customers want and how best to provide it. For example, by obtaining suitable information about the needs of the short-break family market, Center Parcs has dominated the year-round holiday centre market since the 1980s. Such information led to the identification of a need for all-weather facilities, quality accommodation and facilities, and breaks based on a range of booking options such as weekend, mid-week and full-week stays.

Identifying markets

Before offering a new product, most organisations carry out research to identify the market at which the product should be aimed. For example, an hotel may identify its potential market as business, conference, leisure or overseas visitors. This is clearly important information, since it allows the hotel to target its products precisely. Alton Towers theme park has undertaken marketing research and identified its main markets as general customers (individuals and families) and trade customers (group organisers, coach operators, corporate companies, school parties and hotels).

▲ The main market at Alton Towers includes general customers and trade customers

Trends

Marketing research can be used to identify trends and therefore to predict future markets. For example, a great deal of research has been conducted into the way shopping activities have become part of the tourism experience. For many tourists, the availability of good shopping facilities is a key factor in their decision about which destination to choose. The customer profile of Meadowhall near Sheffield shows that there is a continuing trend for younger shoppers to use the centre, whereas older shoppers make up a higher proportion of the shopping market in the UK generally.

Figure 4.16: Visitors to Meadowhall			
	1997	**1998**	**1999**
Age			
16–25	23	23	26
25–44	55	55	46
45+	23	23	29
Social grade			
ABC1	62	62	63
C2DE	36	36	36

▲ Snowboarding is an example of new product development

Changes in markets

Trends usually result in changes in the market or in some cases the creation of entirely new markets. The leisure shopping market is a relatively new one that has been encouraged by the development of large, out-of-town shopping malls. Travel and tourism providers have been quick to recognise this and to develop their own products to fit in. For example, many shopping malls contain facilities such as catering outlets and specific transport links. Some of the UK's major tour operators have also realised the potential of this market and offer special shopping trips to cities such as New York.

Opportunities for market and product development

By identifying markets and their characteristics, and the influence of trends, organisations are able to identify the opportunities for developing new and existing products and markets. For example, tour operators have developed the traditional winter skiing holiday market by offering snowboarding and short-break skiing holidays to their core markets.

Tour operators are continually developing new products to meet changing consumer needs and take advantage of opportunities for development. For example, in the early 1990s, the relaxation of travel restrictions to many Eastern European countries, together with rapid growth in the short-break market, resulted in the on-going development of new city-centre destinations such as Prague, Budapest and Warsaw.

Competitors

Marketing research can be used to identify an organisation's main competitors and the way they affect its products and markets. This information is important when identifying opportunities for developing new products and markets, as organisations must be able to gain a large enough market share to meet their financial performance targets. Research involves identifying the type of products offered by competitors, the people who buy them, their share of the market and their pricing strategy.

You need to understand that the travel and tourism industry is highly competitive and providers are unlikely to be successful if they fail to identify and respond to the marketing activities of their competitors. For example, charter airlines have been quick to identify that they need to provide extra in-flight services if they are to remain competitive. Pre-booked seats, a choice of meals, children's packs and in-flight entertainment are some of the ways in which charter airlines have all developed their products and services to keep pace with their competitors.

Effectiveness of promotion

Most organisations use some form of promotion to help sell their products and this can often be expensive. It is therefore important to identify how effective the promotion is in meeting its objectives. For example, did it attract new customers, and if so how many? Did it improve the customers' perception of the product and organisation? Which types of promotion were the most cost-effective? For example, an organisation may ask customers how they heard about the product and services offered, in order to evaluate which of their promotional techniques were the most effective in attracting new customers.

ACTIVITY

Questionnaires

Obtain a questionnaire from a travel or tourism organisation. They are often freely available at the reception desk for customers to complete and many organisations will supply copies of past questionnaires. Discuss what you think the objectives of the questionnaire might be. For example, if the questionnaire asks for details of how customers heard about the facility, product or service, one objective of the research may be to evaluate the effectiveness of promotions.

Classifying customers

Although it is vital to identify markets, it is equally important to understand the characteristics of customers within the market, so that products can be developed which meet their needs. Market research plays a key role in identifying customers and **classifying customers** into key market segments through a process known as market segmentation. **Market segmentation** involves dividing the overall market into segments or groups of customers who are

sufficiently alike to suggest that they will have similar needs for products or services.

Markets can be segmented in several ways, including by:

- socio-economic grouping

- age

- family circumstances

- lifestyle.

Socioeconomic grouping

In marketing, social class (or **socioeconomic segmentation**) is often used to differentiate groups according to income and occupational status. One of the most widely used classifications based on socio-economic class is that developed by the Institute of Practitioners in Advertising. This divides the population into six groups.

- **Class A.** Senior managers and professionals, such as managing directors of large firms, doctors and lawyers.

- **Class B.** Intermediate or middle-level managers and professionals, such as managers of leisure centres, teachers and accountants.

- **Class C1.** Supervisory or junior management, administrative or clerical positions, including office managers, receptionists, computer operators and qualified fitness advisers.

- **Class C2.** Skilled manual workers, such as electricians and carpenters.

- **Class D.** Semi-skilled and unskilled manual workers, such as cleaners and construction workers.

- **Class E.** Others in low incomes, including casual workers and those dependent on State benefits and pensions.

In broad terms, people in these groups tend to have similar tastes, preferences and lifestyles; for example, As and Bs generally buy *The Times*, whereas C1s and C2s prefer the *Daily Mail* and the *Daily Express*, while C2s and Ds choose *The Sun* and similar tabloid papers. Many travel and tourism products are seen to be attractive to a particular class. Butlins is seen as a mainly working-class holiday, for example, while Center Parcs and Oasis are targeted at As and Bs. However, in recent years, many traditional preferences have become blurred, in part due to changing income patterns. Some manual workers have high earnings and can afford luxury holidays, whereas public sector professionals including teachers and nurses may have to take more modest holidays and pursue cheaper pastimes.

ACTIVITY

Socioeconomic and demographic segmentation

The table below provides a breakdown of the demographic characteristics of people taking short breaks and main holidays in the UK in 1997.

Compare the two columns of figures and discuss the main differences between the demographic market segments for the short-break market and the main holiday market.

	Secondary	Main
Total trips (commercial accommodation)	18.1m	19.3m
	%	%
Social class		
AB	32	20
C1	33	30
C2	21	23
DE	15	25
Age		
15–24	11	10
25–34	21	23
35–44	25	25
45–54	19	14
55–64	13	12
65+	11	17
With children	37	47
Lifecycle		
15–34 C	14	22
15–34 NC	19	12
35–54 C	22	25
35–54 NC	21	14
55+	24	29

C = children, NC = no children

Source: UKTS 1997

Age

Many products and services are aimed at people in a particular age group. Shearings Coach Holidays, for example, caters mainly for the over 50s, while Escapades aims to attract the youth market. Carrying out market research into the age segments using particular products and services can help an organisation to develop products and services to meet its customers' needs. Frequently, this means adapting existing products or developing new ones to meet the needs of new and different age groups of target customers. For example, cruise holidays have traditionally been seen as a product that appeals to older people in particular. However, recent research shows that the actual consumer market attracted to cruising is becoming increasingly young (see Figure 4.17). Whereas the over 65 market has halved in four years, the 35–54 market has nearly doubled.

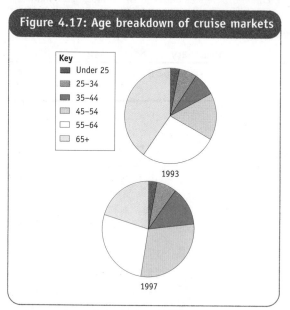

Figure 4.17: Age breakdown of cruise markets

Key
Under 25
25–34
35–44
45–54
55–64
65+

1993

1997

Family circumstances

Customers frequently experience travel and tourism products and services with friends, partners or family members rather than on their own. This means that the market segment for many travel and tourism products is not an individual but a group of customers, each with a range of individual needs. **Family circumstances** market segmentation classifies customers according to their stage in the family life cycle. These stages vary, but generally include most of the following for the majority of people at some stage in their life:

- child
- young adult
- young couple
- young couple with a baby or young children
- couple with a growing family (aged 5–18 years)
- empty nesters, retired couple whose children have recently left home
- elderly couple
- single elderly person.

ACTIVITY

Age segments

The graph compares the numbers of visitors to the UK using the Channel Tunnel in 1994–96 and 1996–97, based on age segments.

As a group, discuss which particular segments you think the Channel Tunnel operators should be targeting and say why. Bear in mind that the best strategy is not necessarily to target segments showing growth. For example, segments showing a sudden and unexpected decline in demand could become loyal customers again with the right marketing mix.

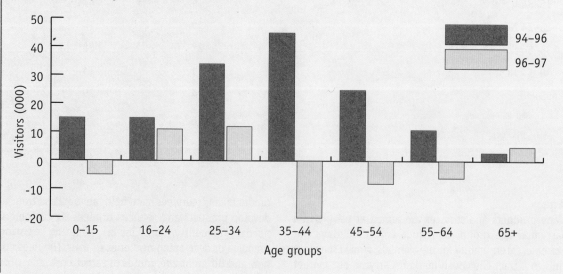

Travel and tourism organisations may find through market research that their customers are predominantly from specific life cycle segments and therefore tailor their products and services to meet these segment needs. For example, over the last 10–15 years there has been a large increase in the number of young couples with babies and couples with growing families using travel and tourism products as family groups. This has led many tourist attractions to introduce special family-priced entrance tickets and to the development of children's areas and facilities in pubs and hotels. Similarly, there has been a growing trend for people in their 50s to take early retirement which has created the empty nesters segment. These people have more time to pursue travel and tourism interests. (Perhaps this is one of the reasons for the changing market segments attracted to cruise holidays discussed earlier.)

ACTIVITY

Life cycle segments

Get a copy of a leading tour operator's main summer package holiday brochure. Look through the brochure and identify all of the life cycle segments that the company aims to attract and discuss how it achieves this.

You will need to think carefully about the actual customers within each segment who actually buy the holiday. For example, Thomson's T- Club may be a hit with young children but young children do not generally decide where the family is going on holiday. Therefore the target market for the T -Club is likely to be the parents in the couple with growing family segment.

Lifestyle

A more complicated method of market segmentation is to identify how customers' lifestyle influence the types of products that they buy. This is particularly useful when looking at travel and tourism products because they often form an integral part of customers' lifestyle. For example, in recent years there has been an increasing tendency for people to take second, third or even more holidays. This has created a huge market for short-break holidays and out of season holidays such as winter breaks at Center Parcs.

The concept of **lifestyle segmentation** has led many organisations to give titles to their main segments that describe the general way in which they work, spend their money and use their leisure time. You have probably heard of one of the first, generally used lifestyle segments to be identified; the yuppie. The term arose in the 1980s and describes a young (25–35 year old), urban, professional person who is single and successful, who earns a high salary and spends his or her money on expensive products, including extensive travel.

One of the more recently identified lifestyle segments in travel and tourism is the juggler. Typically, a juggler is a 35–45 year-old woman who has a full-time and demanding career. She usually has a partner in a high-profile job and a number of school-aged children, as well as a large house to run (albeit, often with help from cleaners, gardeners, and so on). In other words, this type of lifestyle customer is continually juggling the many aspects of her busy life.

ACTIVITY

The juggler

As a group, discuss what particular travel and tourism products and services the juggler will be attracted to. Bear in mind that she will often experience them with others, such as a partner and/or children.

In this activity you might also like to consider another lifestyle concept – money-rich, time-poor. This describes people who earn large salaries but who have such demanding jobs and commitments that they have very little leisure time.

Market segments may be differentiated on the basis of several other factors, such as:

- gender
- place of residence
- personal characteristics.

It is important to remember that identifying market segments is only an approximate way of targeting customers. However, increasingly sophisticated market research is allowing the definition of market segments to become more and more precise.

Conducting market research is a systematic and highly-skilled process. There are two basic types of market research:

- primary (or field) research
- secondary (or desk) research.

Let's look at each of these approaches to research in detail.

Primary research

Primary market research is also known as **field research**. The term refers to any research that involves contact with past, existing or potential customers. Primary market research is what most people think of as market research and includes methods such as:

- surveys
- observation
- focus groups.

Before looking at each of these in further detail it is important that you understand the difference between qualitative and quantitative research.

Qualitative and quantitative research

The difference between qualitative and quantitative research is that **qualitative research** looks in depth at consumers' feelings, attitudes, desires and perceptions, whereas **quantitative research** provides more structured information that is statistically measurable.

Although qualitative research can provide more detailed in-depth information, it is often difficult to present statistically or to come to any general conclusions. For example, if you asked 200 people how the customer service provided by a resort representative could be improved, you could receive 200 different answers. Using all of this information could be difficult.

Quantitative research on the other hand can enable researchers to draw specific conclusions from the results. For example, if you asked if customers were satisfied with the customer service, it might lead you to find that, of those surveyed, 43 per cent were satisfied with the customer service and 57 per cent were dissatisfied. However, quantitative research does not give any detailed information that explains the results. For example, why those 57 per cent were dissatisfied with the customer service.

Generally speaking, quantitative research results become more accurate the larger the sample size. Qualitative research, on the other hand, works better with a small sample size. Many organisations use a combination of both. Questionnaires, for example, are often used to produce quantitative information. Group discussions and in-depth interviews are usually used to produce qualitative information.

Marketing research questions can be phrased as open or closed questions. Closed questions require a single word or brief answer. Open questions require an explanation as an answer. In the Thomson Holidays survey (see Figure 4.18), most of the questions are closed, producing a wide range of quantitative information. Respondents are also given opportunities to make detailed comments on certain aspects of their holiday through the use of open questions,.

Surveys

Surveys are usually conducted as a quantitative research method based on a questionnaire given to a large sample, such as the Thomson Holidays example in Figure 4.17. Questionnaires are one of the most widely used research methods in the travel and tourism industry because they are relatively quick and easy to administer and analyse.

The success of a survey depends to a large extent upon the quality of the questionnaire used. A well-designed questionnaire, including structured questions with answers classified into predetermined categories, is quick to administer and the resulting data easy to process. By contrast, a questionnaire made up of open questions creates problems of interpretation and analysis, as well as in recording the data.

Questionnaires

Compiling a questionnaire is a skilled process that needs careful consideration. You need to consider:

- how you are going to frame the questions
- how long the questionnaire should be
- how the questionnaire should be laid out
- how you are going to record the answers.

Framing questions

One of the most difficult aspects of compiling an effective questionnaire is writing questions that are easily understood and that are interpreted in the same way by all respondents. General rules to writing questions are as follows.

- Keep language simple yet specific.
- Avoid jargon, slang or local terms.
- Do not ask more than one thing in a single question.
- Make sure questions are unambiguous; in other words, that they cannot be interpreted in different ways by different respondents.
- Do not ask respondents to make complicated calculations or recall events that happened a long time ago.
- Only include questions that are totally relevant; it is easy to get side-tracked and forget what you are actually trying to find out.
- Do not ask respondents to speculate on or imagine something that they have not experienced; their answer will only be a guess and will not be very helpful.
- As a general rule, avoid very personal questions; people will either refuse to answer or lie!

Figure 4.18: Thomson Holidays survey

Thomson Holidays

HOLIDAY SURVEY

The opinions of returning holidaymakers are extremely important in helping us to improve the standards and quality of future holidays. If you are 16 years of age or over, we would be pleased if you would complete this holiday questionnaire.

At the end of the questionnaire there is a section for you to fill in your name and address. Should you not wish to receive any information about future holidays then please leave this section blank.

No replies can be given to individual questionnaires. However if you have any specific comments to make to which you would like a reply, please write to the Passenger Relations Department at the address given below.

Thank you for your help and co-operation.

For each question please tick appropriate box or where requested write in the answer.

1 YOUR HOLIDAY DETAILS

A The name of your **Resort**:
   (Two-centre clients name both)
   or full name of **Tour**:

B The name of your Hotel/Villa/Apartment:

C Board arrangements: Full board [1]   Half board [2]   Bed/Breakfast [3]   Self Catering [4]   (24)

D Holiday length (write in number of nights)

E Departure from the UK: Date ___ Month ___ 198_

F How long before the start of your holiday did you book?   More than 6 months before [1]   3-6 months before [2]   1-2 months before [3]   Less than 4 weeks before [4]   (94)

G Which of the following holidays was this one?
   A La Carte [1]   Square Deal [2]   Winter Sun [3]   Tours [4]   Villa/Apartment [5]
   Young at Heart [6]   Air Fares [7]   Ski Thomson [8]   Cruise and Stay [9]
   Other [99]   Please Specify   (109-110)

H Are there any children aged 11 or under in your personal holiday party?   Yes [1]   No [2]   (103)

Thomson Holidays, Greater London House, Hampstead Road, London NW1 7SD.

ACTIVITY

Framing questions

Look at the extract from the questionnaire below. Its market research objectives are to identify the types of holidays taken by respondents and the reasons for their choice. All of the questions break some of the rules of framing questions. Can you rewrite the questions to make them more effective?

1 How much do you earn?

2 Have you taken a long-haul holiday in the last two years?

3 If you were asked to summarise the main features that you and your family look for in a package holiday what would your three main priorities be?

4 How much do you spend on holidays each year?

5 Have you ever used a GDS to make a holiday booking?

6 In your opinion, which tour operator offers the best service?

7 How old are you? Under 18, 18–25, 25–40, 40–55, over 55?

8 Who decides where you go on holiday and what factors do they consider?

9 If you won the lottery, where would you go on holiday?

10 Do you own/drive a car?

If you really want to ensure that your questionnaire is effective, you need to carry out a pilot survey. This means testing the questionnaire on a small group of respondents to make sure that all of the questions are easily understood and not misinterpreted. Once you have carried out the pilot you will probably find that some of the questions will need rewording to make them more effective.

Length of questionnaire

When designing a questionnaire you need to consider how long it should be. There is no definitive answer to the question of length because it depends on the situation in which someone is replying. For example, someone stopped in the street may only be willing to spare a couple of minutes for a face-to-face interview, but a passenger on a long-haul flight may be willing to spend half an hour filling in an in-flight survey.

Layout of questionnaire

The way that a questionnaire is laid out is very important. Questions need to be organised into a logical sequence, so that one question leads directly on to the next. This helps respondents to focus their thoughts and to concentrate on each section.

ACTIVITY

Questionnaire layout

Look at the questions below from a questionnaire given to visitors to a tourist attraction and rearrange them so that they are in a more logical sequence.

1 How did you hear about the Oceania Aquarium?

2 Will you recommend friends to visit Oceania?

3 Have you enjoyed your visit to Oceania?

4 Is this your first visit to Oceania?

5 Have you seen our newspaper advertisements?

6 If you have visited before, how many times have you been in the last year?

7 Did a friend recommend the Oceania to you?

8 Have you used discount vouchers from the local newspaper for your visit?

9 Have you seen copies of our brochure at a tourist information centre?

10 Will you visit Oceania again?

Recording answers

The method used to record answers depends on whether the research is qualitative or quantitative. In qualitative research, answers are usually detailed written explanations. However, in quantitative research there are a number of possibilities. By far the easiest to deal with are yes/no answers, but these can only be used for a limited number of questions and they obviously also give limited information. Multiple choice is a widely used method, in which respondents are given a range of answers and asked to tick the one or ones that apply to them. An example of this type of question is shown in Figure 4.19.

Figure 4.19: Extract from national research survey

12 Do you subscribe or would you consider subscribing to any of the following?

	Currently subscribe	Would consider		Currently subscribe	Would consider
Which?	01 ☐	17 ☐	The Softback Preview	09 ☐	25 ☐
Gardening Which?	02 ☐	18 ☐	Books for children	10 ☐	26 ☐
New Scientist	03 ☐	19 ☐	Time	11 ☐	27 ☐
New Statesman	04 ☐	20 ☐	Disney Book Club	12 ☐	28 ☐
Newsweek	05 ☐	21 ☐	Red House Books	13 ☐	29 ☐
Britannia Music	06 ☐	22 ☐	House of Grolier	14 ☐	30 ☐
Reader's Digest	07 ☐	23 ☐	National Geographic	15 ☐	31 ☐
Spectator	08 ☐	24 ☐	The Economist	16 ☐	32 ☐

13 Does anyone in your household buy, or would anyone consider buying books/videos/magazines/software in the following interest areas:

01 ☐ History	06 ☐ New Age	11 ☐ Railway
02 ☐ Ancient History	07 ☐ Mystery/Myth	12 ☐ Classics
03 ☐ Science Fiction/Fantasy	08 ☐ Crime/Thriller	13 ☐ Art
04 ☐ Military/Aviation	09 ☐ Health Foods	14 ☐ Computers
05 ☐ Children's Interests	10 ☐ Slimming	15 ☐ Golfing

14 Please tick all the newspapers that are REGULARLY read by your family: 99 ☐ None

	Daily	Sunday		Daily	Sunday
Express	01 ☐	21 ☐	Financial Times	10 ☐	
Independent	02 ☐	22 ☐	Guardian	11 ☐	
Mail	03 ☐	23 ☐	Star	12 ☐	
Mirror	04 ☐	24 ☐	Sun	13 ☐	
Sport	05 ☐	25 ☐	News of the World		29 ☐
Telegraph	06 ☐	26 ☐	Observer		30 ☐
Times	07 ☐	27 ☐	People		31 ☐
Other/Local	08 ☐	28 ☐	Post		32 ☐
Daily Record	09 ☐		Sunday Mail (Scotland)		33 ☐

15 From the list above, please write the number of your main newspaper: Daily: | | | Sunday: | | |

16 Is your main daily newspaper delivered? 1 ☐ Yes 9 ☐ No

17 On what day(s) do you buy your main daily newspaper?
(If not everyday, please tick all that apply) 9 ☐ Do not buy

1 ☐ Every day	3 ☐ Tuesday	5 ☐ Thursday	7 ☐ Saturday
2 ☐ Monday	4 ☐ Wednesday	6 ☐ Friday	

18 How often do you buy your main Sunday newspaper?
1 ☐ 3-4 times a month 2 ☐ 1-2 times a month 3 ☐ Less often

19 How often do you use the following to plan your TV viewing?
(Please tick all that apply)

	Every week	Most weeks	Occasionally	Xmas	Never
Daily Paper	01 ☐	06 ☐	11 ☐	16 ☐	21 ☐
Weekend Newspaper Supplement	02 ☐	07 ☐	12 ☐	17 ☐	22 ☐
Radio Times	03 ☐	08 ☐	13 ☐	18 ☐	23 ☐
TV Times	04 ☐	09 ☐	14 ☐	19 ☐	24 ☐
What's on TV/Other paid for listings	05 ☐	10 ☐	15 ☐	20 ☐	25 ☐

This method is only effective if all of the possible options are included. In the example in Figure 4.19 there may be a problem with respondents whose main holiday is visiting friends and relatives (Q2) or who went to Slovenia (Q4). This problem can often be overcome by adding the option: 'Other; please specify'.

Another way of recording answers is to use a method known as semantic differential, in which respondents select the phrase or word that most closely describes their opinion. An example can be seen in Figure 4.20. which asks respondents to rate the importance of facilities on board cruise ships.

Sometimes this method is used with a numerical scale, where respondents circle a number on a scale from 1 to 5. For example:

How often do you require the provision of a children's club at your resort hotel? Please rate on the scale: (1 = never, 2 = occasionally, 3 = quite often, 4 = nearly always, 5 = always).

In selecting a method of recording answers, it is important that the researcher considers the reaction of the respondent. If he or she uses a range of different methods, respondents are likely to become confused and may give inaccurate answers.

Figure 4.20: Cruise ship facilities

	No opinion				Must have →
Beauty salon	◉	○	○	○	○
Casino	◉	○	○	○	○
Child programme	◉	○	○	○	○
Fitness centre	◉	○	○	○	○
Indoor pool	◉	○	○	○	○
Jacuzzi	◉	○	○	○	○
Laundry	◉	○	○	○	○
Library	◉	○	○	○	○
Outdoor pool	◉	○	○	○	○
Shops	◉	○	○	○	○
Showroom	◉	○	○	○	○
Spa	◉	○	○	○	○

ACTIVITY

Designing a questionnaire

Design and implement a short survey questionnaire to identify the main market segments using a local travel or tourism facility or survey. You could base your survey on a travel agency, restaurant or tourist attraction, for example. Once you have completed the survey, discuss with the rest of the group how your questionnaire could have been improved. For example, did all respondents understand the questions, were there questions that you should have added or left out?

▲ Face-to-face interviews produce a high response rate

Contact methods

There are three main ways, or **contact methods**, by which survey information can be gathered:

- by mail
- by telephone
- by personal contact.

Many organisations send questionnaires through the post. The advantage of this contact method is that it is quick to administer and a large sample can be reached relatively cheaply. The drawback is that the reply rate can be very poor (as low as 3 per cent in many cases). Ways of encouraging people to reply include enclosing a stamped addressed envelope and offering incentives for respondents who reply, such as entry into prize draws. Even when this is done there is a problem that certain types of people are more likely to reply than others, making the sample unrepresentative.

Some organisations carry out surveys by asking respondents questions over the telephone. This is more expensive and time consuming than using the mail but usually has a higher response rate. However, because so many organisations use the phone as a sales tool, respondents are often suspicious, thinking that the purpose is to sell them something.

Many surveys are carried out through personal contact between the researcher and the respondent. Face-to-face contact is clearly more time consuming and therefore expensive, but the response rate is usually higher than those of mail and telephone surveys.

It is extremely important that the researcher is fully trained in research techniques and understands the ways in which his or her behaviour and attitude should be controlled. For example, if the researcher appears to agree or disagree with answers or prompts respondents, he or she may influence the way that respondents answer further questions.

The contact method used depends largely on the type of research being conducted and the amount of time and money available. A further consideration is the skill of the people who are going to carry out the research. Above all, the information collected needs to be objective, unbiased and truly representative of the sample if it is to be of any real value to the organisation.

Observation

Observation is a research method in which information is obtained by observing customers' behaviour or events taking place. For example, much research into road traffic is conducted by researchers placed at strategic road junctions who count the number of cars that pass at specific times.

In travel and tourism there are many situations in which observation methods can be used to provide valuable information. For example, observation at marine exhibits has shown that customers want and enjoy physical contact with the fish and other sealife, rather that simply viewing them in glass tanks. This has led some providers, such as Sea Life Centres to provide touch pools where visitors can actually stroke the fish, and special demonstrations that allow customers to handle live exhibits.

ACTIVITY

ACTIVITY

Observation

Observe and record how customers decide what to eat in a cafeteria or self-service restaurant. Do they for example:

■ look at the menu and then decide?

■ go straight to what they want?

■ ask the counter staff for advice?

■ look at all of the dishes on offer and then make their decision?

■ choose in another way?

You will need to design a suitable form to record your observations.

If your college or school has a self-service canteen you can carry out this activity there. Alternatively, you could visit a local self-service restaurant, but remember to get the permission of the manager first!

Focus groups

In **focus group** research, a group of people is encouraged to discuss their opinions and feelings about a particular organisation, product, service or topic that affects an organisation's marketing activities.

This method has the great advantage that the information collected is qualitative and therefore very detailed. However, it is extremely expensive and the information collected is based on a very small selection of respondents. You should also appreciate that focus group research is a highly skilled research technique that is often carried out by qualified psychologists. This is because researchers must be able to encourage the respondents to talk freely about the topics that are of interest without leading them to say something that they do not really mean. In other words, researchers need to be a part of the discussion group but must ensure that their own feelings and opinions do not influence those of the respondents.

ACTIVITY

Focus group research

Carry out focus group research into the brand image of a selection of tour operators. You will need up to seven tour operators' brochures, which target a range of market segments such as families, youth, older people and special interest groups.

Find at least five volunteers to make up your focus group. They should be people that you do not know very well, such as other students or tutors. Set a time limit for the group session of 20 minutes.

At the beginning of the session explain to the group that you are interested in their ideas about the type of customers each tour operator is trying to attract. Give them a few minutes to look at the brochures, then ask them to discuss the customers targeted by each brochure and explain what it is about the brochure that appeals to this type of customer.

You need to think of a few prompt questions that will ensure that you get the information that you want. These are useful if the group become side tracked!

■ Which brochures do you think are aimed at young people/older people/families. Why?

■ Can you find examples of photographs in any of the brochures that particularly appeal to young people/older people/families?

■ What types of customer do you think the front cover of the brochure might appeal to? Why?

■ Are the descriptions of optional excursions particularly attractive to certain types of customer? Why?

After the focus group session evaluate its success.

■ Was the information that you collected useful?

■ Were there anything that reduced the effectiveness of the session, such as one member dominating the discussion or influencing other members?

■ How difficult did you find it to resist the temptation to voice your own opinion or lead the respondents' answers?

■ How would you conduct the session differently if you had to do it again?

CASE STUDY

National Centre for Popular Music

On pp. 237–8 we looked at the PEST analysis carried out by the National Centre for Popular Music in Sheffield. The centre also carries out extensive primary research.

Quantitative research

The centre commissioned Sheffield Hallam University to carry out systematic quantitative research in six towns within a two-hour travel radius of Sheffield. The sample was selected on the basis of age, gender and socioeconomic grouping and involved face-to-face interviews. The findings included the following.

- The most likely people to visit the centre were couples (25.2 per cent), groups of friends (35.8 per cent), students (11.7 per cent) and families (30.6 per cent).

- The most likely common leisure interests of those likely to visit the centre were visits to pop and rock concerts, indoor sports events, nightclubs, jazz and outdoor sports events. Sports events and music-related activities have therefore been target areas for marketing the centre.

Sheffield Hallam University also designed an exit questionnaire for visitors to complete after their visit to the centre. An extract from the three-page questionnaire is shown below.

More recently, the centre has produced its own short feedback questionnaire, which is available at points throughout the centre.

Qualitative research

After the results from the quantitative research were analysed, Sheffield Hallam University conducted a number of focus groups. The quantitative research had identified adults aged 19–45, parents with children aged 5–14 and educators as three target market segments. Two focus groups were constructed for each of these three market segments (a total of six). Each focus group was made up of 20 people who were prompted with material to encourage discussion. Much insight was gained from the focus groups on the overall product of the centre, proposals for a newer and shorter name, responses to exhibition areas, main considerations when planning visits, motivations for visiting and on benefits sought from visits.

The centre also carried out observational research before opening by inviting 200 local schoolchildren to visit and use the exhibits. This research revealed a number of issues, including the fact that the 'unbreakable' interactive exhibits were all promptly broken by the visiting children! This was a very valuable piece of observational research, since it allowed the centre to redesign the exhibits to be truly unbreakable before it opened its doors to the general public in 1999.

THE NATIONAL CENTRE FOR POPULAR MUSIC

VISITOR SURVEY
SHEFFIELD HALLAM UNIVERSITY

WIN £50 HMV VOUCHERS AND A GUINNESS ROCKPEDIA

Dear Visitor

Welcome to The National Centre For Popular Music. We would be very grateful if you would take the time to answer some questions about your visit. The questionnaire should only take a short while to complete. Most questions only require you to mark a box like this [X] against the option which most closely represents your answer. The information will help us to improve our service.

All completed questionnaires will be entered in a **free prize draw** to win one of two prizes of a **£25 HMV music voucher and a Guinness Rockpedia book.**

Source: NCPM Student Pack

ACTIVITY

National Centre for Popular Music

As a group, discuss how you think the information gained from the NCPM's research might affect its marketing mix in terms of product, price, place and promotion.

Secondary research

Secondary market research is also known as **desk research** and refers to getting information from sources that are already published or easily accessible. Desk research is economical and comparatively quick to undertake. It has the advantage that it can be conducted with complete confidentiality; in other words, without competitors finding out! On the other hand, because the information yielded by desk research is not generated for the particular purposes of an organisation, it may not be sufficiently relevant and more specific (primary) research may be required.

There are two main sources of secondary research:

- internal

- external.

Internal sources

Organisations can avoid the need for expensive market research if they use internal sources of information wisely. For example, a large hotel in north Wales identified that most of its customers came from areas of Greater Manchester by checking guest registration cards. A promotional campaign was then targeted specifically at newspapers local to these areas, such as the Bolton Evening News.

Let's look at some of the most commonly used sources of internal market research.

Sales records

Sales records provide information on the quantity and frequency of products sold over a given period and can often be used to provide a comparison between current and past performance. Some organisations maintain detailed sales records showing combinations of products bought by customers.

This information is available from a number of sources, such as customer bills and cash till records. This is one of the reasons that loyalty cards are so useful, since they allow the organisation to evaluate the combinations of products and services purchased by customers.

Information from sales records can be useful in a number of ways. For example, it is possible to identify the average spending of customers, the type of customer who spends the most, peak sales times and which products have the highest sales.

Many organisations maintain information about the number of people using a facility rather than sales figures. For example, tourist information centres provide many of their services free of charge, so they keep usage rather than sales figures. In complex facilities where a range of products and services are provided, usage figures are particularly useful in giving overall information about the number of customers. For example, Meadowhall has an electronic counting device on all the main entrances so that figures can be kept on how many customers visit at any time (Figure 4.21).

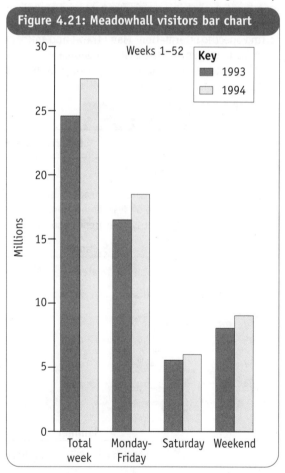

Figure 4.21: Meadowhall visitors bar chart

Many organisations compile financial information and customer databases. Financial information includes information on customers' accounts, methods of payment and credit arrangements. Much of this information is stored on computer and many organisations have their own computerised databases that include a range of information on past and present customers. For example, organisations such as hotels maintain records of occupancy figures. Information includes the number of guests staying, how long they stayed and the type of accommodation they used. Much of this information is obtained when customers fill in booking forms or registration forms. Details from these forms would provide general information on the organisations that visit, their location, the type of people in each group and so on.

The amount of internal information that an organisation has varies according to the type of product and the ways in which customers buy and use it. A bus company may have limited information because customers purchase tickets over the counter, usually without giving any personal details. However, a tour operator or travel agent would have considerably more information because customers have to complete detailed booking forms.

A great deal of information can now be stored on computer and easily accessed if staff are aware of how to find specific information. Many travel and tourism organisations keep detailed customer databases so that they are able to use internal sources of information when planning their marketing activities.

External sources

There are many external sources of information including:

- government publications
- trade journals
- periodicals
- professional associations
- national organisations
- organisations which specialise in collecting market data in a particular business sector, such as Mintel and Key Note.

Government publications

Both central and local government carries out research and publishes the results. The Office for National Statistics (ONS) publishes several very useful volumes of statistics, trends, demographic and census related data. This includes the *Annual Abstract of Statistics, Family Expenditure Survey, Regional Trends and Social*

ACTIVITY

Internal sources of information

Look at the two tables below from a tour operator's database. They compare package holiday accommodation and type of destination from 1985 to 1998. As a group, discuss what trends you can identify and suggest how you think the tour operator could use this information. For example, should the operator be looking to develop more self-catering package holidays to long haul destinations?

	Summer				Winter		
	Hotel	Self-catering	Flight only		Hotel	Self-catering	Flight only
1985	70%	20%	14%		73%	12%	15%
1990	55%	33%	12%		61%	24%	15%
1995	45%	43%	12%		52%	32%	16%
1997	47%	40%	13%		54%	30%	16%
1998*	47%	42%	11%		56%	31%	13%

*These 1998 figures from latest estimates

	Summer		Winter	
	Short haul	Long haul	Short haul	Long haul
1985	97%	3%	94%	6%
1990	91%	9%	88%	12%
1995	90%	10%	83%	17%
1997	87%	13%	78%	22%
1998*	89%	11%	80%	20%

*These 1998 figures from latest estimates

Trends and the annual *General Household Survey* (Living in Britain). It also operates an internet service(www.ons.gov.uk) that provides information about travel and tourism. In all, the government publishes 400 series of statistics and many publications have specific sections on travel and tourism.

Local government also publishes information collected through research. This may include information of direct interest to travel and tourism providers, such as visitor numbers or use of facilities.

Trade journals

A trade journal is a publication that is produced for a particular occupation or industry. Many, such as *Caterer and Hotelkeeper*, *Travel Weekly* and *Travel Trade Gazette* carry out research and publish the results. Figure 4.22 shows the results of some research carried out by *Travel Weekly* on the way travel and tourism providers see the leisure travel market developing in the future.

Travel survey

Look at Figure 4.22. What are the main growth and decline areas? How do you think research like this might influence the type of products developed by tour operators?

Associations

Professional associations are organisations that perform a coordinating, informing or leadership role. Within the travel and tourism industry they include the Association of British Travel Agents (ABTA), the Institute of Travel and Tourism (ITT), the Civil Aviation Authority (CAA) and the Tourism Society. Members of these associations pay a subscription charge in return for a range of services, which frequently includes marketing research information.

National associations, often set up by government, manage various functions relating to different industries. In travel and tourism they include the British Tourist Authority, the national tourist boards and the regional tourist boards. These bodies are a further source of information. For example, the British Tourist Authority publishes the *Tourism Intelligence Quarterly*, which reports on current trends in tourism.

Commercial data

Extensive research is carried out by market research organisations such as Mintel and Gallup.

Figure 4.23: Mintel research

Attitudes to UK short breaks

Which if any of these statements do you agree with?

Short breaks are good for:

Relaxing, treating myself	41%
Visiting different parts of the UK	30%
Visiting specific places, e.g. seaside, city	22%
Specific occasions, e.g. anniversary	16%
Special events, e.g. wedding, festival	14%
Trying out new activities, e.g. rock climbing	9%

Cross section of British adults. Based on responses from 18 per cent who regularly take UK short breaks.
Source: MINTEL/BMRB 1998

Figure 4.22: Travel Industry Digest leisure travel survey

Over the next three years how do you see growth in the following?

	Strong	Weak	Static	Falling	Don't know
The seat-only market	40	23	11	3	17
Long haul	46	17	17	3	11
Ski	20	20	46	0	14
Cruise	49	23	9	0	11
Short breaks	69	14	3	6	3
The cross-Channel market	34	26	9	9	17
Direct booking/direct-sell market	86	3	6	0	0
Bookings through the internet	54	26	11	0	9

Travel and tourism providers can commission research organisations to carry out research for them or buy information that has already been collected.

Analysing the findings

Analysing market research findings means extracting the relevant information and reaching some conclusions where possible. This is known as **data analysis**. One of the dangers in the analysis of market research data is that researchers are often so eager to prove something that they may come to a conclusion that is not wholly supported by the findings.

Survey results

Once the research data is analysed it must then be organised into a usable form to produce **survey results**. With quantitative information, such as that gained from a questionnaire, this usually means analysing it to produce statistical data. This information can then be presented in a number of ways so that it is easier to evaluate. It can be shown as a chart with various columns, as a pie chart, a line graph or a bar graph.

A pie chart is often a good way of showing the distribution of response because it is easy to see the largest shares. Look at the pie charts in Figure 4.24 which show the age and social class characteristics of visitors to Madame Tussaud's. A pie chart is useful so long as there are not too many categories that make it complex and therefore confusing.

Figure 4.24: Visitors to Madame Tussaud's	
Origin	
Domestic:	30%
Overseas:	70%
Europe	60%
North America	15%
Rest of the World	25%
Age	
Under 16	20%
16–24	26%
25–34	23%
35–44	17%
45–54	7%
55+	7%
Social Class	
AB	20%
C1	44%
C2	25%
DE	11%

ACTIVITY

Data analysis

Look at the research information below and decide which, if any, of the statements that follow is absolutely true.

Research information

Seventy-five per cent of respondents said that they went on at least one foreign package holiday a year.

Of the respondents who went on a foreign package holiday, 17 per cent went on their own; 34 per cent went with a friend and 59 per cent went with their family.

Twenty-seven per cent of respondents were not satisfied with the service offered by the tour operator.

Sixty-one per cent of respondents had been on a short-haul package holiday and 14 per cent on a long-haul holiday.

Twelve per cent of those who had been on a foreign package holiday had booked directly with the tour operator whilst 63 per cent had booked through a travel agent.

Statements

1 Twenty-seven per cent of short-haul package holiday customers were not satisfied with the service provided by the tour operator.

2 Twenty-five per cent of respondents did not go on a foreign package holiday.

3 Sixty-three per cent of customers who went with their family booked through a travel agent.

4 Forty-one per cent of people with families did not go on a foreign package holiday.

5 People who went on a package holiday on their own were less likely to be dissatisfied with the service provided by the tour operator.

Bar charts are used in a similar way to pie charts and allow comparisons to be made easily. A bar chart is usually a better choice if there is a large number of categories. Figure 4.25 shows the information from the pie chart on the age characteristics of visitors to Madame Tussaud's as a bar chart.

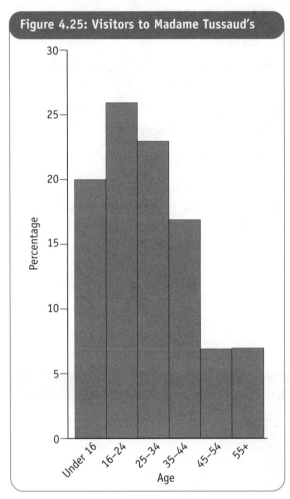

Figure 4.25: Visitors to Madame Tussaud's

Line graphs (see Figure 4.26) are used to show how something rises or falls; for example, an organisation's sales over a week.

Any information that can be shown as a line graph can also be shown as a pie chart or bar chart but the reverse in not true. For example, it would be meaningless to show the age bar chart as a line graph, because each point on the graph is a separate piece of information, unrelated to the others.

Although qualitative research can sometimes be represented in one of these graphical formats it is unusual. Collating and presenting qualitative information normally requires a technical presentation in which the results are explained as a summary of opinions. This is because the responses are in-depth and highly personalised and therefore difficult to express graphically.

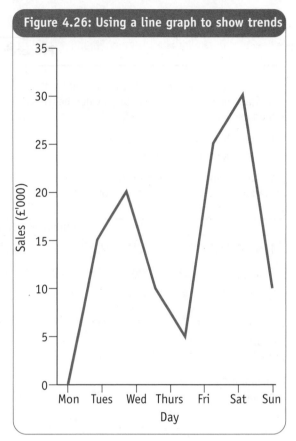

Figure 4.26: Using a line graph to show trends

Whatever method of research is employed, in nearly all cases a written report is produced, providing a summative analysis of the findings. Let's look at some research findings and see how they could be analysed and presented as a written report.

Figure 4.27 shows the results of research into UK residents' tourism based on the number of trips, the number of nights and the average spending of four main market segments: holiday, visiting friends and relatives (VFR), business and other.

From these findings we could produce the following analysis. The largest single sector for trips (58 per cent), nights (75 per cent) and spending (76 per cent) is the holiday market. The VFR market is the second largest market for trips (26 per cent) and nights (14 per cent) but only has 6 per cent of the spending. The business market is the second largest spending market (16 per cent) and trips market (12 per cent) but only has 12 per cent of the total number of nights.

What we could not say in our analysis is that the reason that the VFR market has a large share of the trips but a low share of the spending is because customers do not need to spend as much money when they stay with friends and relatives. Whilst this may well be true there is no evidence in the research to support it. You would need to carry out further research to find out why the VFR market spends less money on tourism before you could make any further statements.

ACTIVITY

Presenting survey results

Imagine you are the marketing manager at a heritage museum. Use the data provided below to produce:

- a pie chart showing the breakdown of admissions by type of visitor
- a line graph showing the total number of admissions during each month of the year

- a bar chart showing the total number of visitors in each category for the whole year
- a brief written summary of the main market segments and trends in admission levels over the year
- recommendations on how the data could be used to influence the museum's marketing mix.

Number of admissions: by month												
Type of visitor	Jan	Feb	Mar	Apr	May	June	July	Aug	Sept	Oct	Nov	Dec
Adult	190	367	566	940	1,070	1,108	1,670	1,890	762	788	512	401
Child	78	290	203	1,363	992	876	1,761	2,445	535	734	269	276
OAP	38	192	314	410	435	512	420	412	396	304	188	58
Coach group booking	40	126	328	764	645	960	1,320	1,526	1,710	596	162	124
School group booking	68	160	522	496	570	610	382	145	62	242	208	95

Figure 4.27: Purpose of UK residents' tourism in the UK, 1997

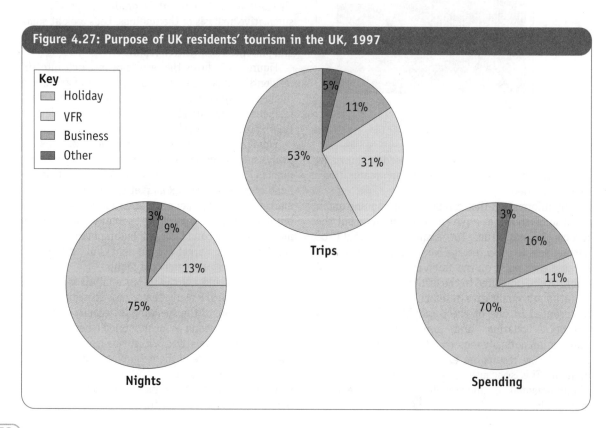

Key
- Holiday
- VFR
- Business
- Other

Trips

Nights

Spending

Analysing attendance data

The table compares visitor attendance figures in 1997 and 1998 at the top 20 UK visitor attractions that charge admission. Write a brief analysis (approximately 200 words) outlining the main findings from the figures. You might choose to analyse the figures generally or to compare specific types of attraction, such as theme parks or historic attractions.

You may find it helpful to begin by calculating the percentage increase or decrease in attendance for each to give you a better basis for evaluation. For example, Alton Towers = change (80,055) divided by 1997 figures (2,701,945) multiplied by 100 = 2.96 per cent increase in attendances. (Figures for 1999 can be found on p. 61.)

Attraction	1998	1997	Change
1. Alton Towers	2,782,000	2,701,945	+80,055
2. Madame Tussaud's	2,772,500	2,798,801	−26,301
3. Tower of London	2,551,459	2,615,170	−63,711
4. Natural History Museum	1,904,539	1,793,400	+111,139
5. Chessington World of Adventure	1,650,000	1,750,00	−100,000
6. Science Museum, London	1,599,817	1,573,151	+62,666
7. Legoland	1,510,363	1,297,818	+212,545
8. Canterbury Cathedral	1,500,000	1,613,000	−113,000
9. Windsor Castle	1,495,365	1,129,629	+365,836
10. Edinburgh Castle	1,219,055	1,238,140	−19,085
11. V&A Museum	1,110,000	1,040,750	+69,250
12. Flamingo Land, N.Yorks	1,105,000	1,103,000	+2,000
13. St Paul's Cathedral	1,095,299	964,737	+130,562
14. London Zoo	1,052,000	1,097,017	−45,637
15. Drayton Manor Park	1,003,802	1,002,100	+1,702
16. Kew Gardens	1,000,000	937,017	+62,983
17. Windermere Lake Cruises	950,000	1,131,932	−181,932
18. Chester Zoo	920,000	829,800	+90,200
19. Royal Academy, London	912,714	858,854	+53,860
20. Royal Baths and Pump Room, Bath	905,426	933,489	−28,063

Choosing research techniques

Clearly, there are many techniques available for collecting market research information. Travel and tourism organisations need to identify which techniques are the most suitable for their particular research needs. A number of factors need to be considered when selecting a method. These are:

- cost
- time
- accessibility
- validity and reliability
- fitness for purpose.

Cost

Research methods that use a lot of personal contact, such as interviews, are generally more expensive than those that do not, such as postal questionnaires. Costs to consider include the expense of staff time, producing materials, postage and telephone charges. The larger the sample size, the higher the costs will be, both in collecting and analysing information.

Time

The amount of time spent in preparing, conducting and analysing marketing information can vary enormously according to the method used and is directly related to cost. If a travel and tourism organisation has limited time to conduct research then techniques such as simple, self-completion questionnaires or telephone surveys may be most effective. Alternatively, secondary research may provide quick and relevant information.

Accessibility

The extent to which the sample is accessible also influences the research methods that are selected. For example, if a local travel agent wants information about its current customers, the sample can easily be accessed because the company has contact details on its customer database. However, if the travel agent wants information on potential customers it would need to use alternative methods, such as mailing questionnaires to a sample of the local population or conducting household interviews.

Validity and reliability

Depending on the type of information required, some methods are more valid than others and .therefore produce more reliable information. For example, a questionnaire would be a more valid method of obtaining quantitative information than a group discussion.

Generally, the reliability of information collected depends less on the method used and more on the way in which it is used. A badly worded questionnaire will not produce reliable information and it would be foolhardy to base marketing decisions on it. Similarly, if the sample used is not truly representative of the market the information cannot be used for general marketing decisions.

Fitness for purpose

The research method selected should be fit for the purpose that is intended. In other words, it should achieve the objectives set by producing reliable information. It is often possible to use simple, inexpensive methods and still produce reliable information. For example, comment cards placed on tables in restaurants are a simple way of evaluating the level of customer satisfaction.

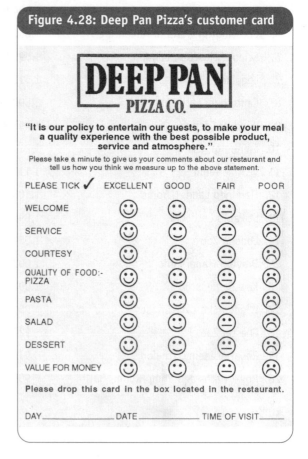

Figure 4.28: Deep Pan Pizza's customer card

Look at the table listing the different types of research techniques and the main strengths and weaknesses of each (Figure 4.29).

Travel and tourism organisations usually have a wide range of information needs and need to use more than one research technique.

Figure 4.29: Comparing the strengths and weaknesses of research techniques

Research technique	Cost	Time	Accessibility	Validity and reliability	Fitness for purpose
Survey	Cost depends on survey and sample size, can be very low	Can be very quick to implement	Can access a wide geographical area	Good if survey questions are well constructed	Especially good for quantitative research
Observation	Cost can be low for quantitative research but rises for qualitative	Time consuming for qualitative, fairly quick for quantitative	Usually fairly limited accessibility localised area only	Good if well-controlled	Can be used for qualitative and quantitative research
Focus group	Very high in terms of time and the need for researchers	Very time consuming	Usually fairly limited accessibility to localised area	Good if well-controlled, but requires highly skilled researchers	Usually only used for qualitative research
Internal secondary	Minimal since data is usually readily available	Can be very quick if accurate internal records are kept and are computerised	Very accessible	If records are accurate, will be highly valid and reliable	Good for quantitative, may also provide some qualitative data
External secondary	Much data is freely available but can be expensive	Can be very quick, purchasing commercial data is instant	Wide access to regional, national and international data	Dependant on source	Can provide quantitative and qualitative data

ACTIVITY

Choosing market research techniques

Clubscene Travel specialises in European budget holidays aimed at the 18–25 market. It has successfully sold package holidays in Spain, Greece and Turkey for the last eight years. It is now planning to introduce a similar package at selected resorts in Slovenia and plans to carry out research to evaluate the market potential of this new destination. The company has set these market research objectives.

■ To identify existing Clubscene customers who may be interested in a holiday in Slovenia.

■ To identify the product characteristics of similar package holidays offered in Slovenia by other tour operators.

■ To identify the specific product characteristics that are valued by our existing customers with a view to extending the characteristics to the Slovenia packages.

■ To evaluate customers' reaction to the proposed brochure for the Slovenia package holidays.

■ To identify other Eastern European destinations that might be developed by Clubscene after the introduction of the Slovenia packages.

As a group, discuss which market research techniques would be suitable to achieve each objective. You should consider primary research methods (surveys, observation and focus groups) and secondary research methods (internal and external sources).

In each case, give the reasons why you think your chosen research technique is the most effective (in terms of its strengths) compared with (the weaknesses of) other techniques.

BUILD YOUR LEARNING

Keywords and phrases

You should know the meaning of the words and phrases listed below. If you are unclear about any of them, go back through the last 22 pages of the unit to refresh your understanding.

- Classifying customers
- Contact method
- Data analysis
- Desk research
- Family circumstances
- Field research
- Focus group
- Lifestyle segmentation
- Market segmentation
- Marketing research
- Observation
- Primary research
- Qualitative research
- Quantitative research
- Secondary research
- Socioeconomic segmentation
- Survey
- Survey results

End of section activity

Select a travel or tourism organisation and investigate and evaluate the market research techniques that it uses by carrying out the following tasks.

1 Identify how the organisation uses market research to identify market segments such as socioeconomic groupings, age, family circumstances and lifestyle.

2 Identify the range of primary research techniques that it uses such as surveys, observation and focus groups. Your evaluation should explain how and why the research is carried out and be supported with examples such as questionnaires.

3 Identify the range of internal and external secondary research that the organisation uses. Find out if it uses secondary research and provide examples, such as details held on customer databases.

4 Explain how the organisation analyses research findings and uses the results when formulating its marketing mix. You need to give detailed examples of action the organisation has taken as a direct result of market research. For example, its effect on:

- the development of new products or services
- pricing strategies
- decisions on location and channels of distribution
- promotional methods.

5 Critically analyse the market research techniques used by the organisation and suggest how they could be improved. For example, could questionnaires be redesigned to be more effective; would a different contact method be better, such as a telephone rather than a postal survey, or could the organisation use a different technique, such as observation? Justify your recommendations by explaining why they would be appropriate.

Marketing communications

MOST TRAVEL AND TOURISM ORGANISATIONS use a number of **marketing communications** channels in order to make customers aware of their products, influence customers' purchasing decisions and gain beneficial publicity to enhance the organisation's image. The choice of these channels of communication (known as media) varies with the type and size of the organisation, the nature of its operations and the budget it has available.

The most common marketing communication media are:

- advertising
- holiday brochures
- direct marketing
- public relations (PR)
- sales promotion
- sponsorship.

Let's look at each in turn.

Advertising

Advertising is one of the most common marketing communication techniques used by travel and tourism organisations, and ranges from national television advertisements costing many thousands of pounds to small classified ads in local newspapers costing just a few pounds. Figure 4.30 compares the amount spent on a range of advertising channels between 1988 and 1997.

Nearly all travel and tourism organisations undertake some form of advertising so it is important to understand the basic concepts involved in this type of marketing communication.

Advertising can be used to achieve a number of objectives including to:

- make a new product or service known
- create awareness of an existing product or service
- inform customers of price changes
- combat competitors' advertising
- describe services available and benefits associated with using them
- create favourable attitudes towards the organisation
- correct false impressions and other obstacles to sales.

Travel and tourism organisations must select the most effective and efficient type of advertising media to achieve their objectives. The main media used by travel and tourism organisations are:

- press
- television
- radio
- magazines
- internet
- leaflets
- point-of-sale material
- posters.

Press

The British are avid readers and buyers of newspapers. In the UK there are approximately 1,300 local and regional newspapers and 21 national dailies and Sunday newspapers. On average, over 27 million people read at least one national daily newspaper and 30 million read a national Sunday newspaper. The press therefore provides significant opportunities for travel and tourism organisations to communicate with existing or potential customers.

Figure 4.30: Advertising expenditure (£m)					
Year	Press	TV	Poster	Radio	Cinema
1988	4,548	2,127	244	138	27
1989	5,131	2,288	271	159	35
1990	8,137	2,325	282	183	39
1991	4,884	2,295	287	149	42
1992	4,957	2,472	284	157	45
1993	5,085	2,805	300	194	49
1994	5,800	2,873	330	213	53
1995	5,979	3,103	378	296	69
1996	8,413	3,333	428	344	73
1997	8,987	3,851	800	383	88

There are many advantages associated with advertising in newspapers. As we have already discussed in the section on market segmentation, newspapers have specific readership profiles that can enable advertisers to target and position their promotional messages to specific groups.

National press advertisements are cheaper than other forms of mass media, such as television advertising, and large national audiences can be reached. Alternatively, press advertisers can reach audiences in individual localities or regions by using local and regional paid or free newspapers.

Advertising in newspapers is very flexible. Advertisements can be placed or changed at relatively short notice, while the advertising message can be read at leisure, reread and even cut out and kept for future use. Press advertisements can be used for direct customer response and mail order sales as well as for special purchase offers using cut-out coupons. Sometimes they are accompanied by editorial coverage in supplements or special features that provide added impact.

There are a few disadvantages to press advertising, however. The advertisements are static, lack movement and an ability to show products or services in use. With many travel and tourism products this is an important consideration because they are intangible experiences. For example, a product such as a holiday in America has greater visual impact on colour television than in a black and white newspaper advertisement. This is why tour operators and travel agents often provide free videos for their customers in addition to glossy colour holiday brochures.

▲ Examples of local and national press advertisements

ACTIVITY

Press advertising

Look at the newspaper advertisement for Whitney Houston's 1999 arena tour. How effective do you think it is? Why do you think the tour promoters chose to advertise in Sunday newspapers rather than on television?

Television

The greatest advantage of television advertising is that it can show products working and the use of music, dialogue, personalities, colour, special effects and animation can help to create a stunning visual impact on a mass audience. However, unlike printed advertising, the exposure is very short, usually 10–60 seconds at a time. This means that the amount of information that can be given is limited and can be missed altogether if the advertisement fails to attract the attention of the viewer.

Research showing that electricity use escalates during commercial breaks indicates that many viewers use the break in programmes to make a hot drink rather than watch the advertisements. A further problem for advertisers is the use of remote control devices that allow viewers to zap between channels when advertisements appear.

ACTIVITY

Television advertising

Adwatch carries out weekly research to identify which television advertisements viewers remember seeing from the previous week. The table shows the results of one such survey.

Over a week, list ten advertisements that appear on television frequently. Carry out a survey of at least 30 people to see which of the advertisements that you have listed are remembered. Try to get a cross section of people of different ages, gender and occupation. When you have completed the survey, rank the advertisements in order of how many people remembered each.

	Last week	Account	Agent/TV buyer	%
1	(1)	Asda	Publicis/Carat	70
2=	(2=)	BT	Abbott Mead Vickers BBDO/The Allmond Partnership	69
2=	(2=)	Andrex	Banks Hoggins O'Shea FCB/MindShare	69
4	(–)	B&Q	Bates Dorland/Zenith Media	68
5	(–)	SkyDigital	In-House/Universal McCann	67
6	(–)	McDonald's	Leo Burnett	64
7	(–)	Somerfield	RPM3/Universal McCann	56
8	(–)	Kellogg's Rice Krispies	J Walter Thompson/MindShare	55
9	(–)	Nescafe	McCann-Erikson/Universal McCann	53
10=	(–)	Surf Tablets	Ammirati Puris Lintas/Initiative Media	52
10=	(–)	Nissan Primera	TBEA GGT Simons Palmer/Carat	52
10=	(–)	Pepsi	Abbot Mead Vickers BBDO/BMP OMD	·52
13	(4)	Persil Colour Tablets	J Walter Thompson/Initiative Media	51
14	(–)	Weetabix	Lowe Howard-Spink/Western International Media	49
15	(–)	Boots	J Walter Thompson/BMP OMD	47
16=	(–)	Burger King	Ammirati Puris Lintas/Carat	44
16=	(–)	National Savings	BMP DDB/BMP OMD	44
18=	(–)	Wella Shockwaves	Abbot Mead Vickers BBDO/New PHD	43
18=	(–)	Maybelline – Wonder Curl Mascara	McCann-Erikson/Universal McCann	43
20	(–)	Teletext	St Luke's/Manning Gottlieb Media	41

Cinema has all the benefits of television advertising. Although the audience is much smaller, it is also more passive and remains seated throughout the commercial break.

Much of the advertising that appears on television is hugely successful and has a tremendous influence on buyers' decision-making processes. It is well planned and targeted, and can reach huge audiences of potential customers. Television advertising is often backed up by teletext services that direct viewers to sources of further information. Tour operators and travel agents make very effective use of the teletext system, providing details of special offers and late availability deals.

For many travel and tourism providers, the single greatest disadvantage of television advertising is the expense. A 30-second advertisement at peak time on one of the larger ITV stations such as Carlton currently costs around £50,000. Many smaller providers, such as health and fitness clubs, and council-owned leisure facilities, cannot afford to consider any form of television advertising.

Radio

Some travel and tourism providers use local commercial radio stations to promote products to the local population. It is a much cheaper medium than television and has the advantage that music, dialogue and sound effects can be used. However, since radio is not a visual or printed medium, the messages rely totally on the effectiveness of oral communication. This is often a drawback for advertisers because of the tendency in listeners to use radio as verbal wallpaper. For many, the radio is something that is on in the background that is ignored unless it is particularly interesting. That said, radio advertising is often an effective means of promoting specific products and local events, particularly when it can be linked to public relations activities such as live radio coverage of an event.

Magazines

Advertisements in magazines have similar advantages and disadvantages to newspapers since they are also a printed medium. Print quality varies but in nearly all cases it is vastly superior to newspapers and the use of full colour is commonplace. As many magazines are

▲ A travel advertisement in a magazine

published weekly, monthly or quarterly, advertisements in them tend to have a longer lifespan than those placed in newspapers. A vast selection of special interest magazines is available aimed at particular hobbies, interests or travel and tourism activities. Examples include *Homes and Gardens, Holiday Which, English Heritage, New Musical Express* and *Theatre Print*.

Perhaps the most useful aspect of advertising in special interest magazines is that travel and tourism organisations can target the specific audiences most likely to buy or use their products.

Trade newsheets, journals and magazines also provide opportunities for travel and tourism organisations to communicate with the trade and inform them of new product and service developments.

The internet

Rapidly increasing use of the internet has meant that many travel and tourism organisations have realised the benefits of using it as an advertising channel. The internet combines many of the advantages of both printed and visual advertising media. Customers have the opportunity to browse through a large amount of information at their own speed and can print out any information that they are interested in. In addition, many travel and tourism websites incorporate video

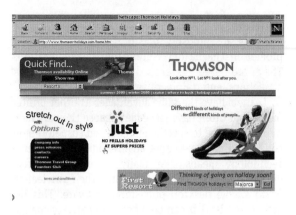

▲ Many travel and tourism operators now have websites

footage and sound to enhance the products that they are promoting. A further advantage is that customers are frequently offered the opportunity to buy products on-line.

Of course, the internet is not without its disadvantages as an advertising medium. Many people do not have access to the internet or are simply reluctant to give the personal details required to make an on-line purchase or reservation. A further disadvantage is that there is such a large amount of information on the internet that it can sometimes be difficult for customers to locate what they are looking for.

ACTIVITY

Internet advertising

Obtain a copy of a tour operator's brochure that also contains its website address. Visit the website and compare the relative strengths and weaknesses of the website information with the information in the brochure.

■ Was it quicker to find information in the brochure or on the internet?

■ What could the internet offer that the brochure could not?

■ Which of the two media made it easiest for a customer to book a holiday?

Leaflets

Leaflets are probably one of the most important promotional media for travel and tourism organisations. They are used extensively to promote tourist attractions, entertainment venues and special events.

Leaflets have the same advantages as other printed media, but often have the edge because they are more highly targeted to specific markets and (usually) more colourful than newspaper advertisements. Computer technology means that many travel and tourism organisations are now able to produce their own leaflets using simple desktop publishing software. This has meant that leaflets can be produced relatively cheaply for specific market segments and products.

▲ Leaflets are used to promote many visitor attractions

ACTIVITY

Leaflet advertising

Visit a tourist information centre, tourist attraction or hotel that has a leaflet rack. Collect examples of leaflets for tourist attractions and compare the relative features that make leaflets effective. For example, you might consider each based on the following criteria:

- overall design
- use of colour
- pictures, diagrams and photographs
- text and use of fonts
- layout
- type of paper and way in which the leaflet is folded.

▲ Point-of-sale promotion

Point-of-sale material

The term point-of-sale refers to the place that the customer actually buys a product, such as a ticket or reservation desk, a shop counter or a travel agency. It has the advantage that it is targeted at customers who are clearly interested in the product. Its main disadvantage is that it rarely reaches new markets. It is often used when the marketing objective is to develop existing markets or products. For example, a point-of-sale promotion might be used in a travel agency to inform customers about special holiday deals. The materials used can include displays of products, posters, leaflets and brochures, and sales staff are often present to answer customers' questions and enquiries.

Posters

▲ Posters can be displayed in a variety of locations

The use of posters is the oldest form of advertising and is still used extensively by travel and tourism organisations. They are often used in combination with other advertising media to reinforce a particular message. This is because the amount of information that they contain is limited by the fact that people often only glance at them in passing.

Posters can be displayed on billboards, bus shelters, on transport such as underground trains, at sports stadiums or simply on the wall of the provider's own facility. One of the main considerations with poster advertising is that its effectiveness depends largely on where it is located. The choice of location should be based on three factors:

- how many people will see it

- which people will see it

- how long they will see it for.

For example, a poster advertisement on London Underground will be seen by a lot of people and they will probably have time to read it properly during their journey. However, it will be a very broad market. A poster outside a tourist attraction such as a museum will have a limited audience but the targeted market may stop to read it fully.

CASE STUDY

Poster campaign: Victoria and Albert Museum

In 1999 the Victoria and Albert Museum (V&A) launched a new advertising campaign on London tube trains, which was supported by advertising in popular tourist guides. The main objectives of the campaign were to increase visitor numbers during the summer months, to establish the V&A as a vibrant and relevant place to visit, and to create a fun and feel good factor about visiting the museum.

The campaign was aimed at tourists in London as well as Londoners, particularly:

- 25–54 year olds

- ABC1s

- those with broad cultural interests

- those who may have visited in the past.

The campaign slogan 'Find yourself at the V&A' was intended to create a sense of urgency in visiting and to encourage visitors to start looking for the beautiful things in life amongst the exhibits.

The following six advertisements were designed for the campaign:

- a genteel lady exclaiming next to the rather racy Yves Saint Laurent Mondrian-inspired cocktail dress

- a large man, hands on hips, grinning next to the awesome plaster reproduction of Michelangelo's David

- a cheeky child wearing a set of 3D glasses next to a stunning stained glass window of Joanna of Aragon

- an older lady hugging her much loved cat next to one the famous Tippoo's Tiger which shows a tiger devouring an English solider

- a happy builder taking time out for a mug of tea next to one of the most fancy silver teapots of the 1700s

- a man in a pinstripe suit having a hair-raising experience next to the classic smooth curve of the 1920s MT8 table lamp.

ACTIVITY

V&A poster campaign

As a group, think of a seventh poster advertisement that would fit the general objectives and image of the V&A's promotional poster campaign.

Holiday brochures

Holiday brochures are one of the most widely used promotional mediums for travel and tourism organisations. They are used extensively to promote package holidays, travel services, hotels and many tourist attractions. The most obvious advantage of brochures (booklets at least eight pages long) is that a great deal of specific information can be included that potential customers can read at their leisure. In addition, since the organisation issues the brochures directly to customers, it can produce separate brochures for different target markets based on the product and market needs. For example, a mass market tour operator such as Thomson publishes separate brochures for different market segments such as summer sun, winter sun and skiing. The information in each is clearly focused on the needs and expectations of the specific target markets.

▲ Thomson holiday brochures

Despite their size, holiday brochures are actually relatively cheap to produce in comparison with many other forms of advertising. However, you need to remember that many customers take a brochure but do not actually buy any of the holidays that they see in it. Therefore, organisations which use brochures as an advertising technique usually calculate the cost of producing a brochure based on the number of sales it generates. Figure 4.31 shows the average cost per brochure, per holiday sold in 1998. As you can see, for some brochures it can work out as high as £30 per brochure.

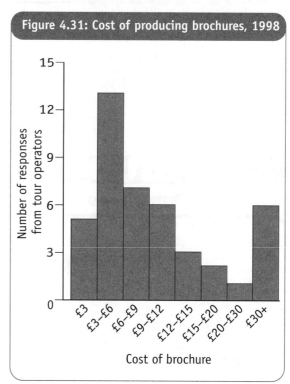

Figure 4.31: Cost of producing brochures, 1998

Because brochures are used so extensively in the travel and tourism industry the techniques used in producing them are becoming increasingly sophisticated. For example, some providers produce a brochure in the form of a file with pull-out sections. Others concentrate on the use of pictures, layout and graphics to create an instant impact and to get their message across. For example, Club 18–30 uses a comic-strip layout in its brochures to appeal to the youth market, whereas Neilson Ski uses a more traditional layout with diagrams and details of slopes to appeal to the serious skier.

As we saw earlier, one of the great advantages of using brochures as an advertising medium is that they can contain a lot of information. However, this can sometimes be one of their disadvantages, since they may appear too complicated to the customer unless they are laid out effectively.

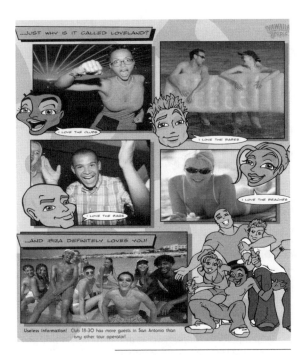

▲ Page from Club 18–30 brochure

ACTIVITY

Holiday brochures

Get a selection of tour operators' brochures and compare the way they present and lay out information. As a group, discuss which brochures you think are the most effective as an advertising technique. Which would be most likely to persuade you to book a holiday?

All the information in a travel brochure must be 100 per cent accurate. Apart from the legal implications of inaccurate information, tour operators also need to consider the likelihood of customers booking a further holiday with the company if they feel that they have been misled by information in the brochure.

Direct marketing

Direct marketing is so called because it operates through personal channels of communication where the target market is, in effect, a single customer. It is one of the fastest growing methods of marketing communication and can be used either as the sole method of promotion or in combination with other methods. One of its main benefits is that it enables organisations to target products at specific markets, as when a theatre sends a list of its forthcoming productions to past customers, for example.

Direct marketing can be carried out in a number of ways, such as by:

- direct mail
- telemarketing
- door-to-door distribution
- media direct response.

Direct mail

The process of sending promotional material to a potential or existing customer is known as **direct mail** or a **mailshot**. The number of direct mail letters rose by 126 per cent between 1987 and 1997 and now represents 11.8 per cent of all advertising. Figure 4.32 compares the numbers of people who made a purchase following different types of advertising. As you can see, direct mail is the second most effective medium after press advertising and a long way ahead of leaflets, radio and the internet.

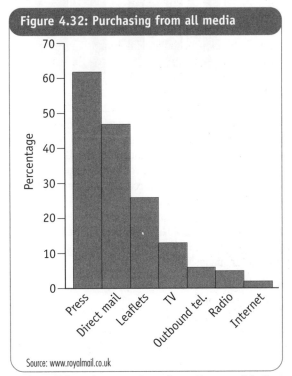

Figure 4.32: Purchasing from all media

Source: www.royalmail.co.uk

One of the misconceptions about direct mail is that everyone throws it into the bin without reading it. In fact, research shows that this is actually not true (see Figure 4.33).

However, it is not enough for the customer to simply open a direct mail letter and read it. The promoter also wants the customer to buy the product as a result of reading the mailshot. The Consumer Direct Mail Trends Survey (1997) found that the average response rate to direct mail letters was 5.2 per cent, which works out at an advertising cost of £8.72 per customer who made a purchase. It is common practice to include a letter in the mailshot explaining the content of sales literature. The letter may include some form of sales promotion, perhaps offering a discount or prize if an order is placed within a certain period.

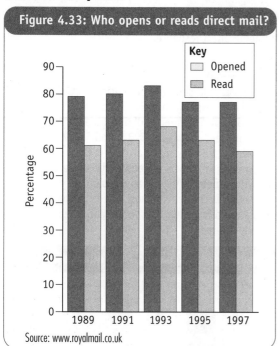

Figure 4.33: Who opens or reads direct mail?

Source: www.royalmail.co.uk

Direct mail must be carefully designed to encourage customers to read the literature. Research has shown that including power words increases the likelihood of a mailshot's success. Power words are terms like new, free, announcing, special, successful, exclusive, limited number, selected and important.

Yale University in the USA conducted research into the power of words. Their conclusion was that the following 12 words were the most powerful in the English language:

- you
- safety
- money
- love
- health
- easy
- proven
- save
- results
- free
- guarantee
- new.

Use of these words can have a positive and persuasive effect on the reader.

ACTIVITY

Direct marketing

Look at the mailshot below and rewrite it using as many of the power words as are appropriate.

Dear Valued Customer

This year we have opened an additional beauty therapy centre at Cramford Grange Health farm offering a wide range of treatments. We are sure that customers will feel the benefits of the services offered – research shows that many of the treatments help people to relax and feel better as well as looking good!

In addition, we are continuing to offer our high standard of accommodation and catering as well as an extensive range of activities and exercise classes.

Early booking (by the end of April) entitles existing customers to a 20 per cent discount on all treatments at the beauty therapy centre as well as a complimentary Indian head massage.

Yours sincerely

K.R. Holdsworth

Manager

Mailshots are also more effective if they appear to have been written to an individual rather than to dozens of customers. Using the word you is effective, as is addressing the recipient by name rather than as Sir or Madam. Finally, it is important to remember the phrase 'The more you tell, the more you sell!'. Mailshots need to include all of the relevant details about the product but to describe it in such a way that customers perceive it as meeting their needs and expectations.

Mailshots are often very successful because they are sent to past customers who, the organisation knows, have bought products before and are therefore likely to be interested in similar ones in the future. But how does an organisation know to whom to send mailshots?

Mailing lists are compiled by using information already held about people who have either bought or enquired about a product or by targeting specific groups of people, for example, by using the postcode system. A computer based system known as ACORN (a classification of residential neighbourhoods) uses postcodes to provide a profile of the types of people likely to be living in any given postal code. So, for example, an organisation could use the ACORN system to create a mailing list and target specific geographical areas, where the population had the particular characteristics that make them likely to be customers.

By analysing past purchases or enquiries it is possible to identify other products that customers might be interested in and to send them relevant direct mail material.

Mailing lists are usually held on a computer database, so it is a very efficient way for many organisations to communicate with existing or potential customers. Direct mail is a particularly important promotional medium for direct sell tour operators such as Eclipse and Portland.

Telemarketing

Like direct mail, **telemarketing** is an increasingly common marketing technique. It suffers from the same kind of drawbacks; many potential customers are suspicious of unsolicited sales calls and therefore unwilling to engage in conversation. However, telemarketing, in which customers are contacted by telephone with the aim of promoting a particular product, can be successful if properly conducted and targeted. This means selecting customers who are likely to be genuinely interested and explaining the reason for the call in such a way that they will want to listen to what you have to say.

In telemarketing, the opening lines are the most important, since many customers will realise that it is a sales call and may say that they are too busy to talk. The trick is get the customer to talk to you by asking them questions, so that they are more likely to listen to you. For example: 'Good morning, Mrs James, this is Paula from Skyborn Travel. I am just calling to see if you enjoyed your holiday in Tenerife that you booked with us'. This opening is likely to encourage an answer from Mrs James, so that Paula can go on to talk about other holidays offered by Skyborn.

In the travel and tourism industry, telemarketing is used more for trade promotions than as a means of reaching individual consumers.

Door-to-door distribution

Rather than mail materials to customers or contact them by telephone, many organisations deliver direct marketing materials to their customers' homes in person (**door-to-door distribution**). This can work out a lot cheaper than mail or telephone. It also provides the opportunity for personal, face-to-face contact with potential customers which can encourage customers to try a product or service. For example, a restaurant may send staff out to local houses with discount vouchers, to make contact with residents and ask them if they would be interested in using the restaurant.

One of the disadvantages of this method is that it can lack the personal touch and be ignored. For example, in large-scale leaflet drops when standard material is posted through a lot of letterboxes, many people simply throw the materials away. As a general rule people are far more likely to look at direct mail material if it is addressed to them personally.

Media direct response

Media direct response allows customers to place direct orders for products without having to go to an intermediate supplier such as a shop. It can be used in any medium such as television, radio, newspapers and magazines. Customers can call a fax or telephone number, write to a given address or contact the organisation over the internet to place their orders.

Apart from persuading customers to buy products immediately, direct response also allows organisations to evaluate how effective each advertisement is by logging the number of responses they receive. The advertisement for Irish Ferries gives potential customers three ways to respond directly; a telephone number, a website address or a visit to a local travel agent. You will notice that if customers choose to use the travel agent option they are asked to quote reference A118. This is so Irish Ferries can identify which bookings made via the travel agent were as a direct result of the customer seeing the advertisement.

▲ Irish Ferries uses media direct response

ACTIVITY

Spectrum Travel

Read the conversation between Carla Andrews, manager of Spectrum Travel and Jason Barnes, her newly appointed marketing manager.

Carla: 'Well Jason, you've had a few weeks to find your feet at Spectrum Travel. I'd like to start thinking about promotional ideas for some of our new products and services.'

Jason: 'I'd welcome that opportunity Carla. I've had plenty of time to get to know the company and its products. Where do you think we should begin?'

Carla: 'Well, I'm particularly keen to promote the new airport hotel booking service that we are now able to offer. As you know, we have recently negotiated an excellent rate of commission for all bookings that we make with three large airport hotel organisations.'

Jason: 'I agree. I think that there is huge potential in this market. Many of our package holiday and flight-only customers have early morning or late night flights and probably arrange hotel accommodation at the airport themselves. Not to mention customers who have booked with other travel agents but may be persuaded to book hotel accommodation with us if they know that we offer

it. If we can offer to make all of the arrangements for them at a competitive price I'm sure that it would be a big seller. How about using newspaper advertisements?'

Carla: 'That might work, but I'm not sure that it is necessarily the most effective means of advertising. I was thinking more of using direct marketing, such as mailshots, telemarketing and perhaps media direct response advertising in the local press. We have a customer database covering the last nine years that should be a good starting point. Get back to me with a some ideas in a few days on how we could achieve this.'

Imagine that you are Jason. What suggestions would you return with? You should include details of who you intend to contact and the contact method.

Draft a mailshot and specify what additional information you would include. If you decide to use telemarketing as one of your methods, outline what sales staff would say as an opening statement.

If you opt to also use media direct response, produce a draft of the advertisement and show how you will be able to evaluate the response rate.

The use of credit and charge cards has resulted in more direct response promotions and more customers able to make instant purchases of many travel and tourism products, such as flights, theatre tickets and excursions.

Public relations

The Institute of Public Relations (IPR) defines **public relations** as:

the planned and sustained effort to establish and maintain goodwill and mutual understanding between an organisation and its public.

In this definition, public means the whole range of people who come into contact with the organisation, not just its customers and employees. These may include trade unions, suppliers, press, shareholders or councillors, for example. In 1999, the IPR extended its original definition to:

PR is about reputation, which is the result of all you say, all you do and what others say about you.

In other words, organisations continually communicate messages to the public, whether they want to or not. Let's look at some of the ways in which this is done.

In many cases public relations (PR) involves positioning information about an organisation to obtain favourable presentations of its activities on radio, television, in the press, or elsewhere. Public relations can include:

- media inclusion
- press releases
- community relations
- lobbying
- corporate communications.

Media inclusion

The term **media inclusion** refers to the inclusion of a travel or tourism product in a screened or broadcast film or programme. An obvious example is the featuring of a particular resort, tour operator or tourist attraction in one of the many holiday programmes.

Media inclusion is usually welcomed by travel and tourism providers and used as part of their marketing communications. For example, the tourism trade in Torbay is partly promoted through the PR benefits of being used as a film and television programme location.

WEBSTRACT

TV and film productions made in Devon

The beautiful scenery of the English Riviera has long attracted film and television companies to use the area as a backdrop. In recent years, Torbay has been the setting for several major TV programmes including *Brookside, GMTV, Songs of Praise, Noel's House Party* and *Working Lunch*. In addition, the English Riviera is frequently featured on travel related programmes such as *Travel Show, Wish You Were Here* and *Holiday*.

Other TV productions include:

Edward the Seventh

Location: Oldway Mansions, Paignton

Starring Anette Crosbie as Queen Victoria, Robert Hardy as Prince Albert, John Gielgud as Disraeli with Timothy West in the title role.

Monty Python's Flying Circus

Locations include Paignton beach, Broadsands beach as well as open-top bus ride to Babbacombe by John Cleese.

Fawlty Towers

It was while John Cleese was filming with the Monty Python team at the Gleneagles Hotel, Torquay that he was inspired to write *Fawlty Towers*.

Source: www.swtourism.co.uk

This is a growing trend, as local tourism authorities realise the great PR benefits using their towns, cities or areas as the backdrop for productions. *The Full Monty* encouraged a large increase in visitors to Sheffield and *Little Voice* had a similar effect in Scarborough.

Individual organisations have benefited similarly from being the subject of fly-on-the-wall documentaries, such as the Adelphi Hotel in Liverpool,

ACTIVITY

Media inclusion

Media inclusion can have negative PR results, as for many of the travel and tourism products featured in consumer programmes like the BBC's Watchdog.

Watch a few consumer or travel programmes on television and identify examples of travel and tourism providers who may not have benefited from inclusion in the programme.

Blackpool Pleasure Beach, Butlin's, RyanAir and London Zoo. Some travel and tourism companies maximise the effectiveness of this media inclusion by prompting potential customers to watch programmes featuring the organisation.

For organisations with a limited promotional budget, PR activities often form an extremely important part of the promotion mix. For example, a small tourist attraction may not be able to afford to pay for expensive advertising but finds that the public relations exposure of, say, sponsoring a local fund-raising event, is an effective way of promoting the organisation.

▲ Butlin's got good exposure from a television documentary

One of the ways in which organisations ensure that the public are aware of their public relations activities is by issuing press releases.

Press releases

A **press release** is a statement written by an organisation describing a particular event, occasion or piece of interesting news which is sent to the media in the hope that editors will consider it of interest and publish it. In many newspapers, particularly local ones, a large proportion of the editorial (articles) is in fact made up of stories based on press releases, rather than articles written by reporters.

The decision about whether or not to use a press release depends not only on its content but also on the relationship that the organisation has with the paper. Therefore, PR organisers must maintain a good relationship with media staff to ensure that the latter look favourably on news items submitted.

Apart from the fact that it is free, the main advantage of getting editorial coverage based on a press release rather than, say, advertising, is that people are likely to read it properly without thinking that it is trying to sell them something.

ACTIVITY

Writing a press release

Read the press release from Virgin Trains about disruption to train services due to refurbishment. The press release does not contain any quotes from Virgin staff. Can you add some quotes to make the press release even more effective, exciting and enthusing? Compare your quotes with those written by other members of the group and identify any key words and phrases that are effective in conveying excitement and enthusiasm.

Bringing customer benefits to North Wales

Customers on some of Virgin Trains' Holyhead to London Euston services, may have noticed that the type of train they catch is different from usual. This means that on certain days, journey times may be extended to compensate for a locomotive change at Crewe.

As part of the £100 million fleet refurbishment programme currently underway, trains used for this route are receiving a facelift, prior to the introduction of the brand new fleet due to come into service from the early part of the new millennium.

On top of the refurbishment, further exciting news is that with effect from the introduction of the Summer timetable, the current 0850 departure from Holyhead to London Euston will be retimed to depart at 0919 with an arrival time in London of 1346 – a 13 minute journey time improvement.

Note to editors

The refurbishment programme forms an integral part of Virgin Trains continuing commitment to customer comfort.

Customers wishing to make enquiries about train times and prices, may contact National Rail Enquiries on 0345 484950.

Customers wishing to purchase tickets by debit or credit cards may now do so by contacting the new website at www.thetrainline.com or by ringing The TrainLine number on 0345 222 333.

Virgin Trains press release

There are a few simple guidelines to writing an effective press release.

- Provide a contact name and number for further information if required.

- Include all of the necessary details, such as times, prices and special features.

- Make the title and first line interesting and eye-catching to draw readers' attention.

- Write an introduction, middle and conclusion so that the piece appears to be a proper news story. Make sure you get the main newspoint in the first paragraph.

- Keep it short, to-the-point and interesting.

- Always try to include at least one quotation, as this makes the story more realistic and enables you to say a lot in a few words. It also lets you sound really enthusiastic and excited about the subject. For example: Joe Shepherd, waiter said, 'We are all really excited about the new restaurant and menu. It has been a challenge getting everything ready for the opening, but we are sure that customers will love it.'

- Give a date to the press release and indicate whether there is a date before which it cannot be used.

Community relations

A good relationship with the local community (**community relations**) is an important part of PR. This is often achieved by providing support to various groups or participating in events. For example, a hotel may allow its premises to be used free of charge by a group of retired people for their Christmas party, give guided tours of the premises to schools and colleges or participate in local events, such as entering a float in a street carnival parade.

Lobbying

When a group of people with a common interest join together in an attempt to influence or change opinions or policies this is known as **lobbying**. For example, in the last few years reports of polluted British coastal areas have resulted in many seaside travel and tourism providers joining forces and lobbying for action to clean up beaches.

Some large organisations lobby independently on specific issues, like the Ramblers' Association's campaign on access to the countryside for recreational use. From a PR perspective, the benefit of lobbying is that the organisation can be seen by the public to care about wider issues than simply making a profit.

Corporate communications

Many organisations establish their corporate image in part through their communications. **Corporate communications** use consistent and recognisable formats and images such as logos, colours and typefaces on leaflets, bills, faxes and advertising. The logos on this page are all well known to consumers because each of these organisations has invested huge sums of money to establish a high-profile corporate identity, despite the fact that they target similar market segments.

▲ Established corporate identities

The establishment of effective corporate communications is important for most organisations, not just major companies. Although some methods of PR, such as providing extensive free use of facilities, may be too expensive for smaller businesses, most can afford some form of PR activity to ensure that they maintain a positive corporate image and good relationship with the public.

It should be mentioned at this point that sponsorship is frequently seen as a key part of an organisation's public relations activities. We look at sponsorship in detail on pp. 302–3.

ACTIVITY

Corporate communications

Hanworth Grange is a privately owned stately home in Norfolk. It attracts visitors from a wide geographical area and targets both resident markets and tourists visiting the area. Research has shown that its main market segments are:

- families (35 per cent)
- couples (21 per cent)
- school groups (17 per cent)
- special interest groups (15 per cent)
- other (12 per cent).

Based on the fact that at least 52 per cent of Hanworth Grange's market includes groups with children (families and school groups), it has recently invested £12,000 in the development of a children's outdoor play area in the grounds.

With a very limited advertising budget and the opening of the play area set for the beginning of June, the owners are keen to maximise the PR opportunities available. It has been decided that the opening should be marked by a special event to be covered by the local newspaper and staff have been asked to provide suggestions. The following suggestions have been received.

- A famous actor lives in the nearby village and would officially open the play area for a fee.
- A selection of past customers could be invited for a free barbeque and firework display to view the new play area.
- A competition could be held in the local newspaper to invite selected guests to the opening. The newspaper has agreed to print the competition entry forms free of charge.
- All the local primary school children from the nearby village could be invited to attend the opening and use the facilities free of charge.
- A sponsored playtime could be held for the longest time spent on a swing, to raise funds for the local hospice. Local GNVQ college students have said that they would be willing to organise the event.

As a group, discuss which of the options offers the best PR opportunities. Based on the option that you select, see if you can think of any other ways in which the event could be improved at minimal cost to the owners. Then write a press release for the local paper, outlining the opening event.

Sales promotions

A **sales promotion** is a short-term activity aimed at generating sales or improving public perception. It can be aimed either at consumers or trade clients. Sales promotions are often undertaken in response to the activities of competitors so that an organisation can keep its market share.

Sales promotions targeted at consumers

Sales promotions usually form part of a campaign and are supported by advertising, personal selling, direct mail and public relations activities. In the travel and tourism industry, a wide variety of sales promotions is commonly used.

- **Price reductions (discounting).** Discounts are offered to increase sales or usage, often at periods of low demand. For example, look in the window of any high street travel agency and you will find discounted late availability holidays on offer.

HOT HOLIDAYS. COOL PRICES.

ALL INCLUSIVE IN THE CARIBBEAN WITH VIRGIN HOLIDAYS

	Prices from	Savings up to
ANTIGUA	£669	£130
BARBADOS	£749	£170
ST. LUCIA	£719	£130

TEL: 01293 61 71 81

OR SEE YOUR TRAVEL AGENT
www.virginholidays.co.uk

▲ Using price reductions as an incentive

▲ Special offers are a type of discounting

■ **Free gifts and incentives**. These are used to encourage consumers to purchase products or services. Travel and tourism organisations often forces with providers outside the tourism industry to provide incentives. For example, booking a holiday at Going Places provides Tesco customers with Clubcard points that are redeemable against products at Tesco supermarkets.

▲ Loyalty schemes are a popular form of sales promotion

■ **Special offers**. This is another form of discounting. Special offers are often run in conjunction with some form of advertising campaign in which consumers have to produce the advertisement (or coupons) to qualify for the offer. For example, many travel and tourism organisations provide money-off vouchers in both local and national press. Customers often have to collect several tokens or coupons in the newspapers over a period of time to qualify for the special offer.

▲ Euro Sites special offer coupon

■ **Competitions**. Many travel and tourism organisations run free competitions to encourage consumers to buy their products and services. Prizes include a wide range of products, services, memberships, activities, holidays and cars. Some work together with other organisations.

▲ A competition for Club Med holidays

■ **Loyalty incentives**. Many organisations use a range of loyalty incentives to retain their customers. For example, Drayton Manor theme park offers regular customers the chance to buy a year-round VIP pass that includes a number of price concessions as well as reduced entrance charges.

▲ VIP passes can be offered as loyalty incentives

■ **Extra products.** This is another form of special offer. Customers are provided with extra products or services at no extra charge. A free bottle of wine with a meal, or three weeks holiday for the price of two, are just two examples of extra products being used as incentives to persuade consumers to purchase products.

▲ Escape, the travel book club, offers extra products as a sales promotion

Sales promotions targeted at the trade

Trade clients are those who work in the travel and tourism industry and who are in a position to recommend or sometimes sell an organisation's product to customers. For example, someone working in a tourist information centre recommends local accommodation, catering and attractions. Organisations often use sales promotions to encourage the trade to recommend their products to customers by offering discounts, allowances and free products and gifts. For example, tour operators provide free educational visits to their resorts for travel agency staff, so that they can provide customers with detailed product information.

Tour operators also offer bonus payments to travel agencies that achieve a certain level of sales. These payments are usually paid in the form of extra commission on sales of holidays (for example, 12.5 per cent instead of the normal 10 per cent commission). This type of trade sales promotion is commonplace in the retail travel industry and has an impact on brochure racking policies in travel agencies. Those operators offering the best trade incentives are generally given the most prominent display areas to attract sales.

Theatres use similar sales promotions by giving free press passes on opening nights, together with complimentary refreshments, in the hope that critics will recommend the performance in their newspapers.

Trade shows are another way in which organisations promote their products to other staff within the trade. For example, the World Travel Market and Hotelympia are both aimed at trade customers. The exhibition industry is a rapidly growing area of travel and tourism and there is now a wide range of specialist exhibitions. Figure 4.34 gives some examples of major trade and public exhibitions in the travel and tourism industry.

By now you should understand that there are many examples of sales promotion in use in the highly competitive travel and tourism industry. As with all other forms of marketing activity, it is vital that organisations can accurately measure the effectiveness of sales promotions. This involves measuring results against predetermined objectives such as to increase sales by 10 per cent, or to increase an organisation's market share over a specific period.

ACTIVITY

Sales promotion

Look at the extract opposite from the *Grantchester Evening News*. The editorial was supplied by Pizza Park as a press release and has been printed alongside its advertisement. How many examples of sales promotion can you identify in the extract?

Figure 4.34: Selected trade and public exhibitions

Exhibition and venue	Type of show	Duration	Number of exhibitions	Visitor attendance figures
BBC Holiday Line Olympia	P	6 days	230	13,000
Holiday World. The Kings Hall	TP	5 days	119	31,400
International Holiday Travel Show Bournemouth International Centre	P	2 days	78	41,500
Northern International Holiday and Travel Show, Manchester	TP	4 days	287	41,000
World Travel Market, Earls Court	T	4 days	3,254	11,069
International Food and Drink Exhibition, Earls Court	T	4 days	550	3,897
International Boat Show	TP	12 days	546	172,813
British Craft Trade Fair, Harrogate Exhibition Centre	T	3 days	667	n/a
Boat Caravan and Leisure Exhibition, National Exhibition Centre, Birmingham	P	9 days	386	112,455
Daily Mail International Ski Show, Olympia	P	9 days	175	96,700
Leisure Industry Week	T	4 days	538	16,279

Source: The UK Exhibition Industry Federation, 1994

Note: T = trade only, P = public show, TP = trade and public

Pizza park set to open

Grantchester's newest restaurant is all set to open on 1 August 2000. Housed in the former library building on the High Street, Pizza Park's owners have completely redesigned the interior to bring a touch of Italy to the East of England. The exciting new menu features a range of pizza, pasta and seafood dishes as well as a mouth-watering choice of desserts. Reasonably priced Italian wines and soft drinks are also offered to compliment the meal. In addition, throughout August they are offering a free children's meal for every child accompanied by two adult diners.

Pizza Park is able to offer Evening News readers a tremendous offer available for the entire month of August. Simply cut out and collect 10 vouchers from the evening news and you can have two main courses for the price of one. The first two vouchers are printed above and further vouchers will appear during the next two weeks.

Grantchester Evening News
17 July 2000

ACTIVITY

Promoting Pizza Park

Read the article on p. 301 about Pizza Park. Three months later in early November, Pizza Park is already a success but there is strong local competition for the Christmas market of office parties. The company has decided to run a new series of sales promotions. Can you suggest suitable sales promotions and redesign the newspaper spread based on your suggestions? You will need to write a new press release, bearing in mind that the restaurant is now well established with a number of loyal customers.

Sponsorship

Organisations provide financial support to other organisations, individuals or events in order to gain prestige and status from their association with them. **Sponsorship** is often included in an organisation's public relations activities since it indirectly enhances customer perceptions of the organisation, its products and services.

There are many examples of sponsorship in the travel and tourism industry where organisations provide financial support for an event, service or product in return for linking their name with it. For example, Air 2000 operates a scheme that sponsors young people who want to become airline pilots.

As part of the airline's expansion plans, Air 2000 is looking to sponsor a number of young men and women into an airline pilot career. A unique sponsorship scheme has been devised, the details of which are set out in a prospectus available from Cabair College of air training. Applicants for this scheme must be aged between 18 and 28 on the start date for the course. To apply you must hold two A levels, preferably in science subjects but most of all you must have a passion to fly! Recruitment has now ended for 1999, but we will be seeking applicants for the 2000 scheme. Keep an eye on the aviation press for details of our next recruitment.

On a smaller scale, a small business may gain PR benefits by sponsoring local or regional organisations, events, facilities or services. For example, many local businesses sponsor local charitable causes that can lead to enhanced community relations for the sponsor.

The main concern with sponsorship is that an organisation needs to have a clear idea of what it wants

ACTIVITY

Sponsorship

Golden Years Travel is a small, privately owned coach operator specialising in day trips for the elderly in Scotland. It has a very small marketing budget but has decided to use £100 for sponsorship of a local cause that will enhance its public relations image.

Having received a number of requests for sponsorship, Golden Years Travel has shortlisted the three below. As a group, discuss which you think Golden Years should sponsor and write a press release for the local paper outlining the details of the sponsorship. You should bear in mind that none of the causes are directly related to the company's target market (elderly people) and therefore your press release needs to be worded in a way that is attractive to this segment. For example, might they have grandchildren who would be affected by one of the causes?

Sponsorship requests

1 The local college has requested Golden Years Travel sponsors an annual trophy for the best Travel and Tourism student to be awarded at the prizegiving ceremony at the town hall. The ceremony is usually featured on the front page of the local newspaper along with the list of prizewinners.

2 St Margaret's Hospital has sent details of its fund-raising campaign to provide a day room for relatives visiting patients on the children's ward. All sponsors who contribute £100 or more have a plaque with their name on in the new day room.

3 Rachel Chiltern, a local teenager, is hoping to go on a trip to Ecuador with a charitable organisation. She has passed the interviews and been selected from more than 50 local applicants. However, she needs to raise £2,000 for the trip and has so far only managed to secure £1,325 of sponsorship. Her fund-raising campaign has been constantly reported in the local press, which has already contributed £300 itself in sponsorship.

to achieve and how it is going to achieve it. So, for example, it might ask:

- how much can we afford to pay out in sponsorship?

- which sponsorship causes do we want our name associated with?

- will these causes create a positive image for existing and potential customers?

- how are we going to ensure that existing and potential customers know about our sponsorship activities?

Many travel and tourism organisations receive a large number of requests for sponsorship. The amount of money requested may vary from thousands of pounds to just a few pounds and organisations must decide how best to spend their sponsorship funds.

All of the marketing communications that we have looked at here help organisations to achieve their marketing objectives. In particular, effective marketing communications can:

- be an effective tool to increase consumer awareness

- prompt sales and take-up. In other words encourage consumers to actually buy the product or service.

While each type of marketing communication has its individual benefits and uses, most organisations use a range of different communications to achieve their marketing objectives. This is because different types of communication influence different customer segments. Similarly, different products and services benefit from different types of marketing communications. For example, a tour operator may use:

- brochures to target customers who go to a travel agency or book directly when selecting a holiday

- press advertisements to attract new customers

- TV advertisements to raise general consumer awareness of the products on offer

- point-of-sales posters for sales promotions

- direct marketing to past customers.

The use of a range of marketing communications is known as the **promotions mix**. The case study shows how Cadbury World uses marketing communications.

CASE STUDY

Marketing communications at Cadbury World

Cadbury World in Birmingham was one of the first organisations to realise the potential of turning a consumer product into a tourist attraction. Apart from generating a great deal of revenue from the attraction itself, the creation of Cadbury World also helps to promote the company's core product of chocolate.

Cadbury World does not have a large advertising budget and feels that it cannot justify national advertising. Therefore marketing communications are focused on the Midlands area. When identifying the promotions mix, Cadbury World aimed to achieve four marketing objectives:

- to communicate what Cadbury World is

- to communicate what Cadbury World is not

- to highlight new developments at Cadbury World

- to encourage return visits based on the new developments.

The promotions mix encompasses six main forms of marketing communications.

Brochures and leaflets

Brochures and leaflets designed for consumers have grown from 600,000 in the early days to a current 1.25 million. Whilst still providing basic product information and details on how to organise a visit, each new print run of leaflets has included details of new developments.

Regional press advertising

Cadbury World uses regional newspapers to advertise its facilities, products and services. Through experience, it has decided that discount vouchers in the press are largely ineffective as they take up a large amount of advertising space but do not guarantee that readers will necessarily decide to visit.

Radio

Initially, the effectiveness of radio advertising was marginal. However, more recently, Cadbury World has found this to be a highly effective advertising medium – to the extent that some radio advertisements have resulted in a huge increase in visitors which has been difficult to deal with.

One of the further advantages identified by Cadbury World when using radio advertising is that visitors are asked to provide their phone number as part of the evaluation of its effectiveness. This means that phone numbers can be used to identify which radio areas are attracting the most visitors.

Poster advertising

Cadbury World uses both four and six-sheet posters, as well as posters on the sides of local buses. The effectiveness of posters as an advertising medium has been supported by word-of-mouth and observation, although it is difficult to evaluate precisely how effective this form of advertising is.

Public relations

Public relations was used extensively in the pre-launch of Cadbury World and a great deal of television coverage was gained, outlining the new tourist attraction and the products and services offered. This was particularly useful in launching Cadbury World into the introduction and growth stage of its product life cycle.

Sales promotions

Half of the Cadbury World advertising budget has been used on sales promotions, with offers linked to discounted admission charges. Sales promotions are primarily used to increase customer awareness and to support the other marketing communications used. Sales promotions were also used on Cadbury's chocolate product wrappers.

ACTIVITY

Cadbury World

As a group, discuss any further marketing communications that you think would be effective for Cadbury World. For example, could it use direct marketing or sponsorship?

We have already seen that the most appropriate type of marketing communication depends on the products and services offered and the target market, as well as the amount of money that the organisation can afford. However, there are three further, very important considerations when using marketing communications. These are:

- AIDA
- timing
- legal requirements.

AIDA

Identifying suitable communication channels is only the first step in successful marketing communications. The next stage is the actual design of marketing communications materials. For example, local press advertisements may be identified as the best way of communicating with certain local market segments. However, unless the actual advertisement is well written and eye-catching it is unlikely to be successful.

Most advertisers use a model known as AIDA which stands for:

Attention

Interest

Desire

Action.

The **AIDA approach** to advertising is designed to draw attention and create interest in order to produce a desire and demand for the product or service in the target audience. The aim is that this desire should be translated into action as customers purchase the product or service. Advertisers applying AIDA to the design of advertising material frequently attract attention through the use of slogans, bold headlines, well known personalities or celebrities, vivid use of colour and eye-catching graphics. The message is kept clear, concise and understandable to maintain interest.

Highlighting the benefits and incentives of purchase creates desire for the product. Prompt action is encouraged by providing instructions on how to purchase or use the product, providing booking information or directions and opening times.

ACTIVITY

AIDA

Look at the leaflet about the Dinosaur Museum and identify how it achieves AIDA.

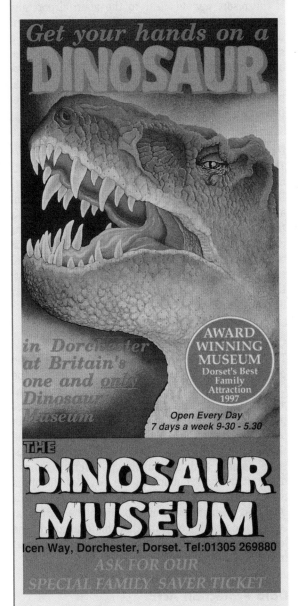

Get your hands on a **DINOSAUR**

in Dorchester at Britain's one and only Dinosaur Museum

AWARD WINNING MUSEUM
Dorset's Best Family Attraction 1997

Open Every Day
7 days a week 9-30 - 5.30

THE **DINOSAUR MUSEUM**

Icen Way, Dorchester, Dorset. Tel:01305 269880

ASK FOR OUR SPECIAL FAMILY SAVER TICKET

Timing

One problem that many travel and tourism providers face is that demand for their products fluctuates in the course of the year and is therefore subject to seasonality. For example, cinemas and theatres have peak demand at weekends. The demand for European sunseekers' package holidays peaks in July and August, whereas the demand for European skiing holidays peaks between January and March. Travel and tourism organisations need to time their market communications to fit in with the particular seasonality of their products and services.

The important issue that you need to bear in mind is that the chosen marketing communication method needs to be timed for when consumers actually decide to buy the product, not necessarily when they actually experience it. So for example, many summer package holiday customers decide on their summer holiday in the preceding November to February. Therefore, the majority of tour operators spend a large amount of their advertising budget at this time, issuing the next year's brochures and launching extensive press and TV campaigns. A further advertising drive is usually run from May through the summer, featuring special offers to enable tour operators to sell the remaining package holidays.

Any number of external factors may alter the timing of consumers' decisions to buy a product and therefore affect the timing of promotions. For example, the hype surrounding the millennium celebration meant that many travel and tourism providers advertised new year packages as much as three years in advance.

With other travel and tourism products, the decision to buy may be much nearer the time of actually experiencing the product or service and the timing of promotions needs to reflect this. For example, the decision to go to a particular film may be made during the week before the visit by reading a review in a local paper. Alternatively, the decision to visit an art gallery may be made on a rainy day by a tourist in a local tourist information centre who is looking for something to do. Travel and tourism organisations need to have a clear idea of when consumers decide to purchase their products, so that promotional material can be made available at the appropriate time to influence the buying decision.

ACTIVITY

The Regal Hotel is a privately owned, 115-bedroom hotel offering a wide range of products and services to a number of distinct market segments. Its promotional mix includes brochures, leaflets for special events and sales promotions, advertisements in the local press and on local radio, point-of-sales promotions and direct marketing.

Some of the main products and services that the Regal intends to promote in the next 12 months include:

- bargain break weekends throughout the year
- residential conference facilities (the main conference market is October-April)
- a three-day Christmas package
- a Valentine's night dinner dance
- bar snacks to non-residents
- discounted membership rates for locals wanting to join the hotel's health and fitness club.

As a group, discuss what the hotel should consider when deciding on the timing of promotions for each of the above. When do you think each target market segment decides to buy the product or service? For example, at what time of the year are people most likely to think that joining a health and fitness club is a good idea?

Legal requirements

When designing marketing communications materials it is important to remember that there are restrictions on what can and cannot be included. A number of laws restrict what advertisers can include in promotional materials. These include the:

- Trades Description Act 1968
- Package Travel Regulations 1992
- Consumer Protection Act 1987
- Data Protection Act 1984.

Some of these acts affect activities other than just marketing, but let's look at their impact on the way travel and tourism organisations are allowed to use marketing communications.

Trade Description Act 1968

This Act states that any description of a product or service must be truthful at the time that it was written and that if circumstances change, the organisation must inform customers of the changes. Therefore it would be a contravention of the Act to describe a holiday destination as quiet and peaceful in a brochure if the resort was adjacent to the main airport and frequently subject to aircraft noise. Similarly, a tour operator could not state that a resort hotel had a swimming pool if the pool was simply being constructed at the time of writing the description. This would have to be made clear in the brochure and customers would have to be informed if the promised swimming pool failed to be ready in time for their holiday.

Package Travel Regulations 1992

These are European Union regulations (their full title is the Package Travel, Package Holidays and Package Tours Directive) which give consumers increased protection and compensation when something goes wrong with a travel product or service (see p. 34). The regulations cover tour operators, hotels, conference organisers, tourist information centres, coach operators and local resort offices. In terms of marketing communications, the main impact is created by the requirement that brochures and leaflets provide accurate information.

Consumer Protection Act 1987

The Package Travel Directive has covered much of the provision of this Act since its introduction. The Consumer Protection Act requires that organisations accurately display prices for products and services. Sales promotions offering discounted holidays which are in fact more expensive than advertised would contravene this Act. In 1998–9 there was a lot of controversy about travel agents and tour operators offering holiday discounts without publicising the fact that the offers were only available to customers who took out the tour operators' own travel insurance. Often the additional cost of the insurance meant that the total cost of the holiday was higher than the non-discounted rate plus insurance from an independent broker.

Data Protection Act

The Data Protection Act has particular implications for direct marketing. The Act affects all organisations that hold personal details on customers. There are eight general principles to the Act. In particular, organisations are only allowed to keep relevant information on customers for the purpose for which it was collected and not longer than is necessary. So, for example, a tour operator which collects names and addresses of customers when they enter a competition cannot keep the data and use it for other promotional activities unless the customers give permission. The tour operator is not allowed to sell the data to another organisation either.

ACTIVITY

Legal requirements

The Hotel Splendide is a 457-bedroom hotel in Ibiza in the centre of the resort of San Antonio. The hotel is built on 14 floors with some rooms having seaviews of the harbour. The Spanish owners are currently considering a number of major improvements, including a refurbishment of the swimming pool, a new poolside bar and restaurant, and a fitness centre which they hope will be completed by 2001. Thirty per cent of the bedrooms have been recently redecorated and a further 30 per cent are due for redecoration during the next two years.

The resort of San Antonio is a bustling town, particularly popular with young people because of the large number of bars and night-clubs. There is a large number of high-rise hotels throughout the town and outlying area. Bars and restaurants tend to cater for the British market.

Espania Travel, a large tour operator, has included the hotel in its new summer brochure. The package is based on a fully-inclusive deal that includes all meals and drinks (local wines, beers and spirits) as well as unlimited ice creams and snacks for children. There is free children's club, although advance booking is necessary as it is always full when the hotel is busy.

During the off-peak months of April and May, Espania offers three weeks for the price of two to increase bookings. The offer is only available to customers who also book a hire car.

Customer feedback on the hotel has been mixed, with a number of complaints about the poor standard of food in the restaurant.

Look at Espania Travel's brochure description of the hotel and resort and discuss whether it might be contravening any laws. You might like to get hold of some tour operators' brochures and see how they describe San Antonio before you start the activity.

SAN ANTONIO

San Antonio is a cosmopolitan resort maintaining much of its historical Spanish charm. Gently winding streets awash with colour from exotic plants and flowers make the town a joy to explore. There are many good restaurants offering traditional Ibizan dishes and wines. Ideally suited to families and couples looking for a relaxing and laid-back holiday at one of its many first class hotels.

Hotel Splendide ★★★★

Our customer's ratings: 100%

Accommodation:

Restaurants:

Resort:

Facilities:

The Hotel Splendide is a family-run hotel offering many personal touches. The newly refurbished swimming pool is ideal for families with young children, whilst the beach is only 5 minutes walk away.
The excellent bedroom accommodation has been recently up-graded and offers stunning seaviews across the harbour.

Facilities include:

* Swimming pool with poolside bar
* Fitness Club
* Self-service, buffet style restaurant
* Children's Club
* TV lounge
* Three bars

Fully-inclusive:
* All meals
* All beer, wine, spirits and soft drinks
* Unlimited ice cream and snacks
* Afternoon tea

SPECIAL OFFER
Three weeks for the price of two in April and May

Regulatory bodies

Travel and tourism organisations need to conform to regulations set down by advertising bodies such as the:

- Independent Television Commission (ITC)
- Advertising Standards Authority (ASA).

The Independent Television Commission

The Independent Television Commission (ITC) regulates all advertising on commercial television and sets over 40 different standards that advertisers must comply with. If you are interested in looking at some of these standards you can find a detailed description of them on the ITC website: www.itc.org.uk

Here are some examples of standards that could affect travel and tourism providers.

- Advertising must comply with the Race Relations Act and Sex Discrimination Act.

- Advertisements for alcohol, the Lottery, the football pools or bingo cannot be directed at people under the age of 16 years (18 for bingo and alcohol) or use treatments likely to appeal to them.

- Advertisements cannot unfairly attack or discredit other products or services.

- Products cannot be described as free unless there is no cost other than postage and packing.

- No advertisement may suggest that drinking alcohol is an essential attribute of masculinity.

- No advertisement may lead children to believe that if they do not have a product or service they will be inferior to other children.

The Advertising Standards Authority

The Advertising Standards Authority (ASA) is responsible for ensuring that all advertising conforms to the British Code of Advertising Conduct. If an advertisement is found to contravene the code it has to be withdrawn.

WEBSTRACT

The Advertising Standards Authority

The Advertising Standards Authority (ASA) requires all advertising materials to be legal, decent, honest and truthful.

Below is the ASA definition of these four words.

Legal

Advertisers have primary responsibility for ensuring that their advertisements are legal. Advertisements should contain nothing that breaks the law or incites anyone to break it, and should omit nothing that the law requires.

Decent

Advertisements should contain nothing that is likely to cause serious or widespread offence. Particular care should be taken to avoid causing offence on the grounds of race, religion, sex, sexual orientation or disability. Compliance with the authority's codes will be judged on the context, medium, audience, product and the prevailing standards of decency.

Advertisements may be distasteful without necessarily conflicting with the above. Advertisers are urged to consider public sensitivities before using potentially offensive material.

The fact that a particular product is offensive to some people is not sufficient grounds for objecting to an advertisement for it.

Honest

Advertisers should not exploit the credulity, lack of knowledge or inexperience of consumers.

Truthful

No advertisement should mislead by inaccuracy, ambiguity, exaggeration, omission or otherwise.

Source: www.asa.org.uk

Look at the four cases below which were referred to the ASA and decide in each case whether the travel and tourism organisations contravened ASA rules. You can find the correct answers on p. 311.

1 Is it legal?

Organisation: P & O Stena Line Ltd

Medium: Brochure

Complaint: Objection to the front cover of a holiday brochure entitled self-drive holidays. It featured a photograph of a car being driven through a field of flowers. The car had two adults sitting in the front seats with three children in the back. None of the children wore seat belts and no other safety restraints were visible. The complainants objected that the photograph encouraged a dangerous practice.

2 Is it decent?

Organisation: Air New Zealand

Medium: National press

Complaint: Objection to an advertisement, in The Sunday Telegraph, that was headlined 'Smartarse...The only comfortable economy class seat in the air'. The complainant objected that the headline was offensive.

3 Is it honest?

Organisation: Destiny Fairs

Complaint: Complainant objected to a local press advertisement for the Psychic Festival. The complainant challenged the claims 'accuracy guaranteed', 'ten per cent of all door money to Princess Diana's memorial fund' and 'top psychics/healers'.

4 Is it truthful?

Organisation: Airtours plc t/a Airtours Holidays Ltd

Medium: Brochure

Complaint: Objection to a holiday brochure, entitled Golden Years, that claimed 'Thousands more holidays for the over 50s' on the front cover and contained photographs of groups of middle-aged and elderly people. The complainant, who found that the age of the guests at her resort ranged from 10 months to 86 years, objected to the misleading impression that holidaymakers at the resorts featured would be over 50 years old.

BUILD YOUR LEARNING

End of section activity

1 Each member of the group should select a different travel or tourism organisation and investigate how it uses marketing communications including:

- advertising (press, TV, radio, magazines, internet, leaflets, posters, point of sale promotion)

- brochures

- direct marketing (direct mail, telemarketing, door-to-door distribution, direct response advertising)

- public relations

- sales promotions

- sponsorship.

2 Collect as many examples as you can of your organisation's marketing communications materials.

3 As a group, make up a display board of your marketing communications materials, using the six categories above as headings.

4 Evaluate how effective you think the various materials are and make recommendations about how they could be improved.

Keywords and phrases

You should know the meaning of the words and phrases listed below. If you are unsure about any of them, go back through the last 27 pages to refresh your understanding.

- Advertising Standards Authority (ASA)

- AIDA approach

- Community relations

- Corporate communications

- Direct mail

- Direct marketing

- Door-to-door distribution

- Holiday brochures

- Independent Television Commission (ITC)

- Leaflets

- Lobbying

- Mailshot

- Mailing lists

- Marketing communications

- Market direct response

- Media inclusion

- Point of sale

- Press release

- Promotions mix

- Public relations

- Sales promotion

- Sponsorship

- Telemarketing

- Trade clients

Answers To ASA activity

1 **Adjudication: Complaint upheld.** The advertisers said they would not use the picture again and they would take more care in their choice of photographs in future. The Authority reminded the advertisers that the Codes require advertisements not to show or encourage dangerous practices except in the context of promoting safety. It welcomed the advertisers' assurance that they would not use the picture again.

2 **Adjudication: Complaint not upheld.** The advertisers thought research they had carried out suggested that the advertisement would be accepted as being light-hearted and amusing. They believed the word "Smartarse" was not rude. They said the campaign had ended and they had no intention of using the advertisement again. The publishers acknowledged that the word was coarse but thought it acceptable because it was relevant in an advertisement about the comfort of seats on long-haul flights. The Authority considered that the word "Smartarse" was in common casual parlance and noted that its use in the advertisement was relevant to the advertised message. It concluded that the advertisement was unlikely to cause serious or widespread offence.

3 **Adjudication: First complaint upheld.** The advertisers said they had taken the claim from another advertisement but then realised that they could not substantiate it and had withdrawn it before the Authority had started its enquiry. The Authority welcomed the advertisers' action.

   Second complaint not upheld. The advertisers submitted their latest quarterly accounts, which showed £150 doormoney had been collected at the Kingston Fair and £15 had been donated to charity. The advertisers also submitted a cheque that showed the advertisers had donated £85 to the Princess Diana Memorial Fund on 10 October 1997. The Authority accepted the claim.

Third complaint upheld. The advertisers argued that all the psychics mentioned in the advertisement have large followings and were "good crowd-pullers". The Authority considered that this did not substantiate the claim and asked the advertisers to remove it from their advertisements.

4 **Adjudication: Complaint upheld.** The advertisers explained that the apartments and hotels in the brochure were chosen because they were more suitable for those in or near retirement and that the holidays were specifically designed for that age group. They stressed that they had not claimed in the brochure that the accommodation would be exclusive to an older age range. They pointed out that the brochure offered long-stay, low-season holidays, which would usually better suit retired people, and activities and entertainment that generally appealed more to retired people. The advertisers asserted that their method of presentation was similar to that of other major tour operators' brochures and was common industry practice. The Authority noted that the Golden Years product was intended for older people but considered that the photographs in the brochure could give readers the overall impression that the accommodation was exclusively for the over-50s. The Authority asked the advertisers to include a brief explanation in future brochures that the resorts were not age-restricted and include photographs that showed the likely variety of holidaymakers at the resorts.

The main focus of all travel and tourism organisations, whether they operate to make a profit or are non-profit making, is on ensuring that customers want and, therefore, buy their products and services. One of the main ways organisations can ensure this is by offering excellent customer service. Excellent customer service achieves a high level of customer satisfaction and encourages customers to return and to recommend the organisation to others. In this unit, we explore the various ways in which travel and tourism organisations and you, as a member of staff, can provide excellent customer service. The portfolio assessment for this unit is on pp. 456–7.

Customer service in travel and tourism

The importance of excellent customer service

CUSTOMER SERVICE IS BROADLY concerned with looking after customers. However, this is a very general definition and we need to be more exact about what we mean by customer service. The components of customer service are set out in Figure 5.1.

Customer service is very much a team effort and it is vital that all team members recognise the important contribution that they are expected to make. This is why many travel and tourism organisations provide staff with training in customer service skills.

Providing excellent customer service is an important part of everybody's job then. It is particularly important in the travel and tourism industry, as there are many organisations which provide similar products or services and it is often the quality of customer service which distinguishes one from another. Good customer service leads to customer loyalty, which in turn increases repeat business.

Most major airline operators offer incentives for regular customers, for example. They might offer free tickets, special check-in facilities, first-class seats and other perks to encourage customer loyalty. Many travel and tourism organisations outline their customer service strategy in what is known as a customer promise or charter.

The term **customer service** embraces all elements of the customer interface and includes all direct and indirect contact with the customer as well as the products, services, systems and strategies that support the customer service process.

The attitude and behaviour of staff is the foundation of all excellent customer service. It means that staff really have to care about their customers and try to anticipate and satisfy their needs. To achieve this, staff need to be able to put themselves in the position of their customers and see the service from a customer's point of view.

- How would you feel if you were kept queuing for half an hour?

- What would your attitude be if your train was late?

- How would you react if a waiter was off-hand?

What would you expect staff to do and say in any of these service situations? If you can put yourself in the customer's position, most aspects of excellent customer service will come easily to you.

You probably already have some ideas about what customer service is, based on your own experience. You

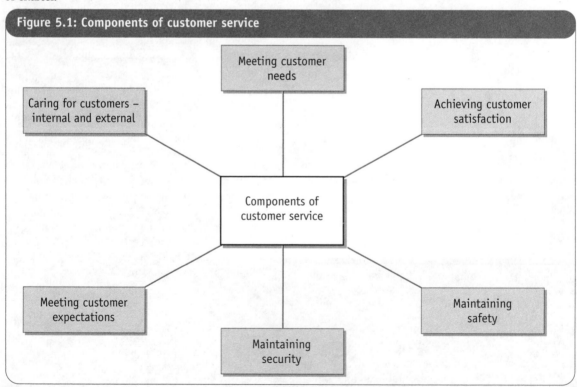

Figure 5.1: Components of customer service

Meeting customer needs

Caring for customers – internal and external

Achieving customer satisfaction

Components of customer service

Meeting customer expectations

Maintaining safety

Maintaining security

may have experienced excellent service that is worth copying or you may have received bad service and therefore recognise what you should not do.

Customer service is the most important part of a travel and tourism organisation's business because, quite simply, without customers there would be no business. But what are the specific benefits to an organisation of training its staff in good customer service skills? There are many, but seven key and interlinked benefits can be highlighted:

■ increased sales

■ more customers

■ a better public image

■ an edge over the competition

■ a happier and more efficient workforce

■ satisfied customers

■ customer loyalty and repeat business.

Before we go on to look at these in detail, read the case study on the English Tourist Board's Welcome Host programme, which will give you a general overview of the benefits of providing excellent customer service to customers.

CASE STUDY

ETB Welcome Host programme

The Welcome Host programme was developed by the English Tourist Board (now known as the English Tourism Council) in association with the regional tourist boards to improve the level of customer service in the leisure and tourism industry. Its aim is to improve levels of hospitality throughout the industry by encouraging staff to take professional pride in their work. The one-day course covers a range of topics including communication skills, complaint handling, making a positive first impression and providing information and guidance to customers. In 1998, almost 28,000 people successfully completed Welcome Host.

Successful course attendees receive a Welcome Host certificate and badge on completion of the course. If you visit a tourist information centre you will probably see most, if not all, of the staff wearing their Welcome Host badges.

The English Tourist Board offers a number of other Welcome programmes including:

■ Welcome Line, which focuses on telephone skills

■ Welcome All, which deals with customers with specific needs or disabilities

■ Welcome Management, aimed at managerial and supervisory staff with responsibility for customer service

■ Welcome International, which focuses on the needs of foreign visitors.

Training shows taxis the route to more profit

Are you good enough to become an ambassador for Bristol? This is the question being asked of 420 registered taxi drivers in the famous West of England city, in an initiative which has captured the attention and support of local people.

Based upon Welcome Host, the programme has been drawn together by Bristol Tourism in an initiative which will shortly spread to Bath through the tourism department.

Cab drivers are being encouraged to complete two days of learning, the first hinging on the Welcome Host for transport variation of Britain's most popular customer service award, whilst the second is devoted to Bristol

Awareness, with presentations from some of the city's top attractions.

The initiative began in January led by Carol Wager of Bristol Tourism, with the enthusiastic support of local taxi driver leaders.

Approximately ten drivers are recruited on each programme, which is free thanks to European funding.

'At the beginning everyone was pretty sceptical,' said Carol, 'But those opinion formers on the original programme worked hard in spreading the message that the training is worthwhile and the feedback indicated that they had learned a lot.'

Trailblazer magazine

The Welcome Host programme is available to any leisure and tourism organisations with specially adapted programmes, being tailored to the needs of individual providers, as the article above shows.

In 1999, the English Tourist Board commissioned independent research to look at the benefits to organisations of offering the Welcome Host programme to their employees. The results were overwhelming, both in terms of enthusiasm for the programme and in listing a number of very important benefits. The chart shows the results of the research.

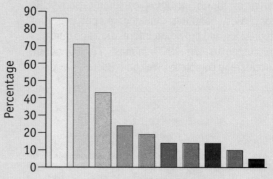

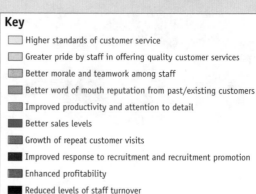

Key

- ☐ Higher standards of customer service
- ☐ Greater pride by staff in offering quality customer services
- ☐ Better morale and teamwork among staff
- ☐ Better word of mouth reputation from past/existing customers
- ☐ Improved productivity and attention to detail
- ■ Better sales levels
- ■ Growth of repeat customer visits
- ■ Improved response to recruitment and recruitment promotion
- ■ Enhanced profitability
- ■ Reduced levels of staff turnover

ACTIVITY

Selling the benefits of training

The article in the case study on page 315 states that everyone was pretty sceptical about attending the Welcome Host programme at the beginning. If you were leading the initiative, how would you have persuaded the taxi drivers that the training would be beneficial to them and other travel and tourism providers in the area?

Increased sales

Sales are one of the key measurements of success. Excellent customer service mean that customers will both buy more and also recommend an organisation's products and services to others which will, in turn, increase sales.

More customers

Whilst sales are clearly very important to travel and tourism organisations, many also measure their success by the number of customers that they attract. This is particularly true of non-profit making organisations. For example, a public library does not charge customers for its services, but aims to increase the use of the facility.

The way customer service plays a part in attracting customers is twofold. First, and probably most important, is the powerful influence of word of mouth. Existing customers who are impressed by the customer service that they receive tell others about it. This means that the organisation keeps its existing customers and attracts new ones. Research shows that the single, greatest influence on customers' decisions to buy or use one travel and tourism product as opposed to another is the recommendation of people they know. This influence is far greater, in fact, than that of any amount of expensive advertising.

ACTIVITY

What are your customers worth?

The quiz in the cutting opposite is given to staff in a tourist attraction to show them how important customer service is in ensuring sales. Have a go at it and find out how much a single member of staff might contribute to sales by providing excellent customer service.

- C = £
- D = £
- E = £
- F = £
- Final total = £

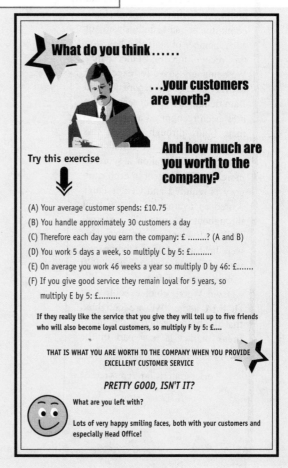

What do you think......

...your customers are worth?

Try this exercise

And how much are you worth to the company?

(A) Your average customer spends: £10.75

(B) You handle approximately 30 customers a day

(C) Therefore each day you earn the company: £ ....? (A and B)

(D) You work 5 days a week, so multiply C by 5: £.........

(E) On average you work 46 weeks a year so multiply D by 46: £.......

(F) If you give good service they remain loyal for 5 years, so multiply E by 5: £.........

If they really like the service that you give they will tell up to five friends who will also become loyal customers, so multiply F by 5: £....

THAT IS WHAT YOU ARE WORTH TO THE COMPANY WHEN YOU PROVIDE EXCELLENT CUSTOMER SERVICE

PRETTY GOOD, ISN'T IT?

What are you left with?

Lots of very happy smiling faces, both with your customers and especially Head Office!

Center Parcs wins major customer service accolade

Center Parcs is the first company in the short-break sector to receive Hospitality Assured accreditation, in recognition of its high standards of guest service and management.

Hospitality Assured is the quality marque developed by the Hotel and Catering International Management Association (HCIMA) to recognise and reward commitment to and achievement of service excellence. It is a new industry standard and is awarded only to organisations in the leisure and hospitality sector – hotels, restaurants and catering establishments – which demonstrate the highest standards of service across all areas of their business.

Peter Moore, managing director of Center Parcs comments: 'Without doubt, it is the professionalism, commitment and enthusiasm of each member of staff that has won this recognition for Center Parcs. We genuinely strive for excellence in every facet of our experience, and I am delighted that our teams have now been recognised as leaders in their fields through gaining this Hospitality Assured accreditation.'

To gain accreditation a score of more than 50 per cent in each category is required and Center Parcs scored an average of 81 per cent throughout. During the external audit, individual on-site interviews were held with staff and the process was communicated to its 3,000 company wide staff.

David Wood, chief executive of HCIMA adds: 'We are delighted that the brand leader in the short-break market is now part of the Hospitality Assured stable.'

Extract from HCIMA press release

The second way excellent customer service helps to attract customers is by reassuring them that they can expect the highest standards. Many organisations emphasise their customer service policies and make them a major part of any promotional material and information. Center Parcs, for example, uses the coveted Hospitality Assured marque on all of its promotional materials to reassure customers that they can expect the highest standards of customer service.

Improved image

The overall effect of an effective customer service policy is that customers see the organisation and the products or services that it offers in a positive way. This means that its image is enhanced by the customer service provided.

An organisation's image is very important for:

- attracting new customers
- retaining existing customers
- reinforcing customer satisfaction
- securing repeat business
- gaining an edge over the competition.

But what is meant by an organisation's image? An **image** is the mental picture that you have of an organisation. This can be based on your own experience of the organisation, what others have told you about it or what the organisation itself has told you through marketing activities such as advertising and public relations.

ACTIVITY

Public image

In small groups, discuss the image you have of each of the following organisations and the factors that have influenced your image:

- Alton Towers
- Centre Parcs
- Railtrack
- Disneyland, Paris
- McDonald's
- Madame Tussaud's
- Club 18–30 holidays
- London Zoo.

WEBSTRACT

Ticketing trauma

Did you know that British Airways has a four-letter rule? If it prints the wrong name or gets more than three letters wrong on your APEX plane ticket you may have to pay for a new one. Correcting the ticket is the same as transferring the ticket to another person. Tickets are strictly non-transferable, you cannot buy the ticket in one name and give it to someone else. APEX tickets are also non-refundable.

On 22 April 1999, Dr Terry Gourvish, a business lecturer at a London university, flew with BA from Heathrow to Vienna to take part in a seminar. Flying with him was his colleague, Sonia Copeland and her husband Dr Basil Copeland.

Mrs Copeland booked the three return flights from Heathrow to Vienna through Trailfinders travel agent. But when the tickets arrived there was a mistake. BA had sent one for Mr B Copeland, one for Mrs S Copeland and one for a Mr T Copeland – a mystery man! Mrs Copeland rang Trailfinders to say that the ticket for Dr Gourvish needed to be changed. Trailfinders told her it was not easy to reissue a ticket to Dr Gourvish because BA would not authorise a name change. It was not just a spelling error on the ticket, the entire name on the ticket was wrong. They told her nothing could be done and she would have to buy an entirely new ticket for Dr Gourvish.

Trailfinders insist that it must have been booked under the name of Mr T Copeland, even though Mr and Mrs Copeland say they know no one with that initial. Dr Gourvish had to pay for another ticket for the same flight out and because the return was full, he had to get a later flight back to London, delaying him for four hours.

BA says its policy and indeed the policy of all airlines, is that once air tickets have been booked, names on them cannot be changed.

Trailfinders say that when it confirms tickets it checks back all names with the purchaser to make sure they are spelt correctly.

Source: www.bbc.co.uk/watchdog/stories

Customer service can enhance the image of an organisation's individual products or services. For example, customers may have a positive image of a hotel company but also have a positive image of individual services such as the reservations system and restaurant facilities.

Competitive advantage

Customer service is vitally important in giving an organisation a **competitive advantage**. This is an edge over the competition, in that the organisation offers something that its competitors do not. If an organisation has a similar product to its competitors, it can gain an advantage by offering a better quality of service or by advertising its product at a lower price. If it can achieve a competitive advantage it has a greater chance of attracting customers from its competitors.

Physical resources play a large part in gaining competitive advantage. For example, a small local swimming pool has little chance of competing with a large leisure pool providing water flumes, slides and wave machines. However, where the facility is similar to that of its competitors, the importance of customer service becomes crucial. In some circumstances, such as the case study about Getaway Travel, the use of good customer service has been successful in achieving a competitive advantage, even where the physical resources of the company are inferior to those of its competitors.

CASE STUDY

Customer service and competitive advantage

Getaway Travel is a single operation, privately owned travel agency. The agency is situated on the main street of a northern town. In the same street there are offices of travel agencies owned by most of the major UK companies. The national companies have large premises, impressive shop displays and national publicity campaigns on television and in newspapers. Getaway Travel has a much smaller shop, advertises only in the local newspapers and is unable to afford the high-quality displays used by the nationally owned travel agents. Getaway Travel and the other agencies offer a similar range of holidays and additional services such as insurance and car hire.

The owner of Getaway Travel was convinced that, despite the apparent competitive advantage of the national companies, he could gain an advantage over them if he could offer a better level of customer service. He visited all of the competitors in the guise of a potential customer to discover if Getaway's service could be improved upon. Over a period of two weeks he called in at various times, sometimes on his own, sometimes with his wife and two young children, enquiring about family holidays.

The owner of Getaway Travel soon realised that at peak times, the queue to see a member of staff in the competitor businesses could mean waiting as long as 45 minutes. This time was spent standing next to a brochure rack, often worrying that his wife was getting restless and with the children running riot in the shop.

Having put himself in the position of a customer, the owner of Getaway Travel saw an opportunity to secure a competitive advantage. He went back to his own shop and reorganised the way it was laid out. Although space was limited, there was enough room to create a small seating area, where he put some comfortable chairs and a coffee table. He bought a coffee machine and asked a member of staff to ensure that coffee, milk, sugar, biscuits and clean cups were always available. Next he went out to the newsagents and bought colouring books and crayons. He put the books and crayons on the coffee table, together with an assortment of magazines.

The owner of Getaway Travel placed a new notice at the entrance to the shop. It read: 'Welcome To Getaway Travel. If we cannot serve you straight away, please make yourself comfortable in our reception lounge. Relax with free coffee and biscuits while you are waiting. Please help yourself. Children: enter our colouring competition. The best colouring each month wins a children's video. Colouring books and crayons are on the table – hand your entry in to a member of staff. We promise that our service is worth waiting for!'

Three months later, Getaway's owner was able to congratulate his staff on record sales. The manager of one of the national travel agencies remarked to her staff, 'Getaway Travel seems to be stealing our customers. Put some more offers in the window. I want to see people queueing in the street.'

ACTIVITY

Competitive advantage

Compare two similar facilities you know of, such as two transport providers, two tourist attractions or two travel agencies. Identify which, in your opinion, has achieved a competitive advantage, giving reasons for your choice.

A happier workforce

A further benefit of excellent customer service is that it creates a much more pleasant working environment. If you have worked in a customer service situation you will already know how much more enjoyable the work is when customers thank you for the good service that you have given them. Similarly, if you treat your colleagues well, they will treat you well in return. Figure 5.2 shows the link between good customner service and staff satisfaction.

Figure 5.2: Customer and staff satisfaction

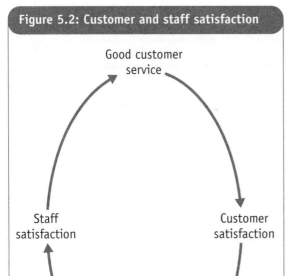

Good customer service → Customer satisfaction → Appreciation and recognition of staff → Staff satisfaction → Good customer service

ACTIVITY

Woburn Safari Park

As a group, identify the ways in which the customer service initiatives at Woburn Safari Park could help to create a happier, more efficient workforce.

CASE STUDY

Woburn's 1999 season preparations

Preparations for the 1999 season at Woburn Safari Park are accelerating in a visitor attraction with a remarkable record of growth and awards recognition.

For the second consecutive time in 1998, the park was named as the East of England Tourist Board Visitor Attraction of the Year.

The seeds of achievement are people, performance and the responsiveness of staff in putting customers first without sacrificing any of the vital responsibilities in the care and well-being of a variety of animals.

Six years ago there was a culture of resistance to training among employees and Chris Webster found himself having to impose a three-line whip to get the participation of all in identifying needs and prioritising.

'It was clear that both communication and customers services were areas where improvement was necessary to help lift the business, improve the customer experience and provide better value for money,' said Mr Webster.

Today at least two-thirds of the growing staff of 51 full-time and 120 part-time employees claim to enjoy the training and over the last three winters a total of at least 18 days have been devoted to the running of courses.

The process has been assisted by job swaps introduced in 1996, giving more people greater levels of skills in the different specialisms of work and understanding the business as a whole.

In 1997 the first comprehensive market research into customer attitudes to their visits to Woburn was completed and results were widely shared internally. This form of benchmarking, repeated up to four times a year, is now linked to the park's quality measurement scales, with a linkage to both appraisals and individual job performance measurement. This includes input into a bonus scheme for seasonal staff, who can earn bonus payments of up to £70 every six months if they are clearly shown to be contributing to the success of the totality of Woburn Safari Park through their customer service skills.

Source: *Trailblazers* magazine

Satisfied customers

The main aim of providing excellent customer service is to make sure that customers are totally satisfied by the service that they receive. This is known as **customer satisfaction**. This means that the service provided must meet the customers' **needs** and **expectations**. The terms needs and expectations are often used interchangeably, as if their meaning is the same. In fact, there is a subtle difference. A need is the reason why a customer is buying a product or service. An expectation is what he or she expects that product or service to be like. For example, a customer's need might be for an airline ticket to Paris. The customer's expectation of the flight will be influenced by a number of factors, such as past experience, advertising or what friends have said about the airline. Clearly, it is just as important to meet customers' expectations as it is to meet their needs. This is why British Airways, for example, has spent large amounts on portraying itself as the world's favourite airline.

Which? magazine evaluates all of the letters that it receives and identifies the top ten tips for providing excellent customer service. This provides a good insight into the general needs and expectations of customers and the factors that contribute to customer satisfaction. The results can be seen in the webstract.

WEBSTRACT

Keeping customers happy

Here are ten tips on how organisations can keep their customers happy.

- Ensure that staff are well informed, polite, and attentive.

- Introduce customer-friendly after-sales service systems.

- Provide easy and quick access to tills and customer service points in stores.

- Provide reliable guarantee and warranty clauses, without any exclusions hidden in the small print.

- Make sure that phone lines are easy to get through to.

- Phone queuing systems should let callers know how many people are being kept waiting.

- Label goods clearly.

- Ensure that promised levels of service are honest and clear. Charters and pledges are good, but they should come without disclaimers and small print.

- Keep people informed about how their complaint is progressing, and ensure that phone calls are returned and letters answered.

- Avoid piped music.

Source: Which on-line

ACTIVITY

Customer needs

Decide what the needs of customers might be when they buy the following services or products. Remember, most customers have more than one need when buying a service or product.

Product or service	Needs
A foreign package holiday	For example, a resort rep to deal with emergencies
A meal in a fast food restaurant	
A visit to a stately home	
Information from a tourist information centre	
A cheap stand-by flight to Paris	
Information about holiday availability on the internet	

ACTIVITY

Keeping customers happy

Look at the ten-point checklist in the webstract on page 322 and think of two examples in travel and tourism where each one particularly applies. You will find that some of them, such as the first one, would apply to any travel and tourism situation. However, others are more specific to certain types of organisation. For example, which travel and tourism organisations use piped music? Does it improve or hinder customers' experience?

Discuss why you think these ten points are particularly important in ensuring customer satisfaction.

Customer loyalty

Excellent customer service provides the opportunity to reinforce **customer loyalty** with each visit that customers make and ensure that they will return. This is known as **customer retention**.

WEBSTRACT

The Royal Mail and customer loyalty

It used to be thought that a good product backed with good service would automatically lead to repeat sales. Nowadays research tells us that those customers who pronounce themselves as satisfied are often the most fickle when it comes to brand loyalty. That's why it pays to communicate with your customers – to build relationships with them. Just because a customer has bought something from you once doesn't mean that they'll buy from you again. There are dozens of reasons why customers might not buy from you again, and only really two why they would.

The first is a negative reason. He or she can't be bothered to look elsewhere (but they might well in the future). The second reason for staying with you is positive. You give the customer a reason to stay loyal. Not just by selling a good product or service, but by initiating a relationship, by taking the trouble to communicate, and by finding out what he or she wants and then offering it.

Source: www.royalmail.co.uk

It is estimated that it costs five times as much to attract a new customer as it does to retain an existing customer, so it makes sound business sense to adopt a customer service approach that aims to keep existing customers by encouraging their loyalty. This loyalty is based on the knowledge that:

- the organisation can satisfy their needs
- they will not be pressurised to buy something that they do not want
- they are made to feel important and valued whenever they visit
- the advice and information they get is accurate and tailored to their requirements
- they can trust the staff to meet their expectations of the organisation on each and every occasion.

Even if a customer has been dissatisfied with some aspect of an organisation's service, that need not mean that the organisation should lose that business. Survey evidence shows that 82 per cent of customers are likely to return if their complaints are answered successfully. However, failure to deal with complaints can have severe consequences. Research indicates that, on average, satisfied customers tell three people of their experience, whereas dissatisfied customers share their experience with an average of 15 others.

If customers are loyal they are likely to return. A repeat customer is someone that you know. You know their needs and expectations and are therefore able to satisfy them better. At best, you will have created loyal customers who would not consider going anywhere else because they know that their needs and expectations can be totally met by the service that you provide. Think of a popular restaurant in your locality – it will probably be popular because, in achieving customer satisfaction, it has built up a high number of regular customers. Figure 5.3 shows the reasons why customers chose a particular hotel. As you can see, more than a third are either repeat customers or have heard about it from loyal customers through word of mouth recommendation.

We have looked at why customer service is important to an organisation and focused on the benefits that can be gained. However, it is important that you do not view these benefits separately for, in reality, they are all closely related. For example, customer satisfaction results in repeat business, increased sales and more customers. This in turn leads to an enhanced image and competitive advantage. All of these benefits are likely to create a happier and more efficient workforce.

Figure 5.3: How accommodation is chosen

Word of mouth	19%
Stayed before	19%
Travel agent	10%
Guidebook	9%
Arranged by holiday company	8%
Tourist board/tourist information centre	7%
Brochure	6%
Saw a sign	6%
Newspaper/magazine	3%

Source: ETB *Insights* magazine, March 1999

Effects of poor service

We have looked at the main benefits to travel and tourism organisations of providing excellent customer service, however, what about the effects of poor customer service? Organisations which provide poor customer service are likely to suffer from:

- decreased sales
- fewer customers
- a poor public image
- a lack of competitive advantage
- an unhappy and less efficient workforce
- dissatisfied customers
- lack of customer loyalty and repeat business.

ACTIVITY

Effects of poor service

The article opposite raises a number of interesting issues about the effects of poor customer service, such as the fact that customers aged 15–34 are the most dissatisfied. As a group, discuss these questions.

- Why do you think these customers might have particular grounds for complaint?

- What could the long-term effect of alienating this group of customers be? Consider the volume of sales and customers as well as public image, competitive edge, customer satisfaction and loyalty and repeat customers.

It is the question posed by shop staff millions of times every week: 'How can I help you?'

The answer, according to many customers, is this: 'Buck up your ideas.'

A survey published today reveals that one in six shoppers has been put off making a purchase because of the way they were treated by staff. The poll found that poor staff attitudes damage consumer relations and that businesses need to improve service standards.

MORI questioned over 1,000 consumers over the past three months.

Younger and more affluent consumers appeared the most dissatisfied. Nearly a quarter of those aged 15–34 and a similar number with an annual household income of more than £30,000 said that they had left a shop empty-handed after being badly treated by staff.

In describing their dealings with shop staff, only 20 per cent of consumers said that employees showed appreciation that they were buying something from their shop and just 12 per cent said staff were enthusiastic about their products or services. Consumers who feel that staff feel an interest in helping them are more than twice as likely to make a repeat purchase and more than three times as likely to recommend the company to others.

The survey also tried to determine the main factors influencing repeat purchases.

Whilst quality and price came out top, the third most important factor was how customers were treated by staff. This came out well ahead of advertising and brand reputation.

The report also found that only one in 26 customers complained before shopping elsewhere – because customers only complain when they want to have a continuing relationship with the company.

Daily Mail, 28 May 1999

Figure 5.4: Elements of poor and excellent customer service

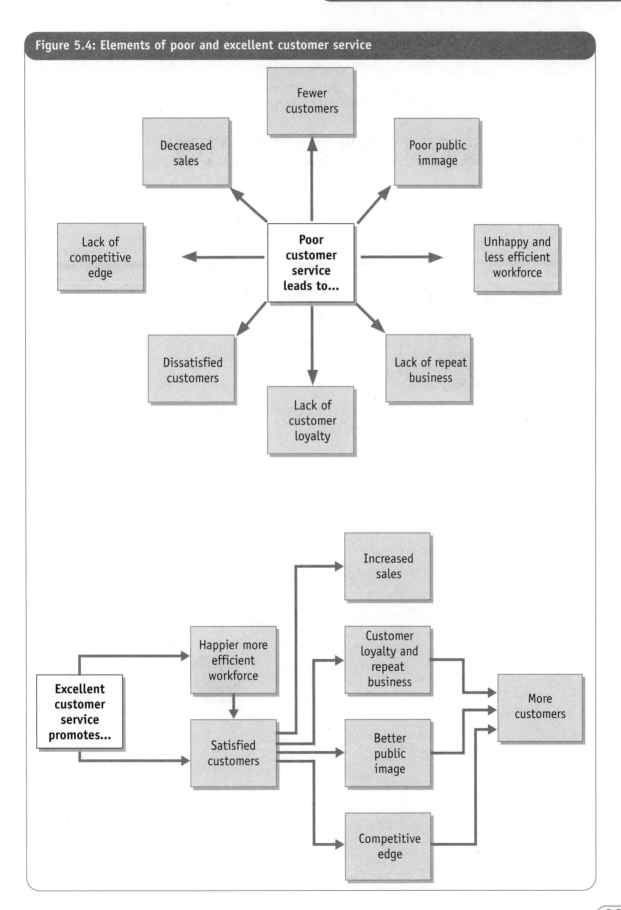

We have now looked at the key reasons why customer service is so important to travel and tourism organisations and the benefits that can result. We have also seen that these benefits are closely linked and often result simultaneously. For example, satisfied customers usually generate more sales, customer loyalty and repeat business. It is important, therefore, that you understand excellent customer service as an overall approach that creates a wide range of benefits for the organisation, its customers and the staff.

BUILD YOUR LEARNING

Keywords and phrases

You should know the meaning of the words and phrases listed below. If you are unsure about any of them, go back through the last 13 pages to refresh your understanding.

- Competitive advantage
- Customer loyalty
- Customer retention
- Customer satisfaction
- Customer service
- Image
- Increased sales
- Needs and expectations

End of section activity

Select two travel and tourism organisations and identify why customer service is important for each of them. You should give specific examples of how the following benefits are achieved through the effective use of excellent customer service:

- increased sales
- more customers
- a better public image
- a competitive edge
- a happier, more efficient workforce
- satisfied customers
- customer loyalty and repeat business.

If you feel that the organisations could increase the benefits by offering even better customer service, give examples of how they could achieve this.

Personal presentation

YOU WILL BE AT THE CENTRE of customer service delivery when you work in the travel and tourism industry. The way you present yourself (**personal presentation**) to customers will have a direct influence on the level of customer satisfaction as well as the image of the organisation you work for.

You never get a second chance to make a first impression. The **first impression** that you give to customers communicates a great deal about yourself, what you think of them and how you view your job and the organisation that you work for. It sets the tone of customers' dealings with the organisation and its staff and their enjoyment of the experience. Customers' impression of you and the organisation you represent is formed within the first 30 seconds of contact.

ACTIVITY

First impressions

Think about an organisation that you used for the first time recently. This could be a shop, a restaurant or a tourist attraction. What were your first impressions when you met a member of staff? What influenced that impression? If you cannot remember your first impression, this is just as important. Why do you think the member of staff failed to make any impression?

Discuss your ideas and experiences with the rest of the group.

Personal presentation includes four key areas:

- dress
- personal hygiene
- personality
- attitude.

Let's look at each in turn.

Dress

Dress and appearance covers everything from clothes and footwear to hairstyle, make-up and jewellery. Why do you think so many travel and tourism organisations provide their staff with uniforms? From a customer service point of view there are many advantages.

- It helps create a positive first impression.
- Staff are instantly recognisable.
- It is easy to find a member of staff when a customer needs advice or assistance.
- It can indicate which department a member of staff works in.
- It helps to create a professional corporate image.

This is Mr Perkins. He deals with all our Spanish holidays.

BARCELONA

It is becoming more common for organisations to provide some sort of uniform. However they also rely on the good judgement of their staff in deciding what is and is not acceptable. Some organisations set ground rules and to a large extent these reflect the nature of the organisation and the types of customer it serves. For example, flight attendants have to conform to strict rules on how they can style their hair and some airlines even specify the required shades of lipstick for female staff. Other travel and tourism organisations have less stringent requirements such as those for a travel agency shown in the case study on p. 328.

CASE STUDY

Dress code for a travel agency

The company uniform must be worn at all times when staff are representing the company. This includes training sessions, meetings, promotions, etc. Uniforms must be kept in a clean and tidy condition. Standard uniform jackets should be worn and not jumpers/cardigans and pullovers.

Shoes must be black, navy or red (red with summer uniform) and should be businesslike.

Jewellery may be worn but should be subtle and suitable to an office environment – ladies should not wear too much jewellery and it should blend with the uniform. Gentlemen are restricted to watch, ID bracelet and wedding or signet ring.

Hair accessories (if worn) should be chosen to match the uniform. Hair should be well groomed, professional and businesslike.

Name badges **must always be worn** and visible when on duty. Only first names are required. If badges are lost or damaged this must be reported to Head Office which is responsible for ordering a replacement.

Nail varnish and make-up (when worn) must be well maintained and businesslike.

The most important consideration with dress and appearance is that it should suit the job, the organisation and customers' expectations. Travel and tourism organisations should also ensure that uniforms are comfortable, easy to maintain and equally appropriate for staff of all builds.

Personal hygiene

It goes without saying that anyone who is serving customers should ensure excellent standards of **personal hygiene**. No customer will be impressed by a flight attendant who breathes garlic fumes over them or a waiter with dirty fingernails, and dousing yourself with perfume or aftershave when you have not had time for a shower, or chewing gum after a curry, is just as off-putting for the customer.

ACTIVITY

Personal hygiene

Look at the drawing below and identify the key personal hygiene concerns.

Who wanted the burger?

ACTIVITY

Uniform

Yannis Demetriopolus is about to open his own travel agency and wants to provide all staff with a uniform. He has a limited budget but has decided to spend a maximum of £175 per uniform. The colour scheme of the shop front and fittings is red and dark blue. Yannis employs three female and two male travel consultants.

Use some mail-order clothes catalogues to suggest a suitable uniform that does not exceed Yannis's budget but that fits in with the general image of his company. Bear in mind that if you choose shirts, staff will need more than one! You are not expected to buy shoes, socks, tights etc. Present your ideas in a file together with a checklist of general requirements for staff appearance. You should also include a breakdown of the total cost.

Some jobs in travel and tourism have stricter requirements for personal hygiene than others, because of the nature of the work. For example, people employed in food preparation are expected to wash their hands dozens of times a day between separate food preparation activities to avoid cross contamination.

Personality

The first impression that you give to customers also depends on your **personality** and the way in which you project it. Your personality will influence the image that the customer has of the whole organisation.

Only you can actually influence your personality and determine whether the customer is going to see it positively, but the importance of projecting a good personality is summed up by the following extract from a training session given by a personnel and training manager for Forte Hotels:

Most of us spend our social lives trying to be attractive, friendly and likeable people – we want others to like us and to see our best side. So why should we behave any differently at work? Treat every customer as the person you most want to impress and impress them totally! Make sure that they walk out of the door wanting to come back because they liked you!

Of course, different jobs in travel and tourism require different types of personality. The sort of personality required to work as a Club 18–30 resort representative is likely to be very different to that of a representative employed by SAGA holidays, for example.

ACTIVITY

Personality

Identify the particular personality traits that a Blue Badge Guide needs, based on the details given in the webstract below.

WEBSTRACT

The Blue Badge for tourism guides

All members of the National Association of Tourist Board Registered Blue Badge Guides hold the coveted Blue Badge, the British national standard guiding qualification and internationally recognised standard of excellence.

Blue Badge Guides are selected, trained and examined by the official British tourist boards. The training is detailed and comprehensive, the examinations rigorous and registration an achievement. In London the course lasts for eighteen months.

Originating in London, this has been awarded by regional Tourist Boards since 1969, so that every guide will have the same background of national core knowledge combined with in-depth local knowledge. As well as acquiring knowledge, Blue Badge Guides are trained in the selection and presentation of material. This has been so successful that English trainers have trained guides all over the world, and the Blue Badge is recognised internationally. Blue Badge Guides have a wide range of languages (40!), specialities and interests, and can guide on foot, in cars, on coaches, on trains and on boats. They take pride in constantly updating their knowledge to enable their visitors to enjoy Britain's immense, unique and varied heritage. They are practical, punctual, reliable and thrive on the unexpected, welcoming individuals or groups, here on business or for pleasure.

Source: www.blue-badge.org.uk

Attitude

Your **attitude** towards the customer is crucial to your ability to deliver excellent customer service. All customers are sensitive to the way you feel about them. For example, imagine that you go into a tourist information centre and ask for advice and the information assistant informs you that she is just going off duty. As you require a lot of information, she will hand you over to the assistant on the next shift who starts in five minutes. In this situation you might feel that:

- you are asking for too much

- the information assistant does not care about you enough to handle the enquiry herself

- she does not really care about the job or the customers because she wants to go off duty.

In short, the assistant gives the impression by her **attitude** that she is not interested in you, the customer.

Your attitude towards customers may vary according to the situation. For example, it may be acceptable to be less formal with a child than you might be with an adult; you might address children by their first name but call adults sir or madam. However, there are some general rules on attitude that should apply to all customers, whatever their age or circumstances. These include being:

Attentive

Thoughtful

Tolerant

Individual

Thorough

Unflappable

Dependable

Enthusiatic

ACTIVITY

Attitude

Your attitude towards and understanding of particular customer service situations says a lot about your attitude generally. Here is a quick quiz to see how you score on the attitude scale! Consider the following statements and decide whether they apply **always, never or sometimes**. If you decide the answer to a question is 'sometimes', explain the situations in which this would apply.

1 It is all right to call customers by their first name.

2 A member of staff should always stand up when dealing with customers.

3 It is acceptable to chew gum when talking to a customer.

4 You should always wait for a customer to start a conversation.

5 You should maintain eye contact when dealing with a customer in a face-to-face situation.

6 It is old fashioned to address a customer as sir or madam.

7 It is acceptable to get angry with a very difficult customer.

8 It is wrong to complain about one customer to another customer.

9 Customers will understand if you are tired or unwell and make allowances.

10 All customers are equally important.

11 Your attitude and behaviour towards customers affects the extent to which they are satisfied.

12 The customer is always right.

Score rating

- 8–12 correct answers: an excellent attitude

- 4–7 correct answers: not bad, but you probably need a bit more practice, try some of the role play exercises in this unit

- 0–3 correct answers: oh dear, perhaps you should read this chapter again. Slowly!

Answers are given on p. 395.

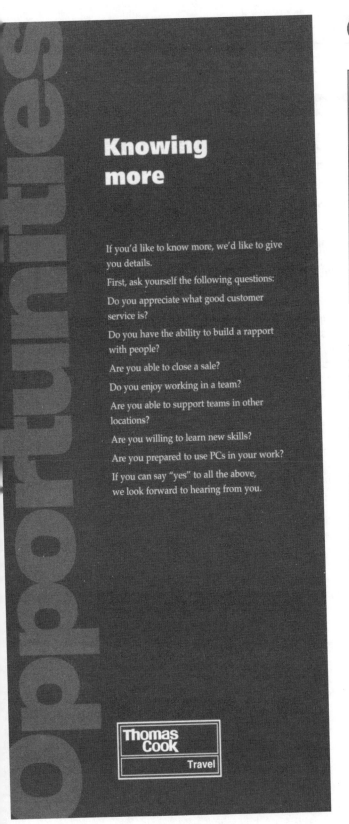

Knowing more

If you'd like to know more, we'd like to give you details.

First, ask yourself the following questions:

Do you appreciate what good customer service is?

Do you have the ability to build a rapport with people?

Are you able to close a sale?

Do you enjoy working in a team?

Are you able to support teams in other locations?

Are you willing to learn new skills?

Are you prepared to use PCs in your work?

If you can say "yes" to all the above, we look forward to hearing from you.

Thomas Cook
Travel

▲ Extract from Thomas Cook's career opportunities leaflet

ACTIVITY

Positive attitude

Look at the extract from Thomas Cook Travel's career opportunities leaflet.

Imagine that you are at an interview for the position of a travel consultant and the seven questions in the leaflet are the basis for the interview questions. Think of some examples that you could give to show that you could give a positive answer to all of the questions. For example, for the first question you might say, 'Good customer service is the ability to put yourself in the position of the customer and treat them in a way that you would like to be treated yourself. It means not only meeting but also exceeding their expectations'.

Personal presentation is important in any situation where you have contact with customers whether face to face, in writing or over the telephone. On pp. 351–66 we look at the specific features of these three methods of communication in detail.

ACTIVITY

Personal presentation role play

Think of a situation involving a customer in a currency exchange bureau. Be as inventive as you can. For example, the customer might be complaining, unable to speak English, have special needs or have an unusual request.

Take it in turns to role play the customer and the member of staff in the currency exchange. Do not tell the staff member what your request is going to be, as it is important that it is a surprise! You might like to plan this role play in advance and arrange to dress in a way that would be suitable for someone working in a currency exchange. You may be able to use this exercise for your unit assessment.

It would be useful if you could video each role play in this activity. At the end, you should play back the video to give group members an opportunity to evaluate the way their personal presentation affected the service they gave.

BUILD YOUR LEARNING

1 Select two travel and tourism organisations from different components of the industry. Visit them as a customer and evaluate the staff's personal presentation based on the following criteria:

- first impressions
- dress
- personal hygiene
- personality
- attitude.

2 As a group, write a letter to and telephone each organisation to ask for details of their products and services. Think of a reason for your visit/letter/telephone call, such as asking a travel agency about travel insurance. Identify the areas of good practice in staff presentation skills and make recommendations about how it could have been improved.

Keywords and phrases

You should know the meaning of the words and phrases listed below. If you are unsure about any of them, go back through the last five pages to refresh your understanding.

- Attitude
- Dress and appearance
- First impression
- Personal hygiene
- Personal presentation
- Personality

Types of customer

WE HAVE ALREADY SEEN HOW important it is to meet the needs of customers and achieve customer satisfaction. However, the needs of customers vary, depending on who they are and the situation that they are in. For example, a visitor to London has different needs when visiting on business than when on a week's sightseeing holiday. It is important to be able to identify the different types of customer that use a service, product or facility and understand how their needs may vary.

Let's begin by making a distinction between internal and external customers. **Internal customers** are members of staff within an organisation or outside suppliers who contribute towards the service that is provided to external customers. They include the following.

- **Colleagues.** These are the people that you work with directly and who have a similar status to you.

- **Management and supervisors.** Most employees have a direct line manager in the organisation, either a supervisor, head of department or manager.

- **Staff teams.** These are groups of staff who form a team to undertake specific functions or jobs. For example, a tourist attraction may have a health and safety team made up of staff from different departments and many hotels have a fire evacuation team which works together to evacuate the building if the fire alarm sounds.

- **Employees.** If you are self-employed or own a company you may employ people to work for your organisation.

- **Staff in other functional departments or organisations** who do not work directly with you but contribute to the job that you do. These people are also internal customers. For example, the personnel, finance, administration and maintenance departments in a local authority provide services to employees in the authority's tourism facilities such as the tourist information centre, museum, art gallery and so on.

Organisations must provide effective customer service to internal customers in order to establish good working relationships between colleagues, managers and staff teams.

External customers are the people who actually buy or use an organisation's products and services. There are many ways of categorising external customers. To a large extent the way this is done will depend on the type of organisation and the nature of the business it operates. Common methods of identifying particular types or groups of customer include by:

- individual

- group

- age

- culture

- language spoken

- specific needs, such as wheelchair access or people with young children.

Individuals and groups

It is important to recognise that although customers may use a product or service on an individual basis, they may also become part of a group. For example, customers on a singles holiday may go hoping to meet and socialise with others.

Other customers may appreciate the fact that they are on their own and prefer to be treated individually rather than grouped together with others. Guests at a private health clinic such as Champneys in London, for example, pay for the privilege of individual and personal service.

Many organisations identify specific types of individual and group that use their products and services, in order to provide the kind of service that meets their needs and expectations. For example, Crest Hotels recognised that the number of businesswomen who travel and stay in hotels on their own was rapidly increasing. The chain introduced Lady Crest rooms, furnished and decorated with feminine fabrics, ornaments and pictures. An extended range of toiletries, magazines and provisions was provided to appeal to female guests, in addition to the facilities that businessmen receive, such as a desk with stationery and a mini-bar. The scheme was a success because the level of service exceeded customer expectations and therefore gave Crest Hotels a competitive advantage over its rivals.

ACTIVITY

Jane's internal customers

Jane is the front-of-house manager in an hotel that is part of a national chain. She supervises three receptionists, a telephonist, a cashier and two hall porters. The hotel has a general manager and a deputy manager to whom Jane reports. She liaises on a day-to-day basis with other heads of department. She is part of the hotel's quality review group and also the front-of-house representative for the hotel's staff consultative committee which meets once a month to discuss general issues. Many reservations come from the company's central reservations department at head office or through recommendations from the local tourist information centre.

Jane works closely with the hotel's marketing manager on promoting the hotel's facilities, but receives most of the promotional leaflets and brochures from the head office marketing department. She has recently set up a customer service advisory group in the hotel, meeting with a member of staff from each department to discuss how customer service could be improved. Jane carries out most staff training within her department herself but sends key members of staff to residential training courses run by the company's training office.

Fill in the following boxes to show all of Jane's internal customers. Be specific, for example, under 'colleagues', specify the departments concerned.

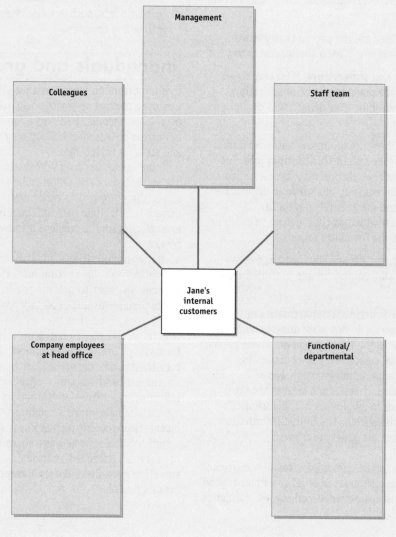

In 1999, the *Mail on Sunday* carried out a consumer test on a range of airlines to evaluate how good their in-flight customer service was. It evaluated six different airlines. The newspaper article below gives the verdict on three of these providers; British Airways, easyJet and Virgin Atlantic.

ACTIVITY

Individual customers

From the three evaluations in the newspaper article, discuss what flight attendants should (and should not!) do when providing excellent customer service to individual customers. Can you think of any further ideas for ensuring that individual customers are treated well?

▲ In-flight service

Testing the merits of in-flight service

British Airways

Welcome: Warm reception from two female flight attendants at the plane entrance – men stationed further up the aircraft offer a more dour greeting – if they were in a Beano cartoon they would have a bubble over their heads with 'Oh no, passengers!' written on it. Since this followed an hour's wait to check in, I hardly felt I was being swept off my feet by the warmth of corporate kindness.

In flight, BA cabin crew were capable of kind gestures but I felt we were treated like unruly four year olds at a posh friend's party and needed to be kept firmly but politely in our place.

Efficiency: In-flight service was briskly efficient but rather charmless. An American passenger who asked for caffeine-free ginger ale was told it was not available and that she had better get used to it not being available because we didn't bother about caffeine-free and diet drinks over here.

Verdict: Service was never more than adequate and occasionally the attendants were indifferent and rude.

SCORE: 37 per cent

easyJet

Welcome: As I boarded I was offered a friendly, smiling greeting by the female attendant at the top of the steps. Impressively, she made time to chat with passengers about their destination (most people seemed to be going to a Celine Dion concert).

Efficiency: No-frills services mean that you pay for any drinks or snacks: this could be tedious and time-consuming, but the service was performed with rapid good humour. My request for an aspirin was smilingly declined ('we're not allowed to give out anything on board').

Verdict: easyJet's service has been transformed since I last flew with them almost a year ago.

SCORE: 63 per cent

Virgin Atlantic

Welcome: A bright, cheerful greeting as you board is fundamental in making you feel welcome (and a crucial relaxant for the fearful traveller). There were two smiling attendants at the door eager to inspect my boarding card and direct me to my seat. Virgin has its fair share of snappy crew – I've encountered them on other flights – but here crew were unstressed, cheerful and approachable. Ringing the call button produced a hastily delivered aspirin and glass of water.

Efficiency: The job of flight attendant is a dull grind – as a passenger the best you can hope for is that this dull grind is performed with swift dispatch and good humour. Virgin did this and a bit more. Handing out choc ices during the film is one of the small details that helps define the overall difference in quality and service.

Verdict: Love him or hate him, even Richard Branson's sternest critic would have to admit his airline rates among the best – particularly in the quality of its flight attendants.

SCORE: 80 per cent

One of the problems encountered when dealing with groups of people is satisfying all of their individual needs. The customers may have chosen to experience a travel or tourism product or service as part of a group, but they often expect some personal recognition and attention as well. For example, a visitor on a guided tour of a stately home may well have interests and questions that the tour guide will need to deal with on a personal level. Similarly, holidaymakers on a package holiday will expect the resort representative to speak to them personally and answer their specific questions.

Cruise holiday operators are essentially dealing with a large group of customers on each voyage. In the early days of cruising, one of the most frequent complaints from customers was that they felt herded around, with rigidly set meal times at pre-arranged tables and an itinerary of organised activities and excursions whilst in port. Fortunately, most of today's cruise customers can expect a more personalised approach although the old image of cruising still exists amongst many potential customers.

Look at the webstract from P&O Cruises and identify the ways in which it reassures cruise groups that they will not be treated as one of a herd.

People of different ages

Customer age groups can be broken down into:

- children – babies, toddlers, older children and teenagers
- adults – young adults, middle-aged adults, senior citizens.

However, it should be remembered that customers are often in the company of friends or relatives and that the group may therefore be made up of a combination of people of different ages. Some common combinations are:

- parents with young children and/or babies
- parents with teenage children
- adults with grandchildren
- adults with senior citizen parents.

Although the age of customers is important, it is equally important not to make assumptions about customers' needs based solely on their age.

WEBSTRACT

P&O Cruises

Cruising has always been a people business and the rapport between the passengers and team on board our ships is as important to the success of a cruise as the smooth running of the engines, calm seas and hot sunny weather.

Our captains are not just unseen figureheads up on the bridge, but men who thrive on day-to-day contact with their passengers, listening to their comments and often acting on them. Each of our passengers is the special guest of the captain at a champagne reception, a great chance to chat with your captain and get to know him.

Your cabin steward is there to make sure you are totally comfortable. He has the very important task of being there to answer all your questions, carry up your luggage and ensure your cabin is looked after. He will even turn your bed down at the end of the day.

There are plenty of friendly faces on a P&O cruise, all ready to help you enjoy your holiday to the fullest. You will find many a friendly member of the purser's staff who will be happy to answer your questions.

Among the most popular staff members are the Goanese stewards, recruited via our special training school in Bombay, who have been an integral part of P&O passenger ships since the mid-1800s.

Source: www.pocruises.com

Many travel and tourism organisations promote specific facilities and services for people of different ages, particularly young children and babies. This can be particularly effective in encouraging customers to visit by reassuring them that their needs will be met. The extract from an Alton Towers' leaflet opposite shows the special services offered to parents with babies and toddlers who visit the attraction.

Dealing with older customers also requires specific skills, as the newspaper article below shows.

Babies and toddlers

Baby changing faclities are available across the park – see the map for details. A free milk warming service is available in the Medical Centre and nappies are sold in Towers Street and Festival Park – see the map for locations.

Why not hire a pushchair from the Guest Facilities Office at the top of Towers Street? There's a lot of walking to do. As proud winners of the Tommy's Campaign 'Parent Friendly' award for 1995, Alton Towers tries to make sure that the needs of guests with babies and toddlers are well catered for.

Extract from Alton Towers leaflet

Years that add golden touch for tour hosts

Life has been one long party for Tony and Yvonne Francis since they were made redundant in 1994. They are using their customer-orientated skills as former managers with British Gas to help the growing number of older customers have fun in the sun.

Tony and Yvonne are hosts for Airtours' Golden Years holiday programme for the over-55s that runs from October to March, a job that takes them to one of many Mediterranean hotspots each year. Yvonne says: 'We like the variety that the job brings. No two days are the same. We are with the customers for most of their holiday, organising activities such as bowling, dancing and rambling. And we are their contacts if they have any queries or problems. It is hard work but addictive, and our previous skills come in useful; for example, presentation skills for the welcome meetings at hotels, organising skills for preparing and carrying out activity programmes and communication and customer service

skills to ensure that the holidays go as smoothly as possible.'

Airtours believes that British hosts are best suited to the demands of keeping the more mature customers entertained for every minute of their holiday. Hosts must be full of energy for all kinds of activities and must understand what excellent customer service entails. They must take time to listen, have a caring approach and enjoy being with people.

Applicants for jobs as activity hosts are asked to fill in an application form. If they meet Airtours' requirements they are invited to an assessment day when their skills and experience are put to the test. Successful candidates are then invited for an interview. Those who clear this second hurdle are given a six-day training course that includes how to prepare for being a host and how to organise activities as well as administration and paperwork.

Mail on Sunday, 7 November 1999

ACTIVITY

Customer age groups

Look at the following list of customers and discuss what you think their specific customer service needs might be.

- Young, single adults on a package holiday in Spain.

- Two elderly grandparents taking their three young grandchildren to a theme park.

- Two 50-year-old women on their first holiday abroad on a sightseeing tour of Italian cities.

- A couple with a six-month-old baby on a long haul flight to Singapore.

- A 70-year-old woman on a week's coach tour of Scotland.

Different cultures

It is often important to recognise types of customer by their cultural background in order to provide effective customer service. **Cultural background** influences people's traditions, tastes, preferences and opinions, and therefore has an impact on the type and level of service that people need and expect. For example, some cinemas show films in different languages to cater for the demands of large ethnic populations in their area.

As with different age groups, the cultural background of customers is useful in identifying their needs, but it is equally important not to make assumptions based on culture. At best, this may result in customer dissatisfaction; at worst, it may offend and upset the customer. However, it is very useful to have an understanding of some of the more common cultural differences, such as the way different cultures use gestures (see Figure 5.5).

Language

Foreign visitors are an increasingly large part of the UK tourism market. Many such visitors speak little or no English, but expect staff to be able to deal with their needs despite the language barrier. Large organisations often employ multilingual staff to communicate with visitors who do not speak English (see Figure 5.6).

Figure 5.5: Watch your hands

In Greece, Spain and Turkey the fig gesture (fist with thumb protruding between index and middle fingers) is considered very rude

In Egypt the right hand over the heart means 'no thank you'

In Greece an open palm and extended fingers (like a 'five' sign) can be insulting

In Japan, Korea and Mexico making a circle or semi-circle with forefinger and thumb is a symbol for money; in France the same gesture means something worthless; in Brazil it is very rude; in the US it means OK

In Morocco and parts of the Middle East the thumbs-up sign is an obscenity

Figure 5.6: Languages spoken at UK airports

Heathrow Airport

- Middle East Visitors Service – Arabic
- Iranian Visitors Service – Farsi
- South Asian Visitors Service – Hindi, Punjabi, Marathi, Gujerati, Bengali, Syheti, Tamil, Telegu
- Sri Lankan Visitors Service – Sinhalese
- Japanese Visitors Service – Japenese
- Chinese Visitors Service – Cantonese, Mandarin
- Thai Visitors Service – Thai
- Korean Visitors Service – Korean
- Mexican Visitors Service – Spanish
- Filipino Visitors Service – Tagalog
- Aremenian Visitors Service – Armenian

Gatwick Airport

- Latin American Visitors Service – Spanish, Portuguese
- African Visitors Service – Twi, Ga, Fante, Yoruba, Shona, Ndau, Nyanja, Luganda, Swahili
- Russian Visitors Service – Russian
- Middle East Visitors Service – Arabic

Manchester Airport

- Pakistani Vistors Service – Urdu

Even if you are not proficient in other languages, there is still a great deal that you can do to help the communication process. This includes:

- using gestures, as when pointing out directions
- using diagrams and pictures
- keeping dictionaries in order to translate key words
- making the effort to learn a few simply phrases in some common languages. Being able to say hello, goodbye, please and thank you in two or three foreign languages will please your foreign guests and show that you care enough to make the effort.

You should not forget that even foreign visitors whose native language is English may still have difficulty in understanding some words. For example, Americans have a range of different words and phrases from us which can lead to confusion. The British Tourist Authority provides a guide to the English language for visiting American tourists called *Talk Like A Brit!*

ACTIVITY

American English

Look at the 14 words below. If an American asked you for these, would you know what he or she meant? Answers appear on p. 395.

- traffic circle
- divided highway
- freeway
- sidewalk
- second floor
- faucet
- jelly
- check
- liquor store
- chips
- restroom
- ATM
- pocket book
- band aid

Specific needs

Some customers have **specific needs** which may require special customer service in addition to that provided to meet the general needs of customers. This may be because of:

- sensory disabilities, such as visual impairment, hearing impairment or speech impairment

- mobility problems, such as the need for a wheelchair, Zimmer frame or walking stick

- learning difficulties

- dietary requirements, such as vegetarian, nut allergy or religious restrictions

- people with young children.

There is often a lot of misunderstanding about people with specific needs and this can lead to inappropriate service delivery. Many people are even unsure how to refer to customers' special needs and may use terms that are offensive. Look at Figure 5.7 for some key dos and don'ts.

People with specific needs require tailored customer service but they do not want to be made to feel different, stupid or a nuisance. They want the same level of customer service that every customer gets and a little extra care and consideration of their particular needs. Try to remember that people are often disabled not by their impairment but by the environment and the attitudes of the people they encounter.

You need to understand that there are legal requirements and guidelines covering people with disabilities or specific needs. For example, the government's national tourism strategy emphasises the need for England and Wales to improve the way the tourism experience is provided to people with disabilities and specific needs. One of the main reasons for this is to attract more foreign visitors and to improve the quality of the tourism experience for the aging population in the UK.

The **Disability Discrimination Act 1995** was introduced to end the discrimination that many people with impairments face. Of particular relevance to the travel and tourism industry is the section that deals with access to goods, facilities and services. Some of the main requirements of this section are as follows.

- Since 1996, service providers cannot refuse a service or offer a worse standard or terms of service to a person with an impairment for a reason related to their impairment.

- Since 1999, providers must consider making changes to the products or services that they offer so that customers with impairments are not excluded.

- From 2004, providers must take reasonable steps to remove any physical barriers that make it unreasonably difficult for customers with impairments to access goods and services.

Figure 5.7: Avoiding offensive language

Don't say	Say instead
A cripple	Disabled person
Invalid	Disabled person
Handicapped	Disabled
Mentally retarded/handicapped	Person with learning disabilities/difficulties
Deaf aid	Hearing aid
The disabled	People with impaired mobility/a disability
Spastic	Person with cerebral palsy
Suffering from/afflicted by/a victim of Confined to a wheelchair/wheelchair bound	Wheelchair user
Deaf and dumb	Profoundly deaf
Disabled toilet	Accessible toilet

Figure 5.8: York Theatre Royal's guide at a glance

A guide at a glance

- There is level access from St Leonard's Place into the Box Office, Foyer and Stalls and a wheelchair lift to the Café Bar and payphone.

- Car parking spaces are available nearby in Bootham Row, Union Terrace and Marygate car parks.

- Spaces for up to 10 wheelchair users are available in the Stalls.

- There is a toilet suitable for wheelchair users.

- There is a Sennheiser infrared system for deaf people and those who are hard of hearing.

- There are sign language interpreted and audio described performances for each of the Theatre Royal's own productions and for many visiting companies.

- Taped and large print copies of the theatre's season brochure are available.

- Guide and hearing dogs are welcome at the theatre.

- If you would like to be kept up to date on the Theatre Royal's facilities and services for disabled people, please let us know and we will place you on our free mailing list.

- Disabled people can claim the concessionary ticket price for themselves and one other person.

It is important to realise that, while removing physical barriers is a positive move, the attitude of staff serving customers with specific needs is much more significant. An excellent example of the way specific needs can be met through caring customer service is shown by York's Theatre Royal which provides a special leaflet outlining the wide range of facilities and services offered to customers with specific needs (Figure 5.8).

People with specific needs also include customers with young children. In recent years, travel and tourism organisations have been quick to respond to the growing pressure to provide better facilities and services for this type of customer. Designated and well equipped changing and feeding rooms, baby foods and bottle warming services and free pushchair loans are offered by many organisations. When dealing with customers with specific needs, it is not only the provision of extra facilities that is important. Staff need to be trained in appropriate skills so that they can advise and help customers to use the facilities. For example, the Scottish Tourist Board produces an excellent book entitled *Tourism for All* that gives clear advice on meeting the needs of customers with specific needs. The following extract gives guidance to reception staff.

- Assume that all guests will wish to register for themselves.

- Be aware that the reception area may not be accessible for all guests; be prepared to take registration details to the guest, provide a chair or whatever is required.

- Offer a member of staff to accompany guests with disabilities to their bedroom.

- Ask guests if they would like the housekeeper to meet them in their bedroom to rearrange or remove furniture.

We have looked at the different types of customer and ways their specific needs and expectations can be met through excellent customer service. Of course, it is often very different in real life, particularly when you begin your career and may be apprehensive about how best to deal with a situation. Practice and experience are the only route to effectively dealing with customer service situations and you will discover that with time your confidence and expertise will grow. The activity on (p. 343) gives you the opportunity to start gaining some experience by carrying out some realistic role plays and evaluating how well you perform.

ACTIVITY

How Eurostar provides for: Specific needs

1 Look at the extract from Eurostar's brochure and identify all of the customers with specific needs that the company caters for.

2 Visit a travel and tourism facility such as a tourist attraction, travel agency or station. Make a list of any special facilities or services for people with visual or hearing impairments, who are foreign visitors, who cannot speak English or who have mobility problems. Do you think the facilities and services provided meet the specific needs of these customers?

What is it like on board?

On board you can relax in the air-conditioned carriages and stretch out in your comfortable seat.

Eurostar has been designed for comfort and speed and travels at up to 186 mph during the journey.

If you want a change of scene you can wander down to one of the two bar-buffet cars for a drink, or a snack. If you wish to make a call there are telephones on board that take credit cards. You can also use your mobile telephones (except in the tunnel). Multi-lingual staff are on hand to help you in any way and will show you the baby changing and bottle heating facilities and handout games and puzzles for older children. Wheelchairs can be accommodated on board in two of the First Class carriages.

These role plays cover all of the different types of customer that we have discussed in this section. Each member of the group should select and perform a range of role plays, to ensure that they practice dealing with different types of customer. You may be able to use this activity for your assessment evidence (see pp. 456–7)

Role plays

1 Mr Jones is an elderly gentleman on a coach trip. He likes to sit in a front seat because there is more room. When he gets on the coach, the front seats have already been taken by two by other passengers and by two couriers who say that they are sorry but they cannot move because they have to be next to the microphone which is situated at the front of the coach.

Roles: Mr Jones, two passengers, two couriers.

2 Lizzie is three years old and very excited about staying in an hotel for the first time. One quiet afternoon she is running around the lounge and collides with a waiter carrying a tray of tea. Luckily she is not hurt.

Roles: Lizzie, Lizzie's mother and father, the waiter.

3 Wayne is on holiday in Benidorm. The holiday company's courier has taken a party of holidaymakers on a karaoke night. Wayne has had too much sangria and is trying to start a fight with another man whom Wayne claims has stolen his girlfriend.

Roles: Wayne, other man, courier.

4 Maureen is a guide at a stately home. She is showing a group of visitors around when one of the guests faints. A cleaner is working nearby.

Roles: Maureen, fainting visitor, cleaner, rest of tour group.

5 An American couple make the restrooms their first visit at a theme park but are disgusted to find them dirty with no soap or towels. They complain to a member of staff who tells them to go to the customer service desk.

Roles: American couple, member of staff, customer service clerk.

6 A party of visitors arrives at a museum. One of their number is in a wheelchair. They have written in advance asking for assistance in gaining access. When the party arrives, the main car park is full and the only available parking spaces are on a lower level reached by 30 steps.

Roles: visitor in wheelchair, car park attendant.

7 The fire alarm has sounded at 10.30 p.m. in an hotel. All of the guests have evacuated the building, apart from Mrs Simcox, an elderly lady who is standing at reception in her dressing gown and slippers refusing to go outside because it is snowing.

Roles: Mrs Simcox, receptionist.

8 Mr and Mrs Rodriguez are from Spain and speak very little English. They have gone to the tourist information centre to ask for directions to the train station.

Roles: Mr Rodriguez, Mrs Rodriguez, tourist information clerk.

9 Mr and Mrs Cohen are interested in booking a wedding reception for their daughter at an hotel. As devout Jews, they have to abide by strict dietary requirements. They would like the hotel to allow an outside chef to oversee the food preparation to ensure that it is kosher. The hotel's chef is not very keen on the idea of an outsider running his kitchen, even if it is only for one day.

Roles: Mr and Mrs Cohen, hotel manager, hotel chef.

10 Miss Carmichael has gone to a travel agency to find out about holidays in Greece. She has a profound hearing impairment but can lip read.

Roles: Miss Carmichael, travel sales consultant.

BUILD YOUR LEARNING

Select two travel or tourism organisations. Identify the different types of customer that they serve and evaluate how each organisation meets the particular needs of different customers including:

- individuals
- groups
- people of different ages
- people from different cultures
- people who do not speak English
- people with specific needs, for example, people with sensory disabilities and people with young children.

You will need to identify the criteria that you are going to use for your evaluation. For example, you might identify some of the specific needs of people with young children as pushchair access, changing facilities, bottle warming facilities, children's menus and so on.

Make recommendations about how each organisation could improve the service that it offers to these types of customer and compare the two organisations in terms of their effectiveness in meeting specific customer needs.

Keywords and phrases

You should know the meaning of the words and phrases listed below. If you are unsure about any of them, go back through the last 11 pages to refresh your understanding.

- Colleague
- Cultural background
- Disability Discrimination Act 1995
- Employee
- External customer
- Internal customer
- Management and supervisors
- Specific needs
- Staff in functional departments
- Staff teams

Selling skills

SELLING SKILLS ARE AN IMPORTANT part of customer service and providing good customer service should always be more important than simply selling a product to the customer. As a member of staff, your main objective should be to satisfy customers by meeting their needs and expectations. In doing this you will almost inevitably sell the customer a product. But the selling aspect of your relationship with the customer should be the end result of giving good customer service.

In many situations you will not even have to consider whether or not you are using selling techniques, because if you provide good customer service you are also using selling techniques. For example, the bus driver who smiles at customers as they board, helps an elderly lady to her seat, advises foreign visitors about where they want to go and shows that nothing is too much trouble is providing good customer service. The driver is also demonstrating excellent selling techniques (even if he or she does not realise it) because customers are likely to be impressed by the service and use it again.

Selling is not just the responsibility of designated sales staff – all staff need to understand the importance of effective selling skills and put them into practice. Every time a customer asks you for advice or information you are probably in a selling situation. The advice or information that you give is part of both selling and customer service. In many selling situations, you may not realise that you will be selling something until the customer approaches you. For example, a customer may approach a resort representative and ask about car hire.

Clearly, your task is easier if you know about the situation beforehand because you can make sure that you have all the necessary information ready. However, in any selling situation there are certain steps you can take to ensure that you meet the customer's needs and expectations.

In order to carry out your duties and responsibilities, you need certain personal qualities together with detailed knowledge about your organisation's products and services. Figure 5.9 shows some of the personal qualities required.

Let's look at some of these qualities in more detail.

- **Enthusiasm**. Showing that you are enthusiastic about your job, the organisation, its products and the customers.

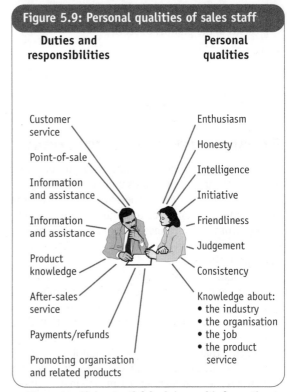

Figure 5.9: Personal qualities of sales staff

Duties and responsibilities	Personal qualities
Customer service	Enthusiasm
Point-of-sale	Honesty
Information and assistance	Intelligence
Information and assistance	Initiative
Product knowledge	Friendliness
After-sales service	Judgement
Payments/refunds	Consistency
Promoting organisation and related products	Knowledge about: • the industry • the organisation • the job • the product service

- **Honesty**. Giving truthful advice and information to customers to ensure that the product will meet their needs and expectations.

- **Intelligence**. Showing that you have really thought about the customers and that you understand the way you can meet their needs.

- **Initiative**. The ability to react quickly and efficiently on an individual basis.

- **Friendliness**. Showing that customers are wanted and welcome and not a nuisance or an interruption.

- **Judgement**. The ability to assess each situation and the needs of the customer so that the service is appropriate.

- **Consistency**. Ensuring that you always give the same high level of customer service regardless of the situation or needs of the customer.

- **Knowledge**. Knowing enough about the travel and tourism industry, your organisation, your job and the products and services that you offer, that you can provide any advice, information or assistance that customers require.

The travel and tourism industry uses a number of selling skills, including:

- raising customer awareness
- establishing rapport with the customer
- investigating customer needs
- presenting the product or service
- closing the sale
- delivering after-sales service

Let's look at each in turn.

Raising customer awareness

Often, customers do not buy particular products and services from an organisation simply because they are not aware that they exist. Therefore, one of the key selling skills that you need to acquire is the ability to **raise customer awareness** by highlighting products and services that you think might satisfy their needs and expectations.

For example, a travel agency clerk might offer to arrange foreign currency and travellers cheques for a customer booking a package holiday. Bar staff in a theatre bar might suggest to theatregoers that they order their interval drinks in advance. However, you must ensure that you only highlight suitable products, or you risk giving the impression that you do not understand the customers' needs and are merely trying to increase sales. Disneyland, Paris produces a sales manual for staff to enable them to sell the park to customers. The case study opposite shows an extract from the section dealing with answering customer questions and raising awareness about what is on offer.

Establishing rapport

Establishing rapport with customers means communicating on the same level and indicating that you are sympathetic to their needs. This requires good judgement for, while no customer likes to be ignored, people do not like to feel that they are being pressured or rushed by over enthusiastic sales staff either. It is usually possible to read from customers' body language and behaviour whether they feel comfortable talking to you and want to pursue the conversation. However, in any situation it is important to greet each customer and ask if you can be of help.

CASE STUDY

Disneyland Paris sales manual

What is Euro Disneyland, Paris?

Euro Disneyland Paris is more than just a theme park, it's a complete destination. The exciting and unique theme park is complemented by top quality entertainment and dining, excellent sport and leisure facilities, 27 holes of golf, a state of the art convention centre, and six beautifully themed hotels.

Isn't Euro Disneyland, Paris just for kids?

No, Euro Disneyland Paris is not just for children. It's a fun destination for all age groups. It is designed to have something for everyone, sparkling shows, themed architecture, fascinating technology and, of course, thrilling rides. With hotels ranging from economy to luxury, and self-catering, there is something to fit every taste and budget.

Why go to Euro Disneyland, Paris?

People go to Euro Disneyland Paris to have fun and nobody has more experience in providing fun than Disney. Euro Disneyland Paris is perfect for a short-break and it's a great place to celebrate a birthday, anniversary or some other special event. It is also an ideal add-on to a longer trip to France or Europe.

When should we go to Euro Disneyland, Paris?

Euro Disneyland Paris is open 365 days a year, so it can fit into everybody's schedule. The entertainment changes seasonally so there's always something new to see. Some 80 per cent of the attractions are covered and almost all facilities are well adapted to cooler seasons, plus seasonal pricing means even better value for money for your clients.

Identifying customer needs

The most direct way of **identifying customer needs** is to ask, 'Can I help you?' The reply will indicate what further questions you need to ask to establish the customer's specific needs. For example, if a customer expresses an interest in booking a holiday in Portugal, you might ask about preferences for resorts, accommodation or time of year. Thomas Cook trains all of its travel consultants in selling skills and suggests 15 key questions that can help when investigating the needs of customers booking a package holiday. These are set out in Figure 5.10.

Figure 5.10: Thomas Cook's key questions when selling

- What do you like to do on holiday?
- What do the children like to do on holiday?
- What does the other person like to do on holiday?
- What age and sex are the children?
- What type of self-catering accommodation would you like, for example, studio, apartment?
- How many bedrooms would you like?
- What type of resort would you like, for example, quiet, lively?

- What on-site facilities would you like?
- What amenities would you like close by?
- What time of day would you prefer to fly?
- Would you like to be close to the airport?
- Do you intend to travel around while you are there?
- Are you flexible with your dates and departure airport?
- Did you have a country or resort in mind?
- What kind of temperature are you looking for?

ACTIVITY

Identifying and satisfying customer needs

1 Ask a colleague, friend or relative to complete the Going Places questionnaire (you may want to design your own or photocopy the Going Places example). Role play the travel agent, with your friend playing the customer.

2 Select a suitable holiday package and destination based on your client's needs. Talk through the proposal with your client. Can you sell him or her the product?

Going Places

Holiday Match ✓
Your guide to your ideal holiday

Help us to help you

How can you be confident that the holiday you've chosen will be right for you? Going Places and Holiday Match can help. To begin with think about which of your previous holidays you enjoyed most. Which were the plus points that made it a success? You might also like to consider recommendations from friends and relatives. Then just fill in the questionnaire below and take it into any of our shops. Holiday Match is as easy as 1, 2, 3. . . .

1. The Holiday Match Enquiry Form helps to identify your key personal holiday requirements.
2. The Holiday Match Resort Guide will help to find those resorts that best match your needs – pick up your free copy at any Going Places shop.
3. The Holiday Match Fact Sheets give details of suggested hotels and apartments for your chosen resort – ask our staff for the Fact Sheet that is right for you.

Use one, two or all three elements – Holiday Match is totally flexible.

Name _____

Address _____

_____

Day/Evening phone number _____

Number in party _____ Adults _____ Children _____

Preferred departure dates

1. _____ 2. _____ 3. _____

Holiday duration (no. of nights) _____

Do you have any particular destination in mind?

_____

Preferred departure points/airport

_____

Accommodation type (Please circle)

Self catering — Villa/Apartment
or Hotel — Half board/Bed and breakfast/Fully inclusive
Room Type — Twin/3 bedded/4 bedded/Other _____

Interests and Activities
(please tick those that are important to you)

- ☐ Close to beach
- ☐ Beach activities (e.g. pedaloes, watersports, volleyball etc)
- ☐ Children's Club/Teenage Club at hotel
- ☐ Children's pool at hotel
- ☐ Hotel pool
- ☐ Hotel located close to night life/restaurants/shops
- ☐ Lively night life
- ☐ Quieter resort
- ☐ Hotel located outside resort centre
- ☐ Good opportunities for sightseeing nearby
- ☐ Other

_____

_____

_____

How much approximately are you planning on spending on your holiday in total?

£ _____

Any other specific holiday requirements?

_____

_____

_____

_____

_____

Presenting the product

Staff need to be able to **present the product** or service to the customer in a way that satisfies the customer's needs. This process usually involves considering the available options and possibly suggesting compromises. For example, a customer may want to book two weeks in a luxury hotel in Greece but be unable to afford the brochure price. The travel agent may suggest a less expensive hotel, a different resort, or a one-week stay instead of two weeks.

Customers also expect to see examples of the product or service that they are considering buying. For example, travel consultants might show customers package holiday brochures or give them videos to watch at home.

ACTIVITY

Presenting the product

Mr and Mrs Butler have recently retired. They have never been abroad before but have decided to spend some of their savings on a foreign holiday. They have both always wanted to see Spain and have dreams of sleepy fishing villages with quaint, white, matchbox houses, winding roads and friendly locals sharing a bottle of wine as the sun goes down. Having visited their local travel agent, they have been recommended (and agreed to) a two-week package in Benidorm in August. The travel consultant showed then some general photographs of Spain and assured them that Benidorm would live up to their dreams. When the Butlers returned from Benidorm they complained that the resort was not at all what they were expecting and felt disappointed that the travel consultant had not presented a more realistic image of the resort.

1 Obtain a copy of a brochure offering holidays in Spain and discuss the extent to which you think the travel consultant could have avoided the complaint by presenting the resort of Benidorm more accurately.

2 Can you suggest a more suitable holiday for the Butlers? Role-play your alternative suggestion by presenting your chosen resort, using the brochure pictures and information.

Closing the sale

Closing the sale means getting the customer to buy the product. Not all sales can be closed straight away. Often customers want to go away and think about it or discuss it with someone else. In these circumstances, it is often acceptable to suggest that you reserve the product or service for the customer until he or she decides whether or not to buy it. You might suggest that you contact the customer in a few days for a decision.

A further aspect of closing the sale is taking the **customer's payment**. It is a duty of staff to ensure that customers pay the correct amount for products and, from a service point of view, it is important to consider the way payment is asked for and handled. American Express uses the advertising slogan: 'That will do nicely'. This phrase sums up the sort of attitude that the company wants projected when accepting payments from customers; cheerful, friendly, polite and grateful.

There are four basic steps to accepting payment from customers.

Calculate accurately. Make sure that the bill is added up correctly and laid out clearly so that the customer understands it.

Ask politely. Saying, '£4.50' is not polite. A far better request might be: 'That will be £4.50 please, madam.'

Say thank you when the customer hands you payment.

Hand over the change and a receipt.

Closing the sale points spell out the word cash, but there are many other ways that customers can pay, including by cheque, traveller's cheque, credit card, debit card and company account. You will need to know how to deal with all of these forms of payment, since a mistake can prove very costly for your organisation and create a dissatisfied customer.

After-sales service

Good customer service does not end when customers hand over their money. The service should continue after the sale has been made to show that you care about the customer.

Sometimes, **after-sales service** is immediate, such as asking customers if they have enjoyed their visit to a museum and listening to the comments that they make. In other situations, there may be a need for service a long time after the sale has been made. For example, a customer buying a time-share apartment may need after-sales service for many years.

It is important to remember the maxim, once a customer, always a customer. In other words, once you have established a relationship with a customer, he or she is entitled to receive good service from you in the future, even if you are not in the position of being able to sell something.

AIDA

The AIDA technique which we discussed in Chapter Four is of equal value when considering effective selling techniques. You will remember that **AIDA** is a mnemonic that stands for:

Attention

Interest

Desire

Action.

This mnemonic is useful because it expresses the process of selling in simple terms. The first stage of selling is to ensure that you have the full attention of the customer. Having achieved this, you need to create interest by describing the product in a way that sounds attractive. This will result in the customer desiring the product and therefore taking action to buy it.

ACTIVITY

After-sales service role play

Go-Europe is a tour operator offering a wide range of package holidays to popular destinations in Europe and Africa. A broad cross-section of tourists travel to resorts in Tunisia, including senior citizens, singles, young couples and families with young children.

Go-Europe offers a number of excursions to customers in its resorts including:

- Bedouin feast night with Arabian entertainers
- beach barbeque at night with meal and unlimited free wine
- karaoke night and disco
- half-day excursion to the camel market at Nabuel
- three-day safari in the Sahara desert
- full-day cruise along the coast
- half-day visit to a carpet factory
- introductory half-day visit to local town
- full-day tour of ancient monuments, ruins and historic landmarks
- full-day of water sports and picnic.

Some guests have come to the introductory cocktail party on their first day abroad and are interested in booking some excursions.

Guests attending the cocktail party are:

- Mr and Mrs Jacob, senior citizens, who have never visited Tunisia before

- Miss Shogbesan and Miss Adanouga, both 18 years old, who have limited spending money
- Mr and Mrs Wallis and their five-year-old twins
- Miss Carruthers, 75 years old, who has been to Tunisia on holiday for the last two years
- Mrs Walton and her 19-year-old daughter, Louise
- Mr and Mrs Khan, both 30 years old, who booked one week's holiday at the last minute (they usually go to America for their holidays)
- Mr Nagana, 25 and Mrs Wong, 26, who usually go on sporting or adventure holidays
- Mr and Mrs Lloyd and their two children, Ruby, 15 and Zita, 12. The 15 year old did not want to go on holiday with her parents.

Take turns at playing the customers and the holiday representative, advising each customer on the most suitable types of excursions. You should try to:

- establish a rapport with each customer
- raise customer awareness about the different excursions that might meet their needs
- investigate each customer's specific needs
- present the excursions
- close the sale.

After the role plays, identify what after-sales service might be needed for the customers who have booked excursions.

We have seen that selling is an important part of excellent customer service because it helps to ensure that customer needs and expectations are met. However, it is equally important to understand that gaining a sale is never the only objective in a selling situation. Pressurising customers to buy a product or service that they do not really want may result in a short-term gain but the end result is almost certainly a dissatisfied customer who will probably not return.

BUILD YOUR LEARNING

Keywords and phrases

You should know the meaning of the words and phrases listed below. If you are unsure about any of them, go back through the last five pages to refresh your understanding.

- After-sales service
- AIDA
- Closing the sale
- Customer's payment
- Establishing rapport
- Identifying customer needs
- Presenting the product
- Raising customer awareness
- Selling skills

End of section activity

1 Select two travel or tourism organisations and evaluate the selling skills of their staff by visiting each as a customer. For example you could:

- go to a tourist information centre and say that you are interested in going to local museums and art galleries
- go to a train station and ask about the cheapest fares for a certain destination
- visit a travel agency and ask about getting foreign currency for a trip abroad
- telephone a tourist attraction and ask about discounted rates for student groups.

2 For each organisation, identify and evaluate how the staff used the following sales skills:

- raising customer awareness
- establishing rapport with customers
- investigating customer needs
- presenting the products or services
- closing the sale.

You should use AIDA to identify the effectiveness of the selling skills of staff in each organisation.

3 Give examples of how the staff could deliver after-sales service.

4 Following your investigation, suggest ways in which the staff could have improved their selling skills.

Dealing with customers

NEARLY EVERYONE WHO WORKS in the travel and tourism industry is required to deal with customers on a regular basis. The contact might be face-to-face, on the telephone or in writing.

Face-to-face communication

Face-to-face communication has many advantages but only if you understand how to use it well. For example, your appearance can help to create a positive impression. You can also use facial expressions and gestures to help you to communicate more effectively. Different communication skills are required for situations involving groups and individuals. For example, when communicating with a group you must ensure that all group members understand you. This can often be difficult with mixed groups, such as a tour group with adults and small children; the adults may want detailed information whereas the children will quickly become bored if the tour is too formal and factual.

ACTIVITY

Appealing to children

Look at the text below from the leaflet for the Mysteries of Egypt exhibition at Goodwood House.

Most young children are fascinated by ancient Egypt and study it in depth at primary school. However, this leaflet is clearly written for adults. Imagine that you are a tour guide for the exhibition and have a school party of 15 nine-year-olds to show around. Can you rewrite the leaflet so that it would appeal to this group? You can make up some stories and details if you like, but try to keep them realistic! Try role playing the tour, using your new text with the rest of the group.

Mysteries of Egypt at Goodwood House

The Regency splendour of Goodwood's Egyptian State Dining Room is guaranteed to make visitors catch their breath.

Soon after Napoleon's campaign on the Nile, the third Duke of Richmond decorated his dining room with this striking scheme.

Now, 200 years later, it can be seen again. Thanks to the Earl of March, who now lives in Goodwood House, we can marvel at this dramatic recreation of the Egyptian scheme after two years of intensive restoration.

The stunning scagliola marbled walls reflect the light both by day and by night, making this a room full of beautiful, exotic mystery exactly as the 3rd Duke had planned. Majestic purple drapes highlighted by flashes of Egyptian turquoise frame the windows beneath their gilded temple pelmets while golden scarabs, cobras, vultures and crocodiles add exotic interest to the stunning cornice.

Goodwood House has taken on new life. The grand Yellow Drawing Room forms a glowing heart to the house with its ottomans, sofas and French chairs beautifully covered in newly-woven yellow silk. Every painting from the vast collection has been rehung. The Ballroom arrangement faithfully follows a sketch laid down – but never realised – by the Duke before his death in 1806. The English paintings, including works by Van Dyck, Stubbs, Canaletto and Reynolds are unrivalled as a group and the Sèvres porcelain dinner service has been superbly redisplayed.

The family's French descent is reflected in the 18th century furniture and tapestries while the Scottish history can be seen in portraits and landscapes. New gilding provides the perfect setting for these old favourites.

Today, whilst still being used by Lord and Lady March for private entertainments, especially during the world-renowned Festival of Speed in June and for Raceweek in July, the State Apartments are available throughout the year for private parties, weddings or corporate functions.

Once experienced, visitors will never forget the unmistakable atmosphere – both friendly and grand – which permeates the Goodwood Estate.

Telephone communication

Most organisations use the telephone to provide part of their customer service. Indeed, some organisations such as hotel central reservations offices use the telephone as the main method of communication when dealing with customer enquiries.

ACTIVITY
Telephone communication

1 Make a list of the things that annoy or frustrate you about telephoning organisations based on your own experience. You should consider criteria such as the way the call is answered, the telephone manner of the person answering, the process of being connected to someone else within the organisation, how delays are dealt with, the way in which the call is terminated and the effectiveness of message taking.

2 Look over the list you have made and note how many items on it are due to technical factors, (such as a bad line or a wrong number) and how many are due to poor customer service. You will probably find that most of the things that annoy you could be avoided with better staff communication skills and customer service.

With good telephone skills, it is usually possible to meet or exceed the standard of service that customers expect. Many of the skills needed are the same that you would use in any customer service situation. For example, you need to be polite, friendly, attentive and efficient. However, additional skills are needed when using a telephone because the customer cannot see you and you cannot see the customer. This means that you cannot use expression or gesture to help the communication process but must rely totally on your voice and your ability to listen carefully.

Here are some basic rules for using the telephone effectively.

- **Speak clearly.** Do not eat, drink, chew gum or smoke while on the telephone, as this will distort or muffle the sound of your voice.

- **Take notes.** Always write down full details of what the customer wants, particularly if the message is for someone else.

- **Identify the caller's needs.** Remember that the caller is paying for the call and wants to be dealt with quickly and efficiently.

- **Listen carefully.** Do not interrupt when the caller is talking.

- **Explain what is happening.** If you transfer the caller to someone else, state what you are doing.

ACTIVITY
Telephone communication role play

In pairs, role play a caller and telephonist. Decide who is going to be the caller and who the telephonist.

With your backs to each other, role play the following telephone calls made by the caller to a tour operator's reservations switchboard.

- A customer who wants to know what holidays are offered to the USA.

- A customer who has not received confirmation for his flight to Athens next week.

- The mother of a member of staff who wants to talk to her daughter (who is on her lunch break).

- A student who wants some general information about the company.

- Someone ringing up about a recent job advertisement for a reservations clerk.

- A travel agent who wants to change a customer's itinerary.

For each role play, the telephonist should record all necessary details and say what action he or she would be taking after the call.

After the role plays, identify the extent to which the information recorded was sufficient. For example, did the telephonist record the full name, telephone number and extension number (if appropriate) of the caller, the time of the call and establish whether it was a matter of urgency?

Written communication

Written communication is the main way in which some organisations keep in contact with customers. For example, many customers rarely visit a branch of their bank to talk to staff; they get money from a cash dispenser and receive details of their accounts by letter. Much of the image that they have of the service offered by the bank therefore depends on written communication.

Examples of written communications used by travel and tourism organisations include:

- menus
- tariffs or price lists
- letters
- bills
- brochures and leaflets
- advertisements
- signs
- notice boards
- programmes
- tickets
- faxes
- e-mail
- the internet
- timetables.

The same standard of care needs to be given to written forms of communication as to any other aspect of customer service; the quality of written communication affects customers' image both of you and of the organisation. For example, a guest in an hotel may be very impressed by the friendly, enthusiastic attitude of the receptionist but that impression may change if he or she is handed a crumpled and badly photocopied bar snacks menu. If the menu is presented in a professional and attractive manner, however, the previous positive impression will be confirmed.

ACTIVITY

Written communication

Imagine you are a resort representative in Spain.

1 Write a letter welcoming guests to the resort. The letter is to be handed to everyone as they arrive in their hotel.

2 What other information could you provide for visitors? You may find it useful to visit an hotel to obtain examples of information provided.

Most travel and tourism organisations use a combination of communication methods and it is important that all staff are trained appropriately. Even if it is not a normal part of the job, they may still need the skills on occasions, such as when a cleaner answers an early morning call from an anxious customer.

Every form of communication used by an organisation must be professional. This is because contact with the organisation may take place through different communication channels on different occasions. For example, a customer may write to a tourist attraction requesting information and then telephone or call in person to clarify the details. On each occasion the communication needs to be excellent. Some organisations excel at certain types of communication but let their overall service down by not ensuring that all of their communications meet the same standards.

WEBSTRACT

Foreign tourist offices: Communication

Holiday Which? magazine carried out research to see which of the foreign tourist offices in London are best at dealing with inquiries through the following channels:

- in writing
- face-to-face
- on the phone
- by e-mail
- via the internet.

Some of the research results are summarised here.

Australia

Commended: Australia has a great website; easy to get around, fun to use, and packed with ideas and useful links to accommodation and sights. It also had the best e-mail response, going into more detail than any other office.

Could do better: Personal visits are discouraged, and we found that our specific enquiries by post were met with a standard, if wide-ranging, package of information.

Mail: Becket House, 60–68 St Thomas Street, London SE1 3QN
Telephone: 0891 070707 (premium rate)
E-mail: atc@acxiom.co.uk
Website: **www.aussie.net.au**

Cyprus

Commended: This office did well in every test. The mailing showed that our letter had been read, with information covering each specific request. On our visit the staff showed that their knowledge was good, but they were also prepared to look things up if they didn't know.

Could do better: It's a shame there's no e-mail or website.

Mail/personal callers: 213 Regent Street, London W1R 8DA

Telephone: 020 7734 9822

Germany

Commended: A hefty envelope filled with information included some good leaflets on walking and children's activities, though the response was rather slow (16 working days). The e-mail response was good, and the website was comprehensive, if a little dull.

Could do better: Although our visit to the office was useful for picking up leaflets and timetables, the assistant didn't seem very interested in our specific requirements.

Mail/personal callers: Nightingale House, 65 Curzon Street, London W1Y 8NE

Telephone: 0891 600100 (premium rate)

E-mail: German_National_Tourist_Office@ compuserve.com

Website: **www.germany-tourism.de**

Greece

Commended: The safety advice we received by telephone was quite helpful – though we had to wait 105 rings for someone to answer.

Could do better: This was one of the worst mailings we received – an uninspiring booklet of general information that wasn't tailored to the requests in our letter. On our face-to-face visit, the assistant was dismissive and appeared to take little interest in our enquiry.

Mail/personal callers: 4 Conduit Street, London W1R 0DJ

Telephone: 020 7734 5997

E-mail: EOT-greektouristoffice@btinternet.com

Italy

Commended: Our visit to the office rescued what was otherwise a miserable performance. We were given plenty of useful information to plan a trip to the Neapolitan Riviera using public transport.

Could do better: The information sent by post took 19 days to reach us and tackled only our questions on facilities for visitors with disabilities. Telephoning the enquiry line was tedious: if the line wasn't constantly engaged, the phone often remained unanswered for several minutes, and when we did get through, the recorded message was unhelpful.

Mail/personal callers: 1 Princes Street, London W1R 8AY

Telephone: 0891 600280 (brochures, premium rate) 020 7408 1254 (enquiries)

Netherlands

Commended: The main drawback of a personal visit is the fleeting opening hours (1–3 p.m.). Once there, we found the staff relaxed and prepared to take their time to produce extra information. The website is excellent.

Could do better: The telephone service is absolutely hopeless. You will end up in a maze of options on the recorded message that is likely to end in exasperation.

Mail: PO Box 523, London, SW1E 6NT

Personal callers: 18 Buckingham Gate, London SW1E 6NT

Telephone: 0891 717777 (premium rate)

E-mail: info@nbt.org.uk

Website: **www.nbt.nl/holland**

Source: *Holiday Which?* on-line

ACTIVITY

Communicating

Select a travel and tourism information desk at a tourist information centre, railway station, hotel, or elsewhere. Evaluate how good the staff are at dealing with customers face-to-face, in writing and over the telephone. You will need to think of a reason for your inquiry first. For example, you might try to find out what attractions for are available in the area.

Verbal communication

Verbal communication is central to many of the communication methods that we have already considered. For example, it is part of face-to-face, group and telephone communication and it influences your personal presentation and the first impression that you give to customers.

The ability to speak well need not mean that you have to use a posh accent. Of far greater importance is the ability to speak in a way that is comprehensible and acceptable to your customers. Comprehensible means that you need to speak in a way that is meaningful and easily followed by the customer. Acceptable means that the way you express yourself should fit the personal image that you are trying to create. As a quick guide, the following points are worth considering.

- **Express your thoughts clearly.** Do not mumble or ramble.

- **Beware of slang and jargon.** Use language that is likely to be familiar to the customer.

- **Vary your tone of voice.** It makes it more interesting and shows that you are interested.

- **Listen to the customer.** Good communication skills also involve the ability to listen carefully to customers' requests and to respond to their needs.

- **React with interest** by using suitable facial expressions as well as your voice.

Effective verbal skills are often a matter of experience and practice. One situation that frequently makes staff nervous is making a speech or presentation. You may have experienced this already on your course if you have been required to give a presentation to other students. You will know that it can be a nerve-racking experience but have hopefully learned that good planning and preparation gives confidence and helps you to communicate effectively.

The same advice can be applied to any situation in which you have to speak to a number of customers at the same time. For example, many organisations such as hotels and cinemas use public address systems or tannoys. The steps set out in Figure 5.11 will help you to create a professional and calm impression.

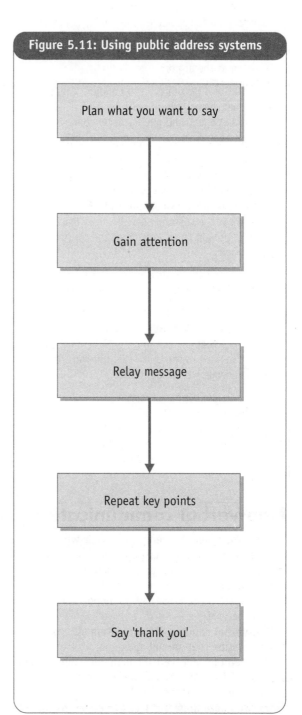

Figure 5.11: Using public address systems

Plan what you want to say

↓

Gain attention

↓

Relay message

↓

Repeat key points

↓

Say 'thank you'

ACTIVITY

Verbal communication skills

Practice your verbal communication skills by role playing the following tannoy messages. It will help if the rest of the group have their backs to the announcer, to make it more realistic.

1 Flight AL 371B to Alicante has been delayed due to its late departure from Spain. The new estimated departure time is in three and a half hours. Make the announcement to passengers waiting at the airport.

2 The platform for the train to London, King's Cross has changed from platform 3 to platform 15b. Passengers who need assistance moving their luggage can get help from the customer service assistants. Make the announcement to passengers waiting for the train.

3 Staff have found a five-year-old boy called Tom in a tourist attraction. He is waiting for his parents at the customer service desk. Make the announcement to all visitors at the tourist attraction.

4 Give a standard security warning at a ferry terminal advising passengers not to leave luggage unattended.

5 The receptionist at a holiday centre is asked to announce that the evening's entertainment is about to start in the Gaity Theatre. Make the announcement to all guests.

6 A blue Renault Espace, license plate L177 HRO has been parked in the bay for emergency vehicles at an art gallery. Make the announcement to visitors and staff at the art gallery.

Non-verbal communication

There is a widespread tendency to focus on what we say or write and overlook the importance of what we communicate non-verbally. However, research has shown that as much as 80 per cent of communication is non-verbal, so it is clearly an important part of customer service.

Non-verbal communication covers all aspects of communication that are not spoken or written down. Another term for non-verbal communication is **body language**. This means the way we use our body to send out messages to someone else. It can include posture, mannerisms, gestures and facial expressions, all of which communicate messages about what we really think and feel.

The subject of body language is too complex to discuss in detail here. However, from a customer service point of view it is useful to look at what is known as open and closed body language. **Open body language** persuades customers that you are interested in them, that you are not hostile or aggressive and that you want to listen to them and please them. **Closed body language** suggests the opposite – that you are uninterested, may be hostile or aggressive and are unwilling to listen to them or satisfy their needs. Figure 5.12 gives examples of open and closed types of body language.

Figure 5.12: Open and closed body language

Open	Closed
Smiling	Frowning
Standing up straight	Slouching
Arms loosely at your side or behind your back	Arms crossed in front of you, or hands on your hips or in your pockets
Head held with chin level to floor	Chin up or down
Eye contact with customer	Avoiding eye contact with customer
Remaining in a comfortable position	Fidgeting, moving from foot to foot, crossing and uncrossing legs
No obvious mannerism	Fiddling with your hair, hands, clothes
Using gestures that help you to explain what you are saying	Using gestures excessively or for no apparent reason
Showing interest	Showing no feeling at all
Showing concern	Showing lack of concern

Smiling is the single most important aspect of non-verbal communication. It says that you like and take pride in your job and that you like the customer and want to meet and satisfy his or her needs.

Good communication skills, both verbal and non-verbal, are important in all situations, whether face-to-face, over the telephone or in writing. However, dealing with customers covers a wide range of different situations that include:

- providing information
- giving advice
- taking and relaying messages
- keeping records
- providing assistance
- dealing with problems
- handling complaints.

Providing information

Most travel and tourism customers expect you to be able to **provide information** about the products and services your organisation offers. The type of information provided largely depends on what customers ask you. They may want to know about products, services or holiday destinations. Alternatively, they may require information on what prices include or directions on how to get to somewhere. Many organisations include detailed information on how to get to them in their promotional materials, as the very thorough example from London Zoo shows.

Because travel and tourism is such a diverse industry, customers' information requirements are equally diverse.

ACTIVITY

Providing information

Here are some questions frequently asked by American visitors to the UK. See how many of them you can answer. You might need to use reference books, manuals, guides or the internet.

- How do I get from Heathrow to Gatwick?
- What's the most convenient airport if I want to visit Shakespeare country and the Cotswolds?
- How can I fix to stay in a bed and breakfast?
- How can I book theatre tickets in the USA for London shows?
- I am arriving at Southampton on the QE2; how can I get to London?
- When does the Ceremony of the Keys take place and how can I get tickets?
- How can I claim back the VAT on my purchases?
- When does the circus start in Piccadilly?
- What's the weather like in York during July?
- We would love to see those shaggy brown cows while in Scotland. Where can we find them?

Answers can be found on the British Tourist Authority's website at www.usagateway.visitbritain.com

---

Getting There

London Zoo is open every day – except Christmas Day – from 10 a.m. To get to the Web of Life use the map and instructions below.

Using London Transport

By Underground – The nearest station is Camden Town (Northern Line). Follow the signs up 'Parkway' to the Zoo (12 minute walk).

By British Rail – the nearest station is Euston. Take the Underground (Northern Line) from Euston to Camden Town.

By Bus – Services run from Oxford Circus and Baker Street (no. 274), to Ormonde Terrace. Pick up the C2 from Oxford Circus or Great Portland Street, to Gloucester Gate.

By Waterbus – The London Waterbus Company runs a scheduled service along the Regent's Canal between Camden Lock or Little Venice and London Zoo. For full details call the London Waterbus Company: 020 7482 2550.

By London Pride Sightseeing Bus – Hop on a 'No. 1 for Attractions' London Pride Sightseeing Bus oin the centre of London, at any London Pride bus stop. All-inclusive price. Arrives at the Zoo every 15 minutes. For full details call London Pride: 01708 631122.

By Car – The Zoo's Main Gate is situated on the Outer Circle of Regent's Park, NW1. Parking is available in the Zoo's Gloucester Slips car park at £5 per car, per day. £12 is payable at the car park, with £7 when paying to get into the Zoo.

▲ Directions to London Zoo

Of course, no one can be expected to know the answers to all questions. However, what is expected is that you know where and how to find out information so that you can answer customers' questions. A wide range of information sources is available, including:

- manuals and travel guides
- brochures and leaflets
- reference books
- guide books
- computerised information systems
- timetables and schedules
- recorded telephone information lines
- tourist information centres.

Knowing where to find information quickly is an essential part of excellent customer service.

ACTIVITY

Finding information

The left-hand column in the table below lists some sources of information. The right-hand column lists some examples of typical requests for information. Can you match the information request with a suitable source? There may be more than one source for some of the requests.

Source of reference	Request for information
Yellow Pages	Telephone number of Gatwick Airport
Tourist map of area	Five-star hotels in London
Directory enquiries	Film showing at local cinema
Railway timetable	Name of a plumber
Local newspaper	Stately homes in the area
RAC hotel guide	Nearest tourist information centre
Telephone directory	Length of train journey to Bath
National Trust book	Location of local restaurant
What's On magazine	Late opening for the area chemists

In any customer service situation, **product information** should be impersonal, accurate and objective.

- **Impersonal** means that your own tastes and preferences should not limit or restrict the sort of information you give. For example, a customer visiting a travel agency expects product information about a destination that is suitable for his or her needs, not about destinations where the assistant would like to go.

- **Accurate** means making sure that everything you say is true. If you are not sure about something, say that you will check the information and let the customer know the full picture. For example, saying that a cinema film is suitable for young children when you are not really sure could result in some very dissatisfied customers.

- **Objective** means including all the information that customers need to know, even if you think that it might put them off buying the product. Sometimes this may mean referring potential customers to a competitor, but the reputation that you gain for good customer service means that they will come back.

Impersonal, accurate and objective information is important if you are to satisfy customers' needs and ensure that they return. Sometimes giving the wrong information can mean that customers are not able to buy a product or service at all.

The need for accurate information is a key issue for customers using rail services, particularly at larger stations. This includes information before departure on topics such as fares, timetables, departures, and delays, and information given on board the train, such as approaching stations and delays. *Which?* magazine compared the effectiveness of the information services of four main rail companies both in terms of platform and on board information. The results are shown in the case study.

ACTIVITY

Train companies compared

Look at the results of the survey in the case study and identify the main strengths and weaknesses of the provision of information from rail companies.

CASE STUDY

Train companies compared

Connex South Central

Commuters' rating: 77 per cent

Satisfaction with information:

on the platform 85 per cent

on the train 81 per cent

Good for: information during the journey

Bad for: giving departure times

General comments:

On the specific journeys we asked about, Connex South Central was the best of the four companies at giving information. Connex South Central was good at giving platform announcements about where trains were due to call, but it was poor at stating the departure time. It also did well for warning passengers when stations were approaching, doing so in four out of five cases.

South West Trains

Commuters' rating: 62 per cent

Satisfaction with information:

on the platform 81 per cent

on the train 67 per cent

Good for: details on the platform

Bad for: information on the train

General comments:

SWT was average at giving information. It was better at giving train details on the platform than giving information on the train. SWT gave more information than ScotRail on the journeys our respondents reported on, but it got the worst rating from regular travellers for information provision.

ScotRail

Commuters' rating: 66 per cent

Satisfaction with information:

on the platform 58 per cent

on the train 67 per cent

Good for: not particularly good for anything

Bad for: information on the platform

General comments:

It's no wonder ScotRail got such low ratings - it gave platform announcements about where trains call and terminate on only about half the journeys in our survey. And on trains, just 9 per cent of passengers said they were given information about connecting services. It wasn't as good as the other companies at announcing where a train would call and when it was approaching stations.

West Anglia Great Northern

Commuters' rating: 88 per cent

Satisfaction with information:

on the platform 86 per cent

on the train 80 per cent

Good for: platform information

Bad for: destination information on station concourse

General comments:

More of WAGN's regular travellers said they were given good information than people who use the other three train companies in our survey. WAGN was good at telling passengers on the train the departure time and where the train calls, before it had left the station. Other companies generally gave this after the train had left the platform, which is not much help if you're not sure you're on the right train!

Source: *Which?* on-line

Giving advice

Giving customers advice is really an extension of giving them information. However, while information may be purely factual, advice requires that you make appropriate recommendations and suggestions. For example, a travel adviser may provide customers with information on package holidays by giving them appropriate brochures and possibly a video. However, customers may ask for additional advice on what would best suit their particular needs. For example, 'Which Greek islands would you recommend for a get-away-from-it-all holiday?' or 'Do you think I should take foreign currency or traveller's cheques to Tunisia?' As with giving information, so with advice: make sure it is impersonal, accurate and objective.

Many travel and tourism products and services are complex and involve a wide range of different elements. First-time customers can find this quite confusing and their enjoyment of the product may be spoiled if they have difficulty in understanding how it is delivered. Therefore, travel and tourism organisations have to make sure that they give customers sufficient advice on the way services are delivered and used. For example, package holiday customers are sent pre-holiday advice about when and where they check in for their flight. Once they arrive they are usually given advice on health and safety issues such as the use of lifts, swimming pools, hotel balconies and so on.

One excellent example of an organisation providing clear and effective advice to its customers is the system used by the Brewers Fayre public houses for customers wishing to have a meal (see case study opposite). This shows a leisure and recreation provider giving advice to customers so that they can fully enjoy the product. In this next activity you are asked to think about customer advice within a different leisure and recreation context.

ACTIVITY

Customer advice

Customer feedback at theme parks indicates that one of the biggest complaints is the length of queues for the big rides. Some parks are introducing virtual queuing, where customers get a ticket with the time that they will be guaranteed a place on the ride. This means that they are then free to go off and see other attractions, rather than waste time in a queue.

Design a form that advises customers on how the system works. You should include blank spaces to allow customers to fill in the times that they are booked on a number of rides at the park.

Taking messages

Taking and relaying messages is an important part of customer service for both internal and external customers. Here are a few examples of occasions when it is necessary to take messages.

- A customer telephones a conference centre and wants to speak to one of the delegates.

- A customer in a tourist information centre complains about the service and wants the manager to contact him about it when he returns.

- Someone wants to leave a package for a guest at hotel reception, to be given to the guest on arrival.

- A member of staff phones to say that she is unwell and will not be in for work.

Failure to take accurate messages and to ensure that they are passed on to the right person promptly can have disastrous effects on customers' perception of the overall level of service offered. For example, a guest in an hotel may be very impressed by the friendly, enthusiastic attitude of the receptionist but that impression may change if he or she is handed an illegible handwritten message on a scrappy piece of paper. However, if the message is in a professional format, the positive impression is confirmed.

Figure 5.13: Good and bad message taking

TELEPHONE MESSAGE

Message for: Mr Sinclair   Date: 26/9/96

Message from: Miss J Collins   Time: 3.40 p.m.

Message:
Please call me at the office before 6:00pm tonight.

Telephone number: 01723 562189 Ext.126

Message taken by: *S Rawlins*

Mr Sinclair
Please call Miss Collins
at the office this afternoon
Tel no. 01723 582189
KR

CASE STUDY

Customer information at Brewers Fayre

Brewers Fayre offer an extensive menu aimed primarily at the family market. Meals are selected from a menu, ordered and paid for at the bar and served at the customer's table by waiting staff. One potential problem is that at busy times customers may order a meal but not be able to find a table. Brewers Fayre uses a simply but very effective system to ensure that this does not happen, however, and provides customers with clear advice on how the system operates.

All tables have menus and a tent card giving advice on how to order food.

Customers then fill in their order and table number on the order form.

TABLE NUMBER	
STARTERS	
SIDE ORDERS	DRINKS
MAIN MEALS	CHOICE OF CHIPS/POTATOES OF THE DAY
WINE	

There are even reminders about drinks, wine, side orders and whether the customer wants chips or the potatoes of the day.

When customers go to the bar to order food they place another tent card on the table to show that the table is already taken, so that another customer does not sit down.

HOW TO ORDER YOUR MEAL

- Find a vacant table and note the table number
- Place your order at the food counter, quoting your table number
- Please pay for your food when you order
- Our staff will serve your order to the table
- Please purchase drinks at the bar

TO SHOW THAT YOUR TABLE IS OCCUPIED SIMPLY REVERSE THIS CARD.

NOWHERE'S FAIRER THAN A BREWERS FAYRE.

BUT THIS TABLE IS OCCUPIED

– we have gone to order our meal

NOWHERE'S FAIRER THAN A BREWERS FAYRE.

ACTIVITY

Taking and relaying messages

Megathrills theme park often receives phone calls to its customer service desk from customers who are due to meet up with friends for the day but who have been delayed. The park can become very crowded, covers several acres of land and has no public address system, so passing these messages on has proved very difficult. The manager has decided to introduce a meeting point notice board at the customer services desk, so that customers will be able to get information about when and where they are to meet up with their friends in the park and what time the friends expect to arrive. Customer service staff will fill in a printed card with each message received and display it on the board.

1 Design the layout of the card, leaving spaces for the customer service staff to fill in the relevant details. Try to think of all of the information that you would want to give if your friends had been delayed.

2 Design a checklist for the staff showing how they should fill in the card and outlining what information is appropriate (the cards are displayed in a public area). You need to consider confidentiality and tact; for example, it would not be appropriate to have a card that read:

Reason for delay:

Your mother has had a heart attack

or

John has been stopped for drinking and driving!

Keeping records

As we have already seen, excellent customer service involves giving information to customers. However, another key part of the process involves **keeping records** of information that is needed by other staff to help them provide good service. For example, a hotel receptionist may record a guest's reservation and include the following information that would be passed on to the relevant staff:

- double room with cot in bedroom – head housekeeper

- table for two for dinner at 8 p.m. – head waiter

- one guest cannot eat any dairy products – head waiter and head chef

- early morning alarm call at 7 p.m. – early shift receptionist

- mini-bus transfer to the airport – hall porter.

All travel and tourism organisations keep records on their customers and understanding how to maintain and use these records is an essential part of excellent customer service.

Customer records can be kept of a wide range of information such as:

- details of financial transactions

- customer details

- details of complaints and compliment letters

- accidents and emergencies.

Most travel and tourism organisations have standard procedures for keeping records, which may be paper-based or stored on a computer. For example, a travel agency may have paper-based customer files which contain copies of booking forms, confirmation letters and payment details. It may also store specific details on a computerised database.

Customer records are vital to ensure that you know who your customers are, what their needs are and how you have satisfied them in the past. They are also a very necessary part of the process of being able to answer a customer's inquiry quickly and efficiently. For example, the customer in a travel agency who says, 'We really liked the charter airline we flew with the year before last but cannot remember who it was', is far more likely to book again if the travel clerk is able to say, 'Let me look, ah yes, it was Monarch. We get a lot of very positive comments about their service'.

ACTIVITY

For this activity you will need some holiday brochures that offer summer package holidays in Portugal.

Imagine that you are a newly employed travel consultant at Sunburst Travel. Mr and Mrs Butler have telephoned to say that they are coming in at 10.30 a.m. tomorrow to discuss possible summer holidays in Portugal. You have not dealt with the Butlers before, but have printed out a copy of their customer record from your computerised database

(see below). This includes a column where the agency enters any comments received from customers following a phone call to them after their holiday

Look at the Butlers' customer details and identify the sort of features that you think they might be looking for in a holiday. Identify some suitable holidays in Portugal that you could suggest to them as options. Write a list of questions that you would ask the Butlers to ensure that you give them the best advice.

Name: Butler
Customers: James (Mr)/Elizabeth (Mrs)
Address: The Ashes, High Street, Chorley, Lancs, MA30 5CH Tel: 01635874162
Customer history:

Date	Destination	Type of package	Cost	Tour operator	Comments
12.05.96	Madeira	4* hotel, full-board	£1,879	Thomson	Required air-con, sea-view and balcony
20.03.97	Prague	Tailor-made	£856	Independent Scheduled flight, British Airways Holiday Inn	Very positive about standard of hotel. Wanted more access to excursions.
17.08.97	Mediterranean	Cruise	£2,472	P&O	Required luxury outside cabin. Praised standard of catering and excursions.
23.06.98	Sorrento, Italy	5* hotel, full-board	£2,105	Italia	Complained about restaurant and no decent swimming pool.
18.07.99	Cyprus	Self-catering	£2,055	Airtours	Disliked lack of maid and local restaurants. Said: 'Never again!'

Providing assistance

We have already seen that some customers have specific needs and looked at the ways in which excellent customer service can meet these needs. In reality, any customer may have a need for extra assistance at any time. For example, the hotel guest who needs help carrying his luggage; the conference organisation which wants assistance in working the overhead projector, the holidaymaker who would like to book a hire car and the mother with young children who needs help in getting a pushchair up a flight of stairs.

In situations such as these, your responsibility is to try to anticipate when customers might need assistance and provide it. For example, if you see a mother struggling with a pushchair you should not wait for her to ask for help – offer assistance quickly to show that you really care and have anticipated her needs.

ACTIVITY

Providing assistance

Sam is having a very stressful day as a resort representative in Corfu. Her base is at the three-star Olympia hotel in the resort of Kavos. During the day she has been called on by a number of guests to provide assistance in the following situations.

1 A guest's young child has become badly sunburned on the beach.

2 A guest's wife has gone on a day's excursion taking the key to their apartment with her.

3 A guest has left her handbag in a local restaurant. It contained her passport, money, traveller's cheques and credit cards. A telephone call to the restaurant has failed to find the missing bag.

4 A vegetarian has complained that, apart from salad and chips, the buffet in the hotel restaurant can offer nothing for him to eat.

5 A couple of guests have spilt a bottle of red wine over the settee in their bedroom. In trying to clear up the mess they have made the stain worse.

6 A guest has brought her hairdryer and heated curlers with her but finds that the plugs do not fit the Greek sockets.

For each situation, say what assistance you think Sam should provide. If you do not know the solution to some of the situations, now is the time to find out! For example, what is the best help for a young child with sunburn; what is the first thing that people should do who lose credit cards?

Dealing with problems

Dealing with customers' problems overlaps with giving assistance. However, the distinction is that the problems frequently lie outside the control of the customer, such as a sudden illness, missing luggage or being robbed. These situations are very stressful for customers and require tactful and careful handling. Often customers are anxious, upset or angry; it is your responsibility to reassure them and show that you are confident and in control of the situation.

Depending on how complex the problem is, the member of staff may need to check on a number of occasions that it has been resolved and that there is nothing more that can be done. For example, if a holidaymaker has a moped accident and ends up in hospital, the resort representative will have a number of different problems to resolve such as;

■ visiting the holidaymaker in hospital to see how he or she is and whether he or she needs anything

■ sorting out medical insurance

■ notifying next of kin if the accident is serious

■ ensuring that others accompanying the injured guest are all right and can get to the hospital.

In any situation, it is vital that you remain calm and listen carefully to what is said, so that you can accurately identify the customers' needs and provide the best possible customer service.

ACTIVITY

Dealing with problems

Two very common problems are for a member of a group, particularly a small child, to go missing, or for personal belongings to be lost or stolen. Discuss how you would resolve the problems listed below and the specific factors you would need to consider in each situation.

■ A six-year-old child has gone missing in a large shopping complex. There are six entrances. The child was last seen outside McDonald's.

■ A teenage son has not met up with his parents as arranged, at the car park of a theme park.

■ A man has been separated from his wife at an airport. His wife has a hearing impairment and he is concerned that she may not have heard the call for their flight.

■ A married American couple in their forties have arrived at Heathrow after a 12-hour flight from Los Angeles but their luggage has been lost en route.

ACTIVITY

Resort representatives

Resort representatives give out a lot of general information at the standard welcome party that is usually held on holidaymakers' first day and throughout the holiday they are available to answer questions and deal with any problems.

As a group, brainstorm a list of problems that you think resort reps are frequently asked to deal with.

ACTIVITY

Customer role play situations

1 Flight attendant

A passenger has already had several drinks from the in-flight bar and is becoming aggressive. He has asked for another glass of wine, which you have refused. For the last five minutes he has repeatedly pressed the call button and shouted at passing flight attendants to get him a drink.

2 Tourist information clerk

An Italian visitor to the area wants a double bedroom with en-suite bathroom for two nights. You have managed to make him a reservation at the St Mark's hotel. He does not speak much English.

3 Travel consultant

A customer would like to visit one of the Greek islands. Her preference is for one that is not too overdeveloped but which has a good range of sights. She is in a wheelchair, so requires a destination that is easily accessible with no steep hills or steps.

4 Hotel receptionist

A hotel guest has just returned to his room and found that his wallet has disappeared. He claims to have left it on the dressing table and is sure that he locked the bedroom door as he left. The only other people with a key to the room are the housekeeping staff and the duty manager.

5 Ride operator

A customer and her two children have been queuing for the Log Flume for 45 minutes. Just as she gets near the front of the queue the maintenance engineer decides that the ride has to be temporarily closed down due to a suspected fault.

6 Travel consultant

A customer is booking a flight to America for himself and his family. His youngest child is 18 months and therefore entitled to a free flight, but will have to sit on a parent's lap. The customer is concerned about the safety of such an arrangement.

7 Conference centre receptionist

A new customer telephones to speak to a delegate attending a conference at the centre. You must make a public address announcement. The delegate does not respond to this, so you must take a message to pass on.

8 Train hostess/host

An elderly passenger would like to sit near the toilets as she has difficulty moving around. The train is very busy and there are no vacant seats in the area that she would like. She did not know that she could have reserved a specific seat in advance.

9 Stately home souvenir shop sales assistant

A customer has returned with a recently bought video of the stately home. There is nothing wrong with it, but he is disappointed that the video only features the house interior and not the grounds. He says this should have been made clear in the description.

10 Fast food assistant

Lucy is having her sixth birthday party at your fast food restaurant. She and her ten friends have finished their meal and become bored. They have started running around the restaurant, disturbing other customers. The manager has asked you to quickly think of an activity that will keep them occupied (and relatively quiet!).

11 Currency exchange assistant

A Swedish visitor would like to exchange some traveller's cheques for English sterling. She has cheques to the value of 1,500 Krona. The currency exchange charges 1 per cent commission for all transactions. The customer would also like a receipt.

12 Hotel night porter

A guest rings down in the middle of the night and asks for some indigestion tablets, claiming that the fish he had in the restaurant has made him ill. It is against company policy to give guests any form of medication. There are no all-night chemists locally.

13 Resort representative

A customer has booked herself and her sister on a day's excursion to some local vineyards. On the day the sister is unwell and both customers want a full refund. The booking form states clearly that no refunds will be given if cancellations occur less than 24 hours before the excursion.

14 Airline check-in clerk

A passenger and her family have arrived to check-in for their holiday flight to Malaga. Unfortunately, they did not realise that their 14-month-old baby needed a passport.

BUILD YOUR LEARNING

End of section activity

For this activity you should select at least four of the situations outlined on p. 365 and role play them in front of the rest of the group. Evaluate your performance with the help of the group and make recommendations about how you could improve your customer service skills in the future. You may wish to record your role plays on a form such as the one on p. 472.

Keywords and phrases

You should know the meaning of the words and phrases listed below. If you are unsure about any of them, go back through the last 15 pages to refresh your understanding.

- Body language
- Customer records
- Dealing with customers' problems
- Face-to-face communication
- Giving customers advice
- Keeping records
- Non-verbal communication
- Product information
- Providing assistance
- Providing information
- Smiling
- Taking and relaying messages
- Telephone communication
- Verbal communication
- Written communication

Handling complaints

STRANGE AS IT MAY SEEM, dealing with customers' complaints is also a part of providing excellent customer service. This is because if a complaint is handled well, a good relationship can be established and the customer may well return in future.

Handling complaints

Research into customer complaints reveals some interesting facts:

- happy customers tell about four other people about the good service that they receive

- dissatisfied customers tell at least 15 people about the bad service they receive

- 94 per cent of customers do not complain, they simply walk away and don't come back

- most organisations lose between 45-50 per cent of their customers every five years through complaints

- replacing lost customers costs a company five times more than keeping them.

If you still need convincing about the huge benefits of **effective complaint handling**, consider the following observation from the Strategic Planning Institute:

Those companies which actively encourage customers to complain can increase customer retention by 10 per cent. Actually responding to that complaint can boost retention by up to 75 per cent. And if the customer is very satisfied, retention increases to 95 per cent.

What this means is that staff need not only to know how to deal effectively with complaints, but also actively to encourage their customers to voice any complaints.

Most organisations have a **complaints procedure** which staff must follow when dealing with customer complaints. This procedure is usually described in the organisation's customer charter. Figure 5.14 shows an extract from the customer charter issued by Newcastle City Council and outlines what action the council will take when dealing with complaints.

Figure 5.14: Newcastle's complaints policy

We will:

- always treat you fairly and with respect
- always offer a friendly and polite service
- see you promptly when you visit our offices
- answer your letters and phone calls promptly
- listen to you and be sensitive to your needs
- do our best to help you and let you know how quickly we can act
- provide easy-to-understand, useful, information
- keep you informed about services we provide
- deal with your comments and complaints positively and quickly
- respect your confidentiality
- make sure our staff have the skills they need to do their jobs properly and considerately
- listen to and consult you as our customers, and be prepared to change our policies and practices whenever possible

Complaints

- we recognise that things can go wrong and that
- we can only put them right if customers complain – so we treat every complaint as an opportunity to improve our service
- we will try to deal with any complaints about our service informally, quickly and through the most suitable person
- you have the right to complain formally if you are not satisfied with the service you have received
- we will investigate your complaint fully, and you will receive a full reply or a progress update in writing within 15 working days of us receiving your complaint
- you can get copies of our complaints procedure from all our offices and receptions

Effective complaint handling

No one likes dealing with customer complaints because it usually suggests that you or a colleague have not done your job properly. In fact, research carried out by the English Tourism Council shows that the top four most common reasons for complaints in the travel and tourism industry are:

- poor service
- delays
- incorrect information
- standards not meeting customers' expectations.

Even when a complaint is about something which is totally out of your control, you may still feel concerned that the customer is disappointed. Sometimes customers may behave angrily or directly criticise you. They may even shout at you. The ability to deal with situations like this is all part of good customer service, although on the first few occasions that you receive complaints you may find them difficult to handle.

The following measures provide some useful tips when handling complaints.

- Listen carefully to the customer.
- Apologise in general terms for any inconvenience caused.
- Let the customer know that the matter will be fully investigated and put right.
- Try to see the problem from the customer's point of view.
- Keep calm and don't argue with the customer.
- Find a solution to the problem or refer the issue to a supervisor.
- Agree the solution with the customer.
- Take action and make sure that what you promised to do gets done.
- Make sure that you record details of the complaint and the actions taken.

Types of complainer

The English Tourism Council's Welcome Host programme identifies four different types of complainant, each of which need handling in a slightly different way:

Aggressive complainers

Aggressive complainers are likely to be angry and to raise their voice and shout at you. Often there will be a very good reason for their anger. The worst approach to the aggressive complainer is to shout back or interrupt,

as this simply makes them angrier. Allowing them to let off steam is the best solution, as they soon calm down if you remain calm and in control. It also helps to suggest that you discuss the complaint in a private area. Apart from preventing other customers from hearing all of the details, you will also find that an aggressive complainer often calms down more quickly if there is no audience.

Once aggressive complainers have calmed down you are then in a position to identify exactly what they are dissatisfied with and to find a solution. Needless to say, if this type of customer is physically aggressive or abusive you would not be expected to deal with the situation on your own and should call for assistance from a supervisor at once.

Passive complainers

Passive complainers are by far the most common. They will often not tell a member of staff about their complaint but simply leave dissatisfied. A typical passive complainer's conversation might go something like:

'Is your meal all right, mother?'

'Not really. I asked for the steak well done and it's still raw in the middle.'

'Why don't you tell that nice waitress? I'm sure that she would get it changed for you.'

'No I don't want to cause a fuss and anyway she is so busy.'

The obvious way that this complaint could have been identified and solved would have been for the waitress to check that the customers were enjoying their meal. Customers must be observed to see whether they appear satisfied with the product or service that they are using; you can usually tell by customers' body language when they are not happy.

Passive complainers often need coaxing to actually voice their complaint and should be made to feel comfortable about the situation rather than a nuisance.

Waiter! Might I suggest that the chef cooks the calamari just a teensy bit longer?

Constructive complainers

Constructive complainers often raise general issues that will be of concern to other customers. Their main reason for complaining is because they want some action taken and they often offer constructive advice on what they think you should do. A typical complaint from a constructive complainer might be:

'Excuse me, I've just used your ladies toilet and it's in a terrible state. Someone's left the taps running and thrown toilet paper all over the floor. You might like to get someone to clear it up before you get any complaints'.

...left our wallet in the hotel room again, sir?

Professional complainers

Unfortunately, not all complaints are genuine. There is a small group of people (**professional complainers**) who complain because they hope to get something free in return. This situation has arisen largely because organisations are becoming very good at dealing with complaints and are keen to ensure that customers leave totally satisfied. Therefore, the customer who has not been charged for his meal on one occasion after complaining might be tempted to see if he can do it again in another restaurant! However, you should always assume that a complaint is genuine and listen carefully to the details before jumping to conclusions.

Dealing with complaints

We have looked at the general guidelines to dealing with complaints in face-to-face situations and some of the specific types of complainers that you may encounter. Two further methods of dealing with complaints are over the telephone and in writing.

Both or either of these methods may be necessary when:

- following up a face-to-face complaint that could not be resolved at the time
- responding to a telephone complaint
- responding to a written letter of complaint.

The decision about which method is preferable depends on the situation. The Strategic Planning Institute found that 95 per cent of customers prefer a letter to a phone call when you are dealing with their complaints. This is because a letter is more personal, it demonstrates a greater commitment by the company and its tangibility suggests that the complaint has been taken seriously and is concrete evidence that something is being done.

However, there are some situations in which a phone call is the most appropriate first method of contact. The great advantage of telephoning a complainer is that it is immediate and ensures that the customer knows that you are taking the complaint seriously. Many travel and tourism organisations have a policy of phoning customers as soon as they receive a complaint letter to confirm that something is being done and of following it up with a letter outlining the action that has been taken.

The benefit of responding to a complaint in writing is that considerable thought can be given to the planning and content of the letter to make sure that it is absolutely right. However, even then some organisations do not seem to get it quite right – as the next activity demonstrates.

ACTIVITY

Handling complaints

The letter below shows the genuine response that a theme park sent to a tutor who wrote complaining about the poor customer service that she and her group of students had experienced on a visit to the park.

Read the letter carefully and discuss the following points.

1 Do you think that it is adequate simply to 'duly note' the complainant's comments?

2 Is it justifiable to argue that it easier to provide good customer service at a smaller tourist attraction because staff morale is higher and staff turnover lower?

3 To what extent is it helpful to suggest that a complainant is being hypercritical because she was part of a leisure and tourism group?

4 Is it acceptable to suggest that because the complainant received a group discount on the admission price she should be grateful for the value for money? (The implication is that she should therefore not complain about poor customer service!)

5 To what extent do you think the complainant shares the theme park manager's confidence that a return visit will more than match her expectations?

Based on your discussion of the five points above, rewrite the letter to make it more effective.

Dear....

I am in receipt of your letter regarding your group's visit to .... Your comments concerning employee apathy and sullenness have been duly noted. I concede that it is sometimes difficult to keep young, part-time staff motivated, however, we have had much success with improved induction courses and staff training. On the whole, feedback concerning staff has been generally good this season.

The comparison which you have used between our operation and other operations in the region has also been noted. I have to say that I find this comparison unrealistic. There is no other leisure facility in the region which is remotely close to the magnitude of [.....]. Running a small concern and keeping staff morale high and staff turnover low is relatively non-complex. The situation becomes more obtuse when an operation grows to become one of the most visited theme parks in the country and attracts in excess of one million visitors per annum. Perhaps being part of a leisure and tourism trip has made you hypercritical. If you were part of a prepaid group you would have enjoyed all of our facilities for £6.50 each. Perhaps the many positives such as the aforementioned value for money should be remembered as well as the negatives.

Please be assured that much effort and resources has been allocated towards improving staff training and in particular customer service. The impression of our staff which you have been left with is by no means our normal operating standard. I am confident that if you make a return trip to ...... our operation will more than match your expectations.

Regards

General manager

Deciding on action

One difficulty that many staff have when dealing with complaints is deciding what action is most appropriate and whether or not they have the authority to take it! For example, a waitress in a new job may be unsure whether or not she is allowed to make a deduction from the bill of a customer who is dissatisfied with his meal. If you are ever unsure about the appropriate action you should always ask a supervisor for help.

The best course of action depends, of course, on the type of customer, the nature and importance of the complaint. It is very important to correctly identify what the customer would find acceptable or you may risk making him or her even more dissatisfied or even causing offence. For example, constructive complainers are usually be satisfied if they know that their complaint has been taken seriously and that something will be done about it. Offering constructive complainers their money back may be totally inappropriate and give the impression that you are trying to get rid of a difficult customer with a bribe.

In many complaint situations customers are given some form of compensation, such as a refund or a complimentary product. The scale of the compensation should reflect the severity of the complaint. For example, passengers whose flight had been delayed for an hour on the runway may be given a complimentary drink but would not expect to have their fare refunded in full. On the other hand, customers whose meal has been ruined by slow service and the wrong order may receive an invitation to return for a complimentary meal at a later date.

There are great advantages to providing compensation in the form of a free return visit, since it ensures that the customer will come back and gives the organisation the opportunity to show that it can get it right. Many travel and tourism organisations use this approach when dealing with customer complaints. For example, Great North Eastern Railways issues travel vouchers to customers who complain about train service delays.

It is often more difficult to decide on an appropriate level of compensation for complex products such as a package holidays where only one element has given rise to dissatisfaction. For example, a holidaymaker may have enjoyed his holiday but complains that the hotel swimming pool was closed. If the provision of a pool was one of the main reasons why the customer chose the holiday this would need to be considered when deciding on a suitable level of compensation.

ACTIVITY

Identifying appropriate action

Read the following case study about a holiday to Egypt and, as a group, identify the key issues of complaint. Discuss what you think the rep should have done about each and identify which of the complaints could actually have been avoided if the rep had been more efficient. Finally, draft a letter from the tour operator to the customer in response to the complaints.

CASE STUDY

Tense times in Egypt

Kuoni coughs up when its reps fail to take charge during tension in Egypt

When Hilary Francis and her daughter Carla booked a 14-night Kuoni package to Egypt, they were looking forward to an exotic combination of sightseeing, cruising, relaxing and snorkelling at a Red Sea resort. The total cost of the holiday was £1,950. This charge included one night in Luxor, a seven-night cruise, four nights in Hurghada, and two nights in Cairo.

The day before Hilary and Carla were due to leave the cruise ship, 58 tourists were massacred at Luxor. When they arrived in Hurghada, their room at the Three Corners Village Hotel turned out to be shabby and smelling of sewage, and had a shower that flooded the bathroom every time it was used. More worryingly, the Kuoni rep who met Hilary and Carla at the hotel the day after their arrival was unable to brief them about possible repatriation and said that the holiday was to continue as planned. They later discovered that Kuoni guests in other Red Sea resorts were being given the option to fly home.

Concerned about the tense situation, Hilary repeatedly tried to contact the rep to ascertain the current position, without success. When the rep eventually came to the hotel, Hilary and Carla, trying to make the best of their holiday, booked an excursion to a local island for snorkelling. But, although they waited at their hotel for an additional 45 minutes after the scheduled collection time, no transportation arrived.

The rep telephoned the hotel later to say that the bus driver had forgotten to collect them. He promised to come to the hotel during the day to refund the money, eventually arriving at 9.30 p.m., when he confirmed that they would be collected at 7.30 a.m. the next morning to be taken to the airport for their transfer to Cairo. On arrival at reception in the morning, they discovered that no transport had been arranged and that the rep was nowhere to be found.

With little alternative, Hilary asked the hotel to call them a street taxi. This arrived in a dreadful condition and was filthy both inside and out. As two women journeying alone, they were understandably terrified about travelling unaccompanied in an unapproved vehicle, especially in light of the recent Luxor shootings.

Back in the UK, Kuoni responded to their catalogue of complaints with a basket of flowers and an offer of £100 (later increased to £200) in compensation.

Source: *Which?* on-line

Despite the cautionary tale in the case study, most travel and tourism organisations are highly efficient at dealing with customer complaints as the example in the webstract shows.

WEBSTRACT

BA's Executive Solution

Mr Ellum wrote to British Airways (BA) Executive Club after encountering a few problems during a trip to Tunis last year. His traveller's cheques, which he had ordered through BA, were not ready at the airport, so he had to wait for them. He had asked if he could pay by credit card, but he wasn't told there would be a surcharge of £7.61. Once on the plane, Mr Ellum found that there were only one-litre bottles of gin available, which cost more than double the price of the 500 cl bottles advertised in the in-flight magazine.

On his return, Mr Ellum wrote to BA. In its reply, BA explained why the problems occurred and sent a cheque for £16 to cover out-of-pocket expenses. Later, it sent him three bottles of wine. He was delighted with BA's response.

Source: *Which?* on-line

BUILD YOUR LEARNING

1 Think of a realistic complaint that a package holidaymaker might have whose accommodation is not up to the standard described in the brochure. For example, it might be unclean, the fixtures and fittings might be poor, it may be noisy or overlook a building site. Try to select several grounds for complaint rather than just one.

2 Write a letter to the tour operator outlining your main areas of complaint.

3 Working with other members of the group, role play the following situations, with everyone taking a turn as both the complainant and the member of staff for each situation.

- The customer outlines the complaint to the resort representative. The resort representative should take steps to solve the problems.

- A telephone call between the customer and the travel agent after the customer's return from the holiday. The customer should outline the complaint and allow the travel agent to deal with it.

- Give your letter to someone else in the group who should write a response on behalf of the tour operator.

After all three role plays, identify how effective the member of staff was in handling the complaint and suggest ways in which his or her complaint handling skills could be improved.

Keywords and phrases

You should know the meaning of the words and phrases listed below. If you are unsure about any of them, go back through the last five pages to refresh your understanding.

- Aggressive complainer
- Complaint handling
- Complaints procedure
- Constructive complainer
- Customer viewpoint
- Dealing with complaints
- Passive complainer
- Professional complainer

Assessing the quality of customer service

FOR MOST TRAVEL AND TOURISM organisations, training staff to provide excellent customer service is not the end of the process. The organisation also continuously monitors, assesses and evaluates its levels of customer service to ensure that it is meeting and, hopefully, exceeding its customers' needs and expectations. If the evaluation identifies areas where service is not meeting customers' expectations, it gives the organisation the opportunity to make any changes that are necessary.

Benchmarking

Many travel and tourism organisations use a system of monitoring and evaluation known as **benchmarking**. This involves setting **quality criteria** or **standards** and then measuring the organisation's performance against those standards. For example, a fast food take-away may set as a benchmark that all customers will be served within four minutes. Sometimes the benchmarks are set according to standards offered by competitors. Rank Xerox defines benchmarking as:

> *The continuous measuring of products, services and practices against the toughest competition of those recognised as leaders.*

Increasingly, many tourist destinations are using benchmarking to ensure that the products and services they provide meet or exceed the quality standards of other, similar, destinations. This system is known as destination benchmarking, and the case study below outlines how the regional tourist boards initiated such a scheme in 1998.

CASE STUDY

Destination benchmarking

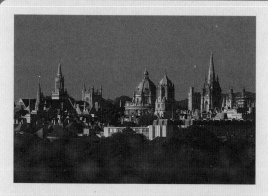

The regional tourist boards introduced pilot destination benchmarking in 1998. The aim is to allow tourist destinations to identify aspects of their products and services that are under-performing in comparison with competitor destinations and therefore do something about it. The initial stage was to interview a large sample of visitors in a range of destinations to identify which factors were important in the visitor experience. Fourteen destinations in three separate types of destination were selected for the research.

- Historic towns (Chester, Oxford, Salisbury and Winchester).

- Seaside resorts (Blackpool, Redcar, Scarborough and Southport).

- Cities/large towns (Bolton, Darlington, Leeds, Liverpool, Manchester, Portsmouth).

The research identified a range of factors that were seen as an important part of the visitor experience. There was some difference in the priority of these factors from one destination to another, as can be seen in the Bournemouth example opposite.

Once these factors have been identified they become benchmarks for all destinations. Subsequent destination surveys asking visitors to rate their level of satisfaction can then be measured against the average national satisfaction ratings or compared to the ratings in similar types of destinations such as seaside resorts, historic cities, or cities and large towns, as can be seen in the charts opposite.

Alternatively, individual destinations can use the results of surveys to compare their performance with past years to measure where improvements have or have not been made.

Source: *Insights* magazine

Top 10 Satisfaction Factors

All destinations	Bournemouth
1 Cleanliness of streets	1 Availability of public toilets
2 General appearance	2 Cleanliness of beach/sea
3 Range of places to visit	3 Range of places to visit
4 Range of shops	4 Cleanliness of public toilets
5 Ease of finding car parking	5 Cleanliness of streets
6 Cleanliness of toilets	6 General appearance
7 Range of places to eat and drink	7 Range of places to eat and drink
8 Availability of toilets	8 Feeling of welcome
9 Feeling of welcome	9 Range of shops
10 Quality of shopping environment	10 Availability of public seating

Key
- Anytown
- Large towns/cities (ave.)
- All destinations (ave.)

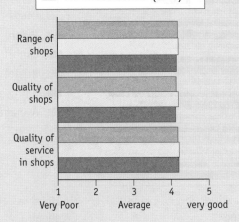

Source: ETB Insights

Key
- Anytown
- Historic cities (ave.)
- All destinations (ave.)

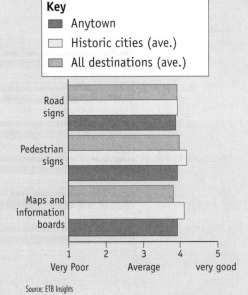

Source: ETB Insights

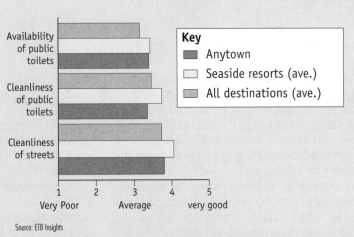

Key
- Anytown
- Seaside resorts (ave.)
- All destinations (ave.)

Source: ETB Insights

ACTIVITY

Benchmarking

Crescent Hotels owns 45 hotels throughout England and Wales. In 1999, the company introduced a benchmarking system to enable each hotel to measure its performance against other hotels in the company and identify where improvements need to be made. The system involves sending postal questionnaires to samples of customers from each hotel and asking them to rate a range of factors on a scale of 0 (poor) to 10 (excellent). The results from six of the hotels, plus the average rating for all 45 hotels are shown in the chart below.

Imagine that you work in the company's customer service department at head office. Your manager has asked you to write a brief report outlining the hotels and specific areas that need immediate attention.

For example, the hotel in Oxford appears to have a serious problem with its reservations system that needs addressing. Your report could take the following structure.

- Introduction explaining what is included in the report and its purpose.

- Main areas of concern, listing the hotels involved and the issues specific to each.

- Examples of good practice, again listing the hotels that scored highly in specific areas.

- Conclusion. Summarising the main issues that generally scored badly or scored highly throughout the company.

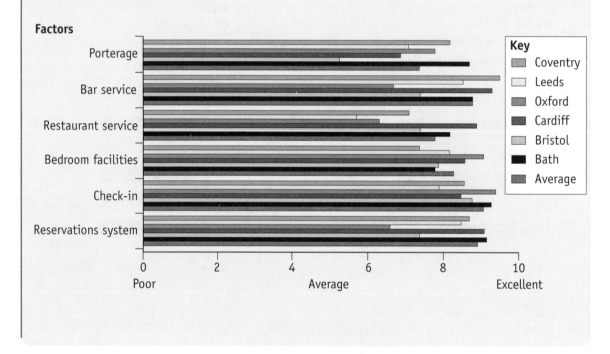

Different travel and tourism organisations identify different quality criteria that are important for their particular products and services. For example, providing personal attention to individual needs would be one of the main criteria for a private health spa, whereas providing value for money to groups may be one of the main criteria for a theme park.

Many travel and tourism organisations partly rely on evaluating and monitoring the quality of their customer service by using quality criteria identified by independent organisations. In the last activity we looked at the way the Crescent Hotel group used its own

internal benchmarking system to evaluate customer satisfaction. However, smaller hotel companies often do not have the resources to carry out this type of large-scale evaluation and may rely on organisations such as the AA, RAC, English Tourism Council (ETC), Egon Ronay and Relais Routiers to help them evaluate the service that they offer.

For example, the AA introduced the first hotel rating scheme, based on stars, in 1906. This was followed a considerable time later by the English Tourist Board's Roses scheme in 1974 and Crown scheme in 1987. In 1998 the ETC joined forces with the AA and RAC to develop a single rating system based on Diamond and Star signs which was introduced nationally in England in 1999. The new scheme rates hotels on a 1–5 star rating (Diamonds are used for guest accommodation such as bed and breakfast houses) based on 71 individual quality criteria which cover all aspects of guests' experience.

Before deciding on suitable criteria for the scheme, extensive research was carried out by a number of independent research organisations including MVA. MVA's research in 1995 indicated that hotel guests had clear ideas of what was important to them when staying in an hotel. The top criteria are shown in Figure 5.15.

The first stage in using a benchmarking system is to identify the most important aspects of service delivery.

ACTIVITY

Rating scheme for accommodation

Identify which of the criteria on the list in Figure 5.15 are directly related to customer service delivery. Give five examples for each, showing how a hotel could ensure that it achieved a high rating.

These will vary depending on the organisation and the nature of the product and service being offered. Figure 5.16 shows the eight quality criteria that can be applied to many travel and tourism facilities, products and services.

Figure 5.15: Essential features in hotel accommodation

Category	
Staff attentive and efficient	78
High standards of cleanliness throughout	76
High quality and well maintained bathroom/and fittings	65
High quality bed, mattress, linen	63
Quiet bedroom, no disturbance	63
Attractive and pleasant bedroom to be in	63
Lighting in room and at bedside, good enough to read by	63
Well furnished bedroom, mirrors, chairs etc.	63
Efficient and easy booking service	61
Well regulated temperature and atmosphere	60
Prompt and efficient check-in/out	60

Source: MVA 1995

Figure 5.16: Quality criteria

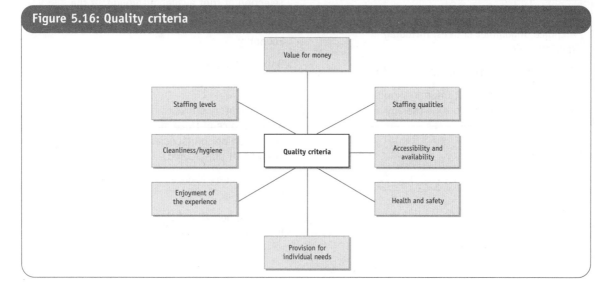

Value for money

Most customers have clear expectations about what they must pay for a particular service and will be dissatisfied if the price charged does not meet their expectations by providing value for money. This means that organisations need to be fully aware of customers' expectations of price and set standards that meet these expectations. For example, if a theme park increased its entrance price from £12.50 to £25, it is likely that past customers would feel cheated by the unexplained rise.

The concept of **value for money** is closely related to price but also involves other quality criteria. Value for money does not mean cheap but rather that the customer is satisfied that the service provided is worth the money that is paid for it. Many people are willing to pay considerably more for a first-class train seat

ACTIVITY

Value for money

Many travel and tourism providers offer a different range of prices for their products and services. For example, transport providers offer different fare categories to distinguish between the level of service that the customer can expect. It is important that customers appreciate exactly what is included so that they understand how the prices charged represent value for money and can make an informed choice about the level of service they want. Look at the three classes of air travel provided by Virgin Airways below and identify the main differences between each.

Virgin Atlantic Upper Class

Onboard facilities

Pre take-off champagne, bucks fizz or fruit juice.

Reclining first class sleeper seat with up to 60" seat pitch, giving 10–20 per cent more legroom than leading competitors.

Cabin crew to passenger ratio of 1:7.

Sleeper service on all night flights, giving a comfortable duvet, pillow, snoozesuit, eyeshades and a darkened cabin with flexible meal options.

Upper Class comfort kit.

Onboard lounges and stand up bar (on most aircraft).

A choice of gourmet entrées, including speciality dishes.

Complimentary drinks throughout the flight.

Inflight beauty therapist offering shoulder, neck and scalp massage, hand zone therapy and manicures on most flights.

Premium Economy

Onboard facilities

Once on board, enjoy a separate cabin where you'll be welcomed with complimentary pre take-off drinks, including champagne, and newspapers.

Priority meal and duty free service is offered to all Premium Economy passengers.

Stretch out and relax in a larger seat with 38" seat pitch, leg rests and adjustable headrest. It's the perfect way to enjoy our award winning inflight entertainment system.

Enjoy the benefits of cleaner, fresher, smoke-free flights on all routes.

Selection of fruit available throughout the flight.

Economy

Onboard facilities

Comfortable seats.

Complimentary drinks throughout the flight with a choice of three meals including a vegetarian option (special dietary meals available if pre-ordered).

Complimentary headset and comfort kit full of useful items.

Enjoy the benefits of cleaner, fresher, smoke-free flights on all flights.

because of the increased levels of service offered; these customers feel that they are getting good value for money.

In understanding value for money, it is important to understand why the customer feels that the product or service is good value. A guest staying at the Savoy Hotel in London may pay several hundred pounds but feel that it is value for money because of the high quality service. Those setting standards in such a situation need to identify exactly what aspects of the service contributed towards the guest's impression that he or she is getting value for money.

Consistency and accuracy

Consistency is concerned with ensuring that customers always receive the same level of service so that they are not disappointed that it does not meet their expectations. Accuracy means that the customer is given correct information about the products and services offered. So, for example, customers want accurate information on train timetables, with the trains departing at the published time. They also expect the service to be consistent, providing clean and comfortable carriages, friendly and knowledgeable staff and an efficient buffet service.

Reliability

Reliability is perhaps one of the most important quality criteria, because it influences all of the others. Reliability means that customers can rely on the service being the same every time they use it. Therefore they can be confident that it will provide value for money, be enjoyable and ensure excellent staffing levels. For example, customers who use the same tour operator every year probably do so because they know that they can rely on the organisation to maintain past standards of service. This might include:

- the accuracy of brochure descriptions
- the friendliness and efficiency of staff
- the value for money
- the pre-holiday information
- the quality of in-flight service.

For transport passengers, a key issue in reliability is the punctuality of services. Poor punctuality can often ruin the entire experience for customers, no matter how good other aspects of the service or product are.

CASE STUDY

Coach Marque

There are a large number of professional organisations that allow membership on condition that organisations meet and maintain quality criteria. This membership can then be used to reassure customers of the consistency of their service. Coach Marque was launched in 1999 and provides reassurance to passengers that coach companies bearing the marque conform to a set of quality standards.

What does Coach Marque mean?

This sign displayed on the side of a vehicle means that the coach company has been awarded the Coach Marque status by passing a series of qualification standards:

- seat-belts on all vehicles
- high standards of customer service
- 75% of the coach fleet under 10 years old
- approved high-quality staff and driver training programmes
- an annual assessment of standards
- full compliance with financial protection legislation
- a commitment to focus on high levels of passenger safety and comfort
- an efficient complaints procedure.

ACTIVITY

However hard airlines try to improve the punctuality of their flights there are inevitably times when flights are delayed due to unforeseen circumstances such as poor weather or aircraft faults.

Look at the five different passengers below, all of whom have had their flight delayed.

- An unaccompanied child of 11 years travelling home to Athens for the holidays from her English boarding school.

- A businesswoman travelling to Brussels for the day for a conference.

- A couple going on a two-week holiday to Hong Kong for their silver wedding anniversary.

- An elderly lady travelling by plane for the first time to Sydney, Australia, to visit her sister.

- A businessman flying to Paris to catch a connecting flight to Washington.

In each case, discuss why you think the customer will be particularly dissatisfied at a delay to their service and suggest what the service quality criteria might be.

Pushing airline punctuality to record levels

British Airways is seeing great results from its ongoing punctuality push, with record levels of on-time departures being achieved.

British Airways is beating its competitors in getting flights away from London on time on 80 per cent of its routes.

Mike Street, British Airways' Director of Customer Service and Operations, said: 'Getting flights away on time is a vital part of our customer service. The latest results are encouraging, but we aim to continue to improve our punctuality levels to be the most punctual airline in Europe.

'We have introduced a whole range of initiatives in the past year to help achieve this, both "behind the scenes" and involving our customers.'

Departures gates are being closed ten minutes before the flight is due to push back. This 'minus 10' approach will help ensure that passengers are safely seated and ready for take-off by the scheduled departure time, enabling crew to finish last minute preparations and push-back promptly.

This new policy has been tested at Heathrow and Gatwick since November 1998 and British Airways customer services staff have been communicating the new procedures to passengers and explaining that it has been introduced to help them get to their destinations on time.

Other customer initiatives include the introduction of easy-to-read boarding passes which highlight the departure gate and the time that the gate will close. In addition customer service staff are now weighing all hand baggage at check-in to reduce the number of passengers stopped at the gate with excessive carry-on bags, which then need to be tagged and placed in the hold – a process that can further delay departure.

Public Relations Archive,
27 January 1999

Staffing

In any service industry, wages are one of the most expensive overheads because a high level of staffing is required to deliver the service. Because staffing is so costly, organisations tread a fine line between providing the right **staffing levels** to deliver the service and overstaffing a facility and therefore reducing profits.

This balance is often made more difficult to achieve by the fact that it may be impossible to predict the number of customers on some occasions. For example, a coach party arriving unannounced at a motorway service station at 2 a.m. will probably find that there are not enough staff to serve them quickly.

In setting standards for staffing levels, organisations must identify as best they can the number and type of staff required to deliver the service. They adopt different staffing levels for different times of the day, week or year, where they can predict variation in the level of demand.

Staffing levels are often linked to health and safety standards. For example, a hotel swimming pool must have a minimum ratio of lifeguards to swimmers to ensure safety at all times.

Setting staffing levels is not just a matter of determining the number of staff needed to provide the speed of service required. It also involves the types of service that are offered. An organisation may find that

ACTIVITY

Staffing levels and qualities

The owner of a children's museum has received the letter of complaint below.

1 Identify the different ways that the staffing levels and staff qualities were inadequate.

2 Suggest what the manager should do to ensure a similar situation does not arise in the future.

Dear Sir/Madam

Last Saturday I brought a group of 25 scouts to your museum for the day and feel that you should be aware of some of the problems that we experienced. I had telephoned the previous month to establish whether the museum was suitable for boys aged nine to 15 years old. I was told that it was suitable. However, the exhibits and activities were largely geared towards younger children and the older boys quickly became bored.

When we arrived there was already a long queue at the ticket office because there was only one member of staff on duty and, having waited for 30 minutes, I was told that I should have gone to an alternative entrance for group arrivals. Her manner was offhand and discourteous. However, she agreed that the system was poor and said that she had been complaining about it to the management for the last three months.

When we finally got into the museum, I asked about disabled toilet facilities as one of the boys uses a wheelchair. The member of staff was very polite but said that the disabled toilet was locked and had to be opened by the duty manager. He promised to find the key but did not return until 25 minutes later. Apparently the duty manager was now busy helping the girl at the ticket office! When we actually got into the toilet, it was filthy and had clearly not been cleaned for some time. The duty manager apologised for the state of the toilet but explained that the cleaner had not turned up for work that morning.

At lunchtime we visited the cafe and had an enjoyable lunch, although one of the boys was given change for a £5 note rather than the £10 that he had paid. The money was refunded, but the cashier insinuated that it was the boy's fault for not checking his change.

Finally, on leaving, I asked a member of staff for directions for the town centre. The member of staff was new to the area but suggested that I ask at the police station.

I am sorry to have to write this letter, as I feel that the facilities in the museum are first class and offer excellent value for money. However, I feel that you should be aware that your staff are frequently unable to provide an acceptable level of service.

Yours faithfully

R N Scales

---

its service levels vary greatly from one facility to another, and in many cases from one product to another.

A passenger travelling economy class on a plane receives standard check-in service, seats and in-flight meals, but a passenger travelling club class (or first class) receives a better level of service. This may include express check-in, use of the VIP's departure lounge, more extravagant in-flight meals and a higher ratio of flight attendants to passengers. Both situations reflect quality standards but have different service levels because of the needs and expectations of the customers.

In general terms (although there are exceptions) the more that a customer pays for a particular product or service the higher the service level is likely to be. In other words, the service is more personalised, with a higher staff to customer ratio.

The personal qualities of an organisation's staff is also an important quality criterion and it is important to identify the specific aspects of dress, personal hygiene, personality and attitude as well as skills needed by staff in a particular job. Of course, as we have said so often, this varies enormously according to the type of organisation and the actual job. Staff must be accessible to customers so that they can provide information, help and assistance, and all these staff qualities must be seen in the context of consistency and reliability.

Quality standards are only as good as the minimum that is offered. If a member of staff is usually friendly and welcoming but on a bad day is offhand and disinterested, then the bad day sets the standard. This is because the member of staff cannot guarantee to be friendly and welcoming on each and every occasion. When setting quality criteria for staff, it is vital that they will always be able to live up to the standard.

Enjoyment

The reasons why customers enjoy a particular travel and tourism experience is difficult to quantify. Some visitors to the Lake District may only enjoy their stay if the weather is good, the enjoyment of others may be unaffected by the weather. In fact, poor weather can have such a negative effect on many people's enjoyment of a holiday that a lot of tour operators include a question about the weather on their customer feedback forms. This is because bad weather often affect customers' perception of all aspects of their holiday and makes them more critical than they would have been if the weather had been good!

Obviously the weather is outside the control of travel and tourism providers, but there are other factors that affect enjoyment which can be controlled, and which can be assessed in terms of quality. The MGM cinema complex in York identifies many factors that affect its

customers' enjoyment. One factor is that customers like to sit with others in their group rather than being split up. Therefore one quality standard is that the maximum number of seats sold for any one performance in each of its screens is 40 less than the actual number of seats available. This gives the organisation the flexibility to move customers so that they can watch the film in the company of their group.

Sometimes people's enjoyment is derived because of the other people that they are with. For example, parents may take their children to the pantomime not so much because they enjoy it but because of the enjoyment that they get from seeing their children's pleasure. Their enjoyment will be increased by any aspects of the service that increases their children's enjoyment of the experience, such as imaginative merchandising and theatre staff taking the trouble to talk directly to the children.

ACTIVITY

Enjoyment

Consider the following types of customer taking package holidays.

- An elderly retired couple on their first UK coach holiday.

- A group of teenagers on a package holiday to Corfu.

- A couple with two young children on an all-inclusive holiday in Portugal.

- Two 30-year-old men on a week's skiing holiday in the Austrian Alps.

- A middle-aged couple on a Caribbean cruise, who have booked a luxury outside suite.

For each, discuss the specific quality criteria that would affect their enjoyment of the experience. For example, the elderly couple on the coach tour may require a very well organised itinerary, help with luggage and detailed information about travel and accommodation arrangements.

Health and safety

You need to understand that **health and safety** issues are one of the key concerns of all travel and tourism organisations. In fact, failure to comply with health and safety requirements can mean that an organisation is no longer allowed to operate.

Most health and safety standards are set by legal requirements. Health and safety regulations have a varying impact on travel and tourism organisations depending on the type of service and facility provided. For example, COSHH (Control of Substances Hazardous to Health) regulations have a greater significance for hotel swimming pools than for art galleries. However, all organisations must comply with the Health and Safety at Work Act, 1974 which covers four main areas:

- the health, safety and welfare of people at work
- the protection of outsiders from risks to health and safety
- the controlled storage and use of dangerous substances
- the controlled emission of noxious or offensive substances.

Apart from complying with legal requirements, many travel and tourism organisations also provide customers with general health and safety advice as part of their customer service standards. For example, tour operators know that the first few days of many customers' holidays are spoilt by spending too long in the sun and ending up with sunburn or even sunstroke. Therefore, many resort representatives give general advice about safety in the sun at the welcome party. The tour operator First Choice produces a detailed guide to health and safety for holidaymakers (see case study).

Because travel and tourism is an international industry, many providers have to consider the implications of health and safety in foreign countries. For example, in some countries child seats are not provided in rental cars, whereas in the UK they are standard. Similarly, regulations about lifts and balconies in hotels are considerably less strict outside the UK. Whilst tour operators are not always directly responsible if accidents occur due to these differences (although under new EU law they have additional legal responsibilities), most try to ensure that their customers are aware of the potential risks.

CASE STUDY

Health and safety guide for holidaymakers

Part of the fun of any holiday is experiencing different cultures and sampling a different way of life. This will almost certainly expose you to a different hygiene and safety regime than you are used to at home and this is why you need to exercise more care than usual. We want you to have a safe and enjoyable holiday, which is why we have published this health and safety information here.

Accommodation safety

If you have a gas cooker or oven in your accommodation, please ensure that it is always turned off properly. In most cases the gas will be supplied from a bottle located under the oven/burner. Please ensure this supply is turned off at the bottle when not in use. Water heaters should not be supplied by individual gas bottles.

Although all hotels and apartments should have safety stickers on windows and doors, few are equipped with toughened safety glass. Please take extra care when using these, as in bright sunlight it is not always obvious when windows and doors are open or closed. Not all guest lifts have the internal doors that provide protection from the lift wall when the lift is in motion. Please be extra careful when using this type of lift and stand well back from the door. Children should not use lifts unaccompanied.

Swimming pools

As only the largest hotels employ lifeguards, please find out the times (if any) that your pool is supervised, and follow all pool rules. Please do not use the pool after dark or after consuming alcohol. Never dive from the poolside into water less than 1.5 m deep, or where you see a No Diving sign. Do not dive or jump from any raised features around the pool such as decorative rocks, bridges and islands. Remember the pool at your accommodation may have a strange design, so familiarise yourself with its layout, including depths, slopes and children's areas before you or your children swim. As in the UK, children must never use the pool unless supervised by an adult, even if there is a lifeguard. Please do not run around the pool area as floors can be slippery and accidents could occur. Swim before drinking and eating, not after!

Beach safety

Check whether it's a recommended bathing beach and whether there are any hazards such as rocks, currents or tides. Make sure you know the meanings of any warning signs or flags. Check out whether there is lifeguard supervision and what you should do in case of an emergency.

Source: Air 2000 website

ACTIVITY

Health and safety

Another section of the First Choice health and safety booklet in the case study deals with children's safety. Can you suggest the key points that should be included?

Hygiene

Cleanliness and hygiene are often linked to health and safety criteria. For example, a chef would be expected to be clean and work hygienically anyway, but this is also a legal requirement under health and safety legislation.

As we discussed when looking at personal presentation, personal hygiene is a key factor in providing excellent customer service, because it shows that you take pride in yourself and your job and care about your customers. However, travel and tourism organisations also have quality criteria for the cleanliness and hygiene of the products that they offer and the environment in which they are delivered. For example, it is almost impossible to find a piece of litter

WEBSTRACT

Britain's beaches

One area where cleanliness is a key quality criterion is in coastal resorts where the cleanliness of the beaches and bathing water is regularly monitored and assessed.

The Environment Agency monitors the quality of bathing water in England and Wales between May and September. Twenty samples are taken at regular intervals throughout the season at each site, and the results are updated fortnightly on its website. Agency spokesman Rob Thomas, said: 'There have been major improvements at many beaches in recent years and in the last year alone, effective sewage treatment has been provided for the first time at such popular coastal resorts as Benllech, Colwyn Bay and Llandudno. We will be keeping a close eye on the results and investigating the reasons if any samples fail to meet EC standards. A number of other remedial schemes are now in areas such as Harlech and neighbouring Llandanwg and we are hoping to see improvements in water quality at all beaches.'

Source: www.environment-agency.gov.uk

at Disneyland, because the highly efficient staff remove all litter the minute it touches the ground!

Cleanliness and hygiene also extends to general tidiness of the working environment, such as ensuring that reception desks are uncluttered. Many organisations do not allow staff to have drinks or food in areas where they are dealing with customers because it can give an impression of lack of cleanliness.

Beaches that pass a range of tests can gain specific awards such as Blue Flag awards and seaside awards. Blue Flag awards are annual, pan-European awards given to beaches that meet the strictest guideline standard as well as various standards for beach management. Beaches which have won Seaside awards display yellow-and-blue flags. Beaches are classified as resort or rural beaches and have to meet the mandatory (minimum) water quality standard, as well as providing good safety measures and supervision. They must also practice good beach management, such as dog controls, and offer facilities for disabled visitors at resort beaches.

ACTIVITY

Britain's beaches

Select a coastal area in the UK. Investigate how many of the beaches in the area have been awarded a Blue Flag or Seaside award and find out why the area has gained the award.

Accessibility

Making it easy and straightforward for customers to buy a product or service is also an important quality criterion. An art gallery will quickly lose customers if it is not open (available) at the times specified and it will be inaccessible to some customers, if people in wheelchairs are unable to get through the turnstile. Accessibility can also be affected by the provision of car parking.

The timing of a service relates, in part, to availability. It focuses on offering the service at a time that the customer wants to buy it. The success of Sunday trading is an example of how a service has been made available to meet customer needs.

Some travel and tourism organisations offer different prices to increase availability. For example, a tourist attraction such as a theme park that offers an experience that usually lasts several hours may have a reduced admission charge in the late afternoon to encourage customers to experience part of the product or service.

Another factor that greatly affects the accessibility of a travel and tourism product or service is the process that the customer needs to go through to gain further information and actually buy it. The leaflet from the National Centre for Popular Music aims to increase its accessibility by giving a number of booking options, by highlighting how customers can get to the centre and by explaining how the specific needs of visitors can be met.

▲ Information made easy

Individual needs

One of the criticisms often directed at organisations that have well defined quality standards is that it makes the service too inflexible and unable to meet the individual needs of customers. One example is the customer asking for a hamburger without gherkins or mayonnaise and being told that it is not possible because all hamburgers have to be served with the standard garnishes. Fortunately, situations like this are becoming less common, as organisations realise that quality standards are only effective if they truly satisfy the needs of all customers.

In assessing the quality of customer service, therefore, the needs of individual customers must be considered. Often, this may be a matter of identifying the general needs of customers and then asking the question, 'But what if one customer wants something different?'

▲ Open-top bus tours often provide commentary in a variety of languages

For example, a company running open-top bus guided tours of an historic city may identify the general needs of customers as for friendly service, detailed and expert information, comfortable transport and value for money. But individual needs should also be identified, by asking such questions as, 'But what if the customer:

- cannot speak English?
- is elderly?
- is in a wheelchair?
- is a child?
- wants extra information?'

Feedback techniques

Once an organisation has identified the quality criteria on which it is going to monitor and evaluate its customer service it then needs to decide how to go about it. Organisations use a number of **feedback**

techniques to evaluate whether their customers are happy with the level of customer service. These are set out in Figure 5.17.

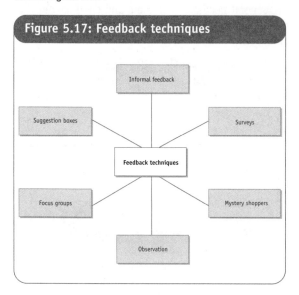

Figure 5.17: Feedback techniques

- Informal feedback
- Suggestion boxes
- Surveys
- Feedback techniques
- Focus groups
- Mystery shoppers
- Observation

Informal feedback

All staff in travel and tourism organisations receive **informal feedback** on a daily basis. They may overhear customers talking or customers may voice their opinions directly to staff. Alternatively, feedback may be from other staff, management or even people who are not customers but who voice an opinion about the products and services offered. For example, someone passing a tourist attraction may comment on how untidy the outside is looking and that the plants need watering.

This type of informal feedback is very important to organisations in helping them to monitor and evaluate the service that they offer. Many customers feel more comfortable making informal comments and may not have the time or inclination to complete formal questionnaires. Remember the passive complainers who are much more likely to make an informal comment than to put their complaints in writing.

Of course, informal feedback can also be positive and it is just as important to listen to this. Positive feedback tells an organisation what it is doing right and allows it to develop these areas to continue to satisfy customers needs and expectations.

All staff who work in travel and tourism organisations need to be receptive to informal feedback and ensure that it is relayed to the appropriate people so that action can be taken. Many organisations have mechanisms to ensure this, such as regular staff meetings where staff can report back on feedback that they may have received.

ACTIVITY

Informal feedback

Jo is a resort manager for a large tour operator in Gran Canaria. One of her responsibilities is to ensure high sales for excursions and her annual appraisal takes this into account. This season, sales have decreased and she is keen to identify the reasons and see if anything can be done. Therefore, she has decided to call a meeting of all of her resort representatives to discuss any ideas that they might have about the decline in interest in excursions. She has asked them to report on any informal feedback that they have received. The five resort reps profiled here attend the meeting.

As a group, take one of the roles each, including Jo, the resort manager. Role play the staff meeting and discuss all of the feedback that you have received and what you are going to do about it. You can repeat the role play if there are more of you in your group than there are roles.

Julie. She is the rep in a large hotel on the outskirts of the resort. One of the main complaints that she gets from her guests is that they are always the first hotel to be picked up by the coach and the last to be dropped off for excursions. This often means that they are on the coach for up to two hours longer than guests at other hotels. She has also had complaints about the fact that children over the age of 12 years have to pay the adult price for excursions, even though they receive a children's discount on the actual holiday up to the age of 16 years.

Robin. He is in a hotel and apartment complex that is used by three other large tour operators. He was speaking to some guests with a rival tour operator yesterday who were unhappy with their operator's excursions. The main complaint was that health and safety was poor, with overcrowded boats with no life jackets and poor standards of hygiene at the restaurants included in the price of excursions.

Dana. Her excursion sales have shown the biggest decline of all of the hotels. She claims that the manager at her hotel is advising guests to book with local excursion operators because it is much cheaper and they have the advantage of being taken by locals. Dana argues that they may be cheaper, but her company's excursions are better organised and the level of service is higher, with air-conditioned coaches and qualified tour guides.

Antonio. His excursion bookings are the only ones to have increased this season. His customers have said that although the trips may be more expensive, you get what you pay for. They are complimentary about the reps who accompany them on the trips and say that they are friendly and well organised.

Sandra. Excursion bookings have remained steady at Sandra's hotel, however, she has overheard some customers on excursions complaining about the inclusion of stops for sales pitches. This is when the excursion stops at souvenir factories and wine producers to allow customers to make purchases. Some of the more sceptical guests believe that this is because the reps get commission from the producers of these goods – a belief that is actually unfounded.

Surveys

Many travel and tourism organisations use **formal feedback** methods such as surveys and customer comment cards. If you have already studied the Chapter Four you will have a good understanding of how questionnaires are designed and used.

Some organisations use open questions that allow the customers to write their own opinions, such as the one in Figure 5.18 for Manchester Airport.

In the example in Figure 5.18, customers are not directed to comment on anything in particular but asked for their general comments and suggestions. This

Figure 5.18: Manchester Airport customer care questionnaire

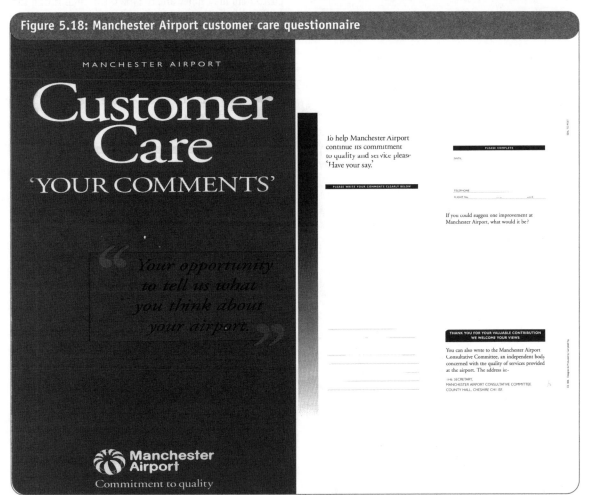

can be useful in ensuring that customers focus on what is really important to them rather than what the organisation feels is important. However, a disadvantage is that customers may not mention something that the organisation particularly wants to know about. For example, if no one mentions the disabled facilities, the airport has no way of identifying whether or not it is meeting customers' needs.

Some organisations are able to use more structured comment sheets yet still obtain useful information. Figure 5.19 shows the customer comment card used by Travelcare.

Figure 5.19: Travelcare customer comment card

YES   NO

1. WERE YOU ACKNOWLEDGED WITHIN A MINUTE OF ENTERING THE SHOP?

2. WERE YOU GREETED BY THE CONSULTANT IN A POLITE AND FRIENDLY MANNER?

3. DID THE CONSULTANT APPEAR INTERESTED IN YOUR ENQUIRY AND WAS HE/SHE POSITIVE IN HELPING YOU MAKE A DECISION?

4. DID YOU FEEL THAT WE PUT YOU FIRST?

5. WOULD YOU BOOK WITH CO-OP TRAVELCARE AGAIN?

WHY DID YOU BOOK WITH CO-OP TRAVELCARE?
_____
_____

HOW COULD WE IMPROVE OUR SERVICE:
_____
_____
_____

NAME
ADDRESS
     POSTCODE
TEL. NO.
YOUR CUSTOMER NUMBER IF KNOWN
NAME OF CONSULTANT
BRANCH VISITED

        T9

☐ If you would prefer not to receive details about the goods and services we offer, please tick this box.

The completion of this sheet could not be made easier for customers; they simply need to tick the appropriate facial expression for each quality criterion listed. There is also a space for customers to make specific recommendations on how the customer service could be improved.

ACTIVITY

Customer comment cards

Go back to the last activity about Jo and her resort representatives. Design a customer comment card to find out customers' opinions of the service offered on the company's excursions. You should bear in mind the results of your role play discussion.

Suggestion boxes

Some travel and tourism organisations provide suggestion boxes for their customers. As with informal feedback, these have the advantage that many customers may not want to spend the time filling in a lengthy questionnaire but would like to make a brief comment on the service that they have received.

One variation on the suggestion box concept is to have a visitor's book in which customers can write comments. Visitor's books are particularly popular at tourist attractions and signing them has become an enjoyable part of the experience for many visitors. For example, in the Anne Frank museum in Amsterdam, visitors queue, not only to write their own comments, but also to read the moving messages from visitors from around the world.

Focus groups

A **focus group** is a group of people brought together to discuss their opinions and feelings about a particular organisation, product, service or topic. As a form of feedback it has the great advantage that the information collected is very detailed, because customers can explain their feelings and opinions in depth. For example, a travel agency may hold a focus group discussion to identify how customers view the customer service that they got when choosing a package holiday.

Mystery shoppers

An increasingly common method of evaluating customer service is to employ a **mystery shopper**. This is someone employed by the organisation, but not known by the staff, who visits the facility as a customer and analyses the extent to which service levels meet quality criteria. The mystery customer usually has a checklist covering what needs to be looked at. For example, the rail company Connex South Central employed a mystery passenger to evaluate the extent to which train services meet the needs of customers in wheelchairs. The mystery passenger tested out both staff and facilities and found problems such as platforms being too low for someone in a wheelchair to disembark from a train.

ACTIVITY

Customer comment books

Pandora Holidays monitors and evaluates levels of satisfaction by asking holidaymakers to complete a questionnaire on their return flight. The annual results of customer satisfaction over the whole season indicate an unusually high level of dissatisfaction with the Las Palmas hotel in Magaluf during the first fortnight of August. Areas that scored particularly badly were:

- resort
- hotel accommodation
- hotel facilities
- resort representative.

The report has been sent to the resort manager who is surprised, as the Las Palmas is usually one of the most popular hotels. On looking in the customer comment book from the hotel she finds the following entries for the fortnight in question.

- Excellent accommodation, but very disappointed that the swimming pool was closed for five days. I cannot see why arrangements could not have been made for us to use the pool at the adjoining hotel.

- Too hot for us – but realise you cannot control the weather! Otherwise great holiday.

- Very good staff – the rep was great when a jellyfish stung our child – thanks! But why aren't there warnings when there are jellyfish in the sea?

- We really liked the hotel, friendly and helpful staff. Pity there were no fans for hire, the brochure said that they would be available. Drinks at the hotel bar very expensive.

- Trust us to come to Spain in the hottest week on record. But we'll come back again, in May next time!

- Brilliant holiday. Thanks for arranging the open-top jeep for us, it was a great way of seeing the countryside and cooling off.

- Very disappointed. Lack of swimming pool for five days meant children got bored and could not cool down. Next year it's Skegness.

Only seven of the 350 guests staying at the hotel with Pandora that fortnight actually made a comment in the visitor's book. However, if you were the resort manager could you identify why dissatisfaction was uncharacteristically high for this period?

CASE STUDY

Cadbury World

Cadbury World in Birmingham uses a range of feedback techniques to evaluate the level and quality of its customer service. In 1993 it introduced a mystery visitor survey which is now run annually. Each mystery visitor is provided with a checklist of points to assess, which include eye contact, smile and wearing of name badges.

Wearing name badges is particularly important, because it allows the organisation to identify which staff need further training in customer service skills.

The mystery visitor scheme is linked to the staff bonus scheme and has resulted in a dramatic improvement in standards. Each department is rated separately, using a points system, and there is healthy competition between departments to achieve the highest score. The mystery visitors usually call during peak times. Interestingly, though, scores tend to be higher at these times than when the attraction is quieter and staff are tempted to stand around and chat.

Source: *Insights* magazine

ACTIVITY

Mystery shopper

Imagine that you have been employed as a mystery visitor evaluating the customer service in souvenir shops. Design a checklist with a rating score and visit at least three shops to assess their customer service. For example:

Greeting: 1 (very poor) 2 (poor) 3 (adequate) 4 (good) 5 (excellent)

You could use a table such as the one shown below to record your findings. Compare your results with the rest of the group.

NAME OF ORGANISATION			
CRITERIA			
1. Greeting	Rating 1–2–3–4–5	Rating 1–2–3–4–5	Rating 1–2–3–4–5
2.	Rating 1–2–3–4–5	Rating 1–2–3–4–5	Rating 1–2–3–4–5
3.	Rating 1–2–3–4–5	Rating 1–2–3–4–5	Rating 1–2–3–4–5
4.	Rating 1–2–3–4–5	Rating 1–2–3–4–5	Rating 1–2–3–4–5
5.	Rating 1–2–3–4–5	Rating 1–2–3–4–5	Rating 1–2–3–4–5
6.	Rating 1–2–3–4–5	Rating 1–2–3–4–5	Rating 1–2–3–4–5
7.	Rating 1–2–3–4–5	Rating 1–2–3–4–5	Rating 1–2–3–4–5
General comments			

Observation

Observation is a research method in which information is obtained by observing customers' behaviour or events taking place. In travel and tourism there are many situations in which observation methods can be used to provide valuable information on customer reactions to customer service. For example, observing the way that holidaymakers react at a welcome party often indicates the extent to which they find it enjoyable and interesting. For this reason most tour operators ensure that resort managers observe new resort representatives at their first few welcome meetings to check that they are meeting customers' needs and expectations. Similarly, a new waiter or waitress will be closely observed by the restaurant manager during training to check that he or she is delivering an appropriate level of service.

ACTIVITY

Observation

For this activity you will need to work in groups of three. Take turns to play the role of a telephone inquirer, a tourist information centre manager and a trainee at the tourism information centre (TIC).

The TIC trainee has been given the following quality criteria for taking telephone messages.

- Answer phone within five rings.

- Say, 'Good morning/afternoon, Anytown Tourist Information Centre. How may I help you?'

- Identify who the message is for. If recipient is not available, make a record of the following details:

  - name of caller

  - telephone number of caller

  - name of person to receive message

  - message

  - time and date of message.

- Thank caller for message and assure them that it will be given to recipient.

- Remain polite, friendly, confident and professional throughout the call.

The TIC manager is observing the trainee taking a telephone message and should give feedback at the end on the extent to which the quality criteria were met. The inquirer needs to make up the details of the message.

Each of you should have a turn at playing all three roles.

Evaluating quality criteria

The quality criteria that can be used to determine the standard of customer service give us a clear idea of what we need to be looking at in terms of assessing customer service requirements. However, it is important to understand how to evaluate the criteria and the quality of customer service provided. In this context, to

evaluate means to identify the value or worth of each criterion in terms of customer needs and expectations. It is vital to understand:

- the perceived importance of each quality criterion to the customer

- how customers would rank each criterion in order of importance.

A customer taking a flight might rank health and safety as the most important quality criterion. Someone visiting a museum might feel that the provision of specialist guides is most important. Of course, both customers will have many other quality criteria that they rank in differing order of importance.

Most organisations evaluate and continually monitor the customer service that they provide. They do this to ensure that their service is meeting the needs of customers, and, if not, that the necessary changes can be made. Evaluation of customer service focuses on:

- the extent to which quality criteria meet customers' expectations

- the extent to which quality criteria are met by the actual level of service being provided.

In setting quality criteria, it is clearly the intention to satisfy customers' needs but ongoing evaluation is needed to ensure that these needs are being met on each and every occasion. Similarly, in setting standards organisations expect them to be met, but in reality this may not always happen. For example, a quality criterion may be that telephones are answered within three rings. In reality this may be impossible if staff are overstretched and trying to meet a number of other criteria at the same time, such as dealing promptly with customers waiting at the reception desk.

In essence, then, an evaluation of customer service seeks to ensure that the level of customer service is meeting the quality criteria, and that these quality criteria are, in turn, satisfying customer expectations.

Service delivered by competitors

Evaluation of the quality of customer service should include an assessment of the level of service offered by organisations in related markets. On pp. 261–2 we looked at the benefits of securing a competitive advantage in the provision of products and services. By analysing the level of customer service in related markets against key quality criteria, it is possible to evaluate the quality of service provided within an organisation. This is another way of benchmarking standards.

Related markets consist of organisations which offer services that may influence customer expectations of your service provision. Organisations in related markets include the following.

■ Direct competitors. Those which offer the same provision, for example, competing, travel agencies, museums or airlines. If a competitor offers customers a better level of customer service, it is likely that it will achieve a competitive advantage which may threaten the profitability of your organisation.

■ Other organisations in the same business. For example, an art gallery is in the same business as a museum, because they both provide entertainment in a similar way.

■ Related service organisations. A tourist attraction could be related to other travel and tourism organisations in terms of customer service. For example, procedures for dealing with credit card payments at a theme park could be used at a tourist attraction.

ACTIVITY

Competitors

1 Use the information in the table to identify:

■ customer service areas for which the attraction received low scores from customers

■ service areas where staff think they are performing better than actual customer perceptions

■ service areas where the attraction has and has not gained a competitive advantage over the competitor attraction.

2 On the basis of these findings, write a brief summary of the level of customer service and make recommendations for possible improvements in service delivery that will meet customers' expectations and gain a competitive advantage in all areas.

Customer service quality criteria	Rank in order of importance	Average customer score	Average employee score	Average customer score for competitor attraction
Wide range of exciting activities	1	8	9	9
Value for money	2	5	6	10
Attraction appropriate	3	5	7	8
Attraction suitable for all weathers	4	5	6	7
Good staff supervision	5	8	8	5
Friendly and helpful staff	6	9	10	6
Attraction well located and easy to find	7	10	10	7
Clean environment	8	10	10	8
Good catering service	9	9	8	7
Sufficient car parking	10	8	8	10

Scoring system used for assessing customer and employee atttitudes based on marks out of 10:
1 = very poor, 5 = average, 10 = excellent

Facilities outside the travel and tourism industry in unrelated service organisations also influence customers' expectations. For example, the use of hole-in-the-wall cash machines by banks reduces queueing times. This may affect customers' expectations of how long they are willing to wait for a travel and tourism service. Many tourist information centres now have a similar facility to that offered by banks, where customers can use a visual display unit to access information without queueing.

Recommending improvements

The final stage of evaluating customer service quality is to summarise findings and make recommendations for improvements to service delivery. This process is summarised in Figure 5.20.

Remember that the evaluation of customer service quality is based on the measurement of key customer service criteria against actual service delivery, together with a comparison of service delivery with organisations in related markets. This evaluation of organisations in related markets focuses on the level of service provided by direct competitors in particular.

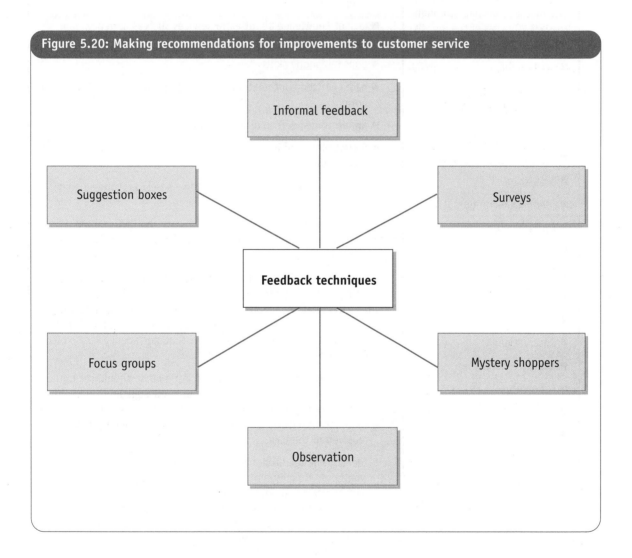

Figure 5.20: Making recommendations for improvements to customer service

BUILD YOUR LEARNING

Keywords and phrases

You should know the meaning of the words and phrases listed below. If you are unsure about any of them, go back through the last 20 pages of the unit to refresh your understanding.

- Accessibility
- Accuracy
- Benchmarking
- Cleanliness and hygiene
- Consistency
- Evaluation
- Feedback techniques
- Focus group
- Formal feedback
- Health and safety
- Informal feedback
- Mystery shopper
- Observation
- Quality criteria
- Reliability
- Staffing levels
- Standards
- Value for money

Linda Bray has recently taken over an independent travel agency. The previous owners had a reputation for poor customer service and many of their customers moved away to use the services of the high street multiples. Past customer records show a high level of customer complaints about:

- insufficient advice from travel consultants resulting in inappropriate holidays
- lack of knowledge about extra services such as currency, insurance and car hire
- poor telephone skills
- badly written confirmation letters with spelling and grammatical errors
- failure to respond to or resolve complaints
- a general lack of interest on the part of the travel consultants in giving advice or information
- badly displayed brochures (or in some cases, brochures being out of stock)
- long queues during busy periods, despite the fact that extra staff were present but engaged in administration work in the back office.

When Linda bought the agency she agreed to continue to employ the existing staff. They are all well qualified and experienced, but Linda thinks that they have probably become used to a very sloppy approach to customers. As a result, Linda realises that she has a lot of work to do to convince the local population that her agency can provide excellent customer service.

1 As a group, discuss what quality criteria Linda should set for her travel consultants. Base this on your knowledge and understanding of customer service as a whole, as well as the information regarding the complaints that the agency has received in the past.

2 Identify the feedback methods that Linda could use to evaluate whether her quality criteria are being met. Explain fully how each method will be used. For example, if you select surveys as one of the methods you need to design a questionnaire or feedback form and explain how it would be implemented. Similarly, if you are going to use a mystery customer you should design the checklist that he or she would use.

Answers to activities

Activity, p. 330

1 Sometimes, but it depends on the situation and type of customer. For example children or young adults on a youth package holiday may prefer to be called by their first name. However, in most situations it is safer to address someone by their surname unless invited to use their given name.

2 Sometimes, again it depends on the situation. Generally if the customer is standing then so should you. However, there are many situations such as when dealing with a customer in a travel agency when it is more appropriate to remain seated.

3 Never.

4 Never. You should take the lead by approaching a customer and asking if you can be of assistance.

5 Always.

6 Never, it is polite and shows respect. However, if you know the customer's surname it is even better to address them as Mr/Mrs....

7 Never, it shows that you have lost control of the situation and is highly unprofessional.

8 Always, it is unprofessional and breaches confidentiality.

9 Never, they expect excellent service every time. If you are so tired or unwell that you cannot do your job properly you should not be atwork!

10 Always.

11 Always

12 Sometimes, but what is important is that you always act as if the customer is right.

Activity, p. 339

1 Traffic circle – roundabout

2 Divided highway – dual carriageway

3 Freeway – motoway

4 Sidewalk – pavement

5 Second floor – first floor

6 Faucet – tap

7 Jelly – jam

8 Check – bill

9 Liquor store – off-licence

10 Chips – crisps

11 Restroom – toilet

12 ATM – cash machine

13 Pocket book – diary

14 Band aid – plaster

Organisations in the travel and tourism industry are constantly undertaking projects to develop and test new products and services. Such projects are responses to ever-changing consumer trends and expectations and are often unique and innovative as a result.

This unit gives you the opportunity to work as part of a team to plan, carry out and evaluate a real project that is of interest to you. Working as part of a group, you will agree on a project (which could be an event or a business project) that is travel and tourism related, and then assess whether it is feasible to run. Once the feasibility of the project has been established, you will put together a business plan and then actually carry out the planned project, rounding it all off with an evaluation of your performance. As part of this process you will produce a written business plan and keep a log of your involvement in the project.

The title of this unit effectively sums up what you need to do to complete your assessment. This is because it requires you to apply the knowledge and skills that you have gathered from topics such as marketing and customer service, to a real project – in other words, to put travel and tourism into action. The portfolio assessment for this unit is shown on pp. 458–9.

6

Travel and tourism in action

Choosing a travel and tourism project

PROJECT DEVELOPMENT AND the staging of events in the travel and tourism industry is widespread, as organisations strive to meet increasing consumer demand for leisure activities and travel to new destinations. The terms **project** and **event** refer here to planned undertakings that are travel and tourism related, and that will run for a designated period of time. The period of time may be short (for example, a week), medium, (a month or so), or long term (several months). The basic planning aspects for both projects and events are the same, so we will use the term project throughout to cover the wide range of events and projects that take place in the travel and tourism industry.

There is an enormous range of examples, from small-scale projects, (such as a farmer diversifying to create a small caravan site on his farm, or a hotel adding a Spanish night to its entertainment programme) to large-scale travel and tourism projects. The latter can involve huge financial investment, extensive planning and many thousands of participants. International events such as the Olympics, FIFA's World Cup, or the World Expo in Hanover, for example, all involve extensive planning over a number of years in order to host the millions of visitors who attend them.

Some other examples of large-scale travel and tourism projects around the world include the:

- completion of new airports in Dominica, Hong Kong and Madeira

- the Millennium Dome and Ferris wheel (London Eye) by the Thames in London

- creation of the new theme park Animal Kingdom in Disney World, Orlando

▲ A large-scale tourism project

There are many examples of much smaller-scale travel and tourism projects such as:

- craft fairs, restoration and conservation work

- open days, exhibitions and promotional campaigns

- rock concerts, day trips and tours.

ACTIVITY

Travel and tourism projects

Make a list of examples of travel and tourism related projects that are:

- of worldwide or national significance

- of regional significance

- of local significance.

When you have completed your list, discuss in groups what features each of these projects have in common in terms of the way they are planned and run.

The assessment for this unit involves planning, carrying out and evaluating your own travel and tourism related project. The flow chart in Figure 6.1 shows you the main stages you must follow in order to complete this task.

Your project team should start out by selecting a few ideas you think might be appropriate for your project and then spend some time assessing each idea in more detail, to see which one is the most feasible (possible). You will then plan the project and put together a business plan. A business plan should normally represent a summary of:

- what the organisation aims to achieve – its objectives

- the methods by which it intends to achieve those aims – such as marketing, project content, etc.

- the tools or resources required – such as people and equipment

- the financial implications – budget

- how success will be measured.

Figure 6.2 shows the link between each of the elements of the business plan.

Figure 6.1: Stages in carrying out a project

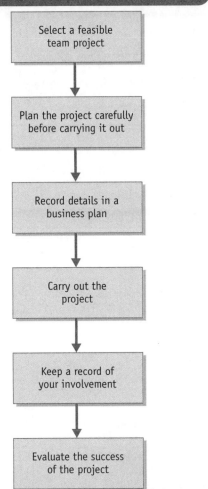

Select a feasible team project

↓

Plan the project carefully before carrying it out

↓

Record details in a business plan

↓

Carry out the project

↓

Keep a record of your involvement

↓

Evaluate the success of the project

Recording your involvement

Although you will be involved in running the project as part of a team, you will also need to produce a **personal log book** or diary. This records your own contribution to the team project from your first meeting through the running of the project to final evaluation.

Figure 6.3 shows a grid of the skills and attitudes you will need to complete the project well. You should keep them in mind throughout.

Keeping a record of your own and the team's contribution to the whole project is an active process which you must engage in regularly. It also represents a vital source of evaluation and review material. You need to decide how you will record this information right at the start of the project. You can use a variety of formats and should prepare these during the planning stage, so that you are familiar with filling out your documentation during the busy project stage as well. Formats might include:

- ring binder divided into sections
- diary with ample pages for notes
- computer disk
- wall planner or flow chart
- video recording
- photographs or tapes
- observer comments
- participant statements
- tutor observations.

Figure 6.2: Planning and implementation loop

Evaluation

Idea

Research

Planning

Gathering resources

Final preparation

Implementing the project

Figure 6.3: Personal skills grid for carrying out a project

- learn by your mistakes
- communicate
- be adaptable
- keep up group spirit

- be proactive
- begin with the end in mind
- prioritise
- synergise

- manage your tasks well
- be a positive influence
- think before you speak
- use logic, not emotion, to decide issues

- respond rapidly
- don't get stressed
- do an equal share
- be part of the team

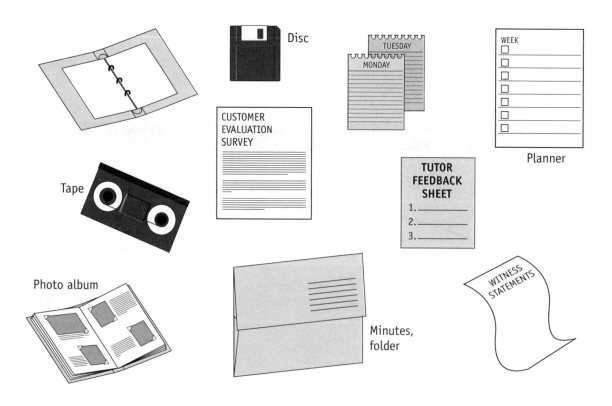

Disc

Photo album

Tape

CUSTOMER EVALUATION SURVEY

MONDAY
TUESDAY

TUTOR FEEDBACK SHEET
1. _____
2. _____
3. _____

WEEK

Planner

Minutes, folder

WITNESS STATEMENTS

▲ Possible recording formats for personal and team log books

Whichever format you select, it has to cover two main areas: process and content. The **process** means all the actions or procedures gone through by the team, such as planning, allocating tasks, customer care and setting deadlines, along with notes on advice sought. The **content** means the topic covered. This must include records of:

- personal and team contributions
- how roles (briefings) were maintained
- how disruptions were handled
- how health, safety and security aspects were maintained
- how well the team cooperated and whether it adhered to the plan.

The format of the log should be discussed with your teacher. For example, you could use individual page headings as shown in Figure 6.4.

Your log should also contain copies of all relevant materials, such as:

- minutes from team meetings
- schedules of tasks
- checklists and briefings
- diary of activities
- reports on research
- costs of resources
- contacts for providers
- contingency plans
- emergency procedures.

All of these go to make up the complex picture of your own and your colleagues' contribution to running the project or event, for assessment purposes. If you are unsure whether to include materials, you can always present them as an appendix. This helps others to cross check and verify your evidence, and shows depth.

It is essential that you fill in your log frequently, while your memory is fresh. There is nothing worse than trying to record information long after the project.

Figure 6.4: Log book headings

Date	Topic	Contribution	Action

Task	Details	By when	Result

Time	Incident	How dealt with	Who informed

Meeting	Subject	Points agreed

ACTIVITY

Creating a personal log book

Create a log book which is capable of recording your own contribution to the running of an event and those of your fellow team members. It needs to have enough space and sections to cover all of the following process and content factors.

Process:

- schedule for the project or event
- reports on progress
- revisions or alterations made
- summary of the business plan.

Content:

- own contribution
- team's contribution
- adherence to role and briefing
- maintenance of health, safety and security
- cooperation with others
- report on how closely the plan was followed
- reports on dealing with disruptions
- advice and guidance from others.

You can use this log book for the activity on p. 451 and the portfolio assessment on pp. 458–9.

▼ Several ideas can come together to form a project

Ideas and options

The starting point for your project is the ideas stage. Without initial ideas or options for a project, you will have nothing to plan and develop.

One of the best ways of identifying ideas and options for your project is to run a brainstorming session with everyone in your team. **Brainstorming** is a technique used to come up with options. Everyone is encouraged to put forward ideas, however bizarre. From the list of options, a short list can be produced of the best three ideas, which can then be investigated further. Here is list of brainstormed options which a local council in a seaside resort might come up with in order to increase off-season tourism in the town.

- Street festival
- Water carnival
- Historic re-enactment
- Sporting event
- Travel and timeshare exhibition
- Jazz festival
- Traditional music concert
- Children's travel event
- Display.

Looking at examples of previous successful projects can also be an effective way of identifying options for your own project. It is a safe route which may not be as creative as an original idea, but which nevertheless offers opportunities for teams to stage their own version

of tried tested formulas. Projects that student groups have successfully run include:

- organised tours, such as around a historic city
- special events, such as children's beach games
- excursions to visitor attractions
- fund-raising ventures for charity
- open days for prospective travel and tourism students
- exhibitions
- conferences.

ACTIVITY

Brainstorming

Carry out a group brainstorming session with your project team to identify ideas for possible projects you could run. When you have come up with a number of ideas, decide on the best three to create your short list. From this shortlist, select the best option for your project.

You will need to consider a wide range of factors in your decision, such as timescale, skills of the team, and potential demand from customers.

Whatever you finally decide to do, it is a good idea to have an alternative project in mind, just in case your first choice is not feasible.

Feasibility

In preparing to carry out your chosen project you will need to investigate its feasibility. Assessing the feasibility of a project involves asking the question, can it be done within the timescale and resources available? The main factors that will determine the feasibility of a project are:

- the market (customers)
- the location(s) to be used
- scale (size of the project)
- cost
- funding sources
- method of production
- plan of operations.

There is a wide range of possibilities to choose from within a travel and tourism context. The choice is yours, as long as the project is sufficient to meet all of the unit assessment requirements.

There are two main benefits in ascertaining the feasibility of the project. First, it helps to think the project through in a logical sequence. Second, a thorough plan ensures that human, physical and financial resources are not wasted unnecessarily on a project that cannot be implemented.

The case study (on p. 404) highlights some of the key feasibility points that Barclays Bank advises for customers starting up a business. The questions that the bank asks can be applied to your own project.

CASE STUDY

Will your idea work?

You may have the best idea in the world for a project – you might even have a product or service that nobody has thought of before – but a good idea alone will not guarantee you success. Before you begin to develop your project idea, there are some key questions you should ask yourselves.

■ Are there people who will want what you propose to offer?

■ Who are they and how will you market your team's idea to them?

■ What will you charge them?

■ Will it meet targets you set?

Personal qualities

■ Self sufficiency – will your team be able to handle pressure from others, make decisions quickly, carry responsibilities?

■ Initiative – can your team spot opportunities and act on them?

■ Determination – can you overcome difficulties and sustain the effort?

■ Resilience – can your team learn from mistakes and keep believing the project will succeed?

■ Responsibility – will you tend to blame everyone else when things go wrong?

■ Imagination – can your team keep the smaller ideas flowing to meet client needs?

Skills

■ Management – can your team control the project, prioritise tasks and meet deadlines?

■ Financial – will your team meet its targets and keep accurate records?

■ Marketing – can you meet your customer needs and cover costs or make a profit for your project?

■ Production – even if you don't actually make a product, but deliver a service instead, can you deliver on time, to the right level and in style?

■ Technical expertise – does your team have access to any specialist knowledge it requires?

Source: Barclays Bank *Starting Your Own Business*

ACTIVITY

Will your ideas work?

Read the case study and summarise the guidance given to produce just six key points your team should consider when deciding the feasibility of your project. Once these are agreed, discuss and evaluate each of the three ideas you shortlisted in the last activity on p. 403 and select the best option.

Planning

Planning for all projects is essential, in order to fit all the pieces together. Two pieces of sound advice given to anyone involved in carrying out a project is are, 'If you fail to plan, then prepare to fail!' and 'Proper planning prevents poor performance'.

In the travel and tourism industry, however large or small the project, the business plan forms the basis of discussions and negotiations with bankers, planners, sponsors and many others when seeking funding, support or permission to go ahead. Your business plan will show if your team has:

■ considered every aspect of your plan

■ budgeted in a logical and realistic manner

■ allocated sufficient resources to fulfil your plans.

CASE STUDY

Planning the Endeavour visit to Whitby

A replica of Captain James Cook's pioneering ship *Endeavour* has just made a successful ten-day visit to Whitby, the place where the original ship was built in 1765.

It was originally named the *Earl of Pembroke* but was renamed three years later when put into service for the Royal Navy. The original ship was one of the eighteenth century colliers known as Whitby cats because of their sturdiness and seaworthiness. The modern museum standard replica was built in Fremantle, Western Australia and was commissioned in 1994 as a travelling tourist attraction. It was from here that the *Endeavour* set sail on 16 October 1996 bound for England and its home port.

On its journey it called in at such exotic ports such as Mauritius, Durban, Cape Town and Madeira, before reaching the port of London in March 1997. From there she set off for a tour around Britain calling at Greenwich, Boston in Lincolnshire and on to Whitby on 9 May.

The ship is captained by Chris Blake, an experienced sailor who had previously commanded four square rigged ships prior to the *Endeavour*. He has kept a log of all aspects of the trip and project, just as Captain Cook would have done. From the information he sent every month, including press releases and a regional advertising campaign, along with leaflets and commemorative brochures, awareness was created of the culmination of the project – the homecoming. This brought many extra thousands of visitors to the area.

In order to make the most of the *Endeavour's* homecoming, Scarborough Borough Council, in conjunction with other bodies, spent months planning the visit. Special committees were set up to coordinate marketing, highways and harbour operations. A week-long festival of events such as exhibitions, street entertainment, guided walks, sea shanty and folk concerts was also planned.

▲ Many organisations provide guidance on planning

Figure 6.5 shows where all the different elements fit into the project planning and delivery sequence, and what needs to go into the business plan.

Organisations such as the Regional Tourist Boards, Barclays Bank, The Prince's Trust and Young Enterprise all provide guidance about the planning process for a business project.

In order to plan, co-ordinate and control the complex and diverse activities of many travel and tourism projects, a process called project management can be used. **Project management** can be used to plan, order and control the tasks involved in large project schemes such as the building of the Channel Tunnel and the Millennium Dome in London. Both of these large-scale projects involved massive amounts of technology and investment, and thus required complex project management techniques.

Project management also helps teams to take economic pressures to deliver to budget, work safely and within the law, give value for money and respect the environment, into account. Your project team will probably face similar pressures, albeit on a much smaller scale.

All projects share one characteristic – they transform a feasible idea into reality. In any project there will always be an element of risk and uncertainty. This means that the steps and tasks leading to completion can never be described with absolute certainty beforehand. Every effort must be made to get the details as accurate as possible – in other words to foresee or predict all of the elements of the project, using the best information available, with back-ups provided should anything unforeseen occur. This brings us to the central concept of business planning, in which each element is meticulously calculated to help reduce uncertainty and make the project run smoothly.

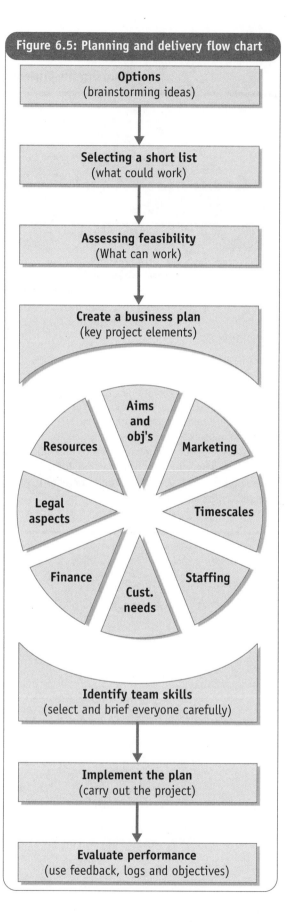

Figure 6.5: Planning and delivery flow chart

Options
(brainstorming ideas)

Selecting a short list
(what could work)

Assessing feasibility
(What can work)

Create a business plan
(key project elements)

- Aims and obj's
- Marketing
- Timescales
- Staffing
- Cust. needs
- Finance
- Legal aspects
- Resources

Identify team skills
(select and brief everyone carefully)

Implement the plan
(carry out the project)

Evaluate performance
(use feedback, logs and objectives)

BUILD YOUR LEARNING

Assess the feasibility of your chosen project. As a team, consider the criteria listed below to debate the pros, cons and logistics of your chosen project.

- Location and availability of facilities.

- Accessibility and suitability.

- Likely customer demand.

- Cost implications and finance available.

- Human resources available, including skills, abilities and numbers.

- Time scale.

- Scale or scope of the project: will it meet all necessary assessment criteria?

- Tutor, school or college and outside organisation approval.

- Health and safety issues.

- Achievable by the team within the time and budget.

This meeting and discussion should be recorded, especially where agreement about action to be taken is reached.

Keywords and phrases

You should know the meaning of the words and phrases listed below. If you are unsure about any of them, go back through the last nine pages to refresh your understanding.

- Brainstorming
- Content
- Event
- Feasibility
- Ideas and options
- Personal log book
- Planning and delivery
- Process
- Project
- Project management

The business plan

WE LOOK NEXT AT EACH of the elements of the business plan (see Figure 6.6) so that you can put together a written team plan for your own project.

Aims and objectives

Devising your group's overall aim(s) can be done through discussion. An **aim** describes what an organisation intends to do. It usually states its overall purpose or direction. It is best, however, if you can keep the aim(s) short and memorable. The overall aim of project teams varies. Some examples could be to:

- complete the project on time and on budget
- provide a first-class service to customers
- ensure participants have a safe and happy time
- use all resources effectively for the benefit of the target group.

In order to achieve the overall aim(s) and give it more measurable dimensions, the project team must set specific objectives. **Objectives** are used as the starting point of the whole business planning process and as the main means by which performance is measured at the end of the project. Objectives must therefore be quantifiable. One of the best known ways to remember how to set appropriate objectives is to use the SMART

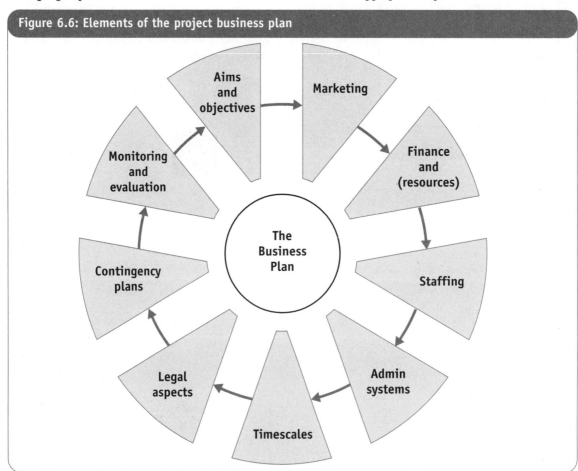

Figure 6.6: Elements of the project business plan

approach (see p. 230). This states that objectives should be:

Specific

Measurable

Agreed

Realistic

Timed

Objectives should usually cover three key areas of the project operation.

- **Performance and quality.** The end result of the project must be fit for the purpose for which it was intended and the specifications given must be satisfied. For example, a new white-knuckle ride must function reliably, efficiently and safely, as well as also meeting the expectations of customers to provide excitement.

- **Budget.** The project must be completed without exceeding the agreed budget. For most commercial projects, failure to achieve this objective may lead to reduced profits, lower returns on capital invested or even losses. Proper attention to the calculation of costs and financial management of a project, however large or small, is essential.

- **Time to completion.** Actual progress must match planned progress, so that all of the significant stages of the project take place no later than their specified date, leading to final completion on or before the planned date. High profile projects for which time to completion has been crucial are the Millennium Dome, which successfully met its objective and the London Eye, which did not open on time and lost its entire first month's income.

Projects in the travel and tourism industry tend to incorporate objectives derived from the overall aims of the organisation involved, the type of service it provides and the sector of the market in which it operates. Let's look at some typical objectives.

- To increase **profitability**. Private sector organisations strive to make a profit. For example, a project team might set a profit objective of 25 per cent from ticket or admission charges.

- To increase **take-up** (numbers of customers). This might be an objective for providers from any sector of the travel and tourism industry. For example, a seaside resort might set a target of 12,500 more visitors as a result of running a series of conferences and exhibitions. Public sector providers sometimes use increasing take-up as an objective when targeting groups which have low levels of participation (take-up), such as ethnic minorities or people with disabilities.

- To increase **consumer interest** in products or services. A number of short-term projects can raise awareness of products and services. Such projects often attract sponsors, who see them as excellent vehicles for promoting their products and services. In this case, a percentage increase in sales, such as a target of 5 per cent, could be used to judge whether increased consumer interest had been achieved.

- To create a favourable **image**. The completion of a project in partnership with a charity group provides an opportunity for an organisation to improve or maintain its public image. The long-term aim is usually to create repeat business and customer/brand loyalty. Success here might be judged by the number of new loyalty cards issued after a successful project, for example.

- To provide **community benefits**. Private sector organisations may try to achieve a good relationship with the local community through sponsorship, the public sector by trying to improve the quality of life for local people, and the voluntary sector by trying to improve conditions for their target groups in the community. Feedback could be gathered from the target group to see how many were satisfied with the changes or improvements.

When you have agreed the objectives for your team project, you should include them in your business plan, so that the outcomes can be measured. This may involve focusing each objective on a specific aspect of the project, for example, setting a target of 100 ticket sales, or of a 10 per cent profit, or of less than five complaints overall, or using a combination of several indicators, to measure success. You should make sure that all of your team members are aware of, and agree with the objectives that are set.

It is also important to decide how your team will collate the evidence and compare objectives to outcomes at the planning stage. Figure 6.7 illustrates this process.

Figure 6.7: Monitoring objectives throughout the project

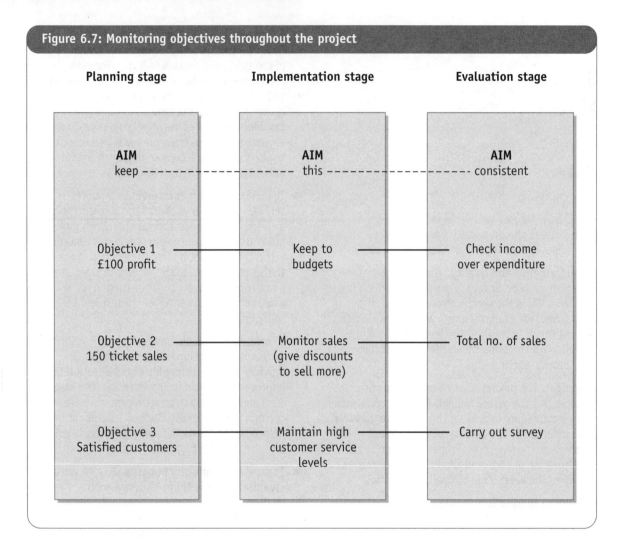

Planning stage	Implementation stage	Evaluation stage
AIM keep	**AIM** this	**AIM** consistent
Objective 1 £100 profit	Keep to budgets	Check income over expenditure
Objective 2 150 ticket sales	Monitor sales (give discounts to sell more)	Total no. of sales
Objective 3 Satisfied customers	Maintain high customer service levels	Carry out survey

ACTIVITY

Setting objectives

With the rest of the people in your project team look at the examples of projects shown in the list below and devise suitable objectives for them, bearing in mind the SMART approach. For each objective you devise, list how you might gather information on how your team performed, or the success of the project, with reference to the objectives set. Some possible sources to get you started include: tickets sales, questionnaires and evaluation sheets.

■ A day-trip to a theme park for the rest of your class.

■ An outing to a museum for a group OAPs.

■ An exhibition of a destination or country with invited exhibitors and guests.

■ A guide book for tourists about local tourist attractions.

■ Hosting a travel and tourism quiz for charity.

Based on your own team project, devise a range of objectives that follow the SMART approach. When your team has agreed these, include them in your business plan. Remember to consider how you will evaluate the project outcomes to determine if you have met each objective set.

Project timescales

The success of your project could depend on people working to a **timescale** (prearranged schedule). The importance of timing cannot be emphasised enough. Quite apart from the effect late running could have on the organisation undertaking a project such as a new product launch, it has a knock-on effect on other resources, budget estimates and business relationships.

The most common delays are caused by:

- lack of information
- lack of immediate funds
- delay in other resources
- waiting for approval and permissions.

Any project, irrespective of its scale or content, costs money during every day of its existence, for a variety of reasons such as the costs of:

- materials
- design time
- construction time
- inflation
- price rises
- wages
- interest on loans
- administration
- accommodation
- buying other services
- use of facilities.

When you tackle your project, it is well worth remembering that 'time is money'.

Deadlines

Projects always have important **deadlines** which must not be missed. The obvious deadline is the actual starting date and time, but there may be a whole series of deadlines before the start concerning a wide range of aspects of the project, including:

- publicity
- finances and resources
- delivery of materials
- confirmation of arrangements
- staff training
- health, safety and security checks.

In order to set and monitor the various deadlines, it is often necessary to establish an **implementation schedule**, which lists actions, responsibilities, dates, times and the resources required to run it all. Establishing this schedule and documenting it is an important aspect of your business plan.

The time scale for preparing for the Sydney Olympics was over eight years and a business plan was submitted to the International Olympic Committee at the bidding stage in 1992. You can see from the webstract that the project managers followed a masterplan covering four main projects which embraced both the sporting needs and the travel and tourism requirements of the project.

WEBSTRACT

Sydney Olympic preparations

The development of the Olympic Games site is actually a re-development of an area called Homebush Bay, and the biggest programme that the state government of New South Wales has undertaken. A masterplan sets out the mixed uses of the massive site, which is strategically located near the heart of Sydney – its long-term uses are for tourism, recreation, exhibitions and entertainment, residential and commerce.

The masterplan divides sites into four main project areas:

- urban core, containing sporting and entertainment facilities, the show ground and exhibition precinct and commercial sites
- urban district, the Olympic village
- a major metropolitan park
- a waterfront development providing public access to the shoreline.

The masterplan has been revised to include changes prompted by the bad experiences of the Atlanta Olympic Games. A huge plaza with room for 300,000 people to circulate has been planned and the natural landscape has been harnessed and improved to include water features.

The spin-off in tourism income will not just be during the games, but for considerable periods after, for it has added another attraction to the ones which Sydney already has to offer the tourist.

Source: webdog.com

Recording time scales and deadlines

Timetables are the simplest form of project time scale plan and are useful at the feasibility stage to roughly assess whether the proposal will fit into the available time scale. However, they are not sophisticated enough for day-to-day progress monitoring and control because they do not display enough detail for a large project. You can see from Figure 6.8 how difficult it is to squeeze information onto a calendar.

Bar charts are a better option. They display the programme more effectively, with the time scale shown along the top and each horizontal bar representing a project task, its length scaled to its expected duration. The name or description of each job is written on the same row at the left-hand edge of the chart (see Figure 6.9).

Bar charts are easy to construct and interpret, and are readily adaptable to a great variety of planning requirements. You may well see them used for staffing rotas and room scheduling in your school or college. A more complex chart might be colour coded to show exactly who is to complete which task. The Alton Towers

Figure 6.8: Calendar style timetable

Week	Monday	Tuesday	Wednesday	Thursday	Friday	Saturday	Sunday
1	First team meeting		Aims & obj's decided		Bus. plan		
2		Marketing commences		Second team meeting	Fund raising days		
3	Third team meeting		Roles decided		Bookings confirmed		
4		Publicity stunt					
5	Fourth team meeting		Final checks				
6	Projects starts					Project finishes	
7	Evaluation						
8	Reports	Logs					

Figure 6.9: Bar chart for travel and tourism event

Task	Week ending (Friday)										
	8 Jan	15 Jan	22 Jan	29 Jan	5 Feb	12 Feb	19 Feb	26 Feb	5 Mar	12 Mar	19 Mar
Agree plan for event	▬	▬									
Design layout			▬	▬							
Identify and book speakers					▬						
Prepare publicity					▬						
Allocate materials and resources						▬					
Agree contingencies						▬					
Check arrangements								▬			
Liaison with exhibitors	▬			▬		▬					
Final press releases									▬		
Stage event										▬	
Gather and evaluate data											▬

event planner in Figure 6.10 uses a flow chart to indicate the key stages of the project in a chronological or prioritised sequence.

Critical path analysis, (CPA) is a planning technique that sets out the master route or sequence of the key tasks. It is widely used for planning where groups of tasks need prioritising and scheduling and uses an arrow system of notation to show tasks, their order and duration. Figure 6.11 shows how a critical path analysis may look when applied to a project planning sequence. This technique is particularly helpful at the more complex stages of a project, when several tasks must be carried out simultaneously or when the completion of some tasks is contingent upon the completion of others.

ACTIVITY

Recording time scales

Your whole project team should attempt this activity, in pairs at first.

1 Look at the set of tasks set out below, for the opening of a small heritage museum.

- Agree promotional activities.
- Schedule regular staff planning meetings.
- Design and order posters.
- Make hospitality arrangements.
- Set up health, safety and security measures.
- Prepare and send out invitations.
- Prepare and send out press releases.
- Carry out a practice or dry run.
- Compile budget.
- Prepare exhibits.

First, put the tasks into the correct order. Then create a bar chart showing the duration of the tasks. Finally, create a critical path analysis diagram of the tasks.

2 As a team, devise a detailed time scale plan for your project. You will need to present it as a chart that all team members can follow. An example of a time scale plan is shown in Figure 6.12 for a project due to run over three months. You could use this example as the basis for your own chart, or devise your own.

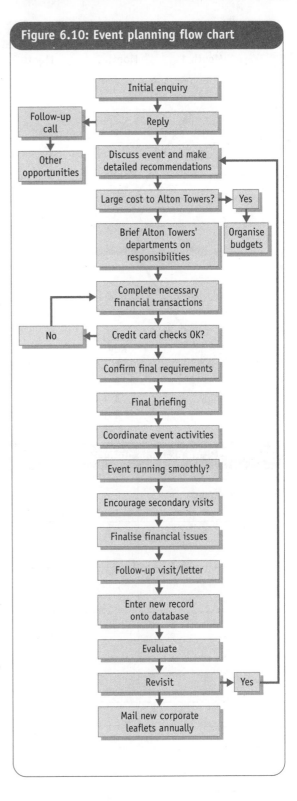

Figure 6.10: Event planning flow chart

Figure 6.11: Critical path analysis

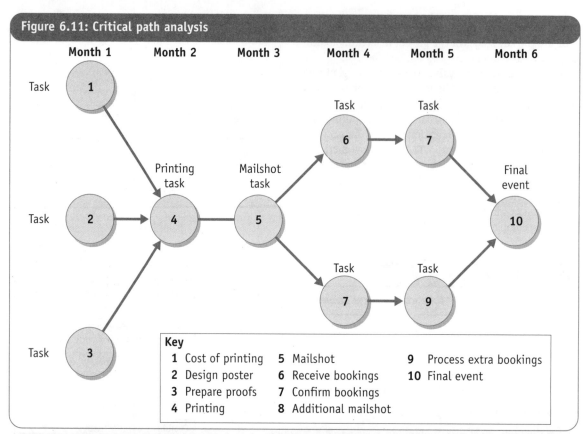

Key					
1	Cost of printing	**5**	Mailshot	**9**	Process extra bookings
2	Design poster	**6**	Receive bookings	**10**	Final event
3	Prepare proofs	**7**	Confirm bookings		
4	Printing	**8**	Additional mailshot		

Figure 6.12: An example project time scale chart

Tasks	January 1 ——————▶ 31	February 1 ——————▶ 28	March 1 ——————▶ 31
1			
2			
3			
4			
5			
6			
7			
8			

Description of the project

Your business plan needs to include a brief description of the project. This should include details of:

- the scale and content of the project – for example, whether it will provide a product or a service, a team profile, a time scale and a list of reasons why you think the project will succeed

- the location and venue – give brief details of the site and its suitability, any constraints or difficulties envisaged.

Target customers

Customers are crucial to any travel any tourism project. An early part of your business planning will involve identifying who your customers are going to be, what their needs are and how the project will actually meet these needs.

You can use the following categories to help you identify your target groups.

- Age. Will you aim for children, teenagers, adults or the over fifties?

- Lifestyle. Will you aim to attract families, couples or singles?

- Location. Will you aim to attract people from a particular area?

The identification of target customer groups allows you to be more exact about whom your project is designed to attract and this will, in turn, guide your marketing activities.

The best summary of the marketing details which are required for a business plan is the four Ps of the marketing mix, namely, product, price, promotion and place. You should refer back to pp. 242–58. Further help is contained in the case study about the Barclays Bank guide to starting and running a business on p. 404. Some of the promotional techniques that your project team could use are shown in Figure 6.13, on p. 416.

CASE STUDY

Planning a new business project

As many as 40 per cent of new business projects are unsuccessful. Studies reveal that a substantial proportion of these failed to undertake adequate market research, both before they set themselves up and after they started their project. Many became complacent about their customers and about rival projects, relying instead on what they thought their customers wanted rather than finding out what they actually wanted.

This kind of knowledge helps to focus efforts in the most effective and profitable ways. Knowing why your customers are interested in your project and checking with them (gathering feedback) on the details of their interest is important too, for it may enable you to:

- offer them a better service

- create additional products

- identify new customers.

A simple example of this involved a young woman who ran a hairdressing salon, which offered beauty treatments too, as a franchise on a cruise liner. Two weeks into the cruise, she decided to analyse her list of customers and the amount they had spent since they left port. She learned that 80 per cent of her sales came from just 20 per cent of her customers. Further analysis revealed that a lot of her profit came from beauty treatments and that these were enjoyed mainly by her more regular customers.

As part of this investigation, the salon owner asked her customers to answer a questionnaire on the kinds of services they would like. A significant number said they would be interested in aromatherapy treatments. Since she was getting to know her customers better, she was able to revise her business plan, focus her attention on the customers who visited the salon most frequently, and increase the space and staff she devoted to beauty and aromatherapy treatments. She then went on to complete the cruise with a very successful project, much to delight of the cruise company, for she had added value to their product as well.

Figure 6.13: Promotional techniques

Promotional techniques	Use for a project
Advertising	All appropriate and affordable means should be used: radio, television (news reports), displays, etc.
Publicity materials	Creation of a specific brochure, based on the business plan, adds to the project's credibility.
Public relations	Free publicity via newspaper stories. Promotional events to publicise the project.
Direct mail	A mailshot or leaflet drop directly to target customers.
Posters	Flyers or large posters positioned at strategic points to catch the eye of likely customers.
Sponsorship	Use of the sponsor's name and logo on all publicity material or letters can greatly boost the project's image and attractiveness.
Personal selling	Telephone calls, presentations, one-to-one contact with key people.

ACTIVITY

Target groups and marketing

Using the suggestions in this section and in the marketing unit (p. 241), carry out the following tasks as a project team.

1 Identify the types of customer that would be interested in your project.

2 Discuss what research techniques you could use to find out what customers' needs are.

3 Determine the price that you intend to charge customers for your product or service. (Remember to ensure that your pricing strategy falls in line with any financial objectives that your team has set, such as to break even or to make a profit.)

4 List the main ways in which you will promote your project to your target customers (see Figure 6.13 for suggestions).

5 Create a chart similar to the one in Figure 6.13, but add a column for costs.

6 Complete each of the three columns in the chart with: promotional techniques; how you will apply them; and accurate costs.

Resources

Identifying the range of resources for a project is an important task and an essential part of your business planning. For the purposes of your business plan you will probably need to consider many types of resources. We shall consider the key resource requirements under the following headings:

- physical resources
- financial resources
- human resources.

Let's look at each in turn.

Physical resources

Physical resources include materials, equipment, venues, premises and facilities. The materials and equipment required for projects and events are as diverse as the projects and events themselves. They can range from the simplest of things, such as paper and pens for a children's party game, to high-tech lasers and computer packages for large exhibitions or shows.

There are a number of ways of identifying all the resources that will be needed. This can be done by:

- visualising each separate section of the project and jotting down the materials and equipment needed to resource it

- listing all the requirements through discussion and consultation

- putting oneself in the customer's place for every stage of the experience

- dividing responsibility for each aspect of the project among the project team and researching the materials and equipment required.

ACTIVITY

Physical resources

Imagine that your group had decided to run a small project in your school or college sports hall on a Saturday morning. The objective is to raise funds (£150) towards hiring a coach to take a local children's playgroup to a theme park. You have invited five teams, each with five players, to compete in a sponsored obstacle race. Your project team will provide some light refreshments afterwards. Each team has worked hard to find sponsors, which will be your main source of income. They will earn money every time a team member completes a circuit of the obstacle course. There is also a prize, donated by your tutors, for the team which gets the most people round in the time set.

Make a list of all the materials and equipment that you would require.

Premises, facilities and venues

Premises or facilities are usually required when undertaking a project, whether this means arranging a field for a car boot sale or booking a room or a hall for an exhibition. The premises selected must be appropriate for the type of project. The factors which influence the suitability of location should be identified at the planning stage and evaluated for inclusion in the business plan. These could include:

- number of participants or spectators who will attend

- parking requirements for staff, spectators and participants

- specialist needs, for example, a high roof, lighting or a stage

- access for people with disabilities

- communications for organisers, press and customers

- permanent catering facilities

- ease of adaptation or alteration

- health, safety and security considerations

- opening and closing times

- accommodation

- hire costs or facility charges.

Most project teams create a checklist to gather all this information and then allocate team members to assess costs, supply, availability and other factors which are specific to the resources identified. You can see an example of this in the Alton Towers event planning extract shown in Figure 6.14.

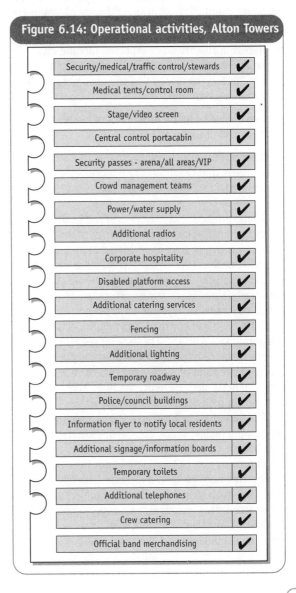

Figure 6.14: Operational activities, Alton Towers

- Security/medical/traffic control/stewards ✔
- Medical tents/control room ✔
- Stage/video screen ✔
- Central control portacabin ✔
- Security passes - arena/all areas/VIP ✔
- Crowd management teams ✔
- Power/water supply ✔
- Additional radios ✔
- Corporate hospitality ✔
- Disabled platform access ✔
- Additional catering services ✔
- Fencing ✔
- Additional lighting ✔
- Temporary roadway ✔
- Police/council buildings ✔
- Information flyer to notify local residents ✔
- Additional signage/information boards ✔
- Temporary toilets ✔
- Additional telephones ✔
- Crew catering ✔
- Official band merchandising ✔

ACTIVITY

Operational checklist

As a team, create a blank version of the checklist in Figure 6.14 and carry out a check of the premises, facility or venue which you intend to use for your project. During this check, identify the resources which might be needed. Opposite each item put a brief description of the action needed to ensure it is ready for the project.

Financial resources

The term **financial resources** refers to the amount of money involved in a project and the ways in which it is made or spent. The control of financial resources involves:

- preparing an analysis of expected **income and expenditure**, (forecasts of the money you hope to bring in and the money you will need to spend to generate the income)

- preparing a **budget** (the amount of money to be spent and in which areas)

- **financial monitoring** (checking and controlling) to ensure that the project's financial objectives are achieved.

Small projects may have very straightforward financial considerations; for example, taking a group on a coach trip or tour of an historic site might only require a small degree of budgeting. Since most of the people organising this type of project usually give their time freely, there are no staffing costs and a small profit could be made. A medium-size project, such as a pageant or parade, would have considerably more budgeting implications. For very large events such as international festivals and exhibitions, budgeting may involve huge sums of money and extensive accounting and financial management, such as that faced by Manchester galleries in the following article.

It is important to keep accurate records (accounts) so that the budget is not exceeded. Projects which go over budget are unlikely to be repeated or supported in the future, or may be terminated prior to completion.

You will need to have a realistic understanding of the costs involved in implementing a project and adopt good accounting practices, especially where cash is involved. The following information on record keeping gives some guidance and examples that you may wish to refer to for your team's financial controls.

Financial record keeping

There are three basic rules to keep in mind:

- record everything

- keep the system simple

- summarise your financial position at each team meeting.

Manchester gets £4.5 million from European Regional Development Fund (ERDF)

Three museums in Manchester are set to get a major cash injection, thanks to the assurance of £4.5 million from the European Regional Development Fund.

A total of £60 million will be divided between the Manchester Museum, the Museum of Science and Industry in Manchester and the City Art Gallery.

The extra funding will be spent on a new building at the Manchester City Art Gallery to display paintings and sculpture. The Manchester Museum will create new galleries to display its collections on ancient Egypt and global natural history. The Museum of Science and Industry will be able to complete the restoration of a warehouse to provide more exhibition space. Two large viaduct arches adjoining the building will be converted into a science theatre for demonstrations, events films and performances, and there will also be a communications laboratory, which will promote an interest in science through radio, recording and virtual reality.

Culture Secretary Chris Smith, who toured the three sites, said this investment is in line with the government's objectives of widening physical and intellectual access to art and heritage collections and promoting education.

Leisure Opportunities

Some general guidance follows to help you decide what is appropriate for your project.

Appoint one or two people as your treasurer or financial management team as soon as possible. As a starting point, you should calculate your **breakeven** point, that is the amount of money your project will need to cover its expenditure compared to the income it is expected to achieve. If one of your objectives is to make a profit, you can then calculate what you need to charge to meet your profit objective by adding that percentage or amount to your calculations. For example, if you need to make £100 to break even, set a profit target of £50 and expect 50 participants, you would have to charge £3 per person to achieve your objective.

You will need to hold a team meeting to agree on budgets for each area of expenditure according to what you can afford. The financial calculations and allocation of money need to be based on accurate research into the costs of every item, for example, the hire of a hall, printing of tickets or production of publicity posters. Your team will then have to decide how much of the budget can be allocated to each item or activity by establishing what is essential spending, what could be gathered through donations, supported by sponsorship, or obtained free of charge from your school or college. An example is shown in Figure 6.15.

Budget estimates made at the planning stage and agreed by the team provide guidance and control throughout the project's organisation and set the limits of spending. Once these are created they should go into your business plan. It is always wise to keep a small amount in reserve for unexpected costs. This is called a contingency fund.

ACTIVITY

Budget control

Study the following scenarios of project teams trying to control their budgets and discuss what they could have done better.

- One member of the team in charge of marketing has overspent on the printing of advertising materials by £40, but has no records of what exactly he spent the money on.

- A group of travel and tourism students has organised a very successful project and gained a lot of publicity and letters of thanks, but it has made a loss of £133, despite its objective to break even.

- With only three weeks to go until the start of the project, a team finds out that the hire charges for the local hall have gone up and taken the project over budget by £150.

- A group of travel and tourism students undertake a sponsored walk to raise money for a trip abroad but many of the participants fail to collect all of their sponsor money, so the team falls short of its target.

At the end of the project, your team may need to produce a balance sheet and use it as part of the evaluation process. The **balance sheet** shows the financial position of the project (see Figure 6.16).

Figure 6.15: An example expenditure budget sheet for a student project

Category	Week 1	Week 2	Week 3	Week 4	Week 5
Marketing	45	40	35	30	15
Printing costs	15	12	11	10	–
Admin. resources	25	18	12	9	–
Hire of premises	–	–	–	28	28
Catering	5	5	5	5	25
Travel	12	12	9	6	7
Fees	15	–	–	–	25

Sponsorship

Many organisations in the travel and tourism industry strive to attract sponsorship to support their projects. Sponsored projects often have a greater chance of success, as the sponsor can pay for additional resources or promotional activities. The sponsor will of course want to be associated with success, which enhances its image and the products or services that it provides.

Project teams working with a sponsor need to ensure they keep accurate accounts, as the sponsor will not only want value for money, but may also want to know how its donation has been spent.

Financial targets

As a group, set appropriate financial target(s) for your project, then devise and draw up a forecast detailing every category of income and expenditure that you envisage will occur during the lifetime of the project.

Human resources

The success of every travel and tourism project relies heavily on the people who run it. These people are known as **human resources**. It is essential to get the right people doing the jobs they are best suited for, and

---

Figure 6.16: Sample of an end-of-project balance sheet

Balance Sheet

	Debit £	Credit £
"Saturn Event" End of project, June 2001 net closing balances		527.74
Bank balance	107.72	
Petty cash	36.43	
Sales account	380.37	
Purchase account		390.34
Sales		311.84
Other income		177.26
Fees	206.67	
Light and heat	76.90	
Travel expenditure	52.90	
Materials	375.68	
Sundries	16.22	
Office	42.50	
Printing and stationery	111.79	
	1407.18	1407.18

to allocate their tasks effectively. The process of matching people's skills to jobs may even mean that adjustments to the tasks or the actual format of the proposals must be made, in order to get the best out of everyone.

▲ Good teamwork is vital

Success very often comes down to individual skills and the time, effort and teamwork put into the tasks which make up the project. The following principle can be applied to any project management team:

success = time and effort + skills and motivation

At the initial planning stage, team members have responsibilities for researching options and considering the feasibility of these options. During the project itself, each team member must undertake specific tasks. In the evaluation phase that follows the project, it is vital to assess how effective both individuals and the team as a whole have been in completing these tasks.

Once all the tasks required to meet the objectives of the project have been identified, the allocation of all the tasks required to complete the project can begin. Team members may have preferences, skills or experience which will help to determine who takes on which tasks. Where skills required for key tasks do not exist within the team, then other people may have to be sought to carry them out. Identifying tasks helps to create your team's operational structure.

Roles and tasks

A **role** is the part or function each team member plays in the project. The following guidelines provide you with some help in allocating roles for your team members effectively.

- Definition of role must be clear, so that team members know what is expected of them – a copy may be put into your log book for reference.

- People need clear guidelines on leadership and coordination within the team.

You can begin to identify the range of tasks likely to be involved your project by doing this activity.

Imagine you are in charge of one of the following aspects of the project:

- finance
- human resources
- marketing
- security
- physical resources.

Now brainstorm every single task, large or small, which you think might need doing. Put these down onto a checklist, then pass the list to colleagues for comment. If everyone in your team participates, you will be able to cover some of the of tasks in your project.

Analyse the final checklist sheets and put the tasks under the headings provided. This exercise can be repeated every time a new planning aspect arises.

When allocating tasks to team members, it is important to ensure that they understand their roles and have a chance to ask questions about their tasks. Once everyone is clear about responsibilities, these should be entered into the business plan, along with the team structure, so that they are recorded to guide each person. More detail about team structures can be found on pp. 435–6.

Allocating resources

One of the most difficult tasks for any project management team is the efficient allocation of its resources. Deciding on the factors that will determine how resources are allocated may involve lengthy discussion at team meetings and consideration of questions such as:

- what resources do we have available?
- what additional resources are needed?
- what skills or abilities are needed to use the resources?
- how long are the resources available for?
- how much finance will the resources require?

There is no single formula for calculating and allocating resources, however, you can use the following guidelines to help your team make decisions.

- Physical resources may well be in short supply and represent a considerable cost, so your team will have to identify exactly what it needs and match that to a definite source, so that its availability and cost can be assessed.

- Your school or college may make a lot of resources available to you at no cost, such as the venue, photocopying, staff and so on. It is important that your team still appreciates what the costs would have been had they not been provided free of charge. Where the cost involved is prohibitive, you may have to negotiate discounts, arrange for free use, or sponsorship, or perhaps change your plans.

- Care needs to be taken not to waste or duplicate resources due to lack of communication. The business plan should itemise the agreed allocations clearly for everyone to see and follow. This record will also provide a source of information for evaluation of the event, by which the efficient use of resources can be judged.

ACTIVITY

Identifying and allocating resources

Imagine that your team is running a day visit programme to your area for a group of visiting foreign students. Devise a one-day programme for them that includes a guided tour of your school or college and visits to at least one attraction in your area. Once you have done this, identify all the resources the programme will need.

Administration

All organisations need clearly established systems (procedures to follow) to support their functions (ways of working) and to allow them to operate smoothly. The two most important systems to consider for the purposes of running your project are administrative systems and communications systems, these are covered in more detail on p. 441.

Administrative systems

A good **administration system** identifies exactly what information needs to be recorded and the most effective method of recording it. Usually, it is the simple systems, which are thoroughly understood by those who operate them, that are most effective.

The overall objective of a project administration system should be to save time and money by helping the people involved to work well together. The procedure for collecting and recording information should be simple and easily applied by all involved.

Administration systems from the travel and tourism industry under two broad categories:

- those that support routine functions

- those that support non-routine functions.

Routine functions are the activities that occur on a regular basis and that constitute a large part of the day-to-day operation of the project team. They include procedures for financial transactions, communications, staffing and customer service. For example, booking systems and sales procedures are routine functions.

Non-routine functions, such as accidents and emergencies, occur infrequently, but still require administrative procedures for dealing with them. These are covered later on pp. 425–430.

When deciding what administrative systems to use for your project, the overall effectiveness of each system can be judged as follows.

- Fitness for purpose – is the system well suited to your needs?

- Value for money – will costs fit your budget?

- Accuracy – will it provide you with accurate records?

- Efficiency – will it take a minimum amount of time and effort to complete ?

- Security – will information be kept confidential with no unauthorised access?

- Ease of use – is the system paper based or computer based and is it easy to use?

- Users' opinion – have you consulted everyone in the team about your choice?

One administrative system you will have to devise for yourself is your personal log book or diary that records your involvement in the project. Whatever format you select, it has to cover all the actions or procedures undertaken by the team, from the start of the project to its completion, as outlined earlier (see pp. 399–401).

Legal considerations

Your team must ensure that any **legal considerations** applicable to the project are fully investigated and actioned, in order to remain within the law and ensure the health, safety and security of the staff and customers involved in the project.

You will have to describe the measures or actions your team has taken within your business plan. All organisations, irrespective of size or type of operation must ensure the health, safety and security of their staff and customers at all times, in order to comply with the law. Failure to do so can have serious consequences. Inadequate procedures can result in injury, prosecution, loss of income, loss of business, large claims for damages and, in extreme cases, loss of life. Figure 6.17 sets out the main benefits of effective health, safety and security policies and procedures for organisations, staff and customers.

Health and safety

The Health and Safety Executive (HSE) provides guidance and information to help organisations to formulate and implement health and safety procedures and to meet their statutory duties.

The health, safety and security legislation which is considered most widely applicable to travel and tourism projects is set out in Figure 6.18.

Depending on the nature of your project you may also need to consider other pieces of legislation, such as:

- Data Protection Act
- Consumer Protection Act
- Disability Discrimination Act
- EC Package Holidays Directive
- Food Saftey Act
- Children Act.

Although you are not required to learn the contents of the regulations and Acts in Figure 6.18, you do need to be able to identify which parts of them may apply to your project.

The aims of health and safety law are to maintain minimum health and safety standards, to control the actions of employers and to secure the health, safety and welfare of those working at or visiting premises. Under the legislation, actions taken to ensure health, safety and security for your project are covered by the principle of 'so far as is reasonably practicable'. In other words, the action taken needs to be balanced against the time, trouble, cost and physical difficulty of taking measures to avoid or reduce the problems. What the law requires here is what good management and common sense would lead organisers to do anyway: that is, to look at the potential hazards and take sensible measures to tackle them.

Figure 6.17: The benefits of effective health, safety and security

The work is carried out within the law

- fewer accidents
- increased productivity
- compensation claims are reduced
- prosecution is eliminated
- company image and reputation is enhanced
- insurance premiums are lower
- fraud and theft can be reduced

The environment

- damage is reduced or prevented
- enhancement is encouraged
- wildlife or plants re-inhabit
- more visitors may result

The staff

- morale and effectiveness can improve
- hazards and risk are reduced
- working conditions improve
- stress or threat level can be reduced
- awareness is increased of health safety and security needs
- training needs are identified

The customers

- suppliers and workmen on the premises are protected
- disabled users can have special provision
- a safe, secure environment is created for visitors
- standards of service may improve.

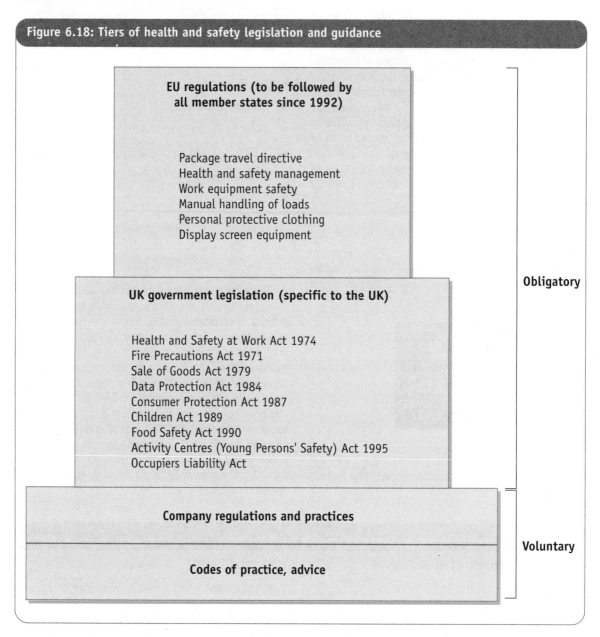

Figure 6.18: Tiers of health and safety legislation and guidance

EU regulations (to be followed by all member states since 1992)

Package travel directive
Health and safety management
Work equipment safety
Manual handling of loads
Personal protective clothing
Display screen equipment

UK government legislation (specific to the UK)

Health and Safety at Work Act 1974
Fire Precautions Act 1971
Sale of Goods Act 1979
Data Protection Act 1984
Consumer Protection Act 1987
Children Act 1989
Food Safety Act 1990
Activity Centres (Young Persons' Safety) Act 1995
Occupiers Liability Act

Company regulations and practices

Codes of practice, advice

Obligatory

Voluntary

As the onus is on organisers to assess health, safety and security hazards and to take measures to eliminate or control them, it is important that the concepts of hazard and risk are clearly understood.

Risk assessment

The term hazard refers to anything that can cause us harm in our everyday lives, such as chemical spillage, fumes, walking across a busy street, fire or undercooked food. The term risk refers to the chance, however great or small, that someone will be harmed by a hazard. The risk of a hazard harming us is obviously increased if we do not identify the hazard and take suitable measures to protect ourselves, for example, by wearing seat belts in motor vehicles, or washing our hands after using the lavatory.

Health and safety measures are precautions that we take to reduce the chance of accidents occurring, or to minimise the harm that an accident can cause. Modern health, safety and security law in all EU countries is based on the principle of risk assessment. This term refers to reasoned judgements about the risks and extent of those risks to people's health, safety and security, based on the application of information which leads to decisions on how risks should be managed.

There are five steps to risk assessment, as shown in the article on page 425.

Any risks must be identified very early in the team plan for your project, so that measures can be taken to eliminate, or at least minimise them. Everyone in a team has a responsibility for maintaining health and safety, and is assessed on how well this is carried out.

The case study on p. 426 shows that although health and safety are in the minds of most project organisers, much could still be done in the conference and exhibition sector of the industry. You may be able to follow the recommendations if you plan to run an exhibition or conference for your project.

The five steps to risk assessment

Step 1: Look for the hazards.

If you are doing the risk assessment yourselves, walk around your venue and look for anything that could reasonably be expected to cause harm. Ignore the trivial and concentrate only on significant hazards which could result in serious harm or affect several people. Ask the owner(s) what they think. They may have noticed things which will affect your project plans. Instruction sheets and notices can often help you spot hazards.

Step 2: Decide who might be harmed, and how.

Think about the range of people who will be using the venue, for example, team members, other staff, cleaners, visitors, children, suppliers, maintenance people and so on. Think also about how they could be harmed, for example, by obstructions; loose fittings; sharp edges or faulty equipment.

Step 3: Evaluate the risks arising from the hazards and decide whether existing precautions are adequate or more should be done.

Even after all precautions have been taken, some risk usually remains. What you have to decide for each significant hazard is whether this remaining risk is high, medium or low. First, ask yourselves whether your team has done all the things that the law requires. Then ask yourselves whether generally accepted standards are in place. But don't stop there – think further and try to imagine the specific hazards which your project might bring. Your real aim is to make risks as small as possible by adding your own precautions where necessary.

Step 4: Record your findings.

You must record the significant findings of your assessment. This means writing down the more significant hazards and recording your most important conclusions – for example, boxes stored in a corridor restrict access and exit.

Step 5: Review your assessment over timeand revise if necessary.

This may well apply if new machinery or new staff are brought in which could lead to new hazards. You don't need to worry about trivial changes, but do remember the changing needs of disabled people if they are involved in your project.

Source: Health and Safety Executive

CASE STUDY

Health and safety at exhibitions

A health and safety survey carried out in 1999 showed that organisers and venue owners were very aware of their responsibilities.

The findings showed that much work still had to be done in raising awareness of health and safety at exhibitions. The Association of Exhibition Organisers and Venues will aim to publish guidelines to help both clients and contractors.

Martin Neale of the Concept centre (an events venue) and Richard Armitage on behalf of the exhibitors agreed that health and safety is ultimately about teamwork between the organisers and the venue.

Fifty-three per cent of the respondents claimed to have a formal safety review policy (see reviews bar chart), while 80 per cent of respondents reported having a safety policy in place (see policies chart). The bulk of the positive statistics on health and safety applied to the organisers who had effective plans in place, often in a written format.

Exhibitors seemed to be less aware of the need to have a formal safety policy.

The overwhelming number of exhibitors expected the organisers to carry the responsibility for health and safety. They were willing to cover the costs of this, but spent much more money on stands.

Martin Neale of the Concept Centre said: 'You have to have risk assessments to define what could be dangerous and develop method statements of how you're going to deal with the potential dangers.'

Trevor Foley, on behalf of the organisers, pointed out that: 'Generally, organisers take the issue of health and safety very seriously and invest in manuals, administration systems, staff training and regular liaison with venues.'

Steve Bagnall, operations manager of London Arena, one of London's most popular event venues, supported these comments, adding: 'Organisers with venues have to take responsibility for the safety of visitors and exhibitors – if these people are not confident that we are covering all angles, it's an added anxiety, which they can do without.'

Richard Armitage, on behalf of the contractors who erect the stands, reported that: 'They are under pressure to continue to ensure safety in the ever decreasing build and breakdown times', and looked forward to the publication of the industry guidelines.

Source: Marketing Event, May 1999

Do you have a formal safety policy?

Key
- ☐ Event specific
- ☐ Written
- ■ No policy
- ■ Don't know

How often do you renew your company's safety policy?

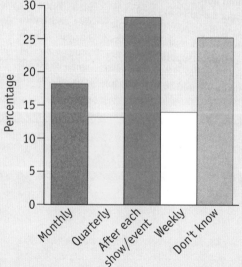

ACTIVITY

Legal considerations

Can you identify which Act or law would apply in the following circumstances? Ensuring:

- the confidentiality of customers' personal information, such as addresses
- that correct equipment is on hand to deal with first aid emergencies
- that adults working with children are properly vetted
- that too many people are not admitted to the venue
- that a hot dog stand is hygienic.

Insurance

It is possible that your school or college insurance policy covers your activities for the project, but you should check what exactly is permitted. If your project involves making travel arrangements for customers, for example, you may need to arrange travel insurance on their behalf or activity insurance if you plan to go skiing.

ACTIVITY

Insurance

Appoint one person in your team to liaise with your tutor to ascertain what insurance cover, if any, your project requires. Assess the impact of any additional insurance cover on your budget. Find out about the insurance cover of your school or college. Compare this to the needs of your project.

Security

In the travel and tourism industry a great deal of investment is made to ensure the security of customers and their possessions. Security measures are necessary because if customers feel unsafe they will not use the products and services or visit the facilities and events provided.

Security measures vary, depending on the organisation and environment and may include use of elaborate entry systems, closed circuit television cameras (CCTV), and the deployment of specialist security personnel.

The security aspects of projects can be complicated because they are one-off activities, which may involve the movement of large numbers of people. As with health and safety, the starting point for organisers is to identify and evaluate the security hazards for the project. Once this is done it is possible to consider the measures necessary to ensure security for both customers and staff.

The hazards which need to be identified depend on the scale of your project. The range of security hazards associated with a small local group going on a day-trip, for example, are far less than those associated with running a major visitor attraction, such as the Millennium Dome or Disneyland, Paris. In these major facilities security hazards involve:

- violence – for example, against spectators, participants, VIPs or staff
- theft – for example, of information, cash, stock, equipment or property
- fraud – for example, by the sale of fake tickets
- acts of terrorism and sabotage – for example, bombs and kidnapping
- damage – either accidental, deliberate or criminal.

Accidental damage is the security hazard you are most likely to face while running your project. Quite simply, the more activities that are going on and the more people involved, the greater is the probability of accidental damage. Staff or customers may drop equipment or misuse it, people may be unfamiliar with how things operate or with the surroundings in which they are working.

Your team will have to try and anticipate where this type of damage is most likely to occur and either have someone on hand to ensure it doesn't happen or propose measures to help minimise the risk. You should make sure that your institution's insurance covers you and any participants or spectators for the project you are going to undertake and for any accidental damage that may occur.

To ensure security at your team's project, you should consider:

- storing valuables in lockable containers or rooms
- patrolling vulnerable areas such as car parks with security personnel
- using premises which are alarmed
- leaving lights on as a deterrent
- restricting access to certain areas.

Your group will have to itemise all the security hazards it identifies, evaluate them and propose measures to counteract them and include this information in your plan. You could use or adapt the format shown in Figure 6.19 to record your findings for all types of security hazards.

You could consult professional organisations such as the police, security firms and consultants for help in all aspects of safety and security assessment, as they will have a great deal of advice and guidance to offer.

ACTIVITY

Security risk assessment

Identify the types of security hazard which might occur with the following projects and events, and give examples.

- A three-day arts exhibition in a local village hall.

- A weekend gathering of vintage cars at a city hotel's open-air car park.

- A residential trip to Paris via Eurostar for a group of 16–18 year old students.

Figure 6.20 shows just a few examples of risk reduction measures used in the travel and tourism industry.

ACTIVITY

Legal risk assessment

You should now have enough information to carry out a risk assessment on all the legal aspects of your project – health, safety, security and liability (insurance). As a group, begin an assessment for each area. Include your completed assessment in your business plan and ensure that everyone is familiar with its contents.

Contingency plans

Contingencies are things which happen by chance, accident or design, but which are not expected by you. Your risk assessment measures and procedures will cover your team for many types of contingency, but your team should expect some contingencies to occur and have plans in place to cope with them.

Figure 6.19: Security risk assessment record sheet

Security hazard identified	Who/what at risk	Probability of happening and importance	Measure to prevent
Violence	Staff or other customers	Low/important	Stewards on patrol
Theft	Cash and equipment	High/important	Locked till and lockable store
Fraud	Tickets	Low/low	Unique design
Damage	Exhibition stands Cars	Low/low High/high	Warning signs Parking attendants
Other			

Figure 6.20: Examples of risk reduction measures for travel and tourism projects

Violence
- Personal alarms and panic buttons
- Radios
- Staff training

Theft
- Alarms
- Sensors
- CCTV

Fraud
- Ultraviolet markers on tickets
- Swipe cards
- ID checks

Damage
- Patrols
- Security lighting
- Fencing
- Durable materials
- Clear signs
- Lockers
- Security guards
- CCTV

Murphy's law is often quoted at this point in planning: 'If something can go wrong it will!'

Effective contingency planning for emergencies is essential to ensure the health and safety of staff, participants and spectators. There have been accidents in the travel and tourism industry in recent years which have been due in part to a lack of effective contingency planning. Such is the concern for tourist safety that ABTA issues its own guidelines on contingency plans for tour operators to follow in the event of a major incident. Incidents are classified under the following headings:

- aircraft crash or hijack
- building collapse or fire
- coach, car, train or boat incident
- civil unrest, war, riot, terrorist action, fire or storm
- serious medical epidemic
- other accidents involving death or serious injury (such as avalanche or flood).

The guidelines include advice on setting up control points and teams to handle enquiries, logging details of all incidents, dealing with the media, repatriation, insurance claims and follow-up procedures.

If your project involves an event, your plan needs to include contingency actions to be taken should things go wrong. Formulating these plans is an important task for any team to tackle, as there can be serious consequences if contingency actions are not planned in advance or fail.

Disruptions at events are either foreseeable or unforeseeable and can range from the trivial and minor, which are dealt with quickly and easily, to the serious and major, which require dramatic action or professional assistance.

Foreseeable contingencies include things that project teams can usually predict, such as adverse weather, running short of something, lost property or late arrivals. Contingency plans for unforeseen circumstances, including emergencies such as fire, accident and crowd control are also required.

The contingency actions that your team decides upon should be capable of being put into operation quickly and communicated to both staff and customers in an effective and professional manner.

One method of preparing contingency plans is for each person in the team to brainstorm all the possible things that could go wrong within his or her area of responsibility. Each team member can then present the most important ones at a team meeting for discussion and seek suggestions for solutions should they occur. Well-organised teams agree and write out the procedures to be undertaken should any emergencies or disruptions occur, so that the whole team knows them and can practice or rehearse them as necessary. Reactions need to be quick and positive to reassure the public that the organisers are in control.

The customers for your project might include quite a diverse range of people, and all of them will have to be considered a likely source of contingencies. Similarly, as organisers, you must not forget to consider your team itself. Some of the team may be in vulnerable positions or have hazardous responsibilities, such as collecting money, controlling access, dealing with complaints, coordinating activities or looking after VIPs. Each team member's role should be evaluated for likely contingencies, such as:

- equipment failure
- theft or loss of essential equipment
- damage or vandalism
- supplies not turning up.

The best preparation is to have good communication between team members and professional support on hand should it be required. Training should also be undertaken to practise safety or security procedures agreed by the team or advised by the authorities, so that the time between any incident and response is minimal.

Review and evaluation

The final phase of planning your project consists of preparing for the final review and evaluation. This is an assessment of how it all went and involves deciding if the objectives set by your team at the outset have been achieved. Travel and tourism organisations should continually monitor and evaluate their performance in order to improve service delivery.

We have already highlighted the need to build evaluation into the plan as early as possible so that outcomes can be measured, so we focus here on evaluation methods. Depending on the type of project, some of the following methods of evaluation might be applicable:

- video
- publicity reports

ACTIVITY

Contingency action

1 Suggest some feasible contingency action for the following scenarios.

- A small child gets separated from her parents during a tour of a historic site.
- A tour bus breaks down in safari park.
- A horse-drawn carriage fails to appear at a hotel for the bride and groom.
- A generator you are using for power packs up and there is no heating in the marquee.
- A field you are using for parking turns into a bog after a torrential downpour.
- The caterer's van breaks down on the way to your venue.
- The coach you are using fails to return to pick your group up.
- A key member of your project team is ill on the day of your event.

2 As a group, hold a contingency planning meeting and keep notes of your discussions. You should consider:

- all components of your business plan
- everyone's specific roles
- whether all tasks have been identified
- details of resources
- health, safety, security and liability
- potential weaknesses in your planning.

- photographs or slides
- witness statements or comments sheets
- questionnaires
- written records of meetings
- feedback from other team members
- tutor assessment
- customer complaints
- customer compliments.

You should view the evaluation process as an essential element in improving both individual and team performance, as you can always learn from the strengths and weaknesses it reveals.

We discussed earlier the need to set specific, measurable and realistic objectives and targets at an early stage and in a form that could be evaluated after the project (see p. 409). We saw that it is not feasible to try to build in an evaluation process once the project is over. Your team will therefore need to set objectives and then monitor progress and results at every stage of project planning and implementation.

Use the checklist in Figure 6.21 to help you verify that you have established ways of measuring performance (performance indicators) in all the areas necessary for evaluation. These headings will also form the basis for your evaluation report.

Gathering feedback

The process of gathering **feedback** (information on performance) should be done continuously; before, during and after the project, either formally through minuted meetings or informally, through discussion. Certainly some evaluation will be needed early in your planning, for example, with the meeting of deadlines, progress towards targets or the suitability of people for roles. Other information, such as customer feedback, can be collected during the project, while some details,

such as the profit made, or take-up numbers, are likely to emerge once the project is over.

It is important to make sure that the information you collect is easily understood, easy to collect and record and helpful in the assessment of your team performance.

Sources of feedback

You can use many sources of feedback when evaluating your team's performance. These might include customer interviews and questionnaires, sales records, occupancy and usage figures, financial information and budget reports. For the staging of very large events, such as the Edinburgh International Festival, feedback will be sought from many other sources too. The Festival has a tremendous impact on the city of Edinburgh each year as it creates a huge influx of thousands of performers and visitors. A very close relationship needs to be built, through the exchange of feedback, between the organisers of the event and residents, travel agents, hoteliers and other tourism businesses and many departments of the city council. The Festival's organising committee keeps records of the feedback from its sources each year as a basis for planning improvements for the next year. Although you won't be organising a project on such a large scale as the

---

Figure 6.21: Project checklist of areas for evaluation

Objectives:
- ☐
- ☐
- ☐

Financial Targets:
- ☐
- ☐

Health & Safety
- ☐
- ☐

Customer Needs:
- ☐
- ☐
- ☐

Staffing Effectiveness:
- ☐
- ☐

Security:
- ☐

Marketing:
- ☐
- ☐

Efficiency of Systems:
- ☐
- ☐

Legal Aspects:
- ☐
- ☐

Use of Resources:
- ☐
- ☐

Timescales:
- ☐
- ☐

Contingencies
- ☐
- ☐
- ☐

Edinburgh International Festival, you will have to use appropriate sources effectively, to gather your feedback.

Feedback can be measured under one of the following headings.

- Quantitative – numbers or volumes, for example, tickets sold, profit made or levels of participation.

- Qualitative – by the features or superiority, for example, benefits, cleanliness or politeness.

- Effectiveness – how well targets were met, (for example, almost met, equalled, surpassed) or how well resources were used.

- Efficiency – best use of financial resources, for example, budgets or donations.

Constructive feedback

Your group may hold a meeting to debrief and provide feedback on the outcomes of the project. It is crucial that any feedback should be given in a constructive and sensitive manner. There is little likelihood of an individual or a team benefiting from inappropriately phrased or hostile feedback, for it is more likely to elicit a defensive or even aggressive response! The aim of giving feedback constructively is to enable people to learn so that they improve their performance next time.

Your team needs to gather feedback from:

- team members

- customers

- your teacher.

It is important that the framework for personal feedback is agreed at the outset. Sample feedback forms are shown in Figure 6.22.

Assessment by others can be in the form of:

- verbal feedback from colleagues given openly or in confidence

- grading or ratings on performance evaluation cards

- observational feedback using review sheets

- customer comments from questionnaires.

Feedback from customers can be presented in many different formats, such as graphs, bar charts, pie charts, reports outlining actions taken, summaries of customer surveys and statistical analysis.

If your team agrees on the types and methods of feedback at the planning stage, members will know what areas need attention and the materials and processes for collection can become a planned task.

Factors which affect performance

It is important during evaluation to identify the factors which have affected the team's performance. Consider some of the following questions.

- How good was teamwork and communications?

- How effective was project planning?.

- How effective was the team leadership?

- Did any factors prevent individuals from carrying out tasks?

- Did any constraints, such as insufficient resources or adverse weather affect performance?

This checklist provides a reminder of what to include in your team's project plan:

- aims and objectives

- description of project

- project timescales

- target customers

- how it will be marketed

- physical resource needs

- human resource needs

- financial resources

- administrative systems

- legal aspects

- contingency plans

- evaluation plan.

Figure 6.22: Sample feedback forms

Task set	Travel date	Actual outcome
Produce a poster	2 weeks by 10 May	1 day late
To sell 10 tickets	by 8 April	9 sole 1 refund
Book hall	for 20 May	Confirmed OK

Performance areas	Rating Poor → Good
	1 2 3 4 5
Politeness	3
Punctuality	5
Coping under pressure	1
Decision making	4

Satisfaction survey

	YES	NO
Comfort	✔	
Choice of food		✔
Staff politeness	✔	

Customer comment card

Comments on the project:

Signature .... Date ....

Action	By whom	By when
Order 15 thank you cards	David	1 May

BUILD YOUR LEARNING

Produce a business plan for your chosen project. The plan should be developed as a group but presented individually. It should include:

- objectives and timescales for the project
- customers and marketing activities
- physical, finance and human resource needs
- administrative systems
- legal aspects of the project – health and safety, security and insurance
- contingency plans
- methods used to evaluate the project.

Keywords and phrases

You should know the meaning of the words and phrases listed below. If you are unsure about any of them, go back through the last 24 pages to refresh your understanding.

- Administration system
- Aim
- Balance sheet
- Breakeven point
- Budget
- Contingencies
- Critical path analysis (CPA)
- Deadlines
- Feedback
- Financial monitoring
- Financial resources
- Hazards
- Human resources
- Implementation schedule
- Income and expenditure
- Legal considerations
- Objectives
- Physical resources
- Risk
- Risk assessment
- Role
- Roles and tasks
- Time scale
- Timetable

Teamwork

TEAMS OF STAFF OPERATE IN THE travel and tourism industry in many different organisations, to deliver an enormous range of products and services to customers. Examples of teams in a travel and tourism context include an air-cabin crew looking after passengers from take-off to landing, staff at a hotel serving guests and charity workers running a fundraising project. We define a **team** as a group of people who work together in an effective way to achieve tasks or goals.

Whatever the nature and purpose of the team, there are several characteristics that it requires in order to be effective. It should:

- work towards a common goal or objective

- display enthusiasm and commitment

- communicate effectively.

Teams can develop informally, as in a social group, or formally, as in a working group put together for a specific task, with a structure (arrangement of its members) for leadership and accepted methods of communication. We will study the features of a formal type of team structure in more detail, as this will provide you with a model to follow for your own project.

The majority of people who work in a port or airport form part of a formal team. Each has his or her own functions, such as check-in, baggage handling, air-cabin crew and so on. Members of such teams know who is in charge, and who to report to, because they are familiar with the structure of their team (see Figure 6.23).

This type of structure can be found in many other travel and tourism contexts. For example, if you check into a large hotel for a few days you will encounter the staff teams carrying out their regular duties, including receptionists, waiters and waitresses, bar-staff, chambermaids, porters, chefs and managers. All of these people work together, perhaps over a long period of time, as an effective team.

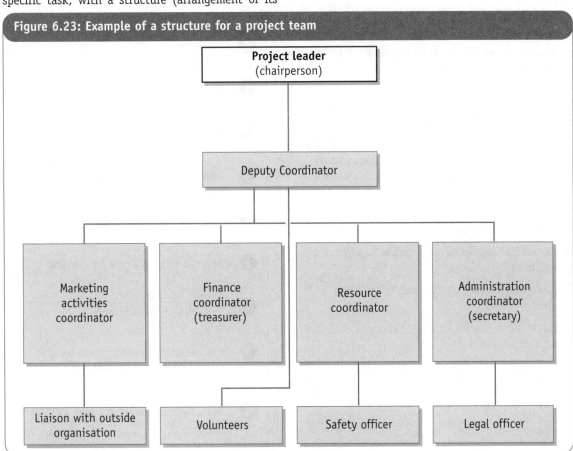

Figure 6.23: Example of a structure for a project team

Good **teamwork** doesn't just happen, it is a cooperative effort and needs to be worked at. Achieving effective teamwork amongst a group of people requires careful consideration, as poor teamwork can ruin a project. The essentials of good teamwork come from:

- a clear purpose and objectives
- an effective structure and leadership
- sharing of roles and responsibilities
- making best use of skills and supporting each other.

The purpose of a team is to achieve the aims and objectives of the project. Your own project's aims and objectives should be very clear to everyone, so that you all share this common purpose and work together to achieve success.

Team structure

Many travel and tourism organisations create **ad hoc teams** to carry out short-term projects or special events. These teams are composed of members whose expertise is needed for that particular project only. Once the project is over, team members may return to other duties such as marketing or finance, or come to the end of their contract, if they are employed on a temporary basis.

Members of ad hoc teams do not have a lot of time to get together and probably only a short time to deliver the project. However, they are usually selected for their ability to get along with others and should have the right blend of skills and talents to complete the task on time.

Ad hoc team members may be selected for their technical or operational talents and skills to solve a problem or tackle a project. In travel and tourism this could be:

- computer skills, for example, to use a spreadsheet or create good graphics
- mechanical knowledge, for example, to repair equipment
- marketing knowledge, for example, to design questionnaires
- communications, for example, to act as a confident announcer.

Your project involves setting up an *ad hoc* team, so a sound structure on which to base your teamwork will be a key requirement.

Committee structures

Most projects are overseen by a single coordinator or leader. However, this role can be performed by a small team with the right combination of skills and abilities.

One form of team structure which may be suitable for your project is that of a committee, with people elected or nominated for certain roles. Normally this would be headed by a chairperson as team leader, with a treasurer in charge of finance and a secretary to carry out the administration. Some advantages of a committee structure are that:

- people are voted into positions
- they make decisions democratically
- they can form subcommittees to tackle certain areas – such as safety or marketing
- their meetings are minuted.

Disadvantages are that decision-making can be slow and the organisation of project tasks cumbersome.

Figure 6.24: Agenda and minutes

Agenda

1. Apologies

2. Welcome and introductions

3. Minutes of last meeting

4. Update on venue and dates

5. Hospitality arrangements

6. Brainstorm programme for evening

7. Roles and responsibilities

8. Any other business (items to be with Chair 2 days prior to meeting)

9. Date, time and venue for next meeting

Throughout your project you will need to record evidence of team meetings. This is probably best done by taking minutes of each meeting. An example of a meeting agenda and minutes is shown in Figure 6.24.

The team leader or coordinator of a formal team structure like the one depicted in Figure 6.23 normally has responsibilities that include:

- liaison with outside organisations
- supervision of other team members
- making decisions on behalf of the team
- calling and running team meetings
- representing the project team at other meetings
- seeking advice or coopting specialists and volunteers to help.

Once the issue of leadership has been decided by the team, **lines of authority** (who is in charge of whom or what) can also be mapped out. The type of structure in Figure 6.23 is usually subdivided into functions, or areas of responsibility, with subsections to cover more detailed areas, such as marketing or safety. Figure 6.23 also represents the team's lines of communication for reporting progress or problems.

In larger project teams, each function leader is likely to have a small team working for him or her which carries out the allocated tasks. Individual team members in the structure know to whom to report, what authority they have in their area and understand the responsibilities appropriate to their role. Areas of responsibility or functions can be expanded to cover all needs, but good communication between team members and the coordinators is vital.

You may find that your team starts out with a much less formal approach to the planning and running of your project, with no one individual acting as leader or coordinator and everyone just responding to needs as they arise. However, you should understand that this arrangement rarely occurs in the travel and tourism industry and that projects with more formal structures are the norm.

Roles and responsibilities

As we have seen, a role is the part or function a team member has to play in the project and is especially significant in any group. Definition of role must be clear, so that team members understand what is expected of them. It is worth remembering the following.

- Each person's role must be set out clearly in **task descriptions**. If this does not happen, team members' perceptions or expectations of their role may diverge from those of colleagues and the team coordinator or leader.

- If someone is uncomfortable or not suited to a role this can create relationship problems within or between teams. One group may want to work as an ad hoc team with freedom of actions, while another may prefer to organise in a structured way.

- Different personal standards within a team can cause problems. For example, an untidy, unpunctual person, or someone who does not pull his or her weight, will not work well in a team which takes pride in punctuality and expects equal contributions from all.

- Conflict may result from giving a person several roles. For example, a person who works in two or three teams may find that decisions that he or she has to make in one team cause conflict with his or her role in another team.

- Team members who haven't been given enough work to do or who feel unchallenged are often discontented. **Delegation**, (the passing on of work) to someone who feels like this is a good way of showing that his or her contribution to the team or organisation is valued.

- When people have too much work to do, or not enough time to do it in, role overload results and the quality of work suffers. Allocating more time to complete tasks, or reducing the workload is the antidote to this problem.

If there is too much role conflict, overload or underload, then team members will suffer stress. Pressure to meet deadlines, sell tickets or fill seats are common stresses for a travel and tourism project. Strain comes from tension, low morale, communication problems and the need to meet exacting or unrealistic targets and will eventually affect team effectiveness.

Once everyone is clear about responsibilities, these should be entered into the business plan, along with your team structure, functions and roles, so that they are recorded to guide each person.

ACTIVITY

Roles and responsibilities

On the basis of the structure that your team has agreed and the functions identified for your project, identify areas of responsibility and suitable team members to carry out the roles required to complete the tasks for that area. Draw up job descriptions for each role and its tasks and put these into a file, so that anyone in the team can refer to them, during and after the project.

Team building

Whatever the team structure, team members all have to go through the process of getting to know each other and working together. A sequence of words created by Tuckman to describe the evolution of a group into an effective team sums up the stages very succinctly.

- **Forming.** At this stage there is very little evidence of teamwork, as people are simply getting to know each other. This stage may occur at the very beginning of your project, as you brainstorm ideas and test the feasibility of options. This is often an uncertain time. It might help the formation of your team if you can do some activities to get to know each other better, such as having a night out or having lunch, together. Building up confidence and trust with one another is the key to passing through this stage.

- **Storming.** This is potentially the most difficult stage of team building, as each person is striving to attain a position in the team with which they feel comfortable. Relationships can be stormy as team members vie for leadership or dominance. Others may object to their role or be a bit lazier and annoy others in the process. Discussion is the key to settling this stormy phase. Everyone must have their say, so that decisions can be made and agreed by all the team. Once people are comfortable with their workload, and have a had a fair chance to discuss roles and tasks, things should settle. One way to help your team pass through this stage is to set achievable aims and objectives and write out (minute) what has been agreed, so that if there is any dispute you can refer to the plans made.

- **Norming.** This is the stage at which relations settle down, work is underway and people are starting to pull together. Standards are set on performance, which everyone tries to attain, such as meeting deadlines or completing tasks to a high standard. Some group pride and team identity emerges at this stage, and individual potential begins to show. You should expect to have your planning completed by this stage. In general, teams seldom leave enough time for planning, so make sure you make the most of this stage.

- **Performing.** This is the most productive phase, according to Tuckman. It is often achieved by teams as they actually carry out their project, since this is when the most energy and perseverance are needed. A high performance team should be able to achieve all its objectives and cope with any contingencies which come along. There will be no room for slackers at this stage, so make sure everyone is really geared up to play their part. Friendships and mutual respect are often built up during this phase. This is the best time to record personal performance in your log book, gather feedback on levels of success and record key skills evidence.

- **Completion.** Although Tuckman does not include this stage in his scheme of group formation, the completion phase involves making the most of the work done. During this stage thanks must be made to everyone who contributed and all information collated for submission. At this stage, when the project is over, it is tempting to relax, but your team needs to maximise the effort it has made to achieve good results and grades – then and only then can you go out and party to celebrate!

The formation of an effective team is vital to the success of any travel or tourism organisation, enabling it to meet the challenging tasks and changing demands of the travel and tourism industry. And don't forget the other benefits of teams which are often taken for granted. They give help and support for members and meet personal needs through sharing. The article opposite shows the importance of building an effective team and the benefits that it can bring.

Sink or swim? BT Global Challenge

Sailing round the world must be one of the ultimate tests and there are some tremendous leadership and team building lessons to be learned by the amateurs who take part in the BT Global Challenge. Volunteers for the 10-month, 33,000-mile race first meet at the London Boat Show to discover who their crew mates will be and to which yacht they are allocated. The essence of the race is that you get who you get, and you get on with it.

Crew members have varying amounts of experience of sailing, so they are allocated to balance out their skills and experience, and give each identical yacht the same chance to win. Any difference between the performance of each crew depends solely on leadership skills and the attention paid to teamwork and personal motivation.

The Global BT Challenge gives a host of challenges to test the best – elements of fear, life-threatening incidents, confinement, interpersonal problems, an unpredictable environment, elation, depression and many more.

Some teams immediately get down to the task of learning to sail their boat and the technical tasks, others however spend some time getting to know each other, building team spirit, and learning about the leadership style of the professional skipper. The latter teams all finish in the top half of the race, showing the value of this approach.

Right from the start it is important to set a strategy and target for each leg of the race which is believable and acceptable to everyone. The winning skipper of the 1996 race avoided telling his crew that they should go all out for victory; instead he emphasised that a consistently high performance would ensure that they did well and that would have a good chance of being successful. Several other skippers adopted this approach and finished in the top three every leg. Skippers who stated publicly that they were going all out to win did not do well.

Consistency was valued highly, along with effective job allocation, especially in the hazardous conditions in which participants often found themselves. Crews which performed a range of tasks were never as effective when under pressure or in unfamiliar situations.

Giving people adequate information also proved to be essential. The more dynamic and complex the situation the greater the need for rapid communication. Knowledge dispels fear and speeds up action. Often when the skipper was off watch (asleep below deck) the crew had complete control of the yacht and the tasks which were essential to keeping alive and racing across the oceans.

Apart from crashing walls of water and the fear of being washed overboard, there were other problems, such as the pressure of relentless pounding and shortage of sleep. With such levels of stress, people often blame others for problems and are unforgiving when disputes develop.

Lives were under constant threat in the southern ocean legs of the race; if someone went overboard, survival was a matter of minutes and depended totally on crew mates' speed of reaction. It was therefore essential that leadership and decision making were carried out quickly. A code of behaviour was developed amongst the crews and an ethos that being a follower was as important as being a leader. This meant that the crews were self supporting on many occasions and did not always need the skipper to settle issues or provide motivation. Tolerance was at premium, punctuality was next, followed by a willingness to apologise quickly for mistakes (saying sorry was seen as a strength and not a weakness). Gossip was not tolerated and idle chatter was outlawed. Yachts returning to Southampton with happy crews were also those with high performance crews made up of team members who were friends for life.

ACTIVITY

BT Global Challenge

Use the case study about the BT Global Challenge yacht race to discuss some key issues for your team. Here are some examples to get you started.

■ How best to develop a teamwork style for your group project and how you will manage your own role and responsibilities.

■ Consider how you could motivate your team.

■ Dealing with personality clashes where value systems are different, or where there is an autocratic style of leadership. This might mean exploring different ideas about resolving conflict.

Group dynamics

Group dynamics are the interactions within teams and with other teams or individuals. Groups evolve into teams as they develop accord amongst their members and with other groups or individuals. The flow of interaction (dynamics) involved is shown in Figure 6.25.

Figure 6.25: Flow chart of group interactions

Accepting

↓

Communicating

↓

Cooperating

↓

Organising

↓

Responding

↓

Delivering

↓

Reviewing

At any stage of the interaction, conflict or problems can arise which may reduce the effectiveness of the group. For example, if a group has too many people who want to lead, this may cause competition, friction and personality clashes. On the other hand, there may be no one able to lead or coordinate, especially if a group is composed of people with no leadership skills. Try the activity below to see how well your team can operate to get you out of a difficult situation.

ACTIVITY

Group dynamics

As a team, stand round in a circle. All reach in with your right hand and grab the right hand of someone opposite you in the circle. Then reach in with your left hand to grab a different person's left hand. Now untangle the hands to recreate your circle, without letting go of anybody's hand.

Team effectiveness

We investigate next some of the factors which can influence the effectiveness of teams, both positively and negatively (see Figure 6.26).

Figure 6.26: Factors on team performance>

Positive factors	Negative factors
Good working relationships	Poor working relationships
Good leadership	Weak leadership
Adequate resources	Lack of resources
Clear roles and responsibilities	Confused roles and responsibilities
A flexible structure	An inflexible structure
A good working environment	Poor working environment
Clear procedures and processes	Lack of clearly defined procedures
Regular feedback and evaluation	No feedback or evaluation of performance

Communication

Groups and teams that do not communicate effectively are destined to fail. They will be unable to discuss issues or to solve problems. Everyone in a team needs to have the ability to listen, so that all points and opinions can be aired and understood. Your team needs to establish **channels of communication** to ensure that vital information is reported in time, such as up-to-date minutes, or accounts. This enables decisions to be made quickly on the basis of good, up-to-date information.

Communication systems have two broad functions. The first is to make links with external organisations and individuals so that appropriate and relevant information is communicated to the necessary people outside the organisation, such as customers, suppliers or the media: in fact, anyone who has an influence on the way the project will run. For example, you may need to put up signs to direct people to your project, you may issue progress reports to the press, or simply advertise tickets sales. Poor external communications, such as not ordering sufficient goods from suppliers, will affect your ability to operate effectively on the day.

The second main function of communication systems is to support the management and operation of the project. This largely serves an internal purpose: effective communication channels (ways of passing messages) between team members or staff on the project help to ensure that the project goes smoothly. Poor internal communication, such as failing to pass on a customer's request, may result in a booking being made twice and therefore affect communication with customers on the day of the project.

ACTIVITY

Communication

List the systems which your group are going to need for the communication elements of your project. Some of these may be manual (paper based) and some electronic. Discuss the pros and cons of each, relative to your budget plans, the ability of the staff or team to use them, customer needs and availability of resources. Agree the internal and external communication procedures and systems you will use.

Leadership styles

The term **leadership style** refers to the way in which a coordinator or leader relates to the team he or she is responsible for. Some teams have dominant leaders who like to be the boss. Their style (which is called autocratic) is characterised by the fact that the leader is the only person who makes decisions. This type of leadership is more often found in small teams.

Some teams have a democratic style of leadership that allows small committees or groups of people (teams) to be involved in decision making, as well as the team leader. You are more likely to adopt this style for your project. In between these two styles we find a leadership style which mixes the autocratic and the democratic style, depending on the task or project involved. This is called a **contingency approach** or flexible style.

Leaders can also select team members for specific jobs or tasks to take advantage of their skills and abilities. This **task culture** often suits project teams.

Project leaders must have the ability to lead and delegate, coordinate and control, support and motivate, but above all, to take an overview of proceedings and make decisions to smooth the progress of the team and the project. The contingency approach is best suited to these needs.

ACTIVITY

Leadership styles

What leadership styles are being used in the following scenario?

A student travel and tourism project team has recently elected its leader, who now insists that all team members must have their log books inspected at every meeting. After several weeks of this, the leader allows a vote to be taken on this practice because of the number of complaints from team members. As a result, the checking of log books is dropped.

Team types

Figure 6.27 shows a chart of Belbin's **team types.** Belbin argued after considerable research, that a range of different types of people was needed to make teams work well. He found that everyone had a dominant **primary team type**, though some might also have a strong secondary type and that each team type had certain typical positive qualities and allowable weaknesses.

Belbin found that too many of some team types, such as more than one shaper, or too many plants, would cause friction in a team. A few team workers and implementers were always required as the core of the team, but perhaps only one resource investigator and completer finisher.

You might like to use some of Belbin's ideas to help select your team. Or you may use the chart to assess whether team members turned out according to the type you thought they were, after the project is over.

Figure 6.27: Belbin's team types

Type	Symbol	Typical features	Positive qualities	Allowable weaknesses
Implementor	IM	Conservative, dutiful, predictable	Organising ability, practical common-sense, hard-working self-discipline	Lack of flexibility, unresponsiveness to unproven ideas
Coordinator	CO	Calm, self-confident, controlled	A capacity for treating and welcoming all potential contributors on their merits and without prejudice, a strong sense of objectives	No more than ordinary in terms of intellect or creative ability
Shaper	SH	Highly strung, outgoing, dynamic	Drive and a readiness to challenge inertia, ineffectiveness, complacency or self-deception	Proneness to provocation, irritation and impatience
Plant	PL	Individualistic, serious minded, unorthodox	Genius, imagination, intellect, knowledge	Up in the clouds, inclined to disregard practical details of protocol
Resource investigator	RI	Extrovert, enthusiastic, curious, communicative	A capacity for contracting people and exploring anything new, an ability to respond to challenge	Liable to lose interest once the initial fascination has passed
Monitor evaluator	ME	Sober, unemotional, prudent	Judgement, discretion, hard-headedness	Lacks inspiration or the ability to motivate others
Team worker	TW	Socially orientated, rather mild, sensitive	An ability to respond topeople and to situations,and to promote team spirit	Indecisiveness at moments of crisis
Complete finisher	CF	Painstaking, orderly, conscientious, anxious	A capacity for follow-through perfectionism	A tendency to worry about small things, a reluctance to 'let go'
Specialist	SP	Single-minded, self-starting and dedicated	Provides knowledge and skills in rare supply	Contributed on only a narrow front, dwells on technicalities, overlooks the 'big picture'

ACTIVITY

Team types

Analyse the different team types presented by Belbin and assess which is closest to you. Your group should then discuss what you think your team types are, and make an assessment of how many of each type you have. Discuss whether you feel you have allocated the right people to the right task areas. This exercise is normally carried out with the help of a sophisticated assessment test, so your judgements will not be conclusive. Nevertheless, it should make you think about people, their nature and the roles in which they can be most effective.

Synergy and motivation

If the team lacks cohesion it will definitely not perform effectively. The term synergy means that the energy of the whole team applied to a task is much greater than if just one or two work hard. Team synergy means that the team achieves a great deal more than it would if everyone worked independently.

Synergy does not just appear. Effort and input is required from everyone if it is to be created. It requires:

- enthusiasm – even when things go wrong

- tolerance – to the views and methods of others

- perseverance – sticking to the task.

The fact that team members have opinions about each other may also determine how well team members work together. If they have low opinions of each other, attitudes may become negative and conflict may occur. A positive atmosphere between team members is the starting point for creating the best environment for effective teams.

Motivation can come in many forms, from within ourselves (intrinsic) or from others (extrinsic). Although motivation is often seen as the responsibility of the leader, this should not be the case. All team members should support each other, especially when someone is struggling.

A good team-working atmosphere is difficult to create, for it encompasses a wide variety of factors, such as personal interests and beliefs and individual attitudes. Teams must also consider personalities. For example, if a person has an abrasive nature or is very quiet this might prevent him or her from getting along with others, and consequently prevent the team from being effective.

The working environment

The working environment for the project team should meet the following conditions. It should:

- be supportive, encouraging staff to innovate and to trust: this favours a democratic approach to leadership and involves staff in some decision making

- be based on clear goals and definite standards with guidelines for teams to follow which are outlined in mission statements, charters or strategic plans

- allow people to measure their performance by evaluating objectives and outcomes using targets and feedback from senior staff and colleagues such as appraisals and reports

- provide rewards and incentives such as bonuses, or consequences for poor performance such as explanations or discipline

- provide opportunities for personal improvement, such as learning new skills.

The most effective organisations in the travel and tourism industry spend a great deal of time trying to create these positive conditions for teams. You should try to follow their example for your project.

The final check

With an agreed structure in place, roles allocated and an idea of what good teamwork and leadership entails, there only remains the painstaking but essential process of going over every detail of planning for the project. This enables everyone to finally check (and make a note) of their exact responsibilities, tasks, contingency plans, use of resources and the desired outcome according to the targets agreed by the team for the event.

Two methods used by travel and tourism project teams that you might be able to adopt to help you complete your team preparations are a final meeting and a dress rehearsal. A final team meeting can be called to which everyone brings their proposals, in order to discuss each stage in turn. The inputs given by each person should piece together the jigsaw puzzle of the plan. This can be a slow process, but it allows amendments to be made as threads are pulled together. It also means that any variations are dealt with by the team at the final planning stage rather than on the actual day of the event. In this method, everyone hears and sees the whole plan as it is brought together by the coordinator(s) into a workable format.

It is often possible to carry out a dress rehearsal of many of the organisational aspects of an event. This provides tremendous feedback on a whole range of aspects important to the smooth running of the event, such as timings, shortages, resources used and communications. Rehearsals can instigate useful changes, such as:

- adjustment of deadlines
- revision of targets
- the addition of a contingency plan
- redefinition of a key factor
- increasing or decreasing a resource
- applying a new budget limit
- identifying other sources of feedback
- ironing out problems.

Because the whole team works together to amend the plan, everyone knows of any changes and agreement can be reached on the final operating version of the plan. This whole process is called **closing the loop**, as shown in Figure 6.2 on page 399.

ACTIVITY

Effective teamwork

Look at the model created by John Adair, a renowned leadership expert, below. Make a list under each of the categories – individual, team and task – of what each category requires to help create effective teamwork and a successful task or project. An example is given in each category to help give you a start.

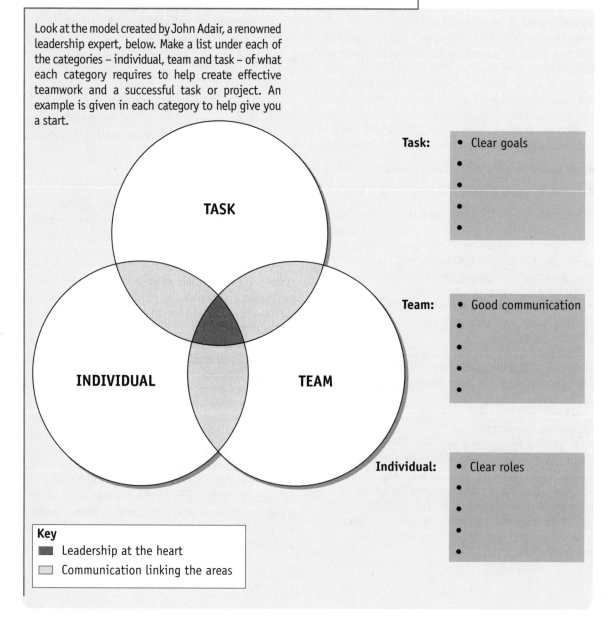

Task:
- Clear goals
-
-
-
-

Team:
- Good communication
-
-
-
-

Individual:
- Clear roles
-
-
-
-

Key
- Leadership at the heart
- Communication linking the areas

BUILD YOUR LEARNING

Make a recommendation about how the project teams in the following scenarios could improve their teamwork.

A student project team has had an argument about who should carry out the role of meeting and greeting two local celebrities who have agreed to appear at the start of the project. The group's leader insists that he should carry out the role as he is the most important person. The student in charge of marketing feels that she should have this responsibility as it is part of her function. A third person, who had suggested the idea because her parents knew the celebrities, wants to greet them. The group is having one of its regular team meetings, but is getting nowhere.

A tourist information centre team has decided to stage a promotional project at a London travel and holiday show. Competition to be on the stand at the exhibition is strong amongst the staff. The manager of the centre says that this should be decided on merit, by deciding what attributes (skills and qualities) the staff who will be on the stand need to have. She asks everyone for ideas about what these attributes might be. What skills and abilities would you identify and how would you then go on to select staff?

The staff from a theme park are asked to undertake an identical event on their site every year, to raise money for charity. They are happy to do this, but every year there are new staff or seasonal workers and many of the preparations have to be gone over several times. What could they could do about the situation?

Keywords and phrases

You should know the meaning of the words and phrases listed below. If you are unsure about any of them, go back through the last ten pages to refresh your understanding.

- Ad hoc teams
- Belbin's team types
- Channels of communication
- Closing the loop
- Contingency approach
- Delegation
- Forming, norming, storming, performing
- Group dynamics
- Leadership style
- Lines of authority
- Motivation
- Primary team type
- Synergy
- Task culture
- Task descriptions
- Team
- Teamwork

Carrying out and evaluating the project

YOU WILL BE EXPECTED TO TAKE on your agreed roles positively and to work with the rest of the team to achieve the agreed objectives while the project is being carried out and evaluated. The following points and guidelines should prove useful.

- **Carry out the tasks and role allocated** to you in the team plan and make sure that everything you do helps the team to achieve the project objective(s).

- **Keep to the deadlines set**. If you personally fall behind with your contribution this will have a knock-on effect for other people such as other team members or suppliers of goods or services.

- **Know when to get help and advice from others**. As soon as you realise, for example, that you are falling behind or overloaded, report this to the rest of the team or to your coordinator, for this is where you will find the most help.

- **Deal politely with customers**, other members of your team and any other people involved with the project at all times. You must try to maintain this approach even when you are under pressure or things are not going as expected.

- **Support other team members** throughout the project. Any assistance is usually appreciated and shows good teamwork.

- **React quickly and confidently to any problems** that arise. You may be the first in line when a problem occurs or need to assist someone else. Your team will have to obtain information on the contingency procedures well before the actual day(s), to ensure that you have an effective sequence planned.

Keeping to the team plan

Your team will have spent a lot of time preparing a plan, so it makes sense to follow it as precisely as possible. A little flexibility does of course need to be allowed, but that should be anticipated through contingency planning, or agreed in advance with the coordinator to keep things under control.

Part of **keeping to the team plan** involves ensuring that all meetings are properly run and minuted throughout all the planning, running and evaluation phases and that all team members record their personal or task objectives in a log book, so that progress can be checked and any differences can be controlled. You should be able to find guidance on how to hold a proper meeting – with an agenda, numbered items for discussion, minutes for a true record and discussion conducted through the chairperson in your school or college library. This will be another important source of evaluation.

CASE STUDY

Woodlands: a tourist project achieved

Peter and Sarah Chichester had been very keen campers and caravaners for 20 years and had toured much of Britain and Europe. Over the years, they had built up a good idea of what made staying at some parks more enjoyable than others. They knew it was not always the location and the tourist facilities that attracted them to a park, but functional and well managed sites with clean toilets and showers, a friendly welcome and helpful advice.

The Chichesters had worked for some years in the Far East and, on their return to England, Peter Chichester had become a director of a company with interests in caravan and marina businesses. Later a successful takeover bid was made for the company, and he was offered compensation to give up his directorship. The couple now only had a small mortgage and some savings, together with the new compensation capital. They now began to consider what options or ideas they could put their resources into as a tourism business venture.

Friends suggested that, as they both enjoyed meeting people, they should buy a pub or open a restaurant in the area. The Chichesters came up with their own idea and decided that they would be far happier operating a caravan and camping park, as a husband and wife partnership, using the knowledge they had gained from personal experience as tourists and Peter's business expertise.

They contacted a few of the best known estate agents specialising in the sale of caravan parks and visited a number of sites which interested them. Many of the establishments that they viewed had very dated facilities and required major capital investment to remain competitive.

While they saw the advantages of taking over an existing business with a track record and goodwill, this was usually reflected in the asking price and would have required them to borrow heavily. They decided to develop from scratch instead. Through contact with the regional tourist board (RTB), they found a site in the adjoining county where a farmhouse and 25 acres of land were for sale with outline planning consent for a touring caravan park.

The RTB was also able to give a considerable amount of tourism business advice on the area. A firm of leisure property consultants was appointed to carry out an appraisal of the site and to assess commercial feasibility. The couple continued to inspect other options, until the consultants gave a positive report on the viability for the farmhouse and adjoining land.

They had to build up a good relationship with the local authority in order to explore planning, transport and environmental considerations, before they submitted their detailed application. They eventually decided upon a scheme to create a 150-pitch touring caravan park with a separate camping field for 40 tents. The project included adaptation of the farm outbuildings to house a reception office, small self-service shop, launderette and children's play room, which could also be used for entertainment events in the main season.

Careful attention was paid to landscaping and enhancing the natural features of the site in the proposal put to the planners. Full approval was granted for the development, which was conditional on some access improvements to the site.

The initial expense of the consultant's report, which made recommendations on layout, estimated costs and cash flow projections, proved invaluable in securing bank support for the project. The construction work was put out to tender to a number of local builders and specialist contractors for roadways and landscaping. A pond was enlarged to create a small lake and is now an attractive feature of the camp site, (with suitable safety equipment on hand). The Chichesters soon settled into the farmhouse, which needed only some redecoration and modernisation.

Total development costs, including the purchase of the farmhouse and land, were within the budget targets set. The bank agreed to make additional funds available if necessary, based on the business plan the Chichesters had submitted.

The project has been a success, and now employs several full and part-time staff. Peter and Sarah Chichester enjoy running the park. While they find themselves exhausted at the end of each season, they do not regret undertaking the project, which provides them with a good standard of living, frequent compliments and a feeling of pride in their work. Much of the business is repeat visits and personal recommendations.

The park, now called Woodlands, advertises in most of the main caravan and camping guides and tourist board publications, and demand for pitches is high. The Chichesters continue to monitor where their customers come from (home and abroad), what they want and enjoy, and how long they stay. They have also carried out an evaluation to determine whether they could expand, based on present performance. This has proved likely, so expansion plans have been made for a further 50 caravans, which might in turn mean they could afford a indoor leisure pool and enlargement of the shop. A visitor survey has identified that a number of customers would like a take-away service on site. The Chichesters' most recent purchase has been a computer to help handle and record booking details, money transactions a mailing list and customer data base.

ACTIVITY

Woodlands tourist project

There are quite a few examples of good practice in the case study which you could draw upon for your project. Identify and discuss them with your team before you carry out your project. Here are two examples to get you started:

- the owners had some first-hand experience in the area of their project
- advice and guidance was sought at an early stage, and from diverse sources.

Health, safety and security

Figure 6.28 uses the example of a tourism awards evening to illustrate some aspects of health, safety and security involved in running the event.

In carrying out the project you must never forget the need for team members to have due regard for health, safety and security requirements, in terms of:

- themselves
- colleagues
- customers
- facilities
- information
- environment.

Figure 6.28: Health, safety and security factors at a tourism awards evening

Self and team	• Emergency procedures practised • Radio communication available	
Audience	• PA system installed • Tickets valid	
VIPs	• Special entrance • Accompanied to seats	
Winners	• Correctly positioned seated • Briefed and rehearsed	
Facilities	• Stage and seating checked • Fire extinguishers checked	• Lights and sound checked • Fire exits lit up
Information	• Do not reveal VIPs home addresses or telephone numbers • Provide suitable signs for amenities and parking	
Environment	• No litter • Low noise levels	

Evaluation

In this context, **evaluation** means finding the true value of your work and the part you played in the project. You should regard the evaluation process as an essential means of improving both individual and team performance.

The performance of your project team will be measured against the objectives contained in the business plan. In order to evaluate the performance and assess whether the objectives have been achieved, you will need to gather a wide range of information. Some of this information will be measurable (quantitative), while other feedback will be more qualitative.

Your team evaluation should:

- measure quantifiable activities, such as financial performance or attendance numbers

- classify information into similar categories, such as customer information or use of resources

- summarise data, so that it is manageable, such as effectiveness of team skills or efficiency of the systems used.

Figure 6.29: Evaluation checklist

Did you meet all your objectives: if not, why not?	✓
Were key deadlines met: if not, what caused then to be missed?	✓
Did your planning prove effective: if not, what would you recommend should be done differently next time?	✓
Was the project or event a success: if not, why not? If yes, what made it special?	✓
What went well and what went badly: can you identify the highs and lows and what caused them?	✓
How well did the team work together: some of the time, all of the time, never?	✓
What did you gain from working in a team – for example, skills or insight into the behaviour of others?	✓

Your team should work its way through each aspect of the business plan and implementation strategy, so that no potential source of feedback is left untapped. You should also discuss the relative advantages of a range of evaluation techniques in order to select the most appropriate. Evaluation techniques could include:

- a team debriefing session after the project with the whole team present to report on their areas of responsibility

- team member questionnaire

- feedback from your teacher

- customer feedback

- input from suppliers or external organisations about what was done well, or badly in dealing with them.

The information obtained, whether positive or negative, will help improve your personal skills, for you can use the feedback to improve strengths and overcome weaknesses.

Some people fail to learn from their experiences and simply repeat the same pattern in another context or situation. You should be able to make use of the feedback given to improve your skills knowledge and abilities.

You should look at the evaluation checklist in Figure 6.29. You may also wish to evaluate your personal outcomes against the skills listed in Figure 6.30, and make recommendations for improvement.

Figure 6.30: Young Enterprise key skills and experience profile

These skills can be acquired through your experience in Young Enterprise.

Team working

- Take part in identifying the team's objectives.
- Agree each team member's task and report on own tasks.
- Work effectively with others to reach goals.
- Use own and colleagues' time effectively.
- Problem solving
- Identify and analyse problems.
- Choose solutions and implement procedures .

Communication

- Take active part in meetings and discussions.
- Negotiate with others effectively to agree objectives and procedures.
- Interact well with customers and colleagues.
- Produce clear concise written work using IT.
- Make presentations.

Marketing

- Create and carry out a market research plan.
- Identify customer target groups and develop the marketing mix.
- Choose strategies to sell to target groups.
- Maintain good public relations with suppliers and customers.

Operations

- Define resource, quality, legal requirements and health and safety requirements.
- Set up procedures to meet targets.
- Develop evaluation systems.
- Maintain systems to meet quality standards.
- Evaluate environmental impact.

Finance

- Identify financial resource needs and fund these from various sources.
- Use budgetary information and justify expenditure on projects.
- Record financial information using IT.
- Select strategies to improve financial performance.
- Carry out an audit.

Personnel and training

- Understand personnel requirements and set up systems to meet them.
- Identify training.
- Seek and make use of feedback to improve performance and motivation.
- Use self-assessment procedures and review personal objectives.
- Develop a personal record of achievement.

ACTIVITY

Evaluating projects

Read the articles about transport projects initiated by the government. For each, suggest how the government might judge the success of the project.

World's biggest mobility event for disabled people

The world's biggest roadshow for disabled people takes place in just over five weeks time.

The project, organised by the Department of Transport, gives thousands of disabled people the chance to try out the widest possible range of mobility products and to test drive the latest production vehicles from major manufacturers.

Transport Minister Glenda Jackson will be attending the launch on 11 July when the roadshow will be opened officially by Her Royal Highness the Duchess of Gloucester.

Welcoming the project, Glenda Jackson said: 'I am strongly committed to making independent travel easier for people with mobility problems. We need to work towards fully accessible public transport systems and to break down the barriers to free movement within the pedestrian environment.

'Personal mobility is also a vitally important part of independent living. The roadshow gives an opportunity not just to see, but also to try out the widest possible range of vehicles and products in the mobility field. I warmly commend this show to anyone who has a mobility problem of any kind either on a personal level, to find solutions for themselves and their families, or as a professional in the transport or mobility fields, to see what is new in the marketplace. I am greatly looking forward to visiting the show.'

Department of Transport press release, June 1997

Strang toasts pedal power at bicycle breakfast

Cycling civil servants were welcomed by Minister of Transport Dr. Gavin Strang with tea and toast as they arrived for work at the Department of Transport (DoT) today.

The Bicycle Breakfast, which offers a free breakfast to DoT employees who cycle to work, is a special project organised to celebrate Bike to Work Day. It aims to promote cycling as a viable transport option and encourage more people to cycle to work.

Commenting, Dr. Strang said: 'Our Bicycle Breakfast is a fun way of raising the profile of cycling amongst employees and encouraging more of them to get on their bikes.

'Cycling is a key element of a truly integrated transport strategy. But to encourage more people to make the switch, cyclists need to be accommodated not only on the road, but also when they reach their destination.

'Bike to Work Day sends an important message to employers. By providing facilities such as changing rooms and secure storage for bikes, cycling to work can be more convenient and attractive – with the added benefits of reduced car use and a healthier work force.

I hope all employers will take steps to improve facilities for cyclists at the workplace.'

A Dr Bike clinic supplied by the Cyclists Touring Club was also available to Department employees today. It offered a free mechanical check of any cycles brought in on the day.

The Department of Transport, like most Whitehall departments, provides staff with a loan to purchase a bicycle and helmet for commuting purposes. Facilties provided at the DoT include secure parking, showers, changing rooms and lockers.

Bike to Work Day is one of numerous projects organised as part of National Bike Week, by the Cyclists Touring Club.

Department of Transport press release, June 1997

BUILD YOUR LEARNING

1 Take part in running the project and produce a record of your involvement. You may be able to use the personal log book (explained on pp. 399–402) as this record. Whatever format you use, your record should include:

- details of the tasks you were allocated

- details of any problems that arose and how you reacted

- details of any time deadlines you were given and whether you kept to them.

2 Evaluate your role in the project and the effectiveness of the team in achieving the project objectives. You may find it useful to base your evaluation on the checklist shown in Figure 6.29 (see p. 448). You will also need to gather feedback from a variety of sources to complete this task, including from:

- your own personal experiences

- other team members

- customers

- your teachers and supervisors.

3 Make valid recommendations for improvements to your own performance and that of the team, based on your critical evaluation of the project.

Keywords and phrases

You should know the meaning of the words and phrases listed below. If you are unsure about any of them, go back through the last five pages to refresh your understanding.

- Evaluation

- Evaluation technique

- Keeping to the team plan

UNIT 1 PORTFOLIO ASSESSMENT

Unit 1 is assessed through your portfolio work. The grade for the assessment will be your grade for the unit. These pages are designed to help you review your work and to check whether you have covered the required tasks to the right standard. The assessment tasks show what your portfolio needs to contain. Your teacher can give you further advice on what you need to do for each task.

If you completed the end of section activities throughout Unit 1, you will already have done a great deal of the work for your portfolio. Sometimes you may need to reorganise or expand upon the work that you have done before it is ready to be submitted for your final assessment. The table below shows which activities from the unit can help you build your portfolio.

Assessment tasks

This assessment is in two parts. The first part (tasks 1 to 4) requires you to undertake an investigation into the UK travel and tourism industry covering:

- reasons for development of the industry since the end of the Second World War
- its scale and significance to the UK economy
- its structure and key features
- how commercial and non-commercial organisations in the industry interact.

The second part of the assessment (tasks 5 to 7) involves an investigation into employment opportunities in the travel and tourism industry. You will identify one job that interests you and produce your own curriculum vitae.

Task 1. Explain the key post-war developments that have supported the growth of the industry and describe the key features of the present industry. You should explain the following past developments:

- changing socioeconomic circumstances
- technological developments
- product development and innovation
- changing consumer needs, expectations and fashions.

You also need to describe the features of the current industry in terms of:

- the domination of the private sector
- its extensive use of new technologies
- its vulnerability to external pressures
- its positive and negative impact on host communities.

To achieve a grade A you will also need to show a thorough understanding of the reasons for the rapid growth of the industry and the factors that will affect its development in the future.

Assessment tasks	Activities
Task 1	Activities on pages 28 and 38
Task 2	Activity on page 71
Task 3	Activity on page 68
Task 4	Activity on page 38
Task 5	Activities on pages 75 and 85
Task 6	Activities on pages 75,82 and 85
Task 7	Activity on page 93

Task 2. Describe the scale of the UK industry and its economic significance, using relevant data accurately in terms of:

- consumer spending in the UK on travel and tourism
- the number of people employed in the industry
- the number of tourists coming into the UK
- the number of UK residents taking holidays in the UK (domestic tourists) and outside the UK (outgoing tourists).

Task 3. Explain the present structure and key components of the UK travel and tourism industry giving suitable examples, and describe the range of commercial and non-commercial organisations that operate in it. You need to investigate the three key sectors, namely: public, private and voluntary. You should also investigate all of these key industry components:

- tour operations
- travel agents
- transportation
- tourism development and promotion
- tourist attractions
- accommodation and catering.

To achieve a grade A for tasks 2 and 3 you must also provide a clear demonstration of your ability to critically analyse information and data in order to draw valid conclusions about the scale and structure of the industry.

Task 4. Evaluate the key features of commercial and non-commercial organisations to illustrate differences in their funding and business objectives.

Throughout your investigations for tasks 1 to 4, **to achieve a grade C** your work must show a logical and well-structured analysis of the industry that effectively summarises key information and data, and an ability to use appropriate terminology. **To achieve a grade A** your work must also show your ability to use a comprehensive range of information sources, showing how you have cross-checked the reliability of each source.

Task 5. Summarise the range of employment opportunities available within the travel and tourism industry.

Task 6. Describe in detail one job that best matches your own aspirations, skills and abilities.

To achieve a grade C you will need to provide additional information in order to critically evaluate why your chosen job best matches your personal circumstances. For example, this additional information could involve contacting employers, interviewing someone that works in your chosen area, obtaining job a description or person specification, or attending a careers event and exhibition.

Task 7. Produce a curriculum vitae (CV) that is appropriate for seeking employment in your chosen job.

Key skills

It may be possible to claim these key skills for this work depending on how you have completed the tasks and presented your work:

- communication (C3.2, C3.3)
- information technology (IT3.2)
- improving own learning and performance
- working with others.

Your teacher will need to check your evidence against the key skills specification.

UNIT 3 PORTFOLIO ASSESSMENT

Unit 3 is assessed through your portfolio work. The grade for the assessment will be your grade for the unit. These pages are designed to help you review your work and to check whether you have covered the required tasks to the right standard. The assessment tasks show what your portfolio needs to contain. Your teacher can give you further advice on what you need to do for each task.

If you completed the end of section activities throughout Unit 3, you will already have done a great deal of the work for your portfolio. Sometimes you may need to reorganise or expand upon the work that you have done before it is ready to be submitted for your final assessment.

You may be able to use the information about selected popular UK tourist destinations contained in the travel file section (see pp. 203–25) to help you complete this assessment. The table below shows which activities from the unit can also help you build your portfolio.

Assessment tasks

You will need to produce an investigation into two tourist destinations in continental Europe and two long-haul tourist destinations. It is important that you chose destinations that are popular with UK tourists, and for which you can access a wide range of relevant and up-to-date information sources.

Task 1. Using an appropriate map, identify and describe the location of each destination.

Task 2. Assess the importance of the destinations in terms of the number of visitors from the UK and the number of major transport principals using the destination.

Task 3. Describe the main travel routes and gateways by which UK tourists enter and leave each destination, and assess the suitability of the most common routes in terms of cost, convenience, journey time and services provided.

Task 4. Explain why people from the UK visit each destination. Describe the range of attractions and suggest how these might appeal to tourists.

To achieve a grade A your work must also show a critical analysis of the appeal of each destination and the contribution of the different features to this appeal.

Task 5. Identify and describe any major trends in the popularity of each destination over the past ten years. You should investigate:

■ economic considerations

■ social and political considerations

■ environmental and geographical considerations.

To achieve a grade A your work must also show that you can draw valid conclusions from the trends in popularity at each destination.

Assessment tasks	Activities
Task 1	Activities on pages 172 and 173
Task 2	Activities on pages 162 and 202
Task 3	Activities on pages 173, 185 and 191
Task 4	Activities on pages 166, 173, 176 and 183
Task 5	Activities on pages 160, 162, 163, 193, 194 and 202

In completing all of these tasks you will need to use relevant information to support your ideas and use appropriate terminology.

To achieve a grade C your work must show independent, well-organised research, through prioritising work and making use of valid information sources. You will need to make effective use of statistics to support your ideas and use them and other information sources to interpret and explain trends and changes in the popularity of the destinations. Your work should be presented in a logical and well structured manner.

To achieve a grade A you must also show that your work involves sustained research and inquiry using accurate, reliable and sufficient data to support your investigations. Terminology should be used appropriately and fluently

Key skills

It may be possible to claim these key skills for this work depending on how you have completed the tasks and presented your work:

- application of number (N3.1)
- communication (C3.2, C3.1b, C3.3)
- information technology (IT3.1, IT3.2, IT3.3)
- improving own learning and performance (LP3.1, LP3.2, LP3.3).

Your teacher will need to check your evidence against the key skills specification.

UNIT 5 PORTFOLIO ASSESSMENT

Unit 5 is assessed through your portfolio work. The grade for the assessment will be your grade for the unit. These pages are designed to help you review your work and to check whether you have covered the required tasks to the right standard. The assessment tasks show what your portfolio needs to contain. Your teacher can give you further advice on what you need to do for each task.

If you completed the end of section activities throughout Unit 5, you will already have done a great deal of the work for your portfolio. Sometimes you may need to reorganise or expand upon the work that you have done before it is ready to be submitted for your final assessment. The table below shows which activities from the unit can help you build your portfolio.

Assessment tasks

This assessment is in two parts. The first part requires you to produce a record of your involvement in a variety of customer service situations (tasks 1 and 2). These situations can be real, such as from a work placement or your part-time job, or could be simulated through role plays. In the second part you need to investigate the effectiveness of customer service delivery in two travel and tourism organisations (tasks 3 to 6).

Task 1. Provide details of your dealings with at least four different types of customers in a variety of customer service and selling situations. This should include at least one situation for each of the following:

- face-to-face (to individuals and groups)
- on the telephone (to include making and receiving calls and taking accurate messages)
- in writing (to include replying in an appropriate format to a letter)
- handling a customer complaint.

On each occasion you must show how you adapted your responses to meet customer requirements.

To achieve a grade E you must show:

- that you can provide accurate and appropriate information/advice to customers
- your ability to use communication and selling skills appropriately, providing customers with the services they require, taking into account specific needs
- your ability to deal with customers on the telephone
- your ability to deal with customers in writing
- your ability to handle customer complaints effectively and sensitively.

To achieve a grade C you will also need to demonstrate thorough product knowledge, that you understand the specific needs of different types of customer, and that you can adapt your responses by meeting these needs in an appropriate manner.

Assessment tasks	Activities
Task 1	Activities on pages 343, 349, 365 and 373
Task 2	Activities on pages 343, 349, 365 and 373
Task 3	Activities on pages 326 and 366
Task 4	Activities on pages 344, 350 and 366
Task 5	Activities on pages 332, 344 and 366
Task 6	Activities on pages 326, 332, 350, 366 and 394

To achieve a grade A you will also need to display excellent communication and selling skills in your dealings with different types of customers in a pressured work situation, and complete task 2.

Task 2. Critically evaluate your performance in dealing with customers, suggesting actions on how you can improve.

Task 3. Identify the key customer service quality criteria in two travel and tourism organisations, giving examples of the procedures and practices used by managers and staff to achieve them.

Task 4. Using appropriate methods for measuring and monitoring, evaluate the effectiveness of the customer service delivery in each organisation.

Task 5. To achieve a grade C you will also need to critically evaluate and compare the effectiveness of customer service delivery in each organisation.

Task 6. To achieve a grade A you will also need to suggest and justify appropriate actions to improve customer service delivery in each organisation.

Key skills

It may be possible to claim these key skills for this work depending on how you have completed the tasks and presented your work:

- communication (C3.1a, C3. 1b, C3.2)
- improving own learning and performance (level 3)
- working with others (level 3).

Your teacher will need to check your evidence against the key skills specification.

UNIT 6 PORTFOLIO ASSESSMENT

Unit 6 is assessed through your portfolio work. The grade for the assessment will be your grade for the unit. These pages are designed to help you review your work and to check whether you have covered the required tasks to the right standard. The assessment tasks show what your portfolio needs to contain. Your tutor can give you further advice on what you need to do for each task.

If you completed the end of section activities throughout Unit 6, you will already have done a great deal of the work for your portfolio. Sometimes you may need to reorganise or expand upon the work that you have done before it is ready to be submitted for your final assessment. The table below shows which activities from the unit can help you build your portfolio.

Assessment tasks

The assessment involves planning, carrying out and evaluating a travel and tourism related team project. The project could take the form of an organised tour to a particular locality or attraction, a special event involving the local community, or a fundraising venture. You could incorporate the project into a school or college residential trip. In this instance, you may be able to use the services of tour operators offering ready-made residential packages if appropriate. Where resources or opportunities are limited, the project can be implemented in-house, such as organising an open day for visitors to your school or college, entering a major competition or taking part in a local event such as a carnival or parade.

Whatever project you decide to do you must ensure that it will enable you to meet the assessment criteria and provide a realistic experience in a travel and tourism context. It must also be large enough to provide all members of your team with an opportunity to take on substantial responsibilities.

Task 1. Produce a logical and coherent business plan for a travel and tourism related project that covers all aspects listed below. The team project must be viable to run in terms of resources available, legal obligations and time. The plan should be developed as a group, but presented individually. This should include:

- objectives and timescales for the project

- description of the project

- human, financial and physical resource needs

- legal aspects of the project (health and safety, security and insurance)

- methods to be used to evaluate the project.

Task 2. Effectively participate in running the team project. You will need to show an ability to use effective planning and communication skills throughout the project. You must also keep a record of your contribution, including:

- details of the tasks you were allocated

- details of any problems you encountered and how you dealt with them

- details of any time deadlines you were given and if you kept to them

- an evaluation of your role in the project.

Assessment tasks	Activities
Task 1	Activities on pages 407, 410, 413, 416, 418, 420, 421, 427, 428, 434 and 437
Task 2	Activities on pages 402, 430, 441 and 451
Task 3	Activity on page 451

Your personal involvement may be recorded in a number of ways, such as a display, report, presentation or diary. You should keep records of team meetings, briefings or other relevant planning materials, such as marketing and contingency plans or financial projections.

To achieve a grade C for tasks 1 and 2 you must make a significant contribution to planning and running the project, and show an ability to use initiative and creativity. All aspects of the project must be completed within an appropriate timescale.

To achieve a grade A your work must also show independence in managing and running the project, and evidence of a high level of communication skills with team members and customers.

Task 3 Evaluate your role in planning and running the project and the effectiveness of the team's performance throughout the project. You should base this on how effective the team was in achieving the project objectives.

To achieve a grade C this evaluation should be a critical analysis of your own performance, and that of the team, while planning and running the project.

To achieve a grade A you must also make valid recommendations for improvements to your own performance and that of the team, based on your critical evaluation of the project.

Key skills

It may be possible to claim these key skills for this work depending on how you have completed the tasks and presented your work:

- communication (3.1a, 3.1b, 3.3)
- improving own learning and performance (3.1, 3.2, 3.3)
- problem solving (3.1, 3.2, 3.3, 3.4)
- working with others (3.1, 3.2, 3.3).

Your teacher will need to check your evidence against the key skills specification.

Resource and internet directory

DURING YOUR COURSE, YOU WILL gather a wide range of information about travel and tourism organisations, facilities, products, services and events. This textbook provides much of the information that you need to complete your coursework. However, you will need to use a range of information sources in order to successfully complete your portfolio assessments. This section provides you with a directory of information sources and websites that you may find useful throughout your course.

Information sources

Magazines, journals and periodicals

- Attractions Management (with Leisure Management)
- Caterer and Hotelkeeper
- Digest of Tourist Statistics
- Which Holiday?
- Leisure Management
- Leisure Manager
- Leisure Marketing (with Leisure Opportunities)
- Leisure Opportunities
- LeisureWeek
- Travel Trade Gazette
- Travel Weekly

Government publications/research

The Office for National Statistics (ONS) is the government agency responsible for the presentation of government statistics. It provides a wide range of information on society, population, health, social trends, the labour market, business and the economy. Useful publications include:

- Social Trends
- Annual Abstract of Statistics
- Family Spending Surveys
- General Household Surveys
- UK Tourism Surveys

ONS also provides a useful booklet, Statistics for Students, to assist students with their research. See its website (www.ons.gov.uk) for further details.

National tourist authority publications

- Sightseeing in the UK (English Tourist Council)
- UK Tourism Facts (British Tourist Authority)
- Regional Tourism Facts (English, Scottish and Wales Tourist Boards)
- Annual British Tourist Authority report (plus the annual reports of the national boards)
- Insights

Market research organisations

- Mintel (see also useful websites)
- Leisure Industries Research Centre (LIRC)
- Henley Centre for Forecasting
- Key Note (see also useful websites)
- Marketscape

Other sources of information

- Company reports of the major travel and tourism organisations
- Yellow Pages
- Thomson Directories
- Holiday brochures
- Travel guides
- Atlases and travel maps
- Newspapers (holiday and travel sections)
- Textbooks

Useful websites

Many organisations involved in travel and tourism provide information on the worldwide web (www). Their websites provide up-to-date information that you can use for your coursework and assignments. When you use the internet, you will quickly find out that there is an enormous amount of information about travel and tourism. To help you save time, you may find this list of websites useful. However, this list does not cover everything and you may need to search further for information on a particular topic, organisation or locality. Happy 'surfing'!

Association of British Travel Agents (ABTA)

ABTA is the premier trade association for UK tour operators and travel agents. ABTA's 600-plus tour operators and 2,300 travel agency companies have over 7,000 offices and are responsible for the sale of more than 90 per cent of UK-sold package holidays. This site provides information about tourist destinations, tour operators, travel agents, types of holidays, careers guidance and qualifications offered in the travel services sector.

- Association of British Travel Agents (ABTA)
  www.abtanet.com

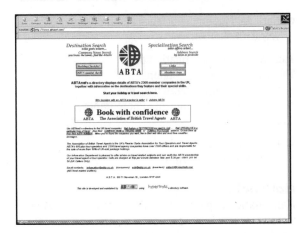

Airlines

Most airlines now have a website. Here a four examples:

- British Airways
  www.british-airways.com

- easyJet
  www.easyjet.com

- British Midland
  www.iflybritishmidland.com

- Virgin Atlantic
  www.virgin.com

Airports

- British Airports Authority (BAA)
  www.baa.co.uk

BAA operates several UK airports including Heathrow, Gatwick, Stansted, Edinburgh and Glasgow.

- Manchester Airport
  www.manairport.co.uk

- Birmingham International Airport
  www.bhx.co.uk

- UK and Ireland Airport Guide
  www.a2bAirports.com

Arts Council

The Arts Council site provides information about the arts in the UK and their funding. Online regional arts pages provide information about the English Regional Arts Boards. Also has links to other arts-related sites.

- Arts Council
  www.artscouncil.org.uk
  www.arts.org.uk

British Tourist Authority (BTA)

Extensive range of information about tourism in Britain including tourist destinations, environments to explore, places to stay, activities and attractions, travel information, tourist boards, interactive images and maps of Britain. The site also contains information about careers in the travel and tourism industry and qualifications.

- British Tourist Authority (BTA)
  www.visitbritain.com

Department for Culture, Media and Sport

This is the central UK government department responsible for government policy on the arts, sport and recreation, tourism, the national lottery, libraries, museums and galleries and film.

- Department of Culture Media and Sport
  www.culture.gov.uk

English Heritage

The 'Places to Visit' site provides information about historic houses, sites and monuments in England. This includes opening times, admission charges, group/school visits, visitor facilities, special events and concerts.

- English Hertiage
  www.english-heritage.org.uk

English and regional tourist boards

The English Tourism Council shares the BTA site listed earlier. For further information about a particular region try the regional tourist boards.

- English Tourism Council
  www.englishtourism.org.uk

- Cumbria
  www.cumbria-the-lake-district.co.uk

- Northumbria
  www.northumbria-tourist-board.org.uk

- Yorkshire
  www.ytb.org.uk

- East of England
  www.eetb.org.uk

- West Country
  www.wctb.co.uk

- South East England
  www.se-eng-tourist-board.org.uk

Holiday Parks

- Butlin's
  www.butlins.co.uk

- Centre Parcs
  www.centreparcs.com

- Oasis
  www.oasishols.co.uk

Leisure Opportunities

This site provides information about job vacancies in the sport and recreation/leisure industries.

- Leisure Opportunities
  www.leisureopportunities.co.uk

Leisurehunt

This extensive database provides information about leisure and tourism facilities in localities throughout the UK, mainland Europe, North America, Canada and Australia. The search of localities within the UK will provide information about hotels, guest houses, hostels, campsites, farms and cottages, art galleries, museums, historic places, restaurants, parks and gardens, golf courses, leisure centres, swimming pools, airports, industrial heritage, libraries, wildlife attractions, racecourses, riding schools and tourist information centres.

- Leisurehunt
  www.leisurehunt.com

Museums

There are many museums in the UK with websites. A good starting point is the '24 Hour Museum', which provides comprehensive information about a wide range of museums. You will find this site useful when researching museums in a chosen locality.

- 24 hour Museum
  www.24hourmuseum.org.uk

- National Museum of Science and Industry
  www.nmsi.ac.uk

This website has information on:
The Science Museum, London
The National Railway Museum, York
The National Museum of Photography, Film and Television

- Royal Armouries
  www.armouries.org.uk

National parks

Many national parks in England and Wales have a website where you can access information about tourism in the Parks. This information may be useful when you investigate the impacts of tourism on the countryside. Here is a selection of National Park websites:

- Dartmoor National Park
  www.dartmoor.npa.gov.uk

- Lake District
  www.lake-district.gov.uk

- North Yorks Moors
  www.northyorkmoors-npa.gov.uk

- Peak District
  www.peakdistrict.org

- Pembrokeshire Coast
  www.pembrokeshirecoast.org

National Tourist Organisations

Most countries/major tourist destinations have national tourist boards/organisations that promote tourism. Examples include:

- France
  www.franceguide.com
  www.paris-touristoffice.com

- Spain
  www.tourspain.es

- Florida
  www.goflorida.com/orlando

- Barbados
  www.barbados.org

- Australia
  www.atc.net.au

National Trust

This site provides information about more than 300 historic buildings and sites to visit. Every week the National Trust receives hundreds of enquiries about its work as the UK's largest land-owning conservation charity. As a major heritage organisation in the voluntary sector, the Trust provides an excellent case study for leisure and tourism students.

The Trust has a designated site for students aged 14+. This provides information about the history of the National Trust, its funding, marketing, access to its properties for disabled visitors and a range of case studies about issues such as nature conservation and the impacts of tourism.

- National Trust
  www.nationaltrust.org.uk

- National Trust education site
  www.nt-education.org.uk

Northern Ireland Tourist Board

- Information about tourism in Northern Ireland.
  www.ni-tourism.com

Rank Group

The Rank Group is one of the leading leisure, tourism and entertainment companies in the UK. The site provides information about the company and its many businesses which include Mecca Bingo, Grosvenor Casinos, Odeon Cinemas, Rank Entertainment, Tom Cobleigh, Haven, Warner, Butlin's, Oasis and Hard Rock Café

- Rank Group
  www.rank.com

Royal Mail

This website provides a range of useful information about customer service and direct mail marketing/promotional activities.

- Royal Mail
  www.royalmail.co.uk

Travel and tourism statistics and research

There is a wide range of research and statistics about travel and tourism available from the following sites:

- www.staruk.org.uk
- www.Keynote.co.uk
- www.Mintel.com
- www.ons.gov.uk

Information on the Office for National Statistics (ONS) website ranges from climate data to unemployment statistics. You can also search for statistical publications to find the subject you are interested in. The most frequently requested datasets and questions are also available on the Biz/ed website: www.bized.ac.uk/dataserv/onsdata.htm

StatBase is an extensive online information resource which can be accessed via the Government Statistical Service: www.statistics.gov.uk

Tourism development

There are many organisations with an interest in tourism development, from National Tourist Boards to environmental groups. Two useful sites include:

- Tourism Concern
  www.tourismconcern.org.uk

- Voluntary Services Overseas (VSO)
  www.vso.org.uk

Theme parks

There are many theme parks in the UK and the majority have websites. Here are four examples:

- Blackpool Pleasure Beach
  www.bpbltd.com
- Alton Towers
  www.alton-towers.co.uk
- Legoland, Windsor
  www.lego.com/legoland/windsor
- Thorpe Park
  www.thorpepark.co.uk

Tour operators

There are hundreds of tour operators in the UK. Two of the largest are:

- Thomson Holidays
  www.thomson-holidays.com
- First Choice
  www.firstchoice.co.uk

You can access information about company history, careers and job opportunities and find out about the holiday products they offer.

Travel agencies

As with tour operators, there are many travel agencies. Two of the best known are:

- Lunn Poly
  www.lunn-poly.co.uk
- Thomas Cook
  www.thomascook.com

There are also many on-line travel agents and services, such as

- LastMinute.com
  www.lastminute.com
- a2btravel.com
  www.a2btravel.com
- uTravel
  www.utravel.co.uk

Travel guides

There are many travel guides available, such as:

www.lonelyplanet.com

www.travelfromHere.com

Travel and tourism jobs

These websites provides information about jobs, type of work in the industry, qualifications needed and career choices.

- Travel and Tourism Jobs
  www.careercompass.co.uk
  www.ilam.co.uk

Virgin Group

Richard Branson's Virgin Group is one of the largest leisure and tourism operators in the UK. The site provides a company history, details of latest developments, career opportunities and information on the various Virgin businesses. These include Virgin Atlantic, Virgin Express, Virgin Trains, Virgin Holidays, Virgin Cinemas and Virgin Hotels.

- Virgin Group
  www.virgin.com

Wales Tourist Board

Extensive information about tourism in Wales including holiday destinations, tours, places to stay and things to do. There is also information about the Rugby World Cup, 1999.

- Wales Tourist Board
  www.tourism.wales.gov.uk

What's on

Britain's national performing arts information and ticketing service. At any one time, the database has information about more than 2,000 performances around the country. 'What's On' provides information about events in the UK, including theatre, opera, music, dance, ballet, and comedy.

- Whats on
  www.whatson.com

Yellow Pages

UK Web is a directory listing of websites in the UK. Organisations are grouped by category, such as travel and tourism, sports and leisure, entertainment and music, education and training.

- Yellow Pages
  www.yell.co.uk

Index

Numbers in bold show the page on which the word is defined or used as a key word.